Alastair **Sawday's**

Special Places
to Stay

British
Bed & Breakfast

"Exceptional places to stay."
The Daily Telegraph

Edited by Nicola Crosse

ipa®

Alastair **Sawday's**

Special Places
to Stay

British
Hotels & Inns

"Filled with the characterful
details we love from the
Sawday's team."
The London Evening Standard

Edited by Tom Bell

ipa®

Alastair **Sawday's**

Special Places
to Stay

Wales

"...trusted guides to high
quality places to stay."
The Daily Telegraph

Alastair **Sawday's**

Special Places
to Stay

Scotland

"Much-loved guidebooks."
The Guardian

ipa®

D0307932

Alastair
Sawday's

Special Places to Stay

Seventh edition
Copyright © 2010 Alastair Sawday
Publishing Co. Ltd
Published in 2010
ISBN-13: 978-1-906136-36-9

Alastair Sawday Publishing Co. Ltd,
The Old Farmyard, Yanley Lane,
Long Ashton, Bristol BS41 9LR, UK
Tel: +44 (0)1275 395430
Email: info@sawdays.co.uk
Web: www.sawdays.co.uk

The Globe Pequot Press,
P. O. Box 480, Guilford,
Connecticut 06437, USA
Tel: +1 203 458 4500
Email: info@globepequot.com
Web: www.globepequot.com

*We have made every effort to ensure the accuracy
of the information in this book at the time of
going to press. However, we cannot accept any
responsibility for any loss, injury or
inconvenience resulting from the use of
information contained therein.*

Series Editor Alastair Sawday
Editor David Hancock
Assistant Editor Claire Wilson
Editorial Director Annie Shillito
Writing David Hancock,
David Ashby, Jo Boissevain,
Allen Stidwill, Mark Taylor,
Claire Wilson, Mandy Wragg
Inspections David Hancock,
David Ashby, Peter Birnie,
Colin Cheyne, Charles Edmondson-Jones,
Jonathan Reynolds, Allen Stidwill,
Mark Taylor, Claire Wilson,
Mandy Wragg
*Thanks to those people who did a few inspections
or had a go at a write-up*
Accounts Bridget Bishop,
Shona Adcock, Rebecca Bebbington,
Christine Buxton, Amy Lancastle,
Sally Ranahan
Editorial Sue Bourner,
Jo Boissevain, Roxy Dumble
Production Jules Richardson,
Rachel Coe, Tom Germain,
Anny Mortada
Sales & Marketing & PR Rob Richardson,
Sarah Bolton, Bethan Riach, Lisa Walklin
Web & IT Dominic Oakley
Chris Banks, Phil Clarke,
Mike Peake, Russell Wilkinson

Alastair Sawday has asserted his right to
be identified as the author of this work

Maps: Maidenhead Cartographic Services
Printing: Butler, Tanner & Dennis, Frome
UK distribution: Penguin UK, London

Alastair
Sawday's

Special Places

Pubs & Inns
of England & Wales

4   Contents

The buildings

Beautiful as they were, our old offices leaked heat, used electricity to heat water and rooms, flooded spaces with light to illuminate one person, and were not ours to alter.

So in 2005 we created our own eco-offices by converting some old barns to create a low-emissions building. We made the building energy-efficient through a variety of innovative and energy-saving building techniques, described below.

Insulation   We went to great lengths to ensure that very little heat can escape, by laying thick insulating board under the roof and floor and adding further insulation underneath the roof and between the rafters. We then lined the whole of the inside of the building with plastic sheeting to ensure air-tightness.

Heating   We installed a wood-pellet boiler from Austria, in order to be largely fossil-fuel free. The pellets are made from compressed sawdust, a waste product from timber mills that work only with sustainably managed forests. The heat is conveyed by water throughout the building, via an under-floor system.

Water   We installed a 6,000-litre tank to collect rainwater from the roofs. This is pumped back, via an ultra-violet filter, to the lavatories, showers and basins. There are two solar thermal panels on the roof providing heat to the one (massively insulated) hot-water cylinder.

Photo: Tom Germain

Lighting   We have a carefully planned mix of low-energy lighting: task lighting and up-lighting. We also installed sun-pipes to reflect the outside light into the building.

Electricity   All our electricity has long come from the Good Energy company and is 100% renewable.

Materials   Virtually all materials are non-toxic or natural. Our carpets are made from (80%) Herdwick sheep-wool from National Trust farms in the Lake District.

Doors and windows   Outside doors and new windows are wooden, double-glazed and beautifully constructed in Norway. Old windows have been double-glazed.

We have a building we are proud of, and that architects and designers are fascinated by. But best of all, we are now in a better position to encourage our owners and readers to take sustainability more seriously.

What we do

Besides having moved the business to a low-carbon building, the company works in a number of ways to reduce its overall environmental footprint.

Our footprint   We measure our footprint annually and use it to find ways of reducing our environmental impact. To help address unavoidable carbon emissions we try to put something back: since 2006 we have supported SCAD, an organisation that works with villagers in India to create sustainable development.

Travel Staff are encouraged to car-share or cycle to work and we provide showers (rainwater-fed) and bike sheds. Our company cars run on LPG (liquid petroleum gas) or recycled cooking oil. We avoid flying and take the train for business trips wherever possible. All office travel is logged as part of our footprint and we count our freelance editors' and inspectors' miles too.

Our office Nearly all of our office waste is recycled; kitchen waste is composted and used in the office vegetable garden. Organic and fairtrade basic provisions are used in the staff kitchen and at in-house events, and green cleaning products are used throughout the office.

Working with owners We are proud that many of our Special Places help support their local economy and, through our Ethical Collection, we recognise owners who go the extra mile to serve locally sourced and organic food or those who have a positive impact on their environment or community.

Engaging readers We hope to raise awareness of the need for individuals to play their part. Our Go Slow series places an emphasis on ethical travel and the Fragile Earth imprint consists of hard-hitting environmental titles. Our Ethical Collection informs readers about owners' ethical endeavours.

Ethical printing We print our books locally to support the British printing industry and to reduce our carbon footprint. We print our books on either FSC-certified or recycled paper, using vegetable or soy-based inks.

Our supply chain Our electricity is 100% renewable (supplied by Good Energy), and we put our savings with Triodos, a bank whose motives we trust. Most supplies are bought in bulk from a local ethical-trading co-operative.

For many years Alastair Sawday Publishing has been 'greening' the business in different ways. Our aim is to reduce our environmental footprint as far as possible, and almost every decision we make takes into account the environmental implications. In recognition of our efforts we won a Business Commitment to the Environment Award in 2005, and in 2006 a Queen's Award for Enterprise in the Sustainable Development category. In that year Alastair was voted ITN's 'Eco Hero'. In 2009 we were given the South West C+ Carbon Positive Consumer Choices Award for our Ethical Collection.

In 2008 and again in 2009 we won the Independent Publishers Guild Environmental Award. In 2009 we were also the IPG overall Independent Publisher and Trade Publisher of the Year. The judging panel were effusive in their praise, stating: "With green issues currently at the forefront of publishers' minds, Alastair Sawday Publishing was singled out in this

category as a model for all independents to follow. Its efforts to reduce waste in its office and supply chain have reduced the company's environmental impact, and it works closely with staff to identify more areas of improvement. Here is a publisher who lives and breathes green. Alastair Sawday has all the right principles and is clearly committed to improving its practice further."

Becoming 'green' is a journey and, although we began long before most companies, we still have a long way to go. We don't plan to pursue growth for growth's sake. The Sawday's name – and thus our future – depends on maintaining our integrity. We promote special places – those that add beauty, authenticity and a touch of humanity to our lives. This is a niche, albeit a growing one, so we will spend time pursuing truly special places rather than chasing the mass market.

That said, we do plan to produce more titles as well as to diversify. We are expanding our Go Slow series to other European countries, and have launched *Green Europe*, bold new publishing projects designed to raise the profile of low-impact tourism. Our Fragile Earth series is a growing collection of campaigning books about the environment: highlighting the perilous state of the world yet offering imaginative and radical solutions and some intriguing facts, these books will keep you up to date and well-armed for the battle with apathy.

Photos: Tom Germain

It is hard to write about pubs without lamenting the demise of so many of them. The cull continues, with pub chains dumping the least profitable, drinkers deserting them in droves in favour of cafes and clubs, and the sheer harshness of the economic climate making life impossible for so many of them. Who would be a publican?

Well, some are brave (and mad?) enough to keep at it, and this book provides a refuge from the storm – awash with stories of landlords who have turned the tables on the chains, seduced people back and re-invented the pub. I had a particularly uplifting pub experience recently in the Royal Oak near Swindon. I walked straight into a throbbing hub of humanity: people eating, drinking, reading by the fire, chatting – all as if they were sharing a big sitting room with a convenient bar in it. To top it all, the food came straight from the landlord's farm in the same village, award-winning and organic.

Talking of food, there is more fine food than ever in this edition. The story above is no longer unusual; lots of landlords grow their own or buy food in from allotments. They buy from their own customers, err only rarely beyond their immediate areas in search of the finest quality, refuse to cook beans flown in from Africa, and are eager to promote the latest local brew. They work hard to earn our loyalty.

Are there any limits to how far the modern landlord will go to serve his community? Some pubs, such as the Shoulder of Mutton, now act as village stores. The Dabbling Duck is owned by the villagers, serves Norfolk produce, runs quiz and poker nights and has a library of books to borrow. In some villages the pub is all that is left to serve a once-convivial community. The Mason Arms has a micro-brewery, fine rooms as well as a camp site, and even goes so far as to run fetes and dog shows.

The trick to survival, then, is for landlords to reach deep into their imaginations and find new ways. The sky is the limit. Why not have local musicians playing, artists displaying, children cavorting and adults consorting in an infinite variety of ways? One of my favourite pub moments was emerging into a scruffy garden and finding an all-women Big Band from Weston blasting the ears of a disorderly collection of drinkers. It was riotous, funny, eccentric – and heart-lifting.

Alastair Sawday

In the face of recession, with pub closures, in January 2010, reaching 52 a week, this edition of *Pubs & Inns of England & Wales* – Sawday's seventh – has had our team trawling the country in search of pubs that have bucked the trend. The result? Over 900 places that stand out from the crowd: community locals, inns with rooms, little-known 'gems' and pubs that take their food seriously – fine dining pubs and gastropubs, ever on the rise. All have been chosen because we believe them to be special, and we hope you will too.

Some pubs have disappeared from the guide. Others have moved sideways to the Worth a Visit sections, and await re-inspection as landlords change and chefs move on. Over 80 places with that special something – authenticity, atmosphere, looks, setting, beds, food, real ale, wine – have made it into the guide for the first time.

2009: a challenging year

In my introduction to Edition 6, I lamented the speed at which pubs were closing as the recession took hold in late 2008, at 39 closures a week. Closure rates – as I said – now stand at an astonishing 52 a week; a total of 2,400 pubs closed down in 2009. High rents and increasing government regulation, such as 2007's smoking ban, must take some of the blame. But it is the small communities that have suffered the most, those places whose pub has often outlasted the village shop as the last remaining venue for social interaction. These non-dining pubs have

been the most vulnerable but the impact across the board has been huge, with 24,000 jobs lost across the industry and a tax loss to the government of some £254m, a loss that is increasing by £5.5m each week. With consumer confidence low and beer sales falling – partly the result of cheap supermarket booze – the government has added further pressure, increasing beer taxes by 20% during 2009. In 2010 the government presses ahead with the mandatory code of practice on alcohol retailing, adding £30m of red tape costs on pubs in the first year alone.

Winners and losers

The giant and once powerful pub companies, reliant on a buoyant economy and high property values making such investment worth their while, have been hit hard as property values have tumbled. To fund mounting debts, Punch offered their licensees the opportunity to buy their pubs in early 2009; by the autumn, more than 400 deals had been completed. And the best deals are happening in the food-led pubs, which tend to receive lower valuations because they have fewer ties with the pub company (beers, gaming machines etc). The winners are those landlords who have developed gastropubs; also those who have introduced pubs with rooms. What's more, successful tenants are being offered great deals by breweries and pub companies to expand to a second or third pub.

Pub is the Hub – a positive outlook

The publicity given to pubs' closure has

sparked an upturn in interest in 'Pub is the Hub', a scheme run by a national advisory body that provides grants for rural regeneration and pub diversification. Local authorities, once little interested in assisting pubs, are now more willing to help pubs diversify as they witness village communities dying after pub closures. Summer 2009 saw the scheme working on 33 projects in 21 council areas in England and Wales, including the opening of seven post offices in pubs in the south east. An increasing number of pubs are doubling up as shop and post office; others are throwing themselves into finding space for farm shops and farmers' markets, parish meetings, art exhibitions, cinema clubs, theatre performances, supper clubs and village fetes.

Cask ale renaissance

Despite declining beer sales and being in the teeth of a recession, 2009 saw the first year of growth in the UK cask-beer market since the early 1990s. With a growing number of cask ale drinkers (7.9 million), a rise of over 3,000 more pubs serving cask ale, and a huge growth in the membership of the Campaign for Real Ale (CAMRA), the future looks bright for real ale.

In the first edition of *Pubs & Inns*, published in 2004, I commented on the flowering of over 400 independent / craft breweries across the country, brewing beer on farms, on industrial estates, even in pub sheds. There are now, astonishingly, over 700 independent breweries in business, providing firm evidence that the

Government's Progressive Beer Duty, introduced in 2002, had a beneficial effect. Regional, local and independent brewers now account for 78% of cask-ale volumes and 81% of value, while the four multi-national brewers concentrate on building national and international lager brands.

Passionate micro-brewers have been innovative and experimental, tapping into and promoting the rich vein of different beers that can be brewed without compromising on quality. There are now fantastic milds (dark and light), cracking bitters and a whole host of other beers, stouts, porters, fruit beers, wheat beers and craft lagers for the discerning beer drinker to discover. The ever-increasing interest in regional, seasonal produce in pub kitchens now extends to the locally produced beers on tap, with lovers of real ale eager to understand the provenance of a beer. There are now more than 150 beer

Photo: Waggon & Horses, entry 526

festivals around Britain, with an estimated combined attendance of half a million. Many pubs are also organising their own mini beer festivals to promote local brews – and are seeing a much increased turnover as a result.

Not surprisingly, a growing number (around 200) of these thriving small brewers are snapping up bargain freehold pubs from struggling large tenanted pub companies. Likewise, there are multiple pub operators that have started brewing their own high-quality beers, supplying their own mini-estates of pubs as well as local pubs. Excellent examples are Paul Tickner at the Flower Pots in Hampshire (Flower Pots Brewery), Cliff and James Nye at the Jolly Sailors in Norfolk (Brancaster Brewery), and Michael Thurlby at the White Hart in Cambridgeshire (Ufford Ales). It's a win-win situation. Not only does it tap into the trend for pubs to think local, but there's a profit to be made from selling your own beer in your own pub.

Responding to the credit crunch: how pubs are surviving

The survival of Britain's rural ale houses increasingly depends on the provision of good food and/or comfortable bedrooms. Many pubs are now places to eat, drink and sleep, and the most successful thrive because their operators are hands-on, consistently aim for high standards and genuinely believe in value for money.

But, as the credit crunch bites deeper into our pockets, and pub-goers continue to be choosy about where they eat out, landlords have had to find ever more imaginative ways to draw punters through the foodie door. To promote their passion for produce from local suppliers (and their very own farm), the Mill Race in Herefordshire supplies luxury gift hampers; in the first half of 2009 they sold 120 for every occasion. At The Pigs in Norfolk, an innovative and very successful barter scheme encourages customers to bring in homegrown fruit, vegetables and herbs and swap them for pints of beer or vouchers for meals; growers also get a mention on the menus. Half the garden at The Pigs has been turned over to allotments for customers to use; similarly, local families grow their own food on the free community vegetable patch at the Potting Shed in Gloucestershire.

Some enterprising landlords are coming up with great value two- and three-course menus at lunchtimes or in the early evening; the cuts of meat may be cheaper but the dishes reflect the quality of the

Photo: The Sun at Northaw,, entry 353

main menu. At the Michelin-starred Hand & Flowers in Buckinghamshire, chef Tom Kerridge offers a two-course lunch for £10, allowing him to introduce pub-style classics such as coq au vin *and* fill the place at lunch times.

Pubs are also becoming more flexible as far as Sundays go, with many serving roasts up to 4pm – or later. What nicer than a lie-in and a late breakfast, a blustery walk and a slap-up lunch? Tim Bilton at the Butchers Arms in West Yorkshire is in tune with his locals' needs, offering Sunday brunch from 11am to 1pm, and a free Sunday newspaper to those who book a table. (A thoughtful touch when the nearest shop is a 15-minute drive away.) To encourage customers to stay longer on a Sunday, some landlords are offering jazz afternoons accompanied by dessert boards, champagne-by-the-glass promotions, film clubs, and, at The Compasses in Essex, a professional magician to entertain the children during lunch.

Other pubs are opening early and rustle up breakfasts and all-morning cappuccinos, others serve food all day, particularly at weekends. Yet others, such as The Millbrook Inn in Devon, have started guest-chef nights in winter: a local chef cooks a three-course meal for £7 a head, to cover the cost of the produce. It creates goodwill, packs the place out on a winter's night and increases wet sales (a 400% increase on a Monday). Ready meals to take away, fresh or frozen, have been successfully introduced at The Compasses in Essex and this trend too is likely to grow – along with pub deli-counters and farm shops.

Creating an art trail along a track from a local gallery to The Bull in Cheshire has been a hit with families and boosted business at weekends. A free customer taxi service (within a five-mile radius) has brought £32,000 worth of business to the very rural Royal Oak in Wiltshire. Taking inspiration from supermarkets, The Bull in Cheshire and The Gun in Sussex have developed customer loyalty or privilege cards, offering regular diners discounts on drink or food on certain nights – or a bottle of champagne on birthdays if you book a table for six.

Then there's the added appeal of a few cosy bedrooms above – or a flurry of super new ones out the back. An ever-growing number of pub owners are investing in new rooms or refurbishing old ones. Even letting out one room can generate £9,000 per year. As customers become choosier about where to spend their hard-earned cash, increasing numbers are spending a weekend away at a cosy country pub or a classy inn rather than a pricier country-house hotel. This trend is reflected in the number of pubs and inns wishing to include their bedroom details here; this edition includes 190 wonderful pubs where you can eat, drink and be merry – and stay the night.

David Hancock

The notion of 'special' is at the heart of what we do, and is highly subjective. We also recognise that one person's idea of special is not necessarily another's so there is a big variety of places in this book, from dog-walker friendly to contemporary chic. Those who are familiar with our Special Places series know that we look for originality and authenticity, and disregard the anonymous and the banal. We also place great emphasis on the welcome – as important to us as the setting, the architecture, the atmosphere and the food.

Inspections and subscriptions

We visit every entry in this guide. We pick up those details that cannot be gleaned over the internet or the phone, and we write the descriptions ourselves, doing our best to avoid misinterpretation. If a pub is in, we think it's special, and the write-up should tell you if it's your sort of special.

Owners pay for their bedrooms to be mentioned but it is not possible for anyone to buy their way in; their fee goes towards the cost of the inspection process and includes a presence on our website.

Feedback

Things evolve at an astonishing pace in the pub world, so between inspections we rely on feedback from our readers as well as our staff, who are encouraged to visit properties across the series. Feedback is invaluable to us and we always follow up on comments.

Do tell us if your visit has been a joy or not, if the atmosphere was great or stuffy, or whether the staff were cheery or bored. The accuracy of the book depends on what you tell us. Occasionally misunderstandings occur, even with the best of intentions; if something is awry, please say something at the time! The landlord or owner will be keen to put things right, if they can.

A lot of the new entries in each edition are recommended by our readers, so keep telling us about new places you've discovered. You can use the forms on our website (www.sawdays.co.uk) or at the end of this book.

Disclaimer

We make no claims to pure objectivity in choosing these places. They are here simply because we like them. Our opinions and tastes are ours alone and we hope you will share them. We have done our utmost to get our facts right but apologise unreservedly for any mistakes that may have crept in.

You should know that we don't check such things as fire alarms, kitchen hygiene or any other regulation with which owners of properties receiving paying guests should comply. This is the responsibility of the owners.

Finding the right place for you

Drink, eat, sleep A growing number of pubs and inns combine atmosphere with good food and bedrooms to match – and at lower prices than many hotels. It's true that some pubs are virtually indistinguishable from some small hotels, but a lively bar serving real beer should put them into the classic inn category. Some pubs with rooms are more modest village affairs where the enthusiasm to get things right in the bar extends upstairs. (If you are worried about noise at weekends, you can ask for a room at the back or a room across the way.) So the next time you take a weekend or business break, dismiss those roadside lodges and impersonal hotels in favour of a friendly country inn.

Gastropubs and country dining pubs Our best pubs are luring foodies away from pricier restaurants as a wave of casual dining enfolds the nation. Many backstreet boozers have been transformed, the fruit machines and beer-stained carpet being replaced by chalked-up menus and chunky tables. In the countryside, too, old-fashioned locals are being rejuvenated by landlords and chefs who believe that gastronomy is rooted in the soil and that food should be fresh, seasonal and sourced from the best local suppliers.

Our favourite food pubs in England and Wales are described within these pages; all strike a happy balance between restaurant and pub. (Note that booking is not always a given and you may have to take your chance with a table.)

Old boys and ale Expect few frills and modern-day intrusions, just real ale tapped from the cask, a game of shove ha'penny and a packet of pork scratchings. Some of these town or country gems are simple in the extreme, others offer more in the way of food and facilities (newspapers, piano, real fire) but remain genuine examples of the British boozer. We have unearthed a much-loved crop.

Pub as hub Despite the rate at which pubs are closing across Britain, with the right landlord at the helm a pub can thrive. With a big welcome, a roaring fire, tasty food and fine beer such a pub can draw a community together, spawning darts, pool, football and cricket teams, raffles, and comedy and quiz nights. A growing number are taking on a wider community role, becoming part-time post offices, shops and delicatessens as village stores close, even venues for farmers' markets, polling stations, theatre performances and exhibitions of art.

Maps and directions

The maps at the front of the book show the approximate position, via a series of coloured flags, of each of our pubs and inns. Mauve flags indicate pubs with rooms, gold flags the award winners, blue flags the Worth a Visits. The maps are for guidance only; use a detailed road map or you could lose yourself down a tangle of lanes. There are directions on each guide entry, but these are also for guidance only.

Symbols

Below each entry you will see a line of symbols, which are explained at the very back of the book. They are based on the information given to us by the owners but things do change, so use the symbols as a guide rather than an absolute statement of fact. Please note that the symbols do not necessarily apply to the bedrooms. Double-check anything that is important to you. A fuller explanation of some symbols is given below.

Children – The 🏃 symbol is given to pubs that accept children of any age.

That doesn't mean that they can go everywhere in the pub, or that highchairs and special menus or small portions are provided. Nor does it mean that children should be anything less than well-behaved! Call to check details such as separate family rooms, whether children are allowed in the dining room and whether there is play equipment in the garden.

Dogs – The 🐕 symbol is given to places where your dog can go into some part of the pub, generally the bar and garden. It is unlikely to include eating areas.

Wheelchairs – We use the ♿ symbol where we have been told that those in wheelchairs can access both the bar and the wc. The symbol does not apply to accommodation.

Pub awards

Every year we choose those pubs that we think deserve a special mention. Our categories are: pubs serving local, seasonal and organic produce; authentic pubs; community pubs; and pubs with rooms. More details are given on page 20, and all the award winners have been tinted and stamped so you can spot them easily.

Opening times

We list the hours pubs are closed during the afternoon and whether or not they are closed during particular lunchtimes and evenings. We do advise that you check before setting out, especially in winter.

Meals and meal prices

We give the times meals are served and the approximate cost of main courses in the bar and/or restaurant. Note that some pubs charge extra for side dishes, which significantly increases the main course price. Where set menus are mentioned, assume these are for three courses unless stated. Note that many pubs do fixed-price Sunday lunches, and that prices in general may change. Check when booking.

Bedrooms, bathrooms and breakfasts

If you're thinking of staying the night in a simple pub or inn, bear in mind that an early night may not be possible if folk are carousing below. A few bedrooms do not have en suite bathrooms – please ask on booking – and pub room check-ins are often late, eg. from 6.30pm. Breakfasts are generally included in the room price, and most places serve breakfast between 8am and 10am.

Bedroom prices

Prices are per room for two people sharing. If a price range is given, then the lowest price is for the least expensive room in low season and the highest for the most expensive room in high season. The single room rate (or the single occupancy of a double room) generally follows. Occasionally prices are for half board, ie. they include dinner, bed and breakfast. Do check.

Photo left: The Freemasons Arms, entry 405
Photo right: The Swan, entry 554

Bookings and cancellations

Tables – At weekends, food pubs are often full and it is best to book a table well in advance; at other times, only tables in the dining rooms may be reserved. Tables in the bar may operate on a first-come, first-served basis. Some of the best gastropubs do not take reservations at all, wanting to hold on to their pubby origins – so arrive early! Always phone to double-check meal times.

Rooms – Most pubs and inns will ask for a credit card number and a contact phone number when you telephone to book a room for the night. They may take a deposit at the time of booking, either by cheque or credit/debit card. If you cancel – depending on how much notice you give – you can lose all or part of this deposit unless your room is re-let. Ask the pub to explain their cancellation policy clearly before booking so you understand exactly where you stand; it may avoid a nasty surprise.

Payment

Those places that accept credit or debit cards are marked with a credit card symbol.

Tipping

It is not obligatory but it is appreciated, particularly in pubs with restaurants.

Some cancellation policies are more stringent than others. It is also worth noting that some owners will take the money directly from your credit/debit card without contacting you to discuss it. So ask them to explain their cancellation policy clearly before booking so you understand exactly where you stand; it may well avoid a nasty surprise. And consider taking out travel insurance (with a cancellation clause) if you're concerned.

Photo left: George & Dragon, entry 149
Photo right: The Sun Inn, entry 139

Local, seasonal & organic produce award

Hearts soar when our inspectors find chalkboard menus promoting regional, seasonal produce: farm meats, village-baked bread, locally shot game, fish from local catches, organic wines and local brewery ale. A passion for actively sourcing seasonal foods from high-quality local suppliers now extends to deli counters by the bar, farmers' markets in pub car parks and poly-tunnels and vegetable plots bursting with home-grown produce. Our champions of local, seasonal and organic produce are:

The Mill Race
Herefordshire
entry 340

The Pigs
Norfolk
entry 478

The Potting Shed Pub
Wiltshire
entry 754

Authentic pub award

We have visited scores of simple, authentic, unadulterated pubs and they are a diminishing breed. Those that we found particularly special are:

White Hart Inn
Cumbria
entry 141

The Square & Compass
Dorset
entry 226

The Royal Oak
Hampshire
entry 301

Pubs with rooms award

With an increasing number of pubs wishing to promote their rooms above the bar – or in the converted barn, coach-house or stables across the way – our inspectors have visited more bedrooms than ever for this edition. Our eclectic bunch of inns-with-rooms get full-page entries and include bedrooms that range from swish suites with plasma TVs to simple but good rooms overlooking the sea. Our winners are good 'all-rounders', too, serving excellent food, beers and wines.

Lord Poulett Arms	**The Crown at Woodbridge**	**The Black Horse**
Somerset	Suffolk	Yorkshire
entry 609	entry 655	entry 827

Community pub award

Within these pages you will find some great little locals run by enterprising, hard-working landlords who have succeeded in making their pub the hub of the community. Our shining examples are:

The Three Tuns	**The Hollist Arms**	**The Shoulder of Mutton**
Shropshire	Sussex	Yorkshire
entry 591	entry 687	entry 852

Shepherd Neame – local food from local people

Shepherd Neame is Britain's oldest brewer and our pubs are special places to relax, unwind and enjoy distinctive local food and ale in warm, comfortable surroundings.

We purchased our first pub in 1711 and have become the custodians of an impressive range of historic buildings in some of the most attractive places in the South East. Our chefs take real pride both in serving classic produce such as Romney Marsh lamb, Dover sole and Kentish apples and in working closely with the county's farmers and fishermen to serve the best seasonal, local produce from the Garden of England.

Many of our pubs and hotels are ideally placed to retreat to and sample that delicious regional food after days out at, say, Canterbury Cathedral, Leeds Castle, the White Cliffs of Dover and Sissinghurst Castle Garden.

more traditional feel to the boutique hotel and brasserie. The George's history can be traced back to 1300 and Queen Elizabeth I visited the inn in 1573. The hotel's Portuguese chef, Paulo Fernandez, came to The George via Harrods, Smith's of Covent Garden and the Green Park Hotel. Paulo delights guests with local dishes like Kentish rump of lamb with horseradish mash and Spitfire beer-battered cod with hand cut chips, alongside his personal favourites that include piri piri chicken and paella.

To mention some shining examples: built in 1760, the Royal Albion in Broadstairs sits on a clifftop with a multi-levelled Rivera-style terrace overlooking the sands of Viking Bay. We have spent £1 million on refurbishing it and installing 21st-century comforts such as the luxurious bathroom suites and opulent soft furnishings that now complement the building's historic character. On the ground floor, the stylish restaurant takes in terrific sea views while Ballard's coffee lounge, with its period illustrations and crystal chandeliers, transports guests back to a more gracious and elegant age. The Royal Albion was a favourite of Charles Dickens. He stayed regularly (one off his letters is on display) and each year the hotel takes part in a festival celebrating his associations with the town.

In the Weald market town of Cranbrook we have also refurbished the 14th-century George Hotel, introducing a

In the centre of the county, the 15th-century Woolpack Inn, in Chilham, has oak beams, an inglenook fireplace, and 14 en suite rooms, two with four-poster beds. The inn is a short walk from the Tudor market square and tea rooms and antique shops.

Visitors to the 17th-century Dog and Bear, in Lenham's medieval village square, can take it easy by an open fire in

the oak-beamed bar, after dining on seasonally inspired classic English dishes in the à la carte restaurant.

Back on the coast, flanking the shingle beach, the Royal at Deal, overlooking the sheltered anchorage of the Downs, was used by Lord Nelson and Lady Hamilton as the British fleet guarded against a Napoleonic invasion. The Marine, on Tankerton cliffs, is another with commanding sea views, and is a short walk from Whitstable with its art galleries and gift shops. Both pubs serve the freshest seasonal seafood, usually landed by local fishermen earlier in the day.

The garden of the New Flying Horse in Wye has a unique feature – a recreation of Chelsea Flower Show winner Julian

Dowle's *A Soldier's Dream of Blighty*. This 17th-century posting house, with its roaring log fire and oak beams, serves a wide range of seasonal specials and classic dishes that make the most of Kentish ingredients.

Echoes of Chaucer and Thomas Beckett resonate at the Millers Arms, in the shadow of Canterbury Cathedral, close to the city's great variety of independent shops, cobbled lanes and Tudor-beamed buildings.

Whichever Shepherd Neame pub you choose, you are sure to find a great welcome, comfortable rooms, fresh, seasonal, local food and distinctive Kentish ales such as Spitfire and Bishops Finger.

www.shepherdneame.co.uk/accommodation

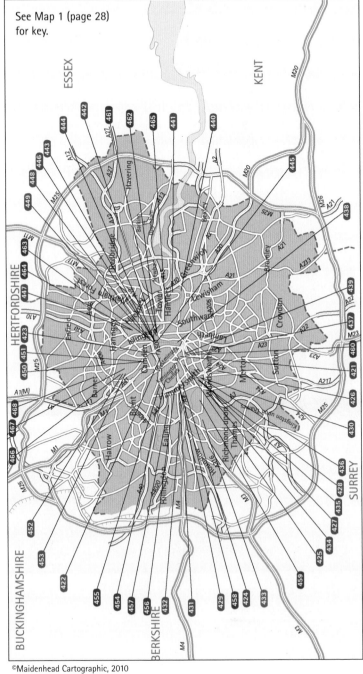

See Map 1 (page 28) for key.

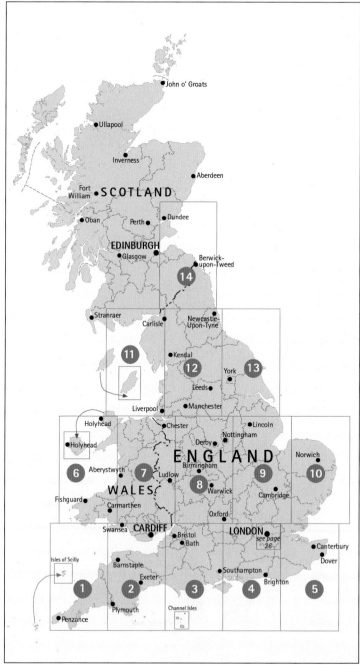

©Maidenhead Cartographic, 2010

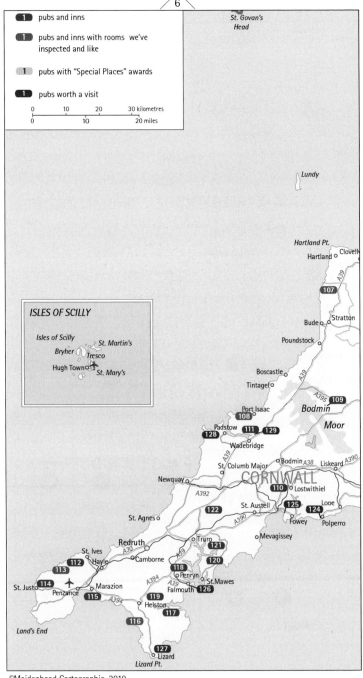

6

pubs and inns

pubs and inns with rooms we've inspected and like

pubs with "Special Places" awards

pubs worth a visit

| 0 | 10 | 20 | 30 kilometres |
| 0 | | 10 | 20 miles |

St. Govan's Head

Lundy

Hartland Pt.
Hartland o   Clovelly

A39

107

Bude o   o Stratton

Poundstock

ISLES OF SCILLY

Isles of Scilly   St. Martin's
Bryher   Tresco
Hugh Town o   St. Mary's

Boscastle o
Tintagel o

A395 109

Port Isaac   Bodmin
108
Padstow   111   129   Moor
128
Wadebridge

A39

St. Columb Major   o Bodmin A38 Liskeard A390

Newquay o   CORNWALL
A392   110 o Lostwithiel
St. Agnes o   122   St. Austell   125   Looe
A390   124
Fowey   Polperro
Redruth   o Truro   o Mevagissey
St. Ives   A30   121
112   Camborne   A39   120
113   Hayle   118
A394   o Penryn
St. Just o   114   Marazion   A39   St. Mawes
Penzance   115   A394   Falmouth 126
119
Helston
117
116

Land's End

127
o Lizard
Lizard Pt.

©Maidenhead Cartographic, 2010

Map 2 29

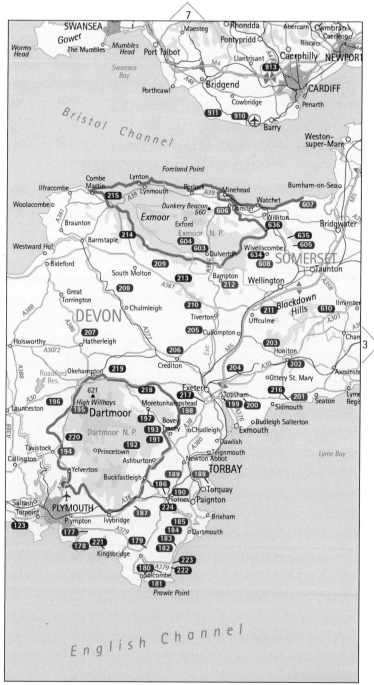

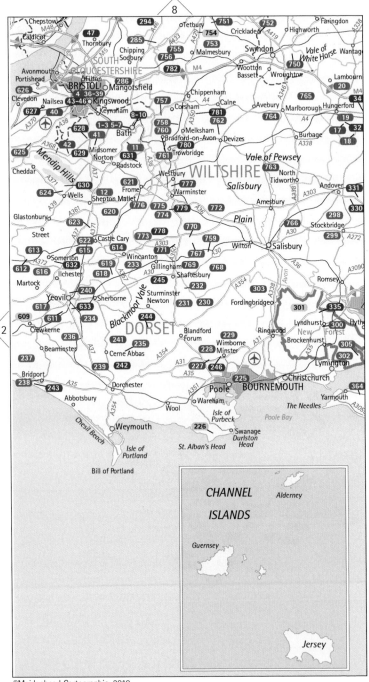

Map 4   31

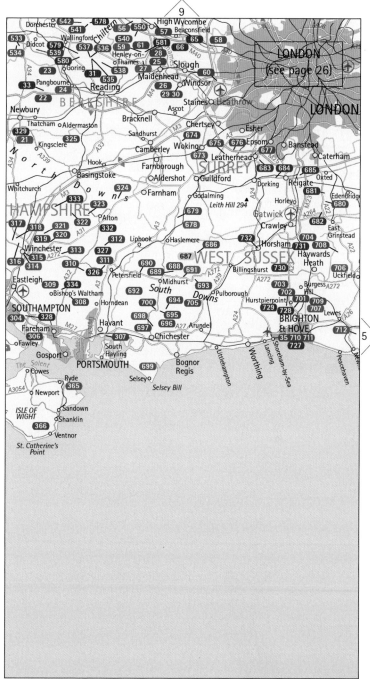

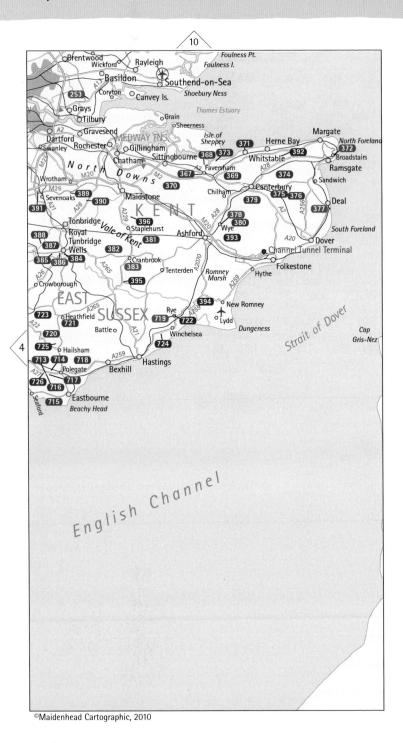

Map 6   33

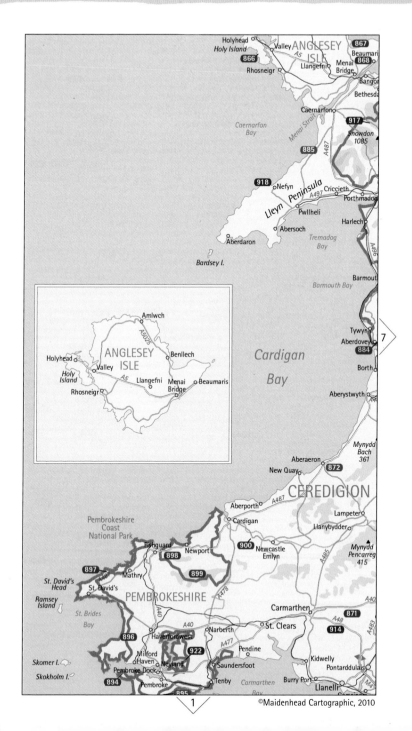

©Maidenhead Cartographic, 2010

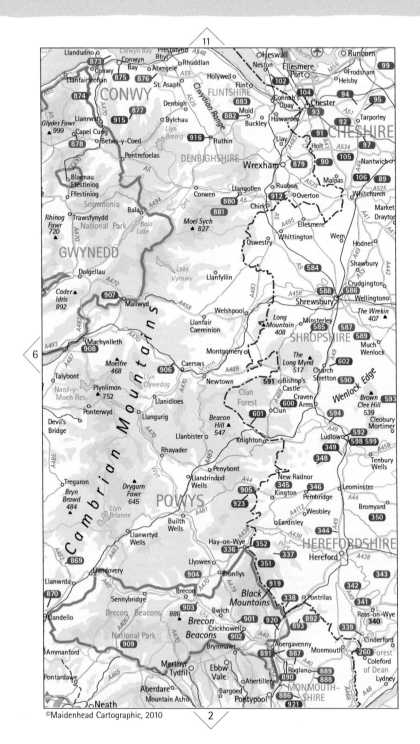

Map 8

35

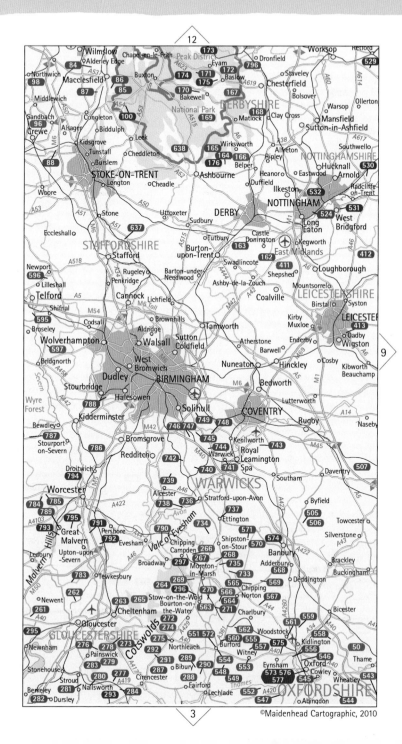

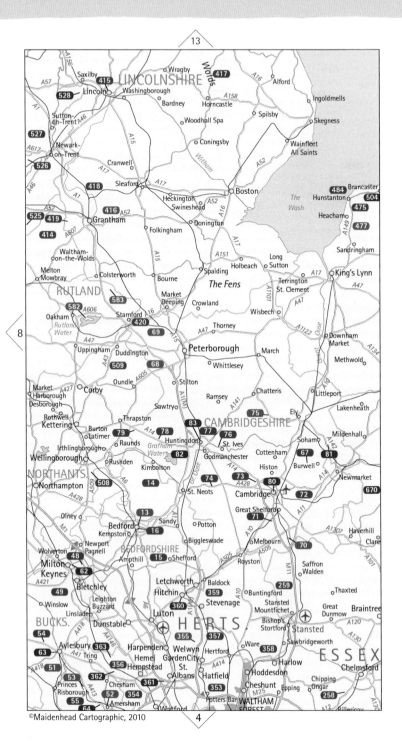

Map 10

37

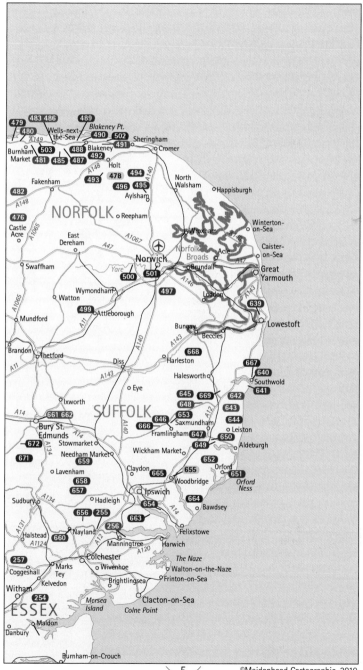

©Maidenhead Cartographic, 2010

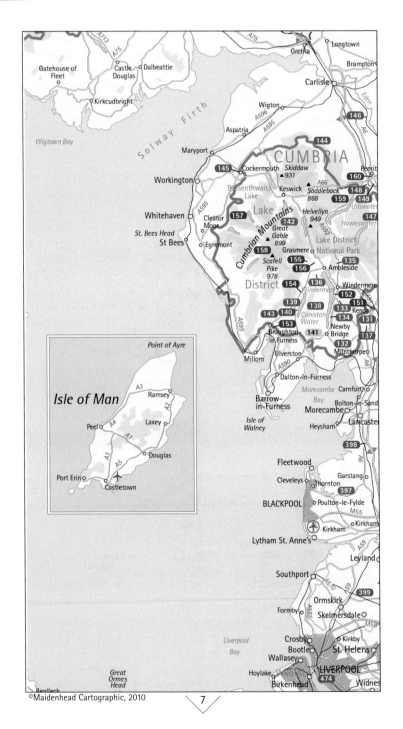

Map 12   39

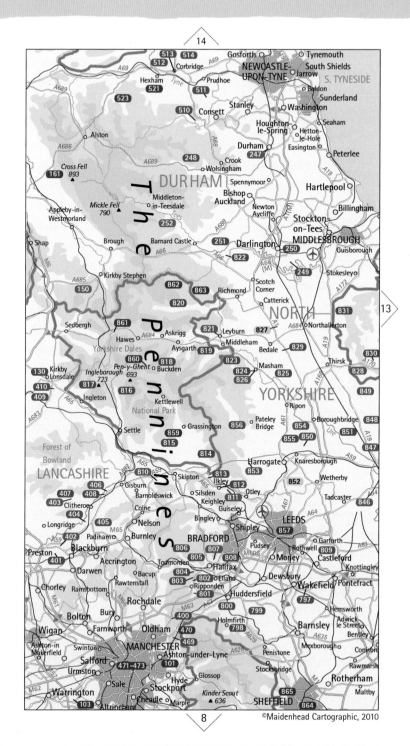

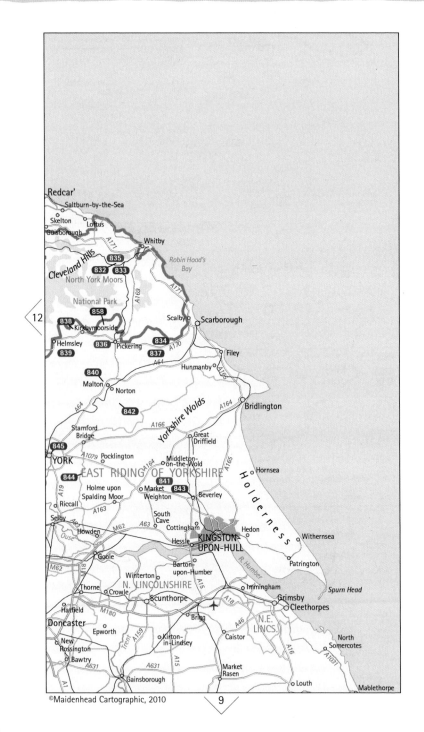

Map 14 41

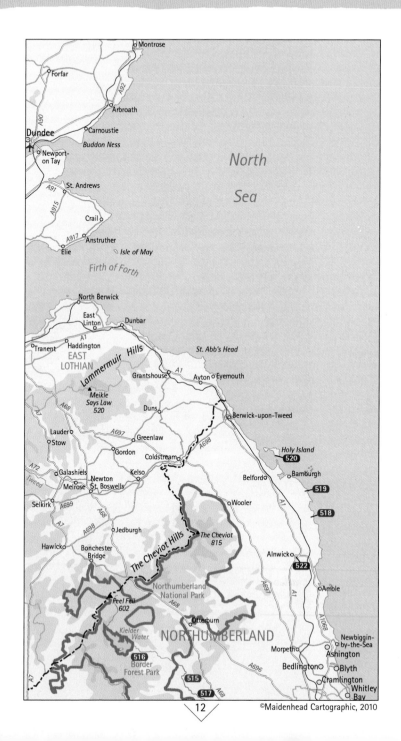

©Maidenhead Cartographic, 2010

England

The Garricks Head
Bath

The famous pub by the Theatre Royal, a refuge for actors and a theatre since 1720, has become a second success story for the proprietors of the King William. Enter a lovely lazy sofa'd bar, with a chic utilitarian dining room to the side. The drinking side of things is important still but the food is something special. Chef Charlie used to work at the Anchor & Hope in Waterloo so the style is robust English. Top produce and seasonality are paramount and the dishes pay a debt to Clerkenwell's celebrated St John's: in one critic's words, "a paragon of everything British eating is heading towards." Just try the snails with braised oxtail and mash, and the rib of beef with goose fat chips. The beers change all the time with the emphasis on small breweries and the cider comes from Julian Temperley at Burrow Hill. Great value.

Gascoyne Place
Bath

"Functional yet ornate" is how Marty Grant and Wayne Taylor hoped Gascoyne Place would be – and so it is. And, bang opposite the Theatre Royal, it's steeped in history. The old city wall intrudes on the lower floor, there's a Georgian hoist near the main staircase and an Edwardian match-board ceiling. This sympathetic restoration includes vivid green hand-glazed tiles over the chimney breast, a Victorian mahogany bar from an East End pub and 1930s opaline lights. There are five seating areas in all: a snug, a small public bar, a mezzanine area and two fine-dining rooms. Food is modern, British and based around produce sourced from local farms. Pluck a pint of Butcombe Bitter to accompany your Joe Baker Farm sirloin steak with roast garlic mash, or one of 90 delicious wines. A thoroughly contemporary space.

Meals	12pm-3pm; 5pm-10pm. Main courses £8.50-£15.
Closed	Open all day.
Directions	5-minute walk from Bath railway & bus stations, next to Bath Theatre Royal.

Meals	12pm-3pm (4pm Sun); 5.30pm-10pm (10.30pm Sat); bar menu available all day. Main courses £7.95-£17.50; bar meals up to £9.95. Sunday lunch £10.95.
Closed	Open all day.
Directions	5-minute walk from Bath railway & bus stations, next to Bath Theatre Royal.

Charlie & Amanda Digney
The Garricks Head,
8 St John's Place,
Bath BA1 1ET
Tel   +44 (0)1225 318368
Web   www.garricksheadpub.com

Entry 1 Map 3

Marty Grant & Wayne Taylor
Gascoyne Place,
1 Sawclose,
Bath BA1 1EY
Tel   +44 (0)1225 445854
Web   www.gascoyneplace.co.uk

Entry 2 Map 3

The Old Green Tree
Bath

Right in the centre, the cosy pub, whose staff are fanatical about ale (at least six guest beers chalked up on the board), hums with life even before midday. Deep in conversation, old regulars clutch pint jars to their chests as you squeeze through the narrow planked bar into a cabin-like room. Undecorated since the panelling was installed in 1928, the pub is part of our heritage and has no intention of changing – Tim and Nick refuse any form of modernisation, and it's all the better for it. In three little, low-ceilinged rooms, a mosaic of foreign coins are stuck up in frames behind the bar – along with artists' work. The menu includes hearty old English dishes and a daily chef's special; homemade chutneys and pâtés too. They have a devoted following and drink is not limited to beer: there are malts, wines and hot toddies.

The Marlborough Tavern
Bath

The old down-at-heel boozer, a pint's throw from the Royal Crescent, was rescued by Cussens and Sleath in 2006. Now it is one of Bath's best food pubs. An airy, high ceilinged room with a central bar, the 18th-century tavern ticks all the gastropub boxes with its sage green paintwork, velvety wallpapers, standard lamps, sofas and village hall furniture. Wines include a fashionable palette of rosés, perfect for sipping in the garden. As for the food, it is driven by the produce, so seasonal and local are the buzzwords and producers and provenance are listed. There's Chew Valley smoked salmon, Neston Park Farm beef, local woodland pork and fruit and veg from seventh generation Eades, just up the road. Fish arrives daily from Cornwall and Devon, Sunday lunches are the stuff of legend and booking is pretty much essential.

Meals	12pm-3pm.
	Main courses £5.50-£10.
Closed	Open all day.
Directions	Green Street, off Milsom Street. Bath city centre.

Meals	12.30pm-2.30pm; 6pm-9.30pm.
	12.30pm-9.30pm Sat (9pm Sun).
	Main courses £8.50-£15.95.
Closed	Open all day.
Directions	A 2-minute walk from the Royal Crescent, the pub is on the corner of Marlborough Buildings opposite the Approach Golf Course.

	T Bethune & F N Luke
	The Old Green Tree,
	12 Green Street,
	Bath BA1 2JZ
Tel	+44 (0)1225 448259

Entry 3 Map 3

	Joe Cussens
	The Marlborough Tavern,
	35 Marlborough Buildings,
	Bath BA1 2LY
Tel	+44 (0)1225 423731
Web	www.marlborough-tavern.com

Entry 4 Map 3

The Star Inn
Bath

Listed on the National Inventory of Historic Pubs, a serious boozer and museum piece wrapped into one. A pub since 1760, it is partitioned off into three numbered rooms, each with rough planks, panelled walls, ancient settles and opaque toplights. A real coal fire pumps out the heat and you can still get a free pinch of snuff from the tins on the ledge above the wall... you can almost imagine the Victorian regulars pressing their lips to their pewter tankards. To this day Bass is served in four-pint jugs which you can take away for a small deposit. There are no meals, just the odd bap from a basket on the bar. What counts is the beer, so much so that Alan has started his own brewery and has since scaled the heady heights of the real ale world to win several awards for his Bellringer tipple. A jewel.

Meals	Fresh rolls served all day. Rolls from £2.
Closed	2.30pm-5.30pm. Open all day Sat & Sun.
Directions	On A4 (London Road) in Bath.

Alan Morgan
The Star Inn,
23 Vineyards,
Bath BA1 5NA
Tel +44 (0)1225 425072
Web www.star-inn-bath.co.uk

Entry 5 Map 3

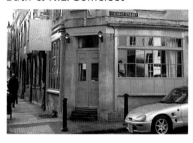

King William
Bath

Named after the king who was on the throne when the Duke of Wellington passed his Beer Act (in a bid to wean people off nasty foreign spirits, anyone with two guineas could open a beerhouse), the little corner pub known as the King Billy has a chilled café/bar feel and a terrific range of wines and beers. They get into gastropub gear at lunch; the food's so popular Charlie and Amanda have created extra space in the intimate dining room upstairs (booking advised). Ingredients are locally sourced and largely organic, dishes are simple, rustic and modern – terrine of pigeon and rabbit, wild bass with roast fennel, local unpasteurised cheeses. Bare boards, village hall furniture, gold flock velvet curtains and background reggae and soul pull in an art-funky, Walcot Street crowd. And the staff couldn't be nicer.

Meals	12pm-3pm (Tues-Sun); 6pm-10pm (Mon-Sun). 2-3 courses £24-£29; bar meals £6-£18.
Closed	3pm-5pm. Open all day Sat & Sun.
Directions	Short walk from Walcot Street, off London Road.

Charlie & Amanda Digney
King William,
36 Thomas Street,
Bath BA1 5NN
Tel +44 (0)1225 428096
Web www.kingwilliampub.com

Entry 6 Map 3

Bath & N.E. Somerset

White Hart
Bath

A short walk from Bath Spa Station, in sought-after Widcombe, this large detached pub has a pleasant courtyard garden and a backpackers' hostel above. Despite its reputation as one of the best places to eat in town, it still feels pubby, with a jolly bar, a pleasingly plain dining room and a mixed bag of tables. On rugby day it heaves, as pints of Butcombe Bitter and RCH Pitchfork are downed. Chef Rupert Pitt has worked in some of Bath's best restaurants and his menu is short and to the point, with five starters and six mains. The food, well-priced and following the seasons, is delicious. Try the marinated feta with Mediterranean bulgur wheat salad, the baked sea bass with lemon and saffron butter, and the tender slow-braised pork belly with mashed potato and cider gravy.

Bath & N.E. Somerset
Worth a visit

8   The Salamander 3 John St, Bath BA1 2JL
    +44 (0)1225 428889
    A fine Bath Ales pub without the spittle. The main bar, like a Victorian apothecary, is stacked with bottles on a Welsh dresser and hand pumps gleam under glass fluted lights. Head upstairs for traditional dishes from an open kitchen.

9   The Raven 7 Queen Street, Bath BA1 1HE
    +44 (0)1225 425045
    Ordinary looking Bath pub in wonderful cobbled street that seduces you with its cosy atmosphere, great beer (try the Raven Ale) and excellent pies. Much-loved by the locals.

10 The Hop Pole 7 Albion Buildings,
    Upper Bristol Road, Bath BA1 3AR
    +44 (0)1225 446327
    Gently sophisticated boozer with a polished feel, a verdant summer courtyard and a modern British menu. An easy pedal from the Bristol-Bath cycle path for tip-top Bath ales.

Meals	12pm-2pm; 6pm-10pm. No food Sun eve. Main courses £10-£13.
Closed	Open all day. Closed Sun eves in winter.
Directions	Where A3604 becomes Claverton Street, pub is on right, at Widcombe Hill & Prior Park Road junction.

Jo Parson
White Hart,
Widcombe Hill,
Bath BA2 6AA

Tel	+44 (0)1225 338053
Web	www.whitehartbath.co.uk

Entry 7 Map 3

The Wheatsheaf Combe Hay

Combe Hay

A hidden valley, a pretty village, a gorgeous inn, three fabulous rooms. Views from the lush terraced garden – replete with veg plot and hens – stretch across to a fine ridge of trees, the manor house and church jutting out of the woods below. In summer there are barbecues, lazy lunches, horses clopping by. This is a 15th-century farmhouse with later additions – it's all but impossible to notice the join – whose exterior comes clad in Farrow & Ball creams. Outside there are Indian benches with seagrass cushions; inside, big sofas in front of the fire. Gastropub interiors have neutral colours to soak up the light, sandblasted beams, halogen spotlights and Lloyd Loom wicker dining chairs. Steps outside lead down to three deeply comfy bedrooms in a stone building. All come in contemporary rustic style with light wood furniture, flat-screen TVs, Egyptian cotton and deluge showers; there are White Company oils and bathrobes too. Climb back up for seriously good food, perhaps pork belly with quince purée, skate wing with beetroot, parmesan and capers, and Valrhona chocolate fondant. Bath is a hike across the fields.

Rooms	3 doubles. £105–£140.
Meals	12pm–2pm; 6pm–9.30pm (10pm Fri & Sat). Main courses £16.50–£26; set menu £14.95 (2 courses) & £18.95 (3 courses).
Closed	3pm–6pm, Sun eve & Mon all day.
Directions	South from Bath on A367, then left in Combe Down onto B3110. Straight ahead for 1.5 miles, then right for Combe Hay.

Ian & Adele Barton
The Wheatsheaf Combe Hay,
Combe Hay,
Bath BA2 7EG

Tel   +44 (0)1225 833504
Web   www.wheatsheafcombehay.com

Entry 11 Map 3

Oakhill Inn
Oakhill

The Digneys, owners of the inimitable King William and the Garrick's Head in Bath, have given the old village inn a sympathetic brush up and a fresh look since they took over in 2007. Expect rugs on bare boards, bold red and green walls lined with local artwork, old sofas and rustic tables, and a cosy corner by the blazing log fire. Now families and food and ale-lovers flock in for the raft of local ales from the likes of Newmans and Stonehenge breweries, and the well-priced menu of robust British dishes. Tuck into rump steak and horseradish sandwiches; beef and ale stew with curly kale; pot-roast partridge; beer-battered pollock and triple-cooked chips; and the most comforting of comfort puddings – warm treacle tart and winter nut crumble with custard... served seasonally, of course. The eclectic, very individual feel extends upstairs – the purple-painted master bedroom sports a big brass bed, crisp linen, bold lamps, a feature fireplace, quirky paintings and old furnishings, and a wood-floored bathroom with claw-foot bath, candles, thick towels, and a walk-in shower. A cracking inn.

Rooms	5: 4 doubles, 1 twin/double (2 rooms connect to form suite). £70–£100. Suite £150. Extra bed £15.
Meals	12pm-3pm; 6pm-9pm. No food Sun eve. Main courses £10–£15.
Closed	3pm-5pm. Open all day Sat & Sun.
Directions	Just off A367 between Bath & Shepton Mallet, 3 miles north of Shepton Mallet.

Charlie & Amanda Digney
Oakhill Inn,
Fosse Road, Oakhill,
Radstock BA3 5HU
Tel   +44 (0)1749 840442
Web   www.theoakhillinn.com

The Embankment
Bedford

Peach Pubs snapped up this faded town-centre hotel in 2008; now it's their flagship inn. Built in 1891, the strikingly timbered neo-Tudor building overlooks the leafy embankment of the river Great Ouse. The style of its late Victorian heyday has been recreated inside, so expect period fireplaces, big mirrors, wooden floors, leather wall benches and a semi-retro feel from the airy front bar to the rear dining rooms. Now a vibrant inn – no hotel or residents' lounge here! – with a buzzy, laid-back bar and a modern all-day menu, the Embankment draws a lively young crowd, here to drink, eat and make merry; business types like it too. Call in for breakfast, order delicious coffee and cake, graze from tempting deli-boards; or chomp your way through the daily roast – or the salmon fishcakes with tomato and basil sauce – from the seasonal menu. Retro styling extends to the bedrooms, with their bold wall coverings and their leather chairs, and their huge comfy beds topped with crisp linen. Room 101 has river views and a grand bathroom with both tub and walk-in shower. The riverside walks are gorgeous.

Rooms	20: 5 doubles, 15 twins/doubles. £79–£120.
Meals	Food served all day. À la carte 12pm-3pm; 6pm-10pm Mon-Fri & all day Sat & Sun. Main courses £9.80-£16.50; deli boards £9.50.
Closed	Open all day.
Directions	On the Embankment by the River Great Ouse, east of the town centre.

Kelly McKenzie
The Embankment,
6 The Embankment,
Bedford MK40 3PD
Tel   +44 (0)1234 261332
Web   www.embankmentbedford.co.uk

Entry 13 Map

Bedfordshire

The Plough at Bolnhurst
Bolnhurst

A tavern has stood here since the 1400s, but nearly 20 years ago the last one burnt down; tradition lives on in this happy reincarnation. The Plough holds on to its heritage, with reclaimed blackened beams and cast-iron chimney. Overlaying this is a modern touch – stripped boards, hewn-wood bar and crisp white walls. Food is equally sophisticated; chef-patron Martin Lee's grounding was with Raymond Blanc. Crab risotto with chilli and parsley, Denham Estate venison, caramel soufflé with Armagnac ice cream... "gutsy flavours but restrained formulation" are the order of the day, and, going by the heaving crowd of happy foodies, they've got it right. Come to dine rather than pop in for a pint – the wines are impressive, though the well-kept Village Bike bitter also slips down a treat. A bright light in the desert that is Bedfordshire.

Bedfordshire

The Black Horse
Ireland

In Ireland – in Bedfordshire – is a wonderfully welcoming gastropub. Stone dogs guard the front door, bollards linked by ships' rope divide terrace from car park and the door opens to a sweep of open-plan, split-level space. There's floor to ceiling glass at one end – looking out to palms, sculptures and ferns – and more formal dining areas at the other. The bar top is solid slate, smart banquettes edge tables both sides of a wood-burning stove but, in spite of the modernity, traditional features remain: fireplaces in excellent order and refurbished beams from which downlighters shine. More geared towards dining than casual drinking, the food ranges from chicken on the griddle to pollock with a tiger prawn brochette, the puddings are superlative and Michael Winner, we are told, loved his Sunday roast.

Meals	12pm-2pm (2.30pm Sun); 6.30pm-9.30pm (6pm-10pm Fri & Sat). Main courses £13.50-£25; bar meals £7.50-£12.95; Sunday roast from £14.95.
Closed	3pm-6.30pm, Sun eves & all day Mon.
Directions	On B660 north of Bedford; pub in village centre.

Meals	12pm-2.30pm; 6.30pm-9.30pm (12pm-5pm Sun). Main courses £8.95-£15.95.
Closed	3pm-6pm & Sun eve.
Directions	Pub signed from the A600 Shefford to Bedford road.

	Martin & Jayne Lee & Michael Moscrop The Plough, Kimbolton Road, Bolnhurst, Bedford MK44 2EX
Tel	+44 (0)1234 376274
Web	www.bolnhurst.com

Entry 14 Map 9

	Darren Campbell The Black Horse, Ireland, Shefford SG17 5QL
Tel	+44 (0)1462 811398
Web	www.blackhorseireland.com

Entry 15 Map 9

Bedfordshire

Hare & Hounds
Old Warden

The food may be fabulous but the Hare & Hounds is first and foremost a pub. There's always a welcome and a buzz, you can drop by for a glass of wine and the aromas from the kitchen mingle irresistibly with the woodsmoke from the fire. The beer's good too (Eagle Bitter, Young's Bitter). On a Sunday in summer, when they fly a Shuttleworth Spitfire from the grass airstrip next door, you could find the ice rattling in your G&T; otherwise the garden is blissfully quiet. No barbecues, just a few drinkers' tables and a smokers' gazebo. Inside are low timbered ceilings and four distinct areas: a funky snug with sofas, two rooms for eating, and a family room beyond. Game and poultry come from the village estate, veg and herbs from the allotment, cheeses are proudly British and the puddings are a treat.

Meals	12pm-2pm (3pm Sun); 6.30pm-9pm. No food Sun eve. Main courses £10-£18.
Closed	3pm-6pm & Mon (except bank hols).
Directions	Off B658 & A6001 3 miles west of Biggleswade; next to village hall.

Jane & Jago Hurt
Hare & Hounds,
The Village, Old Warden,
Biggleswade SG18 9HQ
Tel +44 (0)1767 627225
Web www.hareandhoundsoldwarden.co.uk

Entry 16 Map 9

Berkshire

The Dundas Arms
Kintbury

The Dalzell-Pipers have run this delightfully old-fashioned inn for over 40 years. At the junction of river and canal, dabbling ducks entertain diners while narrowboats glide by and summer crowds fill the waterside patio. People come mainly for the food. The carpeted small bar has a traditional feel; the restaurant to the side is comfortable with polished wooden tables; both are a stage for some wholesome country cooking. Using fresh ingredients, notably estate game and prime meats from local dealers, David's lunchtime blackboard menus support old favourites like Cumberland sausages with mash, onion gravy and peas, steak and ale pie, and bread and butter pudding. There's a decent wine list and Ramsbury Brewery, Adnams and West Berkshire's beers. The little station stands right opposite: in an hour you could be back in London.

Meals	12pm-2pm; 7pm-9pm. No food Mon eve or Sun all day. Main courses £12-£18; bar meals £4.95-£13.50.
Closed	2.30pm-6pm & Sun eve.
Directions	1 mile off A4 between Newbury & Hungerford.

David Dalzell-Piper
The Dundas Arms,
53 Station Road,
Kintbury RG17 9UT
Tel +44 (0)1488 658263
Web www.dundasarms.co.uk

Entry 17 Map 3

Crown & Garter
Inkpen

An unreformed country local hidden down lanes beneath Inkpen Beacon, run with passion by Gill Hern. Gamekeepers and village footballers drop by for a pint of Good Old Boy, Mr Chubbs and Timothy Taylor's Landlord, cockerels crow in the fields and in summer life spills onto a stone terrace and into a pretty garden. Inside are wooden floors, thick red curtains and a huge settle by the fire. There's a small restaurant serving steak and kidney pudding, lamb shank with mint gravy and bubble-and-squeak, and fish and chips with mushy peas; tuck in here, or in the bar, or, on sunny days, on the patio. James II is said to have visited, which might account for the wooden throne by the front door. Bedrooms, in a single-storey annexe built around a garden with a pergola and fish pond, are spacious and airy and have painted floorboards, blended voiles and brass or wooden beds. Two rooms interconnect for families, piping hot water flows in super little bathrooms. You can walk from the front door, try your luck at Newbury Races or watch the early morning gallops at Lambourn.

Rooms	8: 6 doubles, 2 twins. £99. Singles £69.50.
Meals	12pm-2pm (2.30pm Sun); 6.30pm-9.30pm. No food Sun eve. Main courses £9.95-£19.95; bar meals from £7; Sunday roast from £10.95.
Closed	3pm-5.30pm (5pm-7pm Sun), Mon & Tues lunch.
Directions	A4 for Hungerford. After 2 miles, left for Kintbury & Inkpen. In Kintbury, left at corner shop onto Inkpen Road; inn on left after 2 miles.

Gill Hern
Crown & Garter,
Great Common, Inkpen,
Hungerford RG17 9QR
Tel   +44 (0)1488 668325
Web   www.crownandgarter.com

Entry 18 Map 3

Pheasant Inn
Shefford Woodlands

The Pheasant has been spruced up, the once peeling façade has been given a lick of paint, a bedroom wing has been tacked on the back, and still it's a cracking old pub with a reputation among the horse-racing set – and old-school landlord Johnny Ferrand is still at the helm. The much-loved shabby gentility (rustic tiling, blood red walls, big mirrors, pine tables, heavy drapes) has been retained and the TV remains tuned into the racing – often drowned out by the hubbub of jockeys and trainers. Loddon Hoppit and Wadworth 6X help charge the atmosphere, backed up by several wines by the glass. As for food, good ingredients are used in comfortingly familiar ways. A short menu delivers simple but careful home cooking: game terrine with homemade piccalilli and excellent meaty burgers; local partridge with tomato and pancetta jus, halibut with pea and mint risotto. Contemporary rooms have modern furnishings and wall coverings, colourful throws and cushions and big comfortable beds; five have balcony doors to views across fields. It's the best M4 pit-stop for miles.

Rooms	11 twins/doubles. £95-£120. Singles £85-£110.
Meals	12pm-2.30pm; 7pm-9.30pm (9pm Sun). Main courses £11.50-£19.50; baguettes (lunch only) £7.50.
Closed	Open all day.
Directions	400 yards from M4 exit 14; A338 towards Wantage; 1st left onto B4000 for Lambourn; inn on right.

John Ferrand
Pheasant Inn,
Ermin Street, Shefford
Woodlands, Hungerford RG17 7AA

| Tel | +44 (0)1488 648284 |
| Web | www.thepheasant-inn.co.uk |

Entry 19 Map 3

The Queen's Arms Hotel

East Garston

Deep in horse training country, so expect to rub shoulders with owners, trainers, jockeys and locals. The main bar is steeped in character and warmth, the wood-burner blasts out the heat, fat church candles flicker and there are lots of paintings and prints. Plonk yourself on a leather chair and consider the menu while sipping something nurturing from Willy Mason's witty wine list – or a real ale. Bar snacks are not tiny – ploughman's, steak sandwich, fresh fish and hand-cut chips; hungrier folk can eat royally in the deep-red restaurant. Try oysters with sweet and sour red onions, local pheasant with a jug of gravy, and rice pudding with quince. There are bridleways and footpaths to woods, water meadows and rolling farmland; you can stride the Ridgeway too. Return to super smart and themed bedrooms with well-chosen antiques and artwork, checked rugs and throws, soft carpets, feathery beds and a mini-bar if you can't be bothered to go downstairs. Spoil yourself in toasty warm bathrooms with slate tiled floors, walk-in showers, thick towels and an easy chair for those who like to get cosy.

Rooms	8 doubles. £95–£150.
Meals	12pm–2pm (4pm Sun); 7pm–9pm. Reduced menu Sun eve. Main courses £11.90–£18.50; bar snacks from £5.
Closed	Open all day.
Directions	Inn signed off A338 Wantage to Hungerford road at Great Shefford.

Lucy Townsend
The Queen's Arms Hotel,
Newbury Road,
East Garston,
Newbury RG17 7ET
Tel   +44 (0)1488 648757
Web   www.queensarmshotel.co.uk

Carnarvon Arms
Burghclere

Fears that the beloved old pub would become another nondescript restaurant have proved to be unfounded. There are still ales on tap, wines by the glass, a bar menu listing bangers and mash (locally sourced, naturally) and a friendly welcome. The thoroughly modern renovation of this once rambling coaching inn near the gates of Highclere Castle is a spruce, stylish and upbeat affair. Expect fresh vibrant colours, bare boards and deep sofas in lounges, and a swishly traditional bar. In the light, high-vaulted dining room are painted beams, rug-strewn boards, a feature fireplace and Egyptian motifs inspired by collections at the Castle. The menu covers dishes such as braised shoulder of venison with a beetroot and goat's cheese gratin, and grilled fillet of sea bream with sun-blushed tomato and a basil cream sauce. Bedrooms are equally smart, dressed in fashionably neutral fabrics and tones, accompanied by plasma screens, free WiFi connections and top-quality toiletries in super bathrooms.

Rooms	23 twins/doubles. From £89.
Meals	12pm-2.30pm (6pm Sun); 6pm-9.30pm (8.30pm Sun). Main courses £8.95-£19.95; bar meals £4.50-£16.95; set lunch £12.95 & £14.95; Sunday lunch £17.95-£22.95.
Closed	Open all day.
Directions	Leave A34 at Tothill Services south of Newbury; signs to Highclere Castle; pub on right.

Carnarvon Arms,
Winchester Road,
Whitway, Burghclere,
Newbury RG20 9LE

Tel	+44 (0)1635 278222
Web	www.carnarvonarms.com

Entry 21 Map 4

Berkshire

The Pot Kiln
Frilsham

TV chef Mike Robinson drank his very first pint in this remote and determinedly old-fashioned ale house – and jumped at the chance to buy it. A sprucing up of the scrubbed pine tables has not altered the character a jot, and you still find thirsty agricultural workers crowding the tiny, basic bar (bare tables, dartboard) for foaming pints of Brick Kiln Bitter and a beef and roe deer burger. Perfectly lovely in summer – the front garden looks onto fields – it's also a treat in winter, when log fires and a menu strong on game come into their own. In the restaurant it's "European country cooking": fallow deer (most likely shot by Mike) with peppercorn sauce; roast partridge with braised lentils and cider sauce; passionfruit soufflé. The wine list is serious and affordable and the service is all it should be.

Berkshire

The Bell Inn
Aldworth

The Bell has the style of village pubs long gone and has been in the Macaulay family for over 250 years. Plain benches, venerable dark-wood panelling, settles and an outside gents: it's an unspoilt place that visitors love. There's an old wood-burning stove in one room, a more impressive hearth in the public bar, and early evening drinkers cluster around the unique glass hatched bar. Fifty years ago the regulars were agricultural workers; today piped music and mobile phones are fervently opposed. The food fits the image and they keep it simple: choose from hearty warm rolls filled with thick slices of home-baked ham, ox tongue or good old cheddar, treacle sponge and winter soups of the day. Drink prices are another draw; the ales come from the local Arkell's and West Berkshire breweries. There's also a great big garden.

Meals	12pm-2.30pm (2.45pm Sun); 7pm-9pm. Main courses £12.50-£16; bar meals £3.95-£10; set lunch £15 & £20.
Closed	3pm-6pm. Open all day Sat & Sun.
Directions	In Yattendon, pick up sign for Frilsham & The Pot Kiln on main road through village; over motorway, continue for 0.5 miles.

Meals	11am-2.45pm (from 12pm Sun); 6pm-9.30pm (7pm-9pm Sun). Bar meals £2.80-£6.50.
Closed	3pm-6pm (7pm Sun) & Mon (except bank hols).
Directions	Off B4009, 3 miles west of Streatley.

	Mike & Katie Robinson The Pot Kiln, Frilsham, Thatcham RG18 0XX
Tel	+44 (0)1635 201366
Web	www.potkiln.org

	H E Macaulay The Bell Inn, Aldworth, Reading RG8 9SE
Tel	+44 (0)1635 578272

Entry 22 Map 4

Entry 23 Map 4

The Elephant at Pangbourne
Pangbourne

Elephants everywhere – all benign, including those in the Ba-bar. This is a super hotel on the edge of town, renovated in unremitting style, with huge sofas in front of the fire, a tongue-and-groove bar for Sunday brunch, a cocktail lounge where candles flicker and a deeply elegant restaurant. It's a big hit with the locals, with much to draw them in: a supper club on Thursday nights (delicious food and a glass of wine for a song), a cinema club on Sunday afternoons (a classic movie and popcorn for a fiver). Eclectic bedrooms come fully loaded and spin you round the world in style: an Indian four-poster in Viceroy; collage wallpaper in Charlestown; colonial chic in Rangoon. Beds are dressed in crisp cotton, there are custom-made soaps and bubblebaths, perhaps leather sofas, regal colours and rugs on stripped floors; bathrooms are mostly in charcoal grey. Back downstairs eat informally in the bar (mussels, steak frites, Elephant burger) or in the restaurant for something fancier, perhaps pea and ham soup, saddle of venison, plum and almond tart.

Rooms	22: 18 doubles, 2 twins, 2 singles. £140-£160. Singles from £100.
Meals	12pm-3pm; 7pm-9pm; bar meals 6pm-10pm. All day Sat & Sun. Main courses £8.50-£13.50 (bar); £11-£20 (restaurant).
Closed	Open all day.
Directions	M4 junc. 12, A4 south; then A340 north. In village on left at r'bout.

Annica Eskelius
The Elephant at Pangbourne,
Church Road, Pangbourne,
Reading RG8 7AR

Tel	+44 (0)1189 842244
Web	www.elephanthotel.co.uk

Entry 24 Map 4

Hind's Head
Bray

When the Tudor tavern across the road from Heston Blumenthal's legendary Fat Duck came on the market, Heston snapped it up. Now the old Hind's Head is the poshest of village pubs (polished panelling, wing-back armchairs, open fires) with one striking difference: terrific food. Expect a short slate of British classics... pea and ham soup, potted shrimps with watercress salad, wild boar and apple sausages, the trademark thrice-cooked chips, and revivals of historic puds (Quaking Pudding, Eton Mess). Clive Dixon heads the kitchen and never loses the focus: to maximise the taste of the finest materials. Side dishes are extra so it ain't cheap; bar food includes Scotch quail eggs, coffee comes with chocs. Book if you want a table in the restaurant, or a private room, suitable for parties.

The Royal Oak
White Waltham

Modest at first glance, it has star quality inside. Nick Parkinson (son of Michael) may have given this small inn a contemporary and stylish lift, but he has cleverly managed to keep much of the traditional character. There are scrubbed wooden floors and stripped beams, timbers and panelling, the occasional music night. The bar is cosy and inviting, with solid wooden furniture, an open fire and a couple of armchairs. The dining room's food, beautifully cooked by Dominic Chapman, is modern and classy, with a good choice of wines. Tuck into pickled South Devon mackerel with beetroot and watercress, peppered haunch of venison and creamy spinach, Yorkshire rhubarb trifle. And you can get a lovely pint of London Pride. The Royal Oak is friendly and well-run, opening its door to drinkers and diners with equal enthusiasm.

Meals	12pm-2.30pm (4pm Sun); 6.30pm-9.30pm. No food Sun eve. Main courses £12.95-£19.50; bar meals £1.50-£7.50
Closed	Open all day.
Directions	On B3028 in Bray.

Meals	12pm-2.30pm (3.30pm Sun); 6.30pm-9.30pm (10pm Fri & Sat). Main courses £12.50-£24.
Closed	3pm-6pm & Sun eve.
Directions	On B3024 west of Paley Street, between A330 south of Maidenhead & Twyford.

Heston Blumenthal
Hind's Head,
High Street, Bray,
Maidenhead SL6 2AB
Tel   +44 (0)1628 626151
Web   www.thehindsheadhotel.com

Nick Parkinson
The Royal Oak,
Littlefield Green, White Waltham,
Maidenhead SL6 3JN
Tel   +44 (0)1628 620541
Web   www.theroyaloakpaleystreet.com

Entry 25 Map 4

Entry 26 Map 4

The Olde Bell
Hurley

The ancient timber-framed inn first opened its doors in 1135 as a guest house for visitors to the priory down the road. Rescued from chain-hotel ownership, serenely restored by Dhillon Hotels, it marries history with simplicity and charm. Step back centuries in the delightful bar, to rugs on worn terracotta tiles, limewashed beams, board games and crackling fires. In the rustic-chic dining rooms are fur rugs on Ercol chairs, Welsh blankets on old settles, fresh flowers in pewter pots and a modish antler chandelier; thick blackened beams and inglenooks, too. Full-flavoured British food, washed down with local Marlow ales, draws on local produce and the inn's kitchen garden. Try wild mushroom soup, baked duck leg, grilled lemon sole with leeks and mussels, sticky toffee pudding. Rooms in the main inn have a cool, rustic feel: wonky walls, sloping floors, huge beds, natural materials and quirky-elegant touches like red Roberts radios and rocking chairs. The spacious Malthouse suites have roll top baths, and there are new rooms by the Tithe Barn still to come. Close to the Thames Path, a class act.

Rooms	47: 40 doubles, 7 suites. £115–£150. Suites £200.
Meals	12.30pm–3pm (4pm Sun); 6.30pm–10pm (9pm Sun); bar meals all day. Main courses £12–£20; bar meals £2–£8.80.
Closed	Open all day.
Directions	From Maidenhead A4 dir. Reading. At Thicket r'bout merge onto A404 then A4130. Turn onto Hurley High St; Olde Bell is half mile on right.

Neil Irvine
The Olde Bell,
High Street, Hurley,
Maidenhead SL6 5LX
Tel   +44 (0)1628 825881
Web   www.coachinginn.co.uk

Entry 27 Map 4

Berkshire

The White Oak
Cookham

Henry and Katherine Cripps have snapped up the old Spencers Restaurant by the common – in lovely, upmarket Cookham. Transformed in just 12 weeks, the White Oak (sibling to the Greene Oak near Windsor) immediately found favour with the local foodies. Wooden floors, thick oak beams, soft heritage colours, plush cushioned banquettes, bold artwork, big mirrors and cool piped jazz set a swish but relaxed scene for plates of duck leg confit with roasted root vegetables and jus; braised blade of beef with roast garlic and pearl barley risotto; and pan-fried cod with tiger prawns and lemon and herb gnocchi. Chocolate brownie and ice cream, impeccable wines and friendly service complete the pleasing picture. Enjoy coffee in a leather wing chair by a crackling fire, then walk it all off with a Thames path stroll.

Meals	12pm-2.30pm (3.30pm Sun); 6.30pm-9.30pm. Main courses £12-£22.
Closed	Sun eves.
Directions	West side of Cookham Common and village on B4447 towards Maidenhead.

Henry & Katherine Cripps
The White Oak,
The Pound, Cookham,
Maidenhead SL6 9QE
Tel   +44 (0)1628 523043
Web   www.thewhiteoak.co.uk

Entry 28 Map 4

Berkshire

Two Brewers
Windsor

In the royal town, next to the Cambridge Gate and the famous Long Walk, small rooms meander around a tiny panelled bar and come quaintly decked with dark beams and wooden floors. One room with big shared tables reveals deep red walls and matching ceilings; the other two have more intimate seating areas. There are magazines to dip into and walls crammed with posters, press-cuttings, pictures and mirrors. On a blackboard above the fire, anecdotes commemorating each day are chalked up in preference to menu specials. Reserve a table and you won't go hungry: the compact menu follows a steady pub line, with daily specials, roasts on Sundays, and informal tapas on Friday and Saturday evenings. Beer, champagne, fine wines… and a sprinkling of pavement tables to tempt you after the rigours of the Big Tour. *No under-18s.*

Meals	12pm-2.30pm (5.30pm Sat; 4.30pm Sun); 6.30pm-10pm (tapas menu only Fri & Sat eve). Main courses £11-£19.50; tapas £4-£7.50; Sunday roast £12.50.
Closed	Open all day.
Directions	Off High Street, by Cambridge Gate entrance to the Long Walk.

Robert Gillespie
Two Brewers,
34 Park Street,
Windsor SL4 1LB
Tel   +44 (0)1753 855426

Entry 29 Map 4

Berkshire

Greene Oak
Windsor

With a background in London gastro-pubbery, Henry and Katherine Cripps could not fail at their first solo venture, a swishly renovated dining pub close to Windsor, Ascot and foodie Bray. Enter an interior of wood and slate floors and soft green hues, antique French light fittings and big country mirrors. Most people come to eat and the style is traditional with a contemporary twist, a mix of British classic dishes and fashionable modern. Lunch may include pheasant and pistachio terrine with chilli jam and Caesar salad, or homemade beefburger with tomato and chilli relish. In the evening, potted crab and brown shrimp, roast belly pork with wok-fried Asian greens, fillet steak with béarnaise – polished off by a Valrhona chocolate pot with mascarpone. Service, wines and beers are as elegant as the rest.

Meals	12pm-2.30pm (4pm Sun); 6.30pm-9.30pm. No food Sun eve. Main courses £11-£16.90.
Closed	Open all day.
Directions	On B3383 south of A308, 2 miles west of Windsor.

Henry & Katherine Cripps
Greene Oak,
Dedworth Road,
Windsor SL4 5UW

Tel	+44 (0)1753 864294
Web	www.thegreeneoak.co.uk

Entry 30 Map 4

Berkshire
Worth a visit

31 **New Inn** Chalkhouse Green Road, Kidmore End, Reading RG4 9AU
+44 (0)118 972 3115
More well-behaved gastro than quaint country pub, with bags of traditional character in the bar, and simple, robust British cooking – this feels a zillion miles away from the bustle of nearby Reading.

32 **The Swan Inn** Lower Green, Inkpen, Hungerford RG17 9DX +44 (0)1488 668326
Rambling 17th-century inn run by an organic beef farmer who supplies both kitchen and farm shop. Traditional dishes on blackboard menus, excellent ales from local Butts and Maggs breweries, and great walks.

33 **The Royal Oak Hotel** The Square, Yattendon RG18 0UG +44 (0)1635 201325
It comes brimful of surprises and a dash of class – everything you might expect of an English inn on the attractive square of a postcard-pretty village. New owners arrived in December 2009 – we expect good things here.

34 **The Red House** Marsh Benham, Newbury RG20 8LY +44 (0)1635 582017
Thatched gastropub near the Kennet and Avon Canal with French owner and chef. Modern brasserie-style food lives up to the surroundings – in the bistro-bar, the smart book-lined restaurant or on the front terrace.

Brighton & Hove

The Foragers
Hove

The laid-back Forager in residential Hove combines the conviviality of a boozer with classy food from a talented team — you can glimpse the chefs at work from the front bar. Blackboard specials and printed menus reflect the seasons and raw materials are sourced from Sussex producers. There's a definite preference for organic, especially concerning meat (the Sunday roast always is). Everything bursts with flavour, from braised wild rabbit with buttered greens to Jerusalem artichoke and mushroom suet pudding; mash might be truffled or roast onion'd. There are sandwiches too, perhaps salt beef with dill pickle or steak with mayo, and Sussex Best Bitter to wash it all down. The interior revamp has created two distinct rooms with a relaxed, casual air — and the smart, decked all-weather garden is a popular draw.

Bristol

Cornubia
Bristol

This characterful inn, one of central Bristol's best-kept secrets, used to be two Georgian houses; now, after several recent changes of ownership, it has been rescued by Wiltshire's Hidden Brewery and given a new lease of life. Out goes the brown paintwork and the notoriously threadbare and sticky carpet, in comes a fresh lick of paint and a function room upstairs. Surrounded by modern office blocks, this is a drinkers' pub at heart with up to eight ales available at any one time; stout's on draught and there are always a couple of West Country ciders on tap. Food is basic — pies, baguettes, sandwiches — but with so many local beers to chose from, the Cornubia is driven more by conversation than gastronomy. A boozer with soul — and popular with office workers and *Evening Post* scribes.

Meals	12pm-4pm; 6pm-10pm. Main courses £7.50-£13 (lunch), £10.50-£17.50 (dinner); sandwiches £5.95-£6.90; Sunday roast £9.90-£14.90.
Closed	Open all day.
Directions	From A259 turn into Hove Street, cross Church Road (B2066); second right into Stirling Place.

Meals	12pm-2.30pm Mon-Fri. No food Sat & Sun. Main courses £4-£5.60.
Closed	Open all day.
Directions	5-min walk from Temple Meads station. From Victoria St, right into The Countershop, right again into Temple St.

Bek Misich & Paul Hutchison
The Foragers,
3 Stirling Place,
Hove BN3 3YU

Tel	+44 (0)1273 733134
Web	www.theforagerspub.co.uk

Entry 35 Map 4

Luke Daniels
Cornubia,
142 Temple Street,
Bristol BS1 6EN

Tel	+44 (0)117 925 4415
Web	www.thecornubia.com

Entry 36 Map 3

Bristol

The Albion
Bristol

Like Bath but without the tourists: Clifton village is Georgian to the core. Restaurants and delis abound but no-one had, until 2005, quite mastered the gastropub idea. Step forward Owain George who has given the student boozer down the pretty cobbled alley the classiest of makeovers. Outside, vast parasols; inside, a long stylish bar serving Butcombe and monthly guest ales, a winter log fire and a discreet wooden staircase leading to a restaurant that feels like a private room. A chef with a pedigree has been installed and the place attracts Clifton's loudest and proudest, but the Albion is still a pub, its menu available at every table. There are light bites at lunch and posh nosh at dinner (Jerusalem artichoke soup, roast tranche of turbot, Yorkshire grouse, pig's trotter). Book ahead at weekends.

Bristol

Kensington Arms
Bristol

Tucked away at the end of a quiet street in leafy Redland, this Victorian corner pub with its decked front terrace – abuzz in summer, from lunch till late – is a popular place with well-heeled locals and a youthful crowd. Stylish and unpretentious, its painted panelling and plain planked floor are complimented by big mirrors and quirky touches. Fresh flowers and daily-printed menus sit on scrubbed tables so tuck into swordfish carpaccio in the bar – accompanied by delicious warm bread – or settle down to several scrumptious courses in the restaurant. This is modern food of the best kind, with a focus on provenance: pan-fried duck livers with bone marrow toast and persillade, home-smoked salmon fishcakes, pumpkin and pinenut gnocchi, hot chocolate fondant. Everything about the 'Kenny' is lovely, and that includes the staff.

Meals	12pm-3pm; 7pm-10pm. No food Sun eve & all day Mon. Main courses £12-£22.50; bar meals £6-£10.
Closed	Open all day. Mon after 5pm.
Directions	In centre of Clifton village. (Tricky) on-street parking.

Meals	12pm-3pm; 6pm-10pm. Main courses £9.50-£14.
Closed	Open all day.
Directions	From B4468 Redland Hill, 2nd exit at r'bout; right at Clyde Road; left at Elliston Road. On to Stanley Road, pub on left.

Owain George
The Albion,
Boyces Avenue, Clifton,
Bristol BS8 4AA
Tel +44 (0)117 973 3522
Web www.thealbionclifton.co.uk

Entry 37 Map 3

Kensington Arms, 35-37 Stanley
Road, Redland, Bristol, BS6 6NP
Tel +44 (0)117 944 6444
Web www.thekensingtonarms.co.uk

Entry 38 Map 3

Robin Hood's Retreat
Bristol

An ordinary red-brick pub on bustling Gloucester Road; inside is special. Owner and chef Nathan Muir started his career working under Simon Hopkinson at Bibendum and his beautifully executed food is delivered from a broom cupboard-sized kitchen at the back. The refurb is classy, the cuisine modern European with occasional Asian influences, the menus driven by the seasons and the best produce available. Muir majors on bold flavours, often conjured from the humblest of ingredients, be they lambs' tongues with salsa verde or slow-braised mutton. Desserts include a much-loved treacle tart with English custard. Accompany these with a pint of real ale from a constantly changing selection of up to a dozen, mainly from West Country breweries, or an excellent wine. Sunday lunches are fabulous.

The New Inn
Backwell

In a sought-after commuter village between Bristol and the Mendips is the New Inn, Backwell's oldest pub. In 2009 it received the full gastro makeover as chef Nathan Muir, of Bristol's Robin Hood's Retreat, took over the reins. In the main bar: sage tongue and groove, slate flagstone floors, smart leather sofas. In the smaller drinking area: a real fire and high stools. In the stone-walled restaurant: farmhouse tables, church candles and a mocha carpet. Now the pub attracts both locals in for a pint of Butcombe ale and city dwellers escaping for lunch or dinner – and Muir has been sensible enough to offer comforting bar food alongside the full-on à la carte. So pop in for potted beef and a pint or stay longer for rib-eye of Clevedon beef with duck fat-fried chips, and prune and Armagnac tart. The food is fabulous.

Meals	12pm-3pm; 6pm-9.30pm. Main courses from £10; set lunch, 2 courses, £13.50, 3 courses £15.50; Sunday lunch £16.50 & £19.50; Sunday dinner £14.50 & £16.50.
Closed	Open all day.
Directions	North of the city centre on the main Gloucester Road.

Meals	12pm-2.30pm; 6pm-9.30pm. Main courses £11-£18.
Closed	Open all day.
Directions	A370 far south side of main road. Opposite the Rising Sun.

Nathan Muir
Robin Hood's Retreat,
197 Gloucester Road,
Bishopston, Bristol BS7 8BG
Tel   +44 (0)117 924 8639
Web   www.robinhoodsretreat.co.uk

Entry 39 Map 3

Nathan Muir
The New Inn,
86 West Town Road,
Backwell BS48 3BE
Tel   +44 (0)1275 462199

Entry 40 Map 3

The Hunters Rest Inn
Clutton

Astride Clutton Hill with fine views over the Cam valley the inn began life in the 1750s – as a hunting lodge. Eighty years later it became a smallholding and tavern. It's a big place, rambling around a large central bar, part wood, part stone, its bar topped with copper. There's plenty of jostling space so get ready to order from the Butcombe, Otter and guest ales and the Original Broad Oak and Pheasant Plucker ciders. Get cosy amongst the old oak and pine settles, the odd sofa and the tables to fit all sizes, the quirky wine-label wallpaper, the horse and country paraphernalia, the fires crackling away. Food is hale and hearty: shepherd's pie, pickled beetroot, crusty bread, salmon steak. Children are well looked after and there's a miniature railway out in the garden. The fun continues upstairs with rooms that range from traditional four-poster with antiques to contemporary chic. All are distinctive, all have views, several look south to the Mendips; others have private terraces. Stylish bathrooms have bold tiles, roll top baths and thick towels. We like this 'sprack and spry' Somerset hideaway very much.

Rooms	5: 4 doubles, 1 twin. £90–£125. Singles £65–£75.
Meals	12pm–2pm; 6pm–9.30pm (12pm–10pm Sat & Sun). Main courses £8.25– £17.95. Sandwiches from £4.25.
Closed	3pm–6pm. Open all day Fri–Sun.
Directions	A37 south from Bristol. At r'bout with A368, left for Bath; next right (100m), then at T-junction left to top of hill.

Paul Thomas
The Hunters Rest Inn,
King Lane, Clutton Hill,
Clutton BS39 5QL
Tel   +44 (0)1761 452303
Web   www.huntersrest.co.uk

Entry 41 Map 3

Bristol

The Pony & Trap
Chew Magna

Just outside pretty Chew Magna, a short drive from Bristol and Bath, this 200-year-old pub has built up a good local reputation ever since ambitious young chef Josh Eggleton arrived in 2006. The conservatory dining room and the large sloping garden share stunning views across the rolling fields and Somerset hills, while the bar is super-cosy with an abundance of wood panelling, old cider flagons and a cast-iron range. The food may be the draw but muddy-booted walkers are made welcome too, popping by for a pint of Butcombe Bitter and a generous plateful of ham, egg and chips. Foodies will seek out such contemporary delights as pan-seared pigeon breast with walnut salad or chargrilled rib-eye steak (local, naturally) with chunky chips — washed down by one of a short but thoughtful selection of wines.

Meals	12pm-2.30pm (3pm Sun); 7pm-9.30pm. Main courses £8-£15; Sunday roast from £9.95.
Closed	Mon all day & Sun eves in winter.
Directions	From A37, right on A368 for Weston-super-mare at Chelwood r'bout, right after 1.5 miles, signed Chew Magna; pub 1 mile on right.

	Josh Eggleton
	The Pony & Trap,
	Knowle Hill,
	Chew Magna BS40 8TQ
Tel	+44 (0)1275 332627
Web	www.theponyandtrap.co.uk

Entry 42 Map 3

Bristol
Worth a visit

43 Old Duke 45 King St, Bristol BS1 4ER
+44 (0)117 927 7137
There's a New Orleans speakeasy, British-pub feel to this shrine to jazz and blues not far from Bristol Old Vic. Music is served up nightly along with the occasional curry or stew.

44 The King's Head 60 Victoria Street, Bristol BS1 6DE +44 (0)117 927 7860
In Bristol's heart, untouched Victorian inside, 1660 out. A rare period narrow bar and an entirely panelled rear snug, a splendid mirrored back bar, photos of old Bristol and gallons of Smiles.

45 The Hare on the Hill Dove St, Kingsdown, Bristol BS2 8LX +44 (0)117 908 1982
Bath Ales took on this corner boozer for a total overhaul and served it up in unpretentious Bath Ales style — wooden floors, a low-key charm, a pint of Bath Gem and roasts on Sundays.

46 The Merchants Arms 5 Merchants Road, Hotwells, Bristol BS8 4PZ
+44 (0)117 907 3047
Bare-boarded and real, done-up without a whiff of modern pretension. Simple, friendly, civilised and Bath Ales-owned, with excellent beers and good snacks.

47 White Hart Littleton-on-Severn, Bristol BS35 1NR +44 (0)1454 412275
Hops hang from old beams; chairs, tables and a cushioned settle are scattered across flagged floors; fires blaze in grand fireplaces in this 16th-century former farmhouse. Lovely garden, peaceful views, Youngs beers and traditional pub food complete the picture.

Buckinghamshire

Swan Inn
Milton Keynes

A 13th-century gem in the heart of a sprawling New Town; across roundabouts and through housing estates you arrive at the clearly signed 'Milton Keynes Village'. Recently spruced up in gastropub style, keeping its beams, fireplaces and layout, the Swan has cool colours, scatter cushions and pews, chic chairs in its snug and a glowing wood-burner in its bar. In the cosy dining room – wooden floors, chunky tables, open-to-view kitchen – Italian cured meats with chutney and homemade bread are on the menu alongside English pot-roasted chicken and cottage pie. Some produce comes from local allotments (in return for a pint or two), while imaginative evening meals include the likes of venison carpaccio with sweet onion jam. In summer you may eat outside, on the covered sun terrace or in the orchard garden.

Meals	12pm-10pm.
	Main courses £7-£16;
	Sunday lunch £11.50.
Closed	Open all day.
Directions	Follow signs to Milton Keynes Village off V11 between junctions H6 & H7, 5 mins from town centre.

Tyrone Bentham
Swan Inn,
Broughton Road,
Milton Keynes Village MK10 9AH
Tel   +44 (0)1908 665240
Web   theswan-mkvillage.co.uk

Entry 48 Map 9

Buckinghamshire

The Crooked Billet
Newton Longville

The twin talents of a former Sommelier of the Year, John Gilchrist, and head chef Emma have put the 16th-century pub on the county's culinary map. With innovative menus and a 400-bin wine list (all, astonishingly, available by the glass), you may imagine it's more restaurant than pub but it's an exemplary local with a great bar, weekly-changing ales, a log-fired inglenook and a great pubby atmosphere. Munch sandwiches, salads or steak and chips in the beamed bar at lunch; or pan-fried turbot fillet, Palourde clams and artichokes, goat's cheese and tomato soufflé and apple spotted dick in the restaurant – inviting with its deep red walls, candles and country prints. Delicious cheeses come with fig and walnut cake and Emma's seasonal menus make full use of produce from first-class suppliers, villagers included.

Meals	7pm-10pm (12.30pm-3pm Sun); bar meals 12pm-2pm Tues-Sat. No food Sun eve.
	Main courses £10-£20; bar meals £5.75-£10; tasting menu £55.
Closed	2.30pm-5.30pm; Mon lunch.
Directions	From Milton Keynes A421 for Buckingham, left for Newton Longville.

John & Emma Gilchrist
The Crooked Billet,
2 Westbrook End, Newton Longville,
Milton Keynes MK17 0DF
Tel   +44 (0)1908 373936
Web   www.thebillet.co.uk

Entry 49 Map 9

Buckinghamshire

The Mole & Chicken
Long Crendon

Midsomer Murders was filmed here: it's in the middle of nowhere, hardish to find and absurdly picturesque. Come on a damp Sunday and settle in for the day; in summer there's a decked area with fabulous views, a big barbecue and a children's play area. Inside, lovely low beams, a vast fire and squishy leather sofas: a perfect pub for a dog. It's that sort of a bolthole, relaxed, pubby, with ales on tap and 12 wines by the glass. The restaurant feel takes over in several little rooms with chunky pine tables, 60s art and gleaming glasses, and we hear great reports of the food: woodland mushroom risotto with poached egg and truffle oil; grilled plaice with caper and parsley butter; a superb Sunday roast (thick tender beef, fiery horseradish sauce, creamy celeriac, the best Yorkshire pudding). With food this good it's worth staying the night and here you get peaceful rooms in the adjoining cottage. Named after the colours used in them, they are immaculate, stylish and serene; Strawberry (the smallest) is Victorian, Mustard has a roll top tub in the bedroom, Duck Egg is dreamy.

Rooms	5: 4 doubles, 1 family room. £95. Singles £70. Family room £125.
Meals	12pm-2.30pm (4pm Sun); 6.30pm-9.30pm (6pm-9pm Sun). Main courses £11.50-£19.50; bar lunches £6.95-£9.50; set lunch £12.95 & £15.95.
Closed	3pm-6.30pm. Open all day Sun.
Directions	North from Thame on B4011 to Long Crendon. Right on main street opp. the Gurkha, signed Chilton. Left at T-junction; pub on left after 0.5 miles.

Steve Bush
The Mole & Chicken,
Easington Terrace, Long Crendon,
Aylesbury HP18 9EY

Tel	+44 (0)1844 208387
Web	www.themoleandchicken.co.uk

Entry 50 Map 8

The Dinton Hermit
Ford

A Grade II-listed local in a peaceful hamlet with long lawns that run down to the road and fields which stretch out beyond. Hanging baskets and wooden tubs add colour to the garden, while inside, both bar and restaurant are small but sweet, a cosy contemporary kingdom that comes complete with timber-framed walls, roaring fire, the odd wooden pillar and a fine settle. Here you eat great food served off a short menu, perhaps homemade fishcakes with a sweet chilli sauce, venison stew with roasted vegetables, Bramley apple crumble with clotted cream. Breakfasts are delicious. Bedrooms are scattered about the place: those in the main house are bigger but more traditional (two have four-posters) while those in the refurbished barn have a clean, contemporary style (suede headboards, neutral colours, pretty fabrics, robes in bathrooms). The gardens draw a crowd in summer and Sunday lunch is popular with locals. Further afield, bridle paths lead into the hills and Oxford's spires are close. The Aylesbury Vale cycle route passes outside so expect a few cyclists in summer.

Rooms	13: 11 doubles, 2 four-posters. £90. Four-posters £130. Singles from £70.
Meals	12pm-2pm (3pm Sat & Sun); 6.30pm-9pm. Sandwiches all day. Main courses £8.95-£16.90; sandwiches from £6.75.
Closed	Open all day.
Directions	M40, junc. 7, then A418 for Aylesbury. Through Thame, then right after a mile for Haddenham. Through village, right after a mile for Ford. On left in village.

Mary O'Hara
The Dinton Hermit,
Ford,
Aylesbury HP17 8XH
Tel   +44 (0)1296 747473
Web   www.dinton-hermit.com

Buckinghamshire

The Crown Inn
Amersham

Celebrated designer Ilse Crawford has reinvented the English inn. Behind the beautiful timber framework of this 16th-century building is an understated new look, Shaker-simple and full of personality. In the classic bar and timbered dining areas, old planked floors, thick beams, inglenook fireplaces and charming furniture blend with soft muted colours, fur rugs on Ercol windsor chairs, fresh flowers in pewter pots and Welsh blankets on ancient settles. For summer: a cobbled courtyard grill. The emphasis is on heart-warming comfort and restorative food. Short daily menus list English dishes bursting with local produce: Old Spot pork terrine; chicken and butter bean stew; plum crumble. Stay the night. A labyrinth of corridors leads to wonky beamed rooms with sloping oak floors and a décor that is elegant, contemporary, rustic, understated: big beds with crisp linen and Jakob's wool blankets, Robert's radios, seagrass mats. Modern bathrooms have vast walk-in showers; Room 12 has a 16th-century hand-painted wall; the modern-build bedrooms are a tad more traditional. A chic Chiltern's bolthole for city escapees.

Rooms	35: 27 doubles, 1 twin, 2 four-posters, 5 suites. £109–£119. Four-posters from £185. Suites from £149.
Meals	12.30pm–3pm (4pm Sun); 6pm–10pm; bar meals all day. No food Sun eve. Main courses £12–£20; bar meals £2–£8.80.
Closed	Open all day.
Directions	Leave M40 at J2 signs Beaconsfield.

Joe Kelly
The Crown Inn,
16 High Street,
Amersham HP7 0DH

Tel   +44 (0)1494 721541
Web   www.thecrownamersham.co.uk

The Nags Head Inn
Little Kingshill

This was Roald Dahl's local – it features in *Fantastic Mr Fox* – half a mile out of Great Missenden. It's a beautiful place built of red brick and flint under bright red pantiles, framed by the rolling hills of the Chilterns. At the back is a vast garden with plenty of trees under which to dream and picnic tables with umbrellas. Inside, a classic refurbishment from owner Alvin Michaels of the award-winning Bricklayers Arms; the beloved 15th-century boozer has become a great foodie pub. Now low dark beams and big inglenook blend with modern oak and lemon hues, there are salt and pepper mills on shining tables and boxed shelves guarding armagnacs. Our meal was faultless: various smoked fish with lemon coriander butter, and trio of pheasant in a red wine and shallot sauce. Drinks cover every aspect of the grape and globe, plus London Pride; bedrooms above are equally good. Modish creams and whites complement ancient timbers, there are ironing boards, toiletries and full-length mirrors, and the bed linen is delicious.

Rooms	7: 5 doubles, 2 twins. £90–£110.
Meals	12pm-2.30pm (3.30pm Sun); 6.30pm-9.30pm (8.30pm Sun). Main courses £10.95-£19.95.
Closed	Open all day.
Directions	A413 Amersham to Aylesbury. Left onto London Road, past the Children's Hospital.

Alvin Michaels
The Nags Head Inn,
London Road, Little Kingshill,
Great Missenden HP16 0DG

Tel	+44 (0)1494 862200
Web	www.nagsheadbucks.com

Buckinghamshire

Five Arrows Hotel
Waddesdon

Spires, turrets, ornamental ironwork outside; woven carpets, antique furnishings and paintings from Lord Rothschild's collection within. It is part of the model village built in 1887 by the Baron – along with Waddesdon Manor. The recent Pugin-style refurbishment creates an indulgent mood with lofty ceilings and open fires. No bar to prop up but, from a wing-back armchair or a leather chesterfield, pints of London Pride or a glass of champagne may be savoured. In the dining room, carefully sourced produce is transformed into escalope of pork with cream and wild mushroom sauce, roasted sea bass with fennel and parmesan crisps, and honeycomb ice cream. In the shadow of the vast mock-Elizabethan barley-twist chimney stacks is the exceptional garden, all manicured lawns and gravelled pathways. And the service is impeccable.

Meals	12pm-2.15pm (3.30pm Sun); 7pm-9.15pm (8.45pm Sun). Main courses from £13.50; bar meals from £6.50.
Closed	Open all day.
Directions	In village on A41, 6 miles west of Aylesbury.

Alex McEwen
Five Arrows Hotel,
High Street, Waddesdon,
Aylesbury HP18 0JE
Tel   +44 (0)1296 651727
Web   www.thefivearrows.co.uk

Entry 54 Map 9

Buckinghamshire

The Polecat Inn
Prestwood

A quirky place packed with character. Chintzy curtains, low lighting and beams, button-backed chairs, cosy corners, rugs and a fireplace stacked with logs make the 17th-century Polecat Inn feel more home than pub. The unusual flint bar serves several real ales, including Morland Old Speckled Hen and Marstons Pedigree, and there is an impressive selection of malts, and 16 wines by the glass. Among ticking clocks and happy banter, walkers and families tuck into tempting dishes such as steak and kidney pie, seafood hotpot, or roast duck with orange and cognac sauce. The chocolate and hazelnut tart with fudge sauce might just finish you off, so take one of the walking maps thoughtfully provided by John and work off any over-indulgence in the Chiltern Hills. It's a beautifully run place, and has a gorgeous garden.

Meals	12pm-2pm; 6.30pm-9pm. Main courses £9.90-£15.20; bar meals £4.10-£6.25.
Closed	2.30pm-6pm & Sun after 3pm.
Directions	On A4128 between Great Missenden & High Wycombe.

John Gamble
The Polecat Inn,
170 Wycombe Road, Prestwood,
Great Missenden HP16 0HJ
Tel   +44 (0)1494 862253

Entry 55 Map 9

Three Horseshoes Inn
Radnage

London may only be an hour's drive, but this is lost down a leafy lane. Red kites circle a deep bowl of countryside, smoke curls from cottages below, and the inn surveys the idyllic scene from on high. Inside are flagstones and an open fire in the tiny bar, and exposed timbers and pine settles in the restaurant. Simon, chef turned patron, has cooked at Le Gavroche and all the best places; dinner is delectable and the homemade piccalilli worth the trip alone. Come for lunch and baked camembert with garlic and rosemary, stay for dinner and tiger prawns, roasted sea bass, bread and butter pudding with marmalade ice cream. If you're here for the night, private stairs lead to super attic rooms (and more in the annexe) with silky quilts, goose down pillows, deluge showers, funky furniture and Farrow & Ball walls. Breakfast indulgently, drink in the views, hike in the hills, walk by the Thames. There's jazz and tapas once a month and in summer you can eat on the terrace at the back while ducks circle a sunken phone box in the pond. Great value set lunches, and sandwiches for passing walkers.

Rooms	6: 2 doubles, 2 garden rooms, 2 suites. £85–£110. Suites £85–£145. Singles £75.
Meals	12pm–2.30pm; 7pm–9.30pm. Main courses £10.50–£18.50; bar meals (lunch) £3.75–£13.50.
Closed	3pm–6pm, Mon lunch, Tues after bank hols & Sun after 8pm.
Directions	M40 junc. 5, A40 south thro' Stokenchurch, left for Radnage. After 2 miles, left to Bennett End. Sharp right, up hill, on left.

Simon Crawshaw
Three Horseshoes Inn,
Horseshoe Road, Radnage,
High Wycombe HP14 4EB
Tel   +44 (0)1494 483273
Web   www.thethreehorseshoes.net

Entry 56 Map 4

Buckinghamshire

Old Queens Head
Penn

David and Becky Salisbury's mini-empire now contains this pub by the green. Dating from 1666 it has character and charm while inside, old beams and timbers in the rambling bar and dining areas blend perfectly with a stylish and contemporary décor – rug-strewn flags, polished boards, classic fabrics, lovely old oak. Food follows the successful formula of the Alford Arms, Frithsden, The Swan at Denham and the Royal Oak at Marlow, innovative seasonal menus and chalkboard specials mixing classic pub recipes with modern British flair. Choices range from 'small plates' – roast fig, red onion and brie tarte tatin – to big dishes of herb-crusted Scottish salmon with curly kale and almond velouté or ox cheeks with smoked bacon and potatoes. Great puddings too, and a glorious summer garden.

Meals	12pm-2.30pm (3pm Sat; 4pm Sun); 6.30pm-9.30pm (7pm-10pm Fri & Sat). Main courses £11.50-£17.25.
Closed	Open all day.
Directions	From High Wycombe (M40 junc. 4), A40 towards Beaconsfield, then left for 1.5 miles into Hammersley Lane; on right, opposite church.

David & Becky Salisbury
Old Queens Head,
Hammersley Lane, Penn,
High Wycombe HP10 8EY
Tel   +44 (0)1494 813371
Web   www.oldqueensheadpenn.co.uk

Entry 57 Map 4

Buckinghamshire

The Swan Inn
Denham

Swap the bland and everyday for the picture-book perfection of Denham village and the stylish Swan. Georgian, double-fronted, swathed in wisteria, the building has had a makeover by David and Becky Salisbury (of the Alford Arms, the Old Queens Head and the Royal Oak). It has been transformed by rug-strewn boards, chunky tables, cushioned settles, a log fire and a fabulous terrace for outdoor meals. Food is modern British. If pressed for time, choose from the 'small plates' list – pan-fried pigeon breast on caramelised fig tarte tatin or beer steamed Scottish mussels. If you've nothing to rush for, linger over slow-cooked pork belly on mustard mash with parsnip crisps and a pint of Courage Best or one of 19 wines by the glass. The owners have thought of everything, and the gardens are large enough for the kids to go wild in.

Meals	12pm-2.30pm (3pm Sat; 4pm Sun); 6.30pm-9.30pm (7pm-10pm Fri & Sat). Main courses £11.75-£17.25.
Closed	Open all day.
Directions	From A412 (M25 junc. 17 or M40 junc. 1) follow signs for Denham Village.

David & Becky Salisbury
The Swan Inn,
Village Road, Denham,
Uxbridge UB9 5BH
Tel   +44 (0)1895 832085
Web   www.swaninndenham.co.uk

Entry 58 Map 4

The Hand & Flowers
Marlow

It's almost Shakespearean. Ludlow's claim to the culinary crown of England is under challenge from prosperous Marlow: instead of arrows falling from the sky, Michelin stars are tumbling down. Chief instigator is Tom, whose incredible cooking has attracted interest in only two years; locals now fill the place day and night. Step into these airy 18th-century cottages and find flagged floors under low beams – it's remarkably easy-going. There's no froth on the menu, no dress code in the restaurant, just ambrosial food that elates. Try perfectly cooked salmon with frozen horseradish, sausages from pigs that munch windfalls in the orchards of a Suffolk estate, vanilla crème brûlée washed down by a honey-sweet beer chaser. Four vastly stylish suites stand 30 paces along the road in two refurbished cottages (expect a little noise). Beth, a sculptor, oversaw their creation; be wowed by exposed beams, cow hide rugs, Egyptian cotton and flat-screen TVs. Two rooms have hot tubs on private terraces, another has a large copper bath and chandeliers. Don't miss Tom and Beth's new bar (Clayton's) along the road.

Rooms	4 suites. £140–£190.
Meals	12pm-2.30pm; 7pm-9.30pm. Main courses £12.50-£21.
Closed	3pm-6pm & Sun eve.
Directions	M4 junc. 9; A404 north; into Marlow; A4155 dir. Henley; on edge of town on right.

Tom & Beth Kerridge
The Hand & Flowers,
126 West Street,
Marlow SL7 2BP

Tel	+44 (0)1628 482277
Web	www.thehandandflowers.co.uk

Buckinghamshire

The Ostrich
Colnbrook

Smartened up a few years back, the Ostrich is an ancient, rambling place, within a mile of the motorways. The wonky timbered façade remains, but step through the huge glass doors and you enter a world in which old blends vibrantly with new. There's a glittering scarlet and steel bar that picks up the colour in the original stained glass, while the floors are slate-tiled and the furniture chunky. There are sandblasted beams, standing timbers and, in the atmospheric dining room, bowed, putty-coloured walls. Food is modern British and the menu wide-ranging, so pitch up for salads and sandwiches, chicken and lobster sausages with creamed leeks, and braised pork cheeks with vegetables. Take a peek upstairs at the lofty, tightly raftered function room or enjoy a Sunday roast and a pint of Doom Bar.

Buckinghamshire

Royal Oak
Marlow

The old whitewashed cottage stands in a hamlet on the edge of the common. It's one of a thriving quartet of dining pubs owned by David and Becky Salisbury (the Alford Arms, Hertfordshire; the Swan Inn and the Old Queens Head, Buckinghamshire) and the relaxed but professional staff make it special. Beyond the terrace is a stylish, open-plan bar, cheerful with terracotta walls, rug-strewn boards, cushioned pews and crackling log fires. Order a pint of local Rebellion ale or one of the 19 wines available by the glass and check out the daily chalkboard or printed menu. Innovative pub grub comes in the form of 'small plates' (smoked salmon with beetroot carpaccio) and main meals (rabbit, gammon and leek roly poly with purple sprouting broccoli): fresh and delicious. The sprawling gardens are perfect for summer.

Meals	12pm-2.30pm; 6pm-9.30pm (6.30pm-9pm Sun). Main courses £8.75-£16.75; sandwiches from £4.95 (Mon-Fri).
Closed	3pm-5pm.
Directions	Colnbrook is signed off M4 (junc. 5) & A4 east of Slough.

Meals	12pm-2.30pm (3pm Sat; 4pm Sun); 6.30pm-9.30pm (7pm-10pm Fri & Sat). Main courses £11.50-£17.25.
Closed	Open all day.
Directions	From Marlow A4155; right signed Bovingdon Green.

Susan Quayle
The Ostrich,
High Street, Colnbrook,
Slough SL3 0JZ
Tel +44 (0)1753 682628
Web www.theostrichcolnbrook.co.uk

Entry 60 Map 4

David & Becky Salisbury
Royal Oak,
Frieth Road,
Marlow SL7 2JF
Tel +44 (0)1628 488611
Web www.royaloakmarlow.co.uk

Entry 61 Map 4

Buckinghamshire
Worth a visit

62 The Swan 2 Wavendon Road, Salford,
Milton Keynes MK17 8BD
+44 (0)1908 281008
Innovative Peach Pubs have revamped
this ordinary village boozer with style
and panache; escape the M1 for great
antipasti nibbles and enjoyable modern
pub food, served all day.

63 The King's Head King's Head Passage,
Market Square, Aylesbury HP20 2RW
+44 (0)1296 381501
Dating back to 1455 and perfectly
restored by the National Trust. Exposed
wattle and daub, stripped boards, high-
backed settles – and a bar run by
Chiltern Brewery. Traditional pub
dishes, too.

64 The Crown Crown Lane, Little Missenden,
Amersham HP7 0RD +44 (0)1494 862571
An unspoilt brick-cottage pub in a pretty
village, run by the same family for over
90 years. Excellent beers, good wines
and sandwiches, a big garden and
walking all around.

65 The Jolly Cricketers 24 Chalfont Road,
Seer Green, Beaconsfield HP9 2YG
+44 (0)1494 676308
New owners have reversed the fortunes
of this Chilterns pub since taking over
in 2008. Now community focused, its
refurbished bars draw locals and
visitors for coffee and cake, a pint by
the fire, regular events, the daily papers
and fresh food.

66 The White Horse Village Lane, Hedgerley,
Slough SL2 3UY +44 (0)1753 643225
Super local in easy reach of the M40
(junc. 2). Swap the service station for
flagstones, inglenook, beamed bar and a
perfect ploughman's lunch. Seven real
ales are tapped from the barrel.

Cambridgeshire

Dyke's End
Reach

In a community hamlet in Fen country is a
"splendid pub" (to quote the Prince of
Wales), rescued from closure by its regulars
in 1997. Now privately owned, the former
17th-century farmhouse is a lovely old place,
with rug-strewn bare boards, glowing log
fires, high-backed settles, scrubbed pine
tables and a relaxing vibe in two refurbished
candlelit bars. Settle in for a pint of Devil's
Dyke Bitter or No 7, brewed in the
microbrewery at the back, and try one of the
seasonal specialities from the oft-changing
lunch and dinner menus. Choose from
linguini with scallops, black pepper and
truffle oil; pork belly with chorizo and
cannellini beans; local sausages and mash;
chocolate mousse with sloe gin jelly. Book
for memorable Sunday roasts and the limited
'Monday Kitchen' menu. Alfresco dining on
the lawn overlooks the village green.

Meals	12pm-2pm; 7pm-9pm.
	No food Sun eve.
	Main courses £10.95-£15.95 (dinner);
	lunch menu £6.95-£10.95;
	Sunday lunch £16.95 (2 courses)
	& £19.95 (3 courses)
Closed	Closed 2pm-6pm & Mon lunch.
Directions	Take B1102 from A14 (junc. with
	A1103) to Swaffham Prior, then
	follow signs to Reach.

	Simon Owers
	Dyke's End,
	8 Fair Green, Reach,
	Cambridge CB25 0JD
Tel	+44 (0)1638 743816
Web	www.dykesend.co.uk

Entry 67 Map 9

Cambridgeshire

The Crown Inn
Elton

Conkers, hundreds of them, harden to a deep russet brown in the late summer sun by the front door and under the towering chestnut tree, beneath which huddles The Crown; the setting is idyllic. The ancient sandstone inn looks across the green of this Wolds village that harbours the equally beautiful Elton Hall. The bar, beamed, and painted in pastel hues, with a huge oak mantel and grate, is the epitome of Old England. Here you may enjoy a pint of Golden Crown and a light meal. In the 'snug', seated by the big log fire on a wintery night, what nicer than to settle in and try chicken liver and brandy parfait with homemade chutney or fillets of seabass and red mullet with prawn and courgette risotto. For something more traditional, there's ale-battered haddock and chips, beef, ale and mushroom pie. Weekend dining is in the circular conservatory, which opens to a large decked area, great for summer. As for the bedrooms, they're gorgeous (plantation-style shutters for privacy, king-size beds, great lighting) with snazzy en suites. Three are tucked upstairs beneath the thatch, two at the rear in the courtyard.

Rooms	5 doubles. £90–£120. Singles from £60.
Meals	12pm-2.30pm (3pm Sun); 6.30pm-9pm. No food Sun eve or Mon lunch (except bank hols).
	Main courses £9.95-£19; bar meals from £4.95; Sunday lunch £13.50-£19.95.
Closed	Mon lunch (bar open in eve).
Directions	A1(M), junc. 17, then A605 west for 3 miles. Right on B671 for Elton. In village, left, signed Nassington.

Marcus & Rosalind Lamb
The Crown Inn,
8 Duck Street, Elton,
Peterborough PE8 6RQ

Tel +44 (0)1832 280232
Web www.thecrowninn.org

Entry 68 Map 9

The White Hart
Ufford

This much-forgotten slip of England is prettier than most imagine. Wash up at the White Hart and join the locals who come for a bar with atmosphere and high-back settles. The ales are good too: Ufford's own, brewed 50 paces from the beer tap. Farmers gather on Fridays, the cricket team drops by on Sundays, in summer life spills onto the terrace. Flags, floorboards and a crackling fire continue the rustic feel; railway signs, wooden pitch forks and hanging station lamps add colour. You can eat simply or more grandly, anything from a ploughman's at lunch to a three-course feast in the evening; there are great cheeseboards, too. Walk through to a conservatory-style dining area, furnished with Lloyd Loom furniture for comfortable dining all year round. Bedrooms (four above the bar, two out by the microbrewery) are simple, spotless and carry an honest price. White is... white, airy and lovely, with period lounge chairs and views across the fields to the church. Red is a dark deep Victorian red and fits a four-poster. All have crisp white linen and feather pillows.

Rooms	6: 3 doubles, 2 twins, 1 four-poster. From £90. Four-poster from £90. Singles from £80.
Meals	12pm-2.30pm (3pm Sun); 6pm-9.30pm (5.30pm-8.30pm Sun). Main courses £10-£15; bar lunches £5.25-£8.75.
Closed	Sun eve from 9pm. Open all day.
Directions	A1, then east on A47 four miles south of Stamford. Ist left, thro' Southorpe & keep right for Ufford.

Michael Thurlby & Ben Larter
The White Hart,
Main Street, Ufford,
Stamford PE9 3BH

Tel	+44 (0)1780 740250
Web	www.whitehartufford.co.uk

Entry 69 Map 9

Cambridgeshire

Red Lion
Hinxton

In pretty, peaceful Hinxton, close to Cambridge, the rambling Red Lion is a popular stopover in an area deprived of good inns. And its secluded garden, replete with dovecote, overlooks the church: a lovely spot for peaceful summer sipping. Another draw is the buzzy atmosphere Alex Clarke has instilled in the beamed bar with its deep green chesterfields, worn wooden boards, cosy log fire and ticking clock. Ales from City of Cambridge, Adnams and Woodforde's add to the appeal, as do eclectic menus that list a range of classic pub dishes and more inventive specials, all at good prices. Pop in for a beef and horseradish sandwich or linger over venison with blackberry jus or wild mushroom fettuccini. And tuck into delicious roast Norfolk chicken on Sunday. Puddings are to die for: sticky toffee pudding with caramel sauce, lemon tart with mango coulis. Named after local beers and ciders, new-build rooms are comfortable and smart with a fresh, contemporary feel – lightwood furniture, wooden floors, crisp cotton on top-quality beds, fully tiled bathrooms. And you can bring the laptop.

Rooms	8: 5 twins/doubles, 3 doubles. £95. Singles £80.
Meals	12pm-2pm (2.30pm Fri-Sun); 6.45pm-9pm (9.30pm Fri & Sat; 7pm-9pm Sun). Main courses £11-£20; bar meals £4.50-£10.50; Sunday roast £10.50-£12.
Closed	3pm-6pm (from 3.30pm Fri); 4.30pm-7pm Sun. Open all day Sat.
Directions	8 miles south of Cambridge, close to M11 & A11; see website for directions.

Alex Clarke
Red Lion,
32 High Street, Hinxton,
Saffron Walden CB10 1QY
Tel   +44 (0)1799 530601
Web   www.redlionhinxton.co.uk

Entry 70 Map 9

Cambridgeshire

The Queen's Head
Newton

David and Juliet Short have run the legendary pub for a quarter of a century and are joined by son Robert. There's a timeless appeal in the almost spartan main bar where clattering floorboards, plain wooden tables and aged paintings are watched over by a vintage clock that keeps the beat; a tiny carpeted lounge with dark beams and well-worn furniture is a cosier alternative when its fire is blazing. The whole interior is unusual and utterly unspoilt, a perfect backdrop for shove ha'penny, cribbage and beef dripping on toast. Yes, the food is simple, but deliciously so: rare roast beef sliced wafer-thin, ripe stilton sandwiches, ham on the bone, a mug of rich brown soup – dispensed with slow deliberation and accompanied by Adnams ales tapped straight from the barrel. A real pub with a loyal following.

Meals	12pm-2.15pm; 7pm-9.30pm. Bar meals £3.50-£6.
Closed	2.30pm-6pm (7pm Sun).
Directions	M11 junc. 11; A10 for Royston; left on B1368.

David, Juliet & Robert Short
The Queen's Head,
Fowlmere Road, Newton,
Cambridge CB22 7PG
Tel   +44 (0)1223 870436

Entry 71 Map 9

Cambridgeshire

Hole in the Wall
Little Wilbraham

Hiding down a hundred lanes, it was just another pretty pub. In the hands of chef Chris Leeton it has been transformed, with Jenny Leeton perfect front of house. It's clearly well-loved; regulars drop by for a swift half in the big timbered bar, and gather for lunch in the country-style restaurant at the back. In the bar are horse brasses and country prints, junk-shop find tables and several winter log fires. In contrast to this old-fashioned rusticity the food is decidedly modern: ingredients are as local and as organic as can be and the blackboard specials change regularly. Chris Leeton's cooking embraces many ideas, from classic lamb hotpot and peppered steak with hand cut chips to wild sea bass with smoked paprika and pancetta risotto, braised fennel and chorizo velouté. On summery days, the front garden is glorious.

Meals	12pm-2pm; 7pm-9pm. Main courses £10.50-£17.50; light lunches £4-£8.50.
Closed	3pm-6.30pm, Sun eve & Mon. 2 weeks in Jan.
Directions	Take the Stow cum Quy turn off A14, then A1303 Newmarket road & follow signs to Little Wilbraham.

Chris & Jennifer Leeton
Hole in the Wall,
2 High Street, Little Wilbraham,
Cambridge CB1 5JY
Tel   +44 (0)1223 812282
Web   www.the-holeinthewall.com

Entry 72 Map 9

Cambridgeshire

Three Horseshoes
Madingley

From the outside, the thatched pub is old; push the door and you embrace the new. It is simple, stylish, open, with pale wooden floors and chocolate and cream paintwork; there is lightness and space yet the familiar features remain. The bar has Adnams bitter and a guest ale on tap, a modern open log fire and a menu packed with Italian country dishes and imaginative combinations – chargrilled lamb with cavalo nero and braised beans; roast pork belly with fagioli beans, lemon and spinach; white chocolate, mascarpone and pistachio cheesecake. Relaxed but excellent service matches the atmosphere of the busy bar while formality and white linen come together in the conservatory dining room, popular with business lunchers. In both rooms the choice of wines is superb – pity the designated driver.

Meals	12pm-2pm (2.30pm Sat & Sun); 6.30pm-9.30pm (6pm-8.30pm Sun). Main courses £12-£28; bar meals £8-£15.
Closed	3pm-6pm. Open all day Sat & Sun in summer.
Directions	Off A1303, 2 miles west of Cambridge.

Richard Stokes
Three Horseshoes,
High Street, Madingley,
Cambridge CB23 8AB
Tel   +44 (0)1954 210221
Web   www.threehorseshoesmadingley.co.uk

Entry 73 Map 9

Cambridgeshire

The Eltisley
Eltisley

Lucky locals. The Eltisley – once a grubby old boozer – looks across the green of this deeply peaceful village but now the style is individual and quirky. The bar has an industrial late-Victorian feel with mock gas lamps, distressed paintwork and brick and flag floors; the restaurant is all shimmering chandeliers, high backed leather chairs and pale walls. You will eat the freshest, most local produce: meat, poultry and eggs from nearby farms, freshly baked bread, fish from sustainable sources. Starters include mussels with vindaloo sauce and pan-fried mackerel fillet with fennel and orange salad; wild boar and local rabbit are braised slowly, and you can polish it all off with quince and almond tart. Sup a pint of the real stuff, or good wine by the glass; spill into the garden in summer, and listen to jazz on monthly Sundays.

Meals	12pm-2pm (3pm Sun); 6.30pm-9pm. Main courses £9.95-£20; bar menu (lunch) from £4.95.
Closed	3pm-6pm, Sun eves & all day Mon.
Directions	In village centre just off A428 between Cambridge and St Neots.

John Stean
The Eltisley,
2 The Green, Eltisley,
St Neots PE19 6TG
Tel   +44 (0)1480 880308
Web   www.theeltisley.co.uk

Entry 74 Map 9

The Anchor Inn
Ely

A real find, a 1650s ale house on Chatteris Fen, run by good people. Wedged between the bridge and the raised dyke, the little inn was built to bed and board the men conscripted to tame the vast watery tracts of swamp and scrub. These days cosy luxury infuses every corner. There are low beamed ceilings, timber-framed walls, raw dark panelling and terracotta-tiled floors. A wood-burner warms the bar, so stop for a pint of cask ale, then pick from a menu that is light, imaginative and surprising: hand-dressed crabs from Cromer in spring, asparagus and Bottisham hams in summer, wild duck from the marshes in winter. Breakfast is equally indulgent. Four rooms up the narrow stairs fit the mood exactly: not posh, supremely comfy, with trim carpets, wicker chairs, crisp white duvets, Indian throws, candles by the bath. The suites have a sofabed each and three rooms have fen and river views. Footpaths flank the water; stroll down and you might see mallards or whooper swans, even a seal – the river is tidal to the Wash. Don't miss Ely (the bishop comes to eat).

Rooms	4: 1 double, 1 twin, 2 suites. £79.50-£99. Suites £129.50-£155. Singles from £59.50. Extra bed £20.
Meals	12pm-2pm (2.30pm Sun); 7pm-9pm (6.30pm-9.30pm Sat; 6.30pm-8.30pm Sun). Main courses £9.50-£19.95; lunch, 2 courses, £11.95 (Mon-Fri).
Closed	3pm-7pm (6.30pm Sat & Sun).
Directions	From Ely A142 west. In Sutton, left on B1381 for Earith. Right in southern Sutton, signed Sutton Gault. 1 mile north on left at bridge.

Adam Pickup & Carlene Bunten
The Anchor Inn,
Bury Lane,
Sutton Gault, Ely CB6 2BD

Tel	+44 (0)1353 778537
Web	www.anchorsuttongault.co.uk

Cambridgeshire

The Cock
Hemingford Grey

Oliver and Richard have stripped the lovely 17th-century village pub back to its original simplicity. Step directly into an attractive bare-boarded bar, cosy with low beams and log-burner, and sup four real ales from local breweries. For food, move into the airy restaurant where buttermilk walls and modern prints sit beautifully with wooden floors and tables. The menu is strong on pub classics and the chef makes his own sausages, served with a choice of mash with horseradish or cheddar and herb and delicious sauces (wild mushroom, wholegrain mustard). Duck parcel with sweet and sour cucumber is a favourite starter, while fish and game dishes reveal a refreshing, modern view. The British and continental cheeses should not be missed, and Sunday lunch is much praised.

Cambridgeshire

The Crown
Broughton

There's been a pub cum saddler's shop in this peaceful hamlet since medieval times; villagers saved the Crown from residential conversion back in 2001 and now you find one of Cambridgeshire's best gastropubs. Huge terracotta floor slabs, oak beams, a long lightwood bar aimed at drinkers, white wines under ice in a vast brass trough bucket. Round the side of the chimney breast is a dining room with fresh blooms, tall wood-burner and orange check curtains – all very 21st-century. If the ham and pea soup with truffle oil, the pan-fried bream with chorizo risotto, and the apricot and almond frangipane tart are anything to go by, David Anderson's food, refined and unshowy, is worth travelling for. Children have capacious lawns to play on in summer, and conkers from majestic chestnuts to plunder.

Meals	12pm-2.30pm; 6.30pm-9pm (9.30pm Fri & Sat, 8.30pm Sun). Main courses £10-£17; light lunch £7-£15.
Closed	3pm-6pm (4pm-6.30pm Sun).
Directions	From A14 south for Hemingford Grey; 2 miles south of Huntingdon.

Meals	12pm-2.30pm (12pm-2.30pm Sun); 7pm-10pm. Main courses £9.50-£16.50; bar lunches £6.50-£9; set lunch £11.50 & £14; Sunday lunch £14.50 & £17.50.
Closed	3pm-6pm; Mon & Tues. Open all day Sun.
Directions	Broughton is signed off A141 north east of Huntingdon.

Oliver Thain & Richard Bradley
The Cock,
47 High Street, Hemingford Grey,
Huntingdon PE28 9BJ
Tel +44 (0)1480 463609
Web www.cambscuisine.com

David Anderson
The Crown,
Bridge Road, Broughton,
Huntingdon PE28 3AY
Tel +44 (0)1487 824428
Web www.thecrowninnrestaurant.co.uk

Entry 76 Map 9

Entry 77 Map 9

Cambridgeshire

The George Inn
Spaldwick

The rambling building dates from the 1500s and overlooks the village green. Wonky walls are hung with contemporary art, leather sofas and chunky wood tables speak 'modern brasserie', old timbers are exposed and floors are bare boarded. The uncluttered styling blends beautifully with the history of the place. Modern variations on traditional dishes fit the bill – roast pumpkin and lentil soup; roast partridge with juniper jus and apple and blackberry parfait; homemade sausages with mash: simple, robust food based on first-rate ingredients. The relaxed feel extends from the several eating areas in the rambling bar – it's still a genuine village local – to the magnificent high raftered restaurant. To drink there's Adnams Broadside or Greene King IPA, or one of 25 wines by the glass.

Meals	12pm-2.30pm; 6pm-9.30pm. Main courses £7.95-£21.50; bar meals £6.95-£13.95.
Closed	Open all day.
Directions	Beside A141, off junc.18 A14, 5 miles west of Huntingdon.

Mark & Louise Smith
The George Inn,
7 High Street, Spaldwick,
Huntingdon PE28 0TD
Tel +44 (0)1480 890293
Web www.georgeofspaldwick.co.uk

Entry 78 Map 9

Cambridgeshire

The Pheasant
Keyston

This textbook country pub does beams, open fires and comfy sofas better than anyone, yet never forgets it's a pub; two or three guest ales are always on hand pump. Chef Jay (ex-Huntsbridge group, ex-Bibendum) bought the leasehold in 2007, along with Taffeta. The menu is English, the cooking is restorative, the meat is reared in the village, there are six chefs in the kitchen... and if the mushroom man turns up with a colony of particularly flavoursome fungi, then the menu will show them. Add an enterprising list of wines and expertly kept ales and you have the Pheasant to a T. The light lunch menu is great value, and if you don't want a full-blown meal – roasted saddle of rabbit stuffed with homemade black pudding; thyme and almond risotto; treacle sponge – there's bar food and beautiful unpasteurised British cheeses. Outstanding.

Meals	12pm-2.30pm; 6.30pm-9.30pm (8.30pm Sun). Main courses £12.95-£19.95; bar meals £8.95-£10.95; Sunday lunch £12.95 & £16.50.
Closed	Open all day.
Directions	Keyston off A14, halfway between Huntingdon & Kettering.

Taffeta & Jay Scrimshaw
The Pheasant,
Village Loop Road, Keyston,
Huntingdon PE28 0RE
Tel +44 (0)1832 710241
Web www.thepheasant-keyston.co.uk

Entry 79 Map 9

Cambridgeshire

Worth a visit

80 Cambridge Blue 85 Gwydir Street,
Cambridge CB1 2LG +44 (0)1223 471680
Away from the centre, this simple local
has a warm atmosphere, stacks of
breweriana and a large garden. A wide
choice of ales, ciders and world beers, and
straightforward pub grub.

81 White Pheasant 21 Market Street, Fordham,
Ely CB7 5LQ +44 (0)1638 720414
Very welcoming dining pub with bare
boards, wooden tables, crackling logs,
fresh fish and farmhouse cheeses.
Handpumped local Milton ales and a
dozen wines by the glass. Reports
welcome.

82 The George High Street, Buckden,
St Neots PE19 5XA +44 (0)1480 812300
In sleepy Buckden off the A1, a
contemporary makeover of a handsome
Georgian coaching inn. Pull off and
unwind in the swish bar and sample
top-notch food in the bustling brasserie.

83 The Old Bridge Hotel 1 High Street,
Huntingdon PE29 3TQ +44 (0)1480 424300
A smart hotel with battalions of devoted
locals who come for the informal pubby
bar (good local ales), the food
(delicious), the wines (exceptional) and
the hugely comfortable interiors.

Cheshire

The Wizard
Nether Alderley

The old coaching inn is backed by
magnificent leafy National Trust woodland –
and there's a wizard's well out there with a
legend to match. You're a world away from
bustling Alderley Edge and this large
rambling pub has many good things to offer:
stone floors with Indian rugs, scrubbed
wooden tables, an eclectic mix of prints,
paintings and photos, great fare. It's a cosy
and intimate place run by a bright and
cheery staff. Ales come in the form of
Thwaite's Original or an award-winning
Storm Brewery's beer (Silk of Amnesia and
Looks Like Rain Dear being just two); all are
magic in a glass. Foodies won't be unhappy
either; we found Gillian Pugh's roast pork
belly, served with mashed potato and apple
compote, and followed by deep-filled treacle
tart with vanilla ice cream, a big treat.
There's also a pretty sheltered patio for
warm days.

Meals	12pm-2pm; 6.30pm-9.30pm (12pm-10pm Sat; 12pm-8pm Sun). Main courses £7–£13.95; sandwiches (lunch) from £5.95.
Closed	3pm-5.30pm. Open all day Sat & Sun.
Directions	On B5087 1.5 miles before Alderley Edge.

	Martin Ainscough The Wizard, Macclesfield Road, Nether Alderley, Macclesfield SK10 4UB
Tel	+44 (0)1625 584000
Web	www.ainscoughs.co.uk

Entry 84 Map 8

Cheshire

Hanging Gate
Sutton

High above Macclesfield, the heather moors of the Dark Peak fracture into steep, finger-like ridges; this very old pub hangs from the western slope. A staircase of tiny rooms drops sharply from a sublime little tap room via brass, copper and watercolour-dressed snugs to the View Room, where picture windows unveil an inspiring panorama that stretches to the West Pennine Moors. Several open fires add to the timelessness created by the wizened beams, flagged or carpeted floors and cosy corners where beers from Hydes of Manchester complement the splendid home-cooked food. Game from local estates, meat and fowl from nearby farms are crafted into unfussy, fulfilling meals with a strong local following. It's popular, too, with ramblers from the nearby Gritstone Trail and Macclesfield Forest. A brilliant place.

Meals	12pm-2.30pm (4pm Sat & Sun); 6pm-9pm (9.30pm Sun). Main courses £7.50-£19.95.
Closed	3pm-5pm. Open all day Sat & Sun.
Directions	From A54 follow signs to Langley at Fairway Motel.

Ian & Luda Rottenbury
Hanging Gate,
Sutton,
Macclesfield SK11 0NG
Tel   +44 (0)1260 252238
Web   www.thehanginggateinncheshire.co.uk

♿ 🏃 🛏 🐾 🍺 🍷 📶

Entry 85 Map 8

Cheshire

Sutton Hall Inn
Sutton

A grand place set in expansive grounds, this astonishing pub has been fashioned from the 480-year-old family home of the Earls of Lucan and a former convent. Inside are dark oak floors and furniture, beams and Indian rugs, crossed swords and racks of muskets – and everywhere pictures, eye-catching and interesting. Charming staff whir between seven different dining areas with effortless efficiency and smiles. Six cask ales will please all, with Weetwood's Cheshire Cat and Thwaite's Original. Honest and unfussy modern British menus deliver in spadefuls: slow-roasted belly pork with baked apple, braised potatoes and wholegrain mustard sauce or pan-fried sea bass with a pea and spring onion potato cake and marjoram butter. A toasty place, with log fires in winter and view-filled terraces in summer; hugely friendly, too.

Meals	12pm-10pm (9.30pm Sun). Main courses £8.50-£15.50; sandwiches from £4.95.
Closed	Open all day.
Directions	A523 south from Macclesfield, left signed Sutton, Langley & Wincle, 0.5 miles pub signed on right; see website.

Neil Gander
Sutton Hall Inn,
Bullocks Lane, Sutton,
Macclesfield SK11 0HE
Tel   +44 (0)1260 253211
Web   www.suttonhall.co.uk

♿ 🏃 🛏 🐾 🍺 🍷

Entry 86 Map 8

Cheshire

Harrington Arms
Gawsworth

This red-brick building started life as a farmhouse in 1663 and could still be part of a working farm. The outside may have grown but the inside has barely changed – and it wasn't long ago that they were serving beer here just from the cask. Off the passageway are a bar and a quarry-tiled snug – big enough to fit a settle, a table and an open fire. Then three more public rooms: the traditionally furnished Top Parlour, the Garden Room with its magnificent baking range and the Tap Room where Friday's folk club sessions take place. The Wightmans took over in 2006 and have changed little. That includes the quality of the ale: it's said you won't get a finer pint of Robinson's than at the Harrington. Home-cooked meals and snacks are of the traditional pork pie, soup and sandwich variety – simple and good.

Meals	12pm-2.30pm (3.30pm Sun); 5pm-8.30pm. Bar meals £2.99-£9.75; Sunday lunch £7.95.
Closed	3pm-5pm (4pm-7pm Sun).
Directions	Off A536 at junc. with Church Lane, 2.5 miles from Macclesfield.

Andy & Caroline Wightman
Harrington Arms,
Church Lane, Gawsworth,
Macclesfield SK11 9RJ
Tel   +44 (0)1260 223325
Web   www.harringtonarms.co.uk

Entry 87 Map 8

Cheshire

The White Lion
Barthomley

An inn since 1614 and a siege site in the Civil War, the character-oozing White Lion – wonky black and white timbers, thick thatched roof – stands beside a cobbled track close to a fine sandstone church. Step in to three gloriously unspoilt rooms, all woodsmoke and charm, wizened oak beams, ancient benches and twisted walls, tiny latticed windows and quarry-tiled floors. No music or electronic wizardry, just the crackling of log fires and a happy hubbub. Lunchtime food is listed on chalkboards as walkers and locals settle down on ancient settles at scrubbed wooden tables for hot beef and onion baguettes with chips, hearty ploughman's and Sunday roasts, washed down with well-kept pints of Marstons and Jennings real ale. Summer seating is at picnic benches on the cobbles, with pretty views onto the village.

Meals	12pm-2pm (2.30pm Sun). No food in eve. Main courses £4.75-£7.95.
Closed	Open all day.
Directions	M6 junc. 16; 3rd exit for Alsager; left for Barthomley.

Laura Condliffe
The White Lion,
Barthomley,
Crewe CW2 5PG
Tel   +44 (0)1270 882242
Web   www.whitelionbarthomley.com

Entry 88 Map 8

Cheshire

Bhurtpore Inn
Aston

The extended old Cheshire-brick village farmhouse trumpets eleven real ales, countless bottled continental beers, one hundred malts, and farmhouse ciders and perry. Whatever you choose, you can soak it up with something excellent from the ever-changing menu. The pub was named after an Indian city besieged by a local army commander, and multitudinous maps, paintings and ephemera spread through the warren of rooms vividly recall this deed. Low beams sag beneath myriad water jugs, and open fires crackle in the cosy lounge, where a mongrel-mix of furniture and seating, settles, a longcase clock and absorbing local bric-a-brac add tremendous character. The home-cooked food is really tasty, with local produce at the fore, the portions generous, the choice vast, and there are curries — galore! One great little place.

Meals	12pm-2pm; 6.45pm-9.30pm (12pm-9.30pm Sat; 12pm-9pm Sun). Main courses £5.95-£13.50.
Closed	2.30pm-6.30pm. Open all day Fri-Sun.
Directions	Off A530, 5 miles south west of Nantwich. Follow signs for Wrenbury from turn in Aston near pottery.

Simon George
Bhurtpore Inn,
Wrenbury Road, Aston,
Nantwich CW5 8DQ
Tel +44 (0)1270 780917
Web www.bhurtpore.co.uk

Entry 89 Map 7

Cheshire

The Bull
Shocklach

Wonders have been worked on this traditional village pub a short hop from Chester. Now there's a spacious open-plan feel with stylish wallpapers, old beams, eclectic furniture and pictures. And the floor in the main bar is a work of tile art in itself — gaze at it over a pint of Stonehouse Station Bitter or Plassey Bitter. The food comes with local and seasonal twists, so try venison bourguignon, creamy garlic mash and braised red cabbage with one of the sturdy red wines from the extensive list — the owner knows them well. Lighter dishes include a homemade fish pie of fresh and smoked fish with spinach, topped with creamy mash and glazed with Cheshire cheese. Puddings are wicked, perhaps chocolate bread and butter pudding with ice cream. A classy and quirky off the beaten track place, run with a light and easy touch.

Meals	12pm-2.30pm; 6pm-9.30pm (10pm Fri & Sat); 10am-8pm Sun. Main courses £9.50-£15.95; bar meals (lunch) £4.95-£9.50.
Closed	3pm-5pm. Open all day Fri-Sun.
Directions	Pub in centre of Shocklach. From Chester follow B5130 through Aldford.

Jon Cox & Lindsay Melling
The Bull,
Shocklach,
Malpas SY14 7BL
Tel +44 (0)1829 250239
Web www.thebullshocklach.com

Entry 90 Map 7

Cheshire

The Grosvenor Arms
Aldford

Pretty Aldford is all prim cottages and farms with barleysugar-twist chimneys and chequerboard brickwork. Not far from the old church and castle is the imposing brick and Victorian half-timber village local rejuvenated by Brunning & Price as their flagship pub. Something for everyone here in this most relaxing and classy pastiche: a traditional taproom and snug with log fire, tiled floor and a wonderful old photo of drunks in the stocks, an imposing part-panelled Library Room and a verdant conservatory. There are rustic kitchen tables on boards, tiles and rugs, a panoply of seating choices and a dark-wood bar groaning beneath hand pumps dispensing local beers. The ever-reliable B&P menu carries something for everyone and you can eat in summer on huge tree-shaded lawns next to the village cricket pitch.

Meals	12pm-9.30pm (9pm Sun). Main courses £7.25-£18.95.
Closed	Open all day.
Directions	6 miles south of Chester on B5130 to Farndon & Holt.

Tracey Varley
The Grosvenor Arms,
Chester Road, Aldford,
Chester CH3 6HJ
Tel   +44 (0)1244 620228
Web   www.grosvenorarms-aldford.co.uk

Entry 91 Map 7

Cheshire

The Pheasant Inn
Burwardsley

After a hike along the Sandstone Trail, come and stand before the largest fireplace in Cheshire with a pint of Weetwood Old Dog. Or sit out on the terrace and gaze across the Cheshire Plain all the way to North Wales. Gloriously positioned up in the Peckforton Hills, the Pheasant has been stylishly re-vamped inside. The old laid-back feel has survived the smartening up of the big, beamed and wooden-floored bars, and food is informally served in both bar and restaurant. Seared scallops with lime and dill dressing, smoked haddock and salmon fishcakes, lambs' liver, smoked bacon and onion gravy, and sticky toffee pudding with toffee sauce should satisfy the most ravenous walker, while lunchtime's hot beef sandwiches are equally hearty. There are four ales and 12 wines by the glass but it's the views that you'll come back for.

Meals	12pm-9.30pm (10pm Fri & Sat; 8.30pm Sun). No food 3pm-6pm Mon. Main courses £8.50-£18.95; bar meals £3.95-£8.50; Sunday lunch £12.95.
Closed	Open all day.
Directions	Follow A5115 Christleton Road; at r'bout, 2nd exit onto A41. Left at Chester Road, left at Burwardsley Road, then left at Harthill Road. Pub on left.

Andrew Nelson
The Pheasant Inn,
Tattenhall, Burwardsley,
Chester CH3 9PF
Tel   +44 (0)1829 770434
Web   www.thepheasantinn.co.uk

Entry 92 Map 7

Albion Inn
Chester

Chester's last unspoilt Victorian corner pub. Many a young man would have spent his shilling in the public bar, before he left to sign up for King and Country. The Albion is dedicated to the memory of those who fought. To a background of William Morris wallpaper, leather sofas and soft glowing lamps there is Great War memorabilia aplenty – and a 1928 Steck Player piano that occasionally entertains. There are four cask ales, a flurry of malts, decent wines and 'Trench Rations' in un-trench-like portions – boiled gammon and pease pudding, sausages from Penrith – often organic and locally sourced. Yummy Staffordshire oatcakes from Tunstall with all sorts of fillings are a house special; desserts include rice pudding with a dollop of jam. Do stay: the bedrooms at the top, reached via a separate entrance, are compact, cosy and en suite, with good antique furniture and super-comfortable beds. You are very welcome to bring the dogs (cold water and sausages available) but not the children. With the same landlord for 38 years, the Albion is that rare thing: a traditional city pub with an individual streak.

Rooms	2: 1 double, 1 twin. £75. Singles £65.
Meals	12pm–2pm; 5pm–8pm (6pm–8.30 Sat). No food Sun eve. Main courses £6.20–£9.70.
Closed	3pm–5pm (6pm Sat; 7pm Sun).
Directions	Opp. city walls between The Newgate & River Dee.

	Michael Mercer Albion Inn, Park Street, Chester, CH1 1RN
Tel	+44 (0)1244 340345
Web	www.albioninnchester.co.uk

Cheshire

The Boot Inn
Willington

Prettily ivy-strewn, a row of country cottages turned pub. Set against wooded hills in the middle of fruit farming country, the village local looks west towards the Welsh Hills and south over the Cheshire Plain. It's a gorgeous, sheltered spot with walks nearby. Inside, the pub has been opened up with the bar at the hub. Old quarry tiles, some panelling, characterful beams and a log-burning stove pull the walkers and talkers in. The stone-flagged dining room opens onto a garden you can spill into on warm days, there's a log fire in winter, and donkeys and cats to keep children entertained. Popular food ranges from sandwiches, baguettes and panini at the bar to local lamb with roast vegetables and sea bass deep-fried in sesame batter. Local Weetwood Ales are on draught, and there are a number of wines.

Meals	10am-2.30pm; 6pm-9.30pm Mon-Thurs (10am-9.30pm Fri-Sun). Main courses £8.50-£12.95.
Closed	3pm-6pm. Open all day Fri-Sun.
Directions	Chester-Manchester A54; right for Willington; 2 miles, left at T-junction for Boothsdale.

Mike Gollings
The Boot Inn,
Boothsdale, Willington,
Tarporley CW6 0NH
Tel   +44 (0)1829 751375

Entry 94 Map 7

Cheshire

The Fox & Barrel
Cotebrook

Legend has it that a kind former landlord allowed a pursued fox to escape to the cellar. Whatever the name, this busy roadside pub buzzes with drinkers and diners in equal measure. Inside, life centres on a large bar ringed by terracotta tiles; beyond, acres of oak boards are dotted with Indian rugs. A brick fire is stacked with logs, pictures and prints fill the walls and there are plenty of snug corners in which to sup a Deuchars IPA or a Weetwood cask ale such as Wags to Witches. Convivial Gary chooses a mean wine list with his monthly favourites on the board; Aspinall's cider is soon to arrive. Generous, crowd-pleasing menus include a fish pie of smoked haddock, salmon and prawns, and Cumberland sausage with bubble and squeak mash and onion gravy. Hearty sandwiches too if time is short. There's a smart patio and pub benches on lawns with pleasant rural views. Tally-ho!

Meals	12pm-9.30pm Mon-Sat; 12pm-9pm Sun. Main courses £7.95-£16.95; sandwiches from £4.95; Sunday lunch £9.95 & £11.95.
Closed	Open all day.
Directions	On A49 near Oulton Park.

Gary Kidd & Richard Cotterill
The Fox & Barrel,
Forest Road, Cotebrook,
Tarporley CW6 9DZ
Tel   +44 (0)1829 760529
Web   www.thefoxandbarrel.com

Entry 95 Map 7

The Bear's Paw
Warmingham

Tucked into a pretty village is a dazzlingly refurbished 19th-century inn. There's an almost baronial feel to the Bear's Paw, thanks to the polished oak panelling, the huge fireplaces, the sweeping floors, the leather bucket chairs, bookshelves and old prints and vintage photos. No stuffiness here, just cheery staff making sure you are well-watered and well-fed. Six cask ales, several from Weetwood, all local, take centre stage on the bar; there are also premium brand spirits, 12 malts and an excellent wine list. At well-spaced wooden tables are menus that blend classics with modern twists. Try game and root vegetable pie served with hand-cut chips and pickled red cabbage; vegetarian lasagne with wild mushrooms, spinach and toasted pine nuts; posh poached egg with truffle sabayon. There are deli boards and fabulous sandwiches too. Staying the night? You have 17 superb bedrooms to choose from, each boutiquey, each flaunting funky fabrics, contemporary wallpapers, media hubs and designer fittings. Bathrooms are sleek with granite tops, rain showers, and the softest towels and robes.

Rooms	17 doubles. £75-£130.
Meals	12pm-9.30pm.
	Main courses £8.95-£17.95;
	sandwiches from £5.50.
Closed	Open all day.
Directions	Village signed off A530 south of Middlewich.

Andrew Nelson
The Bear's Paw,
School Lane, Warmingham,
Sandbach CW11 3QN

Tel	+44 (0)1270 526317
Web	www.thebearspaw.co.uk

The Dysart Arms
Bunbury

It is one of those rare places – all things to all people. And, with separate areas clustered round a central bar, it feels open and cosy at the same time. The 18th-century brick building protects a listed interior of scrubbed floorboards, good solid tables and chairs, pictures, prints, plants, and French windows opening to terrace and garden. There's an inglenook packed with logs, a dining area in a library, and the beers and wines are superb. They're proud, too, of their food, and rightly so: chicken liver parfait with spiced fruit chutney; seafood paella; roast lamb with herb stuffing; strawberry Eton mess. The cheeses are taken as seriously as the cask ales (try the local Weetwood or Eastgate Bitter) and the wines are thoughtfully chosen. Warm, intimate, friendly… the place runs on well-oiled wheels.

The Duke of Portland
Lach Dennis

A recent refurbishment has created something of a style journey at the Duke. Wander between a 1920s Parisian bistro, an arty club lounge – worn leather sofas, a futuristic stone fire – and Victorian formality… before pulling up in front of a glorious carved oak bar to order a pint of Jenning's Cocker Hoop or Ringwood Best. Menus are hearty and inventive and the provenance is impeccable. Start with naturally smoked mackerel pâté flavoured with whisky, parsley and double cream before moving on to Glyn Arthur lamb, its gravy infused with tomato, basil and slow roasted garlic, its accompaniment Cheshire potatoes and spring greens. A solid wine list complements it all and there's freshly ground Illy coffee. Under the lofty dining roof is a village pub with a great sense of style and hospitality.

Meals	12pm-9.30pm (9pm Sun). Main courses £8.25-£17.70; bar meals £4.50-£9.55; sandwiches from £4.85.
Closed	Open all day.
Directions	Off A49, 3.5 miles from Tarporley; opposite the church in Bunbury.

Meals	12pm-2.30pm; 5.30pm-9.30pm (12pm-8pm Sun). Main courses £9.95-£18.95; set menu, 2 courses, £10.95.
Closed	3pm-5pm Mon-Wed. Open all day Thurs-Sun.
Directions	On B5082 in village centre.

Gregory Williams
The Dysart Arms,
Bowes Gate Road, Bunbury,
Tarporley CW6 9PH
Tel   +44 (0)1829 260183
Web   www.dysartarms-bunbury.co.uk

Entry 97 Map 7

Mathew Mooney
The Duke of Portland,
Penny's Lane, Lach Dennis,
Northwich CW9 7SY
Tel   +44 (0)1606 46264
Web   www.dukeofportland.com

Entry 98 Map 7

Cheshire

Chetwode Arms
Lower Whitley

The 400-year-old, Cheshire-brick roadside inn hides a warren of small rooms and passageways. There's the bar room itself, tiny, with an open coal fire, and four more; the snuggest may be used as a private dining room. Expect low ceilings, exposed brick and beams, fresh flowers and mirrors, oodles of atmosphere and tasty food. In the dining room — opening onto a terrace that overlooks the pub's own bowling green — contented locals tuck into local game pie, confit duck with black cherry jus and rosemary mash, chilli crab cakes, roast pork knuckle, and steaks cooked on hot rocks. There are lunchtime sandwiches, salads and ploughman's, four changing guest ales on tap and the wine list favours some top vineyards from Richard's home country — South Africa. Great for judicious drinkers of wine and beer, and a super dining pub.

Meals	12pm-2.30pm; 6pm-9.30pm (12pm-11pm Sat; 8.30pm Sun). Main courses £12.50-£32; Sunday lunch £9.95.
Closed	3.30pm-5.30pm & all day Mon in winter. Open all day Sat & Sun.
Directions	On A49 2 miles from M56 junc. 10.

	Richard Sharnok Chetwode Arms, Street Lane, Lower Whitley, Warrington WA4 4EN
Tel	+44 (0)1925 730203
Web	www.chetwodearms.org

Entry 99 Map 7

Cheshire
Worth a visit

New owners, old pub. Four beers on handpump in the two little taprooms, one with a cast-iron range, and proper English food in the dining room extension.

Only a handful of these charming Victorian establishments survive — this extraordinary, narrow little bar is an integral part of the busy station. Renowned for its choice of real ale, pies and puddings.

Small and unassuming in a stunning spot on the edge of the Dee Marshes. Watch marsh harriers or little egrets as you down real ales and gaze over the estuary to North Wales.

The youngest chef ever to win a Michelin star, Aiden Byrne returns to his Cheshire roots. His modern British menu will seduce you: potted pork and apple rillettes, Cumbrian lamb with sweet onion purée.

A buzzy atmosphere and a great range of microbrewery ales at this converted warehouse down by the canal. Run by Brunning & Price pubs, so expect good modern pub food.

Victorian schoolhouse opposite the Castle: expect an airy 'schoolroom' feel with vaulted ceilings and educational relics. These days the chalkboards list classy bar food.

Hugely popular pub in a beautifully converted watermill beside the Shropshire Union Canal. Local food is ever-present on the imaginative menus. Super alfresco areas.

Cornwall

The Bush Inn
Morwenstow

After a blowy walk along the cliffs this ancient pub makes a hospitable resting place. Rob and Edwina Tape have sympathetically updated The Bush, one of Cornwall's oldest smugglers' haunts. Once a monastic rest house, its oldest parts date back to AD950; note the Celtic piscina carved from serpentine in one wall. Slate-flagged floors, a huge stone fireplace and lovely old wooden furnishings in the bar preserve the timeless character of this immutable place. Food is served all day in two charming, contemporary dining rooms with old pine tables and yellow-washed walls. Picture windows pull in the views of farmland and sea. Menus include beef and lamb from neighbouring farms, Cornish seafood and vegetables from the kitchen garden; we loved our venison bourguignon with mash and roasted root vegetables. Weary walkers are revived by excellent beers, robust snacks and a lively buzz – and the thought of retiring to one of the three bedrooms upstairs, each with seaside-blue walls, simple down duvets, fresh bathrooms and wonderful views across rolling fields to the Atlantic. A fine little place.

Rooms	3 twins/doubles. £79. Singles £45.
Meals	11am–9pm.
	Main courses £8–£18.
Closed	Open all day.
Directions	Follow signs for Morwenstow off A39, 9 miles north of Bude.

Rob & Edwina Tape
The Bush Inn,
Crosstown, Morwenstow,
Bude EX23 9SR
Tel   +44 (0)1288 331242
Web   www.bushinn-morwenstow.co.uk

Entry 107 Map 1

Slipway Hotel
Port Isaac

If the tide is in, leave your car at the top and approach on foot. To arrive unflustered (the streets are narrow) is the best way to appreciate this charming Cornish fishing village. At the Slipway, a modest bar area plays second fiddle to the front terrace with its prime views of the working harbour, beach and sea. Sup Sharp's ales as seagulls wheel overhead before tucking into the freshest of fresh crab sandwiches (we're talking 'food feet' here, not miles!). If walking the coast path or surfing has drummed up more of an appetite then move into the galleried restaurant – once a chandlery – for some serious fishiness. You could start with steamed Fowey mussels with red onion, chilli, parsley and white wine cream before diving into a whole grilled gilt head bream on artichoke hearts. If your appetite is hearty, finish with crème brulée infused with blackberries and cointreau, or a Cornish cheese board with red onion chutney. Bedrooms offer true shelter from a storm, little havens of modernity with stylish bathrooms and wooden furniture. Ask for a balcony and a sea view.

Rooms	10: 8 twins/doubles, 2 family suites. £90–£140. Family suites £130–£180. Singles £67.50–£97.50.
Meals	12pm-2.30pm; 6.30pm-9pm. Main courses £6.25-£10.95 (lunch), £13.25-£18.95 (dinner).
Closed	Open all day.
Directions	Opposite harbour & beach in village centre.

Mark & Kep Forbes
Slipway Hotel,
Middle Street,
Port Isaac PL29 3RH
Tel   +44 (0)1208 880264
Web   www.portisaachotel.com

Cornwall

The Rising Sun
Altarnun

Beginning life as a farm on the edge of Bodmin Moor in the 1600s, the property later became a 'hole in the wall'. The main bar is all no-nonsense Delabole flagstones and oak floors surrounded by wall settles with long padded cushions; add guns and prints, archaic needlework verse, beams, plenty of woodchip and delicately tobacco tinged paint tones – the smugglers' breath perhaps? Things are all very local hereabouts, the barman brews the Penpont Ale just a mile away and there's also Skinner's Spriggan or St Piran's and Greene King IPA. Next door in the old cattle shed is a more contemporary dining area, its exposed stone walls hung with local art. After a blow on the moors the shoulder of pork with mash, market vegetables and olive and thyme braising liquor will put the colour back in your cheeks.

Meals	12pm-2pm (2.30pm Sun); 6pm-9pm. Main courses £8.25-£15; sandwiches from £4.85.
Closed	2.30pm-5.30pm. Open all day Sat, Sun & bank hols.
Directions	Off A30 in Altarnun village, through with church on left; at T-junc. left (pub signed).

Andy Mason
The Rising Sun,
Altarnun,
Launceston PL15 7SN
Tel   +44 (0)1566 86636
Web   www.therisingsuninn.co.uk

Entry 109 Map 1

Cornwall

The Crown Inn
Lanlivery

You are on the bucolic Saint's Way, along which Irish drovers used to 'fat walk' the cattle from Padstow to Fowey before setting sail for France. Walkers still stop by for sustenance. Most of the 12th-century longhouse's flagged floors have been carpeted, but the deep granite-lined clome oven remains and a country mood prevails – the Crown is the hub of the village. Three areas ramble: the largest for dining, the conservatory for the sun, and the classic, granite-floored bar for foaming pints of Betty Stogs or Knocker Ale. Tasty food comes courtesy of fine Cornish produce, and is cooked to order: mackerel pâté with toasted organic bread, crab gratin, braised shoulder of local lamb, Cornish rump steak with pepper sauce and all the trimmings. There's a decent wine list and the pretty garden has a view of the church tower.

Meals	12pm-9pm. Main courses £8.95-£14.95; bar meals £3.95-£10.95.
Closed	Open all day.
Directions	Signed off A390 between Lostwithiel & St Blazey. Pub opp. church.

Andy Brotheridge
The Crown Inn,
Lanlivery,
Bodmin PL30 5BT
Tel   +44 (0)1208 872707
Web   www.wagtailinns.com

Entry 110 Map 1

Cornwall

St Kew Inn
St Kew

Lost down a maze of lanes in a secluded wooded valley, the St Kew is a grand old inn originally built for the masons working on the church. It is an irresistibly friendly, chatty place with a huge range and a warming fire, a dark slate floor, winged settles and a terrific unspoilt atmosphere – no pub paraphernalia here. Meat hooks hang from a high ceiling and earthenware flagons embellish the mantelpiece in the bar. Local St Austell ales are served in the traditional way, straight from the barrel, and the food is bang up-to-date, freshly cooked by Paul, former head chef at Rick Stein's eponymous Padstow restaurant. Try mussels with cider, cream and chives, chicken, leek and thyme pie, fish and chips with pea purée and tartare sauce, warm coconut Bakewell tart. In summer, the big streamside garden is the place to be.

Meals	12pm-2pm; 6.30pm-9pm. No food Sun eve in winter. Main courses £9.50-£22.
Closed	2.30pm-6pm (from 3pm Sun). Open all day in summer.
Directions	From Wadebridge for Bude on A39 for 4 miles; left after golf club. 1 mile to St Kew Churchtown.

Paul Ripley & Sarah Allen
St Kew Inn,
St Kew,
Bodmin PL30 3HB
Tel   +44 (0)1208 841259
Web   www.stkewinn.co.uk

Entry 111 Map 1

Cornwall

Tinner's Arms
Zennor

Under landlords Grahame and Richard, one of Cornwall's most historic pubs thrives in the wilds of West Penwith. Close to the church in the coastal hamlet of Zennor, the 13th-century inn is pretty unspoilt with its flagstone floors, whitewashed walls and fabulously long, well-stocked bar. The food and drink have moved sharply up a gear, with lunch and evening menus changing daily – rabbit stew, roast pork belly, venison with red wine jus, hake with red pepper sauce, ales from St Austell and Sharp's. The Tinner's Arms, bursting with character and open log fires, will always be a popular stop for walkers heading for the nearby coastal paths. It's packed in summer, so spill out in the lovely large garden overlooking the sea; off-season, it could be you and the dog alone in the bar. Worth the walk from St Ives.

Meals	12pm-2.30pm; 6.30pm-9pm. Main courses £9.95-£15.
Closed	3.30pm-6.30pm. Open all day in summer.
Directions	Off B3306 St Ives-St Just road, 4 miles west of St Ives.

Grahame Edwards &
Richard Motley
Tinner's Arms,
Zennor, St Ives TR26 3BY
Tel   +44 (0)1736 796927
Web   www.tinnersarms.co.uk

Entry 112 Map 1

Cornwall

The Gurnard's Head
Zennor

The coastline is magical and the hike to St Ives hard to beat. Secret beaches appear at low tide, cliffs tumble down to the water and wild flowers streak the land pink in summer. As for the pub, you couldn't hope for a better base. It's earthy, warm, stylish and friendly, with airy interiors, colourwashed walls, stripped wooden floors and log fires at both ends of the bar. Maps and art hang on the walls, books fill every shelf; if you can't finish one, take it home and post it back. Rooms are warm and cosy, simple and spotless, with superb mattresses, throws over armchairs, Roberts radios and, in the suite, a lovely big tub. Downstairs, super food, all homemade, can be eaten wherever you want: in the bar, in the restaurant or out in the garden in good weather. Snack on rustic delights – pork pies, crab claws, half a pint of Atlantic prawns – or tuck into more substantial treats: fresh asparagus with a hollandaise sauce, fish stew with new potatoes, rhubarb crème brûlée. Picnics are easily arranged, there's bluegrass folk music in the bar most weeks, and the St Ives-Penzance bus runs right outside – a huge plus.

Rooms	7: 4 doubles, 3 twins/doubles. £90-£160. Singles from £75.
Meals	12.30pm-2.30pm; 6pm-9.30pm. Main courses £4.50-£10.95 (lunch), £4.50-£14 (dinner).
Closed	Open all day.
Directions	On B3306 between St Ives & St Just, 2 miles west of Zennor, at head of village of Treen.

Charles & Edmund Inkin & Julie Bell
The Gurnard's Head,
Zennor,
St Ives TR26 3DE

Tel   +44 (0)1736 796928
Web   www.gurnardshead.co.uk

Entry 113 Map 1

Cornwall

The Star Inn
St Just

Entrenched in the wild landscape close to Land's End is the "last proper pub in Cornwall". This 18th-century gem, owned by the ex-mayor of St Just and its oldest and most authentic inn, proudly shirks the trappings of tourism and remains a drinkers' den. Bands of locals sink pints of Tinners Ale in the low-beamed, spick-and-span bar, old pub games thrive and the place is the hub of the local folk scene, with live music at least ten nights a month, singalongs and joke-telling all part of the Monday evening entertainment. The dimly-lit bar is jam-packed with interest and walls are littered with seafaring and mining artefacts; coals glow in the grate on wild winter days. Come for St Austell ale and the 'craic'. A free juke box, mulled wine in winter and that pub rarity: a great family room.

Cornwall

The Victoria Inn
Penzance

With glorious Mount's Bay (beach and coastal path) down the lane, this striking pink-washed village inn draws the crowds. Arrive early and bag a seat in the stone-walled bar sprinkled with seafaring and fishing memorabilia, or in the sunny sunken garden. Chef-landlord Stewart is making waves locally, using the best Cornish ingredients to produce some delicious pub food. For ale-lovers there's Doom Bar on tap, a perfect match for a lunchtime crab sandwich or haddock and chips. Cooking moves up a gear in the evenings, so start with a seafood and shellfish soup, move on to crispy belly of St Buryan pork with chorizo and haricot beans, and finish with a rhubarb and ginger crumble – or a plate of artisan cheeses. Built to house the masons extending the church in the 12th century, this old, old pub later became a safe house for the clergy.

Meals	No food served.
Closed	Open all day.
Directions	A3071 from Penzance. On right-hand side of square in centre.

Meals	12pm-2pm; 6.30pm-9pm. No food Sun eve or Mon in winter. Main courses £8.95-£16.75; sandwiches from £5.50.
Closed	Sun eves & Mon in winter.
Directions	Pub and village signed off A394 Penzance to Helston road, 4 miles east of Penzance.

Johnny McFadden
The Star Inn,
1 Fore Street,
St Just, Penzance TR19 7LL
Tel   +44 (0)1736 788767

Stewart & Anna Eddy
The Victoria Inn,
Perranuthnoe,
Penzance TR20 9NP
Tel   +44 (0)1736 710309
Web   www.victoriainn-penzance.co.uk

Entry 114 Map 1

Entry 115 Map 1

Halzephron Inn
Gunwalloe

An opera singer running a pub in a remote smuggler's inn – irresistible and only in Cornwall. Looking out across Mount's Bay towards Land's End, the rugged whitewashed inn has been taking in guests (and smuggler's: there's an underground passage) for 500 years. Come for low ceilings, stone walls, log fires and polished brass in numerous cosy eating areas around the bar. There are sea views from the roadside terrace, a lively courtyard for summer afternoons, and a small garden overlooking fields. Lunch on hearty homemade food – perhaps cheese soufflé, seafood risotto or fish pie (there's a tempting menu for juniors, too) – then walk it all off on a clifftop walk to Gunwalloe's 13th-century church down beside the sand. Return to cosy country bedrooms with antique dressers, patchwork quilts, restful florals, bowls of fruit and long views across fields. Each has a refurbished bathroom and there are books galore – from Dickens to Alan Coren. Angela, exuberant and charming, runs this popular coastal inn with aplomb.

Rooms	2 doubles. £95. Singles £55.
Meals	12pm-2pm; 7pm-9pm. Main courses £10.95-£18.50; bar meals from £5.10.
Closed	2.30pm-6pm (6.30pm in winter), Sun eves & all day Mon & Tues Nov-early Dec & Jan.
Directions	From Helston, A3083, signed The Lizard. Pass Culdrose air base, then right, signed Gunwalloe. 2 miles and inn on left after houses.

Angela Thomas
Halzephron Inn,
Gunwalloe,
Helston TR12 7QB
Tel   +44 (0)1326 240406
Web   www.halzephron-inn.co.uk

Entry 116 Map 1

Cornwall

The New Inn
Manaccan

Genuinely unspoilt country pubs in tourist-trade Cornwall are hard to find, but this rustic thatched cottage close to The Lizard is a treasure. Access is via tortuously narrow lanes, which gives Penny's pub that rare 'lost in the old country' feel. Many opt to stroll over from Helford for heart-warming pub grub, refreshing pints of Doom Bar and a natter with the locals. Don't be fooled by the new thatch and a lick of whitewash, the bar remains delightfully unspoilt, with its beam and plank ceiling, built-in wall settles, walls hung with local art, crackling log fire, and time-honoured pub games. Refuel on lunchtime sandwiches or bowls of moules marinière with crusty dipping bread; steak and ale pie or blackboard-listed smoked haddock risotto and lamb shank with redcurrant jus. Head for the rose-filled garden when the sun shines.

Cornwall

The Pandora Inn
Mylor Bridge

Yachtsmen moor at the end of the pontoon that reaches into the creek. The building, too, is special: thatched and 13th-century. Originally The Passage House, it was renamed in memory of the *Pandora*, a naval ship sent to Tahiti to capture the mutineers of Captain Bligh's *Bounty*. The pub keeps the traditional layout on several levels, along with some panelled walls, polished flagged floors, snug alcoves, three log fires, loads of maritime mementos – and amazingly low wooden ceilings. The bar food has something to please everyone, with fresh seafood dominating the specials board. Arrive early in summer – by car or by boat; the place gets packed and parking is tricky. On winter weekdays it's blissfully peaceful, and the postprandial walking along wooded creekside paths easy.

Meals	12pm-2.30pm (2pm Sun); 6.30pm-9.30pm (7pm-9pm Sun). Main courses £8.95-£14; sandwiches (lunch) from £4.50.
Closed	Open all day.
Directions	Manaccan is signed off B3293 between Helston and St Keverne. Follow signs and narrow lanes through Mawgan; in village centre.

Meals	12pm-9pm (9.30pm Fri & Sat). Main courses £8.50-£14.95.
Closed	Open all day.
Directions	A39 from Truro; B3292 for Penryn & follow Mylor Bridge signs; descend steeply to Restronguet.

Penny Williams
The New Inn,
Manaccan,
Helston TR12 6HA
Tel +44 (0)1326 231323

John Milan
The Pandora Inn,
Restronguet, Mylor Bridge,
Falmouth TR11 5ST
Tel +44 (0)1326 372678
Web www.pandorainn.com

Entry 117 Map 1

Entry 118 Map 1

Cornwall

Trengilly Wartha Inn
Constantine

Well tucked down steep and twisting lanes, in the verdant heaven that is the Helford estuary, is this friendly Cornish inn. Grab a pint of Skinner's Trengilly Gold or St Austell HSD and enjoy a stroll in the six acres of old orchard with pond – and a gravelled pergola with ingenious underfloor heating. The main bar is a cracker with a wealth of mini-snugs formed by mid-height wooden settles, beer mats tacked to beams, cricketing memorabilia, local black and white photos, local paintings, and a display of some of the over 150 wines on offer; there are 40 malts too. Chef Nick Tyler has 20 years under his belt here and keeps it fresh, local and seasonal; a shame not to try the Falmouth River mussels with onion, white wine, cream and chips, or the crab thermidor that comes with homemade granary bread.

Cornwall

The Roseland Inn
Philleigh

Beside a peaceful parish church, two miles from the King Harry Ferry, a cob-built Cornish treasure with keen new owners – locals Phil and Debbie Heslip. The front courtyard is bright with blossom in spring and climbing roses in summer. Indoors: old settles with scatter cushions, worn slate floors, low black beams and winter log fires. Local photographs, gig-racing memorabilia and a corner dedicated to rugby trophies scatter the walls. Spotlessly kept, it attracts locals and visitors in search of good food – such as local farm meats and fish landed at St Mawes. Dishes range from decent sandwiches to scallops with belly pork and white onion sauce, and roast duck with raspberry jus. Staff are full of smiles – even when the pub doubles as the Roseland Rugby Club clubhouse on winter Saturday nights.

Meals	12pm-2.15pm; 6.30pm-9.30pm. Main courses £7-£15.
Closed	3pm-6pm.
Directions	Approaching Falmouth on A39, follow signs to Constantine. On approach to village, inn signed left, then right.

Meals	12pm-2.30pm; 6.30pm-9pm. Main courses £8.50-£13.95; sandwiches from £5; Sunday lunch £9.95.
Closed	3pm-6pm. Open all day weekends & in summer.
Directions	Off A3078 St Mawes road or via King Harry Ferry from Truro (Feock) to Philleigh.

	Lisa & William Lea Trengilly Wartha Inn, Constantine, Falmouth TR11 5RP
Tel	+44 (0)1326 340332
Web	www.trengilly.co.uk

Entry 119 Map 1

	Phil & Debbie Heslip The Roseland Inn, Philleigh, Truro, TR2 5NB
Tel	+44 (0)1872 580254
Web	www.roselandinn.co.uk

Entry 120 Map 1

Cornwall

The Kings Head
Ruan High Lanes

A pub with a heart. Niki and Andrew are warm, friendly and love what they do. Find pine-backed stools, a comfy old sofa, a real fire. An impressive collection of tea cups hangs from the ceiling, a window sparkles with coloured bottles and all is quirky and fun. Off the main bar are a second room with hunting prints and wood-burner and a friendly carpeted dining room with gleaming tables and Windsor chairs. Ales are from Skinners in Truro, fish from St Mawes. Tuck into crab pâté, the famous Ruan slow-roasted duck with pepper sauce, and a fabulous Cornish sirloin of beef with tip-top Yorkshire pudding. The quiet little village has a church with a Norman font and a creek that is a haven for waders and waterfowl… behind is the Roseland countryside.

Cornwall

The Plume of Feathers
Mitchell

It was an inspired move to transform the old 16th-century coaching inn where John Wesley once preached into a warm and stylish pub-restaurant. The imaginative cooking draws an appreciative crowd and in summer food is available all day. Low stripped beams, half-panelled walls hung with modern art, fresh flowers, candle-studded pine tables and soothing lighting make this place a pleasure to walk into; it feels novel and fun. Delightful staff serve Scottish beef and local vegetables and fish at sensible prices – take Cornish fishcakes with sweet chilli sauce and dressed leaves, or grilled Dover sole with lemon butter. There are thick bacon sandwiches at lunch and delicious puddings, perhaps chilled vanilla rice pudding with spiced pineapple. The central bar is lively with TV, piped music and Sharp's Doom Bar on tap. Great value.

Meals	12.30pm-2pm; 6.30pm-9pm. No food Sun eve & Mon in winter. Main courses £9.50-£21.50; bar lunches £6-£11.50; Sunday roast from £12.95.
Closed	2.30pm-6pm, Sun eves & Mon all day in winter. Open all day in summer.
Directions	Village signed off A3078 Tregony-St Mawes road.

Meals	12pm-10pm. Main courses £8.95-£15.50.
Closed	Open all day.
Directions	Off junction of A30 & A3076 south of Newquay.

Andrew & Niki Law
The Kings Head,
Ruanlanihorne, Ruan High Lanes,
Truro TR2 5NX
Tel   +44 (0)1872 501263
Web   www.kingsheadruan.co.uk

Pete & Jaqui Fair
The Plume of Feathers,
Mitchell,
Newquay TR8 5AX
Tel   +44 (0)1872 510387
Web   www.theplume.info

Entry 121 Map 1

Entry 122 Map 1

Cornwall

Worth a visit

123 The Finnygook Inn Crafthole,
Torpoint PL11 3BQ +44 (0)1504 230338
Following the success of Devon's Turtley Corn Mill, the Brunning family have worked their magic on this inn. Look forward to a modern all day menu, decent wines and ales, and views across the Tamar and Lynher. Reports please.

124 The Blue Peter Quay Road, Polperro,
Looe PL13 2QZ +44 (0)1503 272743
Unspoilt little fishing pub built into the cliffside by the harbour. Dark and cosy wood-floored bar with hidden corners, nautical artefacts, and tip-top Cornish ales.

125 The Rashleigh Polkerris, St Austell PL24 2TL
+44 (0)1726 813991
A pub *on* the beach, in a tiny cove! The old coastguard station is cosy in winter, unbeatable in summer, so down a pint of real ale and watch the sun set across St Austell Bay.

126 Seven Stars The Moor, Falmouth TR11 3QA
+44 (0)1326 312111
Unchanging, unspoilt and rather quirky town-centre pub with splendid narrow tap room, racked Sharp's and Skinner's ales and snug back bar. Run by a priest for over 50 years.

127 Cadgwith Cove Inn Cadgwith, Ruan Minor,
Helston TR12 7JX +44 (0)1326 290513
Smack on the coastal path, in a fishing hamlet, sits this old smugglers' inn. Decked with seafaring mementos, there's a fishy menu, five ales on tap and a sun-trap terrace.

128 The Cornish Arms Churchtown, St Merryn,
Padstow PL28 8ND +44 (0)1841 520288
Local lad Rick Stein has added a pub to his empire. This ancient boozer remains a traditional village local with slate floors, log fires and classic pub food cooked from the best local produce.

129 The Maltsters Arms Chaple Amble,
Wadebridge PL27 6EU +44 (0)1208 812473
Away from the busy beaches around Rock is this inviting 16th-century pub, with fun and funky eating areas and a good all-round menu including excellent fresh-fish specials. Reports please.

Cumbria

The Sun Inn
Kirkby Lonsdale

Set in a narrow street, with the historic parish church in view of some of the rooms above, The Sun is a fine example of an old inn. Step under the ancient portico and into a low-ceilinged bar of warmth, soft colours and a jolly mix of tables and chairs. Food is lavish, so push the boat out and sit in the smart brasserie-style dining room for wild boar terrine, roast pork belly with bubble and squeak and apple sauce or hake Welsh rarebit… polish it all off with passion fruit mousse or a plate of cheese; all of it is delicious. There are cask ales to keep serious beer drinkers happy, the wine list is sublime (there are organic choices too) and the staff are wonderful. Pootle around Kirkby Lonsdale with its interesting shops or strike out further for some grand walking in the Yorkshire Dales National Park: sublime.

Meals	12pm-2.30pm (except Mon); 7pm-9pm.
	Main courses £6.95-£9.95 (lunch) £12.95-£22.95 (dinner); bar snacks £3.50-£5.95; Sunday lunch £13.95 & £16.95.
Closed	Open all day.
Directions	M6 junc. 36. A65 for 5 miles following signs for Kirkby Lonsdale. In town centre.

Mark & Lucy Fuller
The Sun Inn,
6 Market Street, Kirkby Lonsdale,
Carnforth LA6 2AU
| Tel | +44 (0)1524 271965 |
| Web | www.sun-inn.info |

Entry 130 Map 12

The Punch Bowl Inn
Crosthwaite

You're away from Lake Windermere in a small village encircled by a tangle of lanes that defeat most tourists. A church stands next door; the odd bride ambles out in summer, bell ringers practise on Friday mornings. But while the Punch Bowl sits in a sleepy village lost to the world and doubles up as the local post office, it is actually a seriously fancy inn. It was rescued from neglect by Paul Spencer, and after a top-to-toe renovation it now sparkles. Outside, honeysuckle climbs on old stone walls, inside four fires keep you warm in winter. A clipped elegance runs throughout: leather sofas in a beamed sitting room, candles in vases on dining room tables, an old farmhouse table in the restaurant crammed with brandies and malts. You can dine on succulent roast Cumbrian lamb with duck-fat potatoes, creamed leeks and a mint jus, then retire to a fabulous room with bold fabrics, flat-screen TV, Roberts radio and a bathroom with a heated floor. Four rooms have huge views down the Lyth valley; readers are full of praise.

Rooms	9: 5 doubles, 1 twin/double, 2 four-posters, 1 suite. £125–£225. Four-posters £140–£175. Suite £245–£310. Singles from £93.75.
Meals	12pm–9.30pm. Main courses £11.95–£18.95.
Closed	Open all day.
Directions	M6 junc. 36, then A590 for Newby Bridge. Right onto A5074, then right for Crosthwaite after 3 miles. Pub on southern flank of village.

	Jenny Sisson The Punch Bowl Inn, Crosthwaite, Kendal LA8 8HR
Tel	+44 (0)15395 68237
Web	www.the-punchbowl.co.uk

Entry 131 Map 11

The Derby Arms
Witherslack

Don't be put off by the faded façade of this traditional local. Behind lies a hugely comfortable and very individual pub. Step into a stylish series of candlelit rooms, aglow with rug-strewn floors, cream and red walls, some rather grand paintings, polished period furniture, merry log fires, old stone fireplaces, dogs and booted walkers. The central bar heaves with hand pumps dispensing Cumbrian microbrewery ales (including Dent Aviator), hand-pressed juices from Witherslack, and heaps of wines by the glass. Bag a seat by the fire and settle in for supper; the changing menu announces a crowd-pleasing mix of traditional and modern pub dishes, much prepared from fresh local produce. Start with own-smoked duck breast, follow with sirloin steak with peppercorn sauce or butternut squash risotto, end with sticky toffee pudding. It's super civilised yet nicely laid-back, so stay the night. Upstairs are six refurbished bedrooms with old brass beds, period furnishings, crisp linen, slate-tiled bathrooms, a couple of claw-foot baths, and peaceful country views. After continental breakfast, explore the southern Lakes.

Rooms	6 doubles. £65–£85.
Meals	12pm-2pm (2.30pm Sat); 6pm-9pm (12pm-8.30pm Sun). Main courses £8.95-£15.25.
Closed	3pm-5.30pm. Open all day Fri-Sun.
Directions	Witherslack is signed off A590 midway between Kendal and Grange-over-Sands.

Dan Schrieber
The Derby Arms,
Witherslack,
Grange over Sands LA11 6RN
Tel   +44 (0)1539 552207
Web   www.ainscoughs.co.uk

Entry 132 Map 11

Masons Arms
Cartmel Fell

A perfect Lakeland inn tucked away two miles inland from Lake Windermere. You're on the side of a hill with huge views across lush fields to Scout Scar in the distance. In summer, all pub life decants onto a spectacular terrace – a sitting room in the sun – where window boxes and flowerbeds tumble with colour. The inn dates from the 16th century and is impossibly pretty. The bar is properly traditional with roaring fires, flagged floors, wavy beams, a cosy snug... and a menu of 70 bottled beers to quench your thirst. Rustic elegance upstairs comes courtesy of stripped floors, country rugs and muted walls in the first-floor dining room – so grab a window seat for fabulous views and order delicious food, anything from a sandwich to Cumbrian duck. Suites are contemporary and gorgeous, with cool colours, fabulous beds, gleaming bathrooms and Bang & Olufsen TVs. Self-catering cottages, equally immaculate, come with fancy kitchens (breakfast hampers can be arranged); best of all, you have your own private terrace, so order a meal in the restaurant and they'll bring it to you here.

Rooms	5 + 2: 5 suites. £75–£145. 2 cottages: 1 for 4, 1 for 6. Cottages £130–£175 per day.
Meals	12pm-2pm; 6pm-9pm (12pm-9pm Sat & Sun). Main courses £10.25–£14.95; bar meals from £5.95.
Closed	Open all day.
Directions	M6 junc. 36; A590 west, then A592 north. 1st right after Fell Foot Park. Straight ahead for 2.5 miles. On left after sharp right-hand turn.

John & Diane Taylor
Masons Arms,
Cartmel Fell,
Grange over Sands LA11 6NW
Tel   +44 (0)1539 568486
Web   www.strawberrybank.com

Brown Horse Inn
Winster

Your satnav will wobble en route to this old pub in the neck of the Lyth Valley. But it's worth getting lost trying to find it, now that the talented Edmondsons have taken over the reins. In the bar of the handsome 18th-century coaching inn are stone floors, open fires, beams and traditional oak chairs; in the dining room, monumental candelabra shed dramatic light on quirky painted furniture and contemporary art. On your plate are vegetables from the back garden, poultry and eggs from Steve's smallholding, and meat from Karen's family farm. (There's a farm shop, too.) So tuck into homemade black pudding with quails' egg and mustard sauce as a starter, grilled tuna steak, herb crushed potatoes, confit fennel and aubergine purée to follow, and candied lemon cheesecake with honeycomb ice cream to finish (best plan a walk round the lake before you start!). Four boutique bedrooms have been added to the rest, each with a wall of tinted glass to make the most of the views across the hills – gorgeous. Huge French beds, glamourous textiles, rococo lights and slate bathrooms complete the snazzy picture.

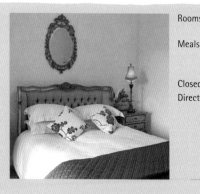

Rooms	9: 7 doubles, 1 twin, 1 family room. £80-£90. Family room £110-£140.
Meals	12pm-2pm; 6pm-9pm (9.30pm Sat). Main courses £9.50-£14.95; bar snacks (lunch) from £4.75.
Closed	Open all day.
Directions	In village on A5074 between A590 west of Levens and A592 south of Bowness-on-Windermere, 4 miles from Bowness.

	Steve Edmondson
	Brown Horse Inn,
	Winster,
	Windermere LA23 3NR
Tel	+44 (0)1539 443443
Web	www.thebrownhorseinn.co.uk

Entry 134 Map 11

Queens Head Hotel
Troutbeck

Nowhere are the views as majestic as on the Kirkstone pass – and there's woodsmoke in the air as you approach this classic old Lakeland inn. Inside: a warren of fascinating rooms and a flagged bar created from a carved Elizabethan four-poster – reputed to have come through the ceiling and never returned. Old instruments hang above beams, stuffed birds and beasts gaze down from mantelpieces, ramblers tuck into their suppers and dogs recover before blazing fires. The dining area is newer and less atmospheric but the food is a major draw: earthy, dependable and chalked up on the boards each day; homemade black pudding; fish pie, slow-braised lamb shank; sticky toffee pudding. There are fine beers, eight wines by the glass, loads of choice, small portions for kids (sausages, mussels), and desserts for hearty hikers. At the front are splendid views; the bedrooms are a treat, too, some peacefully positioned in the barn opposite. Neat, compact, recently refurbished with an elegant farmhouse feel, they sport new four-posters, relaxing colours, unusual fabrics, and wind-up alarm clocks so you don't miss breakfast! *Ask about short breaks.*

Rooms	15: 3 doubles, 2 twins/doubles, 5 four-posters. Barn: 4 doubles, 1 four-poster. £110–£130. Four-posters £130. Singles £70–£80.
Meals	12pm–9pm. Main courses £11.95–£26.95. Baguettes from £7.50.
Closed	Open all day.
Directions	Exit M6 at junc. 36, A591 dir. Ambleside. At mini r'bout right on A592 signed Ullswater & Kirkstone Pass. 3 miles, on left.

Ian Dutton
Queens Head Hotel,
Town Head, Troutbeck,
Windermere LA23 1PW

Tel	+44 (0)1539 432174
Web	www.queensheadhotel.com

Drunken Duck Inn
Ambleside

Afternoon tea can be taken in the garden, where lawns run down to Black Tarn and Greek gods gaze upon jumping fish. You're up on the hill, away from the crowds, cradled by woods and highland fell. Huge views from the terrace shoot off for miles to towering Lakeland peaks. Roses ramble on the veranda, stone walls double as flower beds and burst with colour. As for the Duck, she may be old, but she sure is pretty, so step into a world of airy interiors: stripped floors in a beamed bar, timber-framed walls in the restaurant. Wander at will and find open fires, grandfather clocks, rugs on the floor, exquisite art. They brew their own beer, have nine bitters on tap and the food is utterly delicious: diver-caught scallops, roasted and served with slow confit of pork; fillet of monkfish with crab risotto and sauce gribiche. Bedrooms are dreamy, smartly dressed in crisp white linen, with colours courtesy of Farrow & Ball and peaty water straight off the fell. Rooms in the main house are snug in the eaves; those across the courtyard are crisply uncluttered and indulgent.

Rooms	17: 15 doubles, 2 twins. £95-£285. Singles from £90.
Meals	Dinner 6pm-9.30pm; bar meals 12pm-4pm. Main courses £13.95-£23.95; bar meals £4.50-£8.95.
Closed	Open all day.
Directions	West from Ambleside on A593, then left at Clappersgate for Hawkshead on B5286. After 2 miles, turn right, signed. Up hill to inn.

Stephanie Barton
Drunken Duck Inn,
Barngates,
Ambleside LA22 0NG
Tel +44 (0)1539 436347
Web www.drunkenduckinn.co.uk

Entry 136 Map 11

Cumbria

Strickland Arms
Sizergh

Right beside the gates to Sizergh Castle, this old pub was desperate for attention. Now it is jointly run by Martin Ainscough and the National Trust. Behind the stark stone exterior are two civilised rooms decked out in best NT style: earthy Farrow & Ball colours, rugs on slate and wooden floors, an eclectic mix of antiques. Order a pint of Coniston Bluebird, pick a seat by a glowing coal fire, peruse the papers while you wait, then tuck into delicious food that bears no resemblance to normal pub fare. From local and organic ingredients come baked field mushrooms with concassed tomatoes, sea bass fishcakes with sweet chilli dressing, chump of lamb with port and shallot sauce. There's a lovely flagged front terrace for summer with pretty views (and just a slight hum from the dual carriageway).

Meals	12pm-2pm; 6pm-9pm (12pm-8.30pm Sun). Main courses £9.95-£15.50; bar lunch £5-£8.95.
Closed	3pm-5.30pm. Open all day Sat & Sun & May-Sep.
Directions	Just off A590 north of Kendal, by Sizergh Castle gates.

Helen & Martin Ainscough
Strickland Arms,
Sizergh,
Kendal LA8 8DZ
Tel   +44 (0)1539 561010
Web   www.thestricklandarms.com

Entry 137 Map 11

Cumbria

Tower Bank Arms
Sawrey

Just across from the ferry, next to Hilltop – Beatrix Potter's farm – is Jemima Puddleduck's inn. (She may not have caroused here, but she did waddle by.) Today the National Trust are its sympathetic custodians. Jumbles of whitewashed buildings make up the legendary village of Sawrey; a courteous staff handles the summer crowds. Enter a slate-flagged bar with a grand open range that throws out the heat on chilly days; further in it is carpeted and cosy. Flowers and shining bits and bobs make the place homely; the oak-floored dining room is set with white linen napkins and polished cutlery. Four local ales accompany dishes to please walkers: beef casseroled in ale, Woodall's Cumberland sausages, Cumbrian lamb in various guises. The puddings are scrumptious and the cheeses reflect Cumbria's producers. Special.

Meals	12pm-2pm; 6pm-9pm (8pm Sun). 12pm-2pm; 6pm-8pm (9pm Fri/Sat) Nov-Easter. Main courses £10.50-£17; bar snacks £7.50-£9.
Closed	3pm-5pm. Open all day Sat & Sun & in summer.
Directions	On B5285 2 miles south east of Hawkshead; towards the Windermere Ferry.

Anthony Hutton
Tower Bank Arms,
Sawrey,
Ambleside LA22 0LF
Tel   +44 (0)1539 436334
Web   www.towerbankarms.co.uk

Entry 138 Map 11

The Sun Inn
Hawkshead

Deep in one of the Lake District's prettiest villages, The Sun sits atop stone steps, overlooking the National Trust park and the woodlands beyond. Such is the setting... the pub is having a spruce up, and the the bar will shine just as brightly as the rooms upstairs. The best of the traditional quirkery remains, so expect flagstone floors, rescued oak panelling and hearty fires; outside there are picnic tables and parasols for when the sun's hat comes on. A team of sisters are at the helm, and Diane, Emma and Becky love this place. Food is honest and wholesome, with an emphasis on Herdwick lamb reared by a family friend on Millbeck Farm: order a rack with mash and Cumberland sauce, and settle with a pint of Hawkshead Red while you wait for it to be cooked in the freshest way possible. Emma's deserts are worth the journey alone, but there are walks and mountain bike trails from the door for the adventurous. Return to a cosy bedroom: mind-your-head beams, thick dark fabrics and exposed stone work leave a patina of age, while the bathrooms are new and compact. The locals feel right at home here, and you will too.

Rooms	8: 5 doubles, 1 twin/double, 1 four-poster, 1 family room. £85–£95. Four-poster £94.50–£102.50. Family room £94.50–£104.50. Singles from £52.50.
Meals	12pm-2.30pm; 6pm-9pm. Main courses £8.95–£14.95; sandwiches from £5.
Closed	Open all day.
Directions	Village centre.

Becky Wolf
The Sun Inn,
Main Street, Hawkshead,
Ambleside LA22 0NT

Tel	+44 (0)1539 436236
Web	www.suninn.co.uk

Entry 139 Map 11

Cumbria

Church House Inn
Torver

Michael Beaty arrived in 2006 and injected life into a historic pub, while keeping the best of original features and 15th-century charm. Ceilings are low and heavy beamed, there are slate floors and wood panelling, and locals and visitors steam together by the ever-stocked log fires, swapping tips on the merits of the various ales – perhaps a pint of Whitehaven or Hawkshead before a light lunch? Then set off for a walk: the iconic Coniston Old Man peak surveys the inn, and makes a stunning backdrop to the beer garden, replete with fruit trees and children's play area in summer. Ingredients are as local as can be, and all is made from scratch; join friends for dinner and share a Hot Pot or Game Pie between four or more before devouring a platter of puddings – white chocolate mousse, crème brûlée; there's always room.

Meals	12pm-3pm; 6pm-9pm (9.30pm Fri & Sat). Main courses £11.95-£17.95; sandwiches from £5.45.
Closed	Open all day. Closed Mon & Tue lunch in mid winter.
Directions	Beside A593 Ambleside to Broughton-in-Furness road; in village 2 miles south of Coniston.

Michael Beaty
Church House Inn,
Torver,
Coniston LA21 8AZ
Tel +44 (0)1539 441282
Web www.churchhouseinntorver.com

♿ 🏃 📖 🍴 🍺 📶

Entry 140 Map

Cumbria   Award winner 2010

White Hart Inn
Booth

The main counter drips with brass, hops and beer pumps; walls and shelves are strewn with clay pipes, sepia photos, taxidermy and tankards. It's a sleepy-snoozy village local, friendly too, where regulars cheerfully mingle with visitors over pints of Coniston and Hawkshead Bitter, decent wines and a delicious, no-nonsense menu: rare-breed meat from Aireys of Ayside; steak and Guinness pie; vegetarian chilli; and mallard and pheasant from the shooting parties that gather in the pub car park on winter Saturdays. They source locally, and – yes! – do small portions for children. A sloping flagged floor reflects the light from the window; black leather sofas front stoves at each end, log-fuelled in cold weather. The walking's marvellous and the village fits snugly into the ancient landscape of wooded valleys and tight little roads.

Meals	12pm-2pm; 6pm-8.45pm. All day Sat & Sun. Main courses £10.75-£15.75.
Closed	Open all day.
Directions	Off A590 Barrow road after Lakeside & Haverthwaite Steam Railway.

SPECIAL AWARD
see pages 20-21

Authentic pub

Nigel & Kath Barton
White Hart Inn,
Booth,
Ulverston LA12 8JB
Tel +44 (0)1229 861229
Web www.whitehart-lakedistrict.co.uk

🏃 📖 🍴 🍺 🍷 📶

Entry 141 Map 11

The Langstrath Country Inn

Borrowdale

A magnet for walkers: just a track up the Langstrath to the Lakes' highest peaks. New owners Guy and Jacqui Frazer-Hollins are settling into life here in the "Lake District's fairest valley". Vertical timbers create cosy stable-like corners; carpeting and a crackling fire add warmth; there are fascinating old photos of local characters and fabulous views over the fells from the windows to gaze at. Upstairs, fresh contemporary bedrooms have white linen, brass beds or colourful headboards and gleaming, tiled bathrooms. Wet boots have their own drying room, so you can pick them up warm and cosy again in the morning. The slate-topped bar with its polished brass rail sports four hand-pulls for Jennings, Hawkshead and other local guest ales; good wines are available by the glass; a couple of dozen malts enliven the varnished rack. The dinner menu reveals an enthusiasm for local produce — Keskadale steak and mushroom pudding, Rosthwaite Herdwick lamb with red wine gravy; lunch includes soup and hot baguettes. A popular refuelling stop on the Coast to Coast path and the Cumbrian Way. *No under-5s overnight.*

Rooms	8 twins/doubles. £89-£109. Singles £59.50-£67.
Meals	12pm-2.15pm; 6pm-9pm. Main courses £10.50-£15.75; bar lunch from £4.75.
Closed	Mon all day.
Directions	From Keswick B5289 to Borrowdale. Village on left between Rosthwaite & Seatoller.

Guy & Jacqui Frazer-Hollins
The Langstrath Country Inn,
Borrowdale,
Keswick CA12 5XG
Tel   +44 (0)1768 777239
Web   www.thelangstrath.com

Cumbria

Blacksmiths Arms
Broughton Mills

An utterly unspoilt little local. In the land of rugged hills and wooded valleys, you approach down a winding lane between high hedges; once you are round the final bend, the low-slung farmhouse-inn comes into view. Inside are four small, slate-floored rooms with beams and low ceilings, long settles and several log fires. The bar is strictly for drinking – indeed, there's not much room for anything else; there are three cask ales (two local, one guest) and traditional cider in summer. Across the passage, a room serving proper fresh food, snacks or full meals, and two further dining rooms that sparkle with glass and cutlery. The blackboard advertises dishes with a contemporary slant, plus beef and Herdwick lamb reared in the valley. The food is seriously good, so it gets busy; in summer you can wander onto the flowery terrace.

Meals	12pm-2pm; 6pm-9pm. No food Mon (except bank hols). Main courses £8.50-£13.95; bar meals from £3.95.
Closed	2.30pm-5pm Tues-Fri & Mon lunch (except bank hols). Open all day Sat/Sun.
Directions	Off A593 Broughton-Coniston road.

Michael & Sophie Lane
Blacksmiths Arms,
Broughton Mills,
Broughton-in-Furness LA20 6AX
Tel   +44 (0)1229 716824
Web   www.theblacksmithsarms.com

Entry 143 Map 11

Cumbria

Old Crown
Hesket Newmarket

In a dreamy village and with porter on tap! The old pub is owned by a cooperative of 147 souls and is run by Keith and Edna. Its tiny front room with bar, settles, glowing coals, thumbed books, pictures and folk music (the first Sunday of the month) squeezes in a dozen; a second room houses darts and pool; a third and fourth are dining rooms. Not only is this the only pub where you can sample all of Hesket Newmarket's beers brewed in the barn at the back – ask about tours – but it is the focal point of the community, even supporting the post office whose postmistress repays in puddings and pies. The Old Crown is also known for its fine curries and Sunday roasts. Its authenticity draws people from miles around, Prince Charles dropped by (twice) to launch the *Saving Your Village Pub* guide, walkers come for the Caldbeck Fells.

Meals	12pm-2.30pm Fri-Sun; 6pm-9pm. Main courses £6-£13; bar meals £2.50-£6.50.
Closed	2.30pm-5.30pm Fri-Sun. Open from 5.30pm Mon-Thurs.
Directions	M6 junc. 41 for Wigton on B5305. 6.5 miles turn for Hesket Newmarket.

Keith & Edna Graham
& Joanne Richardson
Old Crown, Hesket Newmarket,
Wigton CA7 8JG
Tel   +44 (0)1697 478288
Web   www.theoldcrownpub.co.uk

Entry 144 Map 11

Cumbria

Kirkstile Inn
Loweswater

Hard to imagine a more glorious setting than that of the Kirkstile Inn, tucked among the fells, next to an old church and a stream, a half mile from the lakes of Loweswater and Crummock. Roger Humphreys is well up to the job of hosting this legendary bar. The whole place is authentic, traditional, well looked after: whitewashed walls, low beams, solid polished tables, cushioned settles, a well-stoked fire, plants, flowers and the odd horse harness to remind you of the past. Come for afternoon tea, or settle down with an unforgettable pint of Loweswater Gold or Melbreak Bitter; they also have their own microbrewery overlooking Estwaite Water near Hawkshead. Six chefs use local produce for unfussy traditional dishes such as steak and ale pie, chicken breast stuffed with Cumberland sausage with an onion sauce, and sticky toffee pudding.

Meals	12pm-2pm; 6pm-9pm. Main courses £8.50-£16.95; bar snacks £4-£7.50.
Closed	Open all day.
Directions	Lorton road from Cockermouth; follow signs to Loweswater.

	Roger Humphreys Kirkstile Inn, Loweswater, Cockermouth CA13 0RU
Tel	+44 (0)1900 85219
Web	www.kirkstile.com

Entry 145 Map 11

Cumbria

Highland Drove
Great Salkeld

Yards from the Norman church with its keep-like tower (protection against marauding Scots), the timber porch leads to a flagged bar – cosy, warm, civilised. There's a bar-dining area with easy leather chairs and pine tables, and a popular games room with pool. With open log fires, tartan, brick and timber, this is a spruce, 21st-century inn that pleases drinkers, diners and walkers. Named after the waters ('kyloes') that the cattle drovers crossed on their way to Scottish market, the dining room has a Highland lodge feel, its great windows gazing to the lush Pennines. Tuck into rack of lamb, pan-fried Nile perch, chargrilled beef fillet with port and thyme jus, and toffee and banana crumble. Beers are from the cask, wines are well-chosen. Or keep things simple with a fresh baguette in the bar.

Meals	12pm-2pm; 6.15pm-7.45pm (5.45pm-7.15pm Sat). Restaurant 6.30pm-9pm only. Main courses £6.25-£10.95 (bar); £9.95-£18.50 (dinner).
Closed	2.30pm-6pm & Mon lunch (except bank hols). Open all day Sat & Sun.
Directions	Just off B6412 in Great Salkeld, off A686 north east of Penrith.

	Donald & Paul Newton Highland Drove, Great Salkeld, Penrith CA11 9NA
Tel	+44 (0)1768 898349
Web	www.highland-drove.co.uk

Entry 146 Map 11

Cumbria

Mardale Inn @ St Patrick's Well
Bampton

Though close to the M6 at Shap, this area east of the Lakes is much overlooked, with its high fells and romantic Haweswater. The hub of the village is its pub – all modern stone flags, exposed stone and brickwork, beams and open fireplaces, nifty lighting and good use of space. Chunky wooden tables and chairs encourage a look at the menu: try potted Morecambe Bay shrimps or sea bass on lemon and coriander mash. Finish with toffee pudding and caramel sauce, or a local cheese platter – nothing a dose of harsh fell walking wouldn't put right. Sebastian oversees proceedings and the feeling is modern, but this is still 'the local' to folk nearby so you'll be rubbing shoulders with Cumbrians quaffing great local beers. Walk the dog to Haweswater where the last breeding golden eagles soar high above its dark surface.

Meals	12pm-9pm. Main courses £9.95-£19.25.
Closed	Open all day.
Directions	Bampton is signed from A6 at Shap or B5320 south of Penrith.

Seb Hindley
Mardale Inn @ St Patrick's Well,
Bampton,
Penrith CA10 2RQ
Tel   +44 (0)1931 713244
Web   www.mardaleinn.co.uk

Entry 147 Map 11

Cumbria

The Gate Inn
Yanwath

It was built as a toll gate in 1683 – hence the name. Known to locals as the Yat, the old pub has gained a reputation for its food, locally sourced and served in hearty portions. The place is immaculate, the young staff are attentive and the landlord remains loyal to the pub's roots, so you may eat anywhere, including the sunny sheltered patio at the back. Walk in to a characterful, dimly-lit bar, all cosy corners and crackling fire, background music and happy chatter. Beyond is a light, airy and raftered dining room. The menu depends on fresh deliveries every day including Cumbrian meat and plenty of fish, and there's homemade food for children, from pizza to beefburgers and fishcakes. Wines come from an excellent merchant's in Kendal, beers include the fruity and full-flavoured Doris's 90th Birthday Ale.

Meals	12pm-2.30pm; 6pm-9pm. Main courses £12-£25.
Closed	Open all day.
Directions	On B5320 south-west of A6 & Penrith; 2.5 miles from M6 junc. 40.

Matt Edwards
The Gate Inn,
Yanwath,
Penrith CA10 2LF
Tel   +44 (0)1768 862386
Web   www.yanwathgate.com

Entry 148 Map 11

George & Dragon
Clifton

Charles Lowther has found a chef who does perfect justice to the slow-grow breeds of beef, pork, chicken and lamb produced organically on the Lowther Estate – and you'll find lovely wines to match, 16 by the glass. Ales and cheeses are local, berries and mushrooms are foraged, vegetables are home-grown… and his signature starter, twice baked cheese soufflé with a hint of spinach – is divine. As for the long low coaching inn, it's been beautifully restored by craftsmen using wood, slate and stone, and painted in colours in tune with the period. Bare wooden tables, comfy sofas, intimate alcoves and crackling fires make this a delightful place to dine and unwind; old prints and archive images tell stories of the 800-year-old estate's history. Outside is plenty of seating and a lawned play area beneath fruit trees. Upstairs are ten bedrooms of varying sizes, perfectly decorated in classic country style. Carpeting is Cumbrian wool, beds are new, ornaments come with Lowther history, showers are walk-in, baths (just two) are free-standing.

Rooms	10 twins/doubles. £85–£135. Singles from £69.
Meals	12pm-2.30pm; 6pm-9.30pm. Main courses & Sunday roast from £9.95.
Closed	Open all day.
Directions	On A6 at end of Clifton village, just south of Penrith and M6 (junc. 40).

Juno Leigh
George & Dragon,
Clifton,
Penrith CA10 2ER
Tel   +44 (0)1768 865381
Web   www.georgeanddragonclifton.co.uk

The Black Swan
Ravenstonedale

Duck under hanging baskets to find a good mix of people in the busy main bar, cosy with red plush stools, exposed stone and soft lighting. Or nip through to the public bar with TV, games of scrabble and newspapers to read. A small lounge is quieter, with comfy seating at bay windows and an open fire. Wherever you land you are looked after by energetic, efficient staff; choose from a simple sandwich to a three-course blow out (try the pie of the day topped with puff pastry). Meat comes from known local farms, the eggs are home-laid, the vegetables are fresh from Kirkby Stephen; visit the thriving village shop and take home some local produce. Bedrooms are comfortable, unfussy, some with views; some are in an annexe, one is next to the bar (not always quiet). All have fine cotton sheets, fresh flowers, large towels, organic soaps from Sedbergh; some have their own sitting rooms with sofabeds for extra folk. A DVD library is available for very lazy lumps but you are deep in the Eden valley and it would be a crime not to explore it!

Rooms	14: 10 doubles, 3 suites, 1 single. £80–£95. Suites £115. Singles from £47. Extra bed £15 (child) £20 (adult).
Meals	12pm-2pm; 6pm-9pm. Main courses £8.95-£15.95; Sunday roast £8.95.
Closed	Open all day.
Directions	Beside A685 between M6 (junc. 38) & A66 at Brough.

Alan & Louise Dinnes
The Black Swan,
Ravenstonedale,
Kirkby Stephen CA17 4NG
Tel   +44 (0)1539 623204
Web   www.blackswanhotel.com

Entry 150 Map 12

Cumbria

Worth a visit

151 The Watermill Inn Ings, Kendal LA8 9PY
+44 (0)1539 821309
The draw of this converted wood mill in prime Windermere country is the mind-boggling range of 16 real ales, including cracking beers brewed in the pub's own microbrewery visible from the bar. Heady farm ciders and 50 malt whiskies, too.

152 Hole in t'Wall Lowside,
Bowness-on-Windermere LA23 3DH
+44 (0)15394 43488
A good old-fashioned tavern, not plain but not plush, packed with Windermere tourists in season and prepared for walkers all year round. Hearty food and a flagged front terrace that's a suntrap in summer.

153 Manor Arms
Broughton-in-Furness LA20 6HY
+44 (0)1229 716286
A modest 18th-century pub in the corner of Broughton's Georgian square that draws ale-lovers for pints of Yates, Copper Dragon, Roosters and more from eight handpumps. Traditional bar snacks all day.

154 The Sun Hotel & Inn Coniston LA21 8HQ
+44 (0)15394 41248
A no-nonsense little pub at the back of an Edwardian hotel, with stone flags and walls, old settles, local ales from the cask and hearty pub food. Great views from the garden.

155 Old Dungeon Ghyll Great Langdale,
Ambleside LA22 9JY +44 (0)15394 37272
To hikers ruddy from the day's exertions, the infamous, barn-like Walkers' Bar serves decent grub, mugs of tea, and God's own beer, Yates. The atmosphere is infectious.

156 Britannia Inn Elterwater,
Ambleside LA22 9HP +44 (0)1539 437210
With Great Langdale Beck tumbling into the tarn, a brilliant starting point for walkers. Return for pints of foaming Cumbrian ale, hearty food, views from the terrace. Being everyone's secret, the pub is always busy.

157 The Three Shires Little Langdale,
Ambleside CA13 0RU +44 (0)15394 37215
Walkers love this friendly pub – for its stunning Lakeland setting, and hearty snacks in the slate-walled public bar or carpeted lounge. Worth calling in after journeying over the high Wrynose and Hardknott passes.

158 The Wasdale Head Inn Wasdale Head,
Gosforth CA20 1EX +44 (0)19467 26229
At the head of Wasdale, in a setting of romantic grandeur – the steep slope of Scafell its dramatic backdrop – is this legendary mountain pub beloved of walkers and climbers. Refurbishment is planned under new owners. Reports please!

159 Brackenrigg Inn Watermillock,
Penrith CA11 0LP +44 (0)1768 486206
The terrace and bay windows of this 18th-century inn have views across Ullswater to the fells – breathtaking. Several local beers on tap in the part-panelled bar and menus with a modern British slant; Sunday lunch is brilliant value.

160 The Cross Keys Inn Carleton,
Penrith CA11 8TP +44 (0)1768 865 588
Donald Newton and son Paul, owners of the successful Highland Drove in Great Salkeld, have refurbished this 16th-century roadside inn close to Penrith. It has a super terrace and fine views – reports welcome.

161 Shepherd's Inn Melmerby, Penrith CA10 1HF
+44 (0)1768 881741
The lovely Lakeland building overlooking the village green reopened in June 2009, offering fresh traditional pub food and six real ales. Combine with invigorating walks on the wild Pennine moors. New owners – reports please.

Derbyshire

Three Horseshoes
Breedon on the Hill

Opposite the old 'village lock up', a listed village inn. Ian Davison and Jennie Ison have revitalised the old place and introduced a relaxed modern feel and a menu to match. Expect painted brickwork, seagrass matting, antique tables, Windsor chairs, an eclectic mix of pictures and masses of space. Smaller rooms include a simple quarry-tiled bar and an intimate red dining room with three tables, while pride of place goes to a handsome Victorian bar counter picked up years ago and stored in anticipation of the right setting. Dishes are chalked up on boards in the bar and the award-winning formula offers halibut with garlic and prawn sauce, lamb shank with mustard mash, and bread and butter pudding. Marston's Pedigree on hand pump should satisfy those in for a swift half. Outside: a garden terrace at the back.

Meals	12pm-2pm; 5.30pm-9.15pm (12pm-3pm Sun). Main courses £8.95-£25.50; bar meals £4.95-£10.95.
Closed	2.30pm-5.30pm & Sun from 3pm.
Directions	Follow signs off A42 between Ashby de la Zouch & Castle Donington.

Ian Davison & Jenny Ison
Three Horseshoes,
44-46 Main Street,
Breedon on the Hill, Derby DE73 8AN
Tel +44 (0)1332 695129
Web www.thehorseshoes.com

Entry 162 Map 8

Derbyshire

The Bulls Head
Repton

Once a derelict shell, this pub was brought back to life by Richard and Loren Pope, with the best of the original features brought to the fore. The downstairs bar is a jumble of connected rooms with wooden floors, stone flags, stripped timbers and designer quirks: chairs upholstered in black and white cow hide, bulls heads made from bicycles, driftwood sculptures, steel pillars. The main restaurant has huge 1930s gilt mirrors that hang on either side of a gas-effect fire; it all works. Energetic staff flit hither and thither to bring you serious dinners or a casual real ale: start with slow-braised Derbyshire belly pork with creamed cabbage, bacon and calvados, finish with lemon posset. A menu of proper food for children means they can come too – and there's a super garden for tearing around in afterwards.

Meals	12pm-3pm; 6pm-10pm. All day Sun. Main courses £7.95-£19.95; sandwiches from £3.95; Sunday roast £8.95.
Closed	Open all day.
Directions	Repton is signed off A38 between Derby & Burton-upon-Trent. Pub in High Street.

Richard & Loren Pope
The Bulls Head,
84 High Street, Repton,
Derby DE65 6GF
Tel +44 (0)1283 704422
Web www.thebullsheadrepton.co.uk

Entry 163 Map 8

Derbyshire

The Barley Mow
Kirk Ireton

Sunlight streams through the stone mullioned windows of this Jacobean pub. Outside, its resplendent sundial is dated 1683. So authentic is the Barley Mow that Sir Isaac Newton could be penning the last words of a thesis in the parlour. The tiled tap room floor is framed by simple wall benches and dotted with old stools; barrels of ale are racked neatly behind the bar; it is austere, dimly lit, addictive. To the side, up a few steps from the front parlours, are adjoining rooms that include the original kitchen with its huge 17th-century working bread oven. A selection of fresh cobs is available at lunchtime while suppers are for residents only. As you sip your Thatchers cider or Whim Hartington IPA, you will notice the slate-topped tables with a missing corner and wonder why? For drinkers, ramblers and historians, sheer delight.

Meals	Rolls available 12pm-2pm, £1.50.
Closed	2pm-7pm.
Directions	Signed off B5023 Wirksworth to Duffield road.

	Mary Short
	The Barley Mow,
	Main Street, Kirk Ireton,
	Ashbourne DE6 3JP
Tel	+44 (0)1335 370306

Entry 164 Map 8

Derbyshire

Ye Olde Gate Inne
Brassington

One of the most exquisite pubs in Derbyshire, built from timber salvaged from the wrecks of the Armada. Furnishings are plain: ancient settles, rush-seated chairs, gleaming copper pans, a clamorous clock, a collection of pewter. In winter a fire blazes in the blackened range that dominates the quarry-tiled bar. In the dim yet wonderfully atmospheric snug are a glowing range and flickering candlelight. There's a short, changing blackboard menu and traditional tucker: ploughman's, baguettes, a hearty and memorable steak and Guinness pie, casseroles, homemade bread and butter pudding. Come too for superbly kept Marston's Pedigree on hand pump and a number of malts. Mullioned windows look onto a sheltered back garden – perfect for the popular evening barbecues that are held from Easter until October.

Meals	12pm-2pm (12.30pm-2.30pm Sun); 6.30pm-8.45pm. No food Sun eve. Main courses £8.25-£13.95; bar meals £4.25-£10.75.
Closed	2.30pm-6pm (7pm Sun); Mon (except bank hols) & Tues lunch.
Directions	Midway between Ashbourne & Wirksworth off B5035.

	Peter Scragg
	Ye Olde Gate Inne,
	Well Street, Brassington,
	Matlock DE4 4HJ
Tel	+44 (0)1629 540448

Entry 165 Map 8

The Bear Inn
Alderwasley

An amazing hilltop position and a fabulous welcome – thanks to open fires and smiling staff. There's a fascinating warren of beamed rooms here on various levels, and wherever you choose to sit, something catches your eye: the place is running over with all manner of quirky ephemera – china, old farming tools, candles and clocks. Food is good value and wholesome; a dense, earthy pâté comes with homemade apple chutney and chunks of bread, and the slow-cooked lamb is tender and aromatic in a red wine and rosemary sauce. There's a snug for a pint and a scan of the paper; well-kept hand-pulled ales are a draw and guest beers change regularly. The lawned garden is a great place to sit in the summer – revel in far-reaching views. Newly refurbished and well-proportioned bedrooms have a touch of the gothic about them and are comfortably stylish, with fat mattresses, crisp white linen and luxuriously dramatic damask fabric at the windows – pull them aside for more stunning vistas. Spotless bathrooms have tiled floors and snowy towels. Choose the grand antique four-poster for a special occasion!

Rooms	6 doubles, 2 four-posters. £75. Four-posters £90.
Meals	12pm-9.30pm (9pm Sun). Main courses £9.95-£22.95; bar meals £3.95-£5.95.
Closed	Open all day.
Directions	From B5025 east of Wirksworth, turn off at Wirksworth Moor at the Malt Shovel pub. Continue for 1 mile.

John & Amanda Stamp
The Bear Inn,
Alderwasley,
Belper DE56 2RD

Tel   +44 (0)1629 822585
Web www.bear-hotel.com

Derbyshire

The Devonshire Arms at Beeley
Beeley

Classic Peak District scenery surrounds Beeley's stone cottages and this public house. Converted from three cottages in 1747, it became a coaching inn that was visited by Edward VII and is popular now because of its proximity to great Chatsworth House. In 2006 it was taken over by the Duke and Duchess of Devonshire. Always a civilised lunch spot for well-heeled locals, it now verges on the opulent. Along with the beams, log fires and settles are candy-stripe tub chairs in vibrant hues and cushions tucked into cosy crannies. In a room where floor-to-ceiling windows overlook the beck are snazzy bar stools, a glass-fronted wine store and more enticing colours. Bar and brasserie serve traditional and modern food and meat from the estate – all delicious – while the wine list reaches the dizzy heights of Château Petrus. In a stone-flagged tap room, walkers are refreshed with expertly kept ales. Bedrooms, equally vibrant, stylish and understated, are full of comfort and joy. The staff are lovely and breakfasts are a treat.

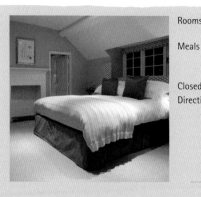

Rooms	8: 4 doubles, 3 twins/doubles, 1 suite. £121–£181. Suite £171–£191.
Meals	12pm–9.30pm. Main courses £9.95–£19.50; bar meals £5.95–£12.95.
Closed	Open all day.
Directions	North from Matlock on A6, then right onto B6012 for Chatsworth and Beeley. Right in village; pub on right.

Alan Hill
The Devonshire Arms at Beeley,
Beeley,
Matlock DE4 2NR
Tel   +44 (0)1629 733259
Web   www.devonshirebeeley.co.uk

Derbyshire

Old Poets' Corner
Ashover

Old Poets' Corner has something for everyone and it has been achieved with effortless style. Inside this mock-Tudor village-centre inn, ideally placed for forays into the Peaks and Dales, is a whirlwind of activity that pulls together live music, eight real ales, one perry, an ever-changing range of five ciders and an Arts and Crafts interior. And, living up to its name, there's a regular poets' night for local rhymesters. From good hefty farmhouse settles and pine tables, music-loving regulars sup ale brewed in the pub's own microbrewery and ciders such as Broadoak Moonshine (8.4% ABV)... And with that in mind the menu is more than substantial, trumpeting chillis, pastas, pies, casseroles and a carvery on Sundays. Sit back, relax and be entertained by the energy and good vibes surrounding you.

Meals	12pm-2pm (3pm Sun); 6.30pm-9pm (curry night Sun from 7pm). Main courses £6.50-£14; bar meals £3.25-£9.50; Sunday roast £7.95.
Closed	Open all day.
Directions	Ashover is just off B6036, between Kelstedge & Woolley Moor.

Kim & Jackie Beresford
Old Poets' Corner,
Butts Road, Ashover,
Chesterfield S45 0EW
Tel   +44 (0)1246 590888
Web   www.oldpoets.co.uk

Entry 168 Map 8

Derbyshire

Druid Inn
Birchover

A strange, enticing countryside of tors, crags, wooded knolls and stone circle-strewn moors erupts high above Matlock. In the midst of this morphological mayhem stands the Druid Inn, its mellow stone exterior disguising an ultra-chic gastropub and a menu drawing on traditional British and the best of European; ham hock, black pudding and stilton terrine, monkfish with tomato, chorizo and butter bean stew, rice pudding with gingerbread ice cream, crab mayonnaise sandwiches. Shadows of the old village local remain: a quarry-tiled snug with open fire, antique seats and beers brewed by the Leatherbritches brewery – but the general atmosphere is that of bistro-in-the-country, with a minimalist décor in the split-level restaurant rooms. Suntrap patios promise village views, and ramblers rub shoulders with epicures.

Meals	12pm-2.30pm (3pm Sun); 6pm-9pm (9.30pm Fri & Sat). Main courses £9-£21; sandwiches from £5-£8.
Closed	Open all day.
Directions	From A6; B5056; signs for Birchover.

Michael & Bryan Thompson
Druid Inn,
Main Street,
Birchover DE4 2BL
Tel   +44 (0)1629 650302
Web   www.thedruidinn.co.uk

Entry 169 Map 8

The Bull's Head
Ashford in the Water

Lovely carved settles, cushions, clocks and country prints – this is pub heaven. There are newspapers and magazines to read, light jazz hums in the background, coals glow in the grate. The busy Bull's Head has been in Debbie Shaw's family for half a century and she and Carl have been at the helm for the past decade. Carl cooks, proudly serving "bistro food, not a laminated menu"; even the bread and the cheese biscuits are homemade. With a strong emphasis on local and seasonal produce, there could be a full-flavoured chicken and pistachio terrine, beef and Guinness sausages with celeriac mash and red wine gravy, monkfish ragôut, sticky toffee pudding with black treacle sauce. Service is swift and friendly and, this being a Robinson's pub, Unicorn Best Bitter, Old Stockport and Double Hop are on hand pump – a brilliant place.

Meals	12pm–2pm; 6.30pm–9pm (7pm–9pm Sun); no food Thurs eve during winter. Main courses £9.50–£16.50.
Closed	3pm–6pm (7pm Sun).
Directions	Off A6, 2 miles north of Bakewell. 5 miles from Chatsworth.

Debbie Shaw
The Bull's Head,
Church St,
Ashford in the Water,
Bakewell DE45 1QB
Tel +44 (0)1629 812931

Entry 170 Map 8

Three Stags Heads
Wardlow

As you weave your way across the moor you could easily miss this collection of cottages, modestly housing a pottery and a pub. The pub is a gem inside, and couldn't be plainer: two small rooms, one heated by a fire, the other by a coal-burning kitchen range, nice for drying out waterproofs. So settle into a pint of Abbeydale's Black Lurcher, the house bitter with an 8% ABV, named in memory of one of the dogs. The menu really is a case of what is available from the surrounding countryside and features a lot of game (it has been known for squirrel to have gone into the pot). Opening times are restricted depending on whether you're here for pottery or a pint, and a plate of something hot and wholesome from the chalked board. Soaked in history it's no museum – the hosts and the dogs see to that!

Meals	12.30pm–3.30pm; 6.30pm–9pm (9.30pm Fri–Sun). Main courses £8.50–£10.50.
Closed	Mon–Thur all day & Fri until 7pm. Open all day weekends & bank hols.
Directions	At junction of A623 & B6465 south east of Tideswell.

Geoff & Pat Fuller
Three Stags Heads,
Wardlow,
Buxton SK17 8RW
Tel +44 (0)1298 872268

Entry 171 Map 8

Derbyshire

The Chequers Inn

Froggatt

The setting is almost alpine in its loveliness – impossible to pass this pub by. Once four stone-built cottages going back to the 16th century, the Tindall's ancient whitewashed inn has been sympathetically modernised, recently refurbished and is full of homely touches. Wooden floorboards, pine and country prints, cottage furniture and interesting objets give character to rooms that radiate off a stone-walled, timber-ceilinged bar. While blackboards promise modern bistro-style dishes – crab and pea linguine, pan-fried calves' liver with celeriac purée and red pepper sauce – the standard menu lists doorstep sandwiches and traditional casseroles and pies. From the raised garden behind, a path leads straight up through woods to stunning Froggatt Edge; the walking is marvellous.

Meals	12pm-2pm; 6pm-9.30pm (12pm-9.30pm Sat; 9pm Sun). Main courses £9-£15; Sunday lunch from £10.50.
Closed	2.30pm-6pm. Open all day Sat & Sun.
Directions	On A625 8 miles northwest of Chesterfield, 9 miles southwest of Sheffield.

	Jonathan & Joanne Tindall The Chequers Inn, Froggatt Edge, Froggatt, Hope Valley S32 3ZJ
Tel	+44 (0)1433 630231
Web	www.chequers-froggatt.com

Entry 172 Map 8

Derbyshire

Worth a visit

173 The Plough Leadmill, Hathersage, Hope Valley S32 1BA +44 (0)1433 650319
The isolated 16th-century inn, once a corn mill, stands in super gardens on the banks of the Derwent, with stunning views to rolling hills. Cosy, plush interior with old beams and log fires, and a posh printed menu with traditional food.

174 The Red Lion Litton, Tideswell SK17 8QU +44 (0)1298 871458
Rooms hemmed in by timeworn, bare-stone walls; shuttered, small-paned windows; huge stone fireplaces warming slab-floored spaces dappled with old kitchen and dining tables – a Peak District classic. Reports please.

175 Eyre Arms Hassop, Bakewell DE45 1NS +44 (0)1629 640390
Traditional pub covered by Virginia creeper, close to Hassop Hall and good walks. Beams, log fires, lamplight, ancient knick-knacks and country cooking that's great value.

176 The Red Lion Inn Hognaston, Ashbourne DE6 1PR +44 (0)1335 370396
Fine old pub for the traditionalist in walking and shooting country. Push open the door to a Pandora's box of artefacts, low beams, pews and settles. Quaff Timmy Taylor Landlord before a huge fire, fill up on hearty pub grub.

Devon

Rose & Crown
Yealmpton

Delicious smells tempt you the moment you enter this big, bustling, open-plan pub. People travel miles for the food; cheerful staff dispatch good-looking dishes to softly-lit tables in one of two dining areas. A step or two down are squashy cow-hide sofas around an open fire, cream-washed open-stone walls and wooden Venetian blinds – perfect simplicity. The best wines represent the best value, and the ales and the menu change seasonally. Old Spot pork with cider and onion jus is just one example of a beautifully executed modern British menu, but you can have potted Salcombe curried crab with fennel salad, sea bream with ratatouille, samphire and tomato coulis, and warm treacle and spice cake. Traditional bar meals and roasts on Sunday complete the picture. Glorious and delicious. *Seafood restaurant in neightbouring barn.*

Meals	12pm-2.30pm (5pm Sun); 6.30pm-9pm. Main courses £9.95-£17.95; Sunday lunch £9 & £15.
Closed	3pm-6pm. Open all day Sun.
Directions	On A379, 7 miles south-east of Plymouth.

Simon Warner
Rose & Crown,
Market Street, Yealmpton,
Plymouth PL8 2EB
Tel   +44 (0)1752 880223
Web   www.theroseandcrown.co.uk

Entry 177 Map 2

Devon

The Ship Inn
Noss Mayo

At the head of a tidal inlet, a 16th-century pub remodelled with a nautical twist. While visiting boats can tie up alongside (with permission!), high-tide parking is trickier. When the tide is in, you enter via the back door on the first-floor level; when out, it's a quick stroll over the 'beach' and in at the front. Downstairs are plain boards, a wooden bar, solid wood furniture and walls heaving with maritime prints. Open fires, books and newspapers add to the easy feel. Upstairs the Galley, Bridge and Library areas have views and a happy, dining buzz. The menu strikes a modern chord: shank of Devon lamb with rosemary and garlic sauce and pan-fried duck breast alongside pumpkin and pea risotto and chocolate mousse. Take your drink to the sunny patio at octagonal tables and relish the watery views.

Meals	12pm-9.30pm (9pm Sun). Main courses £9.75-£17.95; bar meals £5.25-£11.95.
Closed	Open all day.
Directions	South of Yealmpton, on Yealm estuary.

Charles & Lisa Bullock
The Ship Inn,
Noss Mayo,
Plymouth PL8 1EW
Tel   +44 (0)1752 872387
Web   www.nossmayo.com

Entry 178 Map 2

Devon

Fortescue Arms
East Allington

Tom and Werner are the stars here. Canadian Tom is maître d' and has looked after heads of state; Austrian Werner has cheffed in starred kitchens. Double doors fling open in summer and wine corks pop in the bar. Your hosts welcome locals and visitors alike, and provide fabulous food. Portions are generous, quick to arrive, great value and, if the rabbit and pumpkin stew is anything to go by, delicious. Emphasis is on local produce so there's venison steak with red wine and berry gravy; pheasant stuffed with chestnuts; tuna with red wine and caper sauce; apfelstrüdel with crème pâtissière. The dark panelled and flagstoned bar is where Tom holds court, the restaurant is inviting with terracotta walls and glowing candles, and the outdoor decked area is smartly spotlit at night.

Meals	12pm–2pm; 7pm–9.30pm. Main courses £9.95–£19.95; bar meals £4.50–£12.95.
Closed	2.30pm–6pm & Mon lunch.
Directions	Village signed off A361 between Totnes & Kingsbridge.

Werner Rott & Tom Kendrick
Fortescue Arms,
East Allington,
Totnes TQ9 7RA
Tel   +44 (0)1548 521215
Web   www.fortescue-arms.co.uk

Entry 179 Map 2

Devon

The Millbrook Inn
South Pool

Arrive before the boats do. They drop anchor a step away and their first port of call is this inn, known for its food. Perfect ingredients are positively worshipped here, and in the best seasonal and local style. Feast on potted Start Bay crab, confit duck leg with chorizo cassoulet and rhubarb and apple crumble – book for the lively guest chef nights. In winter, a log fire warms the immediate bar area while padded settles and wheelback chairs cluster comfortably around tables in several snugs. The stream-side terrace is tiny but guarantees entertainment in summer once the Aylesbury ducks are at play, so sit back and relax with a pint of West Country ale. The owners have ambition and integrity and succeed in delivering some of the best food and drink in the area.

Meals	12pm–2pm; 7pm–9pm. Main courses £5.50–£10 (lunch), £10–£20 (dinner).
Closed	Open all day.
Directions	From Frogmore on A379 east of Kingsbridge follow signs south to South Pool; pub in village centre.

Ian Dent & Diana Hunt
The Millbrook Inn,
South Pool,
Kingsbridge TQ7 2RW
Tel   +44 (0)1548 531581
Web   www.millbrookinnsouthpool.co.uk

Entry 180 Map 2

Devon

Pig's Nose Inn
East Prawle

Winding lanes with skyscraper hedges weave from the main road to the edge of the world. There are an awful lot of porcine references round these parts (South Hams, Gammon Head, Piglet Stores) and the Pig's Nose is Devon's most southerly pub. Filled with character, a wood-burner and quirky ephemera, it has an atmosphere all of its own. A pie, pint and a paper at lunchtime can give way at night to the entire pub joining in a singalong; Peter's connections entice legendary acts – The Yardbirds, Wishbone Ash – to play in the adjacent hall. Innovations include a flurry of fur 'smoking jackets' hanging in the porch and random pots of knitting inviting punters to 'do a line'. Your hosts have a terrific sense of fun and faithful visitors return again and again. A one-off in a sea-view village that has barely changed since the thirties.

Devon

The Tower Inn
Slapton

A southern belle, loved by all who visit: despite the drawbacks of hidden access and tricky parking, this 14th-century inn attracts not just locals but visitors from Slapton Sands. Standing beside the ivy-clad ruins of a chantry tower, it's a flower-bedecked classic outside. As for the low-beamed and stone-walled interior – all rustic dark-wood tables, old pews and fine stone fireplaces, it is hugely atmospheric by night, thanks to the flickering light from candles and fires. Golden, bitter-sweet St Austell Brewery Tribute from the handpumps could be accompanied by a plateful of black bream with a warm fennel and orange salad, or local beef, seasonal game, venison and lamb; do book at weekends. A lovely, sleepy village setting – and a super landscaped garden at the back with views of the parish church and the tower.

Meals	12pm-2pm; 6.30pm-9pm (from 7pm in winter). Main courses £6.50-£12.50.	Meals	12pm-2pm (2.30pm in summer); 7pm-9pm (6.30pm-9.30pm in summer). Main courses £10-£19.
Closed	2.30pm-6pm (7pm in winter); Sun eve & Mon all day in winter.	Closed	2.30pm-6pm & Mon (winter only).
Directions	A379 Kingsbridge-Dartmouth; at Frogmore, right over bridge opp. bakery; signs to East Prawle. Pub by green.	Directions	Off A379 between Torcross & Dartmouth. Signed.

	Peter & Lesley Webber Pig's Nose Inn, East Prawle, Kingsbridge TQ7 2BY		**Thea Butler, Dan Cheshire & Kevin Tweddell** The Tower Inn, Slapton, Kingsbridge TQ7 2PN
Tel	+44 (0)1548 511209	Tel	+44 (0)1548 580216
Web	www.pigsnoseinn.co.uk	Web	www.thetowerinn.com

Entry 181 Map 2

Entry 182 Map 2

Devon

Kings Arms
Strete

Tempting to visit on a dark and rainy night – but a shame to miss the glorious views of Start Bay. Rob Dawson has revitalised the Edwardian hotel-turned-pub, bringing a natural warmth and a fine menu. A modest bar and a few tables greet you, then up the pine stair to a mezzanine dining room. Delicious smells waft from the kitchen – of seared scallops with pea mousse and serrano ham, brill with red wine glaze and garlic confit, poached pears with Devon Blue ice cream and port jelly. Oysters are gathered from the river Dart, lobsters and crabs come from the bay, the cheeses are local and the wines are wide-ranging with an excellent number by the glass. The Kings Arms and its garden fill up at summer weekends as holiday-cottagers get wind of the place, and return – for the food, the friendliness and the views.

Meals	12pm-2pm (3pm Sun); 6.30pm-9pm. Main courses £9.50-£19.95.
Closed	2.30pm-6pm (3pm-7pm Sun).
Directions	Between Dartmouth & Torcross on the A379.

Rob Dawson
Kings Arms,
Strete,
Dartmouth TQ6 0RW
Tel   +44 (0)1803 770377
Web   www.kingsarms-dartmouth.co.uk

Entry 183 Map 2

Devon

The Normandy Arms
Blackawton

The Commercial of the 1850s became The Normandy 90 years later – named after the landings; some of the sailors who died were buried on a farm in this parish. With its charming slate bar and floor, open wood beams, lovely red corner seating and bright, friendly staff, The Normandy is, in spite of its brilliance with food, still a pub. Peter, who cut a dash at the Dorchester and the Blue Ball at Triscombe, is chef; Sharon does front of house. Both are splendidly hands-on. People come from Kingsbridge, Totnes, Dartmouth for the food. Our meal of pigeon breasts with dauphinoise potatoes and red cabbage, followed by warm plum tarte tatin, was a winning blend of restraint and indulgence. West Country cheeses come with homemade chutney, fish comes from Brixham and the wine list is long. Spoiling all round.

Meals	12pm-2pm (Sun only); 7pm-9pm. Main courses £10.95-£17.95; bar meals £8.50-£14.95.
Closed	Tues-Sat lunch, Sun eves & all day Mon.
Directions	Village signed off A3122 5 miles west of Dartmouth.

Peter Alcroft & Sharon Murdoch
The Normandy Arms,
Blackawton,
Totnes TQ9 7BN
Tel   +44 (0)1803 712884

Entry 184 Map 2

Devon

The Ferry Boat Inn
Dittisham

The only inn right on the river, it used to serve the steamers plying between Dartmouth and Totnes — you can still arrive by boat. Big windows show off the view to the wooded banks of the Greenway Estate (once Agatha Christie's home, now owned by the NT: shake the bell and catch the ferry). Arrive early for the best seats in the rustic, unspoilt little bar with its bare boards, crackling log fire, nautical bric-a-brac and all-important 'high tides' board; if you've missed the village car park, negotiated the steep lane and parked on the 'beach', then check the board before ordering your pint. Similarly, the tide dictates whether or not you can dine outside in summer. Expect a rousing welcome, live music sessions and decent home-cooked pub food. Gents can 'spray and pray' next door in the converted chapel.

Meals	12pm-2pm; 7pm-9pm.
	Main courses £6.95-£14.50.
Closed	Open all day.
Directions	Off A3122, 2 miles west of Dartmouth.

Ray Benson
The Ferry Boat Inn,
Manor Street,
Dittisham,
Dartmouth TQ6 0EX
Tel +44 (0)1803 722368

Entry 185 Map 2

Devon

The White Hart
Totnes

Down a long, long drive past farmland and deer, Dartington Hall finally peeps into view: the college, conference centre, arts centre, dairy farm and 14th-century hall built for a half-brother of Richard II. Tucked into the corner of the courtyard — dotted with picnic tables in summer — is the White Hart. The bar and restaurant is informally 21st-century, with chunky beams, York stone floor, smouldering log fires, round light-oak tables and Windsor chairs. Organic and local produce are the mainstay of the menus, from soups to stews with dumplings. In the trestled dining hall: grilled Capricorn goat's cheese with beetroot and walnut salad; Devon lamb casserole; chocolate and coffee tart. Beers are from Otter Brewery, there are excellent wines and organic juices and ciders. Walk off a very fine lunch with a stroll through the parkland that borders the Dart.

Meals	12pm-2pm; 6pm-9pm; coffee from 10am (11am Sun).
	Main courses £9.50-£15.50.
Closed	Open all day.
Directions	Off A385, 2 miles north west of Totnes on the outskirts of Dartington village.

John Hazzard
The White Hart,
Dartington Hall,
Totnes TQ9 6EL
Tel +44 (0)1803 847111
Web www.dartingtonhall.org

Entry 186 Map 2

Turtley Corn Mill
Avonwick

The mill, revamped in 2005, has six acres sloping down to the lake – space for a multitude of picnic tables: order your hampers in advance. Ducks too… and boules, croquet, Jenga and a ginormous chess set. Inside has been transformed to create a series of spacious inter-connected areas: the bar with its dark slate floors and doors to the garden; the wooden-floored 'library' lined with books; the mill room (turning wheel right outside) with wood-burner, prints on pristine white walls, oriental rugs and newspapers to read. The food is traditional and homemade, be it local game terrine, braised beef in red wine or sea bass with minted pea sauce. A paper menu is printed off every day, there's Princetown Jail Ale on tap and a raft of wines by the glass. Swish new bedrooms are ultra-cosy – light chunky modern furnishings, restful colours, and excellent beds dressed in crispy cotton and goose down. Modernity reigns: sensor lamps, iPod clock radios, spacious showers. The South Hams is close as are the Dartmoor tors; it's also the perfect A38 stopover.

Rooms	4 doubles. £89–£110.
Meals	12pm-9.30pm (9pm Sun). Main courses £9.75–£16.95. Bar meals £5.25–£8.50.
Closed	Open all day.
Directions	A38 eastbound, turn for South Brent & Avonwick; 1st right to Avonwick, on B3372. Bear left following signs for Totnes; pub 100m on left.

Samantha & Scott Colton
Turtley Corn Mill,
Avonwick,
South Brent TQ10 9ES
Tel   +44 (0)1364 646100
Web   www.avonwick.net

Entry 187 Map 2

Devon

The Cary Arms at Babbacombe Bay
Torquay

The Cary Arms hovers above Babbacombe Bay with huge views of water and sky that shoot off to Dorset's Jurassic coast. It's a cool little place – half seaside pub, half dreamy hotel – and it makes the most of its spectacular position: five beautiful terraces drop downhill towards a small jetty, where locals fish. The hotel has six moorings in the bay, you can charter a boat and explore the coast. Back on dry land the bar comes with stone walls, wooden floors and a fire that burns every day. In good weather you eat on the terraces, perhaps seared Brixham scallops, roast partridge, elderflower and lime crème brûlée; there's a wood-fired pizza oven and summer barbeques, too. Dazzling bedrooms come in New England style. All but one opens onto a private terrace or balcony, you get decanters of sloe gin, flat-screen TVs, fabulous beds, super bathrooms (one has a claw-foot bath that looks out to sea). Back outside, you can snorkel on mackerel reefs or hug the coastline in a kayak. If that sounds too energetic, either head to the treatment room or sink into a deck chair on the residents' sun terrace.

Rooms	8 + 3: 6 doubles, 1 twin/double, 1 family suite. 3 cottages for 2-8. £150-£250. Suite £300-£350. Singles from £100. Cottages: £475-£1,250 for 3 nights; £750-£2,500 per week.
Meals	12pm-3pm; 6.30pm-9pm. Main courses £10-£19.
Closed	Open all day.
Directions	From Teignmouth south on A379. 5 miles up hill into St Mary Church, thro' lights, left into Babbacombe Downs Rd. Follow road right; left downhill to hotel.

Jen Podmore
The Cary Arms at Babbacombe Bay,
Beach Road,
Torquay TQ1 3LX

Tel   +44 (0)1803 327110
Web   www.caryarms.co.uk

Entry 188 Map 2

Bickley Mill
Newton Abbot

The microclimate of the English Riviera is never more apparent than in the garden of this 13th-century flour mill. David and Tricia have orchestrated a total refurbishment and their stylish cosy interiors are just great. Come for wood floors, stone walls, hessian rugs, cushioned sofas. Three fires burn in winter, there are Swedish benches, colourful art and a panelled breakfast room in creamy yellow. Everywhere you look something lovely catches the eye, be it a huge sofa covered with mountainous cushions, old black and white photos framed on the walls or the decked terrace at the side, nice for a pint or more in the summer sun. Bedrooms (including a room perfect for families) are stylish, with upbeat art and sculptures, crisp linen and jazzy fabrics, and modern bathrooms are immaculate; at these prices they're a steal. Downstairs you'll find helpful staff, local ales and loads to eat (light bites to three-course feasts) so why not tuck into baked field mushrooms, devilled kidneys, salmon fishcakes, banana and toffee pancakes; there's a menu for children and baby chairs, too. A small inn full of good things.

Rooms	9: 7 doubles, 1 twin, 1 family room. £80–£90. Family room £130–£140. Singles £67.50.
Meals	12pm-2pm (2.15pm Sat; 2.30pm Sun); 6.30pm-9pm (9.30pm Fri & Sat; 6pm-8pm Sun). Main courses £8.50-£15.
Closed	3pm-6pm.
Directions	South from Newton Abbot on A381. Left at garage in Ipplepen. Left at T-junction after 1 mile. Down hill, left again, pub on left.

David & Tricia Smith
Bickley Mill,
Stoneycombe,
Newton Abbot TQ12 5LN

Tel	+44 (0)1803 873201
Web	www.bickleymill.co.uk

Devon

The Church House Inn
Marldon

The old village pub is a civilised place, popular with retired locals and ladies that lunch. With a welcoming bar, several dining areas and a lovely sloping garden, it's a proper all-rounder. The feel is one of a well-crafted, rustic elegance – stonework and beams, original bell-shaped windows, crisp table settings and smiling service. The central bar has been partitioned into three areas, plus one four-tabled candlelit snug, perfect for a party. Food is modern British and locally sourced: baked hake with butterbean and chorizo ragout, Dartmouth smoked fish platter, bramble Bakewell tart with blackberry compote. Others come just for a pint of well-kept Dartmoor Best and a chat by the fire. The pub originally housed the artisans who worked on Marldon Church, and its ancient tower overlooks the hedged garden.

Meals	12pm-2pm (2.30pm Sun); 6.30pm-9.30pm (9pm Sun). Main courses £9-£19.95; Sunday roast £11.50.
Closed	2.30pm-5pm (3pm-5.30pm Sun).
Directions	Marldon off Torquay-Brixham ring road. Pub at bottom of village, signed.

Julian Cook
The Church House Inn,
Marldon,
Paignton TQ3 1SL
Tel   +44 (0)1803 558279
Web   www.churchhousemarldon.com

Entry 190 Map 2

Devon

The Rock Inn
Haytor Vale

Originally an ale house for quarrymen and miners, the 300-year-old Rock Inn stands in a tiny village in a sheltered vale on Dartmoor's windswept slopes. Run by the same family for over 20 years, this civilised haven oozes character; there are polished antique tables and sturdy settles on several levels, a grandfather clock, pretty plates and fresh flowers, cosy corners and at least two fires. Settle down with a pint of Dartmoor Best in the beamed and carpeted bar and peruse the supper menu that highlights local, often organic, produce. All that fresh Dartmoor air will have made you hungry, so tuck into Devon rump steak with garlic butter and chunky chips, then caramelised lemon tart with ginger ice cream. Lunchtime meals range from soup and sandwiches to local sausages in onion gravy. There's a pretty beer garden, too.

Meals	12pm-2pm; 7pm-9pm. Main courses £7.50-£13.95 (lunch), £15.95-£18 (dinner). Set menus £18 & £23.
Closed	Open all day.
Directions	At Drumbridges roundabout A382 for Bovey Tracey; B3387 to Haytor. Left at phone box.

Christopher & Susan Graves
The Rock Inn,
Haytor Vale,
Newton Abbot TQ13 9XP
Tel   +44 (0)1364 661305
Web   www.rock-inn.co.uk

Entry 191 Map 2

Devon

Rugglestone Inn
Widecombe in the Moor

Beside open moorland, within walking distance of the village, is a 200-year-old stone pub whose two tiny rooms lead off a stone-floored passageway. Few of the daytrippers who descend on this idyllic village in the middle of Dartmoor make it to the Rugglestone. Low beams fill the old-fashioned parlour with its simple furnishings and deep-country feel. Both rooms are free of modern intrusions, the locals preferring cribbage, euchre and dominoes. The tiny bar serves local farm cider; Butcombe Bitter and St Austell Dartmoor Best are tapped from the cask. From the kitchen comes proper home cooking, from ploughman's lunches and soups to lamb shanks and fresh fish — and not a deep-fat fryer in sight. Across the babbling brook at the front is a lawn with benches and peaceful moorland views. A little piece of heaven.

Meals	12pm-2pm; 6.30pm-9pm. Main courses from £6.95-£10.95; bar meals from £3.75.
Closed	3pm-6pm. Open all day Sat & Sun.
Directions	250 yards from centre of Widecombe; signed.

Richard Palmer & Vicki Moore
Rugglestone Inn,
Widecombe in the Moor,
Newton Abbot TQ13 7TF

Tel +44 (0)1364 621327
Web www.rugglestoneinn.co.uk

Entry 192 Map 2

Devon

The Cleave Inn
Lustleigh

It's ridiculously pretty, this 15th-century Devon longhouse on the edge of the Dartmoor National Park. Arrive early: seats at the front are like gold dust in summer. Inside, the main bar is classic to the core, the leather armchairs and Windsor chairs forming cosy huddles on a red and gold carpet, with a granite fireplace and a no-nonsense plank bar dispensing Otter Ales and local guests such as Yellowhammer. Ex-River Cottage head chef Mark Lloyd brings passion to the kitchen and his menus are blessed with the finest local and seasonal produce. Bar meals don't get much better than the Cleave Inn pie with fresh vegetables; there are scrumptious pork pies and sandwiches for walkers, and a seriously delicious duck breast boulangère with savoy cabbage and roasted red onion tart. Plenty of dining tables at the back, and good wines poured by cheerful staff.

Meals	12pm-2.30pm (3.30pm Sun); 6pm-9pm. No food Sun eve. Main courses £7.50-£12; set menu £17 & £20; Sunday lunch £9.95-£15.95.
Closed	Open all day.
Directions	Off A382 halfway between Bovey Tracey and Moretonhampstead; pub signed. In village centre, opposite church.

James Smith
The Cleave Inn,
Lustleigh,
Newton Abbot TQ13 9TJ

Tel +44 (0)1647 277223
Web www.thecleaveinn.co.uk

Entry 193 Map

The Elephant's Nest Inn
Mary Tavy

Overseas visitors will give a rapturous smile as they enter the main bar, all polished oak beams, flagstone floors and crackling fires... you almost imagine a distant Baskerville hound baying. This is an atmospheric inn that serves properly home-cooked food -- very local, very seasonal and British with a twist: perhaps antipasto of pastrami, rosette saucisson and Black Forest ham, or South Devon sirloin with mushrooms, vine tomatoes and French fries; sweet tooths can drool over Mrs Cook's fabulous lemon posset with blueberry compote. When suitably sated, slip off to the new annexe and a nest of your own in one of three rather fun, wonderfully quiet and extremely comfortable rooms. Wake to a pretty garden with views to Brentor church and Dartmoor, even, perhaps, a cricket match to watch: the pub has its own ground and club. So settle back to the thwack of willow on leather with a pint of Palmer's IPA – or Doom Bar, Jail Ale from Princetown, and guest ales from O'Hanlon's, Otter, Cotleigh, Teignworthy and Butcombe.

Rooms	3 twins/doubles. £80–£90.
Meals	12pm-2.15pm; 6.30pm-9pm.
	Main courses £8.95-£19.95.
Closed	3pm-6.30pm.
Directions	Pub signed off A386 Okehampton-Plymouth road at the Mary Tavy Inn in Mary Tavy; follow signs for Horndon.

Hugh & Denise Cook
The Elephant's Nest Inn,
Horndon, Mary Tavy,
Tavistock PL19 9NQ
Tel   +44 (0)1822 810273
Web   www.elephantsnest.co.uk

Entry 194 Map 2

The Dartmoor Inn
Lydford

There aren't many inns where you can sink into Zoffany-clad winged armchairs in the dining room, snooze on a hand-painted bed under a French chandelier, or shop for Swedish tableware while you wait for the wild sea bass to crisp in the pan. You can here: the inn is the template of deep-country chic, a fairytale inn dressed up as a country local. True, walkers and dogs stride in from the moors and squeeze into the bar for Dartmoor Best Bitter, organic bottled cider, fish and chips or a hearty steak sandwich, but then again the walls are coated in textured wallpaper, the settles are smartly sandblasted, gilded mirrors sit above smouldering fireplaces and upstairs a soft velvet throw is spread out across a pretty sleigh bed. Add to this wonderful staff and Philip's ambrosial food (saffron scrambled eggs for breakfast, ham hock terrine for lunch, free-range duck for dinner) and you have a very spoiling place. Triple-glazed bedroom windows do their best to defeat the road and the moors are on your doorstep (nearby is the thrilling Lydford Gorge) – so walk in the wind, then eat, drink and sleep.

Rooms	3 doubles. £110-£135.
Meals	12pm-2.15pm; 6.15pm-9.30pm. Main courses £14-£26; bar menu £6.75-£14.75.
Closed	2.30pm-6.30pm, Sun eve & Mon lunch.
Directions	North from Tavistock on A386. Pub on right at Lydford turn-off.

Karen & Philip Burgess
The Dartmoor Inn,
Lydford,
Okehampton EX20 4AY
Tel   +44 (0)1822 820221
Web   www.dartmoorinn.com

Entry 195 Map 2

Devon

The Harris Arms
Lewdown

You are welcomed on the way in and thanked on the way out. The passion Andy and Rowena have for food and wine is infectious and the awards they are gathering is proof of their commitment. Expect a long bar, a woodburner at one end, a patterned carpet, maroon walls and a big strawberry blond cat named Reg. A large decked area at the back has rich rolling views. The Whitemans are members of the Slow Food movement so real food is their thing: cheeses are the West Country's finest, fish, meat, vegetable and dairy produce come from exemplary local suppliers, and wines are chosen from small growers. Flavoursome food is what the chefs deliver and whether it be roast belly pork with cider jus, fish and chips or Devon lamb steak with roasted vine tomatoes and balsamic jus, it is consistently good. Great value, too.

Meals	12pm-2pm; 6.30pm-9pm. Main courses £9.25-£16.95; Sunday lunch £13.95 & £16.50.
Closed	3pm-6.30pm, Sun eve & all day Mon.
Directions	On old A30 between Lewdown & Lifton; leave A30 at Broadwoodwidger exit dir. Lifton then follow signs to Portgate.

Andy & Rowena Whiteman
The Harris Arms,
Portgate,
Lewdown EX20 4PZ
Tel   +44 (0)1566 783331
Web   www.theharrisarms.co.uk

Entry 196 Map 2

Devon

White Horse Inn
Moretonhampstead

Transformed from a biker's boozer to a much-loved local and a foodie's delight, the plain stone 17th-century pub stands in the heart of Dartmoor's 'capital'. The front bar remains suitably rustic; planked floor, stone walls, black beams, worn settles and a stove pumping out the heat – and dogs, locals and jugs of Otter and St Austell Proper Job. Step beyond and you enter another world: a rustic-chic dining room in a stunning barn/stable with a granite slab floor, and doors opening to a cobbled, Italianate courtyard with colourful mosaics. The open kitchen delivers Italian-inspired dishes – cassoulet with Tuscan sausage, pork belly and confit leg of duck; pannatone bread and butter pudding... there's a new pizza oven, and a bistro menu for lighter bites. Excellent espresso and 13 wines by the glass are the icing on the cake.

Meals	12.30pm-2.30pm (summer only); 6.30pm-9pm. Main courses £10.95-£18.95; lunch £9.50-£15.95.
Closed	Sun & Mon. Lunch in winter.
Directions	Village centre, on The Square on B3212.

Nigel Hoyle & Malene Graulund
White Horse Inn,
George Street, Moretonhampstead,
Newton Abbot TQ13 8PG
Tel   +44 (0)1647 440242
Web   www.whitehorse-moretonhampstead.co.uk

Entry 197 Map 2

Nobody Inn
Doddiscombsleigh

Thankfully, little has changed since new owners arrived in 2007. The wine and whisky lists remain 200-strong, and the Devon cheeseboard continues to draw rural winers and diners from afar. Settles and tables are crammed into every corner, horse brasses brighten low beams, there's an inglenook glowing with logs and part of the bar dates from Tudor times. Start with a bowl of Exmouth mussels, move on to rack of lamb with redcurrant and rosemary jus, finish with treacle tart. Or try something from the bar menu, perhaps fish pie, ham, egg and chips, that famous board of cheeses. To wash all this down: Nobody Bitter served in old pint glasses. A rare dram of Islay malt might be an excellent nightcap before retiring to one of five refurbished rooms upstairs, colour-themed according to name: Violet, Rose, Bluebell, Lily and Primrose. Quirky, fun, variously sized and extremely comfortable, they have soft carpets, super beds and decanters of sherry; bathrooms are, bar one, en suite. The village is buried down a maze of lanes but is certainly worth the detour.

Rooms	5: 3 doubles, 1 twin/double; 1 double with separate bath. £60–£95. Singles £45–£70.
Meals	12pm–2pm (3pm Sun); 6.30pm–9pm (9.30pm Fri & Sat; from 7pm Sun). Main courses £9–£16; bar meals £6.95–£9.95.
Closed	Open all day.
Directions	Off A38 at Haldon Racecourse exit, then 3 miles; following pub signs.

Sue Burdge
Nobody Inn,
Doddiscombsleigh,
Exeter EX6 7PS

Tel   +44 (0)1647 252394
Web   www.nobodyinn.co.uk

Devon

The Bridge Inn
Topsham

Unchanged for most of the century – and in the family for as long – the 16th-century Bridge is a must for ale connoisseurs. And for all who love a pub furnished in the old-style: just high-back settles, ancient floors, a simple hatch. (The Queen chose the Bridge for her first official 'visit to a pub'.) Years ago it was a brewery and malthouse; Caroline's great-grandfather was the last publican to brew his own here. This is beer-drinker heaven, with up to ten real ales served by gravity from the cask. There's cider and gooseberry wine, too. Cradle your pint to the background din of local chatter in the Inner Sanctum, or out in the garden by the steep river bank. With bread baked at the local farm, home-cooked hams, homemade chutneys and Devon cheeses, the sandwiches, pork pies and ploughman's are first-class.

Meals	12pm-1.45pm; 6pm-8pm. Sandwiches & pork pies only. Bar meals £3-£6.90.
Closed	2pm-6pm (7pm Sun).
Directions	M5 exit 30; A376 to Exmouth; 2 miles, right to Topsham; Elmgrove Road into Bridge Hill.

Caroline Cheffers-Heard
The Bridge Inn,
Bridge Hill, Topsham,
Exeter EX3 0QQ
Tel   +44 (0)1392 873862
Web   www.cheffers.co.uk

Entry 199 Map 2

Devon

Digger's Rest
Woodbury Salterton

A 500-year-old, fat-walled former cider house built of stone and cob – surely the quintessential thatched Devon inn. A good-looking makeover has revived the timbered interior: mellow walls and an eclectic mix of old dining tables, subtle wall lighting, tasteful prints. Arrive early to bag the sofa by the log fire. In addition to the local Otter and guest ales, the good list of wines and the relaxing atmosphere, there are organic soft drinks, Italian Gaggia coffee, soothing piped jazz, baby-changing facilities, newspapers and a one-hour lunch promise. The brilliant pub menu employs the best local produce, so treat yourself to Diggers fish pie, fine West Country beef and local Kenniford Farm pork, roasted for Sunday lunches; little ones have a menu all of their own. A beautifully landscaped patio garden, too.

Meals	12pm-2.30pm; 6.30pm-9.30pm. Main courses £7.95-£16.95; bar meals £4.75-£16.95.
Closed	3pm-5.30pm. Open all day Sat & Sun in summer.
Directions	Off A3052, 3 miles east of Exeter & 3 miles from M5 junc. 30.

Phil & Shelley Berryman
Digger's Rest,
Woodbury Salterton,
Exeter EX5 1PQ
Tel   +44 (0)1395 232375
Web   www.diggersrest.co.uk

Entry 200 Map 2

Masons Arms
Branscombe

Approach straggling Branscombe down narrow lanes to this creeper-clad inn. The 14th-century bar has a traditional feel with dark ship's timbers, stone walls, slate floor and a fireplace that cooks spit-roasts to perfection. Quaff pints of Otter Bitter or Branscombe Vale Brannoc by the fire; on warm days, head for the sun-trap terrace. Nothing is too much trouble for the staff, whose prime aim is for you to unwind. Local produce, including crab and lobster landed on Branscombe's beach, is the focus of the modern British menu. There's Ruby Red beef casserole with horseradish mash and whole line-caught sea bass, local crab ploughman's and roast leg of organically reared lamb with pancetta and tomato jus. No need to drive home; bed down instead in a room upstairs, or climb the steps to one of the cottages behind. Bedrooms are comfortably traditional while suites are vast and characterful: four-posters, deep sofas, thick carpets, antiques. The pebbly beach is a 12-minute stroll across National Trust land and coastal path walks reward the adventurous.

Rooms	21: 8 doubles, 6 twins/doubles, 4 four-posters, 1 family room, 2 four-poster suites. £80–£130. Four-posters £130. Family room £140–£210. Suites £175.
Meals	12pm–2pm (2.15pm Sat & Sun); 7pm–9pm. Bar meals £10.95–£15.50; set menu, 3 courses, £29.95 (eves only).
Closed	3pm–6pm in winter. Open all day Sat & Sun, every day in summer.
Directions	Branscombe is off A3052 between Seaton & Sidmouth. In village.

Colin & Carol Slaney
Masons Arms,
Branscombe,
Seaton EX12 3DJ

Tel   +44 (0)1297 680300
Web   www.masonsarms.co.uk

Devon

The Holt
Honiton

So named (a holt is the lair of an otter) because the McCaig family own the Otter Brewery in the Blackdown Hills. Young Joe and chef Angus run the pub, and Otter brews (Bitter, Ale, Bright and Head) from a new underground eco-cellar are showcased. But the spruced-up boozer on Honiton's high street is much more than the brewery 'tap', the vibrant bar and contemporary-styled dining room upstairs playing host to live music and film nights when food is off the menu. Angus delivers modern pub food from an open-plan kitchen, the emphasis being on locally sourced produce – farm meats, estate-shot game, smoked meats and fish from the on-site smokehouse. On seasonal menus are beefburgers, confit duck leg and sandwiches for lunch; for dinner, bream with crab and coriander cream sauce, lamb shank with herb dumplings, chocolate brownies. A superb A30 pit-stop.

Meals	12pm-2pm; 7pm-10pm.
	Main courses £5.50-£8.50 (lunch), £12.50-£15.50 (dinner).
Closed	3pm-5.30pm & all day Sun/Mon.
Directions	Exeter end of Honiton High Street. Public car park on Dowell Street.

	Joe & Angus McCaig
	The Holt,
	178 High Street,
	Honiton EX14 1LA
Tel	+44 (0)1404 47707
Web	www.theholt-honiton.com

Entry 202 Map 2

Devon

The Drewe Arms
Broadhembury

Taking pride of place at the crossroads of this pretty cob and thatch Devon village, the low and wide hallway of this 15th-century pub draws you in to a blend of old and new. Golden oak floors lead to a smart well-stocked bar, and there's a calm, leather-chaired dining room in which to enjoy the much talked about food, such as roasted guinea fowl with lentils, bacon, lemon and thyme, and, from the bar menu, ham hock with buttered vegetables, mashed potato and homemade piccalilli. Even if you're just settling down with the paper by the log-fired inglenook for a pint of Otter Bitter, Hanlon's Yellowhammer or one of three ciders you'll be well looked after by Anthony and his team. All wines are by the glass and there's a fruit, vegetable and herb plot planned. Outside is a dreamy garden overlooked by the village church: pure Devon soul.

Meals	12pm-2.30pm; 6.30pm-9.30pm (12pm-8pm Sun).
	Main courses £6-£21; bar meals £5-£15; Sunday roast from £9.50.
Closed	3pm-6pm & all day Mon. Open all day Sat & Sun.
Directions	M5 junc. 28; A373 Honiton to Cullompton; follow signs to Broadhembury; in village centre

	Anthony Russell
	The Drewe Arms,
	Broadhembury,
	Honiton EX14 3NF
Tel	+44 (0)1404 841267
Web	www.thedrewearms.com

Entry 203 Map 2

Devon

The Jack in the Green
Rockbeare

Bustle and buzz in the dark wood bar, and good local brews on tap – Otter Ale, Doom Bar, Butcombe Bitter. But this is more restaurant than pub: "For those who live to eat," reads the sign. In a series of smart, brightly lit, blue-motif carpeted rooms, Devon Chef of the Year (2007) Matthew Mason's bar menu goes in for modern and mouthwatering variations of tried and trusted favourites: braised faggot with creamed potato, steamed venison pudding with port and juniper jus... even the ploughman's is impressive. More ambition on display in the restaurant, where seared fillet of salmon with sorrel and hollandaise sauce and roasted Creedy Carver duck breast with liqueur-soaked cherries make for succulent seasonal choices. Paul Parnell has been at the helm for years and he and his staff do a grand job.

Devon

The Cadeleigh Arms
Cadeleigh

It's a steep climb to get here but the car will drive itself back down the hill – and the sloping garden has wonderful views. From the glittery seats in the ladies' loo to the white wines from Bickleigh a mile down the road, this pub combines fabulous produce with a big dose of fun. The food is done brilliantly, be it moules marinière, risotto of roasted squash, liver and lambs' kidneys or an English pud. The menu varies day to day, according to what is in season. Jane and Elspeth are a great team and a woman's touch is clearly at work here: antique pine tables and modern art, magazines and background jazz, games in the cupboard, logs by the grate. In the skittle alley they hold plays and serve suppers in the interval – and the coffee comes with milk in white china-cow jugs.

Meals	11.30am-2pm (2.30pm Fri & Sat); 6pm-9.30pm (12pm-9pm Sun). Main courses £11.50-£19.50; bar snacks from £4.95.
Closed	3pm-5.30pm (6pm Sat). Open all day Sun.
Directions	5 miles east of M5 (exit 29) on old A30 just past Exeter Airport.

Meals	12pm-2pm (2.30pm Sun); 7pm-9pm. Main courses from £9.95; Sunday lunch £12.95.
Closed	Sun eves & Mon.
Directions	From A396 just after Bickleigh Mill, turn right signed Cadleigh Arms after humped backed bridge. In centre of village.

Paul Parnell
The Jack in the Green,
Rockbeare,
Exeter EX5 2EE
Tel   +44 (0)1404 822240
Web   www.jackinthegreen.uk.com

♿ ⚘ 🖻 🍷

Entry 204 Map 2

Jane Dreyer & Elspeth Burrage
The Cadeleigh Arms,
Cadeleigh,
Tiverton EX16 8HP
Tel   +44 (0)1884 855238
Web   www.thecadeleigharms.co.uk

♿ ⚘ 🖻 🐕

Entry 205 Map 2

Devon

The Lamb Inn
Sandford

Animal paintings brighten the bar, the chef is passionate about provenance and Bob and Tiny (the dogs) are a delight. The old posting inn is the hub of the village. There are three open fires in winter and carpeting for cosiness, stubby white candles on plain tables, tankards filled with roses and, upstairs, a long window seat that looks onto the village below. (Skittles and darts too, a free cinema for films and sporting events, and a brilliant open mic night once a month.) The unplush décor is matched by a blackboard menu free of affectation, the scrumptious-sounding dishes ranging from a platter of West Country cheeses to a Mediterranean cassoulet. All is locally sourced and made from scratch, and that includes the soups, the pastas and the breads.

Meals	12.30pm–3pm; 6.30pm–9.30pm (9pm Sun). Main courses £6.90–£14.50.
Closed	Open all day.
Directions	A377 north from Exeter. 1st right in Credtion, signed Sandford. 1 mile up & in village.

Mark Hildyard
& Katharine Lightfoot
The Lamb Inn,
Sandford, Crediton EX17 4LW
Tel +44 (0)1363 773676
Web www.lambinnsandford.co.uk

Entry 206 Map 2

Devon

Duke of York
Iddesleigh

Built to house the 14th-century stonemasons working on the church next door, the thatched Duke of York is the most genuine of locals, big-hearted and generous. It serves comforting food, real ale and Sams Cider from Winkleigh – along with a great welcome from Andy and Diane King. Scrubbed oak tables carry fresh flowers and candles, there are village photographs on the walls, bank notes on the beams, rocking chairs by the log fire – it's rustic and enchanting. Thanks to fish fresh from Clovelly and Brixham and locally sourced beef, lamb and pork, you tuck into the heartiest home cooking: tureens of homemade soup, steak and kidney pudding, lamb chops with rosemary and garlic gravy, whole baked sea bass with lemon butter, scrumptious puddings. And the all-day breakfasts are not for the faint-hearted.

Meals	12pm–10pm (9.30pm Sun). Set menu, 3 courses, £26; bar meals £4.50–£14.
Closed	Open all day.
Directions	On B3217 between Exbourne & Dolton, 3 miles north east of Hatherleigh.

Andy & Diane King
Duke of York,
Iddesleigh,
Winkleigh EX19 8BG
Tel +44 (0)1837 810253

Entry 207 Map 2

Devon

The Grove Inn
Kings Nympton

The pub is in the heart of old Nympton: a 'natural sacred grove'. A place of celebration for our pagan ancestors, and you should raise a glass to your good fortune in being here. There are paintings of the superb countryside by local artists, a picture gallery of faces past and present, beams hung with bookmarks, stone walls, a slate floor, and a wood-burner. Old and new combine with understated ease. Robert is the perfect host and Deborah his wife uses the freshest local produce to create her menus. Try individual Devon beef wellington served with dauphinoise potatoes, wild rabbit stew, wild venison chop on mash or skate with brown butter with capers. Ales are from local breweries, ciders are Sam's Dry and Poundhouse, wines all come by the glass. As they say round these parts – proper job!

Meals	12pm-2pm; 7pm-9pm. No food Mon (except bank hols) or Sun eve. Main courses £6-£19.50; Sunday lunch £9, £13 & £16.
Closed	3pm-6pm & Mon lunch (except bank hols).
Directions	Off B3226 south of South Molton; pub in village centre.

Robert Smallbone
The Grove Inn,
Kings Nympton,
Umberleigh EX37 9ST
Tel   +44 (0)1769 580406
Web   www.thegroveinn.co.uk

Entry 208 Map 2

Devon

The London Inn
Molland

Persevere down high-banked lanes through the Exmoor foothills to this unpretentious village local. It's a true moorland inn, an oasis for weary walkers and often chock full of farmers, dogs, hunters, shooters and the local gentry, clustered around the log fire and in for the banter. Not forgetting the Exmoor Ale or Sam's heady cider, and the plates of rustic, country food – lamb casserole with thyme dumplings, chicken and smoked bacon pie, treacle tart. Farms within five miles of the pub supply the lamb, beef and pork. Young Toby plans few changes so expect no music, just contented chatter through the rambling flagstoned rooms, unchanged for decades and filled with hunting prints, stuffed birds, country magazines and board games. The sign on the door – "Real ales, real food, real people" – perfectly sums up a rural gem.

Meals	12pm-2pm; 6pm-8.30pm. No food Sun eve or Mon in winter. Main courses £6.80-£11.
Closed	3pm-6pm.
Directions	From A261 exit at B3227 (signed Bampton) within 0.75 miles left (signed Molland).

Toby Bonnett & Deborah See
The London Inn,
Molland,
South Molton EX36 3NG
Tel   +44 (0)1769 550269
Web   www.mollandinn.co.uk

Entry 209 Map 2

Devon

The Stag Inn
Rackenford

Sophie and Matt have left the city for Devon's oldest pub (1197), a thatched, cob-walled beauty in sleepy Rackenford. Unloved and decaying, it was ripe for remodelling, and has lost none of its charm. A cobbled passageway (once used by horses) leads to a timeless bar – Tom Kings Bar – simple and uncluttered with ancient slate floor, black beams, wonky walls, Jacobean panelling and settles by the inglenook. Fat church candles on old pine tables and Farrow & Ball creams and greens add to the atmosphere and keep local farmers happy, along with pints of Exmoor Stag at the bar. Leather chairs and wooden floors add contemporary touches to the dining room where ex-Ramsay chef Matt uses organic produce from Sophie's mother's farm. Expect chicken and duck leg terrine; perfect ham, egg and chips; organic beef sandwiches in the bar. What a find!

Meals	12pm-2.30pm; 6.30pm-9.30pm. Restaurant Weds-Sat eves & Sun lunch. Main courses £11.50-£17; bar meals £6-£13.50.
Closed	3pm-6pm & Sun eves.
Directions	Village signposted off A361, 6 miles west of Tiverton; pub in village centre.

Sophie Bulley & Matt Robinson
The Stag Inn,
Rackenford,
South Molton EX16 8DT
Tel +44 (0)1884 881369
Web www.thestaginn.com

Entry 210 Map 2

Devon

Culm Valley Inn
Culmstock

Richard Hartley's old pub by the lovely river Culm may not be posh but it's warm, easy and charming: deep pink-washed walls, glowing coals, flickering oil lamps and candles. From bar stools the locals sample microbrewery beers while the gentry drop by for unusually good food. Easy-going chef-patron Richard and his merry band make this place zing. Look to the chalkboard for south coast seafood – cod with langoustine broth, halibut with mussels and pesto – Ruby Red Devon beef from nearby farms, tea-smoked venison with tomato relish, spicy Balinese pork, and tapas. From the English elm bar you can order from a fantastic array of rare and curious spirits, French wines from specialist growers and up to ten local beers tapped from the cask. In the words of one reader: "Fantastic host, great wine, superb homemade everything…"

Meals	12pm-2pm; 7pm-9.30pm. No food Sun eve. Main courses £7-£20; bar meals £6-£10.
Closed	3pm-7pm in winter. Open all day Sat & Sun.
Directions	On B3391, 2 miles off A38 west of Wellington.

Richard Hartley
Culm Valley Inn,
Culmstock,
Cullompton EX15 3JJ
Tel +44 (0)1884 840354

Entry 211 Map 2

The Quarryman's Rest
Bampton

There's something for everyone here, at this lively market town inn. Real ale for beer buffs, a dining room for foodies, a fruit machine for gamblers, pool for the football team, and a shelter with cushions in the garden for the smokers. The garden is lovely, and overlooks fields. Back in the pub, it's spacious, with dark panelling and sofas in one area, lightness and sunshine in another, and a separate carpeted dining room for quiet meals. All the produce is local, from the beer and cider (heady Sam's from Winkleigh) to the beef, and you can see the cows from the window. (It's not un-heard of for regulars to swap a pheasant or a box of tomatoes for a pint.) Along with the art on the walls – for sale – you get proper steak and kidney pudding, braised lamb shank with rosemary gravy, roast beef on Sunday – fantastic food, well priced. Upstairs, tucked away at the rear, are three homely bedrooms, the big double with trendy wallpapers, leather sleigh bed, huge plasma screen and bathroom with a corner bath, a walk-in shower and Arran Aromatics. Wild Exmoor walks are on the doorstep.

Rooms	3 doubles. £60-£80. Singles £45-£50.
Meals	12pm-2pm (4pm Sun); 6pm-9.30pm (6.30pm-9pm Sun). Main courses £9.50-£13.95; Sunday roast £8.95.
Closed	Open all day.
Directions	From A396 follow signs to Bampton; pub just as you enter the village.

Paul & Donna Berry
The Quarryman's Rest,
Briton Street,
Bampton, Tiverton EX16 9LN
Tel   +44 (0)1398 331480
Web   www.thequarrymansrest.co.uk

Entry 212 Map 2

Devon

Worth a visit

213 The Masons Arms Knowstone,
South Molton EX36 4RY +44 (0)1398 341231
Arrive through fern or twisting lane to reach Mark Dodson's celebrated 13th-century pub-restaurant. Call in for a pint in the beamed, flagged bar or come for classic French and British dishes cooked with flair and with prices to match.

214 Poltimore Arms South Molton EX36 3HA
+44 (0)1598 710381
An isolated old coaching inn, high on the edge of Exmoor with great Devon views. Very rustic with flagstones, lit with a generator, it attracts farmers and huntsmen with its traditional food and ales.

215 Fox & Goose Parracombe,
Barnstaple EX31 4PE +44 (0)1598 763239
By a stream in a valley between Exmoor and the dramatic coast, an unassuming pub worth seeking out for its big blackboard menus: fish from local boats, meats from surrounding farms, great local ales.

216 Fountain Head Branscombe,
Seaton EX12 3BG +44 (0)1297 680359
Be charmed by big flagstones, wood-clad walls, dim-lit corners, good pub grub and village-brewed beers. No fruit machines, just local babble and possibly a snoozing dog – walking country by the sea.

217 The Turf Hotel Exminster, Exeter EX6 8EE
+44 (0)1392 833128
Reached only on foot (20-min walk), by bike or by boat, a unique, rambling old pub overlooking the estuary mudflats. Bareboard bar with big bay windows for winter wader-watching and top-notch Otter Ales. Closed Dec-Feb.

218 The Drewe Arms Drewsteignton,
Devon EX6 6QN +44 (0)1647 281224
Long, low and thatched, an unpretentious and well-loved village local in a pretty square by the church. Local ales still served from hatchways, and home cooking for walkers. Castle Drogo is nearby.

219 Tom Cobley Tavern Spreyton,
Crediton EX17 5AL +44 (0)1647 231314
Whitewashed 16th-century pub on the northern edge of Dartmoor, popular for its associations with Widecombe Fair and its up to 22 real ales on tap. Traditional, homely bar, tree-shaded garden, home-cooked food – book for Sunday lunch.

220 The Peter Tavy Inn Peter Tavy,
Tavistock PL19 9NN +44 (0)1822 810348
Atmospheric 15th-century inn on the flanks of desolate Dartmoor. Masses of charm in black beams, polished slate, long pine tables and wood-burners in huge hearths. Cracking beer and walks from the door.

221 Pilchard Inn Bigbury-on-Sea,
Kingsbridge TQ7 4BG +44 (0)1548 810514
Walk across the sand or take the sea tractor to this atmospheric smugglers' pub on the tidal island made famous by Agatha Christie. Beams, flagstones, roaring log fires, fresh food, views, cliff walks. Unique!

222 Cricket Inn Beesands,
Kingsbridge TQ7 2EN +44 (0)1548 580215
Unassuming outside, open-plan within, but a real local feel. Yards from the beach, and lots of local fish. Expect jazz with Sunday lunch (that's two fabulous roasts with all the trimmings).

223 The Start Bay Inn Torcross,
Kingsbridge TQ7 2TQ +44 (0)1548 580553
Packed the minute it opens (arrive late at your peril), this modest 14th-century beachside inn serves the best fresh fish and chips in Devon. Dressed crab too. Arrive hungry.

224 Kingsbridge Inn 9 Leechwell Street,
Totnes TQ9 5SY +44 (0)1803 863324
Top-of-the-town treasure dating from the 13th-century, tucked down a narrow street. Cosy beamed bar with wonky walls, blazing fires and worn flagstones, imaginative menus and traditional Sunday lunches. New owners – reports please.

Dorset

The Cow
Parkstone

Off the main road in Parkstone, this sophisticated boozer-bistro is just the ticket for good ales and good food. Owned by David Sax of the Museum Inn, it is spruce with stripped pine floors, scrubbed wooden tables and bright funky prints of their favourite animal (not hard to guess!). The pale woody look continues into the dining room, where dinner and Sunday lunch are served with style: feuillette of smoked haddock, spring onion and sweetcorn perhaps, or rump of lamb with potato gratin, followed by iced vanilla parfait and blackberry and raspberry compote. Diners eat in peace while a friendly, youthful staff keep the bar buzzing at weekends; and they know their stuff when it comes to real ale. All this, and a great room for private parties where you can really let your hair down.

Meals	12pm-2.30pm; 7pm-9.30pm. No food Sun eve. Main courses £11.95-£19.50; bar lunches £8.50-£10.50; Sunday roast from £12.50.
Closed	Open all day.
Directions	Beside Parkstone Station.

David Sax
The Cow,
58 Station Road,
Parkstone, Poole BH14 8UD
Tel   +44 (0)1202 749569
Web   www.thecowpub.co.uk

Entry 225 Map 3

Dorset   Award winner 2010

The Square & Compass
Worth Matravers

The name honours those who cut stone from the nearby quarries. This splendid old pub has been in the family for generations and remains wonderfully unchanged; a narrow, and rare, drinking corridor leads to two hatches from where Palmer's Copper Ale and guest ales are drawn from the cask. With a pint of farmhouse cider and a homemade pastie, you can chat in the flagged corridor or settle in the parlour; find painted wooden panels, wall seats and local prints and cartoons, and a wood-burner to warm you on a wild night. The stone-walled main room has live music; there's cribbage and shove ha'penny and a fossil museum (the family's) next door. Gazing out across fields to the sea this pub and its sunny front terrace – dotted occasionally with free-ranging hens – is a popular stop for coastal path hikers. A national treasure.

Meals	Bar snacks all day. Homemade pasties and pies only £3.
Closed	3pm-6pm. Open all day Sat/Sun & every day July-Sep.
Directions	B3069 east of Corfe Castle; thro' Kingston; right for Worth Matravers.

SPECIAL AWARD
see pages 20-21

Authentic pub

Charlie Newman & Kevin Hunt
The Square & Compass,
Worth Matravers,
Swanage BH19 3LF
Tel   +44 (0)1929 439229
Web   www.squareandcompasspub.co.uk

Entry 226 Map 3

Dorset

Coventry Arms
Corfe Mullen

Hard to beat if you're looking for a great little pit-stop en route to the coast; it's right by the A31. The Coventry Arms may not resemble the 15th-century watermill it once was but the rustic and rambling rooms, the sagging oak beams the worn flagstones and the cosy nooks and crannies lend a clue as to its age. And there's a lovely, comforting, laid-back feel: terracotta walls are lined with tasteful pictures and fishing paraphernalia, logs crackle in the grate, chunky candles glow on old dining tables. The modern British menu focuses on local produce, every small supplier is named and praised on the list of specials, and seafood is a speciality. There are trout and whiting fishcakes with horseradish cream, Angus beef for Sunday lunch, four ales pulled from the cask, and a streamside garden for summer.

Dorset

The Anchor
Shapwick

Little lanes meander through the Stour Valley west of Wimborne to sleepy Shapwick and the Anchor, an unprepossessing 1900s brick-built pub that has been revitalised with style. Expect the unexpected: a classy minimalist feel throughout, with period brick fireplaces, parquet floors and fat radiators alongside rustic scrubbed tables on quarry tiles, earthy heritage greens, chunky candles, fresh flowers and cushioned bow-window seats. Peruse the papers over a pint of local Keystone Bitter and a pork and apple open ciabatta... or tuck into Portland crab soufflé, whole roast partridge with roast root vegetables and red cabbage, and baked stem ginger and mascarpone cheesecake from a short daily-changing menu. Worth visiting after a root around the grand mansion of Kingston Lacy, owned by the National Trust.

Meals	12pm-2.30pm; 6pm-9.30pm. All day Sat/Sun. Main courses £10-£20; bar meals £5-£10.		Meals	12pm-2.30pm (3pm Sun); 6pm-9.30pm. No food Sun eve. Main courses £10-£17 (lunch), £12.50-£17 (dinner).
Closed	3pm-5.30pm. Open all day Sat/Sun.		Closed	3pm-6pm & Sun eve from 4pm.
Directions	A31 between Dorchester & Wimborne; 2 miles west of Wimborne.		Directions	B3082 from Wimborne or Blandford Forum; pub signed.

	John Hugo Coventry Arms, Mill Street, Corfe Mullen, Wimborne BH21 3RH		Mark Thornton The Anchor, West Street, Shapwick, Blandford Forum DT11 9LB
Tel	+44 (0)1258 857284	Tel	+44 (0)1258 857269
Web	www.coventryarms.co.uk	Web	www.anchorshapwick.co.uk

Entry 227 Map 3

Entry 228 Map 3

Dorset

The Bull
Wimborne St Giles

In sleepy Wimborne St Giles in the heart of the Cranborne Chase is Mark Thornton's recently reopened Bull. In spite of refurbishment ongoing in the upstairs bedrooms (watch this space), business has been brisk in the one open-plan, tastefully kitted out bar-dining room – booking is advisable! The chief draw is the food from chef Matt Davey, deliciously on display in an open-to-view kitchen. Choose from fish stew with saffron potatoes; braised pig cheek with cavalo nero and sage; roast lamb shoulder; beer-battered whiting with crushed peas and sauté potatoes... and sweet tooths should leave room for a honey and lavender pannacotta. Wash it all down with a Hall & Woodhouse ale or one of 18 well-chosen wines by the glass. There's a peaceful rambling garden for simple summer supping, and great downland walks for the energetic.

Meals	12pm-2.30pm; 6.30pm-9.30pm. Main courses £9.50-£16.50 (from £6.50 at lunch).
Closed	3pm-6pm.
Directions	From Wimborne, B3078 for approx. 7 miles. Pub signed on left of B3078 (Wimborne St Giles).

Mark Thornton
The Bull,
Wimborne St Giles,
Wimborne BH21 5NF

| Tel | +44 (0)1725 517300 |
| Web | www.bullwsg.com |

♿ 🏃 🖂 🐦 🍷 🔊

Entry 229 Map 3

Dorset

The Museum Inn
Farnham

In a village with roses round every door is one of the finest inns in the south of England. Pub entrepreneur David Sax has kept the atmosphere warm and happy, following a gentle upgrade. The big 17th-century bar has a period feel – all flagstones, inglenook, fresh flowers and a fashionable mismatch of tables and chairs. Popular with the barbour-and-dog set, this inn is quietest out of season. There are cosy alcoves to hide in, a book-filled drawing room to browse and a smart, white-raftered dining room. Sophisticated dishes range from smoked haddock fishcake with creamed leek and split-pea velouté to roasted local estate venison with butternut squash mash and sour cherry jus and steamed turbot with saffron gnocchi and shellfish velouté. Prune and armagnac pudding comes with clotted cream, lemon tart with berry compote. Fabulous.

Meals	12pm-2pm (2.30pm Sat & Sun); 7pm-9.30pm (9pm Sun). Main courses £14-£18.50; bar snacks (lunch) £6.50-£7.50.
Closed	3pm-6pm (7pm Sun).
Directions	From Blandford, A354 for Salisbury for 6.5 miles, then left, signed Farnham. Inn on left in village.

David Sax
The Museum Inn,
Farnham,
Blandford Forum DT11 8DE

| Tel | +44 (0)1725 516261 |
| Web | www.museuminn.co.uk |

🖂 🐦 🍺 🍷

Entry 230 Map 3

The Talbot
Iwerne Minster

Hike to the top of Hambledon Hill and be wowed by the views, then drop down to this excellent roadside pub in little Iwerne Minster for good food and a cosy bedroom. Key to The Talbot's success is that it keeps its locals happy: drinkers come for pints of Badger, pool, darts and screen, and foodies for the lounge and dining room, nicely decorated with rugs and candlelit tables. Monthly menus and daily dishes reflect the seasons and make brilliant use of local supplies – game from surrounding estates, fish from Dorset day boats, meats and sausages from the village butcher. At lunchtime tuck into Hanford Park roast beef and horseradish sandwiches or a platter of charcuterie and cheeses with pickles, or push the boat out with game terrine and pear and walnut chutney, pesto crusted Lyme Bay cod, and sticky toffee, date and walnut pudding with vanilla bean ice cream. Bedrooms are named after local hills and they're as fine as the rest, with crisp cotton sheets and colourful throws, armchairs and painted wooden beds, feature fireplaces and spacious bathrooms. *No under-5s overnight.*

Rooms	5: 4 twins/doubles, 1 family room. £85–£105. Singles from £65. Family room from £120.
Meals	12pm–2pm; 6.30pm–9.30pm. Main courses £9.95–£16.95; bar meals £5.75–£8.95.
Closed	2.30pm–6pm.
Directions	On A350 Blandford/Shaftesbury road, 4 miles north of Blandford.

Lester & Jane Wareham
The Talbot,
Blandford Road,
Iwerne Minster,
Blandford Forum DT11 8QN
Tel   +44 (0)1747 811269
Web   www.the-talbot.com

Entry 231 Map 3

The King John Inn
Tollard Royal

You're on the Dorset/Wiltshire border, lost in blissful country, with paths that lead up into glorious hills. Tumble back down to this super inn. Alex and Gretchen have refurbished every square inch and the place shines. Expect airy interiors, a smart country feel, a sun-trapping terrace and a fire that crackles in winter. Originally a foundry, it opened as a brewery in 1859, and, when beer proved more popular than horseshoes, the inn was born. You'll find three local ales on tap but great wines, too – Alex loves the stuff and has opened his own shop across the courtyard – take home a bottle if you like what you drink. As for the food, it's as local as can be with game straight off the Rushmore estate and meat from over the hill; the sausages are a thing of rare beauty. Country-house bedrooms are the final treat. Some are bigger than others, three are in the Coach House, all come with wonderful fabrics, padded headboards, crisp white linen and super bathrooms (one has a slipper bath). In summer, a terraced lawn gives views over a couple of rooftops onto the woods. A perfect spot.

Rooms	8: 6 doubles, 2 twins/doubles. £100-£150. Singles from £100.
Meals	12pm-2.30pm; 7pm-9.30pm (10pm Fri & Sat). Main courses from £10.95.
Closed	3pm-6pm.
Directions	A30 towards Salisbury. 5 miles to Ludwell, through village, right for Tollard Royal. Pub immed. on left.

Alex & Gretchen Boon
The King John Inn,
Tollard Royal,
Salisbury SP5 5PS

Tel	+44 (0)1725 516207
Web	www.kingjohninn.co.uk

Entry 232 Map 3

Stapleton Arms
Buckhorn Weston

An inn with a big heart. There are no pretensions here, just kind, knowledgeable staff committed to running the place with informal panache. A facelift has brought a streak of glamour back to this old coaching inn, and a delightful garden at the back. Downstairs are sofas in front of the fire, a piano for live music in the bar and a restaurant in Georgian blue with shuttered windows and candles in the fireplace. You can eat wherever you want. Pork pies (to eat in or take out), serrano ham and Tête de Moine cheese all wait at the bar, but if you want a three-course feast you must book – it gets packed out. There are salmon and crab fishcakes, home-baked Dorset ham, banana tarte tatin, even a beer menu; ale matters here. On Sundays groups can order their own joint of meat, and there's always a menu for kids. Rooms above are soundproofed to ensure a good night's sleep. They're comfy-chic with Egyptian linen, fresh flowers, happy colours, perhaps a claw-foot bath. Also: maps and picnics, wellies if you want to walk, games for children, DVDs for all ages. Wincanton is close for the races.

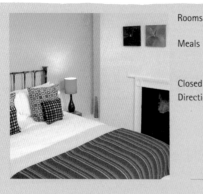

Rooms	4: 3 doubles, 1 twin/double. £72-£120. Singles £72-£96.
Meals	12pm-3pm; 6pm-10pm (9.30pm Sun). Main courses £8.90-£14; bar meals from £5; Sunday roast £12.90.
Closed	3pm-6pm. Open all day Sat & Sun.
Directions	A303 to Wincanton. Into town, right after fire station, signed Buckhorn Weston. Left at T-junction after 3 miles. In village, left at T-junction. Pub on right.

Kaveh Javvi
Stapleton Arms,
Church Hill, Buckhorn Weston,
Gillingham SP8 5HS
Tel   +44 (0)1963 370396
Web   www.thestapletonarms.com

The Chetnole Inn
Chetnole

A cream-painted pub reached by leafy lanes south of Sherborne, half an hour from the wonderful Dorset coast. Opposite the parish church, the up-dated inn has not lost touch with its roots, and is sparklingly run. There's a skittle alley and a dog-friendly bar area with a wood-burning stove and darts; a stone-floored, hop-hung, pine-tabled lounge bar; a restaurant beyond, similarly attractive; and a beer garden with ducks. Dishes range from straightforward, for children, to imaginative, and Mike sources ingredients as locally as possible. A memorable meal might include pan-fried breast of pigeon with puy lentils, black pudding and pancetta followed by duo of duck with red cabbage and redcurrant jus, and an orange and cardamom crème brûlée to round things off. If staying over you'll be comfortable in one of the smart, pale-carpeted bedrooms; all look towards the church, all are prettily dressed. Beds are inviting with thick duvets and feather pillows, so too are the homemade biscuits, the real coffee and the magazines. Gleaming bathrooms have bathrobes and Molten Brown treats. The Chetnole is hard to fault!

Rooms	2 doubles, 1 twin. From £95. Singles £70.
Meals	12pm-2pm; 6.30pm-9pm. Main courses £9-£16; sandwiches £6.25; Sunday lunch from £8.50.
Closed	3pm-6.30pm & Sun eves in winter.
Directions	Chetnole is signed off A37 between Yeovil and Dorchester, 7 miles south of Yeovil, 7 miles south west of Sherborne.

	Mike Lewin
	The Chetnole Inn,
	Chetnole,
	Sherborne DT9 6NU
Tel	+44 (0)1935 872337
Web	www.thechetnoleinn.co.uk

Entry 234 Map 3

Dorset

Brace of Pheasants
Plush

In a sleepy hamlet surrounded by downland, this thatched brick and flint building is Dorset's prettiest pub (or a close contender). Originally two 16th-century cottages linked to the smithy, it became an inn in the 1930s and displays an unusual sign – a brace of pheasants in a glass case. Beyond the latch door, the traditional low-beamed main bar has charm and character, with its inglenook big enough to plonk yourself down in, another impressive fireplace with a winter log fire, and an assortment of tables and chairs. Foaming pints of Doom Bar and Copper Ale are tapped from the cask to accompany plates of warming seasonal food – maybe home-cured duck salad with plum chutney, or venison steak with honey, thyme and red wine jus; then apple and rhubarb crumble. Super-smart rooms in the old skittle alley overlook the peaceful garden and sport painted 'feature' beams, dramatic lamps, ornate drapes and splashes of colour (striking headboards, fancy bed throws, piles of cushions). Expect leather sofas, ceiling speakers, vast tiled bathrooms – and great walks from the door.

Rooms	4 twins/doubles. £95. Singles £85.
Meals	12pm-2.30pm; 7pm-9.30pm. Main courses £9-£16.
Closed	3pm-7pm, Sun eve & Mon.
Directions	Plush is signed off B3143 Dorchester-Sherborne road, just north of Piddletrenthide. In village on left.

Phil & Carol Bennett
Brace of Pheasants,
Plush,
Dorchester DT2 7RQ

Tel	+44 (0)1300 348357
Web	www.braceofpheasants.co.uk

Entry 235 Map 3

The Acorn Inn
Evershot

Perfect Evershot and rolling countryside lie at the door of this 400-year-old inn deep in Thomas Hardy country. Hardy called the inn the Sow and Acorn and let Tess rest a night here; had he visited today he might have let her stay longer. Red Carnation Hotels, under the guidance of chef Jack Mackenzie and Alex Armstrong-Wilson, are reviving its fortunes. This is very much a traditional inn: as much a place for locals to sup pints of Otter Ale and swap stories by the fire in the flagstoned bar, as for foodies to sample some good food sourced within 25 miles. Walk through to the dining room and the atmosphere changes to rural country house with smartly-laid tables, terracotta tiles, soft lighting and elegant fireplaces; food is taken seriously, take scallops with pumpkin and vanilla purée and chorizo dressing and roast pork belly with sherry vinegar jus, or a rare roast beef and horseradish sandwich in the bar. Bedrooms creak with age and style; uneven floors, antiques, bright fabric wall-coverings, beautiful draperies to soften grand four-posters, and smart new bathrooms. Hardy would approve.

Rooms	10: 3 doubles, 3 twins, 3 four-posters, 1 suite. £95–£105. Four-posters £115–£130. Suite £150–£180. Singles £65–£125.
Meals	12pm–2pm; 7pm–9.30pm. Main courses £4–£18.95.
Closed	Open all day.
Directions	Evershot 1 mile off A37 midway between Yeovil & Dorchester.

Jack Mackenzie &
Alex Armstrong-Wilson
The Acorn Inn,
Evershot, Dorchester DT2 0JW
Tel   +44 (0)1935 83228
Web   www.acorn-inn.co.uk

The Shave Cross Inn
Shave Cross

Fancy a pint of Branoc and a spicy salad of jerk chicken? Once a busy stop-off point for pilgrims and monastic visitors (whose crowns were shorn whilst staying), the cob-and-flint pub now sits dreamily off the beaten track at the end of several very narrow lanes. It was rescued from closure by the Warburtons, back from the Caribbean. Life has stepped up a gear and the old tavern thrives – thanks largely to the exotic and delicious cuisine, and the swish bedrooms in a new stone building next door. Where else in deep Dorset can you tuck into Louisiana blackened chicken with cream and pepper sauce? There's simple pub grub for less adventurous palates, while surroundings remain strictly traditional: flagged floors, low beams, country furniture and vast inglenook. Named after the surrounding hills, those seven smart bedrooms flourish big sleigh beds and grand four-posters, stone floors and oak beams and a host of pleasing extras – fresh coffee, plasma screens, bathrobes, posh smellies. The meandering garden, with goldfish pool, wishing well and play area, is gorgeous.

Rooms	7 doubles. £160–£190. Singles £95.
Meals	12pm-2.30pm (3pm Sun); 6pm-9pm (9.30pm in summer). No food Sun eve in winter. Main courses £9.95–£16.50; set menus £28 & £32.50.
Closed	3pm-6pm & Mon (except bank hols). Open all day June-Aug.
Directions	B3162 for Broadwindsor; left in 2 miles for Broadoak. Follow unclassified road for 3 miles.

Roy & Mel Warburton
The Shave Cross Inn,
Shave Cross,
Bridport DT6 6HW
Tel   +44 (0)1308 868358
Web   www.theshavecrossinn.co.uk

Entry 237 Map 3

The Bull Hotel
Bridport

Urban-chic meets rural simplicity at Richard and Nikki's Regency-style coaching inn. Funky and fun sums up this vibrant place and you feel good the moment you step through the door. Escape Bridport's bustle, kick off your shoes and plonk yourself down on a squashy sofa with a pint of Otter Ale. The bar is open all day, for hearty English breakfasts and cappuccino and cake, for lunchtime sandwiches and kids' high tea. For seriously good food, there's a candlelit restaurant; for summer lunches, a Victorian courtyard. Daily menus are contemporary and work with the seasons while organic ingredients are locally sourced: Lyme Bay scallops with black pudding and garlic sauce, Mapperton lamb cutlets with red wine. Enjoy vanilla rice pudding and handmade cheeses. And the bedrooms! Classic period features mix serenely with modern pieces and antiques, there are Designer Guild fabrics and Milo sofas, plasma screens and big comfy beds, Tivoli radios and white waffle robes, roll-top baths and Neal's Yard smellies. A boon for arty Bridport – and the fantastic Jurassic coast is a mile away.

Rooms	15: 7 doubles, 1 twin, 2 family rooms, 1 single, 1 suite. £80–£170. Four-posters £150–£190. Family rooms £155–£205. Single £70–£110. Suite £200–£260.
Meals	8am–10am (3pm Sat brunch); 12pm–3pm; 6.30pm–9.30pm. Main courses £5–£16 (lunch), £12–£24 (dinner); Sunday lunch £10.45.
Closed	Open all day.
Directions	On main street in town. Car park at rear.

Nikki & Richard Cooper
The Bull Hotel,
34 East Street,
Bridport, DT6 3LF
Tel   +44 (0)1308 422878
Web   www.thebullhotel.co.uk

Dorset

The Greyhound
Sydling St Nicholas

Having made a success of The West Bay down by the sea, John and Karen teamed up with friends Ron and Cherry and moved inland to this rambling pub on the Dorset Downs. The hub of an idyllic streamside village, this is a modernised 17th-century inn with a walled front garden – perfect for a pint of Palmers after a downland stroll. Foodies beat a path to the door for fresh Lyme Bay scallops, pea shoots and truffle oil and chicken and lobster ballantine while Dorset-reared meats include fillet steak with cream cabbage and oxtail pudding. Eat in a beamed and carpeted bar, cosy with coal fire, or at clothed tables in a dining room with country décor. Well worth the long valley drive north of Dorchester or as an escape from the Cerne Abbas crowds – and book early for Sunday lunch.

Dorset

Rose & Crown
Trent

In a sleepy estate village is a 15th-century pub – stone-built, thatched and peacefully hidden away next to the church down the lane. Owned by Wadworth and spruced up by tenants Heather and Stuart, it remains refreshingly simple, with a rug-strewn stone floors, winter log fires, soothing colours, glowing church candles on scrubbed tables, ticking grandfather clock, books and newspapers. Expect four gleaming handpumps (try the Bishops Tipple), squashy sofas, impressive artwork in the conservatory dining room and sylvan views from the bar… and a wagging welcome from Archie the spaniel. Food is simple, hearty and homecooked and made from local ingredients – mussels with cider and chive cream, game casserole with thyme-roasted root vegetables, sticky toffee and walnut pudding, and excellent Sunday roasts.

Meals	12pm-2pm (2.30pm Sun); 6.30pm-9pm. Main courses £11-£18.
Closed	2.30pm-6pm, from 3pm Sun.
Directions	Village signed off A37, 6 miles north of Dorchester.

Meals	12pm-2.30pm (3pm Sat/Sun); 6pm-9.30pm (9pm Sat). No food Sun eve. Main courses £7.95-£9.75 (lunch), £8.25-£19.95 (dinner); sandwiches £4.95.
Closed	3pm-6pm Tues-Fri & all day Mon. Open all day Sat/Sun.
Directions	Just off the A30 between Sherborne and Yeovil.

**John Ford & Karen Trimby,
Ron Hobson & Cherry Ball**
The Greyhound, 26 High St,
Sydling St Nicholas DT2 9PD

Tel	+44 (0)1300 341303
Web	www.thegreyhound.net

Entry 239 Map 3

Heather Kirk & Stuart Malcolm
Rose & Crown,
Trent,
Sherborne DT9 4SL

Tel	+44 (0)1935 850776
Web	www.roseandcrowntrent.co.uk

Entry 240 Map 3

Dorset

Gaggle of Geese
Buckland Newton

Having transformed the European Inn into a Piddle Valley favourite, Mark and Emily took on the forlorn Gaggle in the next valley – and worked their magic. Squashy sofas by the fire, bookcases and big flowers, church candles on old pine tables and a lick of Farrow & Ball did the trick in the bar; red walls and rugs soften the rambling dining room. Come for pints of Butcombe and modern pub food – goose leg hash, organic rump steak with pepper sauce, jam roly-poly. Meat comes from Mark's family farm at Cattistock, and allotment vegetables and game are delivered by locals – in return for a pint or two. Skittle evenings, lunch clubs, the village fête, Remembrance dinners, charity goose auctions, takeaway fish and chips... it's the village's adopted hub. Plans for five acres include a kitchen garden, rare-breed livestock and bedrooms.

Meals	12pm-2pm (4pm Sun); 7pm-9pm (6.30pm-9.30pm Fri & Sat). Main courses £8-£14; Sunday roast from £10.
Closed	3.30pm-5.30pm. Open all day Sat & Sun.
Directions	In village centre off B3143, 10 miles north of Dorchester.

Mark & Emily Hammick
Gaggle of Geese,
Buckland Newton,
Dorchester DT2 7BS

Tel   +44 (0)1300 345249
Web   www.thegaggle.co.uk

Entry 241 Map 3

Dorset
Worth a visit

242 The European Inn Piddletrenthide, Dorchester DT2 7QT +44 (0)1300 348308
The inn is a gem, with its beamed bar and dining room and short, seasonal menus that champion local producers, Slow-style... stop by after a day exploring the Dorset coast. New owners early 2010.

243 The Anchor Inn Seatown, Chideock, Bridport DT6 6JU +44 (0)1297 489215
A terrific coastal path watering-hole below Golden Cap. The big sun terrace and clifftop gardens overlook a pebbly beach. Open fires, pints of Palmers, crab sandwiches.

244 Crown Inn Ibberton, Blandford Forum DT11 0EN +44 (0)1258 817448
True old Dorset local in a sleepy village under Bulbarrow Hill. Kick off your hiking boots in the lovely garden, savour local ciders and real ales, refuel on fabulous, well-priced food.

245 Ship Inn West Stour, Gillingham SP8 5RP +44 (0)1747 838640
Spruced up roadside inn with stripped oak boards, scrubbed farmhouse tables, big bow windows and a buzz. Cracking ales on tap and a chalkboard menu listing fish specials and seasonal game.

246 Vine Inn Vine Hill, Pamphill, Wimborne BH21 4EE +44 (0)1292 882259
Former bakehouse run by the Sweatland family for generations, now owned by the National Trust. Two timeless bars, London Pride on tap and sandwiches for sustenance. Close to Kingston Lacy House.

Durham

The Victoria Inn
Durham

In the centre of lovely old-fashioned Durham – all cobbled streets, riverside walks, Cathedral – is a Victorian public house with small rooms, high ceilings, marble fireplaces, three coal fires, etched and cut glass and a collection of Victoriana. Once upon a time, shawled women would pop in for a porter or an errant husband, now it's frequented by builders, students, academics and beer lovers. Virtually unaltered since it was built in 1899, The Vic has been in the Webster family for years and has a strong local following. The three traditional bar rooms are spick and span; above the servery is an unusual gallery with shining figurines and ornaments of Queen Victoria and the Prince Consort. Simple snacks are available but it is the Darwin's Ghost Ale and other local and Scottish beers, the whiskies and the camaraderie that makes this place enticing. Small upstairs bedrooms are warm, cosy, comfortable, traditionally furnished with contemporary touches and good value; breakfasts are relaxed and generous and there's limited off-street parking and garaging. Original, timeless, welcoming.

Rooms	5: 3 doubles, 1 twin, 1 family room. £60-£65. Family room £65-£75. Singles £48-£65.
Meals	12pm-3pm. Toasted sandwiches £1.50.
Closed	Open all day.
Directions	5-minute walk over Kingsgate Bridge from university, cathedral, castle & market place.

Michael Webster
The Victoria Inn,
86 Hallgarth Street,
Durham DH1 3AS
Tel   +44 (0)191 386 5269
Web   www.victoriainn-durhamcity.co.uk

Entry 247 Map 12

Durham

Black Bull Inn
Frosterley

An enticing village pub run as its owners like it. It is atmospherically lit, with solid tables and high-back settles (cushioned for comfort), stone flags, ticking clocks, glowing ranges, warmth and good cheer. No lagers, but coffee and scones from 10.30am, cider from the cask and beers from a few villages away. The hop is treated with reverence here – dark malty porter from Wylam Brewery, bitter from Allendale – and the good value food is a joy. Rather than devising a menu then searching for suppliers, Diane and Duncan source the produce first: local as much as possible, and in tune with the seasons. A shin of Broomhill Farm beef braised in ale on root vegetables with dumplings is the sort of thing they love here. There are regular music sessions where local musicians play classical, folk or jazz… hey, this place even has its own peal of bells.

Meals	12pm-3pm; 7pm-9pm. No food Sun eve. Main courses up to £14.95; Sunday roast £8.95.
Closed	From 5pm Sun. Open all day Thurs-Sat.
Directions	Beside A689 in Weardale between Wolsingham & Stanhope, next to Frosterley steam railway station.

Duncan & Diane Davis
Black Bull Inn,
Bridge End,
Frosterley,
Bishop Auckland DL13 2SL
Tel   +44 (0)1388 527784

Entry 248 Map 12

Durham

The Bay Horse
Hurworth

A pretty, bow-fronted building, painted cream under red pantiles, which sits happily at the end of a terrace with open countryside beyond. Inside is nicely pubby: comforting button-back wall seating, polished oak floor boards, local prints and soft wall lamps, quiet background jazz. At least two good cask ales are served (in dimpled tankards), and truly stunning food from chef Marcus Bennett is brought to you by friendly folk in crisp aprons; you eat in a dining room with antique tables and proper linen napkins. Try wild duck and pistachio terrine with fig chutney, smoked bacon, scrambled egg and toasted mushroom and onion brioche – the eggs come in a shell with a soldier! Puddings are irresistible – try caramelised rice pudding with spiced autumn berries, even the bread is home baked and there are private dining rooms upstairs.

Meals	12pm-2.30pm (4pm Sun); 6pm-9.30pm. No food Sun eve. Main courses £11.95-£21.95; bar lunches from £5.95.
Closed	Open all day.
Directions	Hurworth is signed off A167, 2 miles south of Darlington at Croft. Pub is 1 mile in village centre.

Marcus Bennett & Jonathan Hall
The Bay Horse,
45 The Green, Hurworth,
Darlington, DL2 2AA
Tel   +44 (0)1325 720663
Web   www.thebayhorsehurworth.com

Entry 249 Map 12

Durham

Number Twenty 2
Darlington

It is young, yet it is Darlington's most classic pub. Just off the town centre, the Victorian-styled "Traditional Alehouse & Canteen" looks no different from the neighbouring shop fronts. Inside, a high ceiling and raised areas in the front bays give a vault-like impression; Number Twenty 2 is licensed for the sale of ales, wines and a limited range of spirits. There are five changing guest ales alongside eight regular beers, nine continental beers on tap, and a good choice of wines chosen for easy quaffing; it's a civilised place favoured by local business folk, and the staff know their stuff. At the back of the long bar is a seating area known as the 'canteen' at lunchtimes, and the food is good and uncomplicated. It may be closed on Sundays, but for the rest of the week Darlington has a very fine local.

Meals	12pm-2pm.
	Main courses £4.95-£9.95.
Closed	Sun. Open all day.
Directions	Just west of Darlington town centre. Coniscliffe Road leads into A67 to Barnard Castle.

Ralph Wilkinson
Number Twenty 2,
22 Coniscliffe Road,
Darlington, DL3 7RG

Tel   +44 (0)1325 354590
Web www.villagebrewer.co.uk

Entry 250 Map 12

Durham

Bridgewater Arms
Winston

A Victorian schoolhouse with views rising across fields to distant woods: an unusual setting for a stylish modern bar and restaurant. The memory of the old school is carefully retained in the bar, with its high ceiling, decorative leaded windows, shelves of books and photos of pupils past; the names of the children that took part in 1957's *Jack and the Beanstalk* are inscribed above the bar, adding charm and a touch of history. Adjoining half-panelled dining rooms are warmly decorated and furnished in contemporary style. Blackboards and daily printed menus place firm emphasis on fresh, local supplies with a strong emphasis on fish and game in season – roast grouse with game gravy, sea trout with herb butter sauce – cooked by Paul Grundy, former head chef at the renowned Black Bull in Moulton.

Meals	12pm-2pm; 6pm-9pm.
	Main courses £10-£20.
Closed	2.30pm-6pm, Sun & Mon.
Directions	Just off A67 between Darlington & Barnard Castle; at entrance to village on Staindrop crossroad.

Paul Grundy
Bridgewater Arms,
Winston,
Darlington, DL2 3RN

Tel   +44 (0)1325 730302
Web www.thebridgewaterarms.com

Entry 251 Map 12

Rose & Crown
Romaldkirk

An idyllic village of mellow stone where little has changed in 200 years. The Rose and Crown dates from 1733 and stands on the green, next to the village's Saxon church. Roses ramble above the door in summer, so pick up a pint and search out the sun on the gravelled forecourt. Inside is just as good. You can sit at settles in the tiny locals' bar and roast away in front of the fire while reading the *Teesdale Mercury*, or seek out sofas in the peaceful sitting room and tuck into afternoon tea. Bedrooms are lovely. Those in the converted barn are less posh but have padded headboards and tumble with colour; those in the main house come with stylish furnishings and vibrant colours. They have crisp white linen, Bose sound systems and quietly fancy bathrooms. Delicious food can be eaten informally in the brasserie (smoked salmon soufflé, confit of duck, sticky toffee pudding) or grandly in the panelled dining room (farmhouse ham with fresh figs, grilled sea bass, honey and whisky ice cream). High Force waterfall and Hadrian's Wall are close and there's a drying room for walkers.

Rooms	12: 6 doubles, 4 twins, 2 suites. £140-£170. Singles from £89. Suites £185. Half-board from £100-£125 p.p.
Meals	12pm-1.30pm; 6.30pm-9.30pm (9pm Sun). Main courses £10-£15.25.
Closed	Open all day.
Directions	From Barnard Castle, B6277 north for 6 miles. Right in village towards green. Inn on left.

Christopher & Alison Davy
Rose & Crown,
Romaldkirk,
Barnard Castle DL12 9EB
Tel   +44 (0)1833 650213
Web   www.rose-and-crown.co.uk

Entry 252 Map 12

The Bell Inn & Hill House
Horndon on the Hill

A 600-year-old timber-framed coaching inn, as bustling today with contented locals as it was when pilgrims stopped on their way to Canterbury. Everything here is a delight: hanging lanterns in the courtyard, stripped boards in the bar, smartly dressed staff in the restaurant, copious window boxes bursting with colour. This is a proper inn, warmly welcoming, with thick beams, country rugs, panelled walls and open fires. Stop for a pint of cask ale in the lively bar, then potter into the restaurant for top food, perhaps stilton ravioli, grilled Dover sole, orange and passion fruit tart. Christine grew up here, John joined her years ago; both are much respected in the trade, as is Joanne, Master sommelier and loyal manager of many years. An infectious warmth runs throughout this ever-popular inn. As for the bedrooms, go for the suites above the shop: cosy, individual, very traditional. In the morning stroll up the tiny high street to breakfast with the papers at elegant Hill House, then head north into Constable country, or east to the pier at Southend. Wonderful.

Rooms	15: 7 doubles, 3 twins, 5 suites. £50–£60. Suites £85.
Meals	12pm-1.45pm (2.30pm Sun); 6.30pm-9.45pm (from 7pm Sun). No food bank holiday Mon. Main courses £9.50–£14.95; bar meals £7.95–£10.50.
Closed	2.30pm-5.30pm (3pm Sat; 4pm-7pm Sun).
Directions	M25 junc. 30/31. A13 dir. Southend for 3 miles; B1007 to Horndon. On left in village.

Christine & John Vereker
The Bell Inn & Hill House,
High Road, Horndon on the Hill,
Stanford le Hope SS17 8LD
Tel   +44 (0)1375 642463
Web   www.bell-inn.co.uk

Entry 253 Map 5

Essex

The Swan
Little Totham

In a village of 300 souls with no bus, post office or shop, the highpoint has to be the pub with the award-winning ales. Little Totham is lucky: this listed and very pretty 400-year-old cottage-inn is as friendly as can be, and the beers are fantastic thanks to John's "all-knowing nose" – try Farmer's Pucks Folly, Mauldon's Black Adder and Crouch Vale Brewers Gold. There are quiz nights, live music events (folk, Irish, contemporary) and a choice of old pub games. Lunchtime food ranges from toad-in-the-hole to scampi and chips to roasts on Sundays. No glamour, no frills, just low beams, open fires, soft lighting and bar room chatter. There's a splendid dining room too, ideal for family gatherings, and the front beer garden is a great spot in summer. One of the best real ale pubs in Essex – and one of the friendliest.

Meals	12pm-2.30pm; 6pm-9.30pm.
	No food Sun eve or all day Mon.
	Main courses £9.95-£14.95;
	baguettes £3.25-£4.75
	(lunch only).
Closed	Open all day.
Directions	Leave A12 at Rivenhall dir. Great
	Braxted, right onto B1022, then
	immed. left into Loamy Hill Road;
	2 miles, on right, in village centre.

John & Valerie Pascoe
The Swan,
School Road, Little Totham,
Maldon CM9 8LB

Tel   +44 (0)1621 892689
Web   www.theswanpublichouse.co.uk

Entry 254 Map 10

Essex

The Sun Inn
Dedham

An idyllic village made rich by mills in the 16th century. These days you can hire boats on the river, so order a picnic at the inn, float down the Stour, then tie up on the bank for lunch al fresco. You're in the epicentre of Constable country. As for The Sun, you couldn't hope to wash up in a better place. Step in to find log fires in grand grates, board games on old tables, stripped floors and an easy elegance. A panelled lounge comes with sofas and armchairs, the bar is made from a slab of local elm and the dining room is beamed and airy, so settle in for grilled rib-eye steak with artichokes, fish from British waters, local cheeses and children's portions of whatever they fancy. There's a garden for summer and the inn owns Victoria's Plums, a tiny shop selling locally grown fruit and veg next door.

Meals	12pm-2.30pm (3pm Sat & Sun);
	6.30pm-9.30pm (10pm Sat).
	Main courses £8.50-£16.50;
	bar meals £4.50-£8.50.
Closed	Open all day.
Directions	A12 north past Colchester.
	2nd exit, marked Dedham.
	In village opposite church.

Piers Baker
The Sun Inn,
High Street,
Dedham, Colchester, CO7 6DF

Tel   +44 (0)1206 323351
Web   www.thesuninndedham.com

Entry 255 Map 10

The Mistley Thorn
Mistley

In Constable land: an unexpectedly chi-chi village where Georgian cottages gather around a river estuary with wide, light views of water, bobbing boats and green hills beyond. David and Sherri (who have a cookery school next door) run the place beautifully: staff are young and very good, there are plenty of locals tossed into the mix downstairs and some impeccably behaved children too. The mood is laid-back city wine bar rather than roadside country pub. Colours are soft and easy, the tables are of various shapes, candles flicker, modern art rubs along well with the odd antique and food is taken seriously but with no grim reverence. There's lots of good local fish and seafood – smoked haddock chowder, crab linguine with chilli, chunky fishcakes, brilliant chips – and a pudding list that includes cheesecake from Sherri's mum. Bedrooms are calm with cream carpets, big beds and pale green paintwork; ask for a room with a view over the river. Bathrooms have a Turkish feel with tiny beige and cream tiles, spotless white baths and overhead showers. It's all entirely charming.

Rooms	5: 3 doubles, 2 twins/doubles. £80–£105. Singles from £65.
Meals	12pm-2.30pm (4pm Sat/Sun); 6.30pm-9.30pm (from 6pm Sat & Sun). Main courses £8.95–£15.95; bar meals £4.25–£8.95.
Closed	3pm-6.30pm. Open all day Sat/Sun.
Directions	From A12, Hadleigh & East Bergholt exit north of Colchester. Thro' East Bergholt to A137; signed Manningtree; continue to Mistley High St. 50 yards from station.

David McKay & Sherri Singleton
The Mistley Thorn,
High Street, Mistley,
Manningtree CO11 1HE
Tel   +44 (0)1206 392821
Web   www.mistleythorn.co.uk

Entry 256 Map 10

Essex

The Compasses at Pattiswick
Pattiswick

Jono and Jane Clark's transformation of this old pub is a huge success. Slick and sophisticated bars mix flagstones with floorboards, modern furniture and soft lights with creams and sages. At heart it remains a local, with plenty of space for drinkers in for a pint of Woodforde's Wherry or Abbot Ale. Yet the food is the major draw, served in the bar or the elegantly beamed and spacious restaurant. Old favourites such as British Excellence bangers with mash and onion gravy are founded on well-sourced raw materials, for the kitchen cultivates a network of small local producers. More modern dishes might include chicken breast stuffed with Applewood cheese, and grilled sea bass on wholegrain mustard potatoes; for pudding, who could resist sticky toffee pudding with hot toffee sauce? Outside: a terrace and an adventure play area so children may romp.

Meals	12pm-3pm (4pm Sun); 6pm-10pm. Main courses £6.75-£14.75 (lunch), £9.95-£16.95 (dinner).
Closed	Open all day.
Directions	Take B1024 towards Coggeshall from A12, then left on A120 towards Braintree & take 2nd right for Pattiswick.

Jono & Jane Clark
The Compasses at Pattiswick,
19 Compasses Road, Pattiswick,
Braintree CM77 8BG
Tel   +44 (0)1376 561322
Web   www.thegreatpubcompany.co.uk

Entry 257 Map 10

Essex

The Viper
Mill Green

Isolated, but not lonely, this little pub sits in magnificent woodland on an empty road. The snug, neat, dog-welcome front bar is warm and jolly and the locals will tell you that these plain simple rooms have barely changed for 60-odd years. One blackboard lists a regularly changing selection of East Anglian real ales, such as Mighty Oak's intriguingly named Jake the Snake and Nethergate's Viper Ale, and don't miss the Easter and August bank holiday beer festivals. The classic, good-value bar snacks are served at lunchtime only — sandwiches, pies, soup, chilli, ploughman's — and there's a choice of roasts on Sunday. The setting is so peaceful you can ignore the nearby road. Tables on the lawn overlook a cottage garden, resplendent in summer with flowers and shrubs; excellent walks start from the door. Worth a detour.

Meals	12pm-2pm (3pm Sat & Sun). Main courses £3.85-£7.95; Sunday roast £8.25.
Closed	3pm-6pm. Open all day Sat & Sun.
Directions	From A12 for Margaretting; left up Ivy Barn Lane; pub at top.

Donna Torris
The Viper,
Mill Green Road,
Mill Green,
Ingatestone CM4 0PT
Tel   +44 (0)1277 352010

Entry 258 Map 9

Essex

The Cricketers
Clavering

It achieved fame as the family home and training ground of Jamie Oliver and, as such, draws a few passers-by... but this big 16th-century inn on the edge of Clavering handles its glory with good humour. Trevor and Sally Oliver's pub has low beams, original timbers and a contented, well-cared for air; light floods in, reflected in the highly polished tables and gleaming brass and glass. A serious commitment to seasonal food is obvious the moment you see the printed menu: steamed mussels with white wine and shallots, wild chargrilled venison with quince and redcurrant sauce, organic salmon with a red peppercorn crust on green beans with fresh salsa verde, shank of lamb with root vegetables. Blackboards list daily specials and good value wines of the month, many served by the glass.

Gloucestershire

The Ostrich Inn
Newland

In the village of Newland the Ostrich is where the beer drinkers go to sample eight changing ales. Across from All Saints Church, that 'Cathedral of the Forest', you'll mix with all sorts before a log fire. Huntsmen and trail bikers pile in for the massive portions of delicious food, from the Newland bread and cheese platter to rack of Welsh lamb with lashings of Masala sauce. The nicotine-brown ceiling that looks in danger of imminent collapse is supported by a massive oak pillar in front of the bar where the locals chatter and jazz CDs keep the place swinging. The weekly menu, served throughout the pub, takes a step up in class, and is excellent value. Energetic Kathryn and her team, including Alfie the pub dog, aide the buzzing atmosphere. To the back is a walled garden – and the loos, 'just by there', beyond the coal sacks.

Meals	12pm-2pm; 6.30pm-9.30pm. Main courses £10-£18; set menu £25 & £29.50.
Closed	Open all day.
Directions	On B1038 between Newport & Buntingford.

Meals	12pm-2.30pm; 6.30pm-9.30pm (6pm-9.30pm Sat). Main courses £12.50-£18.50; bar meals £5.50-£10.50.
Closed	3pm-6.30pm (6pm Sat).
Directions	Signed on lane linking A466 at Redbrook & at Clearwell between B4228 Coleford & Chepstow road.

	Trevor & Sally Oliver The Cricketers, Clavering, Saffron Walden CB11 4QT
Tel	+44 (0)1799 550442
Web	www.thecricketers.co.uk

Entry 259 Map 9

	Kathryn Horton The Ostrich Inn, Newland, Coleford GL16 8NP
Tel	+44 (0)1594 833260
Web	www.theostrichinn.com

Entry 260 Map 7

Gloucestershire

The Glasshouse Inn
Longhope

If you are a fan of Fuller's London Pride and Butcombe, Weston's ciders and all good, nature-blessed produce, come here. Ramshackle tables and open log fires are considered modern at this converted 15th-century brick cottage where glass was once blown in wood-fired ovens and cider pressed in the shed. Guinness adverts, cartoons and horse racing prints decorate the place as do autographed England rugby shirts – and the chiming clock never serves as an invitation to leave. Say landlords Steve and Gill: "We buy the best available produce locally, so chefs can provide our customers with generous portions of tasty, interesting, homemade food." Expect authentic Thai curries or pork fillet stuffed with apricots with a cider sauce, a lovely calm atmosphere, a terrific little garden for summer sipping and super local walks.

Meals	12pm–2pm; 7pm–9pm; no food Sun eve. Main courses £7.50–£15; Sunday lunch, 2 courses £13.95.
Closed	3pm–6.30pm & Sun eve.
Directions	North off A40 between Gloucester & Newent at Longhope, signed Clifford Mesne: through Glasshouse, pub at bottom of hill on right.

Steve & Gill Pugh
The Glasshouse Inn,
Glasshouse Hill,
May Hill, Longhope GL17 0NN
Tel +44 (0)1452 830529

Entry 261 Map 8

Gloucestershire

The Boat Inn
Ashleworth

This extraordinary, tiny pub has been in the family since Charles II granted them a licence for liquor and ferry – about 400 years ago! It's a gem – a peaceful, unspoilt red-brick cottage on the banks of the Severn and an ale-lover's paradise. Settle back with a pint of Beowulf, Church End or Archer's in the gleaming front parlour – colourful with fresh garden flowers, huge built-in settle and big scrubbed deal table fronting an old kitchen range – or in the spotless bar. On sunny summer days you can laze by the languid river. Adjectives are inadequate: this place is cherished. Real ale straight from the cask, Weston's farm cider, a bar of chocolate, a packet of crisps... but don't feed Sam the dog, he's on a diet. There's no 'jus' here; lunchtime meals are fresh filled rolls with homemade chutney.

Meals	12pm–2pm. Filled rolls (lunchtime only).
Closed	2.30pm–7pm (3pm–7pm Sat & Sun), Wed lunch & Mon.
Directions	On A417 1.5 miles from Hartpury, between Gloucester & Ledbury.

Ron & Elisabeth Nicholls
& Louise Beer
The Boat Inn, The Quay,
Ashleworth, Gloucester GL19 4HZ
Tel +44 (0)1452 700272
Web www.boat-inn.co.uk

Entry 262 Map 8

Gloucestershire

The Beehive
Cheltenham

There are few pubs of character in Cheltenham but this one shines like a beacon in the bohemian backstreets of Montpellier. Owned by the team in charge of The White Hart in Winchcombe, this is the place to come for lively conversation, well-kept beer and hearty food. It's also very popular with the racing crowd during the Gold Cup. Hidden among antique shops and cafés, the lovely Beehive has a pubby bar and two dining areas, the usual scrubbed floors, mismatched wooden tables and the summery bonus of a courtyard at the back. There are three regular real ales on tap – including the locally brewed Goff's Jouster – and generous portions of gastropub favourites like as Old Spot sausages with mustard mash and gravy – and the more exotic-sounding grilled cod with a merguez, chorizo and chickpea stew.

Meals	12pm-2.30pm (3.30pm Sun); 6pm-9.30pm (7pm-10pm Thur-Sat); no food Sun eve. Main courses £8.50-£16; Sunday lunch £9.50-£17.50.
Closed	Open all day.
Directions	Montpellier Villas is off Suffolk Road.

Matt Walker
The Beehive,
1-3 Montpellier Villas,
Cheltenham GL50 2XE

Tel +44 (0)1242 702270
Web www.thebeehivemontpellier.com

Entry 263 Map 8

Gloucestershire

The Plough Inn
Temple Guiting

Horses from the local stables gallop past, local shoots lunch here, race-goers dine. The pub's rustic walls are lined with photographs of meetings at Cheltenham: this place is dedicated to country pursuits. Cheltenham week is bedlam (a marquee is erected in the garden) but every week is busy. The cooking has a following, the dining room is famous for its asparagus suppers and the Aberdeen Angus fillet in its brandy and black peppercorn sauce tastes as good as it looks. There are local beers, real ciders and well-chosen wines. The building has been an inn since the 16th century and was once a courthouse, so bars are darkly cosy with low beams, flagstones and smouldering fires. In spite of its success, The Plough still pulls in the locals. Children will make a bee-line for the play fort in the garden.

Meals	12pm-9pm. Main courses £8.95-£17.95.
Closed	Open all day.
Directions	B4077 between Stow on the Wold & Tewkesbury.

Craig & Becky Brown
The Plough Inn,
Ford, Temple Guiting,
Cheltenham GL54 5RU

Tel +44 (0)1386 584215
Web www.theploughinnatford.co.uk

Entry 264 Map 8

The White Hart Inn
Winchcombe

In Winchcombe, a stroll from Sudeley Castle, a 16th-century pub for trekkers of the Cotswold Way, and all those who love the Cotswolds. Ongoing changes by owner Peter Austen are slowly returning the old place to its coaching inn roots so, although gastrofied, there are quarry tiles, scrubbed pine tables and framed cricketing memorabilia (including Jack Russell's 1990 Ashes sweater) in the classically pubby front bar. Eat in here or in the intimate little dining room (just five tables); wherever you go, the meal will be a treat. Start with a pint of Goffs Jouster or one of 20 exceptional wines by the glass, move on to succulent Gloucester Old Spot pork sausages with mash and onion gravy, or ham hock terrine and venison stew. The menu is awash with local produce, and lists suppliers. Eight lovely bedrooms should be ready by May 2010, so look forward to Farrow & Ball colours, antique pine, chunky wooden beds and super bathrooms and wet-room showers. Another brilliant touch: if you dine in, there's an organic wine shop that allows you to choose your bottle at cost price, plus corkage.

Rooms	8: 2 doubles, 4 twins/doubles, 2 four-posters. £44.95-£79.95.
Meals	12pm-3pm; 6pm-9.30pm (10pm Fri & Sat). Main courses £8.95-£16.95; bar meals £4.50-£8.95.
Closed	3pm-6pm. Open all day Sat & Sun.
Directions	From Cheltenham, B4632 to Winchcombe. Inn on right.

Peter Austen
The White Hart Inn,
High Street,
Winchcombe, Cheltenham, GL54 5LJ
Tel   +44 (0)1242 602359
Web   www.wineandsausage.co.uk

Entry 265 Map 8

Gloucestershire

Ebrington Arms
Ebrington

The glorious gardens at Hidcote Manor and Kiftsgate Court are a ramble across fields from the Ebrington Arms. This is a relaxed and rustic Cotswold stone pub that has been restored and revived by Claire and Jim. Little has changed in the 17th-century bar, hub of the community, cosy with low beams and winter fires. Bag a seat and share pints of Purity with the regulars, or seek out the dining room next door. Worn stone floors, a delightful mishmash of tables and chairs, cushioned window seats and fresh flowers set the scene for some terrific pub food cooked from mostly local produce. Dishes are simple yet full of flavour, so dive in to spiced lentil and roasted pepper soup, rump of Cotswold lamb with rosemary jus, and walnut tart with vanilla ice cream. No need to negotiate the route home when you can bed down here; bedrooms (up steepish stairs) are quirky and full of charm, with chunky wooden beds, colourful throws and plump pillows, deep window seats with village or country views, and new bathrooms. A properly unpretentious, award-winning pub, run by the nicest people.

Rooms	3: 1 twin, 1 double, 1 four-poster. £90–£120.
Meals	12pm-2.30pm; 6.30pm-9pm (9.30pm Fri & Sat). Main courses £9.50–£14.50.
Closed	3pm-6pm. Open all day Fri-Sun.
Directions	West from Shipton-on-Stour on B4035. Across A429. After a mile, bear right at sharp left-hand bend; village signed.

Claire & Jim Alexander
Ebrington Arms,
Ebrington,
Chipping Campden GL55 6NH
Tel   +44 (0)1386 593223
Web   www.theebringtonarms.co.uk

Gloucestershire

The Churchill Arms
Paxford

On the edge of a pretty village, next to a tiny church and fields of sheep, an authentic Cotswold pub. A wood-burner warms the flagstones, polished wooden tables, chairs and cushioned pews sit beneath a beamed ceiling, and from behind a neat bar, charming staff pull you a well-kept pint of Hook Norton. Sit down, settle in, and look forward to the arrival of something rather special on your plate. Chef Will Guthrie has a gift for delivering unfussy food with wonderful flavours. Our braised pork belly with roasted butternut squash and morel jus was divine, while the Bramley apple and blackberry compote, with nutmeg crème brulée and shortbread, was a beautiful Anglo-Gallic medley. Expect pub classics on the blackboards too, and great cheeses and wines. In the garden, lively teams play traditional Aunt Sally in summer. A near-perfect pub run by new owners.

Meals	12pm-2pm; 7pm-9pm.
	Main courses £10.50-£18.99.
Closed	3pm-6pm.
Directions	A44 through Bourton-on-Hill; right to Paxford, via Blockley; pub in village on right.

Sheridan Mather & Richard Shore
The Churchill Arms,
Paxford,
Chipping Campden GL55 6XH
Tel   +44 (0)1386 594000
Web   www.thechurchillarms.com

文 🖾 🐾 ￥ 🔊
Entry 267 Map 8

Gloucestershire

The Farriers Arms
Todenham

A treasure: a couple of tables in front, a private dining room in the 'library', a restaurant for 25 – and smart tables in the landscaped rear garden, one of many improvements made by Nigel and Louise. It's cosy, cheerful and reassuringly old-fashioned. Polished flagstones, hop-hung beams and an inglenook with a wood-burner; add great beers, real cider, an enjoyable blackboard menu that changes every day and you have one special little pub. The Farriers is jam-packed on Sundays (lunch must be booked), and the draw is the high quality pub food: fresh local ingredients with tasty sauces. There are fresh soups, local sirloin steaks and the likes of apricot and stilton tart, roast duck with rösti and redcurrant sauce, and salmon and spinach wellington. Colouring books welcome kids, and the mellow-stone village is as pretty as the pub.

Meals	12pm-2pm (2.30pm Sun); 6.30pm-9pm (from 6pm in summer).
	Main courses £8-£17.95; bar meals £4-£8; Sunday roast £10.
Closed	3pm-6pm.
Directions	Signed from Moreton-in-Marsh & from A3400.

Nigel & Louise Kirkwood
The Farriers Arms,
Todenham,
Moreton-in-Marsh GL56 9PF
Tel   +44 (0)1608 650901
Web   www.farriersarms.com

文 🖾 🐾 🍺 ￥
Entry 268 Map 8

Gloucestershire

Horse & Groom
Bourton-on-the-Hill

You're at the top of the hill, so grab the window seats for views that pour over the Cotswolds. This is a hive of youthful endeavour, with brothers at the helm; Will cooks, Tom pours the ales, and a cheery conviviality flows. Refurbished interiors mix the old (open fires, stone walls, beamed ceilings) with the new (halogen lighting, crisp coir matting, a cool marble bar), making this a very fine place in which to hole up for a night or two. There are settles and boarded menus in the bar, stripped wooden floors and old rugs in the dining room. Food goes way beyond the pub norm, so tuck into medallions of monkfish with braised haricot beans, Cornish sardines, Dexter beef. Sit back in summer under the shade of damson trees with a mellow pint of Wye Valley Dorothy Goodbody's and watch the chefs raid the kitchen garden – for raspberries and strawberries, broad beans, herbs and more. Bedrooms are nicely plush, smart but uncluttered; those at the front are soundproofed to minimise noise from the road. The deluxe room is huge and comes with a king-sized bed, the garden room has doors that open onto the terrace.

Rooms	5 doubles. £105-£150. Singles from £70. Half-board from £70 p.p.
Meals	12pm-2pm (2.30pm Sun); 7pm-9pm (9.30pm Fri & Sat). Main courses £10-£18; light meals £4-£8.
Closed	3pm-6pm & Sun eve.
Directions	West from Moreton-in-Marsh on A44. Climb hill in Bourton-on-the-Hill; pub at top on left.

Tom & Will Greenstock
Horse & Groom,
Bourton-on-the-Hill,
Moreton-in-Marsh GL56 9AQ
Tel   +44 (0)1386 700413
Web   www.horseandgroom.info

Gloucestershire

The Fox Inn
Lower Oddington

Amid the grandeur of old Cotswold country houses, the Fox evokes a wonderful sense of times past. Low ceilings, worn flagstones, a log fire in winter, good food and an exemplary host... people love it here. The comfortably stylish bar has scrubbed pine tables topped with fresh flowers and candles; newspapers, magazines and ales are on tap; rag-washed ochre walls date back years; no wonder the locals are happy. Eat here or in the elegant, rose-red dining room, or on the terrace, heated on cool nights, of the pretty cottage garden. Imaginative, sometimes elaborate dishes include goat's cheese and roasted red pepper tart, carrot, coriander and ginger soup, sirloin steak with garlic butter, dark chocolate torte. Before you leave, explore the honey-stone village and 11th-century church, known for its magnificent frescos.

Meals	12pm-2pm (3.30pm Sun); 6.30pm-10pm (7pm-9pm Sun). Main courses £10.95-£16.25.
Closed	3.30pm-6pm (5pm-7pm Sun).
Directions	From Stow-on-the-Wold, A436 for Chipping Norton for 3 miles, then 2nd right after VW garage, for Lower Oddington. Inn 500 yds on right.

Ian McKenzie
The Fox Inn,
Lower Oddington,
Moreton-in-Marsh GL56 0UR

Tel	+44 (0)1451 870555
Web	www.foxinn.net

Entry 270 Map 8

Gloucestershire

The Horse and Groom Village Inn
Upper Oddington

Cotswold stone, hanging baskets, hefty beams and flagstone floors, chunky logs around the double fireplace... is this the pub from central casting? It's 500 years old and Simon and Sally Jackson have rejuvenated without losing the traditional charm. There's a good selection of guest ales, some from nearby microbreweries, including Wye Valley Best, Butty Bach and Hereford Pale Ale, Barley Mole and Banks's Best. The menu takes a Cook's tour of Europe, with a good serving of trad-English: rack of lamb with aubergine and tomato confit, shin of beef and root vegetable casserole, fillet of haddock topped with chorizo, lime and parmesan crust, game from the Adlestrop Estate. Produce is organic and local whenever possible, breads and puddings are all homemade. No fewer than 25 wines are available by the glass.

Meals	12pm-2pm; 6.30pm-9pm (7pm-9pm Sun). Main courses £8.95-£19.75.
Closed	3pm-5.30pm.
Directions	Village signed off A436 east of Stow-on-the-Wold.

Simon & Sally Jackson
The Horse and Groom Village Inn,
Upper Oddington,
Moreton-in-Marsh GL56 0XH

Tel	+44 (0)1451 830584
Web	www.horseandgroom.uk.com

Entry 271 Map 8

Gloucestershire

The Plough
Cold Aston

On the High Wold is a charming 17th-century pub on an unspoilt village green. Inside, a lot has been packed into a small space. Low beamed ceilings, flagstones and inglenook greet you, padded benches add a cosy, comfortable feel. From behind the compact bar the deeply hospitable and charming new owners dispense Old Hooky and Donnington Best Bitter and there are well chosen wines by the glass or pichet. The effortless modern English menu comes from a chef with an excellent local pedigree and features grilled whole plaice with prawn, lemon and caper butter, and roast mallard with parsnip purée and ginger, lime and sultana jus; there are good light bites and snacks for those short on time too. With summer seating overlooking a magnificent beech tree on the crossroads, this is a little cracker.

Meals	12pm-2pm Tues-Fri (3pm Sat & Sun); 6pm-9pm (9.30pm Fri & Sat); 6.30pm-9pm Sun. Main courses £9.95-£16; bar snacks (lunch) £4.50-£7.95.
Closed	2.30pm-6pm (3pm-6pm Sat; 3pm-6.30pm Sun) & Mon all day.
Directions	A429, through Fossebridge and take 2nd exit at next roundabout, signed Stow; turn left in 2.5 miles for Cold Aston.

Philip Mason-Gordon
The Plough,
Cold Aston,
Cheltenham GL54 3BN

Tel	+44 (0)1451 821459
Web	www.theploughcoldaston.com

Entry 272 Map 8

Gloucestershire

Five Mile House
Duntisbourne Abbots

In 300 years the interior has changed not a jot. Here are planked floors, open fires, two curving settles, a sunny lounge bar, newspapers and cribbage. There's a flagstoned 'poop deck' of a snug for locals and a galley a few steps below; a more genteel wardroom – once the owner's private parlour – stands across the hall. Here you may review the pick of the day's produce: perhaps splendidly thick sandwiches of roast beef with horseradish, or roast lamb with rosemary jelly. All is cooked to order by Johann and his team. Deserving more consideration than the proverbial swift half, the beer, which includes guests and Taylor's Landlord, is seriously good. There are serene views to the valley below and above, a busy main road, mercifully concealed by a bank and burgeoning hedgerows. You can hardly go wrong here.

Meals	12pm-2.30pm, 6pm-9.30pm; 7pm-9pm Sun (summer only). Main courses £8.50-£16.95.
Closed	3pm-6pm (4pm-7pm Sun).
Directions	On A417, turn at Duntisbourne Abbots Services; pub down the road past the petrol station.

Jo & Jon Carrier
Five Mile House, Old Gloucester Rd,
Duntisbourne Abbots,
Cirencester, GL7 7JR

Tel	+44 (0)1285 821432
Web	www.fivemilehouse.co.uk

Entry 273 Map 8

Puesdown Inn
Compton Abdale

Turn off the A40 and step into a stylish roadside Cotswold inn. Who would not be cheered by the log fires, the fresh flowers, the plump sofas, the scattered magazines and the wandering puss? The owners are charming, the interior is upbeat and the airy shuttered brasserie is a favourite. Chef-patron John creates daily menus of modern British dishes based on high quality ingredients: mutton from the Highgrove estate, game from local shoots, local organic pork, fish delivered daily from Brixham, cheeses from the region. Tuck into warm duck confit salad followed by pork belly with parsley mash and red wine jus with honey and thyme, finish with a bread and butter pudding and homemade ice cream. There are traditional pub favourites too; the quality of the ingredients shines through, the wine list is short but well chosen, and there's Hooky Bitter on tap. Why not stay? Next door are three compact but invitingly contemporary rooms – a leather armchair, a pretty brass bed, Italian showers that drench. The big garden overlooks fields and the road is only busy in the day.

Rooms	3 doubles. £75–£89.50. Singles £50–£60.
Meals	12pm–3pm; 6.30pm–10.30pm. Main courses £10.50–£17; bar meals £4.25–£12.50.
Closed	3pm–6pm, Sun & Mon eve.
Directions	Beside A40, 3 miles west of Northleach, 11 miles east of Cheltenham.

John & Maggie Armstrong
Puesdown Inn,
Compton Abdale,
Cheltenham GL54 4DN

Tel	+44 (0)1451 860262
Web	www.puesdown.cotswoldinns.com

Entry 274 Map 8

Gloucestershire

The Wheatsheaf Inn
Northleach

A well kept Cotswold secret, this small former wool market town is tucked between pretty hills on a crossroads of the Roman Fosse Way. Big smiles from a young staff greet you, and a pint of Hooky Bitter or London Pride will be in your hand before you know it. The wonderfully worn flagstones in the (very well-stocked) bar separate two well proportioned and coordinated dining areas that glow with wooden floors, striking Asian rugs and armchairs fronting crackling fires. Expect a mix of traditional English fare of unpretentious goodness and impeccable provenance, from fish and chips and bangers and mash to fillets of wild sea bass, crushed potatoes, seashore vegetables and cockles. Wine from the best of the old and new worlds has been carefully chosen to suit all budgets. Bedrooms are calm, well-lit and spacious, many with super-king beds, sleek wooden headboards and tasteful period fabrics; most have traditional furniture, though some feel more contemporary. A brilliant little place to return to after a day out exploring the High Wold countryside and villages, with a youthful buzz.

Rooms	9 twins/doubles. £80–£100.
Meals	12pm–2.30pm (3pm Sun); 6pm–9.30pm (10pm Fri & Sat). Main courses £10–£17; set menus £12 & £15.
Closed	Open all day.
Directions	In village centre, off A429 between Stow & Burford.

Sam & Georgina Pearman
The Wheatsheaf Inn,
West End, Northleach,
Cheltenham GL54 3EZ
Tel   +44 (0)1451 860244
Web   www.cotswoldswheatsheaf.com

Gloucestershire

The Butcher's Arms
Sheepscombe

Tracking down this delightful local involves an "are you sure this is the right road?" adventure down narrow winding lanes – to tiny Sheepscombe, one of Laurie Lee's favourite places. If the weather's fine, and you haven't had one too many pints of Otter Bitter, find the most level spot you can in the garden and relish the views. Inside: flowery curtains at mullioned windows, beams, brasses and bentwood chairs. So grab a perch by the wood-burning stove or a table in the tiny dining room; while you tuck into flavoursome food packed with local ingredients – a roast of Pyll House Farm lamb, a 'pie of the day' – you'll find yourself rubbing shoulders with walkers, cyclists and locals. Inside or out, this is a place to savour. No plans for trendification, just a friendly down-to-earth place doing the thing it does best.

Meals	12pm-2.30pm; 6.30pm-9.30pm (12pm-9.30pm Sat; 12pm-9pm Sun). Main courses £7.95-£15.95.
Closed	3pm-6pm. Open all day Sat & Sun.
Directions	Off A46 north of Painswick.

Mark & Sharon Tallents
The Butcher's Arms,
Sheepscombe,
Stroud GL6 7RH
Tel   +44 (0)1452 812113
Web   www.butchers-arms.co.uk

Entry 276 Map 8

Gloucestershire

The Bell at Sapperton
Sapperton

This elegant pub attracts wine-lovers, foodies, ramblers and riders. Inside is a spacious but intimate décor that spreads itself across several levels – stripped beams and wood-burners, modern art on stone walls, old settles and church chairs, fresh flowers and newspapers. Sup on local Uley Old Spot or Otter Amber Bitter, dine on fresh local produce and rare breed meats. Specials are chalked up above the fireplace and the food is generous in its range: pan-fried Madgetts Farm duck breast, lamb from Lighthorne, plum tart with apple sorbet and toasted almonds, a delicious local goat's cheese called Rachel. Not a typical family pub but Sunday roast lunches are hugely popular and the wine list is expertly considered to match the clientele. Summer eating can be outside on the well-tended terrace and spills over into the sun-trapping 'Medditerranean' courtyard.

Meals	12pm-2pm; 7pm-9.30pm (9pm Sun). Main courses £10.50-£20; ploughman's £8.50; Sunday lunch £15.50 & £17.50.
Closed	2.30pm-6.30pm (3pm-7pm Sun).
Directions	Off A419, 6 miles west of Cirencester. Follow signs to Sapperton Village.

Paul Davidson & Pat Le Jeune
The Bell at Sapperton,
Sapperton,
Cirencester GL7 6LE
Tel   +44 (0)1285 760298
Web   www.foodatthebell.co.uk

Entry 277 Map 8

Gloucestershire

Green Dragon
Cowley

Hidden down a sleepy lane somewhere off the A435, this mellow Cotswold stone building, festooned with honeysuckle and hanging baskets, was a cider house three centuries ago. It's still beautifully traditional inside. So settle down with a pint of Hooky in the stone-flagged bar, all warm mustard walls and glowing candles, logs crackling in the inglenook, hops hanging from blackboards and beams. Furnishings are hand-crafted by 'Mouseman' Thompson (look for the mouse trademark signature) and the food is comforting, fresh and delicious. Tuck into a bowl of chilli or a tuna niçoise salad, or, in winter, something more substantial, a hearty mutton stew or a steak and kidney pudding with minted mushy peas. The pick of the courtyard-annexe bedrooms – kitted out in modern pine and named after Gold Cup winners – is the St George's Suite above the former stables, a vast room with deep leather sofas and a king-size bed, a flat-screen TV, books, magazines and a huge tiled bathroom with free standing bath and walk-in shower. Wonderful walks start from the front door.

Rooms	9: 8 twins/doubles, 1 suite. £85–£140. Singles £65.
Meals	12pm-2.30pm (3pm Sat; 3.30pm Sun); 6pm-10pm (9.30pm Sun). Main courses £7.50–£15.95.
Closed	Open all day.
Directions	Cockleford is signed off A435 at Elkstone south of Cheltenham.

Simon & Nicky Haly
Green Dragon,
Cockleford, Cowley,
Cheltenham GL53 9NW
Tel   +44 (0)1242 870271
Web   www.green-dragon-inn.co.uk

Entry 278 Map 8

Bathurst Arms
North Cerney

James Walker has worked hard to breathe new life into this handsome inn on the Bathurst Estate. Once unloved, the 17th-century building now exudes warmth and energy as locals, walkers and travellers drop in for pints of Wickwar Cotswold Way — and unpretentious, delicious pub food. The stone-flagged bar is the hub of the place, warmed by a crackling log fire. Eat here or head next door to James's pride and joy, the revamped restaurant, with open kitchen and a sitting area that displays the wine list — just choose a bottle from the shelf. Allotment vegetables, Cerney goat's cheese, game from Withington and local farm beef are championed... so tuck into wild rabbit terrine, chicken and mushroom pie, Bathurst burgers with barbecue sauce, baked apple crumble with homemade custard. It's the best of British and the two-course set menu (including a glass of wine) is a steal. Spruced-up bedrooms, two with white four-posters, provide a homely base for city folk escaping to the Cotswolds: clean, comfortable, freshly painted and TV-free. Ask for a room with a view.

Rooms	8: 5 doubles, 3 twins. From £77.50. Singles £57.50.
Meals	12pm-2pm (2.30pm weekends); 6-9pm (9.30pm Sat; from 7pm Sun). Main courses £9.95-£16.95; bar meals £3.95-£8.95; set menu (2 courses) £12.50; Sunday roast from £12.95.
Closed	3pm-6pm in winter. Open all day Sat & Sun.
Directions	Beside A435 Cirencester to Cheltenham road, 4 miles north of Cirencester.

James Walker
Bathurst Arms,
North Cerney,
Cirencester GL7 7BZ
Tel   +44 (0)1285 831281
Web   www.bathurstarms.com

Gloucestershire

The Ragged Cot
Chalford

The fine old stone coaching inn stands alongside 600 acres of National Trust common land, opposite Gatcombe Park. Dating from the 17th century, its several popular bars have exposed stone walls, while the conservatory-style dining room overlooks a large garden. Horses graze the fields on the other side of the drystone wall; to the front is the road. You will sleep well here. The nine rooms, named after Penguin classics, are delightfully cosy and rather contemporary with king-size beds, walk-in showers and harmonious fabrics and cushions. The rest of the pub is just as smart; expect quirky touches, framed pictures of film stars and *Tatler* covers, piles of chopped logs and a stag's head or two. In the kitchen, chefs use local supplies as well as herbs and vegetables from the garden for country dishes served at new pine tables. Come for black pudding and mustard croquette with apple purée, pan-fried bream with chorizo braised leeks, venison with game pudding. Wellies, dogs and children are also made welcome.

Rooms	9 twins/doubles. £95-£120.
Meals	12pm-3pm (4pm Sun); 6pm-9pm/10pm. Main courses £10-£15; bar meals from £3.
Closed	Open all day.
Directions	Follow signs to Minchinhampton off A419 midway between Cirencester and Stroud; pub at x-road east of village.

Tom Nunn
The Ragged Cot,
Cirencester Road,
Chalford, Stroud GL6 8PE
Tel   +44 (0)1453 884643
Web   www.theraggedcot.co.uk

Entry 280 Map 8

Gloucestershire

The Lodge
Minchinhampton

Lording it on a high and ancient piece of common ground is this former hunting lodge to Henry VIII. The cattle roam free; you too can wander and gaze on the views of five valleys. Outside is traditional; inside is striking. Expect bold art, classical columns, acres of smooth oak and honey-coloured stone walls; sofas sprawl around low coffee tables, fireplaces crackle, the conversation is lively. Still with a pub feel, albeit an up-to-the-minute one, the bar serves Budding from Stroud Brewery alongside Abbotts, IPA and Otter. In the restaurant, large and open plan with floor-to-ceiling windows for the view, an ancient carved stone lion presides over various freshly sourced delights, such as seared scallops with apple and celeriac truffle dressing, and braised Cotswold pork belly with sauté potatoes.

Gloucestershire

The Old Spot
Dursley

Nudged by a car park and Dursley's bus station is the old and lovely Old Spot. Built in 1776 as a farm cottage, the pub has since gained national recognition among ale buffs who make pilgrimages to sample the brews. Indeed, the Old Spot has become something of a showcase for the beers of Uley Brewery, including Pig's Ear and Old Ric, the latter named after a former landlord. Real ciders include Weston's and Ashton Press. For a pub named after a rare-breed pig it comes as no surprise that there are porcine figurines and pictures dotted around the place, as well as a few old prints and posters. Food is simple and pubby — BLT sandwiches, bangers and mash, home-baked pies with shortcrust pastry lids. Friendly, no-nonsense, traditional, and on the Cotswolds Way. For ale-lovers, sheer joy.

Meals	12pm-2.45pm; 6pm-10pm. Main courses £8.95-£15.95; Sunday lunch £10.95.
Closed	Open all day.
Directions	In the middle of Minchinhampton Common - 300 yds off common road - signed.

Meals	12pm-3pm. Bar meals £3.45-£9.25; Sunday roast £7.95.
Closed	Open all day.
Directions	100 yards from Dursley town centre.

The Lodge,
Minchinhampton,
Stroud GL6 9AQ
Tel   +44 (0)1453 832047
Web   www.food-club.com

Entry 281 Map 8

Steve Herbert
The Old Spot,
2 Hill Road,
Dursley GL11 4JQ
Tel   +44 (0)1453 542870
Web   www.oldspotinn.co.uk

Entry 282 Map 8

Gloucestershire

Woolpack Inn
Slad

The little Woolpack was immortalised by Laurie Lee, who lived in the valley below. It's still a lovely local, packed with rusticity and charm. Now owned by artist Daniel Chadwick and run by Fergus Henderson-trained Michael Carr – and his partner Helen James-Ellett – its regulars include Damien Hirst and actor Keith Allen (father of Lily). Although Lee's portraits are still on the walls and his collection of beer bottles lines the shelves at the back, this is not *Cider With Rosie* themed. Rather, is is the perfect pitstop for walkers, a friendly no-frills pub, a place where the ale from the Uley brewery is as important as the 'nose-to-tail' bar menu. Tuck into the simple best, from Gloucester Old Spot bacon sandwiches to chargrilled rib-eye steak with roast field mushrooms and chips. No wonder it heaves at weekends.

Meals	12pm-2pm (3.30pm Sun); 6.30pm-9pm. No food Sun & Mon eve. Main courses £8.95-£16.50; Sunday lunch from £8.95.
Closed	Open all day.
Directions	Beside B4070 north of Stroud.

Daniel Chadwick
Woolpack Inn,
Slad Road, Slad,
Stroud GL6 7QA
Tel   +44 (0)1452 813429
Web   www.thewoolpackinn-slad.com

Entry 283 Map 8

Gloucestershire

The Tunnel House Inn
Coates

Emerge via the portico tunnel of the Severn & Thames Canal to find a gracious Cotswold stone house in the clearing; it was built in the 1780s to house the canal workers. Its latest conversion has been well considered. There's much to be charmed by: landlord Rupert, the laid-back hospitality, the beef and horseradish sandwiches, the quirky décor: scrubbed tables and huge faded sofas in front of a fire, a cacophony of bric-a-brac in the bar (most on the ceiling!), an Ogygian juke box with decent tunes. In the dining room choose from a seasonal menu: Old Spot sausages with mash and red onion marmalade, crab and watercress tart, roast belly pork on root vegetable mash. Uley Bitter and Hook Norton will keep ale fans happy, and there are several wines. Outside, a big garden with open-field views – great for kids – and a rather smart terrace.

Meals	12pm-2.15pm; 6.30pm-9.15pm. Main courses £8-£14.95.
Closed	3pm-6pm. Open all day Fri-Sun.
Directions	Off A433 Cirencester to Tetbury road; follow brown signs to the pub.

Rupert Longsdon
The Tunnel House Inn,
Coates,
Cirencester GL7 6PW
Tel   +44 (0)1285 770280
Web   www.tunnelhouse.com

Entry 284 Map 8

The King's Arms Inn
Didmarton

The spruced-up roadside village inn sports slate floors, stone lintels, mellow walls, and oak settles in the bar, and a cheekily bright front room adorned with lithographs of the area. In the dining room are terracotta walls, carved panels, chunky wooden tables and high-backed chairs. There's a big old fireplace for winter, darts and dominoes for fun, a walled garden for summer and a boules pitch that people travel some way for. For a light lunch consider a wholemeal sandwich of Wiltshire ham and coleslaw, or rare roast beef and horseradish. 'Classics' on the menu might include haddock in beer batter or roast venison with red wine and juniper berry sauce, while daily dishes could highlight sea bass with tomato and prawn risotto – all delicious. 'If they don't serve beer in heaven, then I'm not going', reads the sign behind the bar, so Uley Bitter stands alongside guest ales. Rooms upstairs, the quietest at the back, are cosy, stylish and inviting, with colourful throws on comfortable beds and spotless shower rooms; the self-catering cottages are in the coaching stable. A perfect place in the Cotswolds.

Rooms	4 + 3: 1 double, 2 twins/doubles, 1 single. 3 self-catering cottages (2 for 4, 1 for 6). £75. Single from £55. Cottages from £90.
Meals	12pm-2.30pm; 6pm-9.30pm (12pm-8pm Sun). Main courses £8.95-£16.95; bar meals £4.95-£9.95.
Closed	Open all day.
Directions	M4 junc. 18, A46 north, then A433 for Tetbury. In village on left.

Alastair & Sarah Sadler
The King's Arms Inn,
The Street, Didmarton,
Badminton GL9 1DT
Tel   +44 (0)1454 238245
Web   www.kingsarmsdidmarton.co.uk

Gloucestershire

The Bull Inn
Hinton

A deep-cut Cotswold lane brings you to this solid stone 17th-century pub in a peaceful village. In good weather, sit on the sunny south-facing terrace and enjoy Wadworth's Bishop's Tipple or Henry's IPA, or wander round to the ample play area at the back where you can see the vegetables and Gloucester Old Spots growing – low food miles indeed. The menus are traditional with a French flavour, the Royal Gloucester steak and ale pie with horseradish pastry has won awards, and the 'trio of French bread and butter pudding' is made from pain au chocolat, croissant and brioche; try it with Marshfield Farm's chocolate ice cream if you dare. Inside the large, beamed and flagged bar are a stone fireplace and some super big oak tables and pews around which to tuck in and chat away an evening. A family run pub with personality.

Meals	12pm-2pm; 6pm-9pm (9.30pm Fri & Sat); 12pm-3.30pm; 7pm-8.30pm Sun. Main courses £8.75– £15.95.
Closed	Mon lunch.
Directions	5 minutes from junc 18 on the M4; A46 to Bath, first right to Hinton

David & Elizabeth White
The Bull Inn,
Hinton,
Chippenham,SN14 8HG
Tel   +44 (0)1179 372332
Web   www.thebullathinton.co.uk

Entry 286 Map 3

Gloucestershire

The Village Pub
Barnsley

An old favourite of locals and faithfuls from far and wide, this civilised boozer has been given a gentle facelift by new owners Calcot Manor Estates, who also own Barnsley House, a chic country house hotel across the road. As before, expect seasonal food based on the best local produce, and good-quality Hook Norton and decent wines. There's even a service hatch to the heated patio at the back, so you can savour the sauvignon until the sun goes down. Cotswold stone and ancient flags sing the country theme; past bar and open fires, quiet alcoves provide a snug setting that may entice you to stay. If you do, tuck into crab and leek tart, rib-eye steak with béarnaise sauce, or whole plaice with crab and parsley butter; pudding-lovers will love the warm ginger cake with rum and raisin ice cream.

Meals	12pm-2.30pm (3pm Sat & Sun); 7pm-9.30pm (10pm Fri & Sat). Main courses £10-£18.50.
Closed	3pm-6pm Mon-Thurs. Open all day Fri-Sun.
Directions	From M4 exit junc. 15. A419 for Gloucester; right onto B4425 for Bibury; village 2 miles.

Neil Williams
The Village Pub,
Barnsley,
Cirencester GL7 5EF
Tel   +44 (0)1285 740421
Web   www.thevillagepub.co.uk

Entry 287 Map 8

The New Inn at Coln
Coln St Aldwyns

The New Inn is old – 1632 to be exact – but well-named nonetheless. The pub stands in a handsome Cotswold village with ivy roaming on original stone walls and a sun-trapping terrace where roses bloom in summer. Owner Christoph Brooke has injected his quirky trademark Indian Empire feel into the refurbished inn – see the Bath Arms (entry 776) and The Elephant (entry 24). Airy interiors have low ceilings, painted beams, flagged floors and fires that roar – perfect for supping pints of real ale with roast beef and horseradish sandwiches, or lingering over seared scallops, pan-roasted duck and baked lemon tart, served in red-walled dining rooms by thoroughly delightful staff. Bedrooms are a treat, all warmly elegant with soft carpets, swish bed throws, perfect white linen and cotton robes in good little bathrooms (a couple with claw-foot baths). There are wonky floors and the odd beam in the main house, while those in the Dovecote come in bold colours and have views across water meadows to the river; walks start from the door. Bibury, Burford and Stow are all close, so spread your wings.

Rooms	13 doubles. £95-£150. Singles from £85. Half-board from £75 p.p.
Meals	12pm-2.30pm (3pm Sun); 7pm-9pm (9.30pm Fri & Sat). Main courses £10-£16; sandwiches £5.25.
Closed	Open all day.
Directions	From Oxford, A40 past Burford, B4425 for Bibury. Left after Aldsworth to Coln St. Aldwyns.

Stuart Hodges
The New Inn at Coln,
Main Street, Coln St Aldwyns,
Cirencester GL7 5AN

Tel	+44 (0)1285 750651
Web	www.new-inn.co.uk

Entry 288 Map 8

Gloucestershire

The Victoria Inn
Eastleach Turville

The golden-stoned Victoria pulls in the locals – whatever their age, whatever the weather – propping up the bar, welly-clad with dogs or indulging in home-cooked grub by the log fire. A simple village hostelry on the outside, it's deceptively spacious inside. The Richardsons, in spite of opening up the interior, have kept much of the character and cosiness intact. The low-ceilinged and flagstoned bar offers darts, conversation and pints of Arkells 3B, while the L-shaped dining room is the setting for delicious platefuls of freshly prepared food: salmon fishcakes; pork and leek sausages; slow-roasted lamb shank with garlic potatoes and red wine sauce. There are picnic tables out at the front, from where you can look down onto the pretty stone cottages of two villages. A lovely spot for a country stroll.

Meals	12pm-2pm; 7pm-9.30pm (9pm Sun). Main courses £7.95-£14.75.
Closed	3pm-7pm.
Directions	Off A361 between Burford & Lechlade.

Stephen & Susan Richardson
The Victoria Inn,
Eastleach Turville,
Cirencester GL7 3NQ
Tel   +44 (0)1367 850277

Entry 289 Map 8

Gloucestershire

The Swan at Southrop
Southrop

A roaring log fire, a sober décor, a relaxed mood and a skittle alley for locals – this is the village inn on the village green that everyone dreams of, and restaurateurs Sebastian and Lana Snow were happy to leave their Shepherd's Bush restaurant in 2008 for this Cotswolds' treasure. The handsome Georgian inn has a much-loved bar but is still a foodie haven. Menus are seasonal and unshowy: a crab, saffron and tomato tart, roast rump of Southrop lamb, Kelmscott pork belly with mushroom fricassé, elderflower panna cotta with autumn raspberries. An excellent wine list matches a tasty selection of local real ales, accompanied by scrumptious bar snacks like ham, egg and chips, beef bourguignon and ploughman's. Come for the great value weekday set lunches. Faultless service comes with a big smile.

Meals	12pm-3pm; 6pm-10pm. Main courses £11.50-£17.25; bar meals £5-£10; set lunch (Mon-Fri) £14 & £18.
Closed	2.30pm-7pm (3pm-7pm Sat & Sun). Closed from 10pm every day.
Directions	2 miles west off A361 between Burford & Lechlade.

Sebastian & Lana Snow
The Swan at Southrop,
Southrop,
Lechlade GL7 3NU
Tel   +44 (0)1367 850205
Web   www.theswanatsouthrop.co.uk

Entry 290 Map 8

Inn at Fossebridge
Fossebridge

A vast two-acre lake, hog roasts in summer, a glorious old bar – such details set the Inn at Fossebridge apart. Inside all is super-rustic and cosy – flagstone floors, stone walls, open fires, beamed ceilings – with a terrific hubbub at lunchtime. Throw in real ales, roast lunches and a welcome for all and you have somewhere worth going out of your way for. The Jenkins family run this gorgeous old coaching inn and draw in lovers of good food with blackboard specials of potted prawns with anchovies and garlic chilli; sausages with bacon mash; sticky toffee pudding. The bar is divided by stone archways; the dining room has a gentler Georgian feel. And there's a cosy sitting room in country-house style. Outside is just as good: a four-acre garden, with mature trees and lake, bordering the river Coln, and a tyre swing for kids. Bedrooms, country-smart, and decorated in Georgian style, range from smallish to spacious, with coordinated fabrics, striped walls, Gilchrist & Soames goodies, flat-screen TVs. The Fossebridge is very well positioned for a Cotswolds break.

Rooms	8: 7 twins/doubles, 1 family suite. £120–£160. Singles £110–£145.
Meals	12pm–3pm; 6.30pm–10pm (9.30pm Sun). Main courses £10.95–£16.95; bar meals £5.95–£8.50; Sunday roast £12.95.
Closed	Open all day.
Directions	Beside A429 between Cirencester & Northleach.

Robert & Samantha Jenkins
Inn at Fossebridge,
Fossebridge,
Cheltenham GL54 3JS
Tel   +44 (0)1285 720721
Web   www.fossebridgeinn.co.uk

Gloucestershire

Seven Tuns Inn
Chedworth

In 1610, and for a few centuries after that, the Seven Tuns was a simple snug; then they diverted the river and built the rest. Part-creepered on the outside, it rambles attractively inside, past open fires, aged furniture, antique prints and a skittle alley with darts. After a gentle walk to Chedworth's Roman Villa, buried in the wooded valley nearby, there's no finer place to return to for a pint of Young's Bitter. Mingle with cyclists, walkers and locals in the little lounge or rustic bar. If you're here to eat you can do so overlooking the garden through two gorgeous mullioned windows; a little further, across the road, is a raised terrace by a waterwheel, babbling brook and new boule court. Pub grub is listed on daily menus, from slow roast pork belly to confit of duck. This is still the village hub, just as it should be.

Meals	12pm-2.30pm (3pm Sat & Sun); 6.30pm-9.30pm (9pm Sun). Main courses £7.95-£14.95.
Closed	3pm-6pm. Open all day Sat & Sun in winter, every day in July & Aug.
Directions	Off A429, north of Cirencester.

Alex Davenport-Jones
Seven Tuns Inn,
Queen Street, Chedworth,
Cheltenham GL54 4AE
Tel +44 (0)1285 720242

Entry 292 Map 8

Gloucestershire
Worth a visit

293 **The Trouble House** Cirencester Road, Tetbury GL8 8SG +44 (0)1666 502206
Everything is done with simplicity and integrity and that includes the interior of bare boards, cream walls and open fires. Chef Martin Caws has a brilliant pedigree. Reports please.

294 **The Gumstool Inn** Calcot Manor, Calcot, Tetbury GL8 8YJ +44 (0)1666 890391
Quietly civilised bar/brasserie attached to the Calcot Manor Hotel. Cosy up by the log fire in the elegant bar; take your pick of local ales, good wines and imaginative food. Westonbirt Arboretum is up the road.

295 **The Red Hart** Blaisdon, Gloucester GL17 0AH +44 (0)1452 830477
A lively little village pub, often packed with locals and wet walkers quaffing pints of Hooky by the fire in the stone-flagged bar. Expect a traditional feel with hop-hung beams, solid, hearty cooking, good value Sunday roasts and a character landlord.

296 **White Hart Inn** The Square, Stow-on-the-Wold, Cheltenham GL54 1AF +44 (0)1451 830674
Refurbished small coaching inn smack on Stow's charming square. Come for a smart eclectic décor, interesting food and quirky compact bedrooms – under new ownership from January 2010.

297 **The Eight Bells** Church Street, Chipping Campden GL55 6JG +44 (0)1386 840371
Tiny Cotswold pub in popular Chipping Campden, with 14th-century beams, flagstones and priest's hole. Walkers in socks wolf down sandwiches and Hooky by the fire. Enjoyable hot dishes too, in the bar, the more formal restaurant or the sun-trap patio. Tricky parking.

The Peat Spade
Longstock

Hampshire is as lovely as any county in England, deeply rural with lanes that snake through verdant countryside. As if to prove the point, the Peat Spade serves up a menu of boundless simplicity and elegance. First there's this dreamy thatched village in the Test valley, then there's the inn itself, packed to the gunnels with lip-licking locals for Sunday lunch in early February (and there's a 4pm sitting to satisfy demand). Behind the lozenge-paned windows a Roberts radio on the bar brings news of English cricket, gilt mirrors sparkle above smouldering fires, candles illuminate chunky tables, and fishing rods hang from the ceiling (a fishing tackle shop is on site). There's a horseshoe bar, a sitting room for those who stay, a roof terrace for summer breakfasts and two bedrooms above the bar. The rest are in Peat House next door, and are as lovely as you'd expect. Fired Earth colours, sisal matting, big wooden beds, crisp white linen – the works. There's no space left to describe how fabulously wonderful the food is, but be assured it is.

Rooms	6: 2 doubles, 1 twin.
	Peat House: 3 doubles. From £100.
Meals	12pm-2pm (4pm Sun);
	7pm-9.30pm;
	no food Sun eve Dec-April.
	Main courses £11.50-£17.
Closed	Open all day.
Directions	A3057 north from Stockbridge,
	then left after a mile for Longstock.
	In village centre.

Lucy Townsend
The Peat Spade,
Longstock,
Stockbridge SO20 6DR

Tel   +44 (0)1264 810612
Web   www.peatspadeinn.co.uk

Entry 298 Map 3

The Greyhound
Stockbridge

Civilised, one-street Stockbridge is England's fly-fishing capital, and the colour-washed Greyhound reels in fishing folk and foodies. The 15th-century coaching inn is a dapper, food-and-wine-centred affair run with charm and panache by Susie Fiducia. Chef Norelle Oberin produces modern dishes based on skill and impeccable produce, served by charming staff. Try confit duck and foie gras terrine with apple and prune chutney; sea bass, brown shrimp risotto and tomato and broad bean velouté; summer berry pudding with clotted cream. Lunchtime bar meals might see wild mushroom, chorizo and goat's cheese risotto and fish pie. In the lounge are low dark beams, modern armchairs and sofas and a big inglenook; in the open-plan dining area, wooden floors, solid trestle-style tables, contemporary leather chairs, more beams. Upgraded bedrooms manage to blend comfort with character, so you'll find spotlights alongside auction antiques, classy bathrooms, books, pictures and mohair throws. A garden at the back overlooks the Test; rest here awhile with a glass of chablis – or cast a line.

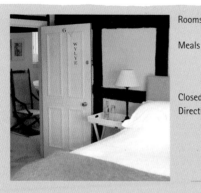

Rooms	8: 4 twins, 3 doubles, 1 single. £95–£125. Singles £70.
Meals	12pm–2pm (2.30pm Fri-Sun); 7pm–9pm (9.30pm Fri & Sat). Main courses £16.50–£21; bar menu £4.20–£15.
Closed	Open all day.
Directions	A303, A34 south, then A30 into Stockbridge. Pub on right on west end of High Street.

Susie Fiducia
The Greyhound, 31 High
Street, Stockbridge, SO20 6EY
Tel   +44 (0)1264 810833
Web   www.thegreyhound.info

Entry 299 Map 3

Hampshire

The Oak Inn
Bank

Aptly named (among the forest oaks), this 18th-century pub, with its double-bay frontage and red phone box outside, is a friendly and traditional little place. It's popular not just with locals but also with walkers and cyclists who pour in at weekends to feast on generous portions of hearty pub grub – much of which has been reared or caught within the New Forest; note the symbols on the menu. Others drop in for a pint of Gales Seafarers in the low-beamed bar, or the little garden sheltered by a big yew. Blackboard specials might include whole baked John Dory or local venison sausages; doorstep sandwiches and homemade steak and ale pie catch the eye of hungry walkers. Come for winter fires, cottagey furniture, old-fashioned comfort, dark red walls and endearing touches like milk-urn bar stalls: everyone loves The Oak.

Meals	12pm-2.30pm; 6pm-9.30pm. Food all day Sun. Main courses £8.95-£16.95; sandwiches from £5.50.
Closed	3.30pm-6pm. Open all day Sat & Sun.
Directions	Bank is signed off A35 one mile SW of Lyndhurst.

Martin Sliva & Zuzana Slivova
The Oak Inn,
Pinkney Lane, Bank,
Lyndhurst SO43 7FE
Tel   +44 (0)23 8028 2350
Web   www.fullers.co.uk

Entry 300 Map 3

Hampshire   Award winner 2010

The Royal Oak
Fritham

Small, ancient, thatched and secluded is this ale-lover's retreat. No fruit machines, just old-fashioned bonhomie. Locals exchange stories around the bar; ramblers and dogs drop by. Huge fires crackle through the winter, demanding you linger. Neil and Pauline McCulloch believe in local produce and deliver honest and unpretentious pub lunches: ploughman's with homemade pâté, French-dressed local crab, sausages from their pigs, no chips. Though rustically simple, the three small rooms are perfect, with pale boards, solid tables and spindleback chairs, darts, dominoes and cribbage, and homely touches. Five local beers are drawn straight from the cask, including Hop Back Summer Lightning and Royal Oak by Bowman ales. And there's more: a large garden for barbecues and a beer and food festival in September. Pub heaven.

Meals	12pm-2.30pm (3pm Sat & Sun). Main courses £4.50-£8.50.
Closed	3pm-6pm. Open all day Sat & Sun. Open all day Jul-Sep.
Directions	M27 junc. 1; B3078 to Fordingbridge; turn for Fritham after 2.5 miles. Signs.

Authentic pub

Neil & Pauline McCulloch
The Royal Oak,
Fritham,
Lyndhurst SO43 7HJ
Tel   +44 (0)23 8081 2606

Entry 301 Map 3

The East End Arms
East End

No London boozer but a good little local hidden down New Forest lanes, winningly unpretentious and owned by John Illsley of Dire Straits. Walkers, wax jackets and locals congregate in the small, rustic Foresters Bar with its chatty community vibe; walls come lined with the famous. The carpeted-cosy dining room, all cottagey furniture and roaring log fire, cocks a snoop at gastropub remodelling, but the menus change twice daily and make the best of seasonal produce. Try seafood casserole with peppers, fennel, saffron potatoes and sauce aïoli, or wild mushroom risotto. A paved terrace invites alfresco drinking, while bedrooms on the back add va-va-voom. Clean-lined and comfortable, in fashionably neutral tones that bring the forest indoors, they sport roman blinds and coordinated soft furnishings. Stylish bathrooms and paintings by John Illsley add warmth and class; fine breakfasts are the cherry on the cake. A great little find for anyone who loves the New Forest – neither new nor a forest, but fine open heathland nonetheless and excellent hiking terrain.

Rooms	5 twins/doubles. £95-£115.
Meals	12pm-2.30pm; 7pm-9.30pm.
	No food Sun eve.
	Main courses £10.50-£19.50.
Closed	3pm-6pm. Open all day Sun.
Directions	Off B3054 signposted Beaulieu; follow signs for Isle of Wight ferry, bear left onto South Baddesley Rd; 2 miles, pub on right.

John Illsley & Jeremy Willcock
The East End Arms,
Lymington Road,
East End, Lymington SO41 5SY
Tel   +44 (0)1590 626223
Web   www.eastendarms.co.uk

Entry 302 Map 3

Hampshire

The Rose & Thistle
Rockbourne

Rockbourne is the kind of village where you might find Miss Marple trimming a rose bush. The pub is dreamy too, and, like many, started life as two thatched cottages – the two huge fireplaces should be no surprise. It is a great mix of oak beams and timbers, carved benches, flagstones and tiles. Add country-style fabrics and tables strewn with magazines and you have an enchanting place to return to after visiting Rockbourne's Roman villa. Kerry Dutton makes use of fresh local produce: estate game in season, pork with champ and black pudding and cider gravy, veal with béarnaise sauce. In summer you can dine in the garden, perhaps smoked trout and scrambled eggs or classic steak and kidney pudding. The changing chalkboard menu favours Cornish fish, such as monkfish wrapped in pancetta.

Meals	12pm-2.30pm; 7pm-9.30pm (no food Sun eve). Main courses £9.50-£19.50; bar meals from £5.
Closed	3pm-6pm (Sun from 8pm Nov-Mar).
Directions	3 miles north west of Fordingbridge, off B3078.

Kerry Dutton
The Rose & Thistle,
Rockbourne,
Fordingbridge SP6 3NL
Tel +44 (0)1725 518236
Web www.roseandthistle.co.uk

Entry 303 Map 3

Hampshire

White Star Tavern & Dining Rooms
Southampton

The old seafarers' hotel has been stylishly revived. Large etched windows carry the White Star logo, while a cluster of lounges at the front come decked with gleaming leather chesterfields. The place is stocked, as is the fashion, with a heady mix of real ales, continental lagers, premium spirits and cocktails. Around the big darkwood bar, to a backdrop of original wood panelling, is booth-like seating for casual dining; shipping photographs and original chandeliers add to the metropolitan mood. The more formal dining area comes with a softer approach: expect stylish wallpaper and sophisticated lighting. The cooking hits all the right notes, with a dedicated bar menu as well as à la carte; dishes include such delights as Hampshire rump steak with wild garlic béarnaise, watercress and hand-cut chips.

Meals	12pm-2.30pm (3pm Fri & Sat); 6.30pm-9.30pm (10pm Fri & Sat); 12pm-9pm Sun. Main courses £9.50-£19; bar meals £4.50-11.
Closed	Open all day.
Directions	M271 into town. Past Ikea, down to docks. Join one-way system & left to Terminus Terrace. 2nd left into Bernard St. 3rd left into Oxford St.

Matthew Boyle
White Star Tavern & Dining Rooms,
28 Oxford Street,
Southampton SO14 3DJ
Tel +44 (0)2380 821990
Web www.whitestartavern.co.uk

Entry 304 Map 4

The Master Builder's House Hotel
Beaulieu

The position here is faultless: lawns roll down to the Beaulieu river, curlews race across the water, a vast sky hangs overhead. The house, built in 1729, was home to shipwrights who served the British fleet and Nelson's favourite vessel, *Agamemnon*, was built here. Inside, newly refurbished interiors mix contemporary flair with classical design. Expect earthy colours and a roaring fire in the yachtsman's bar, then huge sofas and watery views in the sitting room. Bedrooms in the main house are nothing short of gorgeous: huge beds, pots of colour, fabulous views, super bathrooms. Those in the annexe are simpler, but cosy, and getting the same treatment. Back downstairs, the dining room swings to an informal beat. You get wooden booths, smart rugs and doors that open onto a terrace which looks the right way. You can eat here in summer or barbecue on the lawn, perhaps grilled lobster, a rib-eye steak, then custard tart with nutmeg ice cream. Stride out on the footpaths that sweep along the river, dive into the forest to cycle and ride or lose yourself in acres of silence.

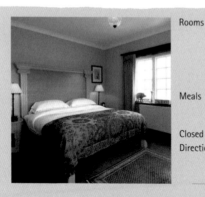

Rooms	25: Main house: 4 doubles, 1 twin/double, 3 suites. Annexe: 16 doubles, 1 twin. Main house: £135-£160. Annexe: £85-£99. Singles from £75. Half-board from £75 p.p.
Meals	12pm-2pm; 7pm-9pm. Main courses £9-£18.50; bar meals from £9.
Closed	Open all day.
Directions	From Lyndhurst, B3056 south past Beaulieu turn; 1st left, signed Bucklers Hard. Hotel signed left after 1 mile.

Michael Clitheroe
The Master Builder's House Hotel,
Bucklers Hard,
Beaulieu,
Brockenhurst SO42 7XB
Tel   +44 (0)1590 616253
Web   www.themasterbuilders.co.uk

Entry 305 Map 4

Hampshire

The Bugle
Hamble

Hamble's famous pub, celebrated by yachtsmen the world over, was saved in 2005 by those behind Southampton's White Star Tavern. Using traditional materials and methods they have remodelled the Bugle's 16th-century heart – so you find new-and-old oak beams and standing timbers, stripped-back brick fireplaces and open fires, natural flagstone floors and polished boards. The atmosphere is relaxed, the bar throngs with drinkers and diners on sailing days, there's a simply adorned dining area for escaping the bustle and a private room upstairs. A wide-ranging clientele informs the style of the food. Sit at the bar with a pint of Bowmans Swift One and tapas-style dishes, or go the whole hog and order mussels and chips or pork belly with leeks and cider gravy. Or slip off to the super front terrace for views of bobbing boats on the Hamble.

Meals	12pm-2.30pm (3pm Fri); 6pm-9.30pm (10pm Fri); 12pm-10pm Sat (9pm Sun). Main courses £8-£12.50; bar meals £4-£7.50.
Closed	Open all day.
Directions	M27 junc. 8; signs to Hamble, right at mini-r'bout & follow cobbled street down to riverside car park.

Matt Boyle
The Bugle,
High Street, Hamble,
Southampton SO31 4HA

| Tel | +44 (0)23 8045 3000 |
| Web | www.buglehamble.co.uk |

Entry 306 Map 4

Hampshire

The Royal Oak
Havant

Twitchers beat a path to the door of this waterside pub. The views across Chichester Harbour are stunning, of rare birds and moored boats, magical on a fine summer's evening. From your bench at the water's edge you can watch the tide ebb and flow and study the waders in the mudflats; at spring tide the water laps the front door. The pub, licenced since 1725, was once a row of 16th-century cottages lived in by workers at Langstone Mill next door; they used to have a 'tidal licence' allowing travellers a drink while waiting for the tide to ebb. When inclement weather forces you in and away from the view you'll find rambling rooms with flagstone and pine floors, beams, an open fire. There are real ales, traditional pub grub (slow to come but rather tasty), roasts on Sundays, sandwiches all day.

Meals	12pm-9pm. Main courses £6.95-£14; bar snacks from £2.95; Sunday roast £7.95.
Closed	Open all day.
Directions	Beside Chichester harbour, off A3023 before bridge to Hayling Island. Parking can be tricky.

Kevin Buck
The Royal Oak,
19 Langstone High Street,
Havant PO9 1RY

| Tel | +44 (0)23 9248 3125 |
| Web | www.royaloak-havant.com |

Entry 307 Map 4

The Bakers Arms
Droxford

Set in the attractive Meon Valley, this small, unprepossessing pub is a bit of a find for lovers of generous British cooking. For locals, there's the added plus of Droxford's Bowman Ales – and the village stores parked on the side. Inside has a relaxed, traditional charm and a winter fire. The L-shaped, opened-up space is light and cheery, the customary miscellany of old wooden furniture sitting alongside a couple of modish leather sofas, but the décor is no slave to fashion. The kitchen's chalkboard menu pleases all with its use of prime local produce and seasonal dishes with punchy flavours and, in this rolling countryside, the local meats are a forte; free-range Droxford Old Spot pork makes an appearance in signature sausages served with crowd-pleasing mash and shallot gravy. An excellent meeting place.

Meals	12pm-2pm; 7pm-9pm.
	Main courses £10.95-£16.95.
Closed	Sun eve & all day Mon.
Directions	In village centre beside A32, 5 miles north of Wickham.

Adam & Anna Cordery
The Bakers Arms,
High Street, Droxford,
Southampton SO32 3PA
Tel +44 (0)1489 877533
Web www.thebakersarmsdroxford.com

Entry 308 Map 4

Brushmakers Arms
Upham

It may be tricky to find, tucked away down country lanes in a small village surrounded by the rolling Hampshire downs, but that's half the joy. And there's not a hint of fashionable gastro pub here: the Brushmakers is a traditional, time-worn pub where pints of beer are as important as food and where locals, walkers – even townies! – are welcomed. Landlord Keith Venton's warm, friendly manner really adds to the convivial spirit. There's a garden out the back, while inside all manner of namesake brushes hang from beams, ceilings and walls: boards, flagstones, tiles and patterned carpet jostle for flooring superiority. Proper pub food comes in hearty portions, from seasonal game (hare in cider) to specials like pork steak with mustard gratin, while a laminated classic's menu offers battered cod, chips and peas as well as light lunch snacks.

Meals	12pm-2pm; 6pm-9pm (7pm-9pm Sun; 9.30pm Fri & Sat).
	Main courses £8.95-£11.95; bar snacks (lunch) £4.50-£6.95.
Closed	3pm-6pm (7pm Sun).
Directions	Upham is off B2177 between Winchester and Bishops Waltham; pub near duck pond.

Keith Venton
Brushmakers Arms,
Shoe Lane,
Upham,
Bishops Waltham SO32 1JJ
Tel +44 (0)1489 860231

Entry 309 Map 4

Hampshire

The Thomas Lord
West Meon

Named after the founder of Lord's, this unpretentious rural gem groans with cricketing paraphernalia. The darkly beamed and half-panelled walls are decorated with old bats, caps, pads and associated prints, while well-used sofas and the odd leather armchair draw up to a fire in winter. There's an endearing miscellany of weathered wooden furniture, big fat candles, drinkers, dogs and a small back room weighed down by books. It's a busy, friendly pub loved by a loyal crowd and the daily menus are crammed with local produce including vegetables and herbs from the pub's own large veg patch; try Grange Farm lamb shoulder with rosemary sauce. A choice of Hampshire ales direct from the cask follows the local theme, while a smart garden and outdoor wood-fired kitchen beckon on sunnier days. A great, rustic country inn.

Hampshire

Harrow Inn
Steep

The 16th-century Harrow is a gem. Unspoilt, brick-and-tiled, it hides down a country lane that dwindles into a footpath by a little stream (not easy to find!). It has been in Claire and Nisa McCutcheon's family since 1929 and they keep it very much as it must always have been. Where nicer to sup a pint than within these two small rooms with their timbered walls, scrubbed elm tables and brick inglenook fireplace aglow in winter. Behind a hatch-like serving counter, barrels of local ale rest on racks, bundles of drying hops hang above. There's a small, wild orchard garden – only the distant hum of the hidden A3 disturbs the bucolic calm. Food is limited to generously filled sandwiches, fresh soups, homemade quiches, a ploughman's platter, treacle tart – served with a smile. Loos are a quick dash across the lane.

Meals	12pm-2pm (3pm Sat & Sun); 7pm-9pm (9.30pm Fri & Sat). Main courses £12.50-£18; sandwiches from £5.
Closed	3pm-6pm. Open all day Sat & Sun.
Directions	Just off A32 between Alton & Wickham. Signed.

Meals	12pm-2pm; 7pm-9pm; no food Sun eve. Bar meals £4.30-£11.
Closed	2.30pm-6pm (3pm-6pm Sat, 3pm-7pm Sun) & Sun eve Oct-May.
Directions	Off A272 at Steep west of Petersfield, left opp. garage; left at church; cross A3 to reach pub.

David Thomas & Richard Taylor
The Thomas Lord,
West Meon,
Petersfield GU32 1LN
Tel   +44 (0)1730 829244
Web   www.thethomaslord.co.uk

Entry 310 Map 4

Claire & Nisa McCutcheon
Harrow Inn,
Steep,
Petersfield GU32 2DA
Tel   +44 (0)1730 262685

Entry 311 Map 4

Hampshire

The Hawkley Inn
Hawkley

In a sleepy village at the end of plunging lanes, a friendly mix of locals, farmers and walkers fill this genuine old inn. The Hawkley's front bars remain delightfully scruffy (a 'listed' carpet, nicotine-stained walls, bare boards, a mad moose head above the log fire) while the rear extension adds a touch of modernity, yet stays true to its roots thanks to sagging old sofas. So bag one of the rustic scrubbed tables and quaff amazing local beers – Ballards Best, Bowmans Swift One – or enjoy some country food. Arrive early at weekends – it's a popular place. Food ranges from soups and ploughman's to sea bream with caper butter and mash, and there are Sunday roasts and hearty weekend breakfasts too (do book). Worth the detour, once you've found it. Chawton, famous for Jane Austen's house, is nearby.

Hampshire

The Flower Pots Inn
Cheriton

Ramblers and beer enthusiasts beat a path to Pat and Jo Bartlett's door, where award-winning pints of Flower Pots Bitter, Goodens Gold and Perridge Pale are brewed in the brewhouse across the car park. Open fires burn in two traditional bars: one a wallpapered parlour, the other a quarry-tiled public bar with scrubbed pine and an illuminated, glass-topped well. Ales are tapped from casks behind the counter hung with hops, and drunk to the accompaniment of happy chat; music and electronic games would be out of place here. In keeping with the simplicity of the place, the menu is short and straightforward: baps with home-cooked ham, sandwiches toasted or plain, home-cooked hotpots, spicy chilli with garlic bread, hearty winter soups.

Meals	12pm-2pm (3pm Sat & Sun); 7pm-9.30pm (9pm Sun). Main courses £7.50-£13.50; bar snacks £5; Sunday roast £10.
Closed	3pm-5.30pm. Open all day Sat & Sun.
Directions	After A3/B3006, thro' Burgates, right into Hawkley Road & back over A3; 2 miles to hairpin bend; next left is Pococks Lane.

James Brushwood
The Hawkley Inn,
Pococks Lane,
Hawkley, Liss GU33 6NE
Tel   +44 (0)1730 827205
Web   www.hawkleyinn.co.uk

Entry 312 Map 4

Meals	12pm-2pm; 7pm-9pm (6.30pm-10pm Weds); no food Sun eve & bank hol eve. Main courses £5-£10.
Closed	2.30pm-6pm (3pm-7pm Sun).
Directions	Village signed off A272 east of Winchester; pub off B3046 in village centre.

Joanna & Patricia Bartlett
The Flower Pots Inn,
Cheriton,
Alresford SO24 0QQ
Tel   +44 (0)1962 771318
Web   www.flowerpots.f2s.com

Entry 313 Map 4

The Old Vine
Winchester

You are in a small square overlooking the cathedral and mature trees. This red-bricked Georgian building has sash windows and pretty hanging baskets – all tickety-boo and smart. Walk straight into the bustling bar with its beamed ceiling, upright timbers, open fires and a partly covered outdoor terrace for sunny days where a cheerful team of local staff serve two permanent ales (Ringwood Best and Timothy Taylor) and two guests on rotation; the wine list has helpful comments and some organic choices, and more on the specials board. If you get peckish after all the quaffing, you can have anything from a hearty sandwich (Hampshire pork sausages and red onion relish) to confit of duck with apple and potato mash, then homemade crumble and custard or some excellent local cheese. Stumble upstairs to a rather posh bedroom; all are generous, with a mix of antique-looking and contemporary furniture. Colour schemes are muted with splashes of bold on throws and cushions, mahogany sleigh beds are deep and comfortable and you can splash about in spoiling bathrooms with fluffy towels and gleaming taps.

Rooms	5: 4 doubles, 1 twin/double. £95-£170.	
Meals	12pm-2.30pm (3pm Sat & Sun); 6.30pm-9.30pm (9pm Sun). Main courses £9.90-£15.95; sandwiches from £4.50.	
Closed	Open all day.	
Directions	Opposite Winchester Cathedral green and the City Museum, just a short walk from the high street. Permit parking available.	

Ashton Gray
The Old Vine,
8 Great Minster Street,
Winchester SO23 9HA

Tel	+44 (0)1962 854616
Web	www.oldvinewinchester.com

Entry 314 Map 4

Hampshire

The Black Boy
Winchester

Quirky pubs with personality, real ale and fine food are worth tracking down. Winchester's example is best reached on foot – following the riverside path from the NT's Winchester Mill. The landlord has created an unassuming tavern that is pleasingly off the wall. Fascinating paraphernalia ranges from fire buckets and old signs to a 'library' crammed with books; oddities greet the eye at every turn. It's the easiest place in the world to while away an hour or three. Choose a pint of Flower Pots Bitter (one of five handpumped ales) and a cosy corner with a deep sofa and a log fire to relish it in. Lunchtime peckish? Tuck into beer-battered cod, shepherd's pie or sandwiches. In the evening, pop across the road to The Black Rat restaurant (also owned by David) and splash out on something a touch more inventive.

Hampshire

Running Horse
Littleton

Littleton saw its old pub close in 2003. The following year saw the horse 'up and running', with a sleek new look and an emphasis on the food. Now this revitalised local is thriving. Pop in for a pint of Flower Pots or Ringwood in the bar with polished boards, leather chairs and subtle uplighting; settle down to a lunchtime ciabatta sandwich or a ploughman's on the fabulous terrace. Or head off to the slate-floored, colonial-styled restaurant extension for some serious dining. The board is chalked up daily – perhaps salmon and crab fishcakes, pork loin with herb risotto and Madeira jus, or beer-battered haddock with hand-cut chips. Finish it all off with iced banana parfait with honeycomb and chocolate ice cream or hazelnut and raspberry crunch with praline tuille. Staff are welcoming and happy to chat.

Meals	12pm-2pm; 7pm-9pm; no food Mon all day, Sun eve & Tues lunch. Main courses £5.50-£8.50.
Closed	Open all day.
Directions	Head south out of city along Chesil Street; Wharf Hill 1st road on right; parking off Chesil Street.

Meals	12pm-2pm (4pm Sun); 6pm-9pm (9.30pm Fri & Sat; 8pm Sun). Main courses £8.95-£17.95; sandwiches from £4.95.
Closed	Open all day.
Directions	Village signed off A272 just west of Winchester.

David Nicholson
The Black Boy,
1 Wharf Hill,
Winchester SO23 9NQ
Tel +44 (0)1962 861754
Web www.theblackboypub.com

Entry 315 Map 4

Charlie & Joanna Lechowski
Running Horse,
88 Main Road, Littleton,
Winchester SO22 6QS
Tel +44 (0)1962 880218
Web www.runninghorseinn.co.uk

Entry 316 Map 4

Hampshire

Hampshire

The Plough Inn
Sparsholt

Children frolic in the flowery garden's wooden chalet and play fort while grown-ups relax and enjoy the views. Walkers drop by for Wadworth ales on draught accompanied by ciabatta sandwiches or a wedge of popular pork pie. Inside, the pub is smart and open-plan, with hop-garlanded beams and an open log fire, while the 200-year-old cottagey front rooms make cosy spots for dinner. After 15 years at the helm, Richard and Kathryn Crawford continue to run this busy pub with enthusiasm and good humour. Blackboards proclaim dishes of the day; old favourites like lamb's liver and bacon are given a modern twist, restaurant-style main courses show imagination and flair. Try venison with celeriac mash and roast beetroot, followed by sticky toffee pudding. Wines are taken seriously with no fewer than 12 available by the glass.

The Wykeham Arms
Winchester

The old Wykeham is English to the core, full of its own traditions and neatly hidden away between the cathedral and the city's famous school. Ceilings drip with memorabilia and bow-tied regulars chat, pints in hand. It's grand too, a throwback to the past and brimming with warm colours and atmosphere. There are small red-shaded lamps on graffiti-etched desks (ex-Winchester College), three roaring fires and two dining rooms. At heart it remains a pub, but it's easy to mistake it for something smarter. Food is not cheap, but certainly reliable, from posh sandwiches and cottage pie at lunch to daily-changing evening dishes, perhaps herb-crusted rack of lamb and fillet steak with pepper sauce. The Fuller's and Gales ales are good, the wine list is interesting (20 by the glass), and the staff young and laid-back.

Meals	12pm-2pm; 6pm-9pm (9.30pm Fri & Sat; 8.30pm Sun). Main courses £10.95-£18.95; bar meals £4.95-£9.95.	Meals	12pm-2.30pm (12.15pm-5pm Sun); 6.30pm-8.45pm (6pm-10pm Sat; 5pm-9pm Sun). Main courses £11.25-£18.95; bar lunch £4.50-£10; sandwiches from £5.75; Sunday lunch £15.50-£19.50.
Closed	3pm-6pm.	Closed	Open all day.
Directions	Off B3149 Winchester to Stockbridge road.	Directions	Immed. south of Cathedral between College & Cathedral. Access via Southgate St & Canon St; call for directions; parking tricky.

Richard & Kathryn Crawford
The Plough Inn,
Sparsholt,
Winchester SO21 2NW
Tel   +44 (0)1962 776353

Jon Howard
The Wykeham Arms,
75 Kingsgate Street,
Winchester SO23 9PE
Tel   +44 (0)1962 853834
Web   www.fullershotels.com

Entry 317 Map 4

Entry 318 Map 4

Hampshire

Chestnut Horse
Easton

In the beautiful Itchen valley, this rather smart 16th-century dining pub is in the capable hands of Karen Wells and the standards of food and service are high. A decked terrace leads to a warren of snug rooms around a central bar, warmed by log fires. At night it is cosy and candlelit; you can eat either in the low beamed 'red' room, with its wood-burning stove, cushioned settles and mix of dining tables, or in the panelled and memorabilia-filled 'green' room. Try the two-course menu (smoked mackerel pâté, sea bream with pesto dressing, apple and walnut pie – all good value). Or tuck into beer-battered fish and chips, lamb shank with broad bean risotto, or rib-eye steak with hand-cut chips and béarnaise. There are great local ales, decent wines and champagne by the glass. A cracking food pub.

Meals	12pm-2pm; 6pm-9.30pm (from 7pm Fri & Sat); 12pm-6pm Sun. Main courses £12.95-£18.95; set lunch, 2 courses, £12 (lunch & before 7.30pm); Sunday roast £12.95; sandwiches from £7.95.
Closed	3pm-5.30pm. Open all day Sat & Sun.
Directions	1 mile off B3047 (Winchester to Alresford), 4 miles east of Winchester.

	Karen Wells
	Chestnut Horse,
	Easton,
	Winchester SO21 1EG
Tel	+44 (0)1962 779257
Web	www.thechestnuthorse.com

Entry 319 Map 4

Hampshire

Bush Inn
Ovington

Down a meandering lane alongside the clear-running waters of the Itchen, a 17th-century jewel in Hampshire's crown. In winter the bar is dark and atmospheric: a roaring log fire, candles on tables, walls gas lamp-lit. In summer, what nicer, in the words of a visitor, than to sit on the bridge with a pint, the evening sun pouring through the trees, the trout hiding in the reeds below. The setting and the cottagey garden are blissful in summer, and you can stroll along the river. Cottage furniture and high-backed pews fill a series of small rooms off the bar; walls are hung with fishing and country paraphernalia. City dwellers come for the atmosphere: cosy and peaceful (though busy in summer). The kitchen is driven by fresh local produce and presents a modern menu, and there are old favourites, too.

Meals	12pm-2pm (3.30pm Sun); 7pm-9pm (8.30pm Sun). Food all day Jul & Aug. Main courses £9-£16; bar meals £6.25-£10.
Closed	3pm-6pm (7pm Sun). Open all day Jul & Aug.
Directions	Off A31 between Winchester & Alresford.

	Nick & Cathy Young
	Bush Inn,
	Ovington,
	Alresford SO24 0RE
Tel	+44 (0)1962 732764

Entry 320 Map 4

The Woolpack Inn
Northington

New owners have revived the fortunes of the old drovers' inn in the Candover valley. In the bar are rugs on wood and tiled floors, logs in a stone fireplace, fat church candles on pine tables, newspapers and the *Tatler*. The vibe is laid-back – dogs doze, walkers and cyclists down pints of Flower Pots Bitter, shooting parties drop by in season, foodies are happy. The smart dining room, replete with striped banquettes and high-backed leather chairs, is the setting for hearty pub classics from Brian Aherne's open-to-view kitchen... simple ham, duck egg and hand-cut chips; shepherd's pie; roast rib of beef on Sundays. Or the more inventive pork and pistachio terrine, slow-cooked lamb with red wine sauce, chocolate and orange tart. Explore the local footpaths, visit The Grange for summer opera, drop into Winchester over the hill. Then return to refurbished cottages out the back, whose contemporary rooms, named after game birds, have exposed brick and flint walls, darkwood and leather furnishings, big beds and gun cupboards; bathrooms come with storm showers and posh smellies.

Rooms	7 doubles. £75–£135.
Meals	11.30am-3pm (4.30pm Sat); 6.30pm-10pm; 12pm-5pm; 6pm-9.30pm Sun. Main courses £11.95-£16.50; bar meals £4.50-£12.50; Sunday roast from £11.95.
Closed	3pm-6pm. Open all day Sat & Sun.
Directions	On B3046 between Alresford and Basingstoke, 4 miles north of Alresford.

Brian & Jarina Ahearne
The Woolpack Inn,
Totford,
Northington, Alresford SO24 9TJ
Tel   +44 (0)845 293 8066
Web   www.thewoolpackinn.co.uk

Hampshire

The Yew Tree
Lower Wield

Tim Gray has totally revitalised this hard-to-find but worth-tracking-down inn. The re-worked, stone-flagged and beamed bar is immediately welcoming: a winter fire, a chiming clock, walls festooned with character prints, a happy mishmash of furniture. There's a slightly more formal note to the dining area off to one side. As for Tim, he is "fuelled by passion and fun." On summer weekends it's especially buzzy as beer flows and the local cricket team play on the pitch opposite; if cricket's not your thing, bag a seat in the peaceful front garden, in the shade of the eponymous yew. Good fresh dishes are chalked up daily, so be cheered by steak, ale and mushroom pudding with rich onion gravy, and sea bass served with parsley and sun-dried tomato butter.

Meals	12pm-2pm; 6.30pm-9pm (8.30pm Sun). Main courses £8.95-£17.95.
Closed	3pm-6pm & all day Mon. Open all day Sun.
Directions	4.5 miles north of Alresford, off B3046, on a small lane between villages of Upper and Lower Weild.

Tim Gray
The Yew Tree,
Lower Wield,
Alresford SO24 9RX
Tel   +44 (0)1256 389224
Web   www.the-yewtree.org.uk

Entry 322 Map 4

Hampshire

The Sun Inn
Bentworth

Timothy Taylor's Landlord, Hog's Back Resolute, Ringwood Best, Fuller's London Pride… a parade of hand pumps pulls the punters in. There's charm, too: this friendly, flower-decked local was once a pair of 17th-century cottages. Surprisingly little has changed. On ancient bricks and bare boards is a rustic mix of scrubbed pine tables and oak benches and settles; beams are hung with brasses, walls adorned with prints and plates; there are fresh flowers, candlelight and newspapers. Cosy, log-fired inglenooks warm the interlinking rooms. Food is mostly perfect English: steak and ale pie, calves' liver and bacon with peas and onion gravy, Sunday roasts, warming puddings. Hidden down a tiny lane on the edge of a village in deepest Hampshire the Sun could scarcely be more rural. Footpaths radiate from the door.

Meals	12pm-2pm; 7pm-9.30pm. Main courses £8.95-£15.95; Sunday roast £10.95.
Closed	3pm-6pm. Open all day Sun.
Directions	Off A339, 2 miles from Alton.

Mary Holmes
The Sun Inn,
Bentworth,
Alton GU34 5JT
Tel   +44 (0)1420 562338

Entry 323 Map 4

The Anchor Inn
Lower Froyle

A super-smart country dining pub, renovated recently in imperious style. The house is Edwardian with 14th-century roots, and its treasure-trove interiors are full of beautiful things: timber frames, wavy beams, oils by the score, trumpets and pith helmets, a piano in the bar. Old photographs of Charterhouse School cover the walls, there are sofas by the fire in the panelled bar and busts on plinths in the airy restaurant, where you dine on proper English food: devilled kidneys, lemon sole, treacle tart with clotted cream. Doors open onto a lawned garden with country views, so come in summer for lunch in the sun. Bedrooms upstairs are seriously indulging. Expect beautifully upholstered armchairs, seagrass matting, fine linen on comfy beds, flat-screen TVs. There are power showers, huge towels and bathrobes, too. One suite is open to the rafters and comes with Nelson and friends framed on the wall; another has an enormous window that opens onto a private balcony. Don't come looking for a gastropub; do come looking for good ales, sublime food and old-world interiors. A treat!

Rooms	5: 4 doubles, 1 suite. £90–£120.
Meals	12pm-2pm (4pm Sun); 6.30pm-9.30pm. Main courses £10.50-£18.50; bar meals from £5.50.
Closed	Open all day.
Directions	Leave A31 for Bentley, 4 miles west of Farnham. West through village, north for Lower Froyle. On left in village.

Lucy Townsend
The Anchor Inn,
Lower Froyle,
Alton GU34 4NA
Tel   +44 (0)1420 23261
Web   www.anchorinnatlowerfroyle.co.uk

Entry 324 Map 4

The Wellington Arms
Baughurst

Lost down a web of lanes, the 'Welly' draws foodies from miles around. Cosy, compact and decorated in style – wall benches, rustic pictures, terracotta floor – the single bar-dining room has just seven tables (do book!). Jason's modern British cooking is first-class and inventive, the boards are chalked up daily and the produce mainly home-grown or organic. Kick off with crispy fried pumpkin flowers stuffed with ricotta and parmesan, follow with a rack of saddleback pork with crackling and sticky red cabbage, finish with a sensational rhubarb, strawberry and elderflower jelly with 'fairy floss'! The mood is easy and there are local ales on tap. Migrate to the huge garden for summer meals and views of the pub's expanding small holding: bees, four pigs and 140 rarebreed chickens; the eggs can be bought at the bar.

Meals	12pm-2.30pm; 6.30pm-9.30pm. Main courses £10.50-£18.50; set lunch £15 & £18 (Wed-Fri).
Closed	3pm-6.30pm, Tues lunch, Sun eve & Mon all day.
Directions	Baughurst is signed off A340 at Tadley, or A339 east of Kingsclere.

	Jason King & Simon Page
	The Wellington Arms, Baughurst Road, Baughurst, RG26 5LP
Tel	+44 (0)118 982 0110
Web	www.thewellingtonarms.com

Entry 325 Map 4

Hampshire
Worth a visit

326 The Trooper Inn Froxfield, Petersfield GU32 1BD +44 (0)1730 827293
Rustic and remote downland inn with a laid-back atmosphere made up of candlelit wood-floored bars, cracking real ale and solidly good, daily changing menus.

327 The White Horse Inn Monkey Lane, Priors Dean GU32 1DA +44 (0)1420 588387
This isolated downland pub may be fiendish to find but it's worth the effort. Candlit Jacobean charm (log fires, old tables, ticking clocks) and a choice of eight real ales. Blissfully cosy in winter, and in summer you can sprawl in the garden.

328 The Jolly Sailor Lands End Road, Bursledon SO31 8DN +44 (0)23 8040 5557
Reached via 45 steps or by boat, this former shipbuilder's house overlooks the river Hamble. Watch all things nautical from the terrace and from big windows in the newly furbished bars.

329 Marco Pierre White's Yew Tree Inn Hollington Cross, Andover Road, Highclere, Newbury RG20 9SE +44 (0)1635 253360
A contemporary and sympathetic makeover stitches the elegant dining room into the old fabric of this building with its inglenooks, timbers and uncluttered walls. With Marco as owner, this is more restaurant than pub, but expect the best of British food.

330 The Mayfly Chilbolton, Stockbridge SO20 6AX +44 (0)1264 860283
Unrivalled river scenes draw summer crowds to this beamed old farmhouse on the banks of the fast-flowing Test. Comfortable bar, good food, splendid riverside terrace. Arrive on foot (or bike) via the Test Way.

Hampshire

Worth a visit

331 The Plough Inn Longparish,
Andover SP11 6PB +44 (0)1264 720358
New owners settling in at this
long-established Test Valley local in
pretty Longparish. Expect a rustic-chic
makeover, local ales and promising
modern pub food.

332 Selborne Arms High Street, Selborne,
Alton GU34 3JR +44 (0)1420 511247
In a charming village – and handy for the
zig-zag climb up to the Selborne Hill
viewpoint (NT). Winter fires, hoppy
beams and hearty food that cranks up a
gear in the evenings. Makes good use of
local produce.

333 The Northbrook Arms East Stratton,
Winchester SO21 3DU +44 (0)1962 774150
Tim Gray, landlord of the Yew Tree at
Lower Wield (also in Hants), took over
this classic estate village pub in 2009 and
has kept things simple. Enjoy a homely,
traditional feel, Hampshire ales and
hearty home-cooked food. Skittle alley
out back.

334 Hampshire Bowman Dundridge Lane,
Bishops Waltham, Southampton SO32 1GD
+44 (0)1489 892940
Rustic, secreted-away country local set
beside a winding lane. Draws an eclectic
crowd for farm cider and Hampshire ales
tapped from the barrel in the time-worn
bar, hearty home cooking, and orchard
garden.

335 The Trusty Servant Minstead,
Lyndhurst SO43 7FY +44 (0)23 8081 2137
Fashionably remodelled New Forest pub
overlooking a classic village green. Open
fires, traditional furniture and a big
garden for summer are the backdrop
for pints of Ringwood Best and good
ol' bangers and mash.

Herefordshire

Old Black Lion
Hay-on-Wye

Heaven for historians, book lovers and
foodies in equal measure. Oliver Cromwell
lodged here while laying siege to Hay Castle
– the main building heaves with oak beams,
ancient artefacts and conspiratorial nooks
and crannies. Dolan Leighton has changed
little at this popular dining pub, where
cheerful staff pull pints of the eponymous
Black Lion bitter. Seasonal bar favourites
keep the kitchen working through every
session as diners feast on creamy peppered
venison casserole with cabbage mash. In the
evening, pick a table in the cosy 20-seat
restaurant to sample a warm salad of pigeon
and smoked bacon and roast salmon with
red pesto and mushroom sauce. There's a
well-priced wine list and a good list of
halves. Don't miss the 13th-century Mappa
Mundi in Hereford Cathedral – or the
town's 30 bookshops.

Meals	12pm-2pm (2.30pm Sat & Sun); 6.30pm-9pm (9.30pm Fri & Sat). Main courses £11.25-£18.95; bar meals from £5.50; Sunday roast £12.95.
Closed	Open all day.
Directions	2-minute walk from centre of Hay.

Dolan Leighton
Old Black Lion,
26 Lion Street,
Hay-on-Wye, Hereford HR3 5AD
Tel   +44 (0)1497 820841
Web   www.oldblacklion.co.uk

Entry 336 Map 7

Herefordshire

The Pandy Inn
Dorstone

Going back to 1165, a half-timbered Herefordshire delight, a contender for 'oldest pub in the land'. Heavy beams, worn flagstoned floors, much smoke-stained stone and a vast oak lintel over the old log grate. This is the county of Dorothy Goodbody and Butty Bach ales, Old Rosie and 'cloudy' scrumpy; no wonder there's a happy buzz. On the menu are big Hereford beef steaks and seasonal British specials like Welsh lamb shank with redcurrant and red wine sauce, and, for walkers, filled baguettes, hearty soups, homemade chicken-liver pâté and first-class bread. Families and dogs are welcome here and children may spill into the garden with its picnic tables and play area in summer. You are in the 'Golden Valley', so set off for Abbey Dore and Arthur's Stone – or bookish Hay-on-Wye, a short drive.

Herefordshire

Carpenter's Arms
Walterstone

A little chapel-side pub in the middle of nowhere, hard to find but worth it, superb in every way. Vera has been dispensing Wadworth 6X and Breconshire Golden Valley from behind the corner hatch for years and everyone gets a welcome: locals, walkers, families, babies. Through an ancient oak doorway is a tiny bar with a log-fired range and a dining area to the side. Floors are Welsh slate, settles polished oak, tables cast iron, walls open stone; it's as cared for as can be. On the menu are fishcakes and salad, chicken breast stuffed with stilton and wrapped in bacon, syrup and stem ginger pudding – proper homemade food, some organic. Beer is served from the drum, cider and perry from the flagon. In summer, spill into the grassy garden and gaze up at the Skirrid, then pull on the hiking boots and climb it.

Meals	12pm-2pm; 6pm-9pm. Main courses £8.95-£16.95; bar snacks £4.50-£9.50; Sunday roast £8.95.		Meals	12pm-3pm; 7pm-10pm. Main courses £10.95-£14.95; bar meals from £5.
Closed	3pm-6pm (6.30pm Sun) & Mon all day in winter (except bank hols). Open all day Sat.		Closed	Open all day.
Directions	Signed from B4348 Hereford to Hay-on-Wye, 5 miles from Hay.		Directions	Village signed from Pandy; Pandy signed from A465 from Abergavenny.

	Bill & Magdalena Gannon The Pandy Inn, Dorstone, Hereford HR3 6AN		Vera Watkins Carpenter's Arms, Walterstone, Hereford HR2 0DX
Tel	+44 (0)1981 550273	Tel	+44 (0)1873 890353
Web	www.pandyinn.co.uk		

Entry 337 Map 7

Entry 338 Map 7

The Saracens Head
Symonds Yat

This is an adventure before you've booked in. The bar staff still, obligingly, run the old, hand-cranked ferry across the lovely limpid river. The old inn dates from the 16th century and became a pub in the 18th but has a 21st-century buzz now, thanks to its friendly young staff and its big choice of dining tables. Dishes are chalked up on the blackboard by the bar – exotic sandwiches and bruschettas, pheasant terrine, wild boar with chive mash, Welsh goat's cheese panna cotta, crème brulée – all so delicious that people travel from far away for the experience. The terraces by the water attract a crowd in summer and lend a seaside-holiday feel; sit back with your Theakston's Old Peculier and watch the canoeists float by. In winter, the public bar is a warm haven; pool tables attract young punters and trippers come for Symonds Yat. A shame not to stay: upstairs and in The Boathouse next door are a flurry of bedrooms, some oak-floored, some carpeted with smart bathrooms. Ask for a room with a view up *and* down the river. Breakfast is one of the best.

Rooms	10: 7 doubles, 2 twins, 1 family room. £79-£130. Singles from £55.
Meals	12pm-2.30pm; 6.30pm-9pm. Main courses £9.50-£16.95 (lunch), £12.50-£19.95 (dinner); bar meals £4.50-£16.95; Sunday lunch £9.95-£15.
Closed	Open all day.
Directions	A40 Ross-on-Wye to Monmouth; exit at Little Chef; signs for Symonds Yat East.

Chris & Peter Rollinson
The Saracens Head,
Symonds Yat,
Ross-on-Wye HR9 6JL
Tel   +44 (0)1600 890435
Web   www.saracensheadinn.co.uk

Herefordshire Award winner 2010

The Mill Race
Walford

As the 'ecclesiastical' door swings open, prepare yourself for a stainless steel kitchen glistening behind a granite-topped bar; this is a stylish place. A wood-burner divides eating areas and there are counter-style bar tables and leather armchairs for aperitifs. A food provenance blackboard shows how seriously food is taken here: local chef Dan Wall chooses the meat and the game from their farm and helps digs the vegetables; the sous-chef catches trout for the table. Linger long over roast red leg of partridge with mash, bread sauce and watercress, or roast Gower pollock with crushed potatoes, wild mushrooms and parsley oil; children may have child-size portions (and that includes yummy garlic bread). Sit on the rear terrace, look across the Wye to the ruins of Goodrich Castle, sip ales from the same valley. Fabulous.

Herefordshire

The Lough Pool Inn
Sellack

The Lough Pool Inn is set deep in the bosky folds of Herefordshire. Expect a hearty greeting from David and Janice Birch, a cosy fire, a glowing bar, hop-strewn and head-ducking beams and a refreshingly unshowy dining room – solid tables, comfortable chairs – in which to enjoy daily-changing dishes. Seasonal menus successfully balance comfort food and modern treatments of superb local ingredients, be it grilled Brixham Market sardines with olive bread, breast of Barbury duck with mustard potato rosti, or confit pork belly with black pudding, sauté cabbage and apple purée. Stock-in-trade are good real ales from Wye Valley Brewery, strong draught ciders, wines by the glass of surprising quality; try the French fizz. A relaxed and civilised place to be.

Meals	12pm-2pm (10am-2.30pm Sat); 6pm-9.30pm (9pm Sun). Main courses £7.50-£16.50; Sunday lunch from £9.
Closed	3pm-5pm. Open all day Sat & Sun.
Directions	Walford is on B4234 3 miles south of Ross-on-Wye.

SPECIAL AWARD see page 20-21

Local, seasonal & organic produce

Meals	12pm-2pm; 7pm-9pm. Main courses £4.85-£12.95 (lunch & specials), £10.95-£18.95 (dinner).
Closed	3pm-6.30pm; Sun eve & Mon (except bank hols & Dec).
Directions	Off A49, 3 miles north-west of Ross-on-Wye; Sellack signed.

	Jane Thompson The Mill Race, Walford, Ross-on-Wye HR9 5QS
Tel	+44 (0)1989 562891
Web	www.millrace.info

Entry 340 Map 7

	David & Janice Birch The Lough Pool Inn, Grove Common, Sellack, Ross-on-Wye HR9 6LX
Tel	+44 (0)1989 730236
Web	www.loughpool.co.uk

Entry 341 Map 7

Herefordshire

The Cottage of Content
Carey

With the Wye Valley on the doorstep and miles and miles of footpaths, you are in fine countryside; for refreshment, you can't do better than pitch up at this cottage pub and country restaurant. The main bar oozes traditional authenticity, with its well-worn wooden tables and pews standing solidly on polished flags and tiles. Fires throw out warmth, night candles flicker. What better place to sup Wye Valley Bitter or Hobsons from the next county, or, in winter, homemade mulled wine and winter Pimms – walkers' manna from heaven. The modern, hale and hearty restaurant menu is a lesson in keeping it simple but delicious; try the tender Rudge Farm beef cooked slowly in spices and local ale, and topped with a savoury herb crumble. The name says it all, so come and settle in for a couple of hours. You'll be well cared for here.

Meals	12pm-2pm; 7pm-9pm. Main courses £9.25-£18.50; bar meals from £3.95.
Closed	2.30pm-6.30pm; Sun eve & Mon all day.
Directions	A40 west of Ross-on-Wye, then A49 towards Hereford; signs for Hoarwithy, then Carey.

Richard & Helen Moore
The Cottage of Content,
Carey,
Hereford HR2 6NG
Tel   +44 (0)1432 840242
Web   www.cottageofcontent.co.uk

Entry 342 Map 7

Herefordshire

The Butchers Arms
Woolhope

Chef Stephen Bull was one of the architects of the modern British food revolution in the 1980s, and he continues to draw foodies to The Butchers Arms, a short drive from Hereford. A splendid 16th-century half-timbered pub tucked down a winding lane in walking country, it is noted for its low beams and smouldering log fires. Bull is in the kitchen as much as he is pulling pints of Wye Valley ale, local ciders, perries and well-chosen wines. The ingredients-driven seasonal menu reads like a 'greatest hits' from his London restaurant days and makes delectable use of local produce: the signature dish of twice-baked cheese soufflé; pork chop with apples, sage and calvados; warm ginger cake with treacle toffee ice cream. In the summer, enjoy the peace of the sheltered garden with its babbling stream.

Meals	12pm-2pm; 6.30pm-9pm. Main courses £9.50-£16.
Closed	3pm-6pm, Sun eve & all Mon.
Directions	Off B4224 between Hereford & Ross-on-Wye.

Stephen Bull
The Butchers Arms,
Woolhope,
Hereford HR1 4RF
Tel   +44 (0)1432 860281
Web   www.butchersarmswoolhope.co.uk

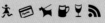

Entry 343 Map 7

The Wellington
Wellington

The austere frontage hides a welcoming bar and memorable food. At banquettes around the fire, Wye Valley HPA, Butty Bach and Hobsons ales can be sampled; beyond is a dining room of exposed brickwork, old beams and Herefordshire hops. A list of suppliers is on show, the chef is a stickler for seasonality and visiting celebrities like Franco Taruschio (ex Walnut Tree) have left their mark. So pitch up for Welsh white pork with apricot and pine nut stuffing, handmade artichoke, lemon and walnut tortellini, pan-fried ducks livers in brandy and pink peppercorn sauce... Puddings might include lemon semifreddo with summer berries or warm chocolate fondant with pistachio ice cream. The cheeses are local and the Sunday roasts magnificent; be sure to book: Wellington is a hungry village.

The Stagg Inn
Titley

In a Herefordshire village lies the first British pub to have been awarded a Michelin star. Gavroche-trained Steve Reynolds took it on and, defying all odds, ended up a Herefordshire food hero. As for provenance: the only thing you're not told is the name of the bird from which your pigeon breast (perfectly served on herb risotto) came. Most of the produce is very local, some is organic, with fresh fruit and vegetables from the kitchen garden or Titley Court next door. Seductive and restorative is the exceptional food: goat's cheese and fennel tart, saddle of venison with horseradish gnocchi and kummel, bread and butter pudding with clotted cream, a cheese trolley resplendent with 15 regional cheeses. The intimate bar is perfect and dog-friendly, there's beer from Hobsons, cider from Dunkerton's and some very classy wines.

Meals	12pm-2pm (12.30pm-2pm Sun); 7pm-9pm. Main courses £10.50-£16.75; bar meals £4.95-£7.95; Sunday lunch £12.50 & £17.50.
Closed	3pm-6pm, Sun eve & Mon lunch.
Directions	Village signed off A49, 4 miles north of Hereford.

Meals	12pm-2pm; 6.30pm-9.30pm. Main courses £14.50-£18.50; bar meals £8.90-£11.90.
Closed	3pm-6.30pm, Sun eve & Mon all day.
Directions	On B4355 between Kington & Presteigne.

Ross Williams
The Wellington,
Wellington,
Hereford HR4 8AT

Tel   +44 (0)1432 830367
Web www.wellingtonpub.co.uk

Steve & Nicola Reynolds
The Stagg Inn,
Titley,
Kington HR5 3RL

Tel   +44 (0)1544 230221
Web www.thestagg.co.uk

Entry 344 Map 7

Entry 345 Map 7

Herefordshire

The New Inn
Pembridge

Perfect for English heritage lovers with big appetites. The food is generously portioned, the building is as old as can be (1311), and Pembridge is a remarkable survivor; its market hall (where you can sup pints in the summer) could be in deepest France. It is a simple but great pleasure to amble in to this ancient inn, order a drink and squeeze into the curved back settle in the flagstoned bar; when the fireplace logs are lit, it's heaven. This is the most timeless of old locals, with photos of village shenanigans up on the wall and a darts board put to good use. Upstairs has floral carpets, books and sofa; it's a reassuring spot in which to tuck into hearteningly familiar smoked chicken and avocado salad, steak and ale pie and seafood stew. Jane Melvin is happy doing what she does best.

Herefordshire

The Bucket of Blood
World's End

Genteel hills and stone footbridges over trout-flecked streams… but don't expect a warm welcome here, this pub reeks of its malevolent past. 18th-century smugglers hid their stashes in the cellars: the notorious Dr Syn and his Devil Riders made merry hell on many a moonless night. A different 'Dr Syn' is served today – a cocktail of rum, brandy, whisky, sheep's milk and sea water from the nearest coast (probably Southend). It may have you seeing scarecrows. The Will-o'-the-Wisp is another lethal brew, with just a hint of methane (and will blow your head off, literally). Tuck into a delicious Cotswold lamb – if you can catch one. Or the mysterious pot-bellied pig that only appears at Christmas, and only to those who can see him. The puddings are seductive too. It's Hell!

Meals	12pm-2pm; 6.30pm-9pm (7pm-8.30pm Sun). Main courses £6.95-£12; bar meals £4.95-£8.50.
Closed	3pm-6pm.
Directions	Just off A44 in Pembridge. In centre next to Market Square.

Meals	Served al fresco or not at all. A few coppers will do.
Closed	Open to the elements.
Directions	Follow the brown tourist signs for Hades.

Jane Melvin
The New Inn,
Market Square, Pembridge,
Leominster HR6 9DZ
Tel   +44 (0)1544 388427

Entry 346 Map 7

Jack O'Lantern
The Bucket of Blood,
World's End,
Mordiford HE1 PME
Tel   +44 (0)1666 666 666

Entry 347 Map 6

Herefordshire

The Riverside Inn
Aymestrey

Edward IV had a celebratory noggin here after a decisive incident in the Wars of the Roses. He was declared King soon afterwards. It is much altered: to an easy mix of antiques, fresh flowers, hops and pine. Menus change with the seasons and the seductive dishes include rack of lamb with fondant potato and red wine jus, and Ludlow venison with spiced red cabbage and walnuts. Wander from the bar into linked rooms with log fires; order a pint of Wye Valley Ale from Stoke Lacy or a house wine from France, Chile, Germany. And look for the map of the kitchen gardens from which so much of the fruit and vegetables come. The setting is bucolic, tucked back from a stone bridge over the river Lugg, alive with river trout, waterside seats and a lovely terraced garden. The Mortimer Trail passes the front door.

Meals	12pm-2pm; 7pm-9pm. Main courses £10.95-£18.95; bar meals from £5.50.
Closed	3pm-6pm; Sun eves & Mon all day in winter (closed Mon lunch in summer).
Directions	On A4110 18 miles north of Hereford.

Richard & Liz Gresko
The Riverside Inn,
Aymestrey,
Leominster HR6 9ST
Tel   +44 (0)1568 708440
Web   www.theriversideinn.org

Entry 348 Map 7

Herefordshire
Worth a visit

A 16th-century timbered pub with a rich history, once a cobbler's, a cider house and a butchers. Cracking quarry-tiled bar with vast open fire and a super garden.

Lost down lanes, it's worth any number of missed turns. Beams and settles, open fires, candles on tables, wonderful menus that brim with local and organic produce. Don't miss the monthly farmers' market.

Down a small flight of steps discover stone floors, a hatch in the wall and real fires; the old drovers' inn has barely changed since the arrival of electricity. Find it down a tangle of lanes in a remote spot below Black Hill. New owners are reviving its fortunes – let us know how you get on!

Beautifully restored with slate floors, oak beams and exposed stone, following a devastating fire in 2005. Hay's oldest pub (16th-century) draws locals and tourist in for tip-top Wye Valley beers and interesting fresh food. We look forward to your reports.

Hertfordshire

The Sun at Northaw
Northaw

The 16th-century pub overlooking Northaw's pretty green shines in this culinary desert north of London. Passionate about food provenance, Oliver ensures his menus bristle with fabulous produce and, as the menu food map shows, most of it is from Hertfordshire and neighbouring Essex. Find rare-breed pork from Mickleford Hall and biodynamic, organic, free-range and artisan goodies, all delicious. Try Suffolk razor clams with smoked bacon and sea purslane; Highbury Farm lamb's liver with braised red cabbage and onion gravy; Sacombe Hill Farm sirloin steak with horseradish and beetroot chutney. The rustic-chic interior oozes charm and atmosphere, all soothing green hues, period fireplaces, board and stone floors, smart antique tables, and crates of fruit and vegetables dotted around the bar and dining rooms.

Meals	12pm-3pm (5pm Sun); 6pm-10pm. Bar food all day. Main courses £9.50-£19.50; sandwiches from £5; Sunday lunch £19.50 & £24.50.
Closed	Sun eve from 7pm & Mon all day.
Directions	M25 junc 24, A111 to Potters Bar, right A1000 along High Street and take B156 right signed to Northaw. Pub on left by green.

Oliver Smith & Sarah Doyle
The Sun at Northaw,
1 Judges Hill, Northaw,
Potters Bar EN6 4NL
Tel   +44 (0)1707 655507
Web   www.thesunatnorthaw.co.uk

Entry 353 Map 9

Hertfordshire

The Bricklayers Arms
Flaunden

Tucked away at a remote crossroads in the exotically named Hogpits Bottom ('hog' is local dialect for shale) is a pretty, ivy-covered 18th-century building with low beams, blazing winter fires and timbered walls. Once a row of cottages and shops, and an ale house since 1832, the rambling pub went 'gastro' a few years ago when Alvin Michaels procured it, eager to restore the fortunes of his run-down local. Now it's rammed with diners daily and his staff are run off their feet. Aided by a French chef, Alvin turns out local fillets of pork with apple compote and cider jus; bream, red mullet and cod in a saffron and juniper bouillon; and good old steak and kidney pie. All are delicious, all are prepared from locally sourced ingredients. There's an excellent range of beers, and over 140 wines, ports and cognacs.

Meals	12pm-2.30pm (3.30pm Sun); 6.30pm-9.30pm (8.30pm Sun). Main courses £9.95-£19.95.
Closed	Open all day.
Directions	M25 junc. 20; A41; 1st left to Chipperfield; 1st right to Flaunden.

Alvin Michaels
The Bricklayers Arms,
Hogpits Bottom, Flaunden,
Hemel Hempstead HP3 0PH
Tel   +44 (0)1442 833322
Web   www.bricklayersarms.com

Entry 354 Map 9

Hertfordshire

The Brocket Arms
Ayot St Lawrence

Welcome to a splendid medieval pub in an equally splendid village, close to Shaw's Corner; George Bernard Shaw lived here for 40 years (pull out your National Trust cards). Little has changed over the centuries, the classic three-roomed interior oozing atmospheric dark oak beams and timbers, a blazing fire in the inglenook, rustic benches and bar tables, and tiled and parquet flooring throughout. At lunch, tuck into beefburgers with fat chips, or a pea, mint and spring onion risotto — nice and tasty with a pint of Nethergate Azzaskunk. Or choose from the 'menu du jour' at dinner; there's confit chicken Caesar salad, braised venison with thyme dumplings, dark chocolate tart. Stay the night to get your full quota of historical charm: six bedrooms have wonky timbered walls, sloping floors, leaded windows, new brass beds and old fireplaces, while modern-day comforts abound — crisp linen, posh toiletries. The four-poster room may have an amazing vaulted ceiling but the simpler rooms in the converted stable block are as comfortable. And there's a super walled garden.

Rooms	6: 5 doubles/twins; 1 twin. £85-£120.
Meals	12pm-2.30pm; 7pm-9pm. No food Sun eve. Main courses £6.50-£12.95 (lunch & early eve); menu du jour £16.95 (2 courses) & £19.95 (3 courses).
Closed	Open all day.
Directions	From Wethampstead, follow signs to Shaw's Corner.

Suzy Sharp
The Brocket Arms,
Ayot St Lawrence,
Welwyn AL6 9BT
Tel   +44 (0)1438 820250
Web   www.brocketarms.com

Hertfordshire

The Alford Arms
Frithsden

It isn't easy to find, so be armed with a detailed map or precise directions before you set out – David and Becky Salisbury's gastropub is worth any number of missed turns. It's in a hamlet enfolded by acres of National Trust common land. Inside, two interlinked rooms, bright, airy, with soft colours, scrubbed pine tables on wooden or tiled floors. Food is taken seriously and ingredients are as organic, free-range and delicious as can be. On a menu that divides dishes into small plates and main meals, there is lamb hotpot with crispy sweetbreads, seared scallops on pear tatin, warm fig chocolate brownie. Wine drinkers have the choice of 19 by the glass, while service is informed and friendly. Arrive early on a warm day to take your pick of the teak tables on the sun-trapping front terrace.

Hertfordshire

The Tilbury
Datchworth

Standing on the village crossroads, the old Tilbury was known as the Inn on the Green. Now smart downlighters illuminate pastel walls and chic wallpaper, there are inglenook fires and chalkboard menus, leather dining chairs and gilt mirrors; this is a sanctuary for ladies that lunch. A fabulous place, too, for a special dinner: the food is a major attraction. Celebrity chef Paul Bloxham and his crew are dedicated to sourcing the very best of local produce and that means free-range pork from Great Dunmow, ducks from Saffron Walden, oysters from Colchester and watercress from Whitwell. So tuck in to red mullet escabeche, fillet Rossini and autumn fruit crumble. You can take home pickles, preserves and terrines as mouthwatering reminders. Coming up for summer: barbecues for the big garden with picnic tables and parasols.

Meals	12pm-2.30pm (3pm Sat; 4pm Sun); 6.30pm-9.30pm (7pm-10pm Fri & Sat). Main courses £11.50-£17.25.
Closed	Open all day.
Directions	A4146 Hemel Hempstead to Water End; 2nd left after Red Lion to Frithsden; left after 1 mile at T-junction, then right; on right.

Meals	12pm-2pm; 6.30pm-9pm. Main courses £9.95-£10 (lunch), £12.50-£18.95 (dinner).
Closed	3pm-6pm.
Directions	A1 to Stevenage, then A602 for Hertford; follow signs to Datchworth, then Datchworth Green.

David & Becky Salisbury
The Alford Arms,
Frithsden,
Hemel Hempstead HP1 3DD
Tel   +44 (0)1442 864480
Web   www.alfordarmsfrithsden.co.uk

Paul Bloxham
The Tilbury,
Watton Road, Datchworth,
Knebworth SG3 6TB
Tel   +44 (0)1438 815550
Web   www.thetilbury.co.uk

Entry 356 Map 9

Entry 357 Map 9

Hertfordshire

The Fox & Hounds
Hunsdon

London chefs quitting fabulous establishments to transforming country boozers are almost two a penny, but few have managed it with the aplomb of James Rix. Enter a comfy laid-back bar with a log fire, leather sofas, the daily papers, local ales on tap and a menu that changes twice daily. Tuck into something simple like a plate of Spanish charcuterie or of tender calves' liver with mash with bacon, or a perfect ploughman's. Things step up a gear in the country-house-on-a-shoestring dining room that throws together polished old tables and a crystal chandelier: a funky backdrop to peppered venison steaks with beetroot and port sauce, tagliolini with clams, garlic and chilli, and apple and amaretti tart. Even the focaccia is homemade. It is a treat to see an old pub in the right hands, and booking is recommended.

Meals	12pm-3pm; 6.30pm-10pm. Main courses £9-£22; bar meals £4.95-£16.50.
Closed	4pm-6pm; Sun eve & Mon all day.
Directions	Off A414 between Harlow & Hertford on B1004.

James Rix
The Fox & Hounds,
2 High Street, Hunsdon,
Ware SG12 8NH
Tel   +44 (0)1279 843999
Web www.foxandhounds-hunsdon.co.uk

Entry 358 Map 9

Hertfordshire

The Fox
Willian

Cliff and James Nye's village pub has a fresh, contemporary feel and a foodie menu that showcases British ingredients, including seafood from the Norfolk coast and local farm meats. It could beat many neighbourhood restaurants into a cocked hat but part of its charm is that it is still a place where beer drinkers are welcome – try a pint of James's Brancaster Best. A cool, formal dining room sits astride a relaxed bar where Brancaster oysters in sesame tempura add glamour to a menu that includes a beef and pork burger with sweet onion and chilli relish. The restaurant is a mix of French bistro and British pub: cod with spring onion and tiger prawn risotto, venison with braised red cabbage and blackberry jus, chocolate orange fondant. With a thriving farm shop full of local goodies out back, this Fox is one you'd do well to hunt down.

Meals	12pm-2pm; 6.45pm-9.15pm; no food Sun eve. Main courses £9.25-£17.50; sandwiches from £5.
Closed	Open all day.
Directions	A1 junc 9 for Letchworth; 1st left into Baldock Lane; pub 0.5 miles.

Cliff & James Nye
The Fox,
Willian,
Letchworth Garden City SG6 2AE
Tel   +44 (0)1462 480233
Web www.foxatwillian.co.uk

Entry 359 Map 9

Hertfordshire

Worth a visit

360 The Highlander Pub 45 Upper Tilehouse St,
  Hitchin SG5 2EF +44 (0)1462 454612
  Run by the Prutton family for 30 years
  and recently renovated, this 300-year-old
  freehouse fuses the atmosphere of a
  traditional pub with the charm of a
  French bistro. Gallic influences on the
  evening menu; classic-British pub
  lunches. Report please.

361 The Holly Bush Potters Crouch,
  St Albans AL2 3NN +44 (0)1727 851792
  An immaculate 17th-century country
  pub elegantly furnished with antiques
  and big oak tables candlelit at night.
  Fabulous Fuller's ales, straightforward
  food, nice garden.

362 The Old Mill London Road,
  Berkhamsted HP4 2NB +44 (0)1442 879590
  A beautifully restored old mill, with
  natural oak furnishings and deep sofas in
  classy rooms, and menus to match — a
  class act from vibrant Peach Pubs. Great
  canal-side terrace.

363 The Valiant Trooper Trooper Road, Aldbury,
  Tring HP23 5RW +44 (0)1442 851203
  Blazing log fires, old-fashioned comfort
  and a good garden. Serving ale since
  1752, this dear little brick and tiled
  cottage high in the Chiltern Hills draws
  booted ramblers, families and diners
  escaping town

Isle of Wight

The New Inn
Shalfleet

Built in 1746, this old fishermen's haunt is
worth more than a passing nod — especially
if you are on the 65-mile coastal path trail.
Or have got here by boat and moored at
Shalfleet Quay. The place now draws a
cheery mix of tourists, walkers and sailors to
a spick-and-span bar with 900-year-old
flagstones, beams and old fireplaces, and a
series of pine-tabled dining rooms decked
with nautical bits and bobs. Refreshment
includes pints of island-brewed ales and
fabulously fresh seafood marked up on the
daily-changing chalkboard. The huge platter
is a treat; other fish choices might include sea
bass cooked with lemon or simply grilled
plaice. The crab sandwiches are memorable,
and carnivores are not forgotten, with prime
steak, game in season and traditional pub
grub. There's a decked garden too for
summer alfresco supping.

Meals	12pm-2.30pm; 6pm-9.30pm. Main courses £6-£20.
Closed	Open all day.
Directions	On A3054 between Yarmouth & Newport.

Martin Bullock
The New Inn,
Main Road, Shalfleet,
Newport PO30 4NS
Tel   +44 (0)1983 531314
Web   www.thenew-inn.co.uk

Entry 364 Map 3

Isle of Wight

Seaview Hotel
Seaview

Everything here is a dream. You're 50 yards from the water in a small seaside village that sweeps you back to a nostalgic past. Locals pop in for a pint, famished yachtsmen step ashore for a meal, those in the know drop by for a luxurious night in indulging rooms. When the weather is warm, have a pre-dinner drink in the front garden and watch the sun go down over the Solent. In the bar, order island-brewed Goddard's Special and the famous hot crab ramekin; if you're here on a Sunday, don't miss the roast. Afterwards, retire to a sitting room for binoculars and views of the sea. The pitch pine bar has a roaring fire and every conceivable nautical curio nailed to its walls, the terrace buzzes with island life in summer, the restaurants hum with the contented sighs of happy diners. Some bedrooms come in country-house style (upholstered four-posters, padded headboards), others are more contemporary (Farrow & Ball colours, fancy bathrooms). Ask for details about wine-tasting, cycling and adventure breaks.

Rooms	28: 14 twins/doubles, 3 four-posters. Seaview Modern: 4 doubles, 3 twins/doubles, 4 family suites. £120–£199.
Meals	12pm-2.30pm; 6.30pm-9.30pm. Main courses £7-£14; Sunday lunch £17.95.
Closed	Open all day.
Directions	From Ryde, B3330 south for 1.5 miles. Hotel signed left.

Andrew Morgan
Seaview Hotel,
High Street,
Seaview PO34 5EX
Tel   +44 (0)1983 612711
Web   www.seaviewhotel.co.uk

Entry 365 Map 3

Isle of Wight

The Taverners
Godshill

A pub for all seasons: in summer take your pint (Taverners Own or a good guest beer) out into a pretty rear garden with petanque, picnic tables, vegetable beds and roaming chickens; in winter hunker down by the front bar with its warming fire, flagstone floor and wooden tables. There's a couple of sofas too for after lunch snoozers, if they can ignore the jazzy background music. Food is straightforward, fresh and local, skilfully cooked by Roger who used to head the kitchen team at The Haymarket Hotel in London; there are plans afoot to convert the family room into a shop selling island food stuffs. Lovely to see hand-raised free-range pork pie, homemade pickles, and 'My Nan's lemon meringue pie' on a simple menu; the wine list is short but well chosen, and there's freshly-squeezed orange juice and real hot chocolate too.

Meals	12pm-3pm; 6pm-9pm (9.30pm Fri & Sat). Main courses £8-£13.50; sandwiches from £3.80.
Closed	Sun eve from 5pm (except bank hol weekends & high summer).
Directions	On A3020 in village centre, opposite model village.

Roger Serjent
The Taverners,
High Street, Godshill,
Ventnor PO38 3HZ
Tel +44 (0)1983 840707
Web www.thetavernersgodshill.co.uk

Entry 366 Map 3

Kent

The Three Mariners
Oare

After a ramble across Oare marshes, a welcoming bolthole full of good things. Food is sourced locally from farms and day boats and is excellent value; it's the sort of place where you wish you could try everything that goes by. Salad of pigeon and wild mushrooms and saddle of venison with sprout tops and celeriac may be contemporary pub classics, but a straightforward slow-cooked leg of lamb (for six to share at Sunday lunch) has that reassuringly timeless appeal. The 400-year-old pub comes with a laid-back medley of furniture and a double-sided log fire, cleverly dividing the bar from the dining room. It's simple and understated with a pleasant informality and lots of bare wood – a place to treasure, and many do. There are Shepherd Neame ales and a modest and thoughtful selection of wines.
A Shepherd Neame pub.

Meals	12pm-2.30pm (3pm Sun); 6pm-9pm (9.30pm Sat). No food Sun eve. Main courses £11.50-£17.50; bar snacks from £4.
Closed	3pm-6pm & all day Mon. Open all day Sat & Sun.
Directions	From A2, take B2045 for Oare, left at T-junction; pub on right in 200 yds.

Claire Houlihan
The Three Mariners,
2 Church Road, Oare,
Faversham ME13 0QA
Tel +44 (0)1795 533633
Web www.thethreemarinersoare.co.uk

Entry 367 Map 5

Kent

Shipwright's Arms
Faversham

It's been called the loneliest pub in the world. Surrounded by salt marshes, the below-sea-level-building and boatyard are protected by a dyke from inundation by the tidal creek above. Its isolation calls for self-sufficiency: water is still drawn from a well and propane gas used for cooking. Plain and simple just about sums up the three tiny bar rooms separated by standing timbers and wooden partitions, all warmed by open fires or stoves, with booths formed by black-panelled settles and there's no shortage of boating paraphernalia. Beers are from Kent brewers Goachers and Hopdaemon and are expertly kept, basic food sustains sailing folk and walkers on the Saxon Shore Way, and Derek and Ruth are lovely people. Join the summer crowd in the garden and sup a pint on the sea wall. Worth the trek.

Kent

The Dove
Dargate

Who could resist a country pub in the gloriously named Plum Pudding Lane? Enter through a series of small rooms with bare floorboards, scrubbed tables and solid chairs, the bar invariably propped up by drinkers with pints of Shepherd Neame's Late Red or Spitfire. Everyone else is here for the food. A decade ago Phillip MacGregor worked as a trainee chef; now he has returned as proprietor and chef, and cooks with great skill and imagination. On the lunchtime blackboard you may find slip sole with herb butter, or a smoked bacon and rocket baguette, or bavette of beef with potato gratin; only the best ingredients are used, and roasted stuffed saddle of Romney Marsh lamb flies the local flag on the carte. Good for both a special meal and a relaxing country lunch, especially in summer when the garden is a draw. *A Shepherd Neame pub.*

Meals	12pm-2.30pm; 7pm-9pm; no food Sun eve. Main courses £6.95-£12.95.
Closed	3pm-6pm & Mon all day in winter.
Directions	From A2 for Sittingbourne. Through Ospringe, right at r'bout on to western link road; right at end (T-junction.). Left opp. school in 0.25 miles. Cross marsh to pub.

Meals	12pm-2pm (2.30pm Sun); 7pm-9pm. No food Sun eve. Main courses £13-£21; bar meals £3-£10.
Closed	Mon all day.
Directions	Off A299, 4 miles south west of Whitstable signed Yorkletts, Dargate, Waterham.

Derek & Ruth Cole
Shipwright's Arms,
Hollowshore,
Faversham ME13 7TU
Tel   +44 (0)1795 590088

Phillip MacGregor
The Dove,
Plum Pudding Lane,
Dargate, Faversham ME13 9HB
Tel   +44 (0)1227 751360

Kent

The Pepperbox Inn
Harrietsham

Off a country lane, surrounded by fields of corn, the 15th-century Pepper Box has far-reaching views across the Kentish Weald from a glorious decked terrace. Once the haunt of smugglers, it takes its name (apparently unique) from their favourite weapon, the Pepper Box pistol. A series of traditional dining areas rambles round the central bar, carpeted, cosy, low-beamed, with a sofa-fronted inglenook and glowing log fire. Drinks include foaming pints of Shepherd Neame Porter and Master Brew, local apple juice and decent wines by the glass. Menus are wide ranging and portions not for the shy! Tuck into a big bowl of chilli or a plateful of monkfish in garlic butter; pot-roasted pheasant or calves' liver in sage butter. And what could be nicer than to sup a summer pint on the terrace as the sun sinks into the Weald? *A Shepherd Neame pub.*

Meals	12pm-2.15pm (3pm Sun); 7pm-9.45pm. Main courses £7.50-£17; sandwiches from £4.
Closed	3.30pm-6.30pm. Closed from 5pm Sun. Open all day Sat.
Directions	From M20 junc 8, take A20 towards Ashford; right for Fairbourne Heath in Harrietsham. Keep ahead at crossroads; pub in 200 yds.

Sarah Pemble
The Pepperbox Inn,
Windmill Hill, Harrietsham,
Maidstone ME17 1LP
Tel   +44 (0)1622 842558
Web   www.thepepperboxinn.co.uk

Entry 370 Map 5

Kent

Pearson's Arms
Whitstable

This 18th-century listed seaside pub has been gastro-furbished and now bare boards, plain tables and comfy sofas deliver a contemporary look. Local ales and cheerful service do the rest. It's not scruffy, not grand, just right, and, under the guidance of chef Simon Wills, the attention to food is amazing. The light-filled restaurant upstairs is the seat of much action: blackboards list modern English dishes where seasonality rules and provenance shines. Game and fish are passions. Be tempted by roast teal and quince, home-smoked sprats and roast saddle of hare – or share a bream baked in salt with roast vegetables and aioli. Stocks in trade are homemade bread, own-smoked fish, hams cured in the cellar, sensational oysters – and, if you are in luck, a ringside seat for one of Whitstable's famous sunsets.

Meals	12pm-3pm; 6pm-9.30pm. Main courses £11-£17.
Closed	Open all day.
Directions	From centre of Whitstable walk 150 yds down Horsebridge Road to Sea Wall.

Simon Wills
Pearson's Arms,
The Horsebridge, Sea Wall,
Whitstable CT5 1BT
Tel   +44 (0)1227 272005
Web   www.pearsonsarms.com

Entry 371 Map 5

The Royal Albion Hotel
Broadstairs

Broadstairs – nicely old-fashioned, with character – held a special place in Charles Dickens's heart. "Our English watering place" he called it and this gloriously situated Georgian hotel played host to the great man for many summers; *Nicholas Nickleby* was written here. Run down in recent years, it has finally been rescued by Shepherd Neame, who have cast their magic wand over the place. Now all sorts come, not just the Dickens Trail tourists but young families and locals, irresistibly drawn by the views of Viking Bay. Catch them from the big light-filled Ballards Lounge or the suntrap double-decked terrace. Light bites in the bar and Sunday roasts are popular, with seafood a speciality in the more formal dining room (crab and prawn risotto, fillet of bass with warm potato salad). This would be a lovely place for a beachy break, so why not stay? Obviously the sea-facing rooms are the ones to go for, but all the renovated rooms are comfortable. Colours are pale with the odd splash of colour from bolster or cushion; bathrooms are slick and modern. And the staff are the best. *A Shepherd Neame pub.*

Rooms	21: 17 doubles, 1 twin, 3 singles. £80–£120.
Meals	12pm–2.30pm; 6.30pm–9.30pm; bar meals 12pm–2.30pm (5pm Sat & Sun) & 6pm–9.30pm. Main courses £10.95–£15.95; bar meals £6.95–£10.95.
Closed	Open all day.
Directions	From London take A299; follow signs to Broadstairs. Continue down High Street until sharp left at bottom. Pub on right.

Shane & Marie Goodwin
The Royal Albion,
6-10 Albion Street,
Broadstairs CT10 1AN

Tel	+44 (0)1843 868071
Web	www.albionbroadstairs.co.uk

Entry 372 Map 5

The Sportsman
Seasalter

Brothers Steve and Phil Harris's pub is a gastronomic haven amid marshland, beach huts and caravan sites with the North Sea somewhere behind. The blackboard menu, short and sweet, promises everything seasonal and local. Meat comes from farms within sight of the front door, Whitstable is just down the road. Order a native oyster or two to slurp while waiting for smoked mackerel with Bramley apple jelly or pork terrine. Roast chicken with bacon, sprouts and bread sauce is an old fashioned treat; apple sorbet and burnt cream makes a stunning finale. There's a tasting menu (book in advance), delicious bread, hams cured in the beer cellar, they churn their own butter and make their own salt. You eat at large chunky tables made from reclaimed wood in any of three airy rooms with marsh views. Exceptional. *A Shepherd Neame pub.*

The Red Lion
Stodmarsh

In an enchanting village, reached down rutted lanes that wind through bluebell woods, is a 15th-century pub with tiny rooms. Walk into an interior of bare boards, log fires, draped hops, prints, menus, old wine bottles, milk churns, trugs, baskets, candles on every table and a very bossy cat. Then there's the landlord, Robert Whigham, a legend in his own time. A basket of freshly laid eggs (chickens roam the garden, of course), chutney and a sign for the sale of locally smoked ham add to the rustic, rural feel. Greene King IPA and Old Speckled Hen are tapped from barrels behind the bar and everyone here is a regular, or looks like one. The blackboard menu changes according to what arrives from the farms and shoots, food comes on huge painted plates and the quality is high. It doesn't get much better than this.

Meals	12pm-2pm; 7pm-9pm; no food Sun eve & Mon. Main courses £15.95-£21.95.
Closed	3pm-6pm.
Directions	On coast road between Faversham & Whitstable.

Meals	12pm-2.30pm (3pm Sun); 7pm-9.30pm; no food Sun eve. Main courses £9.95-£15.95.
Closed	Open all day.
Directions	Off A257 Canterbury to Sandwich road.

Phil & Stephen Harris
The Sportsman,
Faversham Road, Seasalter,
Whitstable CT5 4BP
Tel +44 (0)1227 273370
Web www.thesportsmanseasalter.co.uk

Robert Whigham
The Red Lion,
Stodmarsh,
Canterbury CT3 4BA
Tel +44 (0)1227 721339
Web www.bestofkent.co.uk

Entry 373 Map 5

Entry 374 Map 5

The Fitzwalter Arms
Goodnestone

The 16th-century village pub stands on a sleepy road that dwindles to a footpath bordering Goodnestone Park where Jane Austen was a visitor. There's no standing on ceremony in these two tiny, unspoilt bars. Claire greets you warmly as you rub shoulders with all manner of folk, from local drinkers to walkers and foodies. There are logs fires and delicious bar food – omelettes, mushrooms on toast – all of which wash down nicely with a pint of Shepherd Neame. Then there's an intimate dining room with its own log fire and views through leaded windows to the churchyard. The menu chalks up such delights as wild mallard leg with red cabbage and soured cream, and pork belly with crackling and apple sauce. Chef Dave ensures vegetables are organic, meat free-range and fish delivered daily from Hythe. A gem. *A Shepherd Neame pub.*

The Griffin's Head
Chillenden

Dominated by a log fire in the tiny flagstoned central bar, this is a superb winter pub. Parts of the Wealden Hall House are 13th century so timbers and beams abound, ceilings are low and a maze of beer mugs hangs above the bar. Lovers of fizz know they've come home the moment they step in and spot the blackboard's roll call of champagne. But then longstanding landlord Jeremy Copestake takes his wines seriously; he even offers a chance to taste before committing. Back to back with its doppleganger hearth is a restaurant where good traditional home cooking rules; whether you choose ham, egg and chips or a seasonal partridge casserole, it'll be a perfect match for this simple, affable country pub. While the interior is not suitable for children, they are more than welcome in the gorgeous garden come summer. *A Shepherd Neame pub.*

Meals	12pm-2pm; 7pm-9pm. Main courses £9.50-£17.50; Sunday roast £13.50.
Closed	Sun eve & Tues.
Directions	From Canterbury, A257 to Wingham, then B2046 signed Aylesham; follow signs to Goodnestone.

Meals	12pm-2pm; 7pm-9.30pm; no food Sun eve. Main courses £8.95-£20.
Closed	Open all day. Closed Sun eves.
Directions	A2 from Canterbury; left on B2068 for Wingham; Chillenden signed.

Dave Hart
The Fitzwalter Arms,
The Street, Goodnestone,
Canterbury CT3 1PJ
Tel +44 (0)1304 840303
Web www.thefitzwalterarms.co.uk

Jeremy Copestake
The Griffin's Head,
Chillenden,
Canterbury CT3 1PS
Tel +44 (0)1304 840325

Entry 375 Map 5   Entry 376 Map 5

Royal Hotel
Deal

Whether out on the decked terrace listening to the waves raking the beach, or in the lounge bar cosy with leather chairs, chesterfields and fire, you can follow in the footsteps of Lord Nelson and Emma. They stayed here in the winter of 1801. It was an inspired move by Shepherd Neame – the oldest brewery in the country – to rescue and transform this run-down seaside hotel. The new bedroom look is understated and stylish, and a gentle nautical theme plays. Colours are softly modern, there are flat-screen TVs and modern bathrooms, and the quietest rooms are at the back – though the three most popular come with a sea-view balcony and an in-room claw-foot bath. With food available all day, the Royal has proved a hit with families drawn by the beach and the please-all menu of pub classics – yours to peruse wherever you sit. As for the deckside colonial-style bar, it makes a popular 19th hole inside and out; golfers come to play the celebrated Open Championship course Royal St George's, as well as qualifying courses Prince's and Royal Cinque Port. *A Shepherd Neame pub.*

Rooms	18: 12 twins/doubles, 5 family rooms, 1 single. £100–£170. Single £70. Family room £110–£150.
Meals	12pm–9pm. Main courses £7.95–£15.95.
Closed	Open all day.
Directions	On seafront close to town centre.

Joice & Glen Wisdom
Royal Hotel,
Beach Street,
Deal CT14 6JD
Tel   +44 (0)1304 375555
Web   www.theroyalhotel.com

Entry 377 Map 5

Kent

New Flying Horse Inn
Wye

Nothing is too much trouble for these affable hosts: the day's papers, ales from Shepherd Neame, wines by the glass, a friendly chat. A crackling log fire in the main bar adds to the charm, along with oak beams, timbers and a sprinkling of horse brass and pub paraphernalia. It is a genuine village local, with a difference: in summer you can marvel at Julian Dowle's award-winning Chelsea Flower Show garden, a nostalgic version of wartime Blighty that includes vegetable plots and flower boarders, imported oak trees and a thatched cottage, and a magnificent patio with a flagpole and play area. Food is correspondingly traditional: ham, double egg and chips, perhaps, or beef lasagne, supplemented by a specials board of more exotic offerings such as tempura hake with stir-fry vegetables and noodles with hoisin sauce. The pub was built in the 17th century – as a posting house – so the bedrooms and bathrooms vary in size. They come in neutral colours with the occasional low beam or desk area tucked behind a chimney breast. The quieter, smaller rooms are in the stable block. *A Shepherd Neame pub.*

Rooms	9: 7 doubles, 1 twin, 1 single. £95. Single from £55.
Meals	12pm-2pm; 6pm-9pm (6.30pm-9pm Sun). Main courses £4.95-£8.95 (lunch), £9.25-£14.50 (dinner).
Closed	3pm-5.30pm Mon-Fri in winter. Open all day Sat, Sun & in summer.
Directions	A mile off A28 north of Ashford; follow one-way system into Wye; Upper Bridge St is 2nd turning on right after High Street.

David Little
New Flying Horse Inn,
Upper Bridge Street,
Wye, Ashford TN25 5AW
Tel   +44 (0)1233 812297
Web   www.newflyinghorsewye.co.uk

Entry 378 Map 5

Kent

The Granville
Street End

From the same stable as the Sportsman in Seasalter, the Granville mirrors its older sibling, straddling the divide between restaurant and pub. Rugs are strewn, leather sofas fill one corner and there's a big beer garden outside. It's a pleasure to sit back in this laid-back place, downing rock oysters with shallot vinegar and a pint of stout (or a well-chosen wine). Overseeing it all is Gabrielle Harris, aided by chef Jim Shave heading an open-to-view kitchen that deals in modern uncontrived dishes. Chalked up on blackboards are tried-and-trusted favourites like whole roast wild sea bass with garlic and rosemary. There's homemade bread to dip, and a flourless chocolate cake that will charm those even without allergies. Ingredients are impeccably sourced. Great for walkers, foodies, families – and the Channel tunnel. *A Shepherd Neame pub.*

Meals	12pm-2pm (2.30pm Sun); 7pm-9pm; no food Sun or Mon all day. Main courses £11.95-£19.95.
Closed	3pm-5.30pm. Open all day Sun.
Directions	On B2068 just outside Canterbury.

Phil & Gabrielle Harris
The Granville,
Faussett Hill,
Street End,
Canterbury CT4 7AL
Tel +44 (0)1227 700402

Entry 379 Map 5

Kent

Froggies at the Timber Batts
Bodsham

Winding lanes lead, finally, to Bodsham, with glorious views of the North Downs. Wander into the splendidly rural Timber Batts – built in 1485 – and you are in for a surprise. Along with the bar menu is a slateboard of British and Gallic specialities, chalked up in French, and the Loire house wine comes from the vineyard of the owner-chef's cousin. So sit yourself down at an old pine table and be cheered by platefuls of local game, Hythe Bay fish, free-range egg and crispy thin French fries, confit de canard, roast rack of lamb with herbs, and café Liègoise. In winter, nurse a whisky by one of three fires, in summer enjoy the garden with its lush Kentish views. Wonderful downland walks radiate from the front door.

Meals	12pm-2.30pm (from 12.30pm Sun); 7pm-9.30pm. Main courses £15-£23; set lunch £16 & £20 (except bank hols); Sunday lunch £20 & £25.
Closed	3pm-6.30pm.
Directions	B2068 for Canterbury; left for Wye & Bodsham; 1st left fork; 1.5 miles; right for Wye; right for Bodsham; 300 yds up on top of hill.

Joel Gross
Froggies at the Timber Batts,
School Lane,
Bodsham, Ashford TN25 5JQ
Tel +44 (0)1233 750237
Web www.thetimberbatts.co.uk

Entry 380 Map 5

Kent

The Bell Inn
Smarden

Follow the road through pretty Smarden, between the church and the Chequers pub, to this lovely old Kentish inn. Inside is a rustic yet spick-and-span interior, all low hop-festooned beams, wonky walls, worn flagstones and crackling log fires. Candlelit rooms with rosy brick floors ramble round either side of the snug Cellar Bar, warmed by wood-burners and kitted out with smartly cushioned pew benches at scrubbed wooden tables. Worth a long detour for the atmosphere, the pints of Master Brew and Spitfire, the heady Biddenden scrumpy and the hearty homemade food: thick-cut sandwiches, steak and kidney pudding, lamb shank with roasted vegetables, pork fillet with dauphinoise and red wine sauce, bread and butter pudding. And there's a peaceful, secluded garden where barbecues reign in summer. *A Shepherd Neame pub.*

Kent

The Three Chimneys
Biddenden

Ramble through tiny, unspoilt rooms of stripped brick, faded paintwork, ancient timber and smouldering fires. During the Napoleonic wars French officers imprisoned nearby were allowed to wander as far as the point where the three paths meet (the 'trois chemins' – hence the name)… so, nothing to do with chimneys, of which there are only two. There's farm cider and Adnams Best Bitter drawn straight from the cask, and the cooking is modern and tasty; parmesan and herb-crusted loin of lamb may be followed by chocolate and praline torte with pistachio ice cream. You can eat in the bars (though not the public one) as well as the charming restaurant, replete with a stylish new conservatory extension, or on the sheltered patio. They pretty much get the balance right between pub and restaurant here, so prop up the bar for as long as you like.

Meals	12pm-2.30pm; 6.30pm-9.30pm (8.30pm Sun). Main courses £7.95-£19.95; bar meals from £4.95.	Meals	12pm-2pm (2.30pm Sat & Sun); 6.30pm-9pm (9.30pm Fri & Sat). Main courses £11.95-£18.95; bar snacks £3.95-£8.95.
Closed	Open all day.	Closed	3pm-5.30pm (3.30pm-6pm Sun).
Directions	Pub well signed 1 mile north of Smarden on minor road between Pluckley & A274 near Biddenden.	Directions	On A262 2 miles west of Biddenden.

	Karen Markham & Chris Ralph The Bell Inn, Smarden, Ashford TN27 8PW		Craig Smith The Three Chimneys, Hareplain Road, Biddenden, Ashford TN27 8LW
Tel	+44 (0)1233 770283	Tel	+44 (0)1580 291472
Web	www.shepherdneame.co.uk	Web	www.thethreechimneys.co.uk

🏃 📖 🐾 🍷 📶

Entry 381 Map 5

♿ 🏃 📖 🐾 🍺 🍷

Entry 382 Map 5

George Hotel
Cranbrook

Casual and understated, the pale woods and soft colours of the interior complement 13th-century origins; it may look like a brasserie but The George is Cranbrook's favourite local. While a network of local producers has been assiduously encouraged to add a sense of local identity, it is the consistently high standards that keep the place not just afloat but thriving. The kitchen moves deftly through a repertoire of modern dishes – rump of lamb with horseradish mash and aubergine and tomato confit, sea bass with roast fennel and salsa verde – while the odd pub classic is thrown in: Spitfire beer-battered cod and chips, braised red wine and venison sausages. Well kept Shepherd Neame ales make a matchless accompaniment to a steak and onion ciabatta sandwich, and wines are excellent. Climb "one of the noblest staircases in Kent" to discover hugely stylish and individual bedrooms themed according to colour; the rooms in the old building are full of charm, with wonky floors and exposed timbers; 'Crimson' has a superb four-poster. And Sissinghurst's garden is temptingly close. *A Shepherd Neame pub.*

Rooms	12: 11 doubles,1 twin. £85-£135. Singles £70-£105.
Meals	12pm-3pm; 6pm-9.30pm. Main courses £10-£16.50; bar meals £6-£9; Sunday lunch £8.95.
Closed	Open all day.
Directions	On the main village street.

Martin Lyall
George Hotel,
Stone Street,
Cranbrook TN17 3HE

Tel	+44 (0)1580 713348
Web	www.thegeorgehotelkent.co.uk

Entry 383 Map 5

The Black Pig
Tunbridge Wells

Rustic menus brimming with organic and biodynamic foods put Julian Leefe-Griffiths's George & Dragon on Kent's culinary map. Keen to replicate the success, he took on the Orson Welles in 2007, spruced it up in his own eclectic style and re-named it after a tasty rare-breed pig. Now there's a relaxed informality and a funky feel. In the bar are leather chairs, contemporary wall coverings and a chandelier; in the dining areas, earthy colours and planked floors. From the open-to-view kitchen flow pork sausages with mash and onion gravy, slow-roasted belly pork with roasted vegetables and Three Little Pigs, a board laden with English, Italian and Spanish hams. Non-porcine dishes include crab and scallop fettucine and rump of Sussex Red beef, and there are 13 wines by the glass. Pig heaven in Tunbridge Wells.

The Hare
Langton Green

As you negotiate the town green and the surrounding area in the quest for somewhere to park, you'll see that The Hare is Kent's least well-kept secret. Don't be put off. It may be mighty but it's relaxed and friendly too and the food is some of the best in the area. Large light rooms display gleaming, well-spaced tables on polished boards, and character in old prints, paintings and books. The blackboard menu trumpets pub classics like haddock and chips and posh sandwiches and wraps (try sausage with onion jam), plus more ambitious dishes such as pork fillet with herb and mushroom sauce and slow-cooked beef with garlic and thyme gravy. Chirpy staff dispense Greene King Abbot Ale and guest beers such as Ridley's Witchfinder. Wine is taken seriously too, the well-balanced list announcing 17 by the glass.

Meals	12pm–2.30pm; 7pm–9.30pm (10pm Fri). 12pm–10pm (Sat). 12pm–9pm (Sun). Main courses £7.50–£18 (lunch), £10.50–£18 (dinner).
Closed	Open all day.
Directions	Town centre; Grove Hill Road is almost opp. the railway station entrance, to the right of Hoopers Store.

Meals	12pm–9.30pm (10pm Fri & Sat; 9pm Sun). Main courses £9.75–£18.50; bar meals £6.50–£10.50.
Closed	Open all day.
Directions	On A264 3 miles west of Tunbridge Wells.

Julian Leefe-Griffiths
The Black Pig,
18 Grove Hill Road,
Tunbridge Wells TN1 1RZ

Tel   +44 (0)1892 523030
Web   www.theblackpig.net

Entry 384 Map 5

Andy Mutter
The Hare,
Langton Road, Langton Green,
Tunbridge Wells TN3 0JA

Tel   +44 (0)1892 862419
Web   www.hare-tunbridgewells.co.uk

Entry 385 Map 5

The Beacon
Tunbridge Wells

Everything ticks over beautifully at the Beacon. The spacious late-Victorian interior is a work of art, brimful of magnificent oak panelling, stained glass and ornate plaster ceilings. Good beers, an impressive range of wines by the glass and open fires lure drinkers to the clubby bar; in summer, take to the terrace with its famed panorama of the Weald of Kent – stunning. In every season, the food, served in the bar or the formal dining room, draws people from far and wide. Whether you are here for the Sunday roast, the plaice fillet battered in Harveys Ale or a three-course feast (layered pork and chicken liver terrine with homegrown grape and apple chutney, slow-braised Kentish lamb shoulder, sticky toffee pudding with butterscotch sauce) you should go home happy. And there are beds for the night, in three serene rooms at the top of the grand wooden staircase. In the Georgian Room, elegant colours and a roll-top slipper bath, in the Colonial Room, exquisite African fabrics. Wake to views of spectacular grounds – woods, lakes, wildlife and a genuine Tunbridge Wells chalybeate spring.

Rooms	3: 2 doubles, 1 single. £97. Single £68.50.
Meals	12pm-2.30pm; 6.30pm-9.30pm (12pm-9pm Sun). Main courses £9.95-£15.
Closed	Open all day.
Directions	Tea Garden Lane signed off A264 1 mile west of Tunbridge Wells.

John Cullen
The Beacon,
Tea Garden Lane,
Tunbridge Wells TN3 9JH
Tel   +44 (0)1892 524252
Web   www.the-beacon.co.uk

George & Dragon
Speldhurst

"We buy from people not companies,'" says Julian Leefe-Griffiths — before launching into an exuberant description of the produce he finds in the local woods and the beers that come from Chiddingstone. Meat, game and vegetables are local and often organic; cheeses come mostly from Sussex. Rescuing one of the oldest inns in southern England from years of mediocrity is no easy task, but they've made a fine start. It's a characterful old pub, loved for its massive flagstones, doors, inglenook and beams. Gutsy food is the biggest treat: crisp, salty sea purslane cooked with creamy soft scallops, wood sorrel with seared local wood pigeon breast, smoked eel on toast with poached duck egg and confit garlic, Valrhona chocolate tart. The atmosphere is easy, the staff friendly, and there's a lovely rear garden.

Kent

Spotted Dog
Penshurst

Everyone loves this 16th-century English pub... walkers, grannies, dogs. It is rambling, low-beamed, nooked and crannied to the hilt. But there's nothing traditional about the menu, a well-priced blending of country dishes with current trends. The food is good; there's venison and red wine pie; monkfish wrapped in pancetta with mussel broth; ham, egg and chips. Sit back with an expertly kept pint of Larkins or Doom Bar by an inglenook fire – there are several – and admire the tiny doors and the mullioned windows, the rough hewn beams and the ancient panelling. It's a textbook English pub, and everyone and their dog is welcome. In summer, stroll into one of the tiered beer gardens at the front and back (glorious views), then pop into the pub's wonderful farm shop next door. Fun, friendly and charismatic.

Meals	12pm-2.30pm (3pm Sun); 7pm-9.30pm. No food Sun eve. Main courses £9.50-£15.50; bar meals £5.50-£9.50.
Closed	Open all day.
Directions	In centre of village opposite church.

Meals	12pm-2.30pm; 6pm-9pm (12pm-6pm Sun). No food Sun eve. Main courses £7.75-£14.95.
Closed	3pm-6pm in winter. Open all day Sat & Sun.
Directions	Off B2188, 1.5 miles from Penshurst.

-Griffiths
gon,
, Speldhurst,
TN3 0NN
25

Carl Hood
Spotted Dog,
Smarts Hill, Penshurst,
Tonbridge TN11 8EP

Tel	+44 (0)1892 870253
Web	www.spotteddogpub.co.uk

Entry 388 Map 5

Kent

The Harrow
Ightham

The continuing hands-on approach of John Elton and Claire Butler is reaping rewards. Their Kent ragstone country pub looks the part: cottage garden flowers outside, candlelight and winter fire within. The cooking is based on sound supplies, from local game to wild mushrooms, and the food adds enough spice to provoke interest without being overpowering: citrus sauce with salmon and chive fishcakes, calves' liver and bacon with mash and onion gravy. Some of the starters might make a meal in themselves: spicy vegetable and lentil soup comes with bread, and tomato and anchovy salad is a great heaped pile. A separate restaurant, spreading into a small conservatory, has a more formal feel to match the starched white cloths on the bookable tables. It's first-come, first-served for tables in the bar – and this is a popular place.

Meals	12pm-2pm (3pm Sun); 6pm-9pm. Main courses £9.50-£18.50.
Closed	3pm-6pm, Sun eve & Mon all day.
Directions	Ightham Common signed off A25.

John Elton & Claire Butler
The Harrow,
Common Road,
Ightham,
Sevenoaks TN15 9EB
Tel +44 (0)1732 885912

Entry 389 Map 5

Kent

The Swan on the Green
West Peckham

West Peckham may be the back of beyond – a well-heeled beyond – but there's nothing backward about Gordon Milligan's pub. People are drawn by its reputation for good food and its beer from the microbrewery at the back. The décor is fresh, contemporary and open-plan: blond wood, rush-seated chairs, modern black and white photographs. Under the Swan Ales label, half a dozen brews are funnelled from the central bar: Ginger Swan, Swan Mild, Trumpeter Best, Fuggles, Bewick, Cygnet. Menus are a compendium of updated pub classics and the likes of tomato and root vegetable chowder, red mullet with mussel broth, and crispy duck confit with red wine jus. Gordon and his team have created a balanced mix of drinking bar and dining areas in a 16th-century pub. You may even borrow a rug and eat on the village green.

Meals	12pm-2pm; 7pm-9pm; no food Sun & Mon eve. Main courses £9.95-£15.95; bar meals £5.65-£12.95.
Closed	3pm-6pm; check Sun eves in winter.
Directions	From A26 north east of Tonbridge, north on B2106; 1st left for West Peckham; pub by green & church.

Gordon Milligan
The Swan on the Green,
The Village Green,
West Peckham, Maidstone ME18 5JW
Tel +44 (0)1622 812271
Web www.swan-on-the-green.co.uk

Entry 390 Map 5

The George & Dragon
Chipstead

Not content with two Kent pubs (George & Dragon, Speldhurst; Black Pig, Tunbridge Wells) and unable to resist a bargain, passionate foodie Julian Leefe-Griffiths snapped up this failing boozer in upmarket Chipstead in 2009. Spruced up with style, minutes from Sevenoaks and the M25, it's a 16th-century timbered gem resplendent with log fires, ancient beams and timbers, happy locals and great wines, and a classy daily menu bristling with fresh produce from the larders of Kent and Sussex. At lunch, accompany a pint of Westerham Grasshopper Ale with a steak sandwich or share a deli-board of cured meats, cheeses and chutneys. At dinner, tuck into such delights as pigeon and pancetta salad, seared Chart Farm 'sika' venison, smoked haddock risotto, and chocolate fondant. Shun the motorway services – this is the best pit-stop for miles.

Meals	12pm-9.30pm (8.30pm Sun) Main courses £9-£18.50.
Closed	Open all day.
Directions	2 minutes from junc. 5 M25; off A25 on High Street in centre of Chipstead.

Julian Leefe-Griffiths
The George & Dragon,
39 High Street, Chipstead,
Sevenoaks TN13 2RW
Tel   +44 (0)1732 779019
Web   www.georgeanddragonchipstead.com

Entry 391 Map 5

Worth a visit

392 **The Gate Inn** Church Lane, Chislet, Canterbury CT3 4EB +44 (0)1227 860498
A charming rural local, run for years by a landlord who resists change. Two small, well-worn bars, log fires, Shepherd Neame tapped from the cask, and simple hearty food.

393 **The Tiger** Stowting, Ashford TN25 6BA +44 (0)1303 862130
Hard-to-find, civilised country pub with friendly locals, rugs on bare boards, candles on scrubbed tables, roaring winter fire, real ales and splendid live jazz on Monday evenings. Reports please.

394 **The Woolpack** Brookland, Romney Marsh TN29 9TJ +44 (0)1797 344321
An isolated medieval pub on the edge of windswept Romney Marsh. Seek refuge and warmth by the log fire in the low-ceilinged bar, quaff Shepherd Neame in tip-top condition, tuck into hearty pub food.

395 **The Great House** Gills Green, Cranbrook TN18 5EJ +44 (0)1580 753119
Former Elizabethan cottages with an alluring mix of beams, furnishings and open fires in the rambling bar or cool Orangery dining room. Fresh brasserie food best enjoyed on the Mediterranean terrace.

396 **The Mulberry Tree** Hermitage Lane, Boughton Monchelsea, Maidstone ME17 4DA +44 (0)1622 749082
Contemporary pub-restaurant lost down lanes on the beautiful Kentish Weald. Seek it out for young chef Alan Irwin's impeccable food sourced from Kentish suppliers – and the pub's kitchen garden. The set lunch menu is a steal.

The Cartford Inn
Little Eccleston

Ten miles inland from the bling of Blackpool stands a handsome 17th-century pub on the banks of the river Wyre. Once 'Dirty Annie' ruled the roost; now stylish Patrick and Julie Beaume reign. Enter the etched glass and oak door to find an airy, open-plan space filled with fabulous open fires, polished floors and the bold use of statement wallpaper. Contemporary black and white photographs, candles and huge vases of flowers add to the vibe; locally sourced ingredients shine through the menu. Try Lytham prawns in chilli, lime, garlic and coriander, or leek and creamy Lancashire tartlets. Fleetwood fish pie makes the most of the catch; oxtail and beef in real ale with suet pudding, mash potato and green beans, served with a cold beetroot salad, is richly dense. Seven stunning boutiquey bedrooms have carved French beds dressed in crisp linen, the Beaume's signature wallpapers and sumptuous textured fabrics, and little chandeliers. Bathrooms are bronze-tiled and dramatic. Genteel, historic Lytham is close by... or embrace your inner child, and head for Blackpool Pleasure Beach! Quite a place.

Rooms	7 doubles. £90. Singles from £65.
Meals	12pm-2pm; 5.30pm-9pm (10pm Fri & Sat); 12pm-8.30pm Sun. No food Mon lunch. Main courses £8.50-£19.95; platters from £8.50.
Closed	Open all day.
Directions	From M6 turn off M5; junc. 3 on A535, right at T-junction towards Garstane. Little Eccleston on left; Blackpool Old Road then Cartford Lane.

Patrick & Julie Beaume
The Cartford Inn,
Cartford Lane,
Little Eccleston, Preston PR3 0YP

Tel	+44 (0)1995 670166
Web	www.thecartfordinn.co.uk

Lancashire

Bay Horse Inn
Bay Horse

The Wilkinsons have been in the saddle for a number of years and son Craig takes full advantage of the marvellous Lancashire produce in his modern British cooking — tuck into fish pie with cheese mash, Bowland lamb hotpot with pickled red cabbage, and roast Lune Valley venison with honey sauce. Although the Bay Horse takes its food seriously and is dedicated to quality (right down to its home-grown herbs and veg) it has not lost sight of its pubbiness, so the atmosphere is easy and Moorhouses Pendle Witches Brew and Black Sheep are on tap. Interconnecting areas are comfortably furnished with a mix of old chairs and cushioned seating in bay windows, the dining room sparkles and the red-walled bar is warm and inviting. Gentle background jazz, quirky ephemera and two crackling fires add to the mood.

Meals	12pm-2pm (3pm Sun); 7pm-9.15pm; no food Sun eve. Main courses £11.95-£20.95; Sunday lunch £16.95 & £20.95.
Closed	3pm-6.30pm & Mon all day.
Directions	From M6 junc. 33; A6 for Preston, 2nd left; pub on right.

Craig Wilkinson
Bay Horse Inn,
Bay Horse,
Lancaster LA2 0HR
Tel   +44 (0)1524 791204
Web www.bayhorseinn.com

Entry 398 Map 11

Lancashire

The Eagle & Child
Bispham Green

There's an old-fashioned pubbiness here *and* a sense of style — an informality touched with zing. The candlelit main bar welcomes you in with its rug-strewn flagged floors, hop-decked beams and open fire; another room, just as cosy, has a cast-iron fireplace. Hand pumps line the bar (with beers from lesser-known brewers like Beartown Brewery) while the shelves parade an army of malts and the wine cellar has some fine offerings. The staff seem to enjoy themselves as much as the customers and the food has won awards; there's Lancashire hotpot, roast suckling pig with apple and cider gravy, partridge with porcini and Madeira sauce. The pub's reputation lies, too, with its cask ales, and the beer festival in May packs the place out. Don't forget to stock up in next door's farm shop before you leave.

Meals	12pm-2pm; 5.30pm-8.30pm (9pm Fri & Sat); 12pm-8.30pm Sun. Main courses £10-£16.50; bar meals £3.75-£10.
Closed	3pm-5.30pm. Open all day Sat & Sun.
Directions	From M6 junc. 27, A5209 for Parbold; right along B5246; left for Bispham Green. Pub in 0.5 miles.

Helen & Martin Ainscough
The Eagle & Child,
Malt Kiln Lane,
Bispham Green, Ormskirk L40 3SG
Tel   +44 (0)1257 462297
Web www.ainscoughs.co.uk

Entry 399 Map 11

Lancashire

The Rams Head Inn
Denshaw

High on the moors between Oldham and Ripponden — you're on the border here — with glorious views, the inn is two miles from the motorway but you'd never know. Unspoilt inside and out, there's an authentic, old-farmhouse feel. The small rooms, cosy with winter log fires, are carpeted, half-panelled and beamed and filled with interesting memorabilia. Until recently beer was served straight from the cask; there's still an old sideboard behind the bar to remind you of former days. Blackboards announce a heart-warming selection of tasty and well-priced food cooked to order: game and venison in season, seafood specialities and great steaks. A wonderfully isolated Lancashire outpost, staffed by people who care, and with a farm shop, deli and tea rooms. Well-behaved children are very welcome most evenings — but watch the open fires!

Meals	12pm-2.30pm (Mon); 6pm-10pm (12pm-8.30pm Sun). Main courses £8.95-£21.95; set menu £12.95; sandwiches £4.95-£7.95; deli prices from £2.50.
Closed	2.30pm-6pm Tue-Sat; Sun from 8.30pm & Mon eve. Deli open 9am-late (Tues-Sat); 11am-4pm Sun (2.30pm Mon).
Directions	M62 junc. 22 for Oldham & Saddleworth; 2 miles on right.

G R Haigh
The Rams Head Inn,
Ripponden Road,
Denshaw, Oldham OL3 5UN
Tel   +44 (0)1457 874802
Web   www.ramsheaddenshaw.co.uk

Entry 400 Map 12

Lancashire

The Clog & Billycock
Blackburn

Following the success of the Three Fishes and the Highwayman, Nigel Haworth and his team have another winner. Now the old boozer in a leafy village close to Blackburn has crackling fires, gleaming oak furniture and an eye-catching beamed atrium: a sensitively-lit showcase for a collection of black and white photographs of the pub's esteemed growers and producers. The colour scheme is subtle and calming yet there's a great buzz to the place, as black-aproned staff ferry beautiful food to cosy tables. Tuck into a hotpot from Burholme Farm heather-fed lamb with pickled red cabbage or go totally retro with boiled onions, black pudding, tripe, trotters and English mustard. With a great outside space, an inspiring children's menu, very helpful staff and fine wines and ales, this gloriously named pub is one to get excited about.

Meals	12pm-2pm; 2pm-5.30pm (afternoon light bites); 6pm-9pm (5.30pm-9pm Sat); 12pm-8.30pm Sun & bank hols. Main courses £8.95-£19.80.
Closed	Open all day,
Directions	From M6 junction 3, follow A677 towards Blackburn, then right in 5 miles to follow Billinge End Road to Pleasington. Pub on left in 1 mile.

Craig Bancroft
The Clog & Billycock,
Billinge End Road,
Blackburn BB2 6QB
Tel   +44 (0)1254 201163
Web   www.theclogandbillycock.com

Entry 401 Map 12

Lancashire

Millstone Hotel
Mellor

Modern meets traditional – this time, in a handsome 18th-century coaching inn in a pretty village on the edge of the Ribble valley. There's a welcoming glow in the bar, with its oak beams and panelling, richly patina'd furniture, grandfather clocks and smart carpeting. Get cosy by the roaring fire with a pint of local Thwaites Bitter and a crispy duck spring roll. Or eat in the welcoming dining room, resplendent with chandeliers, red carpeting and white linen. Local ingredients are carefully sourced – poultry from Goosnargh, lamb from Pendle, shrimps from Morecambe Bay. The food is wholesome and unpretentious, including the chutney that bursts with fruit from Balderstone, served with Eccles cake and crumbly cheese. Then there's Ribblesdale goat's cheese and avocado salad, spiced salmon fishcakes with chilli jam and grilled lime, and Farnsworth of Whalley sausages with black pudding, mash and onion gravy. Bedrooms ooze comfort: sumptuous fabrics and luxurious linen, Roberts radios and plasma TVs, top-spec bathrooms, padded coat hangers, umbrellas for wet days. A marvellously popular inn.

Rooms	23 twins/doubles. £95-£125. Singles £109-£124.
Meals	12pm-9.30pm (9pm Sun). Main courses £8.95-£16.95; set menus £25.50 & £31.50.
Closed	Open all day.
Directions	M6 junc. 31; A59 dir. Clitheroe past British Aerospace; right at r'bout signed Blackburn/Mellor; signs to Mellor.

Anson Bolton
Millstone Hotel,
Mellor Lane,
Mellor, Blackburn BB2 7JR
Tel   +44 (0)1254 813333
Web   www.millstonehotel.co.uk

Entry 402 Map 12

Red Pump Inn
Bashall Eaves

Down meandering lanes in the stunning Ribble valley is this handsome roadside pub, its south-facing terrace tumbled with flowers. In the bar: stone floors, an open fire, richly worn oak settles and tables, books scattered here and there, shuttered windows with green views – Jonathan and Martina have transformed the old place into a great country inn. Beers include Moorhouses and Timothy Taylor; pints are downed by the local shoot during the season. For lunch there are two rooms to choose from: one cosy with dark red walls, the other with bare oak tables and settles next to the wood burner. In the evening, sit in the large, beamed, candlelit restaurant. The menu is big in season on local game (with a rare sighting of jugged hare!). There's slow-roasted duck leg with homemade orange marmalade, roasted belly pork in seriously big portions, and their own sausages made with herbs from the garden, served with delicious champ and minted gravy. White-painted bedrooms have golden silk bedspreads, luxurious linens, spic and span bathrooms with thick snowy towels. And those glorious views.

Rooms	3 twins/doubles. £75–£115. Singles £65–£95.
Meals	12pm–2pm; 6pm–9pm (12pm–7pm Sun). Main courses £9.50–£17.95; bar meals from £4.50.
Closed	2.30pm–6pm & Mon (except bank hols). Open all day Sun.
Directions	From Clitheroe, B6243 following signs to Edisford Bridge. Cross bridge & turn right, signed Bashall Eaves.

Jonathan & Martina Myerscough
Red Pump Inn,
Clitheroe Road,
Bashall Eaves, Clitheroe BB7 3DA
Tel +44 (0)1254 826227
Web www.theredpumpinn.co.uk

Entry 403 Map 12

Lancashire

The Three Fishes
Mitton

The producers, suppliers and growers are the heroes of this venture, named and proclaimed on the back of every menu; Lancashire is a hotbed of food artisans. The 17th-century village pub in the lovely Ribble Valley is taking gastropubbery to a mouthwatering new level. The long whitewashed public house has been restyled in rustic-smart 21st-century fashion and is vast: up to 130 people inside, a further 60 out. Walls are pale brick, floors stone, furniture sober, lighting subtle and winter logs glow. Wines are gorgeous, local pints and real ciders are served and the beer-friendly food includes ignored but once-popular British delicacies. Delicious are the treacle baked Middlewhite Garstang ribs, the hotpot from heather-reared lamb, the Apple Valley Pudding and cinnamon custard. Sunday lunch is an institution.

Meals	12pm-2pm; 6pm-9pm (5.30pm-9pm Sat); 12pm-8.30pm Sun. Main courses £9-£17.95; Sunday lunch £15 & £19.50.
Closed	Open all day.
Directions	From M6 junc. 31 onto A677, then follow A59 into Whalley; B6246 for Great Mitton.

Nigel Haworth & Craig Bancroft
The Three Fishes,
Mitton Road, Mitton,
Clitheroe BB7 9PQ
Tel   +44 (0)1254 826888
Web   www.thethreefishes.com

Entry 404 Map 12

Lancashire

The Freemasons Arms
Wiswell

This old village pub has had a facelift; pots, plantings and a gravel drive swish it up. Inside, antique rugs on stone-flagged floors, gleaming oak furniture and beams, leather wing chairs, fires and fresh flowers. A series of rooms upstairs promise more sophisticated dining at antique refectory tables set with white linen and candelabra. Back down in the bar, Pride of Pendle and Blonde Witch are cask conditioned, whilst a staggering cellar (250 wines) awaits. Local lad 'done good' (most recently at Cassis at Stanley House), Steven Smith produces dishes bursting with seasonal ingredients: poached and roast wood pigeon, pressed leeks and hazelnuts, steamed game pudding. Organic salmon is cooked in vanilla oil with Morecambe Bay mussels, fennel & saffron; to finish, Magners cider granita with hot cinnamon doughnuts rounds everything off.

Meals	12pm-2.30pm; 6pm-9.30pm (12pm-8.30pm Sun). Main courses £9.95-£15.95. Sandwiches from £4.95.
Closed	3pm-5.30pm. Open all day Sat & Sun.
Directions	From A59, 2 miles south of Clitheroe, take A671 to Blackburn. After 0.5 miles, 1st left to Wiswell.

Richard Ellison
The Freemasons Arms,
8 Vicarage Fold, Wiswell,
Clitheroe BB7 9DF
Tel   +44 (0)1254 822218
Web   www.freemasonswiswell.co.uk

Entry 405 Map 12

The Spread Eagle
Sawley

With the river Ribble winding its winsome way along one side, and the Cistercian Sawley Abbey 100 yards down the other, the reborn Spread Eagle must be a contender for the 'loveliest location' gong. Martin Clarkson's eye for design has created a pleasing combo of old and new: reclaimed flagged floors, carved settles and antique sofas, kitschy curtains, crushed velvet, funky tartan and a bold wallpaper of books. Retro posters on Farrow & Ball walls proclaim 'Eat your greens', but there's nothing vintage about the menu. To start: air-dried ham with blue cheese pannacotta and quince paste. To follow: wild mushroom, broccoli, smoked garlic and shallot tagliollini with basil cream. And we cannot omit the warm parkin with treacle sauce (just walk it all off later...). Seven striking and stunning bedrooms above have fabulous views over river or abbey. Be seduced by sumptuous textiles and lavish linen, big beds and fat mattresses, cutting-edge showers and a scarlet bathtub in one room. And delightful touches like knitted Arran wool hot water bottle covers. The senses are tickled at every turn.

Rooms	7 doubles. From £80.
Meals	12pm-2pm; 6pm-9.30pm; 12pm-7.30pm Sun; afternoon tea 2.30pm-5.30pm. Main courses £8.95-£15.95; bar meals from £5.95.
Closed	Open all day.
Directions	From Preston, off A59 signed Sawley and Sawley Abbey.

Martin & Veronica Clarkson
The Spread Eagle,
Sawley,
Clitheroe BB7 4NH
Tel   +44 (0)1200 441202
Web   www.spreadeaglesawley.co.uk

Lancashire

The Inn at Whitewell
Whitewell

The old deerkeeper's lodge sits just above the river Hodder with views across parkland to rising fells in the distance. Merchants used to stop by and fill up with wine, food and song before heading north through notorious bandit country. Now barbours and muddy dogs mix with posh frocks and suits. You can eat in the bar but the long restaurant and the outside terrace drink in the view – which will only increase your enjoyment of Bowland lamb with cassoulet of beans and root vegetables, homemade ice cream and fine wines (including their own well-priced Vintner's). In the bar, antiques, bric-a-brac, peat fires, old copies of *The Beano*, fish and chips, warm crab cakes and local bangers. At weekends it gets packed; if you want a table, the more formal restaurant takes bookings. A perfect place.

Lancashire

Duke of York
Grindleton

In the magnificent Ribble Valley Michael Heathcote's roadside pub sits in the shadow of Pendle Hill. In the bar are oak floors, wood-burning stoves and beams – and a gloriously kitsch velvet candelabra. This reformed boozer is littered with quirky touches; a full-length mirror above a leather banquette; designer chairs upholstered in raspberry pink chenille. Heathcote is largely self-taught, and his touch is inspired. Lamb shank potato cake with watercress salad is perfectly judged, a homemade peach chutney offsetting its robust earthiness; poached haddock tagliolini is full of flavour and sublimely silky – the sort of dish you'd choose as a last supper. New season's English plum clafoutis with lavender and honey ice cream makes a strong finish. So, a seriously talented chef in an appealing village – beat a path to his door!

Meals	12pm–2pm; 7.30pm–9.30pm. Main courses £8–£13.75 (bar), £14–£23 (restaurant); bar meals from £3.65–£8.50.
Closed	Open all day.
Directions	M6 junc. 31a, B6243 east through Longridge, then follow signs to Whitewell for 9 miles.

Meals	12pm–2pm; 6pm–9pm (5pm–8pm Sun). Main courses £10.95–£19.95; set lunch £8.95 & £10.95; set dinner (4 courses) £23.50; sandwiches from £5.95.
Closed	3pm–6pm & Mon.
Directions	A59 Clitheroe to Skipton; exit for Chatburn and turn left at post office onto Ribble Lane; Grindleton in 1 mile.

Charles Bowman
The Inn at Whitewell,
Dunsop Road, Whitewell,
Clitheroe BB7 3AT
Tel +44 (0)1200 448222
Web www.innatwhitewell.com

Entry 407 Map 12

Michael Heathcote
Duke of York,
Grindleton,
Clitheroe BB7 4QR
Tel +44 (0)1200 441266
Web www.dukeofyorkgrindleton.com

Entry 408 Map 12

Lancashire

The Lunesdale Arms
Tunstall

A soft, wide, undulating valley, the Pennines its backdrop – this is the setting of The Lunesdale Arms. A traditional pub with a fresh, modern feel: Pimms in the summer, mulled wine in the winter, good ales and good cheer. Comfort is deep: big sofas and wood-burning stoves, cushioned settles, newspapers to browse and oil paintings to consider – even to buy. A big central bar separates drinkers (three local cask ales, whiskies and wines) from diners. Sit down to locally reared produce, home-baked bread and seasonal, often organic, vegetables at tables away from the bar. Chef Richard Price delivers wholesome food full of flavour – spinach, pea and mint soup with home-baked bread, roast Cumbrian smoked ham hock with mash and parsley sauce, chocolate brownie – and encourages children to have small portions.

Meals	12pm–2pm (2.30pm Sat & Sun); 6pm–9pm. Main courses £8.95–£14.50; bar meals £4.50–£14.50.
Closed	Mon all day (except bank hols).
Directions	M6 junc. 34; A683 for Kirkby Lonsdale.

Emma Gillibrand
The Lunesdale Arms,
Tunstall,
Carnforth LA6 2QN

Tel	+44 (0)1524 274203
Web	www.thelunesdale.co.uk

Entry 409 Map 12

Lancashire

The Highwayman
Burrow

Hot on the heels of the Three Fishes at Mitton, the Highwayman was the second pub for Ribble Valley Inns. In this stylishly revamped old stone inn in the beautiful Lune valley, Nigel Haworth raids the rich borderlands of Cumbria and Yorkshire in his continuing pursuit of good produce; his regional heroes are showcased on the menus and the walls. So look forward to heather-reared Bowland lamb Lancashire hot pot, Cumbrian fell-bred rib-eye steak, warm Flookburgh shrimps, and Lancashire curd tart with organic lemon cream. There are a raft of classy wines by the glass and Thwaites Lancaster Bomber on tap. Knowledgeable staff add attentive service to a gloriously informal country interior of stone and wooden floors, eclectic old tables and cosy corners with crackling log fires. For summer: a fantastic terrace and garden.

Meals	12pm–2.30pm; 6pm–9pm (from 5.30pm Sat); 12pm–8.30pm Sun. Light bites 2pm–5.30pm. Main courses £9.95–£19.80.
Closed	Open all day.
Directions	20 mins from junc. 34 on M6; less than 10 mins from junc. 36.

Nigel Haworth & Craig Bancroft
The Highwayman,
Burrow,
Carnforth LA6 2RJ

Tel	+44 (0)1524 273338
Web	www.highwaymaninn.co.uk

Entry 410 Map 12

Leicestershire

The Queen's Head
Belton

Take a church-side village pub by the scruff of its neck and renovate it from top to toe. The result: a cool, relaxed drinkers' bar, all leather sofas, blond wood and low-slung tables, a bistro with a winter fire and a dining room of wood, suede and leather, with a canopied alfresco extension. Add spacious, spotless and warmly carpeted bedrooms with a similarly stylish feel and you have a sleekly, discreetly good-looking coaching inn. (The bedrooms are reached via an unobtrusive door at the side.) The Weldons deserve applause for not losing sight of tradition: the Queen's Head serves its own beer from the local Wicked Hathern brewery, plus outstanding wines. Printed menus and blackboard dishes point to diverse ideas that are beautifully executed, from burgers and relish in the bar to roasted scallops with langoustine risotto, beef fillet with morel mushroom sauce, divine puddings and a good value set menu in the restaurant; there's a proper little kids' menu, too. Watch out for the summer Real Ale and Gourmet Barbecue weekend, and the Champagne and Lobster night.

Rooms	6: 5 doubles, 1 twin. £70-£100. Singles £70.
Meals	12pm-2.30pm (4pm Sun); 7pm-9.30pm (10pm Fri & Sat). Main courses £13.50-£19.50; bar meals £4-£9.50; set menu £12-£16; Sunday lunch £13 & £16.
Closed	Open all day.
Directions	In Belton, just off B5234, 6 miles west of Loughborough.

Henry & Ali Weldon
The Queen's Head,
2 Long Street,
Belton, Loughborough LE12 9TP
Tel   +44 (0)1530 222359
Web   www.thequeenshead.org

Entry 411 Map 8

Leicestershire

The Crown
Old Dalby

Note the small bolted hatch from which stirrup cups were served to the hunt 200 years ago. The pub has a history and a cosy, characterful warren of little rooms with Victorian fireplaces remain. But the hand pumps are new and so is the restaurant, large and light and opening to sweeping lawns and fine terrace. At contemporary oak tables you can dine on seared scallops with Chinese greens or Gressingham duck with potato fondant and Madeira jus, while Sunday lunches are 'Sunday Best' with posh starters and indulging puds – who fancies a trio of crème brulee? Back in the bar, the patterned carpet and wheelback chairs reflect the pubby feel, so enjoy a pint of Batemans or Bombardier or one of 12 wines by the glass. It's a fine pub well-run, and Rachel Higgins is brilliantly hands-on.

Leicestershire

The Cow & Plough
Leicester

A pub-restaurant housed in the former milking sheds of a working farm. The Lounts founded it in 1989 and filled it with good beer and a hoard of brewery memorabilia: the two back bars are stuffed with period signs, mirrors and bottles. It later became an outlet for their range of Steamin' Billy ales (named after Elizabeth's Jack Russell who 'steamed' after energetic country pursuits). When the foot and mouth epidemic closed the farm's visitor centre, they established a restaurant there instead. Most of their dishes are made with local produce such as rib-eye steak with red wine, chestnut and thyme sauce and honey-glazed Tamworth ham. The pub has built up a great reputation, winning awards and becoming a place for shooting lunches. And there's a conservatory with piano and plants and beams decked with dried hops.

Meals	12pm-2pm (3pm Sat & Sun); 6pm-9pm. No food Sun eve or Mon. Main courses £7.85-£17.95; Sunday lunch £14 & £16.	Meals	12pm-3pm (5pm Sun); 6pm-9pm; no food Sun eve. Main courses £7.75-£16.95; bar meals £4.95-£10.95; Sunday lunch £9.95.
Closed	3pm-6pm Tues-Fri. Closed until 5pm Mon.	Closed	Open all day.
Directions	From Nottingham A606; at Nether Broughton right for Old Dalby; there 1st right, then left.	Directions	On B667 north of town centre & A6.

	Rachel Higgins The Crown, 7 Debdale Hill, Old Dalby, Melton Mowbray LE14 3LF		Barry Lount The Cow & Plough, Stoughton Grange Farm, Gartree Road, Leicester LE2 2FB
Tel	+44 (0)1664 823134	Tel	+44 (0)116 272 0852
Web	www.crownolddalby.co.uk	Web	www.steamin-billy.co.uk

Entry 412 Map 8

Entry 413 Map 8

Leicestershire

Red Lion Inn
Stathern

Quirky stylishness and cheerful service. The rambling Red Lion feels like a home, with its books and papers, deep sofas and open fires; gamekeepers frequent the flagstoned bar. A trusted network of growers and suppliers fills the kitchen with game from the Belvoir estate, cheeses from the local dairy, fruits and vegetables from nearby farms. Menus are on blackboards, with a choice that leaps between fashion and tradition: potted prawns and melba toast; village-made sausages with mustard mash; pan-fried halibut with squid ink linguine, olives, pine nuts and saffron dressing; chocolate and pecan pie with apple and cinnamon ice cream. The set Sunday lunch is great value. The wine list is imaginative; beers include village-brewed Brewsters Bonnie and children have homemade lemonade.

Lincolnshire

Wig & Mitre
Lincoln

Sandwiched between the cathedral and the courts, this famous inn draws an eclectic clientele, from journeymen and judges to barristers and bishops. Downstairs has a French café feel: old oak boards, exposed stone, sofas to the side – a civilised spot for late breakfast and the papers. Upstairs, a cosy series of plush carpeted dining rooms and an open fire. In the Seventies it was hard to find decent food in a pub, let alone one in Lincoln. Valerie's kitchen became one of the most exciting in the area, serving a mix of dishes years before the term 'gastropub' was born. Today you'll find the likes of salt cod with celeriac purée and roast lamb with cabbage and bacon. More restaurant than pub, there are also some top of the market wines – available by the case from the Hope's shop next door.

Meals	12pm-2pm (3pm Sun); 7pm-9.30pm. Main courses £10.50-£17.50; Sunday lunch £16.50.
Closed	3pm-6pm; all day Mon & Sun from 6.30pm. Open all day Fri & Sat.
Directions	Off A607 north east of Melton Mowbray; through Stathern; past Plough; pub signed on left.

Meals	9am-11pm. Main courses £9.95-£18.95; set menu £12.50 & £14.95 (lunch); £16.50 & £19.50 (dinner); sandwiches from £4.50.
Closed	Open all day.
Directions	On Steep Hill between Lincoln Cathedral and Lincoln Castle.

	Ben Jones, Sean Hope & Marcus Welford Red Lion Inn, 2 Red Lion St, Stathern, Melton Mowbray LE14 4HS
Tel	+44 (0)1949 860868
Web	www.theredlioninn.co.uk

Entry 414 Map 9

	Michael & Valerie Hope Wig & Mitre, 32 Steep Hill, Lincoln LN2 1LU
Tel	+44 (0)1522 535190
Web	www.wigandmitre.com

Entry 415 Map 9

Lincolnshire

Houblon Inn
Oasby

The word 'civilised' springs to mind, as befits the pedigree of the place. The pub is named after one of the landowners in the area, John Houblon, first governor of the Bank of England – honoured on the back of the £50 note. Hollyhocks round the door and pretty sash windows greet you; low beams, stone walls and a crackling fire wait inside. 'Houblon' is also Flemish for 'hop' and ale-lovers will not be disappointed. Craft brews from Springhead and Everard's breweries will take your fancy as you perch at the bar for a good old chin wag – or to scan the simple but stylish menu. There's venison terrine; cod with tomato and coriander sauce; steak and Guinness pie. Owner Hazel makes this pub special. Quietly passionate about the place, she left 'the smoke' years ago and thrives. Outside is a gravel garden dotted with good wooden furniture and parasols, a boules piste too; across the courtyard, in a converted barn, four recently spruced up and peaceful bedrooms with new bathrooms, new heating, new décor. Bang in the middle of a conservation village, the Houblon Inn is honest, unaffected and intelligently run.

Rooms	4: 3 doubles, 1 twin. £60-£70. Singles £40-£45.
Meals	12pm-2pm; 6.30pm-9.30pm. Main courses £6.95-£18.95; Sunday lunch £12.95 (2 courses) & £14.95 (3 courses).
Closed	2.30pm-6.30pm (3pm-7pm Sun) & Mon (open bank hol lunch).
Directions	From A1, B6703 to Ancaster; right to Welby, follow road to Oasby.

Hazel Purvis
Houblon Inn,
Oasby,
Grantham NG32 3NB
Tel   +44 (0)1529 455215
Web   www.houblon-inn.co.uk

Entry 416 Map 9

Lincolnshire

The Bluebell
Belchford

High in the Wolds, amid the vast openness of the Lincolnshire farms, is the Bluebell in Belchford – warmth and cosiness hit you as you enter. To a traditional backdrop of deep polished oak is a bar sporting chintz curtains with neat ties, floral sofas and wing-back chairs; in one of two dining areas are gilt-framed oil paintings on deep red walls, in the other, an airy modernity. They're proud of their food here, and so they should be: almost all the produce is locally sourced (Lincolnshire Red beef, fish from Grimsby). At lunch there are filled ciabattas and beef and Guinness pie, while things step up a gear at dinner with dishes such as charred calves' liver with roast garlic mash. It's as friendly as can be and as cosy as a steamed sponge pudding with custard – and you might tuck into one of those, too.

Meals	12pm-2pm; 6.30pm-9pm (12pm-2pm Sun). Main courses £9.95-£17.
Closed	3pm-6.30pm; Sun eve & Mon.
Directions	Village signed off A153 between Horncastle & Louth.

Darren & Shona Jackson
The Bluebell,
1 Main Road,
Belchford,
Horncastle LN9 6LQ
Tel   +44 (0)1507 533602

Entry 417 Map 9

Lincolnshire

Brownlow Arms
Hough-on-the-Hill

Standing proudly in the centre of a hilltop village, this magnificent building is said to have been the servants' quarters to the Manor. Now it has the feel of an intimate country house. Winged Queen Anne chairs in autumnal hues invite you to settle in by the open fire amid deep rich oak beams and polished panelling, and regulars sup Marstons Burton ale as chatter flows around the central bar. In the intimate restaurant, the food, revealing a French classical influence, is accomplished as befits such a setting – soufflés, parfaits, lamb with red wine jus, plaice with scallops and chive beurre blanc. Desserts range from refreshing lemon crème brûlée to comforting sticky toffee pudding. It's blowy up here with idyllic open countryside all around, but there is a sheltered, landscaped terrace for a quiet pint and an early supper.

Meals	6.30pm-9.30pm Tues-Sat; Sun lunch 12pm-2.30pm. Main courses £14.95-£22.50; set lunch £20.50 (2 courses) & £23.50 (3 courses).
Closed	Tues-Sat lunch, Sun eve & Mon all day.
Directions	On A607 6 miles north of Grantham.

Paul & Lorraine Willoughby
Brownlow Arms,
High Road, Hough-on-the-Hill,
Grantham NG32 2AZ
Tel   +44 (0)1400 250234
Web   www.thebrownlowarms.com

Entry 418 Map 9

Lincolnshire

The Chequers Inn
Woolsthorpe

A coaching inn for 200 years, the Chequers has built a reputation as a top dining pub in recent years. There's contemporary luxury and deep comfort, a flurry of open fireplaces, three dining areas and two bars, rug-strewn floors, heavy oak tables, leather sofas, linen drapes and Farrow & Ball colours. You have two ales on hand pump, 30 wines by the glass, 50 whiskies, several fruit pressés and a humidor on the bar. Robust dishes – clam, squid and salmon risotto, calves' liver with mash, bacon and onion marmalade, chocolate tart with bitter orange sorbet – taste as good as they look, the weekday evening menu is a steal (three courses, £16.50). In summer the pub hosts the village cricket team on what must be one of the slopiest pitches in England. The Vale of Belvoir and its grand castle are as beautiful as they sound.

Meals	12pm-2.30pm (4pm Sun); 6pm-9.30pm (8.30pm Sun). Main courses £9.50-£19; bar meals £4.95-£8.95; Sunday lunch £11.95; set lunch £11.50 & £15; set dinner £16.50 (Mon-Fri).
Closed	3pm-5.30pm. Open all day Sat & Sun.
Directions	Off A52, west of Grantham. Follow signs to Belvoir Castle.

Justin & Joanne Chad
The Chequers Inn,
Main Street, Woolsthorpe,
Grantham NG32 1LU
Tel +44 (0)1476 870701
Web www.chequersinn.net

Entry 419 Map 9

Lincolnshire

The Tobie Norris
Stamford

Built in 1280, remodelled in 1663 and again, superbly, in 2006, the Tobie Norris draws you in to a warren of stunningly atmospheric rooms and takes you back to the old days – Cromwellian at least. Huge stone flags, oak settles and the smell of woodsmoke assail you as you leave the bustling pavements behind, the weekly market in full flow. Between the main rooms is a staircase leading to three more, each one oozing character and style, with vast exposed timbers, little recesses and cupboard-like doors. Find a church pew or a nice leather armchair and sit back with your Ufford Ales and Adnams – or a tasty wine from a list of 21, each available by the glass. Dogs doze on bare boards, perfect staff ferry pizzas and plates of smoked salmon linguine, there are rotating ales on tap and you could stay here all day.

Meals	12pm-2.30pm (3pm Sat & Sun); 6pm-9pm. No food Fri-Sun eve. Main courses £6.75-£12.95.
Closed	Open all day.
Directions	South on B6403; right at A1. Take A427/A43 exit, left at Kettering Rd. Left at A16, left at St Paul's St; pub on right.

Michael Thurlby & Will Fry
The Tobie Norris,
12 St Paul's Street,
Stamford PE9 2BE
Tel +44 (0)1780 753800
Web www.tobienorris.com

Entry 420 Map 9

London

The Thomas Cubitt
Belgravia

As well-upholstered as Belgravia itself. The handsome ground-floor bar has high ceilings, oak-block floors, tall windows that open to tables in the street, and a bit of panelling thrown in for good measure. A cords and cashmere crowd is drawn by the classic country-house feel, the real ales, the superb wines, and the kitchen, which puts more thought into what it produces than many a full-blown restaurant. In the bar is a reassuring selection of pub favourites — organic beef burgers, grilled sausages with roasted red onion gravy and buttery mash — and the organic Sunday roasts are fabulous. In the über-elegant dining room upstairs the food is fiercely modern (take grilled tuna with red pepper and pearl barley and langoustine bisque). It's popular, and the friendliness of the staff, even under pressure, is a pleasure.

Meals	Bar: 12pm-11pm. Restaurant: 12pm-3pm (Mon-Fri); 6pm-11pm (Sat). Main courses £13.50-£22; bar meals from £8.
Closed	Bar open all day. Restaurant closed Sun.
Directions	Nearest tubes: Victoria; Sloane Square.

Ryan Moses
The Thomas Cubitt,
44 Elizabeth St, Belgravia,
London SW1W 9PA
Tel   +44 (0)20 7730 6060
Web   www.thethomascubitt.co.uk

Entry 421 Map 15

London

Duke of Wellington
Marylebone

An unexpected London find — in a charming backstreet in Marylebone. Until recently it was looking tired, even exhausted; now The Duke is a funky little gastropub. The light, spacious single bar has hung on to its boarded floor, ornate ceiling (painted a deep blood red) and dark wood bar, while a wall of gilt framed mirrors and modern artworks create a bohemian feel (check out the glitter-encrusted bust of the Iron Duke on your way to the loo). While Fuller's London Pride is one of three real ales on tap, the Duke's reputation now rests on its food. The style is robust modern British and the ingredients are the freshest: carrot and coriander soup with cumin, chargrilled 45-day aged rump of beef with mustard and tarragon butter. Upstairs is a wonderfully intimate dining room with a slightly extended menu.

Meals	12pm-3pm (4pm Sat & Sun); 6.30pm-10pm (7pm-9pm Sun). Main courses £12.50-£16 (bar), £13-£19.75 (restaurant).
Closed	Open all day.
Directions	Nearest tube: Marylebone.

Jamie Prudom
Duke of Wellington,
94a Crawford Street, Marylebone,
London W1H 2HQ
Tel   +44 (0)20 7723 2790
Web   www.thedukew1.co.uk

Entry 422 Map 15

London

The Beehive
Marylebone

In the plain wood-floored single bar room of one of London's earliest boozers the old pubbiness remains. And yet… there's been a transformation. Entrepreneurial restaurateur Claudio Pulze, creator of some of the most stylish restaurants in town, has cheerfully accommodated the wishes of the regulars in his first foray into the pub world. Now the quality of the food and drink are a match for civilised Marylebone. The beers are his own – Brew Wharf microbrewery ales – and the wine list a delight to explore. As for the food, it is striking in its simplicity and available all day. Steak sandwiches; burgers with bacon, cheese and egg; Caesar salads; fish and chips with tartare sauce (homemade)… it's gutsy, characterful pub food done brilliantly, and the prices are very fair. A friendly, youthful, Baker Street refuge.

Meals	12pm-11pm; 10.30am-10.30pm Sat, Sun & bank hols. Main courses £5.50-£16.50; bar snacks from £3.90.
Closed	Open all day.
Directions	Just off Baker Street at the Marylebone Road end.

Claudio Pulze
The Beehive,
126 Crawford Street, Marylebone,
London W1U 6BF
Tel +44 (0)20 7486 8037
Web www.thebeehive-pub.co.uk

Entry 423 Map 15

London

Admiral Codrington
Chelsea

It may be hiding down a Chelsea back street, but the savvy know, and love, The Cod. Opened up and remodelled, the Victorian-style central bar is rich in dark woods (panelling, floorboards, furniture) while pale yellow walls are hung with prints, and banquettes, sofas and subtle lighting add softness. The restaurant, by contrast, is a light contemporary space with a retractable glass skylight (amazing in summer), salmon-pink high-backed chairs and wall banquettes, and fishy prints to reflect the nautical name. Tuck into three-cheese macaroni with crispy bacon and a pint of Black Sheep Bitter on the small all-weather terrace, or braised lamb hotpot and ever-popular beer-battered fish and chips in the restaurant. Or even West Mersea rock oysters and Devon crab cake, accompanied by a perfectly chilled bottle of Sancerre.

Meals	12pm-2.30pm (3.30pm Sat; 4pm Sun); 6.30pm-11pm. Main courses £12.75-£46.
Closed	Open all day.
Directions	Nearest tubes: Sloane Square; South Kensignton.

Alexander Langlands Pearse
Admiral Codrington,
17 Mossop Street, Chelsea,
London SW3 2LY
Tel +44 (0)207 581 0005
Web www.theadmiralcodrington.com

Entry 424 Map

London

The Builders Arms
Chelsea

Who would expect such a tasty little pub in the back streets off the King's Road? The country living room feel is so seductive you could happily move in. So settle back with a glass of prosecco or a pint of London Pride among worn leather sofas and mismatched chairs, board games and books, soft green walls and a ruby-red snug behind the bar. 'Never trust a builder without a tattoo' reads the sign on the wall, but you won't find many builders in The Builders: it's stylish at heart (even if labelling the loos 'Builders' and 'Ballerinas' is a touch twee). The food is delicious modern British and well presented: pea and ham soup, roast salmon and basil risotto, and peppered sirloin steak with wilted spinach and mash. The area is a shoppers' dream but don't expect a table on Friday lunchtimes: it's packed!

London

The Pig's Ear
Chelsea

Off the King's Road, a nice little corner pub serving Uley Pig's Ear on tap and a perfect Bloody Mary – drinking is encouraged. In the chattering bar (this is Chelsea) are high ceilings, planked floors, big mirrors, a zinc-top bar and formica tables; upstairs, a cosy sash-windowed dining room with twinkly lights and not a touch of Victoriana. Staff are knowledgeable, casually dressed and perky, in keeping with the spirit of the place. Cooking (from an ex-Aubergine chef) is rousingly rustic – part Mediterranean, part English. The beef brisket and ox cheek casserole, topped with robust Jerusalam artichoke crisps, was deep flavoured and succulent; the orange panna cotta smooth, citrusy and decorated with a perfect sesame tuile. There are cured herrings and rock oysters, and most nights it's rammed. Hurrah.

Meals	12pm-3pm (4pm weekends); 7pm-10pm Mon-Weds; 11pm Thurs-Sat; 9pm Sun. Main courses £8-£15.
Closed	Open all day.
Directions	Nearest tubes: Sloane Square; South Kensington. Behind King's Road, between Sydney Street & Chelsea Green.

Meals	12pm-3pm (12.30pm-3.30pm Sat); 7pm-10.15pm; 12.30pm-4pm; 7pm-9.30pm Sun. Main courses £11.50-£15.95; bar meals £5.75-£16.50.
Closed	Open all day.
Directions	Nearest tube: Sloane Square

Rupert Clevely
The Builders Arms,
13 Britten Street, Chelsea,
London SW3 3TY
Tel   +44 (0)20 7349 9040
Web   www.geronimo-inns.co.uk/thebuildersarms

Entry 425 Map 15

Simon Cherry
The Pig's Ear,
35 Old Church Street, Chelsea,
London SW3 5BS
Tel   +44 (0)20 7352 2908
Web   www.turningearth.co.uk/thepigsear

Entry 426 Map 15

London

Chelsea Ram
Chelsea

A quiet residential street off the Lots Road seems an unlikely place to find a corner pub bursting with bonhomie. It used to be a junk shop; now the fine arched shop windows with etched glass are complemented by soft greens and terracottas, a dark green wooden bar and local art. A carpeted area to the back has small alcoves, soft lighting and thumbed books – an intimate spot for some enticing food. Salmon fishcakes with crab and citrus bisque, perhaps, or confit duck leg on roasted garlic mash and braised red cabbage, all great value. Scrubbed tables see lively card games (bring your own) over coffee, chirpy staff run a fast-paced bar. Close to the large storage depot of Bonhams the auctioneers, this much-loved pub is worth the few minutes' walk from the end of the King's Road.

Meals	12pm-3pm (4pm Sun); 6.30pm-10pm (9pm Sun). Main courses £9.95-£16.50.
Closed	Open all day.
Directions	Nearest tubes: Fulham Broadway; Sloane Square.

James Symington
Chelsea Ram,
32 Burnaby Street,
Chelsea,
London SW10 0PL
Tel   +44 (0)20 7351 4008

Entry 427 Map 15

London

The Harwood Arms
Fulham

Hard to believe you're a pint's throw from the mayhem of Fulham Broadway. 2008 remodelling has delivered an easy-on-the-eye modernity to this big-windowed gastropub on the corner, well-dressed in pastels and pine boards and a Shaker-ish feel. Menus, driven by seasonality and provenance, revel in an intelligent simplicity, with game a speciality. The chef is Ledbury graduate Stephen Williams: you're in very good hands. You might find game 'tea' served with a venison sausage roll; pheasant Kiev with champ and turnips glazed with mead and rosemary; warm Bramley apple doughnuts with spiced sugar; sweet egg custard tart with drunk golden raisins. Hand-pump ales, well-chosen wines, tasty bar snacks and a laid-back but informed staff make this an extremely civilised Fulham bolthole.

Meals	12pm-3pm (12.30pm-4pm Sun); 6.30pm-9.30pm (7pm-9pm Sun). Main courses £14-£18; bar snacks £3-£6.
Closed	Open all day.
Directions	Nearest tubes: West Brompton; Fulham Broadway.

Brett Graham & Mike Robinson
The Harwood Arms,
Walham Grove, Fulham,
London SW6 1QP
Tel   +44 (0)20 7386 1847
Web   www.harwoodarms.com

Entry 428 Map

London

The Atlas
Fulham

Engraved letters on wooden panelling proclaim London Stout, Burton Bitter and Mild Ales. The Atlas is a great little place in which to delve into more modern brews: Fuller's London Pride, Caledonian Deuchars IPA, Adnams Broadside. A glazed wooden partition divides the bar in two, and other Thirties' features remain: floorboards, black and white tiling around the foot of the bar and three brick fireplaces, two of which add a glow in winter. The third has been converted into a serving hatch for superb dishes that change twice a day – grilled sardines and Tuscan sausages, pot-roast poussin – and the wine list trumpets 24 wines by the glass. Doors lead to a walled beer garden where folk flock under the rain cover. Great atmosphere, great food, great staff – a genuine cracker.

Meals	12.30pm-2.30pm (4pm Sat); 6pm-10pm. 12pm-10pm Sun. Main courses £9-£15.50; bar meals £5-£10.
Closed	Open all day.
Directions	Nearest tube: West Brompton.

George & Richard Manners
& Craig Fleeton
The Atlas, 16 Seagrave Rd,
Fulham, London SW6 1RX
Tel   +44 (0)20 7385 9129
Web   www.theatlaspub.co.uk

Entry 429 Map 15

London

The Sands End Pub & Dining Room
Fulham

Down a residential street off Wandsworth Bridge Road the faithful flock. It might have something to do with the fact that one of the business partners was formerly an equerry to the Prince of Wales (sightings of the young Princes are not unfounded) but more of a certainty is the menu, market-based, changing daily and pleasingly affordable. The food zings with flavour – queen scallops with spinach and smoked gubbeen; braised beef, onion and mushroom pie; chocolate brownie – and complements the modern urban rusticity of scrubbed tables, bare boards and displays of bottled produce. While half the place is restaurant, the rest is old-fashioned bar, serving beers, good wine and slices of hand-raised pork pie. Word has spread: at weekends you book. Young staff are friendly and attitude-free.

Meals	12pm-3pm (4pm Sat); 6pm-10pm; 12pm-9pm Sun). Main courses £12-£18; bar snacks from £3.
Closed	Open all day.
Directions	Off A127 (Wandsworth Bridge Road), second turning on left before bridge, heading south.

Eamonn Manson & Mark Dyer
The Sands End Pub & Dining Room,
135-137 Stephendale Rd,
Fulham, London SW6 2PR
Tel   +44 (0)20 7731 7823
Web   www.thesandsend.co.uk

Entry 430 Map 15

London

The Carpenter's Arms
Hammersmith

An unexpected find: an extraordinary distillation of gastropub and local in a charming backwater between King Street and the Great West Road (aka the A4). The glorious single bar has fashionably bare boards, plain tables, a fire that glows on chilly days and doors giving onto a sheltered little garden. And it's done well for itself, being a popular spot for a discerning mix while managing (just) to hold on to its pubby feel, in spite of the emphasis on dining. An ever-changing seasonal menu sees inventive dishes popping up every day. So you get seared scallops with butterbeans, pine nuts and saffron; rib-eye steak with fries and Café de Paris butter; apple tart 'fine' with nutmeg ice cream. Service is exuberant and warm, the atmosphere is laid back. It's a satisfying place to dine.

Meals	12pm-2.30pm (12.30pm-3.30pm Sat; 12.30pm-4pm Sun); 6.30pm-10pm (from 7pm Sat; 7.30pm-9.30pm Sun). Main courses £9.75-£16.95.
Closed	Open all day.
Directions	Off King Street between Ravenscourt Park & Stamford Brook.

Simon Cherry & Matt Jacomb
The Carpenter's Arms,
91 Black Lion Lane,
Hammersmith, London W6 9BG
Tel +44 (0)208 741 8386
Web www.carpentersarmsw6.co.uk

Entry 431 Map 15

London

Cumberland Arms
Hammersmith

The Cumberland hits the mark, when Olympia's full on. It's also a favourite with the locals. Old planked floors and wooden panelling, mellow furniture and candles in the evening: beyond the exuberant baskets and the polished exterior there's a lovely down-to-earth feel. A treat to sit next to the fire with a big glass of wine (many to choose from, each enticingly described) or a pint of Timothy Taylor's (four hand pumps on the bar). You don't have to eat here but it would be a shame not to: the food is rustic, tasty, affordable, the specials change daily and the staff are friendly. The mackerel fillet en escabeche is subtly soused, and comes with a spicy potato and spring onion salad; great Tuscan sausages too, and oxtail casserole with gremolata. Outside is a handful of tables; a small park at the back adds a leafy feel.

Meals	12pm-3pm; 6pm-10.30pm; all day Sun. Main courses £10-£15.50; sandwiches £8-£9.
Closed	Open all day.
Directions	Nearest tube: Kensington (Olympia)

Richard & George Manners & Craig Fleeton
Cumberland Arms,
29 North End Road, London W14 8SZ
Tel +44 (0)20 7371 6806
Web www.thecumberlandarmspub.co.uk

Entry 432 Map 15

The Victoria
London

On a leafy, secluded street in the smart suburb of Richmond with a church and primary school as neighbours, this has been a well established pub for many years, but owners Greg Bellamy and Paul Merrett have swept through the inside and created two stylish bars and a modern conservatory restaurant. The atmosphere is busy, purposeful and fun: find wooden floors, some open brickwork and sofas to flop on while you decide on the bar menu (muffin with smoked salmon, Jersey rock oysters) or if you are really hungry, cured Teruel ham with pan-fried manouri cheese, cumin rubbed lamb loin, then maybe greengage crumble with baked egg custard. The wine list, chosen by Olly Smith, bursts with passion and helpful notes, so it would be a shame not to allow yourself to be led; in an adjacent building there are simple, modern bedrooms, with white walls, light carpets and splashes of colour from pictures and cushions. Bathrooms are smart, fully tiled and well lit. You are within striking distance of a lovely stroll through Sheen Common or Richmond Park, and ten minutes from Twickenham if rugby is your passion.

Rooms	7: 5 doubles, 2 twins/doubles. £115. Singles £105.
Meals	12.30pm-2.30pm; 6pm-10pm. Bar food all day. Main courses £10-£18; bar meals £5-£10.
Closed	Open all day.
Directions	Train: Richmond to Mortlake. Buses: 33, 337, 493. Private car park at rear of hotel.

Paul Merrett & Greg Bellamy
The Victoria,
10 West Temple Sheen,
Richmond, London SW14 7RT
Tel   +44 (0)20 8876 4238
Web   www.thevictoria.net

Entry 433 Map 15

London

Spencer Arms
Putney

They fly the Slow Food flag here – with passion. And it's all so delicious: the roast rainbow trout, the rib-eye steak, the ham hock risotto, the 'English tapas' (venison carpaccio, potted shrimps). The lamb is from Cornwall because it tastes nicer and they love their chutneys; take some home. The stage for all this good humour is a pretty Victorian tavern with a big open room of sturdy tables and painted boards, a blackboard of wines and a sofa by the fire. Add bookshelves and games chest, chilled music for quieter moments, tailormade orders for unfaddy children and cider punch with calvados and you have one amazing place. The staff are brilliant and the food is great value. Finish it off with a walk on Barnes Common.

Meals	12pm-2.30pm (4pm Sat & Sun); 6.30pm-10pm (9pm Sun). Main courses £8.95-£14.95; bar meals & appetisers from £2.95.
Closed	Open all day.
Directions	Nearest rail: Putney; Barnes. Bus no. 22 directly to door.

Jamie Sherriff
Spencer Arms,
237 Lower Richmond Road,
Putney, London SW15 1HJ
Tel   +44 (0)20 8788 0640
Web   www.thespencerarms.co.uk

Entry 434 Map 15

London

Cat's Back
Putney

Down a backstreet, away from waterside development, a gem. There's an appealing eccentricity here, among the cosy-red walls, mix 'n' match tables, African masks, disco glitter ball, portrait of Audrey Hepburn and all manner of flotsam and jetsam – presents from regulars and treasures picked up on the family's travels. It's mellow and fun and everyone and his dog pops by – locals, builders, business folk. At night, moody candlelight, chilled music and good food. The wines are better than the beers but you may expect excellent organic meats and vegetables – try shrimp tempura with oyster sauce and roast shoulder of pork, finish with tiramisu. Coloured lights in the stairwell lead to a lovely sash-windowed restaurant and a small but lavish private dining room beyond. Friendly and much-loved.

Meals	11am-10.30pm. Main courses £8.50-£11.50; bar meals from £4.50.
Closed	Open all day.
Directions	Nearest tube: Putney.

Roger Martin
Cat's Back,
86 Point Pleasant,
Putney, London SW18 1PP
Tel   +44 (0)20 8877 0818
Web   www.thecatsback.com

Entry 435 Map 15

London

The Ship
Wandsworth

Drinking a pint of Young's Special next to a concrete works doesn't sound too enticing, but the riverside terrace by Wandsworth Bridge is a dreamy spot. Chilly evenings still draw the crowds to this super old pub, cosy inside with its warm-red and sage-green walls, and its conservatory with central chopping-board table and wood-burning stove. No music, just happy chat, newspapers, tall blackboards and fresh flowers. Chef Peter Murray sources fresh ingredients to create his seasonal menus which may include crispy pork belly braised oriental style with pak choi, potato spaghetti rösti and star anise jus, or tian of Portobello mushrooms, red onions, mixed peppers and herb cream sauce. The Ship opens its arms to all, there are live music and quiz nights, and families merrily gather in summer.

Meals	12pm–4pm; 6pm–10pm.
	12pm–10pm in bar.
	Main courses £9.95–£19.95.
Closed	Open all day.
Directions	Nearest rail: Wandsworth.

Oisin Rogers
The Ship,
41 Jews Row,
Wandsworth, London SW18 1TB
Tel   +44 (0)20 8870 9667
Web   www.theship.co.uk

Entry 436 Map 15

London

The Fentiman Arms
Kennington

Toffee-coloured walls, a relaxed mood, well-thumbed books and games: a decent place to nurse a hangover on a Saturday morning, along with the Fentiman brunch menu. This busy pub, designed by proprietor Rupert Clevely's wife Jo, echoes the cosmopolitan themes and earthy colours of their beloved South Africa. Smart regulars gather over pints of Bombardier and a menu that stretches beyond the confines of brunch. Chicken liver parfait with red onion marmalade, braised pork belly with apricot and thyme potato rösti, and date and walnut slice with rum ice cream are devoured in cosy corners amongst fat velvet cushions and suede bolsters. The upstairs function room, with high ceilings and large windows, is a popular place for big gatherings; so too is the trendy outdoor terrace. Arrive early on Sundays.

Meals	12pm–3pm (4pm Sat & Sun);
	7pm–10pm (6pm–9pm Sun).
	Main courses £7.95–£15.95.
Closed	Open all day.
Directions	Nearest tubes: Oval; Vauxhall.

Rupert Clevely
The Fentiman Arms,
64 Fentiman Road,
Kennington, London SW8 1LA
Tel   +44 (0)20 7793 9796
Web   www.geronimo-inns.co.uk/thefentimanarms

Entry 437 Map 15

London

The Garrison Public House
Bermondsey

Gastropub veterans Clive Watson and Adam White have taken on an old boozer, kept the engraved glass windows and remodelled the rest into a light, airy, bare-boarded space. The furniture is silver-sprayed, lamps and objects fill every cranny. Fresh food, from apricots to Orkney mussels, arrives from the market down the road. A glass of rioja or a bottle of St Peter's goes down beautifully with rib-eye steak with watercress and roquefort butter, or seabass with crab and baked potatoes. And the pub is open daily for breakfast. The kitchen is open, staff are laid-back, decibels are high, tables are crammed. Forget hushed conversation: the place bounces with bonhomie, and is more eaterie than pub. Do dinner and a movie – there's a cinema downstairs for private hire, and public screenings every Sunday.

London

Anchor & Hope
Southwark

One of the first bistropubs to champion below-stairs food. Come for some of the plainest yet gutsiest cooking in London; chef Jonathan Jones attracts droves. The food is described as 'English bistro', and give or take the odd foreign exception (a chorizo broth, a melting pommes dauphinoise), it is just that. The menu is adventurous yet striking in its simplicity: warm snail and bacon salad, smoked herring with fennel and orange, slip soles with anchovy butter, rabbit with pearl barley and sherry, homemade liqueurs, blackberry merangue. The beer comes from Charles Wells, the wine list has 18 by the glass. Staff are youthful – and may be rushed. Décor is 1930s sober and the restaurant area glows by candlelight. No bookings (bar Sunday lunch) and massively popular, but arrive early or late and you may get a table.

Meals	12pm-3.30pm; 6pm-10pm Mon-Fri; 12.30pm-4pm; 6pm-10pm Sat & Sun (9.30pm Sun). Main courses £11.40-£15.90; lunch menu from £9.50.
Closed	Open all day.
Directions	Nearest tube: London Bridge.

Meals	12pm-2.30pm; 6pm-10.30pm; Sun 2pm (bookings only). Main courses £10-£20; Sunday lunch £30.
Closed	Mon lunch & Sun eve. Open all day Tues-Sat.
Directions	Nearest tubes: Southwark; Waterloo.

Clive Watson & Adam White
The Garrison Public House,
99 Bermondsey Street,
Bermondsey, London SE1 3XB
Tel   +44 (0)20 7089 9355
Web   www.thegarrison.co.uk

Entry 438 Map 15

Robert Shaw
Anchor & Hope,
36 The Cut,
Southwark,
London SE1 8LP
Tel   +44 (0)20 7928 9898

Entry 439 Map 15

Greenwich Union
Greenwich

Master brewer Alastair Hook has turned this Greenwich boozer into a shrine to his lagers and beers. The golds and browns of the interior reflect the hues of the ales he painstakingly creates at the nearby Meantime Brewery; the Raspberry Wheat, London Pale Ale and Wheat beers slip down so easily that Sainsbury's has made them part of their range. (If you're not sure which pairs with which food, helpful staff behind the bar will give you a taster.) And this quirky little pub is a great place to eat, the chef willing to concoct tapas at short notice. He is also a dab hand at roasted chicken breast with sweet shallots, and chestnut gnocchi with porcini mushrooms. Sandwiches include homemade 'piadina' (flat bread from Romagna) served with brie and rocket salad. All are welcome, from families to dogs.

Meals	12pm-4pm (4.30pm weekends); 5.30pm-10pm (9pm Sun). Main courses £7.90-£14.90; bar meals £3.95-£10.50.
Closed	Open all day.
Directions	Exit Greenwich station, left & 2nd right (Royal Hill), pub on right.

Andrew Ward
Greenwich Union,
56 Royal Hill, Greenwich,
London SE10 8RT
Tel   +44 (0)20 8692 6258
Web   www.greenwichunion.com

Entry 440 Map 15

The Gun
Docklands

It's fiendishly difficult to find, but persevere. The front room, dominated by a dark panelled bar, is hugely atmospheric — a planked floor, settles, battered leather sofas, the smell of truffles in the air. The restaurant area is pristine, and a loose nautical theme runs through the prints and paintings. Bag a table by the fire; settle in till the sun sets over the river, on a gorgeously candlelit terrace. There's a reassuring selection of pub favourites — fish pie, beef shin burger with fat chips — in the bar while the restaurant menu is fiercely modern: pan-fried haddock with scallops and a champagne velouté; fillet of veal with dumplings, spinach purée and baby morels. Weekend brunch from 11.30am to 1pm is hugely popular — do book; Portuguese barbecues trumpet Billingsgate fish. Amazing.

Meals	12pm-3pm (11.30am-4pm Sat & Sun); 6pm-10.30pm (9.30pm Sun). Main courses £11.95-£18; bar meals £4.50-£12.50.
Closed	Open all day.
Directions	Just off A1206 (Prestons Road); turn into Managers Street; right turn at the end.

Tom & Ed Martin
The Gun,
27 Coldharbour,
Docklands, London E14 9NS
Tel   +44 (0)20 7515 5222
Web   www.thegundocklands.com

Entry 441 Map 15

London

The Easton
Clerkenwell

Home from home for the Amnesty International crowd, whose headquarters are down the street, this corner pub may look like the classic London tavern but inside it is airy and modern. Bare boards, plain windows, a long bar topped with fresh flowers, funky wallpaper at the far end… drinkers and diners mingle over pints of Timothy Taylor and global house-white and wonder what to pick from the ever-changing chalk board. The kitchen goes in for rustic portions of chargrilled lemon and thyme pork chops; roast tomato and chorizo stew; Springbok sausages with spring onion champ, braised red cabbage and pancetta gravy. It's a godsend for the area, with pub tables spilling onto the pavement and a genuinely local feel. Staff are charming – even on Fridays when the drinkers descend, and hearty dishes are replaced with tapas.

Meals	12.30pm-3pm (1pm-4pm Sun); 6.30pm-10pm (9.30pm Sun). Main courses £9-£16.
Closed	Open all day.
Directions	Nearest tube: Farringdon.

Jeremy Sutton & Andrew Veevers
The Easton,
22 Easton Street, Clerkenwell,
London WC1X 0DS
Tel   +44 (0)20 7278 7608
Web   www.theeastonpub.co.uk

Entry 442 Map 15

London

Coach & Horses
Clerkenwell

Gone are the days when the Edwardian pub was a corner boozer; now it fills with a media crowd. Savour a pint of London Pride in the small panelled bar as you check out a blackboard that lists some of the best gastropub food in London. British dishes are devised with enthusiasm and ingredients burst with flavour: venison and partridge terrine with chutney; sea bream with lentils, fennel and salsa verde; quince and almond tart with clotted cream. Rare-breed meats are reared at Elwy Valley in Wales, fish is delivered daily; there's a good selection of charcuterie and cheese too. The bar specialises in malt whiskies and attentive staff lay on nibbles of toasted pumpkin seeds in keeping with the pub's logo, a pumpkin pulled by four mice. Note: most tables have a reserved sign on them on busy nights, so do book.

Meals	12pm-3pm; 6pm-10pm. Main courses £10.75-£14; bar meals £4-£8.
Closed	Open all day. Closed Sat lunch & Sun eve.
Directions	Nearest tube: Farringdon; Chancery Lane.

Giles Webster
Coach & Horses,
26-28 Ray Street, Clerkenwell,
London EC1R 3DJ
Tel   +44 (0)20 7278 8990
Web   www.thecoachandhorses.com

Entry 443 Map 15

Jerusalem Tavern
Clerkenwell

There's so much atmosphere here you could bottle it up and take it home – along with one of the beers. Old Clerkenwell has reinvented itself and the quaint little 1720 tavern epitomises all that is best about the place. Its name is new, acquired when the St Peter's Brewery of Suffolk took it over and stocked it with their ales and fruit beers. Step in to a reincarnation of a nooked and crannied interior, candlelit at night with a winter fire; come before six if you'd like a table. Lunchtime food is simple and English – bangers and mash, a roast, a fine platter of cheese – with ingredients from Smithfield Market down the road. Staff are friendly and know their beer, and the full range of St Peter's ales is all there, from the cask or the specially designed bottle. Heaven.

Meals	12pm-3pm; 5pm-9.30pm (Tues-Thurs). Main courses £4.50-£8.50.
Closed	Open all day. Closed Sat & Sun.
Directions	Nearest tube/rail: Farringdon.

Colin Cordy
Jerusalem Tavern,
55 Britton Street,
Clerkenwell, London EC1M 5UQ
Tel   +44 (0)20 7490 4281
Web   www.stpetersbrewery.co.uk

Entry 444 Map 15

The White Swan
Holborn

It had spent the previous ten years as the Mucky Duck; then, in 2003, brothers Tom and Ed transformed the old journalists' den. The bar evokes a classic, cramped, city pub feel; at plain tables on fashionably unpolished boards, City traders enjoy real ales and fine wines. Upstairs is a smart restaurant with some unusually good modern European cooking ranging from the robust (roast leg of rabbit with tomato compote, herb dumplings and mustard cream sauce) to the subtle (roast halibut with Savoy cabbage, clams and white wine sauce). Cheese and wine lists are encyclopaedic and regulars get lockers to store their unfinished spirits. The daily bar menu takes in pub classics, perhaps Denham Estate pork sausages with mash and onion gravy, open steak sandwich, brilliant fish and chips.

Meals	12pm-3pm; 6pm-10pm. Main courses £15-£18; bar meals from £8-£15.
Closed	Open all day Mon-Fri. Private parties only Sat & Sun.
Directions	Nearest tube: Chancery Lane.

Tom & Ed Martin
The White Swan,
108 Fetter Lane, Holborn,
London EC4A 1ES
Tel   +44 (0)20 7242 9696
Web   www.thewhiteswanlondon.com

Entry 445 Map 15

London

The Eagle
Clerkenwell

Still mighty, after all these years. No tablecloths, no reservations, just delicious food ordered from the bar. With its real ales and decent choice of wines, the appeal is as much for drinkers as for diners and, in spite of the rustic appeal of scuffed floors, worn leather chairs, mix-and-match crockery, background Latin music and art gallery upstairs, the Eagle's reputation rests on its edible, seasonal bounty. The long bar counter is dominated by a stainless steel area at which Mediterranean vegetables, cuttlefish and pancetta are prepared. Pasta, risotto, peasant soups, spicy steak sandwiches… and vibrant Spanish hustle and bustle. Worth the trek to get here.

London

Drapers Arms
Islington

The name implies a drapery connection, but you'll find few flounces at this new gastropub in Islington. Ben Maschler (son of famed food critic Fay) is a partner. Reborn in May 2009, the pared-back, opened-up Georgian building has high ceilings, bare boards and an eclectic mix of old tables and chairs; there's a relaxed, community vibe. The kitchen, under Karl Goward (one-time head chef at the legendary St John restaurants in Smithfield and Spitalfields) fits the mood and ethic to a tee. Gutsy no-nonsense British dishes appear on twice-daily changing menus: grilled ox tongue with split peas and ham hock; grilled quail with braised chard and aïoli; and lentils with roast shallots, roast butternut squash and goat's curd. Hand-pump ales, enterprising wines, a cooly decorative dining room upstairs and a courtyard garden top a super-charged act.

Meals	12.30pm-3pm (3.30pm Sat & Sun); 6.30pm-10.30pm. Main courses £7.50-£14.50.
Closed	Open all day. Closed Sun eve.
Directions	Nearest tube: Farringdon.

Meals	12pm-3pm (4pm Sun); 6pm-10.30pm (9.30pm Sun). Main courses £9.50-£15.
Closed	Open all day.
Directions	Nearest tubes: Highbury & Islington; Angel.

Michael Belben
The Eagle,
159 Farringdon Road,
Clerkenwell,
London EC1R 3AL
Tel   +44 (0)20 7837 1353

🏃 🖾 🐕‍🦺 ♊ 🍸

Entry 446 Map 15

Ben Maschler
Drapers Arms,
44 Barnsbury Street,
Islington, London N1 1ER
Tel   +44 (0)20 7619 0348
Web   www.thedrapersarms.com

🏃 🖾 🐕‍🦺 🍸 📶

Entry 447 Map 4

London

Charles Lamb Public House
Islington

Everyone's welcome at Camille and Hobby's small pub, hidden down a tangle of Georgian streets behind Camden Passage. It's a dear little place that keeps its pubby feel, with two unshowy bar rooms and well-kept ales on hand pump. So the blackboard menu – fresh, short, ever-changing – is the biggest surprise. Eat informally at plainly set tables in either bar, on serrano ham with celeriac remoulade, or Lancashire hot pot. (Camille is French so there may be a crispy duck confit too.) Best of all is Sunday's all-day roast beef and Yorkshire pudding with all the trimmings. It's brilliant home-cooked food, but you need to get here early: tables cannot be booked. Walk it all off with a stroll along the bosky banks of the Regent's Canal, and seek out the house where essayist and poet Charles Lamb lived, two streets away.

Meals	12pm-3pm Wed-Fri (4pm Sat); 6pm-9.30pm (12pm-6pm Sun). Main courses £9-£12; Sunday roast £10.50-£12.
Closed	Open all day (open from 4pm Mon & Tues).
Directions	Nearest tube: Angel.

Hobby & Camille Limon
Charles Lamb Public House,
16 Elia Street,
Islington, London N1 8DE

Tel   +44 (0)20 7837 5040
Web   www.thecharleslambpub.com

Entry 448 Map 15

London

The Duke of Cambridge
Islington

Thanks to pioneering Geetie Singh, 'organic' and 'sustainable' are the watchwords at London's first-ever organic pub, and British-rustic is the style. Wines, beers, spirits are certified organic and they buy as locally as they can to cut down on food miles. Most of the beers are brewed in nearby Shoreditch, meat comes from two farms, all fish is Marine Conservation Society-approved; impeccable produce and menus that change twice a day. It's a sprawling airy space with a comfortable, easy atmosphere; you could be alone happily here. Sit back and take your fill of lentil and pancetta soup, mussels with chorizo, fennel and chives, game pie with braised red cabbage, venison steak with redcurrant jus, crusty bread, fruity olive oil, quince crumble and cream – in here, or in the large restaurant. Justifiably rammed.

Meals	12.30pm-3pm (3.30pm Sat & Sun); 6.30pm-10.30pm (10pm Sun). Main courses £11-£19.
Closed	Open all day.
Directions	Nearest tube: Angel.

Geetie Singh
The Duke of Cambridge,
30 St Peter's Street,
Islington, London N1 8JT

Tel   +44 (0)20 7359 3066
Web   www.dukeorganic.co.uk

Entry 449 Map 15

London

The Lansdowne
Primrose Hill

Worth crossing postcodes for. It's buzzing, laid-back, open-plan and atmospherically lit, with big wooden tables and dark blue décor – and manages, downstairs, to keep its pubby feel. Upstairs is an elegant and charming 60-seat restaurant where a cool crowd is treated to some adventurous food – homemade pasta dishes, sea bass en papillotte, belly of pork with mash and shallots, juicy rib-eye steak with fat chips and béarnaise. Though the serious dining goes on up here, you can also eat down where the decibels are high, the atmosphere shambolic and everyone loves the pizzas (kids included). There are two draught ales and one real cider, but really this is a wine, lager and olives place. Outside in summer is a little oasis to which you can retreat and leave the city behind.

London

The Engineer
Primrose Hill

Isambard Kingdom Brunel once had an office here, today the place is run by a painter and an actress. Behind the half-stuccoed 1850 edifice lies a cheerful, friendly gastropub with a smart bohemian feel and a reputation for food. It is particularly strong on fish cooked with a touch of the Mediterranean – sea bass with minted couscous and aubergine relish, say – but there are organic steaks with béarnaise, fat homemade chips and creamy and chocolatey desserts to love too. Wines look to the New World and beer is excellent. Eat up or down: the front bar is relaxed, bright and buzzing, the restaurant upstairs has white plates on white cloths, mirrors in gilt frames and art for sale. In summer, the large lush garden catches the sun. The service is often praised, the parking is easy.

Meals	12pm-3pm; 6pm-10pm (9.30pm Sun); pizzas all day. Main courses £11.50-£16; bar meals £5-£7.50.
Closed	Open all day.
Directions	Nearest tube: Chalk Farm.

Meals	9am-3pm (4pm Sat & Sun); 7pm-10.30pm (10pm Sun). Main courses £12.50-£20..
Closed	Open all day.
Directions	Nearest tube: Camden Town.

Amanda Pritchett
The Lansdowne,
90 Gloucester Avenue,
Primrose Hill, London NW1 8HX

Tel +44 (0)20 7483 0409
Web www.thelansdownepub.co.uk

Entry 450 Map 15

Eddie Francis
The Engineer,
65 Gloucester Avenue,
Primrose Hill, London NW1 8JH

Tel +44 (0)20 7722 0950
Web www.the-engineer.com

Entry 451 Map 15

London

Dartmouth Arms
Highgate

Sitting unobtrusively in a Highgate side street, the Dartmouth Arms may look smartly unexceptional but inside is another story. There's personality in the front bar, wooden tables are junk-shop simple and the flat-screen TV attracts fans for the footie. The back room, where champagne bottles hang from a chandelier, is a more peaceful space. Come for three perfectly kept cask ales, loads of small-producer ciders, several wines by the glass and a modern British menu displayed on boards – landlord Nick is passionate about food and beer. Expect something for everyone here: wild mushroom soup, sausages with tomato sauce and mash, steaks, Sunday roasts, croque monsieur, generous salads. The background music is noisy at times, there are quizzes on Tuesdays and an ever-lively crowd.

Meals	11am-3pm; 6pm-10pm (10am-10pm Sat & Sun). Main courses from £7.50.
Closed	Open all day.
Directions	Nearest tubes: Tufnell Park, Kentish Town.

Nick May
Dartmouth Arms,
35 York Rise, Dartmouth Park,
Highgate, London NW5 1SP
Tel +44 (0)20 7485 3267
Web www.dartmoutharms.co.uk

Entry 452 Map 15

London

Holly Bush
Hampstead

Down a Hampstead cul-de-sac, stables once owned by painter George Romney have become a hugely loved pub. A labyrinth of corridors leads to cosy corners, painted settles and big tables set with board games and pints of Harveys Sussex. Ale rules at the Holly Bush, where the chef cooks not with wine but with beer. Through the open kitchen, the aromas of beef and Harveys pie prove a temptation for drinkers to become diners. Adnams rarebit or a pint of prawns – followed by hot chocolate, marmalade and malt whisky fondant – is intended to educate the beer lover's palate. Dishes are seasonal and fresh, with game and organic meats from Winchelsea and a superb selection of English cheeses. Upstairs in the dining room, all pistachio walls and wooden floors, the celebration of all things British continues.

Meals	12pm-10pm (9pm Sun). Main courses £8-£15; bar meals £3.50-£6.
Closed	Open all day.
Directions	Nearest tube: Hampstead.

Jesus Anorve
Holly Bush,
22 Holly Mount,
Hampstead, London NW3 6SG
Tel +44 (0)20 7435 2892
Web www.hollybushpub.com

Entry 453 Map 15

London

Worth a visit

454 Portobello Gold 95-97 Portobello Road,
Notting Hill W11 2QB +44 (0)20 7460 4910
A gastro-hotel: bar, restaurant, internet café and groovy place to stay. In the bar are tiled floors, an open fire, exhibitions of photography and music on Sunday evenings; at the back, a restaurant with a retractable glass roof and jungle planting.

455 The Fat Badger 310 Portobello Road,
North Kensington W10 5TA
+44 (0)20 8969 4500
At the scruffy end of Notting Hill, a good-natured bohemian pub with beaten-up leather chesterfields and funky chandeliers. Works well as a boozer and a place for a plate of something tasty — pork pie and pickle, roast partridge and red cabbage.

456 Havelock Tavern 57 Masbro Road,
Shepherd's Bush W14 0LS
+44 (0)20 7603 5374
No music, no fuss, just plain floorboards and tables squeezed around the main bar, luscious smells from the hatch (the menu changes twice daily!) and a happy, noisy, friendly crowd. As cheap as chips (rather good ones) down the backstreets of Brook Green.

457 The Princess 217 Uxbridge Road,
Shepherd's Bush W12 9DT
+44 (0)20 8749 5886
Revamped Victorian gin palace that has been creating waves across the capital. An impressive interior, robust cooking, exceptional wines — and an artisans' food market on Saturdays.

458 The White Horse 1-3 Parson's Green,
Fulham SW6 4UL +44 (0)20 7731 2183
'The Sloany Pony' may be a hotbed of Fulhamites but it's also reputed to have the best-kept beers in Europe. Comfy sofas, log fires, slatted blinds, a big terrace, and a menu that suggests the best accompanying liquor.

459 The Idle Hour 62 Railway Side,
Barnes SW13 0PQ +44 (0)20 8878 5555
A small haven tucked away down a little alley with a fresh, contemporary décor and a predominantly organic menu. Sundays are legendary, with a winter fire and roasts brought to the table.

460 The Fox & Hounds 66 Latchmere Road,
Battersea SW11 2JU +44 (0)20 7924 5483
A bright little corner pub in Battersea, a foodie destination and a shrine to the golden brew. Mediterranean-style dishes flow from the open-to-view kitchen; a great atmosphere, and a garden for summer.

461 Fox and Anchor 115 Charterhouse Street,
Clerkenwell EC1M 6AA +44 (0)20 7250 1300
The former dawn-drinking hole for Smithfield market has become a gastropub hotel with boutique bedrooms and robust English dishes (prawns by the pint, steak and oyster pie). Ale comes in tankards in the unspoilt Victorian bar.

462 The Gunmakers 13 Eyre Street Hill,
Clerkenwell EC1R 5ET +44 (0)20 7278 1022
In cool Clerkenwell, low ceilings, bare boards and good cheer fill this tiny, unspoilt pub commemorating Hiram Maxin (who produced the first automatic machine gun nearby). Blackboard menus and Wells Bombardier please a mixed bunch.

463 The Peasant 240 St John Street,
Islington EC1V 4PH +44 (0)20 7336 7726
A Victorian gin palace with a reputation for splendid food, wines, beers and cocktails. Tapas, mezze and the daily papers downstairs; pretty restaurant up. Brilliantly positioned for antique shops. the Design Centre and Sadler's Wells.

London

Worth a visit

464 The Albion 10 Thornhill Road,
Islington N1 1HW +44 (0)20 7607 7450
Hidden in leafy, well-to-do Islington,
this wisteria-clad Georgian jewel has
winter fires, period detail and dark
woods… but the big walled garden is the
real draw. Food is important too, and
includes spotted dick and treacle tart.

465 The Narrow 44 Narrow Street,
Limehouse E14 8DJ +44 (0)20 7592 7950
Gordon Ramsay's first pub, in an
Edwardian dockmaster's house on a
gorgeous bend of the Thames. Good
range of real ales and ciders and the best
of gutsy British food. Sensibly short
menu and reasonable prices.

466 The Junction Tavern 101 Fortess Road,
Kentish Town NW5 1AG
+44 (0)20 7485 9400
From the open-to-view kitchen flows
food that is modern European and wide-
ranging. While half the pub is restaurant,
the rest is old-fashioned bar, serving over
ten real ales a week and beer festivals
throughout the year. A joy in laid-back
Kentish Town.

467 The Flask 77 Highgate West Hill,
Highgate N6 6BU +44 (0)20 8348 7346
This Hogarthian warren (he stayed here)
may be 350 years old but its candlelit
crannies have a stylish feel, and all
the ghosts are friendly! Much loved,
mobbed in summer and right by
Hampstead Heath.

468 The Bull 13 North Hill, Highgate N6 4AB
+44 (0)845 456 5033
The plain listed Georgian façade gives
way to an inspired interior for rustic-
simple dishes with huge depth of flavour.
A chic retreat in Highgate – and a
vintage American pool table for a bit
of fun.

Manchester

The White Hart
Lydgate

Decay was setting in at this 18th-century
ale house overlooking Saddleworth Moor
when Charles Brierley took it over a decade
or so ago. It has since been transformed
into a charming restaurant-pub. Relax in
the bar with a glass of Timothy Taylor's
Landlord, toast your toes by the wood-
burning stove and admire the décor – a
sleek backdrop for British cheeses, platters
of oysters, 'Saddleworth' sausages (five,
with five different kinds of mash). Move to
the restaurant, where delicacy combines
with robustness in some unusually fine
cooking: roast pork belly with black
pudding and mustard mash, sea bass with
smoked bacon and mussel risotto, braised
beef with horseradish dumplings. This is a
beautiful village and, on a fine day, you can
stretch your eyes all the way to the distant
Cheshire Plain.

Meals	12pm-2.30pm; 6pm-9.30pm (1pm-7.30pm Sun). Main courses £12.50-£19; sandwiches £6.
Closed	Open all day.
Directions	From Oldham east on A669 for 2.5 miles. Before hill right onto A6050; 50 yds on left.

	Charles Brierley The White Hart, 51 Stockport Road, Lydgate, Oldham, OL4 4JJ
Tel	+44 (0)1457 872566
Web	www.thewhitehart.co.uk

Entry 469 Map 12

Manchester

Worth a visit

470 The Swan 1 The Square, Dobcross,
Oldham OL3 5AA +44 (0)1457 873451
Slabbed stone floors and colourwashed
ceilings pitch like a dinghy in a storm;
rooms warmed by big fires hive off in all
directions from the lobby bar at this
Moors pub on a lovely village square.

471 Circus Tavern 86 Portland Street,
Manchester M1 4GX +44 (0)161 236 5818
In the city centre, one of Britain's
smallest pubs, thrice as deep as wide,
with a tiny under-stairs bar and two
magnificent, panelled roomettes. Twenty
punters (supping Tetleys Bitter) is a
crowd here.

472 Marble Arch 73 Rochdale Road,
Manchester M4 4HY +44 (0)161 832 5914
Marvellous tiled interior, with mosaic
friezes high up in the vaulted roof
and a deceptively sloping floor. A
microbrewery at the rear produces an
enticing array of organic vegan beers.

473 Arden Arms 23 Millgate, Stockport SK1 2LX
+44 (0)161 4802185
A superb tiled lobby bar, hidden snug,
real fires and sublime Edwardian wood
and glass bar, in the shadow of ASDA. The
lunchtime food is of restaurant quality.

Merseyside

The Philharmonic
Liverpool

The Phil was built by Liverpool brewers
Robert Cain & Co in the style of a
gentlemen's club: a place for bodily
refreshment after the aesthetic excitements
of the Philharmonic Hall opposite. There's
ornate Victorian extravagance at every turn,
high ceilings, elaborate embellishment,
etched glass; the gents is decked in marble
and mosaic, its porcelain fittings of historical
importance. Sweep through the columned
entrance into the imposing central bar, gawp
at the scale. Beyond, a succession of small
rooms and snugs separated by mahogany
partitions, then a Grand Lounge with a
stately frieze and table service for lunch:
settle down to baked potatoes or fish and
chips. Very popular with students, the
Philharmonic is a great pub serving
excellent beers, wines and whiskies and a
huge dose of cheer.

Meals	10am-9.30pm.
	Main courses £3.95-£10.
Closed	Open all day.
Directions	City centre; between the cathedrals at corner of Hardman Street.

Marie-Louise Wong
The Philharmonic, 36 Hope
Street, Liverpool, L1 9BX
Tel   +44 (0)1517 072837

Entry 474 Map 11

Norfolk

Gin Trap Inn
Ringstead

An actor and a lawyer run this old English Inn. Steve and Cindy left London for the quiet life and haven't stopped since, adding a conservatory dining room at the back and giving the garden a haircut. The Gin Trap dates to 1667, while the horse chestnut tree that shades the front took root in the 19th century; a conker championship is in the offing. A smart whitewashed exterior gives way to a beamed locals' bar with a crackling fire and the original dining room in Farrow & Ball hues. There are fortnightly quiz nights on Sundays but most come for the food: Norfolk mussels, organic burgers, beer-battered haddock and chips, poached winter fruits; walkers will find great comfort here. Ringstead – a pretty village lost in the country – is two miles inland from the coastal road, Sandringham is close and fabulous beaches beckon.

Lots of landlords grow their own or buy food in from allotments. They buy from their own customers, err only rarely beyond their immediate areas in search of the best and are eager to promote the latest local brew. This is what keeps them alive and competitive; they work hard to earn our loyalty.

Meals	12pm–2pm (2.30pm Sat & Sun); 6pm–9pm (9.30pm Fri & Sat). Main courses £9–£20; sandwiches (lunch) from £5.50.
Closed	2.30pm–6pm. Open all day in summer.
Directions	North from King's Lynn on A149. Ringstead signed right in Heacham. Pub on right in village.

Steve Knowles & Cindy Cook
Gin Trap Inn,
6 High Street, Ringstead,
Hunstanton PE36 5JU
Tel   +44 (0)1485 525264
Web   www.gintrapinn.co.uk

Entry 475 Map 9

The Dabbling Duck
Great Massingham

After a tireless campaign by the villagers to buy their local in 2006, the neglected Rose & Crown became the Dabbling Duck and the pub was revived with panache. The duck egg-blue inn stands prettily by the green and… the dabbling-duck pond. Business has been brisk, the draw being the wonderful food and the beers from the barrel – well-kept Adnams and Woodforde's. As for the mood, it is warmly endearing. The bar has been cut from a single slice of ancient Norfolk oak, there are high-backed settles by a blazing log fire, sober hues, rug-strewn floors, chunky candles on scrubbed tables, and shelves lined with books and board games. Views are to the village. The food includes bowls of Brancaster mussels, roast sea bass with caper butter, sirloin steaks from the Holkham Estate, local-rabbit casserole. The care and attention to detail extends to gorgeous bedrooms with big brass beds, colourful cushions and throws, plasma screens, Roberts radios and wood-floored bathrooms; homemade cookies and fresh coffee on tap. All this, 20 minutes from the beach and the bird-rich saltmarshes. Superb!

Rooms	3 twins/doubles. £80. Singles £55.
Meals	12pm-2.30pm (3pm Sun);
	6.30pm-9pm. No food Sun eve.
	Main courses £8.75-£15.95.
Closed	Open all day (from 10.30am).
Directions	Village signed south off A148 at
	Harpley between King's Lynn &
	Fakenham.

The Dabbling Duck,
11 Abbey Road, Great Massingham,
King's Lynn PE32 2HN
Tel   +44 (0)1485 520827
Web   www.thedabblingduck.co.uk

The Rose & Crown
Snettisham

Roses round the door and twisting passages within, it is gloriously English. Holkham sausages, mash and onion gravy and gammon, eggs and hand cut chips should please the traditionalists; more adventurous diners can tuck into smoked haddock chowder, whole plaice with curly kale and salsa verde, and white chocolate and coconut brûlée. It's great value. In spite of 30 wines on the list, half available by the glass, the Rose and Crown is still proud to be a pub; fine beers on hand pump and a hands-on feel. The walled garden was once the village bowling green and children will enjoy the wooden play fort. Inside are a warren of rooms with low ceilings and uneven floors, old beams and log fires, a family-friendly garden room and a flurry of rather stylish bedrooms, the quietest in the extension off the courtyard. Golfers have Brancaster and Hunstanton, shoppers Burnham Market, birdwatchers Snettisham and Titchwell. For walkers and families the North Coast beaches of Holme and Holkham are stupendous.

Rooms	16 twins/doubles. £90–£110. Singles £70–£90.
Meals	12pm-2pm (2.30pm Sat & Sun); 6.30pm-9pm (9.30pm Fri & Sat). Main courses £9.95-£16.95; Sunday roast £10.
Closed	Open all day.
Directions	Village signed off A149 10 miles north of King's Lynn. Turn right at r'bout into village & then 1st left, 100yds on left.

Anthony & Jeannette Goodrich
The Rose & Crown,
Old Church Road, Snettisham,
King's Lynn PE31 7LX

Tel	+44 (0)1485 541382
Web	www.roseandcrownsnettisham.co.uk

Entry 477 Map 9

Norfolk

The Pigs
Edgefield

If passion and pedigree go hand in hand then The Pigs' patrons are onto a winner. Running the old pub (once known as the Bacon Arms) is a partnership of restaurateurs fighting the corner for real food locally sourced – some of which comes straight from the patrons' gardens. The enterprising menu, a retro version of British classics – tastes and textures long forgotten – includes beef dripping on toast with cock-a-leekie soup, marmalade-glazed ham hock with mustard mash, cauliflower fritters, and a fruity, gingery Norfolk Biffin; also, a tempting little menu for 'piglets'. Homemade pork scratchings, colonial spiced almonds and mixed pickle pots are further lures, along with old-fashioned pub games and decent cask ales. No hushed gastronomic museum this, more of a "traditional bar with continental leanings."

Norfolk

The Jolly Sailors
Brancaster Staithe

In 2009 Cliff and James Nye set about breathing new life into this 200-year-old village pub. 'Eat, Drink and be Jolly' says it all: not only is it a community boozer geared to local drinkers and families but it attracts all those who flock to Brancaster's glorious beach across the road. (Quite different from Cliff's classy White Horse Inn down the road.) In the classic bar, replete with beams, tiled floor, old settles and a wood-burner pumping out the heat, dads can enjoy pints of home-brewed Brancaster Best while kids can watch the pizzas being baked in the open-to-view oven. Hearty traditional pub dishes using fresh local produce include mussels cooked in wine, onion, garlic and cream; pork and cider pie; gammon, egg and chips; and good ol' fish and chips (delicious). A terrific pit-stop for families, beach bums and coastal walkers.

Meals	12pm-2.30pm (3pm Sun); 6pm-9pm. Main courses £9.95-£14.95.
Closed	3pm-6pm; Sun eve & all day Mon.
Directions	Edgefield is on B1149, 3 miles south of Holt; south side of village.

SPECIAL AWARD
see pages 20-21

Local, seasonal & organic produce

Meals	12pm-3pm; 6pm-9pm (12pm-9pm Sat & Sun); pizzas served until 10.45pm (Fri & Sat; every day in summer). Main courses £7.95-£11.95; pizzas from £5.95; Sunday roast £10.95.
Closed	3pm-6pm. Open all day Sat, Sun and in high summer.
Directions	In village centre on A149 coast road, midway between Hunstanton and Wells-next-the-Sea.

Tim Abbott
The Pigs,
Norwich Road, Edgefield,
Melton Constable NR24 2RL

Tel	+44 (0)1263 587634
Web	www.thepigs.org.uk

Entry 478 Map 10

Cliff Nye
The Jolly Sailors,
Main Road, Brancaster Staithe,
King's Lynn PE31 8BJ

Tel	+44 (0)1485 210314
Web	www.jollysailorsbrancaster.co.uk

Entry 479 Map 10

The White Horse
Brancaster Staithe

The setting is magical. Fabulous views reach across the marshes and the water with its moored boats, and dinghies sailing on the evening high tide. The coastal path starts right outside this neat inn with its benches, parasols and troughs of plants and flowers: the perfect spot for a pint after a stroll. Inside, the fishy theme continues but in a modern, crisp way: seascape colours, natural materials, pictures of boats, bowls of pebbles and shells, big windows to the views. Bedrooms are beautiful. Those upstairs capture the ever-changing light; those on the ground floor have flower-filled terraces and a New England feel and lead straight onto the marshes. From here you can spot fishing craft and ringed plovers, several species of tern and, in winter, geese; don't forget your binoculars. Dine by candlelight on mussels and oysters from yards away, homemade bread and ice creams, all of it as local and seasonal as possible. Huge sunsets, fine food, big breakfasts, and a real welcome for both children and dogs, who may stay in your room. Readers are full of praise.

Rooms	15: 11 doubles, 4 twins. £90–£164.
Meals	12pm-2pm; 6.30pm-9pm; bar food 9am-9pm.
	Main courses £10.95–£18.50; bar meals £6.95–£8.95.
Closed	Open all day.
Directions	Midway between Hunstanton & Wells-next-the-Sea on the A149 coast road.

Cliff Nye
The White Horse,
Brancaster Staithe,
King's Lynn PE31 8BY
Tel   +44 (0)1485 210262
Web   www.whitehorsebrancaster.co.uk

Entry 480 Map 10

The Hoste Arms
Burnham Market

Nelson was once a local. Now it's farmers, fishermen and film stars who jostle at the bar and roast away in front of the fire. In its 300-year history the Hoste has been a court house, a livestock market, a gallery and a brothel; these days it's more a pleasure dome than an inn and even on a grey February morning it buzzes with life – the locals in for coffee, the residents polishing off leisurely breakfasts, diligent staff attending a wine tasting. The place has a genius of its own with warm bold colours, armchairs to sink into, panelled walls, an art gallery. Fancy food can be eaten anywhere and anytime, so dig into local oysters, pork belly terrine, sea bass with seafood and shellfish stew, and duck with wild mushroom and truffle dressing. In summer, life spills out onto tables at the front or you can dine on the terrace in the garden at the back. Rooms are all different, the quietest away from the bar: a tartan four-poster, a swagged half-tester, leather sleigh beds in the Zulu Wing, luxury boutique rooms in Vine House, across the village green. And the north Norfolk coast is on your doorstep.

Rooms	42: 12 twins/doubles, 4 four-posters, 4 singles, 7 suites. Zulu Wing: 5 doubles, 3 suites. Vine House: 7 doubles. £104–£255. Singles £69–£133. Suites £170–£312. Half-board from £66 p.p.
Meals	12pm-2pm; 7pm-9pm. Main courses £11.75-£20.25; bar lunches from £5.75; Sunday roast from £10.50.
Closed	Open all day.
Directions	On B1155 for Burnham Market. By green & church in village centre.

Emma Tagg
The Hoste Arms,
Market Place, Burnham Market,
King's Lynn PE31 8HD

Tel	+44 (0)1328 738777
Web	www.hostearms.co.uk

Entry 481 Map 10

The Crown Inn
East Rudham

Kiwi TV chef Chris Coubrough bought his second Crown in 2008 (his first is at Wells-next-the-Sea). Right by the A148, overlooking the village green, it's a handy spot to rest and refuel while exploring the North Norfolk coast. Beyond the charming and spruced-up exterior lies a lovely big open-plan bar with low beams, rug-strewn tiles, fresh contemporary colours, shelves full of books and an assortment of well-scrubbed dining tables. Fishermen and farmers supply the produce for modern dishes listed on daily printed menus – impossible not to be tempted by Houghton Hall venison with braised red cabbage, sea bass with saffron and spring onion risotto, a slate of crayfish, prawns, cockles and brown shrimp (to share), and delicious warm apricot tart. It's all so relaxing and quietly pleasing why not book in for the night? Bedrooms are above, simple and stylish, with white brass beds and painted furniture, modern easy chairs and good quality fabrics, big lamps and lovely bathrooms with wooden floors. Double glazing guarantees a perfect night's sleep.

Rooms	6: 5 doubles, 1 family room. £80–£100.
Meals	12pm-2.30pm; 6.30pm-9.30pm. Main courses £10.95–£13.25; sandwiches from £5.25.
Closed	Open all day.
Directions	Beside A148 between Fakenham and King's Lynn; by village green.

Chris Coubrough
The Crown Inn,
The Green, East Rudham,
King's Lynn PE31 8RD
Tel   +44 (0)1485 528530
Web   www.thecrowneastrudham.co.uk

Entry 482 Map 10

The Globe Inn
Wells-next-the-Sea

Set back a few hundred yards from the bustling harbour at Wells, the Globe sits on leafy Buttlands Green. The 19th-century coaching inn is owned by Tom and Polly Coke, who transformed the Victoria on their family estate at Holkham. It's a big hit with visitors and locals alike, a warm mishmash of old furniture, wooden boards, big wood-burner and antique lighting while the restaurant, done up in New England style, has a reputation for food that's English, unfussy, fresh and modern. Some meat comes from the estate and only the season's best will do: Thornham mussels, rib-eye of Holkham beef with béarnaise, fish chowder, local rabbit, pigeon and estate-reared venison. On sunny days you can take your plates and your pints (Adnams, Woodforde's) out into the red-brick courtyard. Bedrooms have been smartened up and are as fresh and untraditional as can be, with oak floors, iron beds, crisp linen, big baths and monsoon showers. The ones at the front get the views. Children and dogs like it too, what with child-size pies, crabbing on the quay and walks on the hugest beach ever. *Six new rooms open in 2010.*

Rooms	7: 5 doubles, 2 twins. £105–£150.
Meals	12pm–2.30pm; 6.30pm–9pm.
	Main courses £9.95–£15.95;
	sandwiches from £4.95;
	set lunch £9.95 & £12.95.
Closed	Open all day.
Directions	North from Fakenham on B1105.
	Hotel on green in centre of town.

Viscount Coke & Johanna Lissack
The Globe Inn,
The Buttlands,
Wells-next-the-Sea NR23 1EU
Tel +44 (0)1328 710206
Web www.globeatwells.co.uk

Entry 483 Map 10

Norfolk

The Orange Tree
Thornham

This place knows what a contemporary food pub should be. From wicker fencing fronting the garden to sage-splashed walls, the approach from the village green says it all and new owners Mark and Jo Goode plan few changes to this coastal treasure. Step inside – to chunky seagrass floors, light wood, bright walls and log-stuffed fireplaces. Snuggle up at a cheeky *table à deux* at the bar, or retire to one of two relaxed dining rooms. There's a faint waft of Norfolk 'money' on the air, but something for everyone on Philip Milner's innovative menu – from cottage pie or ham, egg and chips in the bar to beef fillet with oxtail ravioli and shiraz jus, and monkfish with risotto Milanese and soy caramelised squid. This is a fabulous area for food, and the pub sources locally and well. Come for urban chic and a particularly happy feel.

Meals	12pm-3pm (5pm Sun); 6pm-9.30pm (9pm Sun). Main courses £9-£17.
Closed	Open all day.
Directions	On A149 in village centre; from Hunstanton, pub on left-hand side.

Mark & Jo Goode
The Orange Tree,
High Street,
Thornham, Hunstanton PE36 6LY
Tel   +44 (0)1485 512213
Web   www.theorangetreethornham.co.uk

Entry 484 Map 10

Norfolk

Carpenter's Arms
Wighton

Regulars and newcomers love this pub for all the right reasons: good beer, good food and hands-on owners. It looks modest enough from the outside, three knocked-together cottages in traditional knicker-pink render. But a courageous hand with the paint pot has transformed the interior: tables and chairs in terracotta, navy and duck-egg blue, a jolly blue in the hallway, and walls in a dining room that would make Barbie blink. Kelims, leather-style sofas and a bold paintings create a happy mishmash of textures, a big double-sided wood-burner heats the bar and dining room and there's a grassy sun-trap around the back. A pint of well-kept Nelson's Revenge slips down a treat with hot crab linguine with mint and chilli, skate wing with buttered samphire, or calves' liver and bacon with red wine jus.

Meals	12pm-2.30pm; 6pm-9pm; no food Sun eve or Mon in winter. Main courses £7.95-£12.95.
Closed	2.30pm-5.30pm. Open all day Sun (open all day Sat in summer).
Directions	Village signed off A149 at Wells-next-the-Sea.

Gareth & Rebecca Williams
Carpenter's Arms,
High Street, Wighton,
Wells-next-the-Sea NR23 1PF
Tel   +44 (0)1328 820752
Web   www.carpentersarmswighton.co.uk

Entry 485 Map 10

The Crown
Wells-next-the-Sea

The interior of this handsome 16th-century coaching inn has been neatly rationalised yet is still atmospheric with its open fires, bare boards and easy chairs. And it's run by Chris Coubrough, an enterprising landlord who knows how to cook. Order pub food at the bar and eat it in the lounges or the lovely modern conservatory: a hearty serving of Brancaster mussels, paella with monkfish, crab claws, squid, clams and chorizo. Or, quite simply, the Crown beefburger with pepper relish and a pint of local Adnams Bitter. Bold colours, modern art and attractively laid tables give life to the restaurant where local ingredients are translated into global ideas: steamed cod with ginger lemongrass and lime; Thai marinated duck breast with seared scallops and chilli jam. Uncluttered bedrooms have a cool, minimalist feel and a fresh white theme – plump pillows and crisp linen on good wooden beds, flat-screen TVs; larger rooms have squashy sofas and DVD players. Beaches and bracing salt marsh walks are mere minutes away.

Rooms	12: 8 doubles, 2 twins, 2 family suites. £90–£155. Singles from £70. Half-board from £75 p.p.
Meals	12pm-2.30pm; 6.30pm-9.30pm. Main courses £9.95–£14.95; set menu £34.95.
Closed	Open all day.
Directions	Wells-next-the-Sea is on B1105, 10 miles north of Fakenham; pub by the green south of town centre.

Chris Coubrough
The Crown,
The Buttlands,
Wells-next-the-Sea NR23 1EX
Tel   +44 (0)1328 710209
Web   www.thecrownhotelwells.co.uk

Norfolk

The Three Horseshoes
Warham

An atmospheric treasure in a rural backwater. This former row of 18th-century cottages hides a mile from the coastal path and glorious salt marshes. Inside, three utterly plain, unspoilt rooms have barely changed since the Thirties – gas lights, rough deal tables, Victorian fireplaces and a pianola that performs.... once in a while. Vintage entertainment includes an intriguing American Mills one-armed bandit converted for modern coins and a rare Norfolk 'twister' set into the ceiling – for village roulette, apparently. The food is in keeping, just traditional English dishes based emphatically on Norfolk produce – locally shot game, hearty casseroles, shortcrust pastry pies – enhanced by great pints of Wherry straight from the cask. Alternatively, sample local cider or homemade lemonade.

Meals	12pm-1.45pm; 6pm-8.30pm. Main courses £8.50-£11.
Closed	2.30pm-6pm.
Directions	Warham off A149 between Wells-next-the-Sea & Stiffkey; 2 miles east of Wells.

Iain Salmon
The Three Horseshoes,
69 The Street,
Warham,
Wells-Next-The-Sea NR23 1NL
Tel   +44 (0)1328 710547

Entry 487 Map 10

Norfolk

White Horse Hotel
Blakeney

The smart hub of this small coastal village attracts its share of switched-on custom; Blakeney is the jewel in north Norfolk's crown. The lamp-lit windows of the bar beckon; Adnams Bitter and Woodforde's Wherry are served to those in search of a pint. But stay for more: parsnip and coconut soup, filled ciabattas and fish pie are all served in the polished bar, while local Morston mussels, roast pollock, partridge and foie gras pie and seasonal ingredients are given a decidedly contemporary treatment in the sunny-coloured restaurant. With its airy conservatory and sheltered courtyard, Dan Goff's friendly inn is a pleasant place to rest weary limbs following a bracing coast path walk. At the bottom of the steep, narrow high street are marshes of sea lavender, natural mussel beds and seals a ferry ride away.

Meals	12pm-2.15pm; 6pm-9pm. Main courses £10.95-£16.95; bar meals (lunch) £4.75-£12.50; set lunch £15 & £20.
Closed	Open all day.
Directions	Just up from quay, in village; off A149 10 miles west of Sheringham.

Dan Goff
White Horse Hotel,
4 High Street,
Blakeney, Holt NR25 7AL
Tel   +44 (0)1263 740574
Web   www.blakeneywhitehorse.co.uk

Entry 488 Map 10

Norfolk

Red Lion
Stiffkey

Tucked into the side of a hill, overlooking the meadows where beef cattle graze, is a cosy inn that's a pleasure to step into: a warren of three small rooms with bare floorboards and 17th-century quarry tiles, 'clotted cream' walls, open log fires and a mix of stripped wooden settles, old pews and scrubbed tables. The pub attracts a loyal crowd for its fresh seafood – crab from Wells boats, mussels from Johnny Dowsing in the village, beer battered cod – or roast partridge with braised red cabbage, and first-rate ales from local brewers: Woodforde's, Yetmans. Locals rub shoulders with booted walkers and birdwatchers recovering from the rigours of the Peddars Way path and Stiffkey's famous marshes. After a day on the beach the large and airy conservatory is popular with families; dogs, too, are welcomed.

Norfolk

The Anchor
Morston

Taste the salty sea – Morston mussels, Thornham oysters, Blakeney crab – and wash it all down with Norwich's Winter Brewery Golden ale... or a nice cup of Royal tea. All a village pub should be, this flintwork and whitewashed building re-opened in 2007 following a serious fire. It's a warren of intimate, loved and lived-in rooms, each with its own story to tell: a random collection of tables and chairs, old fishing pics and faded newspaper clippings. There's even a cosy old 'front room' resplendent with stuffed birds and armchairs. Around every corner are enthusiastic birders, chattering locals and relaxed tourists lapping it up. Honest pub cooking with fine local ingredients matches the decent beers and inexpensive wines. On a sunny day stretch out in the secluded beer garden. Book a seal trip while you sup.

Meals	12pm-2.30pm; 6.30pm-9pm. 12pm-9pm Sun. Main courses £8.95-£14; sandwiches from £4.95.
Closed	Open all day.
Directions	From Wells, 2 miles along coast road towards Cromer.

Meals	12pm-2.30pm; 6pm-9.30pm; 12pm-8pm Sun. Main courses £8.95-£18.95.
Closed	Open all day.
Directions	In the centre of Morston on the A149, 2 miles west of Blakeney.

Stephen Franklin
Red Lion,
44 Wells Road, Stiffkey,
Wells-next-the-Sea NR23 1AJ
Tel   +44 (0)1328 830552
Web   www.stiffkey.com

Nick Handley
The Anchor,
22 The Street,
Morston, Holt NR25 7AA
Tel   +44 (0)1263 741392

Entry 489 Map 10

Entry 490 Map 10

The Wiveton Bell
Wiveton

The pull of the great outdoors led Berni and Sandy, enterprising Nottingham-based restaurateurs, to this Norfolk pub, with a backdrop of village green and church. The setting may be bucolic but Wiveton is no backwater; on highdays and holidays these coastal outposts of North Norfolk get livelier than Chelsea, such is the influx of city escapees. And they will find much to please them here, for a stunning, simple-rustic makeover has transformed the interior of the charming whitewashed inn – beams, chunky tables, polished plank floors – that suits the bistro-pub ethos down to the ground. The menu is seductive, ranging from lamb rump with garlic confit and rosemary sauce or steak bruschetta to Cley smokehouse haddock with mustard sauce. It's all so lovely you'll want to stay the night. Four lovely bedrooms have antique beds with crisp linen and goose down pillows, flat-screen TV/DVDs, mini CD players, iPod docks and books; cosy bathrooms have bathrobes and top toiletries; fresh croissants are delivered to the door.

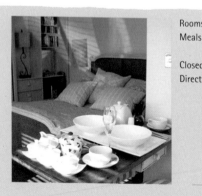

Rooms	4 doubles. £85-£120.
Meals	12pm-2.15pm; 6pm-9.15pm.
	Main courses £8.95-£15.95.
Closed	3pm-5.30pm.
Directions	Wiveton signed off A149 at Blakeney; pub on the green.

Berni Morritt & Sandy Butcher
The Wiveton Bell,
Blakeney Road,
Wiveton, Holt NR25 7TL
Tel   +44 (0)1263 740101
Web   www.wivetonbell.co.uk

Norfolk

The Kings Head
Letheringsett

Chef Chris Coubrough's latest pub venture is his most impressive. In vast gardens close to Holt, this rambling manor-like building has been revamped with panache. Inside, the mood is rustic-chic: rugs on wooden boards or terracotta, warm Farrow & Ball hues, fat table lamps, bookcases crammed with books, big mirrors and feature fireplaces fronted by squashy leather – a cool, civilised feel. Adnams and Woodforde ales, decent wines and classy pub food are further enticements, with menus championing the region's farmers, fishermen and traders. Tuck into smoked haddock, leek and parmesan chowder, confit duck leg with white bean and tomato cassoulet, battered haddock and hand-cut chips, Norfolk cheeses. There's a super sun-trap terrace and an enclosed garden with a fort and play frames. *Bedrooms from Easter 2010.*

Meals	12pm-2.30pm; 6.30pm-9.30pm. Main courses £11.95-££19.95; light lunches £6.95
Closed	Open all day.
Directions	Just off A148 Holt to Fakenham road, 1 mile west of Holt.

Chris Coubrough
The Kings Head,
Holt Road,
Letheringsett, Holt NR25 7AR
Tel   +44 (0)1263 712691
Web www.kingsheadnorfolk.co.uk

Entry 492 Map

Norfolk

The Hunny Bell
Hunworth

The newly-extended 18th-century pub sits by Hunworth's idyllic green in the glorious Glaven Valley. Animal Inns snapped up this North Norfolk gem in 2008 – another upmarket eaterie to add to their collection. Follow a breezy saltmarsh stroll with lunch at long oak tables in the rustic-chic, slate-floored bar. Stuffed owls peer out of cubby-holes by the wood-burner, walls are honey-coloured and flourish country prints, the snug has modish walls and winged chairs, and posh loos wear bee motif wallpapers. Food is fresh, imaginative and locally sourced, so enjoy your potted King's Lynn brown shrimps, steaming Brancaster mussels, Norfolk Wherry beer-battered cod with hand-cut chips, and steak and watercress sandwiches; even the bread is homemade. Illy coffee, Norfolk ales (try a pint of Wolf), and a sweet secret side garden add to the charm.

Meals	12pm-2pm; 6.30pm-9pm (7pm-10pm Sat); 12pm-2.30pm; 6.30pm-8.30pm Sun. Main courses £7.95-£17.95; sandwiches from £4.75
Closed	3pm-5.30pm (6.30pm Sun).
Directions	From Norwich B1149 to Saxthorpe, B1354 to Briston, signposted right for Hunworth. 2 miles, on left of village green.

Henry Watt
The Hunny Bell,
The Green, Hunworth,
Melton Constable NR24 2AA
Tel   +44 (0)1263 712300
Web www.thehunnybell.co.uk

Entry 493 Map 10

Norfolk

Saracens Head
Wolterton

A true country inn with nourishing food, real ale, good wines, a big courtyard garden, and Norfolk's bleakly lovely coast – this is why people come. But it's the food that's the deepest seduction. The team cook up "some of Norfolk's most delicious wild and tame treats". Tuck into Morston mussels with cider and cream, pigeon, scallops, venison. Vegetarians are pampered too, a rare thing. Then they work their magic on old favourites such as bread and butter pudding... The bar with wood-burners is as convivial as could be, a welcome antidote to garish bars with their fruit machines. There's a parlour room that is decidedly civilised: red walls with friezes, a black leather banquette, an open log fire. The whole mood is of quirky, committed individuality – slightly arty, slightly unpredictable and in the middle of nowhere. *New owners 2010.*

Norfolk

Buckinghamshire Arms
Blickling

A Jacobean coaching inn that was originally the estate builder's house for Blickling Hall; it stands close to the grand gates. Later it became the quarters for servants and guests. Like the Hall, it is owned by the National Trust but functions as a self-contained inn, serving the locals in the winter and the crowds in the summer; then the big lawn and sheltered courtyard have an outside servery. Tuck into bangers and mash with red onion gravy and pork pie ploughman's; enjoy a pint of Woodforde's Wherry. In the evening: duck and pistachio terrine, Gunton Park venison casserole, treacle tart. Bars are charming, a cosy red or bold green, with log fires, leaded windows, scrubbed tables, and a cracking snug bar at the front. Walk in the park and admire the lake, the Gothic folly and pyramidal mausoleum; the Hall is open April to October.

Meals	12.15pm-2pm; 7.15pm-9.30pm. Main courses £12.25-£16.75; bar meals £5.50-£8.80.
Closed	3pm-6pm (7pm Sun), all day Mon (except bank hols) & Tues lunch.
Directions	From Norwich, A140 past Aylsham, then left, for Erpingham. Through Calthorpe; over x-roads. On right after about 0.5 miles.

Meals	12pm-2pm; 6.45pm-9pm. No food Mon eve in winter. Main courses £8.95-£9.95 (lunch); £9.25-£13.95 (dinner); ciabattas £7.95.
Closed	3pm-6pm. Open all day in summer.
Directions	From Aylsham B1354; pub opp. Hall.

	Saracens Head, Wolterton, Norwich NR11 7LZ
Tel	+44 (0)1263 768909
Web	www.saracenshead-norfolk.co.uk

Entry 494 Map 10

	Pip Wilkinson Buckinghamshire Arms, Blickling, Norwich NR11 6NF
Tel	+44 (0)1263 732 133
Web	www.bucks-arms.co.uk

Entry 495 Map 10

The Walpole Arms
Itteringham

The Walpole is one of a select band of renowned food pubs in north Norfolk. They like to describe their menu as 'a voyage of discovery' and it certainly is adventurous. The daily chalkboard reflects the seasons and brims with local produce – Cromer crab, Morston mussels, venison from the Gunton estate, farm-fresh fruits and vegetables. Enjoy the likes of Jerusalem artichoke soup with wilted rocket and truffle oil, potato dumpling with Munster cheese, black bream with herb-crushed potatoes and velouté, poached quince and frangipane tart. You can eat in the bar, all rough brick walls, beamed ceilings, standing timbers and big open fire, or in the stylish dining room. There are fine East Anglian ales from Adnams and Woodforde's, a first-class list of wines (and exclusive wine club), and a glorious vine-covered terrace for summer.

Meals	12pm-2pm (12.30pm-2.30pm Sun); 7pm-9pm; no food Sun eve. Main courses £9.95-£17.
Closed	3pm-6pm & Sun eves.
Directions	From Aylsham towards Blickling, then 1st right to Itteringham.

Christian Hodgekinson
The Walpole Arms,
The Common,
Itteringham, Norwich NR11 7AR
Tel   +44 (0)1263 587258
Web   www.thewalpolearms.co.uk

Entry 496 Map 10

The Wildebeest Arms
Stoke Holy Cross

In the 1990s Henry Watt introduced good food to this country inn – a rarity then. Today the Wildebeest is one of the most popular dining pubs in Norfolk. The 19th-century building may be no great shakes on the outside but the atmosphere is special. Modernised to create one long room split by a central bar, there are rich yellow walls, dark oak beams, a winter fire and an African theme to match the pub's name. Ales include Adnams, there's a good choice of wines by the glass and the food is up-to-the-minute and freshly made. Tuck into the rich delights of pan-seared haunch of venison with fondant potato, crispy Parma ham and dark chocolate sauce. Chef Daniel Smith may enjoy a bit of leonine bravura but he is wonderfully at home with old English favourites like sausage and mash and sticky toffee pudding.

Meals	12pm-2pm; 7pm-9pm. Main courses £13.95 & £16.95 (lunch); £16.50 & £19.95 (dinner).
Closed	3pm-6pm.
Directions	Off A140, 3 miles south of Norwich.

Henry Watt
The Wildebeest Arms,
82-86 Norwich Road,
Stoke Holy Cross, Norwich NR14 8QJ
Tel   +44 (0)1508 492497
Web   www.thewildebeest.co.uk

Entry 497 Map 10

Norfolk

The Mulberry Tree
Attleborough

Urbane, contemporary and soothing, this is just perfect for ladies (or shy gentlemen) who lunch, and it wouldn't matter if you arrived alone at this sophisticated pub in the middle of a sleepy market town. There are lots of seating areas in the bar, along with bay windows, high ceilings, huge church candles in glass lanterns and dark leather sofas to guarantee comfort. There's good food, too. Choose from the daily changing bar menu (Suffolk ham with free-range eggs and hand-cut chips) or go the whole hog in the restaurant (potted Cromer crab, pan-fried sea bass). Gooey chocolate squares with butterscotch sauce and vanilla ice cream could finish you off. In summer, simple seating with parasols are set up behind the bar area with its big windows. Forests, beaches, market towns and nature reserves are near to explore.

Meals	12pm-2pm; 6.30pm-9pm. Main courses £10.95-£21.50; bar meals £5.45-£9.50.
Closed	Sun.
Directions	On one-way system around town centre at junction with Station Road.

Philip & Victoria Milligan
The Mulberry Tree,
Station Road,
Attleborough NR17 2AS
Tel +44 (0)1953 452124
Web www.the-mulberry-tree.co.uk

Entry 499 Map 10

Norfolk
Worth a visit

500 King's Head Harts Lane, Bawburgh, Norwich NR9 3LS +44 (0)1603 744977
Unprepossessing yet with a terracotta façade, Anton Wimmer's old pub is full of low-beamed charm. Delight in East Anglian ales, wines by the glass, piped jazz and a heated terrace.

501 Fat Cat 49 West End Street, Norwich NR2 4NA +44 (0)1603 624364
Victorian corner pub and beer drinkers' heaven: 30 real ales with some on hand pump, others tapped from cask. The owners proudly keep this a traditional and simple drinking pub.

502 The George Cley, Holt NR25 7RN +44 (0)1263 740652
The Norfolk Naturalists Trust was formed at this rambling inn overlooking the saltmarshes. Dan Goff (of the White Horse in Blakeney) has completed the refurbishment and menus champion local produce. Reports please.

503 The Lord Nelson Walsingham Rd, Burnham Thorpe, King's Lynn PE31 8HN +44 (0)1328 738241
Ancient benches and settles, worn brick, tile floors, and a serving hatch instead of a bar distinguish this marvellous place. Be tempted by a tot of Nelson's Blood or a pint of Woodforde's. Family-friendly garden.

504 The Lifeboat Inn Ship Lane, Thornham, Hunstanton PE36 6LT +44 (0)1485 512236
The glowing lamps and open fires of this bags-of-character inn beckon. It's been an ale house since the 16th century – and they still serve a decent pint. The sea is a brisk, bracing walk across fields.

Northamptonshire

The Red Lion
Culworth

Culworth has it all: thatched stone cottages, pretty green and church, grand manor – and the Red Lion, a classic old local recently revived by chef Justin Lefevre, landlord of the Royal Oak in Eydon, who has carefully restored the once boarded-up boozer. The unlovely 70s décor has gone; the stone and wood floors, the timbers and the fireplaces have been rediscovered; and there's a fresh rustic-chic feel. Diners mingle with locals, booted walkers quaff pints of Landlord in the bar, and dogs doze. In keeping, the food is hearty and unpretentious, the lunch and monthly-changing dinner menus featuring everyone's favourites – lamb burgers, ham, egg and chips, rump steak with all the trimmings, seafood risotto, sea bass with lemon cream sauce. The garden is huge and has village views.

Meals	12pm-2pm (4pm Sun); 6.30pm-9.30pm. No food Sun eve. Main courses £8.50-£16; sandwiches (lunch) £5.
Closed	3pm-6pm & all Mon.
Directions	Village signed off A361 and B4525 NE of Banbury.

Justin Lefevre
The Red Lion,
High Street,
Culworth, Banbury OX17 2BD
Tel   +44 (0)1295 760050

Entry 505 Map 8

Northamptonshire

Royal Oak
Eydon

Everyone's welcome at this small and unpretentious pub. Walkers drop by to refuel, children are welcome in the games room, dogs amble freely. No music, just the hum of happy eaters. The menu – fresh, short, regularly changing – is the big attraction and you'll find not only the best of British, like rib-eye steak with pepper sauce and chunky chips or monkfish stew, but also a touch of the exotic (crab cakes with lime, chilli and coriander mayonnaise). The pretty, 17th-century pub has old flagstones, exposed stone walls, a wood-burner in the inglenook and a Sunday-papers-and-a-pint feel. The long bar is propped up by ale-quaffing regulars, the rest is made over to the games room and three small eating areas. There are picnic seats out in front and Eydon, though only seven miles from the motorway, feels as remote as can be.

Meals	12pm-2pm; 7pm-9pm; no food Mon. Dinner - 1 course £15.50; 2 courses £21; 3 courses £25; Lunch main courses from £9; 2 course lunch £16.
Closed	2.30pm-6pm (3pm-7pm Sun) & Mon lunch
Directions	Off A361 midway between Banbury & Daventry.

Justin Lefevre
Royal Oak,
6 Lime Avenue,
Eydon, Daventry NN11 3PG
Tel   +44 (0)1327 263167

Entry 506 Map 8

Northamptonshire

The Althorp Coaching Inn
Great Brington

Near Althorp House – home of the Spencers – the pub was once known as the Fox & Hounds. Decked with flowers inside and out, resting in the heart of an multi-thatched estate village, it is a popular place. There's an enclosed courtyard within earshot of the cricket green, a nice spot for a pint of Langton Bowler (alongside many other wonderful ales) and, when the nights draw in, the fires burn brightly in the restaurant and bar, glowingly traditional with its floorboards, flagstones and plentiful bric-a-brac. The regulars appreciate the good value meals and the baguettes from the bar, while the restaurant serves beef and game from the farm estate, cooked in an unfussy manner. Major sporting events – Silverstone is up the road – are shown (discreetly) in the bar, and Tuesday evenings see live music.

Meals	12pm-3pm; 6.30pm-9.30pm (10pm Sat; 8.30pm Sun). Main courses £9.25-£16.75.
Closed	Open all day.
Directions	From Northampton, A428; 1st left after Althorp; near Althorp Hall.

Martin Francis
The Althorp Coaching Inn,
Main Street, Great Brington,
Northampton NN7 4JA
Tel +44 (0)1604 770651
Web www.althorp-coaching-inn.co.uk

Entry 507 Map 8

Northamptonshire

The Wollaston Inn
Wollaston

It was once the Nag's Head: U2 played here and John Peel DJ'd. But then the local Doc Martens factory closed, and when the boots walked, so did the clientele. Chris Spencer's aim was to clean up the pub's act, and the result is as far from spit-and-sawdust as you can get – creamy walls, high ceilings, comfy sofas, glowing fires and a beer garden that's become a courtyard patio with bay trees in terracotta pots. Chris is serious about his food, especially seafood, and the menu changes daily. No pretensions, though, no "drizzling" or "beds" of this or that. Instead, the kitchen does uncluttered food nicely presented: scallops with garlic cream sauce, organic cod with braised oxtail and walnut velouté, roast partridge and venison, pig's cheeks, ploughman's and lemon and thyme panna cotta. And the wine list is one to wade around in.

Meals	11am-10pm (10.30pm Sat & Sun). Main courses £8.50-£25; bar meals from £6.50.
Closed	Open all day.
Directions	Village signed off A509 south of Wellingborough.

Chris Spencer
The Wollaston Inn,
87 London Road, Wollaston,
Wellingborough NN29 7QS
Tel +44 (0)1933 663161
Web www.wollaston-inn.co.uk

Entry 508 Map 9

Northamptonshire

The Queen's Head
Bulwick

A mellow old stone pub in a lovely village — you'll wish this was your local. The simple beamed and flagstoned bar rambles into several country-styled dining rooms that ooze atmosphere and traditional charm. This may be the owners' first pub venture, but their natural friendliness and instinct to keep things simple has worked in their favour. Lunchtime bar food features linguini with crab, chilli, lemon and parsley, or try a smoked chicken and tarragon mayonnaise sandwich washed down with Rockingham Ales from the village microbrewery. The short à la carte menu is full of more extravagant dishes with a distinct Italian flavour: Tuscan-style vegetable and bean soup; seared calves' liver with curly kale, puy lentil cassoulet and pancetta; baked halibut with braised fennel and spicy tomato and roasted pepper sauce.

Meals	12pm-2.30pm; 6pm-9.30pm; no food Sun eve. Main courses £9.95-£19.95; sandwiches from £6.95; set menu £15 & £17.
Closed	3pm-6pm (5pm-7pm Sun) & Mon all day.
Directions	Just off A43, between Stamford & Corby.

Geoff Smith & Angela Partridge
The Queen's Head,
Bulwick,
Corby NN17 3DY
Tel +44 (0)1780 450272

Entry 509 Map 9

Northumberland

The Manor House Inn
Carterway Heads

No wonder it's popular. Cheerful, enthusiastic landlords, tasty food, a good bar with four local cask ales and a cask cider, nines wines by the glass, a raft of malts. The large light lounge bar, with wood-burning stove and blackboard menu, is a great spot for meals, though there's a dining room if you prefer. Tuck into sandwiches and salads, ham hock terrine with piccalilli, local rib-eye steak with béarnaise sauce, or one of the daily seasonal specials – seared pheasant with red wine jus, or, more daringly, pigeon with beetroot and chocolate jus. In the smallish public bar, modestly furnished with oak settles and old pine tables, is a big open fire. Take your pint of Nels Best – from Highhouse Farm Brewery, 12 miles away – into the garden in summer where the eye sweeps over the Derwent valley to the Durham moors.

Meals	12pm-9.30pm. Main courses £6.75-£15; sandwiches from £3.95.
Closed	Open all day.
Directions	Beside A68 at junction with B6278; 3 miles west of Consett.

Neil & Emma Oxley
The Manor House Inn,
Shotley Bridge, Carterway Heads,
Consett DH8 9LX
Tel +44 (0)1207 255268
Web www.themanorhouseinn.com

Entry 510 Map 12

Northumberland

The Feathers Inn
Hedley on the Hill

Since taking over in 2007, Helen and Rhian have built on the Feathers' reputation as a destination for good food, yet this pub keeps its old-fashioned pubby feel. It is a rare treat west of Newcastle to find such an authentic little place. In the two bars are old beams, exposed stone, Turkish rugs, simple furnishings, open fires and a cottagey feel; you'd feel as much at home browsing the papers here as enjoying a fireside chat. Beer is excellent, with four cask beers from local or microbreweries; wines are taken as seriously. The delicious food – wild Holy Island mussels cooked in cider with thyme and parsley; venison and game pie with braised red cabbage; roast Muggleswick grouse with bread sauce and game gravy – is cooked with skill and passion by Rhian from locally sourced produce. A star in the making.

Meals	12pm-2pm; 6pm-8.30pm; no food Mon or Sun eve. Main courses £9-£15; bar meals £3.
Closed	Open all day. Closed Mon lunch.
Directions	From Newcastle cross at Scotswood Bridge; A695 through Balydon towards Prudhoe. B6315 signed Greenside; right in Greenside towards Chopwell along lead road. Continue to village of Hedley.

Helen Greer & Rhian Cradock
The Feathers Inn,
Hedley on the Hill,
Stocksfield NE43 7SW
Tel   +44 (0)1661 843607
Web   www.thefeathers.net

Entry 511 Map 12

Northumberland

Rat Inn
Anick

Tucked into the south-facing hillside, overlooking the Tyne Valley, this hard-to-find old drovers' inn has an irresistible appeal. The bar is cosy, with gleaming dark oak, flagged floor, simple tables and chairs, a roaring fire: sup a pint of something local or a good glass of wine while you toy with the idea of nibbles or a sandwich (try honey roast ham and pease pudding) to appease your rumbling tum. Those who have yomped heartily to get here may be hungrier, so look to the blackboard and its excellent, mostly regional delights: roast Northumberland rib of beef with watercress and golden chips for two is delicious, and maybe rice pudding afterwards. The sun room has grand views of the spectacular valley, and on warm days you can spill out into the little garden with its benches and pretty shrubs.

Meals	12pm-2pm (3pm Sun); 6pm-9pm. Sandwiches only on Mon. Main courses £8.95-£18.95; bar snacks from £1.95; Sunday roast £8.95.
Closed	3pm-6pm. Open all day Sat & Sun.
Directions	Off A69 between Corbridge & Hexham, 2 miles east of Hexham.

Phil Mason & Karen Errington
Rat Inn,
Anick,
Hexham NE46 4LN
Tel   +44 (0)1434 602814
Web   www.theratinn.com

Entry 512 Map 12

Northumberland

The Angel
Corbridge

Even older than Hadrian's Wall, quaint Corbridge is a pretty place with the 17th-century Angel, full of history and character, at its heart. Step straight into the splendid panelled lounge, cosy with its leather armchairs, heavy drapes, big open fire and newspapers to browse. Off to the left, another more modern lounge with deep sofas; to the right, the bar, a big room simply decorated in brasserie style with a bright and contemporary feel. To the rear, the new oak-beamed dining room opens onto a sun-trap courtyard. Five cask beers are available and the menu announces chorizo and black pudding risotto and navarin of lamb as well as more traditional dishes – lambs' liver with bacon and champ, and the Angel's legendary Yorkshire puddings. A comfortable stopover on the long journey from north to south.

Meals	12pm-9pm (9.30pm Fri & Sat; 12pm-5pm Sun); no food Sun eve. Main courses £9.95-£16.95; sandwiches from £5.25.
Closed	Open all day.
Directions	In Corbridge, 2 miles off A69.

John Gibson
The Angel,
Main Street,
Corbridge NE45 5LA
Tel +44 (0)1434 632119
Web www.theangelofcorbridge.com

Entry 513 Map 12

Northumberland

Queens Head Inn
Great Whittington

A warm refuge in a wild country of moors, sheep and vast skies. The mellow bar is charming, its 1930s hunting mural satisfactorily yellowed by open fires. Gleaming beer engines disperse High House Farm Brewery ale from down the road; hunting prints hint at local interests; a background tape plays. Toast your toes from the carved oak settle before the fire, then up steps to a traditional lounge and another log-filled grate for those bitter Northumbrian days. Claire Murray greets all who enter from the cold, staff are still gently charming and people come for the food; chef Steven Murran uses the best available produce, including local beef and lamb. Daily menus may include seared red mullet with coriander and lime dressing, crisp pork belly with apple and cider jus, and dark chocolate steamed pudding.

Meals	12pm-2.30pm; 6pm-9pm; 12pm-9.30pm Fri & Sat (6pm Sun). Main courses £8.95-£15.50; bar meals £7.95-£15.50.
Closed	3pm-5.30pm. Open all day Fri-Sun (closes 10.30pm Sun).
Directions	Off B6318, 4 miles north of Corbridge.

Claire Murray
Queens Head Inn, Great
Whittington,
Newcastle Upon Tyne NE19 2HP
Tel +44 (0)1434 672267
Web www.the-queens-head-inn.co.uk

Entry 514 Map 12

Battlesteads Hotel
Wark

In the land of castles, stone circles and fortified towers is Battlesteads, an old inn given a fresh lease of life by owners who aim to go as 'green' as possible. The boiler burns wood chips from local sustainable forestry, a poly-tunnel produces the salads, the waste composting involves the local school; no wonder the Slades have won a gold award for Green Tourism. Enter a large, cosy, low-beamed and panelled bar with a wood-burning stove and local cask ales on hand pump. A step further and you find a spacious dining area: leather chairs at dark wood tables and a conservatory dining room that reaches into a sunny walled garden. The menus show a commitment to sourcing locally and the food is flavoursome. The home-cured Angus beef with juniper berries, peppercorns and herbs is meltingly tender, the 'two-day duck' with a rich bacon and pea jus is scrummy. Exemplary is the housekeeping so bedrooms are spotless; and spacious, carpeted and comfortable. The newest are mini-suites, and there's wheelchair access on the ground floor. Hadrian's Wall is marvellously close.

Rooms	17: 16 twins/doubles, 1 single. £95-£125. Singles £60-£100.
Meals	12pm-3pm; 6.30pm-9pm (9.30pm Fri-Sun). Main courses £8.95-£22.50; bar meals £4.95-£9.50.
Closed	Open all day.
Directions	From A69 at Hexham, A6079 to Chollerford, then A6320 for Bellingham; Wark is halfway.

Richard & Dee Slade
Battlesteads Hotel,
Wark,
Hexham NE48 3LS
Tel   +44 (0)1434 230209
Web   www.battlesteads.com

The Pheasant Inn
Stannersburn

A super little inn run with an instinctive understanding of its traditions. The stone walls carry old photos of the community: from colliery to smithy, a record of its past. The bars are wonderful: brass beer taps glow, anything wooden has been polished to perfection and the clock above the fire keeps perfect time. The house ales are expertly kept – Timothy Taylor's, Wylam Gold Tankard – and Robin cooks with relish, nothing too fancy, but more than enough to keep a smile on your face: Thai potato soup, fish simply grilled, no chips. As for Sunday lunch, it was once voted one of the best in the North. Bedrooms in the old hay barn are simple and tidy, not grand but cosy and newly refurbished (most with flat-screen TVs) and you'll get a piping hot breakfast the next morning – accompanied maybe by a view of the sheepdogs bringing the flock in for shearing. This is the glorious Northumberland National Park – no traffic jams, no rush – and don't miss the sculpture at Kielder. Then hire bikes and cycle round the lake, or saddle up on a pony and take to the hills.

Rooms	8: 4 doubles, 3 twins, 1 family room. £90–£100. Singles £50–£65. Half-board from £70 p.p.
Meals	12pm–2pm (2.30pm Sun); 7pm–9pm. Main courses £9.50–£14.50; bar meals £7.50–£8.50.
Closed	3pm–6.30pm (7pm Sun); Mon & Tues Nov–Mar.
Directions	From Bellingham follow signs west to Kielder Water & Falstone for 9 miles. On left, 1 mile short of Kielder Water.

Walter, Irene & Robin Kershaw
The Pheasant Inn,
Stannersburn,
Hexham NE48 1DD
Tel   +44 (0)1434 240382
Web   www.thepheasantinn.com

Entry 516 Map 14

Northumberland

Barrasford Arms
Barrasford

Chef/landlord Tony Binks is slowly upgrading this substantial inn with a sheltered garden close to Hadrian's Wall. Expect a mix of locals (the marrow club meet here) and a robust atmosphere, with beers from nearby High House Farm and Allendale Breweries on hand pump. The bar has a high ceiling, deep velour upholstery, various stuffed animals and antlers, local photographs and dark varnished wood. Tony's passion for real food is evident: each week he buys a rare breed pig locally; the shoulder for sausages and the legs for Sunday lunch (with sublime crackling) — even the pickled onions and eggs are local. Try chilli beetroot risotto with a glass of spicy Primitivo del Tarantino Masseria dei Trullan. You eat in one of three dining rooms, popular with farmers and fishermen; you are a stone's throw from the rushing north Tyne.

Meals	12pm-2pm; 6.30pm-9pm. No food Sun eve, Mon lunch & bank hols. Main courses £8.50-£16; set lunch £11.50 & £14.50
Closed	2.30pm-6pm & Mon lunch.
Directions	5 miles north of Hexham, signposted off A6079.

Tony Binks
Barrasford Arms,
Barrasford,
Hexham NE48 4AA
Tel   +44 (0)1434 681237
Web   www.barrasfordarms.co.uk

Entry 517 Map 14

Northumberland

The Ship Inn
Low Newton-by-the-Sea

An authentic coastal inn with tongue and groove boarding, old settles, scrubbed tables and a solid-fuel stove. Step in and step back a hundred years. Landlady Christine Forsyth fell in love with the simplicity of the place and gives you provender to match. The tip-top home-brewed beer (Dolly Daydream, Sandcastles at Dawn) and fairtrade coffee and chocolate blend with a menu built around the best local produce — simple, fresh, satisfying. Local hand-picked crab rolls, lobster from over the way, Craster kippers from two miles down the coast, ploughman's with local unpasteurised cheddar and Turnbulls free-range ham. In the evenings there's often a choice (venison, smoked haddock, sirloin steak) but do book first. Park on a compulsory plot back from the beach and take the short walk to the sand, green and pub. Worth every step.

Meals	12pm-2.30pm; phone for evening opening & food times. Main courses £7-£22; lunch £2-£6.95.
Closed	Phone for details.
Directions	From Alnwick B1340 for Seahouses for 8 miles to crossroads; straight over, follow signs.

Christine Forsyth
The Ship Inn, The Square,
Low Newton-by-the-Sea,
Alnwick NE66 3EL
Tel   +44 (0)1665 576262
Web   www.shipinnnewton.co.uk

Entry 518 Map 14

Northumberland

The Olde Ship
Seahouses

The Glen dynasty has been at the helm of this nautical gem for close on a century. The inn sparkles with maritime memorabilia to remind you of Seahouses' fine heritage and the days when Grace Darling rowed through huge seas to rescue stricken souls. Settle into the atmospheric main bar by the glowing fire with a decent pint – there are eight ales to choose from – and gaze across the harbour to the Farne Islands and the Longstone Light (later, take the ferry). In the smaller 'cabin' bar you can get stuck into the likes of potted corned beef salad, beef stroganoff, apricot chicken, fish chowder and bosun's fish stew, bread and butter pudding... and coffee and mints in the lounge. The place positively creaks with history – retreat here after a bracing coastal walk to Bamburgh Castle.

Meals	12pm-2.30pm; 7pm-8.30pm. Main courses £9-£11.75; lunch £7.50.
Closed	Open all day.
Directions	B1340 off A1 8 miles north of Alnwick; inn above harbour.

A & J Glen, D Swan & J Glen
The Olde Ship,
7-9 Main Street,
Seahouses NE68 7RD
Tel   +44 (0)1665 720200
Web   www.seahouses.co.uk

Entry 519 Map 14

Northumberland
Worth a visit

520 The Ship Marygate, Holy Island, Berwick-upon-Tweed TD15 2SJ +44 (0)1289 389311
Rustic bare boards and beamed bars – a spotless little pub that sits in a terrace of cottages on a fascinating tidal island. Hadrian and Border ales and good seafood.

521 Dipton Mill Dipton Mill Road, Hexham NE46 1YA +44 (0)1434 606577
Former 18th-century mill house in a deep hollow next to a babbling brook a short drive south of Hexham. Squeeze into the single panelled bar for blazing log fires, top-notch Hexhamshire ales (the pub is the brewery tap), and warming home-cooked food. Super summer garden.

522 Blackmore's of Alnwick 24 Bondgate Without, Alnwick NE66 1PN +44 (0)1665 602395
Swish hotel, restaurant and bar by historic town walls overlooking Alnwick Gardens. The Victorian building has been given a stylish makeover, and all-day food from local chef John Blackmore. Reports please.

523 The Crown Catton, Allendale NE47 9S +44 (0)1434 683447
Closed for a decade before the Allendale microbrewery revived its fortunes and re-opened the cosy traditional pub as their brewery tap in 2009. Expect top-notch beers, music and quiz nights, board games and simple fresh food.

Nottinghamshire

The Victoria
Beeston

A large picture of Queen Victoria rules the main bar of this unpretentious and bustling city-suburb pub. It's an ex-Victorian railway hotel with bags of character, and its awesome raft of ales, wines by the glass and malt whiskies pulls in a crowd. The civilised main bar, with fire, newspapers on racks and etched windows, sets the tone for the other rooms, all plainly painted in magnolia with woodblock flooring and scrubbed dark-wood or brass-topped tables. Blackboards give the food and booze headlines. You get Sicilian pork, cottage pie and veggie dishes to delight even non-vegetarians (pasta with goat's cheese and rocket pesto). At the back, there's a heated marquee area for cooler summer nights; dine as the trains go by. Service is efficient and friendly. Try to catch the summer festival of ale, food and music.

Meals	12pm-8.45pm (Sun-Tues); 2pm-9.30pm (Wed-Sat). Main courses £7.50-£12.95.
Closed	Open all day.
Directions	Off A6005 at the bottom of Dovecote Lane. Follow signs to Beeston station.

Neil Kelso & Graham Smith
The Victoria,
85 Dovecote Lane, Beeston,
Nottingham NG9 1JG
Tel   +44 (0)1159 254049
Web   www.victoriabeeston.co.uk

Entry 524 Map 8

Nottinghamshire

Martin's Arms
Colston Bassett

An Elizabethan farmhouse that became an ale house around 1700, and an inn 100 years later. Today it is a deeply civilised pub. The front room exudes so much country-house charm — scatter cushions on sofas and settles, crackling logs in Jacobean fireplaces, 18th-century prints — that the bar seems almost an intrusion. Fresh, seasonal menus change daily. Bar snacks include special sandwiches and splendid ploughman's lunches with Colston Bassett stilton from the dairy up the road (do visit). In the restaurant, highlights include Park Farm Estate game shot by Salvatore, classic jugged hare, turbot with chorizo and pea risotto, and Sunday roast beef. Polish it all off with warm Bakewell tart with cinnamon anglaise. Behind the bar is an impressive range of well-kept real ales, cognacs, wines and malts from Adnams. Superb.

Meals	12pm-2pm (2.30pm Sun); 6pm-10pm; no food Sun eve. Main courses £10.95-£21.95; sandwiches from £5.50; Sunday lunch £16 (2 courses); set lunch £13.95.
Closed	3pm-6pm in winter.
Directions	Off A46, east of Nottingham. Take Owthorpe turning.

Lynne Strafford Bryan
& Salvatore Inguanta
Martin's Arms, School Lane,
Colston Bassett, Nottingham NG12 3FD
Tel   +44 (0)1949 81361
Web   www.themartinsarms.co.uk

Entry 525 Map 9

Nottinghamshire

Waggon & Horses
Halam

Enthused by its fantastic reputation for food, chef Roy Wood jumped at the chance to buy the Whites' share of the business in 2007. Enticing menus change with the seasons and almost everything is sourced locally, while the fish arrives daily from Grimsby docks. So try black pudding and stilton salad, roast sea trout with tomato and rosemary sauce, the renowned Nottinghamshire Pie; even lunchtime's rolls are worth travelling for. Desserts are divine: chocolate and pecan tart, blueberry and vanilla cheesecake. This spotlessly maintained pub is small, oak beamed and softly lit with low ceilings and bold walls; in the cosy but open-plan bar, rush-seated chairs pull up to sturdy tables. It's a Thwaites' tied house, friendly and expertly run. Sit outside and watch the Halam world go by.

Meals	12pm-2pm; 6pm-8pm (8.30pm Fri & Sat). Main courses £10-£16; set menu (lunch & early eve) £12 & £15.
Closed	3pm-5.30pm, Sun eve & Mon all day.
Directions	Halam is signed off A612 or B6386 in Southwell. On road leading to Farnsfield & A614.

Roy & Laura Wood
Waggon & Horses,
The Turnpike, Halam,
Newark NG22 8AE
Tel   +44 (0)1636 813109
Web   www.thewaggonathalam.co.uk

Entry 526 Map 9

Nottinghamshire

Caunton Beck
Caunton

Having hatched the successful Wig & Mitre in Lincoln, the Hopes looked for a rural equivalent and found one in Caunton. The pub was lovingly reconstructed from the skeleton of the 16th-century Hole Arms and then renamed. A decade on and it is a hugely popular pub-restaurant, opening at 8am for breakfast – orange juice, espresso, scrambled eggs. Later, there are sandwiches, mussels with pickled ginger and coriander laksa and pot-roasted guinea fowl; the puddings are fabulous. It's all very relaxed and civilised, the sort of place where newspapers and magazines take precedence over piped music and electronic wizardry. Come for country chairs at scrubbed pine tables, rag-rolled walls and a fire in winter, parasols on the terrace in summer. Well-managed ales are on hand pump, and the village is pretty.

Meals	8am-11pm. Main courses £9.50-£19.95.
Closed	Open all day.
Directions	6 miles NW of Newark past sugar factory on A616.

Michael & Valerie Hope
Caunton Beck,
Main Street,
Caunton, Newark NG23 6AB
Tel   +44 (0)1636 636 793
Web   www.wigandmitre.com

Entry 527 Map 9

Nottinghamshire

Worth a visit

528 Bottle & Glass High Street, Harby,
Newark NG23 7EB +44 (0)1522 703438

Quirky village pub now owned by the Hopes from Lincoln's famous Wig & Mitre. Victorian features blend with soft furnishings and chalkboard menus list soup to Sevruga caviar, all-day breakfast and 38 wines by the glass.

529 Robin Hood High Street, Elkesley,
Retford DN22 8AJ +44 (0)1777 838259

A far better pit-stop than the roadside 'restaurants' on offer: take the Elkesley turning off the A1 for a decent ploughman's or a lamb confit with mint pesto, garlic and thyme sauce.

530 Black Horse 29 Main Street, Caythorpe,
Nottingham NG14 7ED +44 (0)115 966 3520

A tiny, carpeted bar where Sharron Andrews sells beer brewed on the premises and the fish menu is so popular that booking is essential. Dick Turpin once hid in the gents, apparently.

531 Larwood and Voce Fox Road,
West Bridgford, Nottingham NG2 6AJ
+44 (0)115 981 9960

Thriving town-centre 'pub and kitchen' next to Trent Bridge cricket ground. Come for the plush modern bar, cricket on the screen, live jazz and superb gastropub food. On match days the bar throngs.

532 Ye Olde Trip to Jerusalem
1 Brewhouse Yard, Nottingham NG1 6AD
+44 (0)115 947 3171

An amazing place carved into solid rock on which the castle sits, with rickety staircases and an aptly named Rock Lounge... plus a courtyard for those who choose daylight. The Trip serves a mixed crowd – locals, tourists, students – and the food is standard pub grub.

Oxfordshire

The Eyston Arms
East Hendred

The Eyston family have owned this pub at the foot of the Ridgeway since 1443! A renovation by the Daileys has brought a mix of the traditional and the new so step in to find Cotswold flagstone floors and an original water pump, fresh flowers and chunky wooden tables. It's a well-loved local, and the most regular regulars are immortalised in sketches on the dining room's papered walls. Come for happy chatter, a pint of London Pride, and first-class food. Chef Maria Jaremchuck earned her stripes here, left and has returned: the meat is properly hung for thick grilled steaks with triple-cooked chips, and rump of lamb with gratin dauphinoise, and desserts are just as good – try the lemon and saffron pannacotta. Daily specials are chalked up; ask partner Daisy Barton behind the bar for a suggestion. They look after you well here.

Meals	12pm-2pm; 7pm-9pm (12pm-5pm Sun). Main courses £11-£16.95; sandwiches £8; Sunday roast £14.
Closed	3pm-6pm (from 7pm Sun).
Directions	Eeast Hendred is just off A417 between Wantage and Rowstock, 2 miles west of A34; pub in village centre.

George Dailey
The Eyston Arms,
High Street, East Hendred,
Wantage OX12 8JY

Tel	+44 (0)1235 833320
Web	www.eystonarms.co.uk

Entry 533 Map

The Boar's Head
Ardington

A dapper estate village with a church, a pub and a post office, the pub being the home of the village cricket club. It's a civilised place populated by locals and barbour-clad walkers who come for open fires, the daily papers, local ales, upmarket food. Sunday lunch can roll on to six and the bar is lively most evenings, making it the smart spruce hub of this small community. Gilt mirrors and old oils hang on the walls. There are big oak tables in the restaurant and doors onto a terrace for alfresco summer suppers. And the bedrooms upstairs are unmistakably smart. The small double has a beamed ceiling, the big double comes with a claw-foot bath, the suite has a sofa for kids and views over the village. All have good beds, crisp linen and piles of cushions. Much enthusiasm in the kitchen and the food is popular as a result. Everything is homemade: bread, pasta, pastries, ice cream… try scallops with black pudding and roasted foie gras, sea bass with mussels and girolles, Tulwick lamb with garlic confit and mustard sauce, and bread, butter and vanilla pudding. *Check in before 3pm or after 6pm by arrangement.*

Rooms	3: 2 doubles, 1 suite. £95–£140. Singles £85–£95.
Meals	12pm–2pm; 7pm–9.30pm. Main courses £17–£20; bar meals £7.95–£14.95; set lunch £14.50 & £17.50; Sunday lunch (3 courses) £23.50.
Closed	3pm–6.30pm (7pm Sun).
Directions	A417 west from Didcot for Wantage. Through West Hendred & turn left to Ardington. In village, left by bus stop; on left.

Bruce & Kay Buchan
The Boar's Head,
Church Street,
Ardington, Wantage OX12 8QA
Tel +44 (0)1235 833254
Web www.boarsheadardington.co.uk

Entry 534 Map 3

Oxfordshire

Rising Sun
Highmoor

Much-loved landlady Judith Bishop is loving every minute at her creamy cottage-pub, tucked up a gravel track on the edge of the Chilterns. Her magic touch is clearly to be seen... in the rambling dining area and in the cosy bar, with its bare boards, terracotta walls, scrubbed pine tables, deep sofa by the crackling fire and no end of lovely touches – books, magazines and huge vases of flowers. Eager to do something different on the food front, Judith has introduced a seasonal, game orientated menu, as well as French onion soup and garlic aioli, smoked haddock and sweet potato fishcakes, and a rabbit and wild mushroom pie. Great ales and a secluded garden add to the pleasure, best enjoyed following a rural ramble through Chiltern beech woods.

Meals	12pm-2.30pm (3pm Sun); 7pm-9.30pm; no food Sun eve. Main courses £8.95-£15.50.
Closed	3pm-6pm. Open all day Sat & Sun.
Directions	Witheridge Hill is signed off B481 east of Stoke Row.

Judith Bishop
Rising Sun,
Highmoor,
Henley-on-Thames RG9 5PF
Tel   +44 (0)1491 640856

Entry 535 Map 4

Oxfordshire

The Cherry Tree Inn
Stoke Row

A cherry orchard flourished here 400 years ago and farm workers lived in these brick and flint cottages. Five trees survive on the sprawling lawn at the front, so come in spring for the blossom. Beds of lavender lead up to the front door, inside you find ancient stone flagging and low beamed ceilings, plus board games in a cupboard, fairylights in the fireplace and a different colour on the walls in each room. Beers are from Brakspear and there's a very decent selection of wines by the glass but it's the food that's the draw. Huge bowls of mussels and Devonshire crab flow from the kitchen, there are plates of Chiltern lamb with Moroccan spices, butternut squash and goat's cheese risotto, Old Spot pork with mash and black pudding. And updates of classic puddings; our tarte tatin came with a calvados sauce.

Meals	12pm-3pm (4pm Sat); 7pm-10.30pm (6pm-10pm Sun). Main courses £7.50-£13.50 (lunch), £10.50-£15.50 (dinner).
Closed	Open all day.
Directions	A4070 north from Reading. After 4 miles, right, through Checkendon, to the village of Stoke Row.

Richard Coates
The Cherry Tree Inn,
Stoke Row,
Henley-on-Thames RG9 5QA
Tel   +44 (0)1491 680430
Web   www.thecherrytreeinn.com

Entry 536 Map 4

Oxfordshire

The Crooked Billet
Stoke Row

Dick Turpin apparently courted the landlord's daughter and Kate Winslet had her wedding breakfast here. Pints are drawn direct from the cask (there is no bar!) and the rusticity of the pub charms all who manage to find it: beams and inglenooks, old pine, walls lined with bottles and baskets of spent corks. In the larger room, red walls display old photographs and mirrors; shelves are stacked with books... by candlelight it's irresistible. The menu is Italian/French provincial, and long: beef fillet with seared foie gras and red wine jus, venison with roast figs and port and juniper, chocolate tart with mint ice cream. The food is founded on supremely well-sourced raw materials (allotment holders are encouraged!) and bolstered by a satisfying wine list. Occasional jazz, and a big garden bordering the beech woods where children can roam.

Meals	12pm-2.30pm; 7pm-10.30pm (12pm-10.30pm Sat & Sun). Main courses £12.50-£20.
Closed	2.30pm-7pm. Open all day Sat & Sun.
Directions	5 miles west of Henley, off B481 Reading to Nettlebed road.

Paul Clerehugh
The Crooked Billet,
Newlands Lane, Stoke Row,
Henley-on-Thames RG9 5PU
Tel +44 (0)1491 681048
Web www.thecrookedbillet.co.uk

Entry 537 Map 4

Oxfordshire

The Lamb at Satwell
Rotherfield Greys

The fortunes of this 16th-century beamed cottage were revived by Chris & Emma Smith following a period of closure early in 2009. Enter a gorgeously low-beamed bar: scrubbed pine tables on tiled floors, logs crackling in the grate, local ales on hand pump. Arrive early to bag a seat by the fire or settle into the cosy dining room next door; be treated to steaming plates of pork and herb sausages with mash and onion gravy or shepherd's pie from the bar menu. Look to the carte for scallops with sauce vierge, pan-fried foie gras with caramelised apple, venison casserole, and haddock and salmon fishcakes with sorrel hollandaise. Finish with steamed apple and ginger pudding – it's all scrumptiously English – and don't miss the Sunday roasts. There's a secluded garden and roaming chickens, too. Close to watery Henley-on-Thames.

Meals	12pm-3pm; 6pm-9pm (10am-10pm Sat; 12pm-9pm Sun). Main courses £8.95-£18.95; brunch £6.95; Sunday roast £10.95-£13.95.
Closed	3pm-6pm. Open all day Sat & Sun.
Directions	A4130 north from Henley; 3 miles; 1st exit at r'bout near Nettlebed onto B481 to Highmoor; thro' village; 1 mile to Satwell, left at 'Shepherd's Green' sign.

Chris & Emma Smith & Nick Gross
The Lamb at Satwell,
Rotherfield Greys,
Henley-on-Thames RG9 4QZ
Tel +44 (0)1491 628482
Web www.thelambpub.net

Entry 538 Map 4

Oxfordshire

The Sweet Olive at The Chequers Inn
Aston Tirrold

Expect more than a hint of Gallic charm at this homely village local close to the Ridgeway Path: the owners and many of the staff are French, which gives it a great deal of style. In the locals' bar, a central pillar and beam are lined with old wooden wine boxes, there's Brakspear and London Pride on hand pump and first-class French country cooking (with a hint of North Africa) in the rustic bistro dining room with its quarry tiled floor, roaring fire and old oak furniture. The blackboard menu changes daily with much emphasis placed on seasonal and organic food: oxtail in puff pastry with red burgundy sauce, escalope of venison with creamed cabbage and port wine. Children's meals are prepared from the same menu, simple snacks and fresh baguettes are served at lunch time, the wine list is mainly French, and the coffee is perfect.

Meals	12pm-2pm; 7pm-9pm. Main courses £12.95-£19.95; baguettes from £6.
Closed	3pm-6pm; Sun eve & all day Weds.
Directions	Aston Tirrold is signed off A417 between Streatley & Wantage.

Stephanie Brun & Olivier Bouet
The Sweet Olive at The Chequers Inn,
Aston Tirrold,
Didcot OX11 9DD
Tel   +44 (0)1235 851272
Web   www.sweet-olive.com

Entry 539 Map 4

Oxfordshire

The Bull & Butcher
Turville

Landlady Lydia Botha ensures this little pub quenches the thirsts of all who come to visit – and many do – one of the most bucolic film locations in Britain. The Vicar of Dibley has strutted Turville's streets, suspects from *Midsomer Murders* have propped up the bar. There's bags of atmosphere here, and style, in cream walls, latched doors, fresh flowers. It's a jolly place in which to down a pint of Brakspear's finest and indulge is some good modern British food: homemade pies, fresh fish and game in season. No fruit machines, no pubby paraphernalia, just fine 17th-century beams, working log fires, a unique function room, and friendly people. Get there early at weekends when Londoners descend. There's a garden to spill into and great walks through the Chiltern beech woods.

Meals	12pm-2.30pm (4pm Sat & Sun); 6.30pm-9.30pm (6pm-9.30pm Sat; 7pm-9pm Sun). Main courses £10-£14; bar meals £6-£10.
Closed	Open all day.
Directions	M40 junc. 5; through Ibstone; for Turville at T-junction.

Lydia Botha
The Bull & Butcher,
Turville,
Henley-on-Thames RG9 6QU
Tel   +44 (0)1491 638283
Web   www.thebullandbutcher.com

Entry 540 Map 4

Oxfordshire

The Half Moon
Cuxham

Since 2006 Andrew and Eilidh have been at the helm of this thatched house on the main street of the village. Cleverly they have retained the feel of a pub – quarry tiles, floorboards, farm implements, warming fires and a mishmash of settles and rush-seated chairs – while serving the most contemporary of British food (duck hearts or lambs kidneys on toast, local pheasant stew, curly kale and bacon). There are over 20 bins to choose from, or try a pint of Brakspears. Step outside to an area with seating for alfresco dining on sunny days, then a herb garden and a polytunnel where as many vegetables as possible are grown; they also prepare and deliver food to homes in the village to take the hard work out of entertaining. A lovely, informal place – no wonder Harry the springer spaniel makes an appearance most afternoons. *Booking advisable.*

Meals	12pm-2pm (3pm Sun); 6pm-9pm. No food Sun eve. Main courses £9.50-£18.50.
Closed	2.30pm-6pm. Sun eves after 5pm & Mon all day. Open all day Sat.
Directions	M40 junc 6; follow B4009 south to Watlington, then right along B480 to Cuxham.

Andrew Hill & Eilidh Ferguson
The Half Moon,
Cuxham,
Watlington OX49 5NF
Tel   +44 (0)1491 614151
Web   www.thehalf-moon.com

Entry 541 Map 4

Oxfordshire

The Lord Nelson
Brightwell Baldwin

The back-lane setting of Brightwell Baldwin lives up to expectations: cottages tumbling down the hill, a church perched on a bank, a rambling inn festooned with flowers, flags on Trafalgar Day. The creamy façade and front veranda entice you into a civilised and charming interior, wonky beams, logs fires and cosy corners; antiques, fine old prints and Nelson memorabilia keep the eye entertained. Most come to dine and dine well you can, on scallops with lime and coriander dressing, rack of lamb with red wine sauce, and sea bass on crab mash with tomato and black olive tapenade. Retire to the snug (deep sofas, table lamps, a country-house feel) for coffee and a little doze. And there's more – Brakspear on tap, 20 wines by the glass, friendly, smiley service and a wonderful rear terrace for summer sipping.

Meals	12pm-2.30pm (3pm Sun); 6.30pm-10pm (7pm-9.30pm Sun). Main courses £10.50-£18.95; set menu, 2 courses, £12.50; bar meals £10.
Closed	3pm-6pm. Open all day Sun.
Directions	Village signed off B4009 between Benson & Watlington.

Roger & Carole Shippey
The Lord Nelson,
Brightwell Baldwin,
Watlington OX49 5NP
Tel   +44 (0)1491 612497
Web   www.lordnelson-inn.co.uk

Entry 542 Map 4

The Lambert Arms
Aston Rowant

The Lambert Arms is a remodelled pub in several green acres, conveniently close to the motorway. The late 19th-century building has a classic pub interior in which informal rooms ramble around a central bar, with wooden floors, warm walls, leaded windows, crackling fires in three period fireplaces, big lamps and chunky candles on darkwood tables. Locals, travellers and business folk mix contentedly, united by their enjoyment of Greene King beers and decent wines (note the feature wine store). Food ranges from classic liver and bacon and beer-battered fish to modern scallops with bok choi and chorizo, and corn-fed duck with confit leg. Beyond: in a different world entirely lies a land of bedrooms, conference facilities, treatment rooms and a fitness suite. Of course, it's immaculately done: stylish fabrics, muted colours, darkwood furniture, top mattresses. Rooms in the inn are, by contrast, cosier, oozing period character.

Rooms	42 twins/doubles. From £89.
Meals	12pm-2.30pm (6.30pm Sun); 6.30pm-9pm (9.30pm Fri & Sat). Main courses £7.95-£19.95; sandwiches from £5.50.
Closed	Open all day.
Directions	On A40, close to junction with B4009 Chinnor to Watlington road, and M40 (junc. 6).

Neal Tripp
The Lambert Arms,
London Road, Aston Rowant,
Watlington OX49 5SB

Tel	+44 (0)1844 351496
Web	www.lambertarms.com

Oxfordshire

The Mole Inn
Toot Baldon

The Mole Inn continues to wow Oxford foodies – it is packed most days. Expect an impeccable stone exterior, a landscaped garden and a ravishing bar. There are stripped beams and chunky walls, black leather sofas, logs in the grate and a dresser that groans with breads and olive jars. Chic rusticity proceeds into three dining areas: fat candles on blond wooden tables, thick terracotta floors and the sun angling in on a fresh plateful of beef casserole with garlic and bacon dauphinoise. Daily specials point to a menu that trawls the globe for inspiration, and whether you go for light salad and pasta bowl lunches or monkfish and king prawn stir fry with egg noodles and sweet chilli, you'll eat well. Scrumptious ice creams, British cheeses, good wines, local Hook Norton ale and polite staff complete the picture.

Oxfordshire

The Fishes
Oxford

Location, location, location – The Fishes has it all. Three acres of gardens, minutes from the A34, and walking distance from the dreaming spires. It's run by Peach Pubs, the most innovative small pub group in the land; where else can you borrow a rug for the garden, order a Pimms and a picnic basket for two and spread out by a river? Just arrive early on fine days. Order (by midweek) a family roast beef platter for the weekend, on Sunday sit down to it on the veranda. The successful Peach food formula is reproduced here: the deli board selection, the starters of pumpkin and sage risotto and Caesar salad, the main dishes of fish stew, salmon wellington and braised blade of beef with baby onion jus. Greene King ales, decent wines by the glass and a passion for locally sourced produce complete this very rosy picture.

Meals	12pm-2.30pm (4pm Sun); 7pm-9.30pm (6pm-9pm Sun). Main courses £12.95-£18; bar meals £5.95-£9.95.
Closed	Open all day.
Directions	From A4074, 5 miles south of Oxford; turn at Nuneham Courtenay for Marsh Baldon & Toot Baldon. 10 mins from junc. 7 of M40.

Meals	12pm-10.30pm (9.30pm Sun). Main courses £9.75-£16.50; Sunday roast £12.50.
Closed	Open all day.
Directions	North on A34; left junction after Botley Interchange, signed to Rugby Club. From south, exit A34 at Botley & return to A34 south; then as above.

Gary Witchalls
The Mole Inn,
Toot Baldon,
Oxford OX44 9NG

Tel +44 (0)1865 340001
Web www.themoleinn.com

Entry 544 Map 8

Katie Robertson
The Fishes,
North Hinksey,
Oxford OX2 0NA

Tel +44 (0)1865 249796
Web www.fishesoxford.co.uk

Entry 545 Map 8

Oxfordshire

The Anchor Inn
Oxford

Residential North Oxford is an unlikely setting for city's best pub food, but Jamie and Charlotte have defied the odds, and turned a somewhat unattractive Art Deco-styled building into a brilliant dining pub. Weekend walkers escape the city via the canal – the towpath's over the road – while the well-heeled folk of Watton Manor regularly drop by. In two high-ceilinged bars, each embellished with period furnishings and fireplaces, ex-Harvey Nicks chef Jamie delivers seasonal British food using fresh and local ingredients. So there's game terrine, rack of Wytham Wood Farm lamb and treacle tart with ginger cream. Wadworth ales on tap, good house wines by the glass, local book club meetings, sport on the big screen and a 'breakfast club' for mums on the school run ensure, along with the fabulous food, the Anchor's survival.

Oxfordshire

The White Hart
Fyfield

Incredible to think that when Henry VIII came to the throne this building was already 70 years old. Stone mullioned windows, huge oak timbers and a magnificent arch-braced roof are the backdrop for oak settles, wrought-iron candle holders, white linen napkins, fresh flowers and delicious food cooked by Mark. The menu is extensive and modern: beetroot, feta and hazelnut roulade, slow-roasted belly of Kelmscott pork with crackling and cider jus, hot chocolate fondant with pistachio ice cream; suppliers are mentioned on the menu so you can see where everything comes from. Enjoy four real ales and Cheddar valley cider, and staff who are capable and knowledgeable (they were all taken to Hook Norton to see how the beer was brewed).

Meals	12pm-2.30pm (3pm Sun); 6pm-9.30pm (6.30pm-8.30pm Sun). Main courses £9.50-£16; bar snacks £4-£7.85.
Closed	Open all day.
Directions	A34 ring road north; exit Peartree r'bout. 1.5 miles, right at Polstead Road. Follow road to bottom, pub on right.

Meals	12pm-2.30pm (3.30pm Sun); 7pm-9.30pm (Tues-Sat). Main courses £12-£18; set lunch £15 & £18.
Closed	3pm-5.30pm & Mon all day (except bank hols). Open all day Sat & Sun.
Directions	Fyfield is just off A420 Oxford to Swindon road, 6 miles south west of Oxford; pub in village centre.

Jamie & Charlotte King
The Anchor Inn,
2 Hayfield Road,
Walton Manoir, Oxford OX2 6TT
Tel   +44 (0)1865 510282
Web   www.theanchoroxford.com

Entry 546 Map 8

Mark & Kay Chandler
The White Hart,
Main Road, Fyfield,
Abingdon OX13 5LW
Tel   +44 (0)1865 390585
Web   www.whitehart-fyfield.com

Entry 547 Map 8

Oxfordshire

The Rose & Crown
Shilton

Small, cosy, friendly and run with panache. In a mellow Cotswold stone village, the pub's setting could not be more idyllic. The 16th-century Rose & Crown holds just two rooms: the bar room itself, simple and unadorned, and a fractionally larger extension built in 1701. There's an open fire in the inglenook and a medley of kitchen tables and chairs, making the once rundown local a most atmospheric and civilised public house. Be charmed by low beams, exposed stone walls, a terracotta floor, fresh flowers, Old Hooky on tap, and good food. You'll find a happy crowd sitting down to venison terrine, roast partridge with blackberries, or good steak, ale and mushroom pie, and bread and butter pudding. This is a gorgeous, sheltered spot and there's a garden you can drift into on warm days.

Meals	12pm-2pm (2.45pm Sat & Sun); 7pm-9pm; no food Sun eve in winter. Main courses £8.50-£15.50 (lunch), £9-£15.50 (dinner).
Closed	3pm-6pm. Open all day Fri-Sun & bank hols.
Directions	Shilton is signed off B4020, 2 miles SE of A40 at Burford.

Martin Coldicott
The Rose & Crown,
Shilton,
Burford OX18 4AB

Tel   +44 (0)1993 842280

Entry 548 Map 8

Oxfordshire

The Clanfield Tavern
Clanfield

Mellow Cotswold stone, head-cracking timbers, stone-flagged floors and huge log fires set the tone in the rambling bar at this 15th-century village inn not far from the Thames. Add jugs of fresh flowers, posh lamps, colourful canvases and picture lights on bare stone walls, deep sofas, daily papers and a wood-burning stove and you have a very civilised place in which to relax with a morning cappuccino or a lunchtime pint of Ringwood Best (and even a beef and horseradish sandwich). At scrubbed tables in the bar, or in the striking, contemporary conservatory, tuck into sautéed lambs' kidneys, pheasant and mushroom pie, treacle tart with clotted cream. Owner Tom is passionate about produce; he shoots the pheasant, grows the vegetables (in a smallholding beyond the pub garden) and the lamb is reared next door. Set lunches are brilliant value.

Meals	12pm-2.30pm (3pm Sun); 6.30pm-9pm (9.30pm Fri & Sat). No food Sun & takeaway fish & chips 5.30pm-8pm Mon. Main courses £8.50-£15.50; set lunch (2 courses) £10; Sunday lunch £15.95 & £18.95.
Closed	3pm-5.30pm Tues-Fri & until 5.30pm Mon. Open all day Sat & Sun.
Directions	Village centre; at junction of B4020 & A4095 between Witney & Faringdon.

Tom & Lucy Gee
The Clanfield Tavern,
Bampton Road,
Clanfield, Bampton OX18 2RG

Tel   +44 (0)1367 810223
Web   www.clanfieldtavern.com

Entry 549 Map 8

Oxfordshire

The Frog
Skirmett

By the village lane, deep in the beautiful Hambledon valley, the spruced up 18th-century coaching inn is surrounded by open meadows and glorious walks. Head for the secluded garden, pint of Marlow Rebellion in hand, gaze across the valley and watch the red kites wheel. Or retreat inside, mingle with the walkers and the foodies, and bag a deep sofa by the log fire. Wood floors, warm colours, bold mirrors and an eclectic mix of tables and chairs fill the pretty dining areas. Seasonal menus feature pub classics like steak, Guinness and mushroom pie alongside chicken, tarragon and tomato risotto, and roast Hambledon Estate venison with juniper sauce. Don't miss the sticky toffee pudding – or the once-a-month pub 'shop' selling Noelle's luscious savoury pastries, cakes and chutneys.

Meals	12pm-2.30pm; 6.30pm-9.30pm. Main courses £11.95-£16.95.
Closed	3pm-6pm. Open all day Sun (except Sun eve in winter).
Directions	Take Hambleden road off A4155 north eaat of Henley and follow valley road to Skirmett.

Jim Crowe & Noelle Greene
The Frog,
Skirmett,
Henley-on-Thames RG9 6TG
Tel +44 (0)1491 638996
Web www.thefrogatskirmett.co.uk

Entry 550 Map

Oxfordshire

The Highway Inn
Burford

You can sit out on the high street under the shade of a parasol in summer and watch the shoppers haul their bounty up the hill, but this lovely inn comes complete with a small medieval courtyard where honeysuckle and orange blossom roam. The building itself goes back to 1480, with rather lovely interiors where all the architectural gems are to hand: mind-your-head beams, nooks and stairs, ancient flags. Tally and Scott, both locals, spent their wedding night here, then returned to renovate, thus rescuing the inn from years of neglect. They have kept the mood warmly traditional so expect padded window seats, stripped boards, open fires, a good pint and hearty pub food in the bar or private dining room – fishcakes with tartare sauce, Cotswold rib-eye steak with béarnaise, apple and blackberry crumble. This is a very friendly base.

Meals	12pm-2.30pm (3pm Sun); 6.30pm-9pm (9.30pm Fri & Sat). Main courses £9.95-£15.95; bar lunches from £4.50.
Closed	Open all day.
Directions	A40 west from Oxford to Burford. On right in town, halfway down hill.

Tally & Scott Nelson
The Highway Inn,
117 High Street,
Burford OX18 4RG
Tel +44 (0)1993 823661
Web www.thehighwayinn.co.uk

Entry 551 Map 8

The Trout at Tadpole Bridge
Buckland Marsh

A 17th-century Cotswold inn on the banks of the Thames, so pick up a pint, drift into the garden and watch life float by. The Trout is a drinking fisherman's paradise, walls are busy with bendy rods, children are liked and dogs can doze in the flagstoned bars. The downstairs is open plan and timber-framed, there are gilt mirrors and logs piled high in alcoves. Gareth and Helen have cast their fairy dust into every corner: super bedrooms, fabulous modern food, a relaxed style. Bedrooms at the back are away from the crowd; three open onto a small courtyard where wild roses ramble on creamy stone – but you may prefer to stay put in your room and indulge in funky fabrics, trim carpets, monsoon showers (one room has a claw-foot bath), DVD players, a library of films. Sleigh beds, brass beds, upholstered armchairs... one even has a roof terrace. You can watch boats pass from the breakfast table, feast on local sausages, tuck into homemade marmalade courtesy of Helen's mum. Food is as local as possible, and there are maps for walkers to keep you thin. Bliss!

Rooms	6: 2 doubles, 3 twins/doubles, 1 suite. £110. Suite £140. Singles from £75.
Meals	12pm-2pm; 7pm-9pm. No food Sun eve Nov-April. Main courses £11.25-£17.50; bar snacks from £5.95; Sunday lunch £14.95.
Closed	3.30pm-6pm & Sun eve in winter.
Directions	A420 southwest from Oxford for Swindon. After 13 miles, right for Tadpole Bridge. On right by bridge.

Gareth & Helen Pugh
The Trout at Tadpole Bridge,
Buckland Marsh,
Faringdon SN7 8RF

Tel	+44 (0)1367 870382
Web	www.trout-inn.co.uk

Entry 552 Map 8

Oxfordshire

The Fleece
Witney

If you need to be in Oxford, staying at the Fleece is an attractive alternative; a cheaper one, too. Lee Cash and Victoria Moon dug deep into their pockets to buy the lease on the Georgian Fleece – and thus launched the hugely successful Peach Pub Company. Expect a sparkling gastropub interior: wooden floors, plum walls, squashy sofas, low tables – and continental opening hours that start with coffee and bacon sarnies at 8.30am. Moving the bar to the front has worked wonders, drawing in casual drinkers for pints of Greene King. They don't believe a pub is the place for leather-bound tomes either, so what you get is a regularly changing wine list at sensible prices. Thumbs-up too for the all-day sandwiches, salads and deli-board menu: starters of cheese, charcuterie, fish, olive tapenade, marinated chillies, stone-baked pizzas too, and modern brasserie-style dishes such as braised shoulder of lamb with roasted winter roots. Delightful bedrooms are big enough to hold an armchair or two and beds are extremely comfortable; we'd recommend one at the front overlooking charming Witney's green.

Rooms	10: 8 doubles, 1 twin, 1 family room. £80-£100.
Meals	12pm-2.30pm; 6.30pm-9.30pm; all day menu 12pm-6.30pm. Main courses £9.75-£19.50; bar meals £4-£12.
Closed	Open all day.
Directions	Witney is off A40 between Oxford and Burford; pub on green, near church.

Aimee Moore
The Fleece,
11 Church Green,
Witney OX28 4AZ
Tel   +44 (0)1993 892270
Web   www.fleecewitney.co.uk

Entry 553 Map 8

The Swan
Swinbrook

This ancient country pub sits in glorious country with the river Windrush passing yards from the front door and a cricket pitch waiting beyond. It started life as a water mill and stands on the Devonshire estate (the Duchess advised on its restoration). Outside, wisteria wanders along stone walls and creepers blush red in the autumn sun. Interiors come laden with period charm: beautiful windows, open fires, warm colours, the odd beam. Over the years thirsty feet have worn grooves into 400-year-old flagstones, so follow in their footsteps and stop for a pint of Hook Norton at the bar, then eat from a seasonal menu that brims with local produce: deep-fried Windrush goat's cheese, Foxbury Farm chargrilled steak, rich chocolate tart with orange sorbet. Fires roar in winter while doors in the conservatory restaurant open onto a pretty garden in good weather. Bedrooms in the old forge are the most recent addition. Expect 15th-century walls and 21st-century interior design. You get pastel colours to soak up the light, smart white linen on comfy beds and a pink chaise longue in the suite.

Rooms	6: 4 doubles, 1 twin, 1 suite. £110–£180. Singles from £70.
Meals	12pm–2pm (2.30pm Sun); 7pm–9pm (9.30pm Fri & Sat). Main courses £10.95–£17.50; sandwiches (lunch) from £6.50; Sunday roast £14.
Closed	Open all day.
Directions	From Oxford A40, through Witney. Village signed right, off A40.

Archie & Nicola Orr-Ewing
The Swan,
Swinbrook,
Burford OX18 4DY

Tel	+44 (0)1993 823339
Web	www.theswanswinbrook.co.uk

Entry 554 Map 8

Oxfordshire

Royal Oak
Ramsden

Blazing winter fires, piles of magazines and well-thumbed books by the inglenook make this the perfect place for a pint of real ale, so tuck into a corner filled with plump scatter cushions. Some brilliant food can be had in the pubby bar – open-stone walls, cream and soft green windows – as well as in the extension beyond, where glass doors open to a pretty terrace with wrought-iron chairs and outdoor heaters for chilly evenings. Dishes such as roast half shoulder of Westwell lamb with rosemary and garlic sauce, roast cod with tapenade crust and sweet pepper sauce and chocolate and brandy ice cream should put a smile on your face; in winter, there's lots of game. Well-behaved children and dogs are welcome, the staff are delightful and the village is a stunner. You won't hear a bad word said about this place.

Meals	12pm-2pm; 7pm-10pm.
	Main courses £7.50-£18;
	Sunday lunch £16.95.
Closed	3pm-6.30pm.
Directions	On B4022, 3 miles north of Witney.

Jon Oldham
Royal Oak,
High Street,
Ramsden,
Chipping Norton OX7 3AU
Tel +44 (0)1993 868213

Entry 555 Map 8

Oxfordshire

The White Hart
Wytham

Who says the traditional and the contemporary don't mix? At the White Hart, bold colours and modern art mingle with flagged floors and stone fireplaces. And the different areas have distinctive characters: the 'Parlour' room has a French feel with painted floors and furniture and a central bread block laid with fresh loaves; the cosy bar has exotic coloured walls and velvet cushions. The upstairs restaurant is all open brickwork, plain floorboards, log fire and walls bearing framed tomatoes. The walled courtyard terrace is perfect for summer dining. There are real ales and a raft of wines by the glass in the bar and modern cooking from the kitchen. Daily specials might include venison with warm autumn vegetable salad and light balsamic jus, and herb-crusted cod with cauliflower purée and lemon beure noisette.

Meals	12pm-3pm (4pm Sat);
	6.30pm-10pm (12pm-8pm Sun).
	Main courses £13.95-£16.95;
	set dinner, 2 courses, £10.
Closed	4pm-6pm. Open all day Sat & Sun.
Directions	A34 to Oxford, off at Botley interchange.

Colin Royal
The White Hart,
Wytham,
Oxford OX2 8QA
Tel +44 (0)1865 244372
Web www.thewhitehartoxford.co.uk

Entry 556 Map 8

The Bird in Hand
Hailey

A mellow stone inn in a grand position for Cotswold villages (boutiquey retail therapy) and visits to Oxford, but also for quiet country walks. Returning peckish you can wander into the stylish contemporary bar with its wood floors, leather bucket seats, big baskets of logs and muse over the good light lunch menu; try Gloucester Old Spot sausages and mash, or smoked salmon and scrambled egg. The dining room in the old part of the building has exposed stone walls, cushioned window seats and two raised log fireplaces, and the menu sports predominantly British food: ham hock terrine, game stew, plaice with brown shrimp butter; try the rice pudding with boozy prunes afterwards. The gentle hum of chatter, two real ales and an interesting wine list will tempt you to linger beside the roaring fire; there's a terrace for sunny days, too.

Nut Tree Inn
Murcott

The menu reads like a posh London restaurant, but you can get supper and a pint for a tenner on Sunday nights and there are pigs out the back. Imogen and Mike are friendly and fun and operate their own version of 'The Good Life' down here in their idyllic whitewashed, thatched pub, and grow a lot of their own food. The bar is soothing with an open fire, white linen, natural stripped oak beams, stone walls and leather chesterfields. Choose from well-priced bar food (smoked salmon with scrambled eggs, artisan cheeses) or take a look at the specials board: tea-smoked wild goose with mango purée, cucumber and pickled ginger salad; chopped venison steak and wild mushroom risotto. There's real ale, draught cider, a long wine list and a pretty rear terrace for summer days with views over the smallholding.

Meals	12pm-2.30pm (3pm Sun); 6.30pm-9.30pm. Main courses £9.95-£15.95; bar lunches £5-£8.	Meals	12pm-2pm; 7pm-9pm (6.30pm-8pm Sun in summer). Main courses £14-£22; bar meals £4.50-£9.
Closed	Open all day.	Closed	Sun eve in winter.
Directions	On B4022 Witney-Charlbury road, 3 miles north of Witney.	Directions	Murcott is 5 miles south of Bicester, signed off A41 towards Aylesbury.

	Barry Shelton		Michael & Imogen North
	The Bird in Hand,		Nut Tree Inn,
	Whiteoak Green,		Murcott,
	Hailey, Witney OX29 9XP		Kidlington OX5 2RE
Tel	+44 (0)1993 868321	Tel	+44 (0)1865 331253
Web	www.birdinhandinn.co.uk	Web	www.nuttreeinn.co.uk

Entry 557 Map 8

Entry 558 Map 8

Oxfordshire

The Oxford Arms
Kirtlington

A robust 19th-century dining pub tucked away down a lane in a village eight miles from Oxford – the coat of arms above the door shows an Ox walking through a ford. Pretty windows are painted pale green grey and window boxes are coloured with geraniums. The main bar faces south, the floors are flagged and boarded, wood smoke tinges the air; the perfect place to decide what to eat while you sip a half of Hook Bitter or something from the excellent wine list. To one side is a candlelit dining area with large tables and comfy sofas, the other is more pubby and informal with bar stools and farmhouse chairs. Wherever you decide to eat there will be the convivial rumble of chat in the background and the food is a treat: splash out on potted shrimps with toast, then salmon and prawn fish cakes with sweet chilli sauce.

Meals	12pm-2.30pm; 6.30pm-9.30pm. Main courses £9.50-£16.
Closed	3pm-6pm & Sun eve.
Directions	On A4095 between A44 south of Woodstock & Bicester.

Bryn Jones
The Oxford Arms,
Troy Lane, Kirtlington,
Kidlington OX5 3HA
Tel   +44 (0)1869 350208
Web   www.oxford-arms.co.uk

🚶 📇 🐕 🍷 📶

Entry 559 Map 8

Oxfordshire

Lamb Inn
Shipton-under-Wychwood

A gorgeously done-up dining pub tucked down a quiet lane in an idyllic Cotswold village. Centuries-old, with mellow stone walls under a stone-tiled roof, it draws you in to its as-immaculate beamed bar. Tracey and Paul have spruced up the stone-walled bar, injecting a horse racing theme with jockey colours and Cheltenham photos. The polished wooden floor, roaring log fire and scrubbed tables make it a fine setting for homemade food: a steak and mustard mayonnaise sandwich, a cottage pie, or something from the antipasto board. Opt for the cosy dining room at night – chunky candles, log fire in inglenook, local artwork on stone walls – for Kelmscott pork belly, a fine sirloin steak, a rhubarb crème brûlée. And there's a super terrace for a pint of real ale or one of 18 wines by the glass.

Meals	12pm-2.30pm (3.30pm Sun); 6.30pm-9.30pm. Main courses £8.45-£12 (lunch); £9.95-£16.50 (dinner); sandwiches from £5.65.
Closed	Open all day.
Directions	In village centre, off A361 between Chipping Norton and Burford.

Tracey & Paul Hunt
Lamb Inn,
High St, Shipton-under-Wychwood,
Chipping Norton OX7 6DQ
Tel   +44 (0)1993 830465
Web   www.shiptonlamb.com

🚶 📇 🐕 🍷 📶

Entry 560 Map 8

Kings Arms Hotel

Woodstock

Standing proud in historic Woodstock – estate village to Blenheim Palace, one of the country's architectural gems – is the Kings Arms, a refuge from town bustle. David and Sara Sykes's passion for this Georgian building has seen it restored to former glory; old and new combine as airy open-plan interiors drift from one room to another. Tradition can be found downstairs in the classic bar – all boarded floors and leather banquettes – then it's through to the chic, atrium-style dining room with chequered floor, open fire, high-backed leather chairs and huge gilded mirrors. Equally up-to-date are the menus, a typical meal reeling in roast butternut squash and apple soup, braised lamb shank with rosemary mash, port sauce and roast fennel, and apple brûlée with stem ginger ice cream. Lovely bedrooms of all sizes ramble over two floors and have a minimalist feel. Be spoiled by low-slung solid-wood beds with firm mattresses and richly coloured throws, leather bucket chairs, super bathrooms with Molten Brown potions. The staff are great and boutiques abound. *No under-12's overnight.*

Rooms	15: 14 doubles, 1 twin. From £140. Singles from £75.
Meals	12pm-2.30pm; 6.30pm-9.30pm (12pm-9.30pm Sun). Main courses £8.50-10.50 (lunch); £11.50-£19.75 (dinner).
Closed	Open all day.
Directions	On A44 at corner of Market Street in town centre.

David & Sara Sykes
Kings Arms Hotel,
19 Market Street,
Woodstock OX20 1SU
Tel   +44 (0)1993 813636
Web   www.kings-hotel-woodstock.co.uk

The Swan at Ascott
Ascott under Wychwood

The Swan: a spruced-up, mellow Cotswold stone inn rescued from years of brewery decline by Richard Lait. Locals are drawn to the gently refurbished bar for the welcome, the wood-burner and the pints of real ale, while the menu draws foodies from afar. There's chorizo and mozzarella tart with herb and balsamic dressing; local partridge with red cabbage, celeriac and lentil jus; monkfish with mussel and crab chowder; vanilla parfait with roasted plums and shortbread. Walkers enjoy lunchtime's ciabatta sandwiches (steak with red onion marmalade) and the ploughman's — a deli-board laden with cheese, roast ham, egg, coleslaw, fresh leaves and pickles. Peek at the rooms — four upstairs — and you'll have to stay the night... beautifully revamped in contemporary style they have designer fabrics, sleigh beds and crisp linen, colourful throws, modern prints and fat lamps. Cocoon Room, tucked under the eaves, has pale oak beams, a romantic French-style bed, and, at the far end, a subtly-lit bath behind standing timbers. Wake to a hearty breakfast, and explore the Evenlode Valley.

Rooms	5: 4 doubles, 1 twin. £75-£125.
Meals	12pm-2.15pm (2.30pm Sun); 5.30pm-9pm. Main courses £8.50-£15.95.
Closed	3pm-5.30pm, Sun eve & all day Mon.
Directions	Village and pub signposted off A361 south of Chipping Norton.

Richard Lait
The Swan at Ascott,
4 Shipton Road,
Ascott under Wychwood,
Chipping Norton OX7 6AY

Tel	+44 (0)1993 832332
Web	www.swanatascott.com

Entry 562 Map 8

The Kings Head Inn
Bledington

About as Doctor Dolittle-esque as it gets. Achingly pretty Cotswold stone cottages around a village green with quacking ducks, a pond and a perfect pub with a cobbled courtyard. Archie is young, affable and charming with locals and guests, but Nic is his greatest asset – a milliner, she has done up the bedrooms and they look fabulous. All are different, most have a stunning view, some family furniture mixed in with 'bits' she's picked up, painted wood, great colours and lush fabrics. The bar is lively – not with music but with talk – so choose rooms over the courtyard if you prefer a quiet evening. The pretty flagstoned dining room (exposed stone walls, Farrow & Ball paints, pale wood tables) is inviting, there are lovely unpompous touches like jugs of cow parsley in the loo, and you can lunch by the fire in the bar – on devilled kidneys, sausage and mash, local Dexter beef and Guinness pie. They do homemade puds and serious cheeses, too, and breakfasts are huge! Loads to do round these parts: antiques in Stow, walking and riding in gorgeous countryside, even a music festival in June.

Rooms	12: 10 doubles, 2 twins. £80–£125. Singles from £60.
Meals	12pm-2pm; 7pm-9pm (9.30pm Fri & Sat). Main courses from £10; bar meals from £6.
Closed	Open all day.
Directions	East out of Stow-on-the-Wold on A436, then right onto B4450 for Bledington. Pub in village on green.

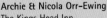

Archie & Nicola Orr-Ewing
The Kings Head Inn,
The Green, Bledington,
Chipping Norton OX7 6XQ
Tel   +44 (0)1608 658365
Web   www.kingsheadinn.net

Entry 563 Map 8

Oxfordshire

The Chequers
Churchill

Eye-catching with an immaculate stone frontage, the 18th-century Chequers stands smartly on the village lane. The Goldings took it on in 2003 and months of refurbishment followed before the reincarnation was unveiled. Prepare for a dramatic, airy and open-plan interior of bare boards and pine tables, cleverly partitioned dining areas, stone walls, roaring wood-burner and stacked logs, and chunky tables topped with candles and flowers. Soaring rafters and a vast dresser racked with wine bottles create an impression in the dining extension. No music, just a buzz when busy, and excellent food – red snapper and shrimp bouillabaisse, rib-eye steak with red wine sauce, lemon and raspberry posset. Book for the crispy duck night (Thursday) and roast Sunday lunches. Upstairs are a lounge and a private dining area.

Meals	12pm-2pm (3pm Sun); 7pm-9.30pm (9pm Sun). Main courses £4-£16.50.
Closed	Open all day.
Directions	On B4450 between Chipping Norton & Stow-on-the-Wold.

Peter & Asumpta Golding
The Chequers,
Church Road, Churchill,
Chipping Norton OX7 6NJ
Tel   +44 (0)1608 659393

Entry 564 Map 8

Oxfordshire

Mason's Arms
Swerford

The village of Swerford was once owned by a unfortunately-named henchman of William the Conqueror, one Robert D'Oily. It may be low on roadside appeal but the Mason's interior reveals a cottagey chic décor: duck-egg blue beams, clotted-cream walls, olive checked curtains, and rugs and seagrass hugging the floors. A wardrobe is stacked with wine bottles, background music plays, candles glow in the restaurant and drinkers nurse their Hooky Best. As for the food, it's locally sourced best-of-British. Chef-patron Bill, who's worked for Ramsay and lives to tell the tale, delivers soft herring roes on toast, braised shin of beef, user-friendly steaks and roast shoulder of Oxford Down lamb. Children are not indulged with nuggets 'n' chips but offered mini-portions of real food – and a garden to romp in.

Meals	12pm-2pm (3.30pm Sun); 7pm-9pm. No food Sun eve. Main courses £10.95-£17.95; bar meals £6.50-£9.95; set menus £15.95 & £21.95.
Closed	3pm-6pm (7pm Sun).
Directions	On A361 north-east of Chipping Norton.

Bill & Charmaine Leadbeater
Mason's Arms,
Banbury Road, Swerford,
Chipping Norton OX7 4AP
Tel   +44 (0)1608 683212
Web   www.masons-arms.com

Entry 565 Map 8

The Kingham Plough
Kingham

Overlooking a pretty green, the perfect Cotswold pub. What's more, the food is exemplary modern British and much of what you eat comes from within ten miles. Scan the chalkboards if you're after a snack: a homemade pork pie with chutney, perhaps, simple and delicious with a pint of Hook Norton or a glass of Weston's pear cider. Up a few steps and you're into the beamed and vaulted dining area, for rustic platefuls of warm pork belly and watercress salad, slow-cooked haunch of venison with port and chestnut sauce, spicy pears poached in mulled wine. Chef-patron Emily Watkins, once sous-chef at the Fat Duck, is another young cook who has swapped the glamour of Michelin stars for her own kitchen in the country – "come here for the gold standard", says food critic A A Gill. Everything is done with simplicity and integrity and that includes the interior of slate, brick and wood floors, exposed stone walls, beams, open fires and wooden tables. Bedrooms (three small) are as fresh and comfy as can be – in one is a magnificent claw-foot bath – while white linen, digital screens and homemade biscuits add to the treats.

Rooms	7 twins/doubles. £85-£125. Singles from £70.
Meals	12pm-2pm (2.30pm Sun); 7pm-9pm. Main courses £12-£22.
Closed	Open all day.
Directions	Off B4450 between Chipping Norton & Stow-on-the-Wold, signed.

Emily Watkins & Miles Lampson
The Kingham Plough,
The Green, Kingham,
Chipping Norton OX7 6YD

Tel	+44 (0)1608 658327
Web	www.thekinghamplough.co.uk

Oxfordshire

The Crown Inn
Church Enstone

Tony was head chef at the Three Choirs Vineyard; now he has his own place. With his wife Caroline, he decided to head for the Cotswolds and found this striking inn. It's a mellow-stone, 17th-century dream, off the beaten track in a sleepy village close to the river Glyme. Step in to a cosy, cottagey bar with old pine tables on a seagrass floor, rough stone walls, and a log fire crackling in the inglenook. At lunchtime, walkers and weekenders drop in for pints of Hook Norton and generous plates of home-cooked pub food; warming soups, steak and Hooky pie, fish and chips are listed on the blackboard. Cooking moves up a gear in the evening and fish is Tony's speciality; sea bass may be on the menu, with scallops, chilli and garlic dressing. Food is locally sourced and Sunday lunch is terrific; be sure to book.

Meals	12pm-2pm; 7pm-9pm. Main courses £8.95-£16.95; bar meals £4.75-£12.95; Sunday lunch £14.95-£17.95.
Closed	3pm-6pm & Sun from 4pm.
Directions	3.5 miles south east of Chipping Norton.

Tony & Caroline Warburton
The Crown Inn,
Church Enstone,
Chipping Norton OX7 4NN
Tel   +44 (0)1608 677262
Web   www.crowninnenstone.co.uk

Entry 567 Map 8

Oxfordshire

Black Boy Inn
Milton

Don't miss this 16th-century gem, next to the parish church in sleepy Milton. The single long room oozes original features and charm: oak beams and exposed stone walls by the bar, a red and black tiled floor, cosy terracotta colours, seagrass matting, scrubbed pine tables – and a log-burning stove in the inglenook. Beyond, a swish conservatory dining area overlooks a small gravelled courtyard. Really good food embraces pub classics like sausages and mash as well as more modern dishes like grilled fillet of seabream with lemon risotto and asparagus, or roasted fillet of sea trout with crab tagliatelle. Heart-warming puds include dark chocolate fondant and sticky toffee pudding; daily papers, real ales and landscaped gardens are further treats.

Meals	12pm-2.30pm (3pm Sun); 6.30pm-9pm (9.30pm Fri & Sat). Main courses £8.95-£19.95; bar meals £4.95-£12.95.
Closed	3pm-5.30pm. Open all day Sat & Sun.
Directions	From Banbury take A4260 towards Oxford; turn right after Adderbury for Bloxham & Milton; pub on right-hand side.

Lee McCallum
Black Boy Inn,
Milton,
Banbury OX15 4HH
Tel   +44 (0)845 4591432
Web   www.blackboyinn.com

Entry 568 Map 8

Falkland Arms
Great Tew

Five hundred years on and the logs still glow in the stone-flagged bar under a low-slung timbered ceiling that drips with tankards and jugs. Tradition runs deep: the hop is treated with reverence, ales are changed weekly, old pump clips hang from the bar and they stock tins of snuff with great names like Irish High Toast and Crumbs of Comfort. In summer Morris Men jingle in the lane outside and life spills out onto the terrace at the front and into the lovely big garden behind. Dig into a homemade burger and ploughman's in front of the fire or hop next door to the tiny beamed dining room for home-cooked delights – try Guiness-baked ham hock with leek and sweetcorn champ. It's all blissfully short on modern trappings: mobile phones meet with swift and decisive action. Perfect pub, perfect village: archetypal Cotswolds.

George & Dragon
Shutford

A typical Cotswold sandstone pub, overshadowed by the church, and well worth roaring down to for good food, real ale, and a rather lively social calendar. Paul encourages darts, a quiz team and robust participation in the celebration of national days. Lean back on high oak settles and enjoy the heat from the roaring fire with its huge grate and dragons' heads made locally – here you can choose bar snacks (very good value) and try the drink the regulars like as a chaser to their Hooky bitter – Dragon's Blood (Navy rum, sloe and spices). The restaurant is quieter with exposed cream and brick walls, a low beamed ceiling and a toothsome British food menu: silver mullet with red onion and parsley salsa to start; confit shoulder of pork with braised savoy cabbage; and a simple lemon tart or homemade ice-cream for pudding.

Meals	12pm-2.30pm; 6pm-9.30pm (restaurant Mon-Sat); bar meals 12-9.30pm Sat & Sun. Main courses £10.95-£20; bar meals £6.50-£12.95.
Closed	2.30pm-6pm. Open all day Sat & Sun & bank hols.
Directions	North from Chipping Norton on A361, then right onto B4022, for Great Tew. Inn by village green.

Meals	12pm-2.30pm; 6.30pm-9pm. No food Sun eve. Main courses £9-£19; bar meals £3-£8.
Closed	2.30pm-5.30pm & Mon all day (except bank hols). Open all day Sat & Sun.
Directions	Village is located off A422, 4 miles west of Banbury.

Paula & James Meredith
Falkland Arms,
19-21 The Green, Great Tew,
Chipping Norton OX7 4DB

Tel +44 (0)1608 683653
Web www.falklandarms.co.uk

Entry 569 Map 8

Paul Stanley
George & Dragon,
Church Lane,
Shutford, Banbury OX15 6PG

Tel +44 (0)1295 780320
Web www.thegeorgeanddragon.com

Entry 570 Map 8

Oxfordshire

Wykham Arms
Sibford Gower

Gordon Ramsay got his first job here. Later, under the name The Moody Cow, it lost some of its popularity; now the listed free house is a thoroughly modern inn. Having seen the Cotswold village, you'd be forgiven for expecting cushions and chintz; instead you get creams and deep reds, flagged floors and farmhouse furnishings. The menu, served through a warren of connected rooms, spills over with local and seasonal produce; flavours are strong, clean and uncomplicated. So tuck into Cornish scallops with celeriac remoulade, salmon with beetroot and marinated artichoke salad, and wild boar and apple sausages with beer mustard mash. Lots of wines by the glass, from a list that is excellent and affordable, and families and dog owners are made very welcome. For summer there's a big patio and a wooded garden.

Oxfordshire

The Carpenters Arms
Fulbrook

Some pubs make you smile as you walk in. This is one of them. Two big blackboards shine above the wood-burner, big chunky candle-topped tables stand on a reclaimed timber floor, exposed stone walls are dotted with prints of animals. Order an Abbot or an Old Speckled Hen at the smart bar; there's even Staropramen (from Prague) on tap for hot days. New head chef Mike Jones trained under Raymond Blanc and is already gathering a following, eager for his roasted pheasant breast with chestnut stuffing, bubble and squeak and red wine gravy. Not to mention his milk chocolate and raisin brioche bread and butter pudding. Claire runs it all with an easy, light touch, there are great lunch deals to be had, and Burford is just down the road. A perfect balance of gastro and pub.

Meals	12pm-3pm; 7pm-9.30pm; no food Sun eve. Main courses £15-£18; bar meals £7.50-£10; Sunday lunch £12.50, £15 & £20.
Closed	3pm-6pm & Mon all day.
Directions	Between Brailes & Swalcliffe; on B4035, follow signs to Sibford Gower.

Meals	12pm-2pm; 6.30pm-8pm; 12pm-4pm Sun. Main courses £11-£15; set lunch, 3 courses for 2 people, £30.
Closed	3pm-6.30pm; Sun from 4pm & Mon all day.
Directions	On A361 2 miles north of Burford.

Damian & Deborah Bradley
Wykham Arms,
Temple Mill Road, Sibford Gower,
Banbury OX15 5RX
Tel   +44 (0)1295 788808
Web   www.thewykhamarms.co.uk

Entry 571 Map 8

Claire Dickson
The Carpenters Arms,
Fulbrook Hill, Fulbrook,
Burford OX18 4BH
Tel   +44 (0)1993 823 275
Web   www.thecarpentersarmsfulbrook.co.uk

Entry 572 Map 8

Oxfordshire
Worth a visit

573 Turf Tavern 7 Bath Place, Oxford OX1 3SU
+44 (0)1865 243235
Classic 18th-century tavern where ale reigns supreme – a dozen on tap and 200 guest beers served annually. A warren of small bars, three flagged courtyards, winter braziers and chestnuts, simple bar food. Generally heaves.

574 Olde Reindeer Inn 47 Parsons Street, Banbury OX16 5NA
+44 (0)1295 264031
Banbury's oldest pub has a reputation for good value, home-cooked lunches and cracking Hook Norton ale, in a cosy bar with polished boards and a magnificent carved fireplace. Don't miss the panelled Globe Room.

575 The Boot Inn Barnard Gate, Witney OX29 6XE +44 (0)1865 881231
Enjoy a pint of Hook Norton and fresh, flavourful food to a backdrop of standing timbers, bare board floors, good country tables, candlelight at night, a huge log fire… and walls covered with a rare collection of celebrity footwear.

576 Rose & Crown 14 North Parade Avenue, Oxford OX2 6LX +44 (0)1865 510551
A characterful, three-room Victorian pub in North Oxford – great ales, traditional lunchtime food, a heated back yard, interesting clientele and no music or mobile phones.

577 The Bear 6 Alfred Street, Oxford OX14EH
+44 (0)1865 728164
Oxford's oldest boozer, popular with town and gown, has a miniscule and shambolic interior, many years' worth of framed, frayed ties (it's a long story), tasty hamburgers and cracking ale.

578 Fox and Hounds Christmas Common, Watlington OX49 5HL +44 (0)1491 612599
Known locally as the 'Top Fox', this 15th-century cottage stands high in the Chiltern Hills. A timeless beamy bar with logs in a vast inglenook, a restaurant with an open-to-view kitchen, glorious walks from the front door. Reports please.

579 King William IV Hailey, Wallingford OX10 6AD +44 (0)1491 681845
Take an OS map to locate this rural treat tucked down single-track lanes in the Chilterns. Spick-and-span traditional interior, the full range of Brakspear ales, grassy front garden with peaceful views – super after a hike in the hills.

580 Black Horse Checkendon, Reading RG8 0TE +44 (0)1491 680418
Persevere up the pitted lane to this old-fashioned country local and enter another age. The pub has been run by the same family for 104 years; come for local ales from the cask, filled rolls, pickled eggs and a peaceful garden.

581 Stag & Huntsman Hambleden, Henley-on-Thames RG9 6RP
+44 (0)1491 571227
The setting's the thing and the picture-book village is popular with film crews. Bars are small and traditional, carpeted and lively; the dining room modern. Hearty food, excellent ale and invigorating walks into the Chilterns.

The Finch's Arms
Hambleton

Alone on its peninsula surrounded by Rutland Water, The Finch's Arms has the greatest of views; Colin Crawford could have sat back and twiddled his thumbs and people would still have poured in. But he has not been idle: he has spruced up the interior, smartened up the bedrooms, and has created a terrific kitchen team led by talented Mark Gough, ex-Hambleton Hall. Décor in the Garden Room is ultra-elegant, with seasonal food to match; choose from peppered hare loin with mulled figs, sea bream with basil mash and chorizo, and rack of Egleton lamb. Round off with glazed rice pudding... the bar and restaurant menus change daily, and look out for Mark's delicious winter game dinners. There's a cracking rustic bar with stripped boards and log fires, a fine selection of local ale and a great wine list. Both the hillside terrace, perfect for summer sipping, and four of the six swish modern bedrooms, one with its own private balcony, have wonderful watery views. Rooms are minimalist rustic-chic with white rugs on wood floors, sleigh beds and flatscreen TVs, and classy bathrooms with huge walk-in showers and roll-top baths.

Rooms	6 twins/doubles. From £95. Singles from £75.
Meals	12pm-2.30pm; 6.30pm-9.30pm (12pm-8pm Sun). Main courses £10.50-£18; set menu £11 & £14.95 (lunch); £14.95 & £18.95 (dinner); Sunday lunch (3 courses) £16.95.
Closed	Open all day.
Directions	Off A606, east of Oakham.

Colin & Celia Crawford
The Finch's Arms,
Oakham Road, Hambleton,
Oakham, LE15 8TL
Tel   +44 (0)1572 756575
Web   www.finchsarms.co.uk

Entry 582 Map 9

The Olive Branch
Clipsham

This is not your usual chi-chi ex-boozer in a sleepy village; a relaxed pub personality is pinned here to a Michelin star. The casual mood is created by old beams, exposed stone walls, loosely arranged tables and a warm medley of books, furniture and roaring log fire – a rustic-chic informality rules and makes a visit here a joy. Chalk boards on tables in the restaurant reveal the names of the evening's diners, while the English food – cauliflower soup, roast rib of beef, caramelised lemon tart – is the greatest treat. So are the hampers of terrine, cheese and homemade pies that you can whisk away for picnics in the country. Bedrooms in Beech House across the lane are impeccable. Three have terraces, one has a free-standing bath, all come with crisp linen, pretty beds, Roberts radios, real coffee. Super breakfasts – smoothies, boiled eggs and soldiers, the full cooked works – are served in a smartly renovated barn, with flames leaping in the wood-burner. The front garden fills in summer, the sloe gin comes from local berries, and bridle paths lead out across peaceful fields.

Rooms	6: 5 doubles, 1 family suite. £120–£170. Suite £170–£190. Singles from £95.
Meals	12pm–2pm (3pm Sun); 7pm–9.30pm (9pm Sun). Main courses £10.50–£22.50; set lunch £19.50; Sunday roast £24.50.
Closed	3pm–6pm. Open all day Sat & Sun.
Directions	2 miles off A1 at Stretton (B668 junction).

Ben Jones & Sean Hope
The Olive Branch,
Main Street, Clipsham,
Oakham LE15 7SH
Tel   +44 (0)1780 410355
Web   www.theolivebranchpub.com

Shropshire

New Inn
Baschurch

Outside, jolly hanging baskets and a plain, whitewashed frontage. Inside, a sensitive stripping back to old brick and beams, a bright and open space. There are comfortable sofas at one end, scrubbed oak dining chairs and tables at the other and a big traditional bar in between. In spite of the 48 covers, a well-placed wall and brick fireplace give the dining areas a certain intimacy; outside, sun shades and decking invite summer drinkers and diners. Five ales on the pump and good house wines are served by Jenny Bean and her charming staff. In the kitchen, Marcus prepares such delights as ham hock and parsley terrine with cheese scone and spiced apple chutney; roast duck breast with sweet plum and star anise jus; white chocolate and mascapone cheesecake. A great all-rounder – all villages should have a pub like this.

Shropshire

White Horse Inn
Pulverbatch

The drive to get here is the biggest treat. And the White Horse, in a village mentioned in the Domesday Book, is an ancient place – parts date back to the 14th century, when it was a farmhouse. There's a more recent restaurant add-on at the back but the old main bar is the most seductive, all wonky flagstoned floors, roaring fire in a big old grate and deep-hued walls. It's the perfect setting for Steve Bruce's excellent, robust cooking. Walkers and cyclists, on their way to the glorious Long Mynd, could do a lot worse than recuperate with a trio of local-farm sausages on whole-grain mustard mash, or a casserole of Shropshire lamb, all washed down with a well-kept ale or a decent wine. There's no garden at the inn – a shame in an area as stunning as this – but there are picnic benches at the front.

Meals	12pm-2pm (3pm Sun); 6.30pm-9.30pm (7pm-9pm Sun). Main courses £9.50-£16.95; bar lunches £4.95-£8.50; Sunday roast £10.25.
Closed	3pm-6pm. Open all day Sat & Sun.
Directions	Pub just off B5067 in Baschurch, 5 miles north west of Shrewsbury.

Meals	12pm-2pm (3pm Sat & Sun); 6.30pm-9pm (6pm-9pm Sat & Sun). Main courses £7.25-£14.95.
Closed	2pm-6.30pm & Mon lunch. Open all day Sat & Sun.
Directions	Pulverbatch signed off A49 south of Shrewsbury & A488 Knighton road south west of Shrewsbury.

	Marcus & Jenny Bean
	New Inn,
	Church Road, Baschurch,
	Shrewsbury SY4 2EF
Tel	+44 (0)1939 260335
Web	www.thenewinnbaschurch.co.uk

Entry 584 Map 7

	Steve & Debbie Bruce
	White Horse Inn,
	Pulverbatch,
	Shrewsbury SY5 8DS
Tel	+44 (0)1743 718247
Web	www.whitehorsepulverbatch.co.uk

Entry 585 Map 7

The Golden Cross Hotel
Shrewsbury

In an ancient hilltop town setting, with the Lady Chapel of Old St Chad's opposite, is a 600-year-old pub — marvellous. All beams, passageways and tunnels, this was once a Royalist meeting place and sacristy. Fortunately today's buzz is more about delicious food and wine than war. Of course delightful Gareth clears tables for those in search of a pint (Salopian Shropshire Gold, Hobson's Twisted Spire) but the emphasis here is on food. The interior has a sumptuous theatrical feel — exotic tablecloths, Venetian masks, quirky chandeliers — and is great fun. But eat one must and Theresa oversees the kitchen with the motto "a good stock is the elixir of all cooking". For proof of this try the duck cooked two ways: a confit leg and seared breast with fondant potato, butternut squash purée, spiced red cabbage and calvados jus — heaven on a plate. Wines from Bibendum and Tanners seal the deal. And if you thought it couldn't get any better, skip upstairs: the suite is sheer indulgence and the attic bathroom is a showstopper. The super king is more contemporary; the two compact doubles have all you need.

Rooms	4: 2 doubles, 1 twin, 1 suite. £65-£150.
Meals	12pm-2.30pm; 6pm-10pm. Main courses £10.50-£18.50; sandwiches from £6.50; set lunch (2 courses) £12.50.
Closed	Open all day.
Directions	From High Street, first left into Milk Street and right into Princess St. Pub on right.

Gareth & Theresa Reece
The Golden Cross Hotel,
14 Princess Street,
Shrewsbury SY1 1LP
Tel   +44 (0)1743 362507
Web   www.goldencrosshotel.co.uk

Entry 586 Map

Shropshire

Feathers Inn
Brockton

Once two Elizabethan cottages built from ship-salvaged timber, the Feathers stands in prime walking country. And the rambling, theatrical interior comes as a surprise. Walk in to tiled and wooden floors, whitewashed stone walls, painted beams, a vast inglenook, stone busts, grand swagged curtains, chunky church candles and colourful art for sale. Order a pint of Hobson's or an excellent wine to accompany some upmarket pub food. Chef-patron Paul Kayiatou comes from London's top kitchens, so try pan-fried Scottish scallops with crispy bacon and Caesar salad, roast belly pork with black pudding and apple and cinnamon chutney, and rack of Shropshire lamb; puddings include warm chocolate fondant. There's a good-value early evening supper menu and local roast beef on Sundays, and if you can't be bothered to go home you can snuggle down here in one of the comfy bedrooms with polished floors, painted vintage beds and snazzy bathrooms – three with roll tops, all with fluffy towels; the family room has magnificent 200-year-old beams. Satisfying to come home to after a long hike along Wenlock Edge.

Rooms	5: 3 doubles, 1 family, 1 single. £75. Singles £50. Family room £130.
Meals	12pm-2pm; 6.30pm-9.30pm. Set menu Tues-Fri before 8pm. Main courses £8.95-£18.50; set menu £13.50 & £15.95; Sunday lunch £9.95, £12.95 & £15.95.
Closed	3pm-6.30pm, Mon all day & Tues lunch.
Directions	On B4378 Much Wenlock to Craven Arms road, 5 miles south west of Much Wenlock.

Paul & Anna Kayiatou
Feathers Inn,
Brockton,
Much Wenlock TF13 6JR
Tel   +44 (0)1746 785202
Web   www.feathersatbrockton.co.uk

Entry 587 Map 7

Shropshire

The Inn at Grinshill
Grinshill

A ridge of pine soars high above the very pretty village; bring the boots and take to Shropshire's wild hills. Down at the inn, a top-to-toe renovation that still shines. Wander at will and you find an 18th-century panelled family room with rugs and games, a 19th-century bar with glass shelves, tiled floors, a crackling fire, and a 21st-century dining room, serene in cream, flooded with light courtesy of glazed coach-house arches. Ambrosial delights pour from the kitchen – try pan-fried pheasant with honeyed root vegetable and red wine glaze, or chicken on a tomato and asparagus salad. A baby grand piano gets played occasionally and life spills out into the garden in summer. Church bells peal, roses ramble, and the Shropshire Way passes by outside. Don't miss the magical follies at Hawkstone Park.

Meals	12pm-2.30pm (3pm Sun); 6.30pm-9.30pm. Main courses £9.95-£24.95; Sunday roast from £10.50.
Closed	3pm-6pm (Sun from 4pm) & Mon.
Directions	A49 north from Shrewsbury. Grinshill signed left after 5 miles.

Kevin & Victoria Brazier
The Inn at Grinshill,
Grinshill,
Shrewsbury SY4 3BL
Tel   +44 (0)1939 220410
Web   www.theinnatgrinshill.co.uk

Entry 588 Map 7

Shropshire

Riverside Inn
Cound

There's a great buzz in this large comfortable huntin', shootin' and fishin' inn – standing on a magnificent bend of the Severn, looking gloriously out to the Wrekin and beyond. It's worth seeking out for its crackling wood-burner in winter and its dining conservatory with views all year round. In summer there's a pretty garden smartly furnished, and you can fish from the bank for salmon and trout. The seasonal monthly menu might start with winter vegetable and lentil broth and move on to roast pork belly with apricot and sage sauce or beef and Guinness pie with shortcrust pastry. There's port to accompany your cheese, and lovely Salopian beers and homemade puddings – try the raspberry and thyme crème brûlée. It's all good value and comfortingly traditional. The service, as in every good pub, is both relaxed and efficient.

Meals	12pm-2.30pm; 6.30pm-9.30pm (12pm-9.30pm Sat & Sun May-Sept). Main courses £7.75-£12.55.
Closed	3pm-6pm. Open all day Sat & Sun May-Sept.
Directions	South from Shrewsbury on A458, through Cross Houses to Cressage; pub on left.

Peter Stanford Davis
Riverside Inn,
Cound,
Shrewsbury SY5 6AF
Tel   +44 (0)1952 510900
Web   www.theriversideinn.net

Entry 589 Map 7

Crown Country Inn
Munslow

Richard and Jane Arnold bought this listed Tudor inn in a parlous state. A courtroom, a doctor's surgery and a jail in its previous lives, it is now a happier place. While locals gather for a chat and a pint of Holden's Golden Glow at dark polished tables in the winter-cosy, log-stoved bar, the secret of the inn's success is revealed on its walls, adorned with food awards and a map of suppliers. Proprietor and chef Richard is passionate about local produce and the menu is stuffed with it. Try crostini ('little toasts') of local black pudding with Wenlock Edge Farm bacon, lamb tagine, and roast smoked chicken with mustard creamed leeks. As for the cheeseboard, it's a treat of lesser-known British cheeses – including the hop-rolled Hereford Hop. And there's a super sun-trap terrace for summer drinking.

The Three Tuns
Bishops Castle

Beer deliveries are a cinch for the Three Tuns. There's been a licensed brewery next door (in a listed Victorian tower) since 1642. Pub and brewery are now under separate ownership but the pub still exclusively sells four of their beers and very good they are too. The place has an unassuming air, like the rest of this time-warp town. The separate snug, public bar and lounge have been simply redecorated with pale green paintwork, scrubbed tables and no airs and graces. (In contrast to some impressive marble loos...) A more recent addition is the oak-framed, conservatory dining room where tasty dishes may feature some unusual touches, such as chargrilled tuna in red Thai curry sauce with fried noodles. A great mix of regulars, from suits to bohemians, a real fire in the stone fireplace, and live music at weekends.

Meals	12pm-2pm; 6.45pm-8.45pm. Main courses £11.95-£16.95; bar meals £4.95-£11.50.
Closed	2.30pm-6.45pm, Sun from 3pm & Mon all day.
Directions	On B4368 to Bridgnorth, at extreme western end of Munslow.

Meals	12pm-3pm; 7pm-9pm; no food Sun eve. Main courses £8.95-£12.95; set menu, 3 courses, £19.50; Sunday lunch £8.95.
Closed	Open all day.
Directions	On B4385 off A488 12 miles N of Knighton; in town centre at top of hill.

SPECIAL AWARD
see pages 20-21

Community pub

Richard & Jane Arnold
Crown Country Inn,
Munslow,
Craven Arms SY7 9ET
Tel   +44 (0)1584 841205
Web   www.crowncountryinn.co.uk

Entry 590 Map 7

Tim & Catherine Curtis-Evans
The Three Tuns,
Salop Street,
Bishops Castle SY9 5BW
Tel   +44 (0)1588 638797
Web   www.thethreetunsinn.co.uk

Entry 591 Map 7

Shropshire

The Unicorn
Ludlow

Ludlow, full of timber-framed houses and artisan shops, looks and tastes delicious. As for The Unicorn, it hides at the bottom end of town on the east bank of the river as you approach the Shrewsbury road and, unlike its more distinguished restaurant neighbours, does not have to be booked weeks in advance. Along with well-priced bar snacks there's proper food and plenty of it (own-recipe sausages with bubble and squeak, chicken roulade with sweet and sour sauce, syrup sponge and custard). You eat at scrubbed tables in the dining rooms or in the beer garden by the stream, or, best of all, before log fires in the panelled, beamed bar where floor and ceiling slope drastically. Ceremony here is about as out-of-place as Formula One tyres on a family Ford and the beer is expertly kept: no wonder it remains popular.

Meals	12pm-2.15pm; 6pm-9.15pm. Main courses £6.75-£12.95; Sunday roast from £7.95; sandwiches from £4.50.
Closed	Open all day.
Directions	From A49, B4361 to Ludlow. After lights & bridge, bear right; bear left up hill. Next right after lights at bottom of hill. 50 yds on left.

Graham Moore
The Unicorn,
66 Corve Street,
Ludlow SY8 1DU
Tel   +44 (0)1584 873555
Web   www.unicorn-ludlow.co.uk

Entry 592 Map 7

Shropshire

Fighting Cocks
Stottesdon

As you tail tractors and horses on the lane to get here, you pass the farm that supplies the kitchen with its excellent meat. Sandra Jefferies wears multiple hats: jolly landlady, enthusiastic chef, manager of the great little shop next door. So step into the bar and choose a velour-topped seat or a settle or a sofa by the fire. The décor is haphazard, the carpet patterned, the piano strewn with newspapers and guides (Shropshire's ancient hills beckon) and the copper-topped bar hung with tankards. Up steps is a room for darts, dominoes and TV; outside, a beer garden. The dining room is as unpretentious as can be and a match for the cooking; you'll love the gamey (and spicy) casseroles, the organic salmon, scrumptious pies and tempting nursery puddings. A true community pub, with a welcome that embraces outsiders.

Meals	12pm-2.30pm Sat only (2pm Sun); 7-9pm. No food Sun eve. Main courses £8-£17.
Closed	Mon-Fri lunch. Open all day Sat & Sun.
Directions	Village signed off A4117 & B4363 east of Ludlow at Cleobury Mortimer.

Sandra Jefferies
Fighting Cocks,
1 High Street,
Stottesdon,
Kidderminster DY14 8TZ
Tel   +44 (0)1746 718270

Entry 593 Map 7

Shropshire

The Clive Bar & Restaurant with Rooms
Bromfield

It doesn't really matter whether you're in the mood for old or new; this pub does both. Inside the old redbrick farmhouse on the Ludlow-Shrewsbury road you discover a chic restaurant on one side and a bar on the other. The bar starts life all chrome tables and blonde wood floors, then turns a corner and changes mood, becoming an elegant collection of antique chairs, rugs and pictures dotted around a huge old stone fireplace. The food remains resolutely modern. Prime ingredients, from Corvedale lamb to Nash venison, are the star players in a menu glittering with talent and clever combinations. It's not just fancy footwork though – the food is terrific, be it wild mushroom, borlotti and pinto bean tagliatelle with roast garlic, basil and gorgonzola, or seared fillet of Shropshire beef with buckwheat noodles, wasabi and oyster sauce. And then there are the bedrooms in converted outbuildings, all of them stylish and impeccable visions of unfussy modern comfort within a framework of gnarled oak beams. Bathrooms are white and pristine, the furniture contemporary, the outlook blissfully rural.

Rooms	14: 13 twins/doubles, 1 family suite. £85-£110. Family suite £110-£200.
Meals	12pm-3pm; 6.30pm-10pm (12pm-10pm Sat; 12pm-9.30pm Sun). Main courses £9.95-£17.95.
Closed	Open all day.
Directions	2 miles north of Ludlow on A49.

	Paul Brooks
	The Clive Bar & Restaurant with Rooms, Bromfield, Ludlow SY8 2JR
Tel	+44 (0)1584 856565
Web	www.theclive.co.uk

Entry 594 Map 7

Shropshire

All Nations
Madeley

The old Victorian pub, spruce and white, could be an extension of the Victorian open air museum on the other side of the bridge. Step across the threshold and you're into timeworn-tavern territory – cast-iron tables, leatherette benches, coal fire at one end, log fire at the other. Old photographs of Ironbridge strew the walls, secondhand paperbacks ask to be taken home (donations to charity accepted), dogs doze and spotless loos await outside. It's a chatty, friendly, ex-miners' ale house and some of the locals could have been here forever. Drink is own-brew, well-kept, low-cost Dabley from the hatch plus three others and a cider, while the menu encompasses several sorts of roll – black pudding perhaps, or cheese and onion, with tomato on request. Catch it before it's gone.

Shropshire

The Fox
Newport

As you wander from room to room you realise just how vast this 1920s pub is. Yet there are plenty of nooks to be private in. Fires crackle in magnificent fireplaces, heavy cast-iron radiators add warmth, Turkish rugs are scattered on stained-wood floors and summer promises a great big garden with rolling views. Pews, solid oak tables and chairs – there's a happy mix of furniture and a bistro feel. It's a grown-ups' pub and attracts a civilised crowd, appreciative of the good selection of wines by the glass and the six regularly changing guest ales. Choose a table, then browse that day's menu: there are ploughman's with local cheeses, salted duck breast with an orange, watercress and fennel salad, venison steak with roasted vegetables, warm chocolate brownies and very good coffee.

Meals	Rolls available all day.
	Filled rolls £1.90–£3.
Closed	Open all day.
Directions	Off Legges Way, near entrance to Blists Hill Victorian museum.

Meals	12pm–10pm (9.30pm Sun).
	Main courses £7.95–£15.95.
Closed	Open all day.
Directions	Just off A41 south of Newport.

Jim Birtwistle
All Nations,
20 Coalport Road,
Madeley, Telford TF7 5DP
Tel   +44 (0)1952 585747

Samantha Forrest
The Fox,
Pave Lane,
Newport TF10 9LQ
Tel   +44 (0)1952 815940
Web   www.brunningandprice.co.uk

Entry 595 Map 8

Entry 596 Map 8

The Hundred House Hotel

Norton

Henry is an innkeeper of the old school, with a sense of humour. As for the inn, having begun its life in the 14th century, it rambles charmingly inside as well as out. Enter a world of blazing log fires, soft brick walls, oak panelling and quarry-tiled floors. Dried flowers hang from beams, herbs sit in vases, and blackboard menus trumpet Hundred House fish pie, roast rack of Shropshire lamb and double chocolate mousse with orange anglaise. You are surrounded by Sylvia's wild and wonderful collage art, which hangs on the walls, and the fun continues in riotously patterned and floral bedrooms upstairs. Just go easy on the ale before you open the door: most have a swing hanging from the ceiling with a colourful velvet seat! When you are not swinging you can lounge on antique beds — large, comfortable and wrapped in lavender-scented sheets. Wander out with a pint of Heritage Mild and share a quiet moment with a few stone lions in the beautiful garden, full of herbaceous plants and a working herb garden with over 50 varieties — a real summer treat. And you can tie the knot in the newly restored Tithe Barn.

Rooms	14: 7 doubles, 2 twins/doubles, 4 family, 1 single. From £65. Singles from £55.
Meals	12pm-2.30pm; 6pm-9.30pm (7pm-9pm Sun). Main courses £8.95-£18.95. Set lunch (2 courses) £11.95.
Closed	3pm-5.30pm.
Directions	In village of Norton, midway between Bridgnorth & Telford on A442.

The Phillips Family
The Hundred House Hotel,
Bridgnorth Road,
Norton, Shifnal TF11 9EE
Tel   +44 (0)1952 580240
Web   www.hundredhouse.co.uk

Shropshire
Worth a visit

598 Charlton Arms Ludford, Ludlow SY8 1PG
+44 (0)1584 872813
A poshed-up old inn slap on the bridge over the Teme with a riverside terrace and glorious views up the hill into Ludlow. Local beers (Wye Valley, Hobson) and decent food add to the attraction.

599 The Church Inn Buttercross,
Ludlow SY8 1AW +44 (0)1584 872174
On one of the oldest sites in Ludlow (Slow Food capital of England), a bustling inn wedged between the old Buttercross and St Lawrence's Church. Ale lovers beat a path to its door. You can eat here, too.

600 The Miners Arms Priest Weston,
Montgomery SY7 8EW +44 (0)1938 561352
On the wild Welsh borders, an unspoilt pub, the hub of hamlet life – they sell dog food, groceries and gas, hold folk nights, marrow competitions and harvest thanksgiving. Wonderful bar with big inglenook and beer brewed in Bishops Castle; food on request.

601 The Waterdine Llanfair Waterdine,
Knighton LD7 1TU +44 (0)1547 528214
The old Welsh longhouse in a hamlet by the river is a fine spot for Ken Adams's innovative modern British cooking. With impeccable local produce and Woods ale on tap, this is more restaurant than pub.

602 The Royal Oak Cardington,
Church Stretton SY6 7JZ +44 (0)1694 771266
At the foot of Caer Caradoc, a 500-year-old pub loved by muddy-booted ramblers who come for its dependable range of real ales, cider and inexpensive daily specials from local suppliers.

Somerset

Woods Bar & Dining Room
Dulverton

It hasn't been a pub for ever – indeed, it used to specialise in tea and cakes – but it is in the centre of a lively village, and wine buffs and foodies have much to be grateful for. Landlords Sally and Paddy are friendly and welcome families and dogs. A stable-like partition divides the space up into two intimate seating areas, beyond which is a smart, soft-lit, deeply cosy bar: two wood-burners, lots of pine, a few barrel tables and exposed stone walls. Ales include Exmoor Gold, Otter and St Austell, but the wines are the thing, and many come by the glass. Expect fine modern British dishes, with an emphasis on sourcing and food in season. There's roast tomato soup with serrano ham, roast Exmoor lamb with confit garlic and rosemary sauce, rich chocolate brownie. Or munch on a stilton and onion marmalade baguette.

Meals	12pm-2pm; 7pm-9.30pm (9pm Sun). Main courses £8.50-£16.50; bar lunches from £5.
Closed	3pm-6pm (7pm Sun).
Directions	From Tiverton, A396 north; left on B3222 for Dulverton; near church & bank.

Sally & Paddy Groves
Woods Bar & Dining Room,
4 Bank Square,
Dulverton TA22 9BU
Tel   +44 (0)1398 324007

Entry 603 Map 2

Somerset

Tarr Farm Inn
Dulverton

Come for rare peace – no traffic lights, no mobile signals, not for miles. Tucked into the Barle valley, a short hop from the ancient clapper bridge at Tarr Steps, this well-established 16th-century inn is surrounded by beautiful woodland above the hauntingly high spaces of Exmoor National Park. The blue-carpeted, low-beamed main bar has plenty of comfy window seats and gleaming black leather sofas; Exmoor Ale and Mayner's cider flow as easily as the conversation. To fill the gap after a bracing walk the menu draws heavily on local game – hunting and shooting are big sports here – so you get venison and rabbit casserole, pan-roasted partridge and a hundred French and New World wines. The garden views are sublime; where better to try the best West Country cheeses followed by perfect coffee?

Somerset

The Rising Sun Inn
Bagborough

In 2002 the Sun rose from the ashes of a fire and shines more brightly than ever. It sits in sleepy West Bagborough on the flanks of the Quantock Hills. Constructed around the original 16th-century cob walls and magnificent door, its reincarnation is bold and craftsman-led, with 80 tons of solid oak timbers and windows and a slate-floored bar. Add Art Nouveau features, spotlighting and swagged drapery and you find one very smart pub. There's Exmoor Fox to sample and, high in the rafters, a dining room with views that unfurl to Exmoor and the Blackdown Hills. It's an impressive setting for impressive food: game and foie gras terrine with quince jelly; saddle of Exmoor lamb with pancetta; ham, duck egg and chips; sticky ginger ale cake. Worth walking down the hill for.

Meals	12pm-3pm; 6.30pm-9.30pm (cream teas 11am-5pm). Main courses £12.95-£17.50; bar meals £6.95-£12.50.	Meals	12pm-2pm (3pm Sun); 6.30pm-9.30pm. No food Sun eve. Main courses £4.95-£17.
Closed	Open all day.	Closed	3pm-6pm.
Directions	From Dulverton, take B3223 north, left to Tarr Steps & inn is signed.	Directions	Off A358 Taunton-Minehead road, 8 miles north west of Taunton.

Judy Carless & Richard Benn
Tarr Farm Inn,
Tarr Steps,
Dulverton TA22 9PY
Tel   +44 (0)1643 851507
Web   www.tarrfarm.co.uk

Jon & Christine Brinkman
The Rising Sun Inn,
Bagborough,
Taunton TA4 3EF
Tel   +44 (0)1823 432575
Web   www.risingsuninn.info

Entry 604 Map 2

Entry 605 Map 2

Royal Oak Inn
Luxborough

Five miles south of Minehead, as the pheasant flies, is Luxborough, tucked under the lip of Exmoor's Brendon hills. This is hunting country, and from September to February the bar hums with the sound of gamekeepers, beaters, drivers and picker-uppers from the nearby Chargot shoot. Often they stay to dine, very well: on potted ham hock; fish from St Mawes; vegetables from local growers; and beef, lamb and venison that's almost walked off the hills. Two low-beamed, log-fired, dog-dozed bars (with locals' own table) lead to a warren of dining rooms kitted out with polished dining tables and hunting prints on deep green walls. (In spate, the river Washford has been known to take a detour!) A shelf heaves with walking books and maps; James and Siân lend them freely, all are returned. The village is small but people have been coming here all their lives, for a pint and a chat over cribbage, backgammon, scrabble. For those lucky enough to stay, bedrooms ramble around the first floor (one below has a private terrace) and are individual, peaceful, homely and great value.

Rooms	10: 7 doubles, 3 twins/doubles. £75–£100. Singles from £55.
Meals	12pm–2pm; 7pm–9pm. Main courses £11.95–£16.95; bar meals £4.95–£10.95; Sunday lunch £7.95–£15.95.
Closed	2.30pm–6pm Oct–May. Open all day June–Aug. Open all day Fri–Sun.
Directions	M5 junc. 25, A358 north, B3224 west. Village signed right, midway between Brendon Hill & Wheddon Cross.

James & Siân Waller
Royal Oak Inn,
Luxborough,
Watchet TA23 0SH

Tel	+44 (0)1984 640319
Web	www.theroyaloakinnluxborough.co.uk

The Hood Arms
Kilve

Be prepared for a lively time at this 17th-century coaching inn, a mile from the fossil beach at Kilve. New landlords Nicky and John are often to be found among the punters, ensuring that the ale and the conversation keep flowing. It does – and how! Horse and hound lovers will feel totally at home among the country artefacts that garnish the beamed interior, so grab a pint of Otter or Exmoor ale and try your hand at bar billiards (one of the few remaining tables in the country?). Then, when hunger bites, consider venison casserole with cranberry and wholegrain mustard mash or sirloin steak with wild mushrooms and port sauce, perfectly matched by well-opened wines; clear tasting notes aid your choice. If you're lucky enough to be staying then the upstairs bedrooms take a more 21st-century turn, thanks to their stylish beds, super linen, upbeat artwork and modern bathrooms. Some look to the road, others to the very pretty garden with boules pitch. A truly comfortable, truly authentic, foot-of-the-Quantock-hills experience. And our inspector left with a brace of pheasants!

Rooms	12: 9 twins/doubles, 3 family suites. From £95; Stag Lodge £125-£250.
Meals	12pm-2pm; 6pm-9pm. Mains from £8.99-£11.50.
Closed	Open all day.
Directions	In Kilve on A39 between Bridgwater and Minehead.

John & Nicky Thompson
The Hood Arms,
Kilve,
Bridgwater TA5 1EA
Tel   +44 (0)1278 741210
Web   www.thehoodarms.com

Entry 607 Map 2

The Rock Inn
Waterrow

Perambulating along the Somerset and Devon borderlands in search of country cooking and a comfortable bed, you could do no better than to chance upon this coaching inn. Lost along the back road between Taunton and South Molton, built into the rock face by the river in a green valley, it is run by a mother and son team. Joanna (chef) and Matt (ex Hotel du Vin) have restored the fortunes of the old timbered inn. Good home-cooked food, served at pine tables in the rustic bar or the bistro-style dining room, draws the farmers from the hills and taps into a network of quality local suppliers: free-range pork, craft cheeses, beef from Joanna's farm down the valley. So tuck into double-baked Jubilee Gold soufflé; beef, red wine and onion pie; Exmoor venison steak with port and berry sauce; and Ladram Bay lobster with salad. Local extends to the ales: very well-kept Cotleigh Tawny and Exmoor Gold. Simple, homely bedrooms are warm and comfortable, with crisp cotton sheets on old pine or brass beds, and flat-screen TVs; the largest has a leather sofa and a wood-burning stove, quite a treat on a winter's night.

Rooms	8 twins/doubles. £75. Singles £50.
Meals	12pm-2.30pm; 6.30pm-9.30pm (7pm-9pm Sun). Main courses £7.50-£15.95.
Closed	3pm-6pm.
Directions	On B3227 between Bampton & Wiveliscombe.

Matt Harvey & Joanna Oldman
The Rock Inn,
Waterrow,
Taunton TA4 2AX
Tel   +44 (0)1984 623293
Web   www.rockinn.co.uk

Lord Poulett Arms
Hinton St George

In a ravishing village, a ravishing inn, French at heart and quietly groovy. Part pub, part country house, with walls painted in reds and greens and old rugs covering flagged floors, it fuses classical design with earthy rusticity. A fire burns on both sides of the chimney in the dining room; on one side you can sink into leather armchairs, on the other you can eat under beams at antique oak tables while candles flicker. Take refuge with the daily papers on the sofa in the locals' bar or head past a pile of logs at the back door and discover an informal French garden of box and bay trees, with a piste for boules, a creeper-shaded terrace, a hammock. Bedrooms upstairs come in funky country-house style, with fancy flock wallpaper, perhaps crushed velvet curtains, a small chandelier or a carved-wood bed. Two rooms have slipper baths behind screens in the room; two have claw-foot baths in bathrooms one step across the landing; Roberts radios add to the fun. Brilliant food includes summer barbecues, Sunday roasts and the full works at breakfast. Great value and friendly to all – dogs included.

Rooms	4: 2 doubles; 2 doubles, each with separate bath. £85-£95. Singles £55-£65.
Meals	12pm-9.15pm. Main courses £11-£22.
Closed	Open all day.
Directions	A303, then A356 south for Crewkerne. Right for West Chinnock. Through village, 1st left for Hinton St George. Pub on right in village.

Steve & Michelle Hill
Lord Poulett Arms,
High Street,
Hinton St George TA17 8SE
Tel   +44 (0)1460 73149
Web   www.lordpoulettarms.com

SPECIAL
AWARD
see pages 20-21

Pub with rooms

Entry 609 Map 3

Somerset

The Candlelight Inn
Bishopswood

Aptly named, this 17th-century flint built pub shines in the heart of the Blackdown Hills. Inside and out are polished woods of all hues, exposed stonework and brick with timber framing, bar skittles and a log fire. Stone flags border the bar behind which a rack holds six gravity-fed casks of Otter Bitter, and guests such as Sharp's or Exmoor, all lovingly looked after by Tom. And there's Sheppy's Farmhouse cider and Weston's Country Perry, perfect for washing down the contents of the sandwich board. Hot dishes? Chef Rodney delivers a great steak and kidney suet pudding, and a chargrilled sirloin steak with brandy and tarragon sauce. It's all homemade bar the ice cream. A former skittle alley makes a super light dining area with views to the pretty garden; its fishpond and covered barbecue look over the river Yarty.

Meals	12pm-2pm; 7pm-9pm (12pm-2.30pm; 7pm-9.30pm Sat & Sun). Main courses £11-£15; bar snacks from £5.50.
Closed	3pm-6pm.
Directions	From A303 between Ilminster and Honiton; signed Bishopswood. In village on right hand side.

Debbie Lush
The Candlelight Inn,
Bishopswood,
Chard TA20 3RS
Tel   +44 (0)1460 234476
Web   www.candlelight-inn.co.uk

Entry 610 Map 3

Somerset

The Helyar Arms
East Coker

Mathieu Eke's gastropub is worth leaving the A30 for – for the atmosphere, the food (lots of produce from local suppliers) and the handsome village it lives in. Daily-updated boards of tasty dishes express the enterprising style: cauliflower soup (when in season, naturally); shin of beef and Guinness stew with thyme dumplings; Somerset pork belly with sage and cider jus; sticky toffee pudding. Real ales, Somerset cider and global wines are well priced. For ploughman's there might be local cheeses, such as Montgomery cheddar served with homemade chutney. Low beams, sofas by the crackling log fire, pictures crowding the walls, flickering candles on old tables, daily papers and board games in the bar, a raftered restaurant in the apple loft, a garden and skittles – this is a great all-round village pub.

Meals	12-2.30pm; 6.30-9.30pm (9pm Sun). Main courses £8.50-£16; sandwiches from £5; Sunday roast £9-£9.95
Closed	3pm-6pm.
Directions	A37, A30 signs to East Coker.

Mathieu Eke
The Helyar Arms,
Moor Lane,
East Coker, Yeovil BA22 9JR
Tel   +44 (0)1935 862332
Web   www.helyar-arms.com

Entry 611 Map 3

Somerset

Rose & Crown Inn (Eli's)
Huish Episcopi

Quirky, unspoilt and in the family for over 140 years. The layout has evolved, gradually taking over the family home. There's no bar as such — you choose from the casks — but who cares when the locals are so lovely, the cider so rough and the beer so tasty. Walk in and you step back to the Fifties. There are worn flagstones, aged panelling and coal fires in five low parlours radiating off a central tap room. The 'gentleman's kitchen' is the oldest and cosiest, the pool, darts and juke box room the largest and newest. They do crib nights and occasional quiz nights and Morris dancers drop by in summer. The food is brilliant value: creamy winter vegetable soup, a tasty pork, apple and cider cobbler, chicken breast with tarragon, chocolate and rum torte. Everyone's happy and children like the little play area outside.

Somerset

Halfway House
Pitney Hill

Somerset's mecca for beer and cider aficionados. No music or electronic wizardry to distract you from the serious business of sampling up to eight ales tapped straight from the cask, heady Hecks' ciders and bottled beers from around the globe. Local clubs gather for chess, music, hockey. In the two simple and homely rooms is a friendly, conversational buzz: there are old benches and pews, scrubbed tables, stone-slabbed floors, three crackling log fires and the daily papers to nod off over. A quick lunchtime pint can swiftly turn into two hours of beer-fuelled bliss — so blot up the alcohol with a ploughman's or a salmon steak straight from the pub's smokery. In the evenings the Halfway's revered homemade curries are gorgeous and go down very nicely with pints of Butcombe, Branscombe and Hop Back ales.

Meals	12pm-2pm; 5.30pm-7.30pm; no food Sun eve. Main courses £6.95-£7.50.	Meals	12pm-2.30pm; 6.30pm-9.30pm; no food Sun. Main courses £4.50-£10.95.
Closed	2.30pm-5.30pm Mon-Thurs. Open all day Fri-Sun.	Closed	3pm-5.30pm (7pm Sun).
Directions	300 yards from St Mary's Church. On left-hand-side towards Wincanton on leaving Huish.	Directions	Beside B3153, midway between Langport & Somerton.

	Steve & Maureen Pittard & Patricia O'Malley Rose & Crown Inn (Eli's), Huish Episcopi, Langport TA10 9QT		Caroline Lacy Halfway House, Pitney Hill, Langport TA10 9AB
Tel	+44 (0)1458 250494	Tel	+44 (0)1458 252513
		Web	www.thehalfwayhouse.co.uk

Entry 612 Map 3

Entry 613 Map 3

Somerset

The Montague Inn
Shepton Montague

The O'Callaghans' 17th-century public house has been a stables, livery, grocery; now it is an inn in the true sense of the word. Small remains beautiful, with Bath Ales and regional guests that may come from Butcombe and Blindman's Brewery, a wood-burner in the bar, candles on stripped pine tables and organic produce from neighbouring farms. Master Chef John McKeever's food is simple yet imaginative. There are lunchtime ploughman's of local cheeses while daily specials could mean a hot pot on Tuesday and fresh fish in beer batter and chips on Friday. And then there's grilled local goat's cheese in a celery, apple and walnut salad, and seared fillet of local beef with garlic cream mash, bacon and lentil jus – all of it brilliant. The restaurant and rear terrace have bosky views to Redlynch and Alfred's Tower.

Meals	12pm-2.30pm; 7pm-9pm. Main courses £4.50-£14.50 (lunch) £12.50-£19.50 (dinner); Sunday lunch £10.50.
Closed	3pm-6pm, Sun from 3pm & Mon (except bank hols).
Directions	A303 to Wincanton, turn offf A359 2 miles east of Castle Cary, towards Bruton.

Sean & Suzy O'Callaghan
The Montague Inn,
Shepton Montague,
Wincanton BA9 8JW

Tel	+44 (0)1749 813213
Web	www.themontagueinn.co.uk

Entry 614 Map 3

Somerset

Red Lion
Babcary

The Red Lion is a Somerset revival that combines the best of pub tradition with excellent food. There is a single central bar with a locals' snug behind dispensing Glastonbury Hedge Monkey ale, local cider and house wines from France and Oz. To one side, hair-cord carpets, sofas and the cast-iron stove give a welcome to the bright bar/lounge, while to the far right a dozen well-spaced country dining tables plainly set out on original flagstone flooring are part of an immaculate reconstruction. Daily menus offer as little or as much as you'd like, from wild boar terrine with red cabbage chutney or wild mushroom soup to pork and herb sausages with mash and mustard jus, chicken with Tuscan bean stew and chorizo, and braised lamb shank. Best to book at weekends.

Meals	12pm-2.30pm; 7pm-9pm (9.30pm Fri & Sat). Main courses £9.50-£16.
Closed	2.30pm-6pm.
Directions	Off A37 & A303 7 miles north of Yeovil.

Clare & Charles Garrard
Red Lion,
Babcary,
Somerton TA11 7ED

Tel	+44 (0)1458 223230
Web	www.redlionbabcary.co.uk

Entry 615 Map 3

The Devonshire Arms
Langport

A lively English village with a well-kept green; the old school house stands to the south, the church to the east and the post office to the west. The inn (due north) is 400 years old and was once a hunting lodge for the Dukes of Devonshire; a rather smart pillared porch survives at the front. These days open-plan interiors are warmly contemporary with high ceilings, shiny blond floorboards and fresh flowers everywhere. Hop onto brown leather stools at the bar and order a pint of Moor Revival, or sink into sofas in front of the fire and crack open a bottle of wine. In summer, life spills onto the terrace at the front, the courtyard at the back and the lawned garden beyond. Upstairs, a flurry of large, light and absolutely fabulous bedrooms, with low-slung wooden beds, seagrass matting and crisp white linen. The hosts are engaging and the food's a joy; choose from ploughman's with homemade chutney or spicy crab and tomato soup, linger over pheasant breast with foie gras, red cabbage and creamy mash. Then take to the nearby Somerset Levels and walk off your indulgence in style.

Rooms	9: 8 doubles, 1 family room. £85-£135. Singles from £75.
Meals	12pm-2.30pm; 7pm-9.30pm (9pm Sun). Main courses £12.95-£23.50; bar meals £4.95-£12.50.
Closed	3pm-6pm.
Directions	A303, then north on B3165, through Martock, to Long Sutton. By village green.

Philip & Sheila Mepham
The Devonshire Arms,
Long Sutton,
Langport TA10 9LP
Tel   +44 (0)1458 241271
Web   www.thedevonshirearms.com

Entry 616 Map 3

The Masons Arms
Odcombe

The old thatched cider house now serves its very own Odcombe Ales; try Spring or A Winter's Tail. All are brewed by Drew, just 20 feet behind the bar; now that's local. Inside all is carpeted cosiness, matched by beams and a former inglenook, now a mini-snug (fires and thatch don't mix!). Owner Paula ferries plates of modern pub food, often with an Asian twist, through the lively crowd who throng here. Try free-range pork loin with dauphinoise potatoes and a cider cream sauce, or game casserole with herb dumplings. The à la carte changes daily, the blackboard specials follow the seasons and you're treated to the best from the markets and the producers nearby. If the sun is out, head to the long, sheltered garden replete with tidy thatched dining hut; views reach over the vegetable plot to pretty fields and pub campsite beyond. Behind the pub, in a single-storey annexe alongside the garden, are six contemporary bedrooms smartly furnished with pale-oak beds and all you might need for business or pleasure. The Masons is a simple, unpretentious pub with a community vibe.

Rooms	6: 4 twins/doubles; 1 single; 1 family room. £85–£105. Single £55.
Meals	12pm–2pm; 6.30pm–9.30pm. Main courses £10–£14.75. Baguettes £5.75.
Closed	3pm–6pm.
Directions	Village signed off A30 and A3088 just west of Yeovil.

Paula Tennyson & Drew Read
The Masons Arms,
41 Lower Odcombe,
Odcombe, Yeovil BA22 8TX
Tel   +44 (0)1935 862591
Web   www.masonsarmsodcombe.co.uk

Entry 617 Map 3

The Queen's Arms
Corton Denham

Stride across rolling fields, feast on Corton Denham lamb, retire to a perfect room. Buried down several Dorset-and-Somerset-border lanes, this 18th-century stone pub has an elegant exterior – more country gentleman's house than pub. Delightful Londoners Rupert and Victoria Reeves have not let it lose its countrified feel. The bar, with its rug-strewn flagstones and bare boards, pew benches, deep sofas and crackling fire, is most charming. In the dining room – big mirrors on terracotta walls, new china on old tables – robust British dishes are distinguished by fresh ingredients from local suppliers. Try smoked haddock and spinach tart with a glass or two of Jim Barry's Aussie shiraz, follow with pan-fried Old Spot pork with balsamic strawberries… and find room for a comforting crumble. The bedrooms above are beautifully designed in gorgeous colours; a duck-egg blue wall here, red and cream checked curtains there. All have lovely views and the bathrooms are immaculate. A friendly labrador, Butcombe on tap, and Gloucester Black Spot bacon at breakfast's communal table. Readers are full of praise.

Rooms	5: 4 doubles, 1 twin. £85-£130. Singles £70-£95.
Meals	12pm-3pm (3.30pm Sun); 6pm-10pm (9.30pm Sun). Main courses £8.60-£14.95; bar meals from £5.25.
Closed	3pm-6pm. Open all day Sat & Sun.
Directions	From A303 take Chapel Crosse turning, through South Cadbury village. Next left & follow signs to Corton Denham. Pub at end of village, on right.

Rupert & Victoria Reeves
The Queen's Arms,
Corton Denham,
Sherborne DT9 4LR

Tel	+44 (0)1963 220317
Web	www.thequeensarms.com

Entry 618 Map 3

Kings Arms
Charlton Horethorne

With three dining pubs and a thriving food company behind them, Tony and Sarah Lethbridge have returned to the world of pubbery – and how! A serious restoration project sees the old boarded-up King's Arms rise from the ashes in 2009, its original – striking – façade opening to a contemporary-chic interior. Step in to wood and stone floors, bold-red and green walls, vintage dining tables, a cheery wood-burner, squashy leather sofas and four real ales in the front bar. The restaurant has a more civilised, less funky feel – a coir-matted floor, arched mirrors, local artwork, and terrace views. From Sarah's daily-changing lunch and dinner menus find ham hock terrine with piccallili; lamb rump with rosemary jus; seared sea bream with chicken broth and herb linguini; banana and ginger pudding. Delicious food for children too. Named after gem stones, each with its own style, are ten bedrooms in the new extension sporting distinctive wallpapers, big beds and marble and mosaic bathrooms with bathrobes, posh smellies and walk-in showers. A class act – and good value, too.

Rooms	10 twins/doubles. From £95.
Meals	12pm-2.30pm; 7pm-9.30pm (10pm Fri & Sat). Main courses £8.95-£16.50; Sunday roast £11.25.
Closed	Open all day.
Directions	In centre of Charlton Horethorne, 3 miles from A303.

Tony & Sarah Lethbridge
Kings Arms,
Charlton Horethorne,
Sherborne DT9 4NL
Tel   +44 (0)1963 220281
Web   www.thekingsarms.co.uk

Entry 619 Map 3

Somerset

The Three Horseshoes
Batcombe

Down a web of country lanes, the Wood's honey-stoned coaching inn sits in a lovely village. Step into a long, low bar, its beams cream, its pine scrubbed, its pink-sponged walls hung with local views. There are cushioned window seats, an inglenook with a wood-burning stove, pretty courtyards and grassed areas, even a play area. It's truly relaxing, a treat for locals, walkers and families. The modern British menu uses local organic produce, much from the vegetable garden, and is full of promise: start with homemade pâté de campagne, move on to shoulder of local lamb with red wine jus or sea bass fillet with tomato and herb salsa, finish with a trio of English puds. *Children welcome at lunchtime.*

Somerset

The Talbot Inn at Mells
Mells

Even in fog the village is lovely. Huge oak doors open to a cobbled courtyard and rough-boarded tithe barn bar on one side, and dining rooms on the other. Inside, a warren of passageways, low doorways, nooks, crannies and beams – all you'd hope for from a 15th-century inn. Butcombe Bitter flows from the cask and there are wines galore including five by the glass; it's a great drinking pub and, with a garden with views, a big draw for tourists in summer. Soak up any excess with battered cod and chips, chargrilled rib-eye steak with roasted red pepper and chilli butter, or local ham, eggs and chips, then head down to the brook and converse with the ducks. Dinner under the hop-strewn rafters highlights fresh Brixham fish such as brill fillets in nut-brown butter. The effortless hospitality is a further plus.

Meals	12pm-2pm; 7pm-9pm; no food Mon or Sun eve. Main courses £9.50-£18.50; lunch from £8.75; bar meals from £6.75.
Closed	3pm-6.30pm (7pm Sun) & Mon (except bank hols).
Directions	Off A359 between Frome & Bruton, 7 miles south west of Frome.

Meals	12pm-2pm; 7pm-9pm. Main courses £11.95-£17.95; set menu (3 courses) £15.95.
Closed	2.30pm-6.30pm (3pm-7pm Sun).
Directions	From Frome A362 for Radstock; left signed Mells.

Bob & Shirley Wood
The Three Horseshoes,
Batcombe,
Shepton Mallet BA4 6HE
Tel   +44 (0)1749 850359
Web   www.thethreehorseshoesinn.co.uk

Entry 620 Map 3

Rob Rowlands
The Talbot Inn at Mells,
Selwood Street,
Mells, Frome BA11 3PN
Tel   +44 (0)1373 812254
Web   www.talbotinn.com

Entry 621 Map 3

The Pilgrim's at Lovington
Lovington

"The pub that thinks it's a restaurant-with-rooms" delivers a unique style. It's thoroughly civilised yet distinctly informal, serving Cottage Champflower on hand pump and good modern dishes that draw on the best local produce. Choose a table in the original part of the building, all low beams, flagstones, rustic walls lined with watercolours and a log fire. Jools is passionate about using the best Somerset has to offer and his menus highlight suppliers and growers. So there's Michael Brown's smoked eel served with Denhay bacon on Charles Dowding's organic leaves, and Dorset-caught sea bass with creamed potatoes and pernod sauce. Local farms supply the meat, ice creams are made in Lovington, veg is organic, bread is homemade using locally milled flour. And then there are the rooms in the converted Cider Store, stunning with their French sleigh or brass bedsteads, plasma screens and touch-activated lamps, fresh coffee and big bathrobes. Ample bathrooms come with roll top baths and 'wet-room' style showers — or both. Wake to delicious breakfasts under posh brollies in summer.

Rooms	5: 4 doubles, 1 twin. £80–£120.
Meals	12pm-2pm; 7pm-9pm.
	Main courses £9-£23;
	Sunday lunch £15 & £19.
Closed	3pm-7pm; Sun eves, Mon all day &
	Tues lunch.
Directions	On B3153 between Castle Cary &
	Somerton. In village by traffic lights.

Julian & Sally Mitchison
The Pilgrim's at Lovington,
Lovington,
Castle Cary BA7 7PT
Tel   +44 (0)1963 240597
Web   www.thepilgrimsatlovington.co.uk

Entry 622 Map 3

Somerset

The Manor House Inn
Ditcheat

Every English village should have as its beating heart a pub such as this. In the bar – large, unscuffed and open plan – there's a good fire blazing. Settle back with something tasty from local breweries – good cider too – and tune into chatter of weather, sump oil and stock. Skittles clatter merrily in the alley that doubles up as a sports bar and function room. In the meantime, enticing aromas encourage you to check out the chalked boards and the game and fish specials. On the regularly changing menus are chargrilled steaks and homemade pies, and pan-fried duck breast with blackberry and rhubarb compote, green beans, parsnip purée and port sauce. Staying the night? Behind the inn and the car park, in the Old Mews, smart and compact bedrooms lie. Named after racehorses trained in the village, all three have a traditional look that's cosy and cottagey; beds are comfortable and modern, bath and shower rooms are a treat. In the morning, after a full English breakfast, you'll discover a picture-perfect village amid gently rolling hills.

Rooms	3: 2 doubles, 1 twin. From £85. Singles £55.
Meals	12pm-2.30pm (5pm Sun); 6.30pm-9pm (9.30pm Fri & Sat). Main courses £9.95-£16.95; bar meals £3.95-£8.95.
Closed	3pm-5.30pm. Open all day Fri-Sun.
Directions	Between A37 & A371, in Ditcheat next to church.

Simon & Kinga d'Offay
The Manor House Inn,
Ditcheat,
Shepton Mallet BA4 6RB
Tel   +44 (0)1749 860276
Web   www.manorhouseinn.co.uk

Entry 623 Map 3

Somerset

Wookey Hole Inn
Wookey Hole

On the edge of the Mendip hills: a traditional façade, a funky décor, excellent food and no end of choice behind the kitsch-with-style bar. The whole place throngs, particularly in summer when the big garden comes into its own. It's also relaxed and properly child-friendly with toys and wax crayons for doodling on (paper) tablecloths. Terracotta tiles, open fires, stripped boards and wooden panelling, splashes of strong colour, arty lamps, photos and interesting objets. The atmosphere is laid-back, the cool levels boosted by live jazz at Sunday lunch times, and the food, which has good local credentials, is seriously tasty and imaginative: onion jam and goat's cheese bruscetta, fillet of beef with Exmoor blue cheese, spiced lamb burgers with smoked cheddar. The puddings are seductive, too.

Meals	12pm-2.30pm (3pm Sun); 7pm-9.30pm; no food Sun eve. Main courses from £5-£14.25 (lunch), £13.75-£24 (dinner).
Closed	Sun eve.
Directions	Follow brown tourist signs for Wookey Hole off A371 or A39 in Wells.

Michael & Richard Davey
Wookey Hole Inn,
Wookey Hole,
Wells BA5 1BP
Tel   +44 (0)1749 676677
Web   www.wookeyholeinn.com

Entry 624 Map 3

Somerset

The Crown
Churchill

Once a coaching stop between Bristol and Exeter, then the village grocer's, now an unspoilt pub. Modern makeovers have passed it by and beer reigns supreme, with up to ten ales tapped from the barrel. For years landlord Tim Rogers has resisted piped music and electronic games; who needs them in these beamed and flagstoned bars? The rustic surroundings and the jolly atmosphere draw both locals and walkers treading the Mendip hills. Find a seat by the log fire, cradle a pint of Butcombe or RCH PG Steam bitter, be lulled by the hum of regulars at the bar. If you're here at lunchtime you'll find a short, traditional, blackboard menu: warming bowls of soup, thick-cut rare roast beef sandwiches, winter casseroles, treacle pud. Evenings are reserved for the serious art of ale drinking, and it's packed at weekends.

Meals	12pm-2.30pm. Main courses £4.25-£6.95.
Closed	Open all day.
Directions	From Bristol A38 to Churchill, right for Weston-super-Mare. Immed left in front of Nelson Pub, up Skinners Lane, pub on bend.

Tim Rogers
The Crown,
The Batch,
Churchill,
Congresbury BS25 5PP
Tel   +44 (0)1934 852995

Entry 625 Map 3

Somerset

The Black Horse
Clapton-in-Gordano

The Snug Bar once doubled as the village lock-up and, if it weren't for the electric lights and the cars outside, you'd be hard pushed to remember you were in the 21st century. With flagstones and dark moody wood, the main room bears the scuffs of centuries of drinking. Settles and old tables sit around the walls; cottage windows with wobbly shutters let a little of the outside in. The fire roars in its vast hearth beneath a fine set of antique guns – so pull off your muddy boots and settle in. Sepia prints of parish cricket teams and steam tractors clutter the walls and cask ales pour from the stone ledge behind the hatch bar. The food is unfancy bar fodder, with daily specials. Ale takes pride of place; beneath a chalkboard six jacketed casks squat above drip pans. There are fine wines too, and plenty of garden.

Meals	12pm-2pm; no food Sun.
	Main courses £3.50-£6.95.
Closed	Open all day.
Directions	M5 junc. 19 for Portbury & Clapton. Left into Clevedon Lane.

Nicholas Evans
The Black Horse,
Clevedon Lane,
Clapton-in-Gordano, BS20 7RH
Tel   +44 (0)1275 842105
Web   www.thekicker.co.uk

Entry 626 Map 3

Somerset
Worth a visit

627 **Blue Flame** West End, Nailsea BS48 4DE
+44 (0)1275 856910
Spartan, well-worn rural local favoured by farmers, philosophers, intellectuals and eccentrics as well as real ale and cider fans. Two basic rooms, a coal fire, barrels on stillage, filled rolls, pub games and a big garden. A one-off!

628 **Carpenter's Arms** Stanton Wick, Pensford, Bristol BS39 4BX +44 (0)1761 490202
Beams and stone walls are jazzed up by a tartan carpet, and the gleaming country style bar bristles with beverages at this classy inn set high above the Chew Valley. Good food and fine wines, too.

629 **Ring O'Bells** Hinton Blewett, Bristol BS39 5AN +44 (0)1761 452239
Snug and cosy village local tucked away by the old church and brimming with cheer and hospitality. Come for cracking Bath ales and honest home-cooked food.

630 **The Hunters' Lodge** Priddy, Wells BA5 3AR
+44 (0)1749 672275
On the windswept crossroads, a stark little treasure. Mr Dors is its proudest fixture, administering ale and just-made bowls of chilli to cavers, pot-holers, hikers and the odd local. An unpretentious treat.

631 **Tucker's Grave Inn** Faulkland, Radstock BA3 5XF +44 (0)1373 834230
An unassuming, almost-unsigned 17th-century stone building, Tucker's is a treasure. Few frills, no bar, just four beer casks and containers of local heady cider in the bay, and a stack of crisp boxes against the wall. Defiantly informal. Up for sale in 2009.

Somerset

Worth a visit

632 Kingsdon Inn Kingsdon, Somerton TA11 7LG
+44 (0)1935 840543
Picture-postcard thatched inn only minutes from the A303 (Podimore roundabout). Charming single bar with bending beams and a blazing fire – the perfect refuge for homecooked meals and pints of Butcombe.

633 Cat Head Inn Cat Street, Chiselborough, Stoke-sub-Hamdon TA14 6TT
+44 (0)1935 881231
Striking hamstone pub in countryside close to Montacute. Spotless flagstoned rooms, fresh imaginative food, Otter bitter on tap and attractive gardens with views over the village.

634 Three Horseshoes Langley Marsh, Wiveliscombe, Taunton TA4 2UL
+44 (0)1984 623763
A proper traditional local and proud of it. Come for Otter and Cotleigh beers tapped from the cask and good food – fish and game from Exmoor, locally reared beef – and best enjoyed in the timeless and bustling front room.

635 Blue Ball Inn Triscombe, Bishops Lydeard, Taunton TA4 3HE +44 (0)1984 618242
The 18th-century thatched barn metamorphosed into a smart dining pub some years back and stands on the slopes of the Quantock Hills, with views from its muti-tiered garden. Reports on the food welcome.

636 The Notley Arms Inn Monksilver, Taunton TA4 4JB +44 (0)1984 656217
A pretty pub in an isolated village with a welcoming intimate feel – perfect for cold nights. Dependable range of local ales and good food.

Staffordshire

The Holly Bush Inn
Salt

Geoffrey Holland came to the Holly Bush some years ago and turned it into a thriving local. Indeed, the entire emphasis is local. Cheeses, vegetables, meat and game come from the region and are almost exclusively organic, herbs are fresh from the garden and some of the recipes, such as the 'oatcakes' (pancakes not biscuits), are strictly Staffs. Only the fish and some of the beers are from further afield. They don't take bookings, so arrive early for dinner; try home-smoked salmon with hollandaise sauce or steak and ale pie. The 'second oldest licensed pub in the country' is a characterful little place, quirky even, with open fires and the odd carved beam and settle. Out on the big back lawn, a wood-oven bakes pizzas in summer. The village, listed in the Domesday Book, should charm you.

Meals	12pm-9.30pm (9pm Sun). Main courses £7.25-£13.95; bar snacks £2.25-£3.25; Sunday lunch £6.25.
Closed	Open all day.
Directions	Off M6 junc. 14, follow signs for Uttoxeter. Straight over 2 r'bouts, 2nd left to Sandon (B5066). 3rd right into Salt, through village; Holly Bush on right.

Geoffrey Holland
The Holly Bush Inn,
Salt,
Stafford ST18 0BX
Tel +44 (0)1889 508234
Web www.hollybushinn.co.uk

Entry 637 Map 8

Staffordshire

The George
Alstonefield

Greensward ripples endlessly in this remote limestone village with its old church, perched on a plateau between the remarkable gorges of the rivers Dove and Manifold. Set amidst this verdant Eden, the handsome George is an ultra-reliable local, in the family for four decades and lovingly managed by Emily. As you walk into the small, timeless rooms of old beams, gleaming quarry tiles and crackling log fire, you know you're in safe hands. It's an unhurried place, where everyone knows everyone else (or soon will), ramblers cram the benches and tables out front, the farm shop bustles and time passes slowly. The welcome is warm, the beer's on song and the food is fab. Young chefs are creative with seasonal produce, so there's potted smoked mackerel, rack of lamb with herb and mustard crust, and pear tarte tatin.

Suffolk

Duke's Head
Somerleyton

The shabby-chic gastropub overlooks the Somerleyton Estate; visit the grand hall, explore the glorious grounds. This 17th-century village inn has been restored in a simple, understated style with a laid-back feel: bare boards and beams, roaring log fire, warmly cosy bar. Next door, in the rambling, simply adorned dining area, good, gutsy, seasonal food is served. Daily menus use produce grown and shot on the estate, ranging from brie and fruit chutney sandwiches to pigeon breast with beetroot relish and Duke burgers with hand-cut chips. Delicious desserts include traditional ginger cake with toffee sauce; at Sunday lunch, listen to live music while tucking into estate-bred roast beef served with all the trimmings. The Duke's Head is great in summer, too, so plonk yourself down on a rustic alfresco bench and relish the views.

Meals	12pm-2.30pm; 7pm-9pm (6.30pm-8pm Sun). Main courses £9-£20; bar meals £4-£14.
Closed	3pm-6pm. Open all day Sat & Sun.
Directions	Village signed off A515, 7 miles north of Ashbourne.

Meals	12pm-3pm; 6.30pm-9pm. Main courses £8.50-£12.50; sandwiches from £4.25
Closed	Open all day.
Directions	Village & pub signed off B1074, 5 miles north west of Lowestoft.

Emily Hammond
The George,
Alstonefield,
Ashbourne DE6 2FX

Tel +44 (0)1335 310205
Web www.thegeorgeatalstonefield.com

Entry 638 Map 8

Andrew Rogers
Duke's Head,
Slugs Lane, Somerleyton,
Lowestoft NR32 5QR

Tel +44 (0)1502 730281
Web www.somerleyton.co.uk

Entry 639 Map 10

The Crown
Southwold

Well-heeled weekenders flock to Southwold most of the year but outside the silly season it's a gem. The chic Crown, stalwart of the dining pub world, oozes metropolitan sophistication. Ceilings are elegantly beamed, walls are colourwashed and uncluttered, the bar is large and laid-back. Adnams, famed for its beers countrywide, is on home turf here, and you would struggle to find a smarter brewery tap. The wood-panelled rear snug is the province of hard-core traditionalists, the brasserie wine bar at the front is beloved of the urbane crowd. Gutsy food travels the world – perhaps Merguez sausages with lemon polenta and gremolata, baked tope fillet in saffron yoghurt, vanilla panna cotta and dried fruit compote. Don't just stick to the palate-quenching ales: the unpretentiously serious Adnams wine list is oenophiles' heaven.

The Anchor
Walberswick

Seeking sea air, beer guru Mark Dorber and wife Sophie are doing wonders at this well-loved pub. To the sound of the sea crashing on the beach beyond, the vast lawn hosts summer barbecues – and the homemade burgers draw an appreciative crowd. Inside, sand, stone and aqua tones are redolent of the sea and open skies and add a contemporary touch, while Sophie's menus overflow with produce sourced from a rich vein of organic farms and top local butchers. They have put fresh food firmly back on the menu, and doubled the allotment at the back. Menus match beer with food: try Adnams Broadside with a melting Irish stew. A summer treat would be tempura rock oysters with a draught wheat beer, out on the sun terrace overlooking allotments, beach huts and distant sea.

Meals	12pm-2pm (2.30pm Sat; 3pm Sun); 6.30pm-9pm. Main courses £12-£17; lunches £9.50-£12.50.	Meals	12pm-3pm; 6pm-9pm (all day Sat in July & Aug). Main courses £10.25-£17.75.
Closed	3pm-6.30pm Mon-Fri in winter. Open all day in summer.	Closed	Open all day.
Directions	From A12, A1095 to Southwold. Inn on High Street.	Directions	From A12 south of Southwold, B1387 to Walberswick.

Francis Guildea
The Crown,
90 High Street,
Southwold IP18 6DP
Tel   +44 (0)1502 722275
Web   www.adnams.co.uk/hotels

Entry 640 Map 10

Mark & Sophie Dorber
The Anchor,
Main Street, Walberswick,
Southwold IP18 6UA
Tel   +44 (0)1502 722112
Web   www.anchoratwalberswick.com

Entry 641 Map 10

Suffolk

The Ship
Dunwich

Once a great port, Dunwich is now a tiny (but famous) village, gradually sinking into the sea. Its well-loved smugglers' inn, almost on the beach, overlooks the salt marsh and sea and pulls in wind-blown walkers and birdwatchers from the Minsmere Reserve. In the old-fashioned bar – nautical bric-a-brac, flagged floors, simple furnishings and a stove that belts out the heat – you can tuck into legendary fish and chips washed down with a pint of Adnams. There's also a more modern dining room, but don't expect fancy food; what you get are traditional dishes in generous portions, bowls of soup with chunks of bread, and big platefuls of ham, egg and chips; in the evening, lamb, pea and mint casserole, or baked megrim in lemon butter. Up the fine Victorian staircase are spruced up bedrooms – simple, uncluttered, with period features, cord carpets, brass beds, old pine, little shower rooms. Rooms at the front have glorious salt marsh views, courtyard rooms are cosy with new pine, and the family room under the eaves is fabulous: single beds, a big futon-style bean bag, and a plasma screen for the kids.

Rooms	11: 7 doubles, 4 family rooms. £85-£135.
Meals	12pm-3pm; 6pm-9pm. Main courses £7.95-£12.95.
Closed	Open all day.
Directions	Village signposted off B1125 between A12 at Blythburgh and Westleton.

Graeme Sims & Chloe Coulson
The Ship,
St James's Street,
Dunwich, Saxmundham IP17 3DT
Tel   +44 (0)1728 648219
Web   www.shipatdunwich.co.uk

The Westleton Crown

Westleton

This is one of England's oldest coaching inns, with 800 years of continuous service under its belt. It stands in a village two miles inland from the sea at Dunwich, with Westleton Heath running east towards Minsmere Bird Sanctuary. Inside, you find the best of old and new. A refurbishment has introduced Farrow & Ball colours, leather sofas and a tongue-and-groove bar, while the panelled walls, stripped floors, ancient beams and spindle-back chairs remain. Weave around and find nooks and crannies in which to hide, flames flickering in an open fire, a huge map on the wall for walkers. You can eat wherever you want, and a breakfast room in the conservatory opens onto a terraced garden for summer barbecues. Fish comes straight off the boats at Lowestoft, local butchers provide local meat. Lovely bedrooms are scattered about and come in cool lime white with comfy beds, Egyptian cotton, flat-screen TVs. Super bathrooms are fitted out in Fired Earth; the most stylish have claw-foot baths. Aldeburgh and Southwold are close by.

Rooms	25: 19 doubles, 2 twins, 3 family rooms, 1 single. £115-180. Singles from £90.
Meals	12pm-2.30pm; 7pm-9.30pm. Main courses £9.50-£22; bar meals from £4.75.
Closed	Open all day.
Directions	A12 north from Ipswich. Right at Yoxford onto B1122, then left for Westleton on B1125. On right in village.

Matt Goodwin
The Westleton Crown,
The Street, Westleton,
Saxmundham IP17 3AD

Tel   +44 (0)1728 648777
Web   www.westletoncrown.co.uk

Suffolk

Eels Foot Inn
Eastbridge

The sign depicts an eel wriggling out of an old boot, and this plain-looking and oddly named backwater village pub lives up to its slightly eccentric reputation. It's a twitchers' pub where you will find watchers and wardens from Minsmere RSPB Reserve swapping stories with walkers, cyclists and holidaymakers. All are drawn to this local for pints of tip-top Adnams ale (the full range is on tap), and hearty food (beer battered cod, steak and ale pie, treacle tart) served in a cosy wood-floored bar, replete with log fire and simple furnishings; there's a homely upper dining area, too. Don't miss the craic on music nights – every Thursday is Squit Night (a folk, country and blues jamming session) and the last Sunday night of the month is folk night. Note – the place is mobbed in summer! *Camping facilities.*

Suffolk

The King's Head
Laxfield

Known locally as the Low House because it lies in a dip below the churchyard, the 600-year-old pub is one of Suffolk's treasures. Little has changed in the last 100 years and the four rooms creak with character – all narrow passageways, low ceilings, wood panelling and tiny fires for cold nights. The simple parlour is dominated by a three-sided, high-backed settle and there's no bar – far too new-fangled a concept for this place. Instead, Adnams ales are served from barrels in the tap room. In keeping with the authenticity, the food is rustic, hearty and homemade, the short blackboard menu listing soup, sandwiches, hot dishes and puddings. It's the sort of place where folk music starts up spontaneously, while summer brings Morris men. The lovely garden overlooking the brook at the back was once a bowling green.

Meals	12pm-2.30pm; 7pm-9pm (6.30pm-8pm Thurs). Main courses £5-£13.
Closed	3pm-6pm. Open all day Sat & Sun.
Directions	Off B1122 between Yoxford & Leiston.

Meals	12pm-2pm; 7pm-9pm. Main courses £6.50-£9.50; bar meals £4.25-£6.
Closed	3pm-6pm. Open all day in summer.
Directions	From Laxfield church, left down hill for 50 yards. Left; pub on right.

	Corinne Webber Eels Foot Inn, Eastbridge, Leiston IP16 4SN
Tel	+44 (0)1728 830154
Web	www.theeelsfootinn.co.uk

	Robert Wilson The King's Head, Gorams Mill Lane, Laxfield, Woodbridge IP13 8DW
Tel	+44 (0)1986 798395
Web	www.laxfield-kingshead.co.uk

Entry 644 Map 10

Entry 645 Map 10

Suffolk

Station Hotel
Framlingham

The railway disappeared long ago, the old buildings are now business units, but the 'hotel' continues to thrive. Cask ales (a classic Victorian bitter, a sweet, wintry porter) are perfect accompaniments for gutsy cooking. Who would imagine, chalked up on the board on the edge of a market town somewhere in Suffolk, creamy baked vacherin cheese or pig's trotters stuffed with apple and black pudding? Or warm almond and orange polenta cake, light as a cloud? Lunch is quiet but it bustles at night, helped along by the master of the kitchen, Mike Jones, and his friendly, laid-back team. The building is pretty in a shabby-boho way, the interior is charming. Expect blackened stripped boards, cream papered walls, a stuffed head, and bone-handled knives partnering paper serviettes – a characterful mix.

Meals	12pm-2pm; 7pm-9pm (9.30pm Fri & Sat). Main courses £4-£14.75; bar meals £3.25-£11.
Closed	2.30pm-5pm (7pm Sun).
Directions	From Wickham Market, 10 min off the A12.

Mike Jones
Station Hotel,
Station Road, Framlingham,
Woodbridge IP13 9EE

Tel	+44 (0)1728 723455
Web	www.thestationhotel.net

Entry 646 Map 10

Suffolk

Crown Inn
Great Glemham

In a sweet hamlet with views of lush parkland over the road, the archetypal 17th-century red brick inn is an easy dash from the A12 and the Heritage Coast. Inside: log fires, scrubbed tables, fresh flowers, a happy feel. The landlords are foodies and their menus sing the praises of the Alde Valley. So there's lamb from the neighbouring estate, Benhall venison and game, Creasey's meats from Peasenhall, Thorpeness salad leaves, Marybelle's Suffolk Meadow ice creams and Buxlow cheeses. Lovers of real ale, too, will go home happy. You may expect the best of the county's Earl Soham and Adnams breweries alongside a regional guest ale, perhaps Norfolk's Humpty Dumpty, while Aspall's cider and James White's juices are a celebration of Suffolk's apples. In short, David and Rhyan serve the cream of the crop.

Meals	11.30am-2.30pm (from 12pm Sun); 6.30pm-9pm (7pm-8.30pm Sun). Main courses £6.95-£12.95; sandwiches from £4.45.
Closed	3pm-6.30pm & Mon (except bank hols).
Directions	Village signed off A12 at Farnham between Woodbridge and Saxmundham.

David Cottle & Rhyan Ball
Crown Inn,
Great Glemham,
Saxmundham IP17 2DA

Tel	+44 (0)1728 663693
Web	www.glemhamcrown.co.uk

Entry 647 Map 10

Sibton White Horse
Sibton

Step through the door of the Masons' unassuming pub and prepare for a surprise. The heart of this thriving village local is 16th-century and the bar is steeped in character: old pews, huge inglenook – aglow in winter – horsebrasses on blackened beams, wonky walls. Ale drinkers will rejoice at the sight of gleaming brass beer engines on the old oak servery; settle in for pints of Adnams and Woodforde's and weekly guests beers. (And don't miss a peep through the window panel into the cellar with a Roman floor.) Food is fresh, seasonal, with local game, meat from the next village, vegetables from the kitchen garden. Try chicken liver brushetta with chilli jam; Docking Hall Farm pork loin with tomato and herb coulis; plum tarte tatin. The bread is homemade, it's all delicious, and on sunny days you can spill onto the lawns. In the annexe, thoroughly modern bedrooms are furnished in old and new pine; beds are comfy; bathrooms spotless; views are to open countryside. You are 20 minutes from Aldeburgh and charming Southwold – perfect for beach cricket, a pint of prawns and a dip in the North Sea.

Rooms	6: 5 twins/doubles, 1 single. £75-£90. Singles £60-£65.
Meals	12pm-2pm (2.30pm Sun); 7pm-9pm (6.30pm-9pm Fri & Sat). Main courses £7.50-£10.50 (lunch), £10-£18 (dinner); Sunday roast £10.
Closed	3pm-6pm & Mon lunch.
Directions	A1120 off A12 at Yoxford; at Peasenhall, turn right opposite Creasey's butchers; pub signed.

Neil & Gill Mason
Sibton White Horse,
Halesworth Road, Sibton,
Saxmundham IP17 2JJ
Tel   +44 (0)1728 660337
Web   www.sibtonwhitehorseinn.co.uk

Suffolk

The Crown Inn
Snape

Forsaking the delights of Aldeburgh's high street and the restaurant where they met as chefs (the renowned 152), Garry, keen forager and shooter and lover of the 'good life', now shares it all with partner Teresa. This wonderful Adnam's inn and smallholding has made it all possible including rearing their own livestock – think Suffolk sheep, Old Spot piglets, egg-incubated quail, and ducks and geese on the flight pond. Inside: a timeless interior of old brick floors, roaring log fires and the finest example anywhere of an 'old codgers' – a double Suffolk settle. The well-bred food naturally homes in on the best 'doorstep' produce: dayboat fish, Campsea Ashe game, their own meats. Families and dog walkers are positively encouraged, even for light bites. As for the wines and beers – they're Adnams' finest.

Suffolk

The Golden Key
Snape

Young Nick Attfield has taken on this civilised little cottage-style pub close to Snape Maltings. Nick's daily menus bristle with local goodies, from Aldeburgh fish and Benhall Estate game to vegetables and salads from an organic smallholding in Sudbourne and Nick's own chickens and rare-breed sheep and pigs; even local allotment produce. So tuck into potted shrimps, venison casserole, rack of Alde Valley lamb and Suffolk Red Poll beefburger. Desserts are the best of traditional: chocolate and walnut brownie, bread-and-putter pudding. The classic bar has quarry tiles, beams and brasses and an ancient curved settle fronting a glowing inglenook. The carpeted dining areas have scrubbed pine tables, log fires and local artwork on mellow yellow walls. There's well-kept Adnams on tap and two terraces for summer supping.

Meals	12pm-2.30pm (3pm Sat & Sun); 6pm-9.30pm (10pm Sat); no food Sun eve in winter & Mon. Main courses £8.50-£13.50.
Closed	2.30pm-6pm (open all day Sat & Sun in summer).
Directions	From A12, A1094 towards Aldeburgh; right at Snape Church onto B1069; follow 'Snape Maltings' sign. Pub on left at bottom of hill.

Meals	12pm-2pm (2.30pm Sun); 6.30pm-9pm (7pm Sun). Main courses £8.50-£15; sandwiches from £4.
Closed	3.30pm (4pm Sat & Sun) - 6pm (7pm Sun).
Directions	Turn off the A12 onto the A1094, signposted Snape and Aldeburgh. Turn right onto the B1069, signposted Snape. Turn left onto Priory Road at the crossroads just before The Crown Inn

	Garry & Teresa Cook
	The Crown Inn,
	Bridge Road,
	Snape,
	Saxmundham IP17 1SL
Tel	+44 (0)1728 688324

	Nick Attfield
	The Golden Key,
	Priory Road, Snape,
	Saxmundham IP17 1SQ
Tel	+44 (0)1728 688510
Web	www.snape-golden-key.co.uk

Entry 649 Map 10

Entry 650 Map 10

Suffolk

The King's Head Inn
Orford

Standing in the shadow of the village church and windswept graveyard, the 16th-century King's Head is steeped in smuggling history: Orford's ancient quay is a stroll away. Adrian and Susan Searing have breathed new life into the place since taking over. This is no gastropub, however, but a proper, no-nonsense village local – children and dogs welcome. A winter fire warms the beamed and carpeted traditional bar, and there are old scrubbed tables on a rug-strewn wooden floor in the rustic-chic dining room next door. Expect classic pub food – sourced entirely from locally sourced ingredients – from fish pie with sautéed french beans and moules and frites to Suffolk ham ploughman's, treacle tart and traditional Sunday roasts. Or drop by for a glass of prosecco or cracking pint of Adnams Broadside – itself a meal in a glass.

Suffolk

The Froize
Chillesford

Impassioned by local produce years before it became fashionable, David Grimwood lives in chef's whites or shooting tweeds – a Suffolk countryman too chivalrous to accept his reputation as East Anglia's best game cook. Off the beaten track, the path to these once charmingly remote 18th-century keepers' cottages is well worn by regulars. Blythburgh pork, Orford and Lowestoft fish, bags of local game (much of it retrieved by the landlord's black labs) combined with retro rustic cooking reflect the 'field, forest and foreshore' landscape The Froize sits in. A perfect joint always stands alongside reworked classics such as devilled kidneys, stuffed skate wing or cider-braised rabbit and prunes, and the homemade puddings are legendary. Ales are the county's best, mostly Adnams, and there's Aspall's cider, too.

Meals	12pm-2.30pm (3pm Sun); 6.30pm-9pm. Main courses £8.95-£12.50; bar meals from £3.95-£7.95; Sunday roast £12.95.
Closed	3pm-6pm (Mon-Fri).
Directions	Leave A12 at Woodbridge; A1152 & B1084 to Orford; pub on main square.

Meals	12pm-2pm; 7pm-9.30pm. Main courses from £13.50.
Closed	Mon all day (except bank hols).
Directions	On B1084 between Woodbridge and Orford.

Susan & Adrian Searing
The King's Head Inn,
Front Street, Orford,
Woodbridge IP12 2LW
Tel   +44 (0)1394 450271
Web   www.thekingsheadorford.co.uk

Entry 651 Map 10

David Grimwood
The Froize,
The Street, Chillesford,
Woodbridge IP12 3PU
Tel   +44 (0)1394 450282
Web   www.froize.co.uk

Entry 652 Map 10

The Dennington Queen
Dennington

Traditional 16th-century features blend with contemporary touches at this beautifully refurbished Tudor inn next to the church in Dennington. If you're heading east to the coast, or west to Framlingham Castle, then head for the family-friendly Queen for a pint of Adnams ale and some great value food. Sink into a leather sofa by the fire with the papers and a coffee, or dine at scrubbed tables in the beamed, timbered and wood-floored dining room. There's lots of good things on the menu: cheddar and chutney ciabattas, salmon fishcakes with grain mustard mayonnaise, roast pork belly with spiced apple sauce, sea bass with smoked garlic, red onion risotto, a nicely gooey treacle tart. Rustic benches in the front garden overlook the church — perfect for summer.

The Ship
Levington

The Levington Ship is a 14th-century thatched beauty overlooking the River Orwell. This alone makes it a popular watering hole, the low-ceilinged bar and flower-festooned rear terrace filling quickly with yachting types, locals and townies escaping to the country for lunch. Naturally, the bar emphasises a nautical theme, with pictures of barges, lifebuoys and a ship's wheel on the walls. Over the past few years chef-patron Mark Johnson's imaginative cooking has made its successful mark, his chalkboard menus listing fresh fish and locally reared meats — notably venison from the Suffolk Estate — as well as seasonal salads and local vegetables. Exemplary French cheeses come from the Rungis Market in Paris and superior real ales from East Anglian brewers Adnams and Greene King. Wonderful riverside walks also await.

Meals	12pm-2pm; 6.30pm-9pm. Main courses £7.50-£12.50; sandwiches from £4.50.
Closed	3pm-6pm.
Directions	On A1120 between Earl Soham and Yoxford, 2 miles north of Framlingham.

Meals	12pm-2pm (3pm Sun); 6.30pm-9.30pm (9pm Sun). All day Apr-Sep. Main courses £8.95-£15.95.
Closed	2.30pm-6pm. Open all day Sat & Sun. Open all day Apr-Sept.
Directions	A12/A14 junction to Woodbridge; follow signs for Levington.

Martin Royal
The Dennington Queen,
Dennington,
Woodbridge IP13 3AB
Tel   +44 (0)1728 638241

Stella & Mark Johnson
The Ship,
Church Lane, Levington,
Ipswich IP10 0LQ
Tel   +44 (0)1473 659573

Entry 653 Map 10

Entry 654 Map 10

The Crown at Woodbridge
Woodbridge

Woodbridge's long wait for a classy inn with great food, urbane bedrooms and a cosmopolitan air is over. The 400-year-old Crown emerged from the shadows in 2009 and it's the talk of the town. Everyone loves the new Crown, from its pastel façade to its cool laid-back interiors and humorous touches: beneath a glass roof a wooden skiff is suspended above a long granite-topped bar. In intimate dining rooms, chef-patron Stephen David's menu trawls Europe for inspiration and draws on Suffolk's natural larder. Look forward to hearty dishes full of flavour and some amazing taste combinations: Cromer crab cakes with pickled ginger; braised shin of beef in chocolate beer; Brancaster mussels; blueberry and almond tart. Wash it all down with Adnams or Meantime beers or delve into the impressive list of wines. Cosseting bedrooms decorated in simple, Nantucket style and themed in white and grey are a further attraction. There are big beds, quirky touches and a host of extras, from fruit, fresh coffee and homemade shortbread to soft bathrobes and heated bathroom floors. A chic Suffolk bolthole – unmissable!

Rooms	10: 8 twins/doubles, 2 family rooms. £140–£180. Singles from £95.
Meals	12pm–2.30pm; 6pm–9.30pm. Main courses £10–£23; light meals from £6.
Closed	Open all day.
Directions	A12 north from Ipswich, then B1438 into town. Pass station and left into Quay St. On right.

Pub with rooms

Stephen David
The Crown at Woodbridge,
Thoroughfare,
Woodbridge IP12 1AD
Tel   +44 (0)1394 384242
Web   www.thecrownatwoodbridge.co.uk

The Crown
Stoke-by-Nayland

A slick operation – and now you can stay! In a smart new-build behind the pub, find rather posh bedrooms with elegant wallpapers, brass beds with superb mattresses and uncluttered bathrooms with storm showers and fluffy towels. All are toasty warm with underfloor heating, thick new carpets (three have French doors leading to a terrace) and country views. Back in the pub, low-ceilinged but rambling rooms are decked in muted colours, and the mood is warm, appealing and refreshingly music-free. There's space to prop up the bar and down a pint from Suffolk brewers Adnams, while the seasonal menu is a sympathetic combination of traditional and contemporary. No fewer than 11 chefs dispatch exuberant renditions of wild Norfolk mussels with bacon and parsley on toast, and locally shot pheasant with bacon, prunes and leeks – topped off with steamed sticky quince and ginger pudding or a plate of five British cheeses. The wine list is outstanding, with wines matched to the food and bottles to take home from the shop. Head to the terrace on sunny days: the views are as fabulous as all the rest.

Rooms	11: 10 doubles, 1 suite. £70-£170. Suite £95-£185. Singles from £70.
Meals	12pm-2.30pm; 6pm-9.30pm (10pm Fri & Sat); 12pm-9pm Sun. Main courses £10.95-£17.95.
Closed	Open all day.
Directions	North from Colchester on A134; B1087 east into Stoke-by-Nayland. Right at T-junction; pub on left.

Richard Sunderland
The Crown,
Park Street, Stoke-by-Nayland,
Colchester, CO6 4SE

Tel	+44 (0)1206 262001
Web	www.crowninn.net

Entry 656 Map 10

Suffolk

The Lindsey Rose
Lindsey

The Lindsey Rose has always been known as a food haunt 'twixt Hadleigh and Lavenham. And the atmospheric feel of the 15th-century Suffolk hall house remains – in the open beamed partitions, the rich red décor, the wooden tables and the planked floors. Recently things have become decidedly posher thanks to the introduction of a retro grill – though the simplicity of the menu belies the quality of the cooking. Choose your own cut and weight of their slow-reared, well-hung estate beef at the meat counter – which will then be cooked to your taste along with some rather good trimmings. For fish-lovers and vegetarians there are Colchester oysters and beer-battered cod, garlic mushrooms with Suffolk Blue cheese and stuffed peppers with couscous, unfussily presented and extremely tasty. Puddings, too, are delicious.

Meals	12pm-2.30pm (3pm Sun); 6.30pm-9.30pm (7pm-9pm Sun). Main courses £8-£16.
Closed	3pm-5.30pm. Open all day Sun.
Directions	Lindsey is signed south off A1141, between Hadleigh & Lavenham.

James Buckle
The Lindsey Rose,
Lindsey,
Ipswich IP7 6PP
Tel   +44 (0)1449 741424
Web   www.redroseinn.co.uk

Entry 657 Map 10

Suffolk

The Swan
Monks Eleigh

The polished, wooden floored interior is not unlike that of a bistro, but Nigel and Carol's 16th-century thatched Swan is still a pub at heart. There's a large bar, Adnams on hand pump and a good line in wines by the glass. The modernised interior is invitingly open with recessed ceiling lights, soft sage tones and a winter log fire. Nigel has created a blackboard menu to please both the traditionalist and the adventurer, so wintry offerings may include potted pork rilettes with apple and sultana chutney, whole roast partridge with braised lentils, bacon and onions, and a fabulously sticky toffee pudding with butterscotch and mascarpone. Fish can be relied upon to be beautifully fresh. Service, by Carol, is a lesson in how these things should be done: efficient, knowledgeable, cheerful and charming.

Meals	12pm-2pm; 7pm-9pm. Main courses £10-£16.75; bar meals £4.25-£7; set menu £13.50 & £17.50 (not Fri or Sat eve).
Closed	3pm-7pm; Sun eve & Mon all day.
Directions	On B1115 between Lavenham & Hadleigh.

Nigel & Carol Ramsbottom
The Swan,
The Street, Monks Eleigh,
Ipswich IP7 7AU
Tel   +44 (0)1449 741391
Web   www.monkseleigh.com

Entry 658 Map 10

Suffolk

The Bildeston Crown
Bildeston

There are flagstones in the bar, warm reds on the walls and sweet-smelling logs smouldering in open fires. The inn dates from 1529, the interior design from 2005. Not that the feel is overly contemporary; ancient beams have been reclaimed and varnished wood floors shine like honey. There are gilded mirrors and oils on the walls, candles in the fireplace, smart locals at the bar. An airy open-plan feel runs throughout, with lots of space in the dining room and smart leather chairs tucked under hand-made oak tables. They're proud of their food here and it ranges from roast Suffolk beef sandwiches with mustard mayo to a theatrically, chicly presented eight-course tasting menu in the evening. There are flowers in the courtyard and Suffolk beers to quench your thirst.

Meals	12pm-3pm; 7pm-10pm (9.30pm Sun). Main courses £14-£24; set menu, 3 courses, £20; Sunday lunch £14; sandwiches from £7.
Closed	Open all day.
Directions	A12 junc. 31, then B1070 to Hadleigh. A1141 north, then B1115 into village & on right.

Hayley Lee
The Bildeston Crown,
104 High Street,
Bildeston, Ipswich IP7 7EB
Tel   +44 (0)1449 740510
Web   www.thebildestoncrown.co.uk

Entry 659 Map 10

Suffolk

Anchor Inn
Nayland

The Bunting family, like many farmers, have had to diversify: they bought the pub next to their land. And they take huge pride in the produce that appears on the menus — pheasant, duck and rabbit from farm shoots, eggs from their bantams, lamb from their fields, vegetables from their kitchen garden. Not only that, the smokehouse at the back produces game, fish and treacle bacon — unmissable! When it came to updating the building they sensibly kept things simple. This pretty butter-coloured pub successfully features soft modern colours in traditional small rooms with open fires; and there's a good big restaurant upstairs. Another draw is the setting, right beside the river Stour with summer barbecues bringing out the best of the garden. At the Buntings Heritage Farm behind, rare Suffolk Punch horses plough the fields in the old way; check their website for times.

Meals	12pm-2pm (2.30pm Sat; 3pm Sun); 6.30pm-9pm (9.30pm Sat; 5pm-8.30pm Sun). Main courses £6.95-£12.95; Sunday roast £9.50.
Closed	3pm-5pm. Open all day Sat & Sun & bank hols.
Directions	From Colchester A134 on Essex & Suffolk border. 300m off A134 where road crosses River Stour.

Daniel Bunting
Anchor Inn,
26 Court Street, Nayland,
Colchester CO6 4JL
Tel   +44 (0)1206 262313
Web   www.anchornayland.co.uk

Entry 660 Map 10

Suffolk

The Fox Inn
Bury St Edmunds

Town centre inns don't get much better than The Fox – a stunning 15th-century building opposite the Abbey Gardens, a stroll from the famous cathedral. Refurbished with style and panache by passionate owners, it draws a small but loyal drinking crowd for tip-top Greene King ales, and foodies for seasonal dishes that champion local produce: free-range farm meats, Bury-baked bread, organic milk and eggs. Escape the shops and bag a table by the fire in the Green Room, replete with fine Jacobean panelling, painted Lloyd Loom chairs and fresh flowers. There's duck liver and tarragon parfait, old Spot pork loin with cider cream sauce, haddock with beetroot and caper relish; or relax over a roast leg of lamb with fresh mint stuffing for Sunday lunch. Beautiful, hugely comfortable bedrooms, crafted from a period barn in 2008, individually styled using locally sourced and reclaimed materials, are the cherry on the cake. Expect oak floors, old brick walls, Cole & Sons wallpapers, brass beds, super-swish bathrooms, and, in the spacious and raftered Hayloft Suite, a super-size contemporary four-poster with a bath for two.

Rooms	6: 3 doubles, 1 twin, 1 family room, 1 suite. £90–£95. Suite £105–£135. Singles from £84.
Meals	12pm-2.30pm (4pm Sun); 6pm-10pm. No food Sun eve. Main courses £9.95–£10.95 (lunch); £8.95–£15.95 (dinner); sandwiches from £5.95; Sunday roast from £9.45.
Closed	Open all day.
Directions	Adjacent to Abbey Gardens in town centre.

Sheila Blackmore
The Fox Inn,
1 Eastgate Street,
Bury St Edmunds IP33 1XX
Tel   +44 (0)1284 705562
Web   www.thefoxinnbury.co.uk

Entry 661 Map 10

Old Cannon Brewery
Bury St Edmunds

Tricky to find down Bury's back streets but well worth the effort, the Old Cannon is an admirable revitalisation of a Victorian brewhouse-pub. Bare boards clatter, wooden tables are simple and plain, the décor is light and airy with splashes of bold colour, and a huge mirror vies with two gleaming stainless-steel brewing vessels smack beside the bar. The atmosphere is youthful, friendly and enlivened by foaming pints of own-brew Gunner's Daughter (5.5%), Blonde Bombshell (4.2%), and a seasonal autumn brew like Rusty Gun (4%). On the chalkboard menu: Elveden Estate venison, mushroom and vegetable stew, steak, kidney and ale pie, local sausages with colcannon and onion gravy, cod in beer batter, and lunchtime cheese ploughman's; good hearty food. A cobbled courtyard beyond the old coach arch has swish tables and chairs for summer sipping; in the former brewhouse are five light, modern and freshly refurbished bedrooms, replete with good-sized shower rooms, curtains at Georgian windows and TVs. And you are a five-minute walk from Bury, hub of East Anglia — and its treasures.

Rooms	5: 4 doubles, 1 twin. £85.
Meals	12pm-2pm; 6pm-9.15pm. No food Sun eve & Mon eve. Bar snacks only Mon lunch. Main courses £8.50-£10.50; bar snacks from £4.25.
Closed	3pm-5pm (7pm Sun).
Directions	From A14, Bury exit, for centre, left at r'bout to Northgate St; right at Cadney Lane & into Cannon St.

Michael & Judith Shallow
Old Cannon Brewery,
86 Cannon Street,
Bury St Edmunds IP33 1JR

Tel	+44 (0)1284 768769
Web	www.oldcannonbrewery.co.uk

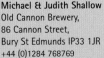

Entry 662 Map 10

Suffolk

Worth a visit

663 Butt & Oyster Pin Mill, Ipswich IP9 1JW
+44 (0)1473 780764
In a charmingly untouristy sailing village, an old estuary pub with settles, tiled floors, summer terrace with barbecue and Adnams tapped from the cask. Arrive early if you want a window seat.

664 The Ramsholt Arms Ramsholt,
Woodbridge IP12 3AB +44 (0)1394 411229
Idyllic — on the shore of the river Deben. Down a pint of Nethergate on the terrace, listen to the calls of the curlew. Cosy fires, game in season and great fish and chips.

665 The Dog Inn The Green, Grundisburgh,
Woodbridge IP13 6TA +44 (0)1473 735267
Quaint Suffolk village with a classic pink-washed inn. Local suppliers and seasonal produce are a basis for modern British cuisine — expect cider-braised local pork, wild rabbit casserole, confit of duck with satsuma sauce. More reports please.

666 Victoria The Street, Earl Soham,
Woodbridge IP13 7RL +44 (0)1728 685758
Inauspicious whitewashed village local by the green, famous for its home-brewed beers (Earl Soham Brewery). Few frills in the main bar but hearty pub food and a proper pint of Victoria Ale.

667 The Randolph Hotel 41 Wangford Road,
Reydon, Southwold IP18 6PZ
+44 (0)1502 723603
As good for a quick bite and a pint of Adnams as for a three-course meal that takes in local fish and game. This late Victorian pub-hotel has sleek modern good looks — and gardens for summer.

668 St Peter's Hall St Peter South Elmham,
Bungay NR35 1NQ +44 (0)1986 782288
The 13th-century moated manor thrives, brewing and bottling an exemplary range of bitters, fruit ales and porters. Take the weekend brewery tour or venture into the medieval hall to eat and drink like kings.

669 The Queens Head The Street, Bramfield,
Halesworth IP19 9HT +44 (0)1986 784214
Chef-landlord Mark Corcoran is passionate about provenance and his menus are filled with local farm meats and vegetables, served in a high-raftered bar with dark timbered walls, scrubbed pine tables and a blazing log fire. Lovely terraced courtyard and Adnams on tap.

670 Star Inn The Street, Lidgate,
Newmarket CB8 9PP +44 (0)1638 500275
The pretty Star was built in 1588. Fire blaze in winter, the garden glows in summer and the rich (French/Spanish) aromas that greet you are delicious all year round. Greene King on hand pump, and Newmarket close by. New owners in the offing.

671 Queens Head Hawkedon,
Bury St Edmunds IP29 4NN
+44 (0)1284 789218
True community pub lost down lanes in a tiny hamlet amid unspoilt Suffolk farmland. The draw is the huge inglenook that glows in winter, the unpretentious atmosphere, the homely food and the six changing regional ales — don't miss the July beer festival.

672 The White Horse Rede Road, Whepstead,
Bury St Edmunds IP29 4SS
+44 (0)1284 735760
The successful landlords of the Beehive in Horringer have refurbished this 17th-century village gem. Expect a stylish interior, local artwork, Suffolk ales, daily menus and seasonal produce. Oh, and a tuck shop selling sweets and ice cream.

The Talbot Inn
Ripley

New life has been breathed into the faded 15th-century coaching inn on Ripley's high street: a thoroughly modern inn that ticks to a historic beat. The untouched bar, all head-cracking beams, log fires and real ales from Surrey Hills, leads to a stunning new dining room, a light and airy space with a copper ceiling, oak floors and an amazing glass extension with garden views. Modern British cooking includes pub classics – haddock with pea purée, local sausages with cabbage and bacon – plus innovative scallops with celeriac risotto, sea bass with oysters and watercress sauce, dark chocolate tart with raspberry compote. Swish bedrooms in the inn itself, named after famous naval figures, combine old beams and wood panelling with designer fabrics. Further rooms cut a dash in the stable block, and in the brand-new mews out back. Traditionally timeless, they have trim carpets and soothing colours, big lamps and comfy beds, thick duvets, crisp linen and posh toiletries. Go for gold and book the four-poster suite, the Trafalgar (Nelson stayed here).

Rooms	39 twins/doubles. From £99. Cooked breakfast extra.
Meals	12pm-2.30pm; 6.30pm-9.30pm (10pm Fri & Sat); 2.30pm-10pm Sun. Main courses £7.95-£19.95; bar meals £4.50-£10.95; set lunch £13.95 & £16.95; Sunday lunch £15.95 & £19.95.
Closed	Open all day.
Directions	Ripley is signposted off A3 just south of M25, junc. 10.

Paul Dixon
The Talbot Inn,
High Street, Ripley,
Woking GU23 6BB

Tel	+44 (0)1483 225188
Web	www.thetalbotinn.com

Entry 673 Map 4

The Inn @ West End
West End

Wine importer Gerry Price draws them in from all over Surrey. Stylishly revamped dining areas are light and modern with wooden floors and fine fabrics. The feeling is relaxed and friendly – quiz nights, film club, boules, barbecues; the homely bar has handpumped ale from Fuller's and Young's and the list of wines is long, with a nod to Portuguese shores. Monthly menus have modern British choices ranging from salmon and dill fishcakes with tartare sauce to pot-roasted pork with cabbage and dauphinoise potatoes – and partridge, pheasant, woodcock and teal in winter. A pastry chef masterminds a select choice of desserts; cheeses are farmhouse best. Add good-value set lunches, lunchtime wine-tasting sessions, an alfresco wood oven and popular wine dinners, and you have a superbly run place.

Black Swan
Guildford

Geronimo Inns' boss must have jumped for joy when he completed the deal on this, his first pub outside London. Minutes from the A3 yet deep in leafy Surrey, the old bikers' boozer got the swishest makeover and its brick façade is now dwarfed by an amazing pavilion extension. Clever design pulls informal and open-plan drinking and dining areas together around a curving bar, with a separate classic bar for pints and an airy high-ceilinged eating area for diners; the place buzzes. Décor may be ultra-modern but, with up to six ales on tap and a flurry of non-bookable tables, the Black Swan still acts like a pub. Good food ranges from the classic chicken Caesar salad and cider-battered haddock and chips to calves' liver with chorizo and sweet pepper mash, or seared tuna with salad niçoise. The Black Swan thrives.

Meals	12pm-2.30pm (3pm Sun); 6pm-9.30pm (9pm Sun). 2 courses £27.95, 3 courses £32.50 (Fri & Sat eve). Set menus from £12.50; sandwiches from £5.25; Sunday lunch £24.95.	Meals	12pm-3pm (4pm Sat & Sun); 6pm-10pm. Main courses £9.50-£16.95; bar snacks £7.95-£10.50.
Closed	3pm-5pm. Open all day Sat & Sun.	Closed	Open all day.
Directions	On A322 towards Guildford, 2 miles from M3 junc. 3.	Directions	Ockham is signed off A3 just south of M25 junc. 10. Pub just north of village at crossroads.

	Gerry & Ann Price The Inn @ West End, 42 Guilford Road, West End, Woking GU24 9PW		Hossey Saghiri Black Swan, Old Lane, Guildford KT11 1NG
Tel	+44 (0)1276 858652	Tel	+44 (0)1932 862364
Web	www.the-inn.co.uk	Web	www.theblackswanockham.co.uk

Entry 674 Map 4

Entry 675 Map 4

The Old Bear
Cobham

Across the road from the river Mole at the end of the High Street, a century-old black-and-white inn. Step in to find a fashionable urban take on the traditional country pub: beautiful old beams and timbers, winter fires and oak floors, and an enomatic wine cabinet on the bar ensuring wines-by-glass are in top condition. The kitchen, headed by Nathan Green – previously of the Michelin-starred Arbutus in Soho – suggests superb gastro credentials. The constantly changing repertoire is driven by seasonal ingredients, interesting combinations and clear flavours. Try game ravioli with shaved chestnuts and braised celery, or roast venison with toasted hazelnuts and turnip gratin. The bar menu offer classics like cottage pie. Four hand-pump ales, a big front terrace, a rear garden, and Sunday lunches to lift the soul.

Meals	12pm-3pm (4pm Sat);
	6pm-10pm (12pm-9pm Sun).
	Main courses £10-£19;
	bar meals £4-£11;
	Sunday roast £14.95.
Closed	3pm-5pm. Open all day Sat & Sun.
Directions	M25 (junc 10); follow A3 towards
	London, then A245 for Cobham;
	pub on left at end of High Street.

	Max Durrant
	The Old Bear,
	Riverhill,
	Cobham KT11 3DX
Tel	+44 (0)1932 862116
Web	www.theoldbearcobham.co.uk

Entry 676 Map 4

The Parrot
Forest Green

Having left their mini-empire of London pubs for a livestock farm in the Surrey hills, the Gottos also run this rambling, 17th-century pub overlooking the village green and cricket pitch. They are passionate about food, its provenance and quality, and The Parrot showcases meats reared on their farm – Shorthorn cattle, Middlewhite pigs, and mutton – both on the short, imaginative menu and in the unique farm shop inside. Surely one of few pubs where you can tuck into game pie, lamb rump with minted pea purée and roast belly pork with mash and braised cabbage, and then buy the produce to take home (farm meats, free-range eggs, sausages, pickles, cheeses, pies). Elsewhere, beams, flagstones and lovely bits and bobs, old settles and blazing fires, Young's on tap and 16 wines by the glass. The value is outstanding.

Meals	12pm-3pm (5pm Sun); 6pm-10pm;
	no food Sun eve.
	Main courses £9.75-£16;
	Sunday roast from £11.75.
Closed	Open all day.
Directions	Opposite the village green, off
	B2127 just west of junction with
	B2126, 5 miles south west of
	Dorking.

	Charles & Linda Gotto
	The Parrot,
	Forest Green,
	Dorking RH5 5RZ
Tel	+44 (0)1306 621339
Web	www.theparrot.co.uk

Entry 677 Map 4

The Crown Inn
Chiddingfold

Beautifully restored in 2008, the Crown is a contender for the oldest hostelry in the country. Thirteenth-century bowed brick walls, warped weathered timbers, plaster ceilings and lattice windows… think yourself back in the days of the highwaymen. The bar's stained-glass leaded lights – for which charming Chiddingfold was once famous – tell of 'the Lion and the Unicorn's fight for the Crown', while the glowing main bar holds a vast flagged inglenook and a crackling log fire. It's a fascinating place so, pint of Hogs Back TEA in hand, take a wander and a gander at the small glass case of coins that date back to 1558. In keeping, the menu lists classic pub food – potted shrimps, steak and kidney pie, roast beef, Eton mess – prepared from excellent ingredients. Historic charm extends upstairs to cosy rooms with wonky walls and madly sloping floors, antique chests and polished wardrobes, carved wooden four-posters (three in all) and beds dressed in crisp cotton. Mod cons include iPod radios, posh tellys, and elegant Penhaligon smellies in smart bathrooms.

Rooms	8: 3 doubles, 3 four-posters, 1 single, 1 suite. £125-£165. Suite £200. Single £100.
Meals	12pm-2.30pm (3pm Sun); 6.30pm-10pm (9.30pm Sun). Main courses £9-£15.
Closed	Open all day.
Directions	On A283 between Guildford and Petworth.

Daniel Hall
The Crown Inn,
The Green, Chiddingfold,
Godalming GU8 4TX
Tel   +44 (0)1428 682255
Web   www.thecrownchiddingfold.com

Entry 678 Map 4

Surrey

Dog & Pheasant
Brook

Safe in the hands of new owners – and sporting a superb and traditional facelift – this popular old roadside inn oozes bonhomie. And, though the food is the driving force, the small bar heaves with upmarket locals in for a pint of Adnams Broadside or a glass of pinot noir. Smart and cosy it is, with black wood ceiling beams, striking wall timbers and warming winter fires; service is both friendly and upbeat. Chef Remi Ravaux's lengthy repertoire should please all with classic and modern dishes, and seafood a speciality. Blackboard specials like pan-fried fillet of rainbow trout with curly kale and roasted garlic sauce complement a main menu that covers all, from roasted shellfish platter to Cumberland sausage with creamed mash and gravy. A front terrace, a big garden and a private dining room upstairs complete the happy picture.

Meals	12pm-2.30pm; 6pm-9.30pm; 12pm-9.30pm Sat (8pm Sun). Main courses £8-£17.
Closed	Open all day.
Directions	On the Haslemere Road (A287) between Godalming and Haslemere.

David Gough & David Hall
Dog & Pheasant,
Haslemere Road,
Brook, Godalming GU8 5UJ
Tel   +44 (0)1428 682763
Web   www.dogandpheasant.com

Entry 679 Map 4

Surrey

The Hare & Hounds
Lingfield

The striking pub may have new owners, Eric and Tracy Payet, but little has changed inside. It's still an idiosyncratic place whose quirky collectables and bold paintings fill every corner and wall. Bar bustle can be surveyed from old cinema seats or one of a pair of throne-like chairs, while cushion-laden banquettes make a cosy spot from which to view Eric's (ex-Club Gascon, London) menus. Look to the chalkboard for daily dishes: rabbit stew with mustard sauce; roast hake with confit fennel. On the printed menu are aged parmesan and pea risotto; honey-glazed pork chop with black pudding and caramelised apple; roast pear clafoutis. Diners are as happy among the hop garlands and the greenery of the main bar as beneath the artwork in the lovely dining room. Nurse a summer pint of Abbot Ale in the partly decked garden.

Meals	12pm-2.30pm (4pm Sun); 7pm-9.30pm. Main courses £7.95-£18.95.
Closed	Open all day (closed Sun from 3pm).
Directions	From A22 towards Lingfield Racecourse into Common Road.

Eric & Tracy Payet
The Hare & Hounds,
Common Road,
Lingfield RH7 6BZ
Tel   +44 (0)1342 832351
Web   www.hareandhoundspublichouse.co.uk

Entry 680 Map 4

Surrey

Worth a visit

681 Red Barn & Snowtes Farm Shop
Tandridge Lane, Lingfield RH7 6LL
+44 (0)1342 830820

Geronimo Inns has transformed this rambling, former Brewer's Fayre pub. Eat enjoyably at scrubbed tables in the high-raftered barn with its central fire. Reports please.

682 The Wiremill Wiremill Lane, Felbridge,
Lingfield RH7 6HJ

Persevere down a pitted lane off the A22 to this secluded 450-year-old mill overlooking its own lake. Beams abound on several floors, the décor is eclectic, the food is fresh, and there are six boutiquey bedrooms. We look forward to feedback.

683 The King William IV Byttom Hill,
Mickleham, Dorking RH5 6EL
+44 (0)1372 372590

Open fires, fresh flowers and amazing views are a few of the reasons people make the steep stepped climb to the little old alehouse on the hill. The steamed puds are a bit of a draw, too. Spill out into terraced gardens in summer.

684 The Jolly Farmers Reigate Road,
Betchworth, Reigate RH3 7BG
+44 (0)1737 221355

Jon and Paula Briscoe's deli-pub concept is thriving at the Jolly Farmers Food Emporium. Tuck into coffee and cake in the all-day café, or fresh lunches and dinners, wines and ales in the pub-restaurant. Then stock up on local goodies in the deli.

685 The Inn on the Pond Nutfield Marsh Rd,
Nutfield, Redhill RH1 4EU +44 (0)1737 643000

Smartly renovated sister pub to The Ostrich in Colnbrook, tucked away by the village cricket pitch and overlooking Nutfield Marsh. Come for local Horsham ales, fresh food, logs fires in eclectic rooms, and a super terrace.

Sussex

The Stag
Balls Cross

The quintessential Sussex pub – some might say (and often do) it's the best pub in the world. Under 16th-century beams by a crackling inglenook, or in the big garden in summer, riders, walkers and locals enjoy a natter over well-kept Badger and Sussex Bitter. Wholesome home-cooked food is another draw, the traditional-recipe pies (steak and kidney), pastries and casseroles (venison with cumberland sauce) being the greatest temptation. A sweet shop in a former life, this little inn still welcomes children: in a set-aside room youngsters may play undisturbed. There is also plenty for adults: The Stag has its own darts team, summer jazz nights and visits from the travelling Mummers at Christmas. There's a 17th-century stone-floored bar and a dining room that's carpeted and cosy. And a useful tethering post for those who come by horse.

Meals	12pm-2pm (2.30pm Sun); 7pm-9pm; no food Sun eve. Main courses £7.50-£18; bar meals £4-£18.
Closed	3pm-6pm (3.30pm-7pm Sun).
Directions	2 miles from Petworth on Kirdford road.

	Hamish Hiddleston The Stag, Balls Cross, Petworth GU28 9JP
Tel	+44 (0)1403 820241

Entry 686 Map 4

The Hollist Arms
Lodsworth

Villager and proprietor George Bristow rescued this lovely pub a few years back, injecting it with a fresh enthusiasm and stuffing the menu with great ingredients. Venison casserole, Moroccan-style lamb shank, and sausages (local, of course) served with mash and onion gravy hit the mark. Villagers prop up the long narrow bar with a pint of King's Horsham Best; old sofas by the big fire encourage others to linger. The smaller, more intimate rooms of this former smithy have been kept: one a cosy private dining room, another a snug with armchairs, blazing fire and tables spilled with magazines and games. From the hand-cut, local-farm potato chips to the striking pink walls, pretty feather-patterned curtains and the cheerful chatter, the Hollist oozes unpretentious charm. Don't miss the village shop in the car park.

Duke of Cumberland Arms
Henley

In the spring the Duke looks divine, its brick and stone cottage walls engulfed by flowering wisteria. Beyond is the garden, with babbling trout pools and huge Weald views. Latch doors lead to two tiny bars that creak with character — painted tongue-and-groove walls, low ceilings, scrubbed tables, log fires in the grate. Gas lamps and old indentures add to the atmosphere, while the quirky, cosy rear dining room makes the most of the view. Choose a pint of Sussex Best straight from the cask, or a glass of farmhouse cider. Rescued from closure by a local in 2007, the Duke has ex-Lickfold Inn chef Simon Goodman as chef-landlord. Popular daily menus rely on fresh local produce, including Goodwood organic rib-eye steak, estate venison, South Downs lamb; delectable Sunday roasts are brought as a joint to the table. A treasure.

Meals	12pm-2pm (2.30pm Sat; 3pm Sun); 7pm-9pm (9.30pm Fri & Sat; 6.30pm-8pm Sun). Main courses £11.50-£17.50; bar meals (lunch) £6.50-£11.50.
Closed	Open all day.
Directions	Off A272 between Midhurst & Petworth.

SPECIAL AWARD see pages 20-21

Community pub

George Bristow
The Hollist Arms,
The Street, Lodsworth,
Petworth GU28 9BZ

Tel   +44 (0)1798 861310
Web   www.thehollistarms.co.uk

Entry 687 Map 4

Meals	12pm-2pm; 7pm-9pm. No food Sun eve or Mon all day in winter. Main courses £9.95-£17.95; organic baguettes £6.95.
Closed	3pm-5pm in winter. Open all day in summer.
Directions	From Fernhurst towards Midhurst; pass pub on right; next left to Henley; follow road, on right.

Simon Goodman
Duke of Cumberland Arms,
Henley,
Haslemere GU27 3HQ

Tel   +44 (0)1428 652280
Web   www.dukeofcumberland.com

Entry 688 Map 4

Sussex

Noah's Ark
Lurgashall

In an idyllic setting – beside village pond and churchyard, overlooking the cricket green – the Ark would restore anyone's faith in the well-being of the English country pub. In this couple's hands, the old village boozer has become a pub of charm; no more darts, but a surprise at every turn. From bar to cosy dining areas – and one barn-like room – are beams, floorboards, winter fires, traditional country furniture and a sprinkling of modern leather. The kitchen's insistence on good-quality local seasonal produce results in a roll-call of British dishes, and the simple lunchtime bar menu is bolstered come evening by the likes of pan-fried wood pigeon breasts with sautéed savoy cabbage and crispy pancetta. A cottagey garden to the side and picnic tables out front complete the upbeat package.

Meals	12pm-2pm (2.30pm Sat & Sun); 6.30pm-9.30pm. Main courses £9.50-£18; bar meals £6-£11.
Closed	3.45pm-5.30pm & Sun eve.
Directions	From Haslemere take B2131. From Chichester follow the A285. From London follow the A3 and exit onto the A283 towards Petworth. Follow signs to Lurgashall.

Henry Coghlan & Amy Whitmore
Noah's Ark,
Lurgashall,
Petworth GU28 9ET
Tel   +44 (0)1428 707346
Web   www.noahsarkinn.co.uk

Entry 689 Map 4

Sussex

The Keepers Arms
Trotton

Nick and Antonia Troth have taken on The Keepers Arms at Trotton. High above the road, with a front terrace and views, it is pleasing outside and in. The warm friendly bar has beams, polished floorboards, characterful tables, leather sofas, a winter fire, and a good range of changing ales from local breweries. Food is good and draws a local crowd, so expect the likes of foie gras and wood pigeon and chicken terrine, seared scallops with cauliflower purée and honey-roasted Gressingham duck; it's more restaurant than pub. You eat at candlelit tables in the dining room next to the bar, its warm colours, light tartan fabrics and modern high-backed chairs giving it an upbeat hunting lodge air. Blackboards announce much-loved pub classics, too.

Meals	12pm-2pm (2.30pm Sun); 7pm-9.30pm (9pm Sun; 6.30pm-9pm in winter). Main courses £11-£21.
Closed	3pm-6pm (7pm Sun).
Directions	On A272 between Midhurst & Petersfield.

Nick Troth
The Keepers Arms,
Trotton,
Petersfield GU31 5ER
Tel   +44 (0)1730 813724
Web   www.keepersarms.co.uk

Entry 690 Map 4

Halfway Bridge Inn
Halfway Bridge

Paul and Sue Carter have created a stylish dining pub/hotel of this mellow old coaching inn on the busy A272. A series of rooms comes with cosy corners and split levels, the bar with a light modern look, the rest more traditional: scrubbed tables, cushioned benches, fat candles. Thirsts are quenched by Sussex beers and wines by the glass, and the food is a satisfying mix of traditional and modern, the menus changing seasonally. Find a seat by the open fire and scan a menu that announces first-rate fish (pan-fried red snapper) alongside lamb rump or pork fillet. For summer there's a sheltered patio with posh tables and brollies. This would be a lovely place for a short break: the old Cowdray barns, 100 yards away over the lane, have been converted into six super rooms where deep beds, leather chairs, plasma screens and PlayStations "for the boys" sit alongside old beams and rustic brickwork. The attention to detail extends to big mirrors, fat fluffy towels, French lotions and potions – and torches attached to key fobs so you don't get lost in the dark!

Rooms	6: 2 doubles , 4 suites. £110–£140. Suites £130–£160. Singles from £75.
Meals	12pm-2.30pm; 6.30pm-9.15pm (8.30pm Sun). Main courses £12.50-£18.25; sandwiches (lunch) from £5.95.
Closed	Open all day.
Directions	On A272 halfway between Midhurst & Petworth.

Paul & Sue Carter
Halfway Bridge Inn,
Halfway Bridge,
Petworth GU28 9BP
Tel   +44 (0)1798 861281
Web   www.halfwaybridge.co.uk

Entry 691 Map 4

Sussex

The Three Horseshoes
Elsted

Low beams, latched doors, red tile or brick floors, high settles, deep-cream bowed walls, big log fires and home-cooked food: all that you'd hope for, and more. Built in 1540 as a drovers' ale house, it has no cellar, so staff pull ales from the barrel instead. The lower bar was formerly a butcher's shop and still has the ceiling hooks. Local seafood, meat and game appear on a tempting country menu – Selsey sea bass, cottage pie, venison goulash, or steak and kidney in Guinness pie – and are served in snug rooms. The main dining room is smarter and less rustic and also comes with its wood-burning stove. In summer sit in the glorious garden and enjoy golden pints and the cracking views over the South Downs. Landlady Sue will look after you here.

Meals	12pm-2pm; 6.30pm-9pm (7pm-8.30pm Sun). Main courses £8.95-£17.95; bar meals £6.95-£9.95.
Closed	2.30pm-6pm (3pm-7pm Sun).
Directions	Elsted is signed off A272 between Midhurst and Petersfield, 2 miles east of Midhurst.

Sue Beavis & Michael Newton
The Three Horseshoes,
Elsted,
Midhurst GU29 0JY
Tel +44 (0)1730 825746

🚶 📖 🐾 🍺

Entry 692 Map 4

Sussex

Welldiggers Arms
Petworth

Once occupied by well-diggers, this rustic 300-year-old roadside cottage has little immediate appeal. But enter and you are greeted by Ted Whitcomb, landlord and larger-than-life persona, pulling pints of Young's and cracking jokes behind the bar for 50-odd years. Surprisingly, this is a dining-orientated pub, its low-ceilinged bar and snug packed with happy eaters at long settles and huge oak tables. Come for classic British food: king prawns in garlic, fresh mussels, whole Dover sole, and properly hung T-bone steaks. Alternatives may include braised oxtail and dumplings, steak, Guinness and stilton pie, black pudding and mash, seasonal game – and magnificent Sunday roasts. Popular with enthusiasts of racing (Goodwood), shooting and polo (Cowdray Park), so be sure to book. At the back is a garden with views over the South Downs.

Meals	12pm-2pm; 6pm-9pm; no food Sun-Wed eve. Main courses £7.50-£22; bar meals from £5.95; Sunday lunch £14.95.
Closed	3.30pm-6pm; Sun, Tues & Wed eve & Mon all day.
Directions	Beside A283 Pulborough road, 1 mile east of Petworth.

Ted Whitcomb
Welldiggers Arms,
Pulborough Road,
Petworth GU28 0HG
Tel +44 (0)1798 342287

🚶 📖 🐾

Entry 693 Map 4

The Star & Garter

Charlton

If fresh fish and seafood appeal then follow the winding Sussex lanes to this 18th-century brick-and-flint pub. Hidden in the folds of the South Downs, with miles of breezy walks from the front door, the old ale house now draws the well-shod from Goodwood and Midhurst. Seafood platters spill over with whole Selsey lobster and crabs, scallops, wild salmon, crevettes and prawns. There are big bowls of mussels, whole baked bass, venison pie and, in season, a mouthwatering game grill, with partridge from West Dean, pigeon from East Dean and local wild boar sausages. Drink fine Sussex ales straight from the cellar in the open-plan, wooden floored room, where hops adorn stripped beams, old village photographs line bare-brick walls and daily papers fill the rack by the door. In summer, head for the sun-trap patio or lawned gardens.

The Fox Goes Free

Charlton

King William III may have stopped off here to refresh his royal hunting parties but this 400-year-old flint pub, secreted away in the South Downs, is now home to some fine ales from small local breweries. Settle down by a big blazing fire under beamed ceilings for a pint of Ballards Best and the pub's own Fox Goes Free; in summer there's a garden with sweeping farmland views. The traditional bar food suits the surroundings, so sit at scrubbed tables and choir chairs for fresh butcher's sausages with mash, onion gravy and veg, followed by a comforting treacle sponge with custard. In the dining room — once a stable for race horses — are less familiar creations, perhaps chicken breast stuffed with banana, curry sauce and basmati rice. Goodwood racecourse is just up the hill and there are downland walks from the door.

Meals	12pm-2.30pm; 6.30pm-10pm. 12pm-10pm Sat (9.30pm Sun). Main courses £11-£19.50; bar meals £6-£9.
Closed	3pm-6pm. Open all day Sat & Sun.
Directions	Village signed off A286 between Midhurst & Chichester at Singleton.

Meals	12pm-2.30pm; 6.30pm-10pm; 12pm-10pm Sat (9.30pm Sun). Main courses £9.50-£19.50; bar meals £9.50-£11.95; Sunday lunch £10.95-£12.95.
Closed	Open all day.
Directions	From Chichester follow A286 towards Midhurst. At Singleton right to Charlton.

Oliver Ligertwood
The Star & Garter,
East Dean,
Chichester PO18 0JG
Tel   +44 (0)1243 811318
Web   www.thestarandgarter.co.uk

Entry 694 Map 4

David Coxon
The Fox Goes Free,
Charlton,
Chichester PO18 0HU
Tel   +44 (0)1243 811461
Web   www.thefoxgoesfree.com

Entry 695 Map 4

Anglesey Arms at Halnaker
Halnaker

Laid back, relaxed, free of airs and graces, a Georgian brick pub in an affluent part of West Sussex. It's not a pie-and-a-pint pub or a chips-with-everything roadside diner, just a cracking local run by George and Jools Jackson, genuinely committed to keeping it charming and old-fashioned. Expect varnished and stripped pine, flagstones, beams and panelling, crackling log fires, locals downing pints at the bar, and a cosier, smarter dining room. Food is fresh and home-cooked using great local produce – crab and lobster from Selsey, traceable meats (organic South Downs lamb and pork, well-hung beef from the Goodwood estate), venison and game from local shoots. Even the ciders, wines and spirits are organic. A great little local, with inter-pub cricket, golf and quizzes and regular 'moules and boules' events in the two-acre garden.

The Earl of March
Lavant

Having been taken over by ex-Ritz executive head chef Giles Thompson, it's no surprise this is a snappy performer, from its upbeat remodelling to the simple handling of excellent ingredients that tick all the right local and seasonal boxes. There are views over the South Downs from terrace and dining area, and lots of sepia prints of old racing cars and aircraft. It's a clean-lined, fashionable space with a positively cosmopolitan vibe; modern leather seating in the bar quarter and high-backed suede chairs in the dining area. Bolstered by specials (there's also a separate bar and terrace menu – delicious sausage, mash and onion gravy) the up-tempo dining roster delivers the likes of seasonal game, or fresh seafood in the summer Champagne and Seafood menu – dressed Selsey crab salad, king prawns with mayonnaise, whole smoked mackerel with saffron rouille.

Meals	12pm-2.30pm; 6.30pm-9.30pm; no food Sun eve.	
	Main courses £10.50-£22 (dinner); £8.50-£13.50 (lunch); sandwiches from £5; Sunday roast £13.	
Closed	3pm-5.30pm. Open all day Sun.	
Directions	On A285, 4 miles north east of Chichester.	

Meals	12pm-2.30pm (4pm Sun); 5.30pm-9.30pm. No food Sun eve.
	Main courses £10.50-£16.95; sandwiches from £6.50.
Closed	Open all day.
Directions	On A286 Chichester to Midhurst road, 2 miles north of Chichester.

George & Jools Jackson
Anglesey Arms at Halnaker,
Halnaker,
Chichester PO18 0NQ
Tel +44 (0)1243 773474
Web www.angleseyarms.co.uk

Entry 696 Map 4

Giles Thompson
The Earl of March,
Lavant,
Chichester PO18 0BQ
Tel +44 (0)1243 533993
Web www.theearlofmarch.com

Entry 697 Map 4

The Royal Oak Inn
Chichester

There's a cheery wine-bar feel to the Royal Oak; locals and young professionals come with their children and it's as countrified as can be. Inside, a modern-rustic look with traditional touches prevails: stripped floors, exposed brickwork, dark leather sofas, open fires and racing pictures on the walls: this was once part of the Goodwood estate. The dining area is big, light and airy, with a conservatory from which you can amble out onto a terrace that's warmed by outdoor lamps on summer nights. At scrubbed-top tables you can tuck into delicious trio of Barbary duck, seared scallops on pumpkin purée, fig tart with pistachio ice cream. Bedrooms are divided between three cottages, a nearby barn and upstairs at the back; ask for a room with a view. All have CD players, plasma screens, a DVD library and top toiletries – the best of modern – along with excellent lighting, brown leather chairs and big beds. Staff are attentive, breakfasts are good and fresh, a secret garden looks over cornfields, and you're well-placed for Chichester Theatre and the boats at pretty Bosham.

Rooms	8: 4 doubles, 1 twin, 3 cottage rooms for 2-4. £90-£165. Cottage rooms £145-£240. Singles from £80.
Meals	12pm-2.30pm; 6.30pm-9pm. Main courses £13.50-£19.50.
Closed	Open all day.
Directions	From Chichester A286 for Midhurst. First right at first mini roundabout into E. Lavant. Down hill, pass village green, over bridge, pub 200 yds on left. Car park opposite.

Charles Ullmann
The Royal Oak Inn,
Pook Lane, East Lavant,
Chichester PO18 0AX

Tel	+44 (0)1243 527434
Web	www.royaloakeastlavant.co.uk

The Crab & Lobster
Sidlesham

The down-at-heel boozer has become a fabulous pub-with-rooms. This one is managed by Sam Bakose. The new-look 'Crab' – backing onto Pagham Harbour and bird-rich marshes – opened its doors in 2007 and the results are stunning. The ancient flagstones and inglenook fireplace blend effortlessly with the upholstered banquettes, the ornate mirrors and the vintage photos on the walls. There's a fishy focus to the menu, as you'd expect – crab and lobster ravioli; organic sea trout with niçoise salad; Cornish sardines with black olive butter – while carnivores can tuck into the likes of Sussex lamb cutlets with roasted garlic and thyme jus. Wash it all down with a pint of local Harveys and choose a seat on the back terrace for those views of sheep-grazed meadows and marshes. Bedrooms are for birdwatchers, particularly Room 4 with its perfectly placed telescope... there are handmade beds, planked floors and walk-in storm showers. We love the heritage colours, fresh coffee and beautiful bathrooms sporting L'Occitane toiletries. A chic Sussex bolthole.

Rooms	4 + 1: 4 doubles. 1 cottage for 4. From £130. Cottage from £200.
Meals	12pm-2.15pm; 6pm-9.30pm. Main courses £13.50-£19.50.
Closed	Open all day.
Directions	Mill Lane is off B2145 Chichester to Selsey road, just south of Sidlesham. Pub close to Pagham Harbour.

Sam Bakose
The Crab & Lobster,
Mill Lane, Sidlesham,
Chichester PO20 7NB
Tel   +44 (0)1243 641233
Web   www.crab-lobster.co.uk

Entry 699 Map 4

Sussex

The Partridge Inn
Singleton

It's a genteel, traditional affair, this 17th-century inn in a quintessential English village on the Goodwood Estate. Now it's in the hands of a former Ritz chef. Giles Thompson also owns the more foodie-styled Earl of March pub in nearby Lavant, and is a man with the Midas touch. While the food matters, the pubby atmosphere is the thing: the Partridge is a local, and a family-friendly one at that. There's heaps of character in old beams, timbers and log fires across a series of rooms. Enjoy Harvey's Sussex Best with a traditional ploughman's in the bar, or one of several accomplished dishes; beer-battered haddock and chips wrapped in newspaper, or pan-fried lamb's liver and bacon with onion gravy. Desserts are the best of old British: treacle sponge, spotted dick. The lovely big garden attracts a crowd in summer.

Meals	12pm-2pm (3pm Sat & Sun); 6pm-9pm (9.30pm Fri & Sat). Main courses £9.50-£19.95; sandwiches from £6.50
Closed	3pm-5.30pm. Open all day Sat & Sun.
Directions	On A286 midway between Midhurst and Chichester. In Singleton village.

Giles Thompson
The Partridge Inn,
Singleton,
Chichester PO18 0EY
Tel   +44 (0)1243 811251
Web   www.thepartridgeinn.co.uk

Entry 700 Map 4

Sussex

The New Inn
Hurstpierpoint

On the High Street and not that new (parts go back 500 years), the New Inn is the sister pub to the Bull Inn in Ditchling. Push open the door, leave bustle behind and step into a cosy, stone-flagged and timbered bar. A pint of Harvey's, a decent coffee, a crackling fire – lovely. There's a rustic-chic feel throughout, with old pine tables and cushioned pews, heritage hues on wonky walls, stacked logs and fat church candles... and dark panelling and leather chesterfields in the intimate snug beyond. Linger over a beef and horseradish sandwich or a 'small plate' of Thai salmon fishcakes with sweet chilli sauce; dig into a chicken and ham pie or a garlic and rosemary beefburger with chips. Leave room for spiced plum tart or a plate of Sussex cheeses. Modern art, a quirky eclectic décor and a secluded terrace complete the scene.

Meals	12pm-2.30pm (9pm Sun); 6pm-9.30pm. Main courses £5-£17.
Closed	Open all day.
Directions	From A23 exit on to B2118. Follow signs for Hurstpierpoint on B2116 for 1.5 miles, pub on right after mini r'bout.

Dominic Worrall
The New Inn,
76 High Street, Hurstpierpoint,
Brighton BN6 9RQ
Tel   +44 (0)1273 834608
Web   www.thenewinnhurst.com

Entry 701 Map 4

Sussex

The Ginger Fox
Albourne

This pretty country pub looks splendidly traditional, its thatch crowned by a fox stalking a pheasant. The second of Ben McKeller's pubs (the first is Hove's Ginger Pig) again adds a contemporary zing. Both the aim (to serve modern British dishes made of fine produce) and the look (armchairs and banquettes, stone and wood floors, open fires) are close to the Hove original, resulting in a cool uncluttered style that blends beautifully with the old. Chalked-up menus are short and to the point: roast breast of pheasant with braised-leg cottage pie; fillet of sea bass with confit shallot potatoes and salsify; tomato risotto with parmesan crisps and pea shoots. There's even Welsh rarebit as an alternative to puddings like chocolate jaffa brulée; team it with a pint of Harveys Sussex Best. Service is friendly and smartly dressed.

Meals	12pm-2pm (12.30pm-4pm Sat & Sun); 6pm-10pm (from 6.30pm Fri-Sun). No food Sun eve. Main courses £10.50-£16.50.
Closed	Open all day.
Directions	From A23 (London Road) take A281; pub is on right in the village.

Ben McKeller
The Ginger Fox,
Albourne,
Hassocks BN6 9EA
Tel +44 (0)1273 857888
Web www.gingermanrestaurants.com

Entry 702 Map 4

Sussex

Royal Oak
Wineham

The part-tiled, part-timbered cottage almost lost down a country road is six centuries old and has been refreshing locals for two. It is unspoilt in every way. In the charming bar and tiny rear room are brick and boarded floors, a huge inglenook with log fires and sturdy rustic furniture, while antique corkscrews, pottery jugs and aged artefacts hang from low-slung beams and walls. Michael and Sharon Bailey have changed little since taking over in 2007, drawing Harveys Best straight from the cask (no pumps) and, in keeping with ale house tradition, offering a menu of good, freshly made pub food using locally sourced produce; new chef Glen Read promises an updated full menu as well as a light lunches: sandwiches, ploughman's and hearty soups. No music or electronic hubbub, just traditional pub games. A heart-warming rural survivor.

Meals	12pm-2.30pm (3pm Sun); 7pm-9.30pm. No food Sun eve. Main courses £8.95-£15.95; light lunches £5-£8.
Closed	2.30pm-5.30pm (3.30pm-6pm Sat, 4pm-7pm Sun).
Directions	Off A272 between Cowfold & Bolney.

Michael & Sharon Bailey
Royal Oak,
Wineham Lane,
Wineham,
Henfield BN5 9AY
Tel +44 (0)1444 881252

Entry 703 Map 4

The Cat
West Hoathly

Gravetye Manor Hotel snapped up the The Cat in October 2009 to add an interesting dimension to their flourishing estate – it's a short stroll away through fields and woods on the High Weald Landscape Trail. The 16th-century building has been comfortably modernised without losing its character; a fine medieval hall house with a Victorian extension. Inside, expect wooden panelling, beamed ceilings, planked floors, splendid inglenooks, and an airy garden room leading out to a garden at the back, furnished with teak and umbrellas. Harvey's ale and fresh pub food attract a solid, old-fashioned crowd: retired locals, well-heeled foodies and walkers. Roast beef and horseradish sandwiches, duck confit with Madeira jus, and sticky toffee pudding show the style. The setting is idyllic: in a pretty village opposite a 12th-century church.

The White Horse Inn
Sutton

Squirrelled away in the South Downs, in the smart village of Sutton, the White Horse Inn is not easy to find. But find it you must! Under new ownership and stylishly revived, the old pub combines an unexpected modernity with a lovely warm feel. More gastropub than local, it sets much store by its food – regional, seasonal and delicious. Find Sussex Down rump of lamb served with roasted vegetables, sautéed potatoes and rosemary jus; chunky Sussex cheddar and pickle sandwiches; hearty mixed-game casserole, good for walkers. All go down a treat with local hand-pump ales such as Harveys Sussex Bitter. The smart, light, opened-up interior is decorated in pleasing neutral tones that blend harmoniously with Indonesian teak furniture, long gleaming wood bar and polished floorboards. Stunning walks start from the door and Goodwood is nearby – visit house and horses.

Meals	12pm-2pm (2.30pm Sun); 6pm-9.30pm. Main courses £9-£18; sandwiches from £6.
Closed	3pm-6pm; Sun eves from 5pm & all day Mon. Open all day Sat.
Directions	Village signed off B2028 6 miles north of Haywards Heath.

Meals	12pm-2pm (4pm Sun); 7pm-9pm. Main courses £9.50-£17; bar meals £4.50-£10.
Closed	3pm-6pm (7pm Sun); Sun & Mon eve.
Directions	Sutton is signposted off A286 south of Petworth and A29 south of Pulborough; in village centre.

	Ian Huxley The Cat, Queen's Square, West Hoathly, East Grinstead RH19 4PP
Tel	+44 (0)1342 810369
Web	www.catinn.co.uk

Entry 704 Map 4

	Mr & Mrs Hajigeorgiou The White Horse Inn, The Street, Sutton, Pulborough RH20 1PS
Tel	+44 (0)1798 869221
Web	www.whitehorse-sutton.co.uk

Entry 705 Map 4

The Griffin Inn
Fletching

A proper inn, one of the best, a community local that draws a well-heeled and devoted crowd. The occasional touch of scruffiness makes it almost perfect; fancy designers need not apply. The Pullan family run it with huge passion. You get cosy open fires, 400-year-old beams, oak panelling, settles, red carpets, prints on the walls... it's aged well. There's a lively bar, a small club room for racing on Saturdays and two cricket teams play in summer. Bedrooms are tremendous value for money and full of uncluttered country-inn elegance: uneven floors, lovely old furniture, soft coloured walls, free-standing Victorian baths, huge shower heads, crisp linen, fluffy bathrobes, handmade soaps. Rooms in the coach house are quieter, those in next-door Griffin House quieter still. Smart menus based on the finest seasonal produce include fresh fish from Rye and Fletching lamb; both food and beers are as local as can be. There's a wood oven on the terrace and, on summer Sundays, a spit-roast barbecue – accompanied by ten-mile views stretching across Sheffield Park to the South Downs.

Rooms	13: 6 doubles, 7 four-posters. £85–£145. Singles £60–£80 (Sun-Thur).
Meals	12pm-2.30pm (3pm Sat & Sun); 7pm-9.30pm (9pm Sun). Main courses £10–£18.50; bar meals £6.50–£14.50.
Closed	Open all day.
Directions	From East Grinstead, A22 south, right at Nutley for Fletching. On for 2 miles into village.

Bridget, Nigel & James Pullan
The Griffin Inn,
Fletching,
Uckfield TN22 3SS

Tel	+44 (0)1825 722890
Web	www.thegriffininn.co.uk

Entry 706 Map 4

The Bull
Ditchling

In a picturesque village, a pretty inn, dark and cosy and warmed by cheery fires and candlelight. The rambling and atmospheric bar hasn't changed for years, there are four ales on tap including Dark Star, and the other areas have been stylishly transformed, with pine and parquet and modern prints on mellow walls. And there's some rather upmarket food to match, like filo-encrusted cannon of lamb stuffed with apricots and cumin. Even the ciabattas are filled with locally smoked salmon and horseradish cream. All of the produce can be traced back to local farms, and the game comes from the Balcombe estate. Similar treats can be found on the separate children's menu, and you can eat or drink wherever you like – including the snug at the back – for as long as you wish. Bring wellies or bikes and try out the high-level trails on the South Downs, then return to gorgeous bedrooms where new and old blend successfully. Expect rain showers, crisp linen sheets, bold silks and fresh lilies. There's even a hot rail in the loos to dry out wet walkers' clothing.

Rooms	4: 3 doubles, 1 twin/double. £80-£120.
Meals	12pm-2.30pm; 6pm-9.30pm (12pm-9.30pm Sat & Sun). Main courses £9.50-£16; sandwiches £6.50.
Closed	Open all day.
Directions	Leave A23 just north of Brighton for Pyecombe. North on A273, then west for Ditchling on B2112. In centre of village, at crossroads.

Dominic Worrall
The Bull,
2 High Street,
Ditchling, Hassocks, BN6 8TA
Tel +44 (0)1273 834608
Web www.thebullditchling.com

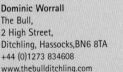

Entry 707 Map 4

The Coach & Horses
Danehill

With ale on tap from Harveys in Lewes, fresh fish from Seaford and lamb from the fields opposite, this is a very fine pub. The central bar is its throbbing hub, original wooden panelling and open fires accompanying the gentle pleasure of mulled wine in winter-cosy rooms. During the rest of the year the big raised garden comes into its own; spread yourselves on the new terrace under the boughs of a spreading maple. Whatever the weather, the food attracts folk from far and wide. In the stable block restaurant a changing seasonal menu from chef Lee Cobb places the emphasis on quality rather than quantity – honey-roasted confit duck leg on chorizo, red pepper and chickpea ragoût, seared queen scallops and tiger prawns with sweet chilli pak choi, broad bean risotto with parmesan and basil oil. A rural pub that is a true local.

The Jolly Sportsman
East Chiltington

Deep in Sussex, a little place with a passion for beers, food and wine. Brewery mats pinned above the bar demonstrate Bruce Wass's support of small breweries, while the food has been described as "robust, savoury, skilled and unpretentious". In the stylish restaurant, where oak tables are decorated with flowers and candles, plates are filled with mussel, prawn and herb risotto, marinated Ditchling lamb rump, peppered red deer fillet. In the bar, dogs doze, the fire glows and there are winter snifters from Bruce's impressive whisky collection to try, including rarities bought at auction. Outside, ancient trees give shade to rustic tables and the idyllic garden has a play area for children. A team of talented enthusiasts runs this pub; the Moroccan-tiled patio tables were even made by the pub's own 'washer-upper'.

Meals	12pm-2pm (2.30pm Sat & Sun); 7pm-9pm (9.30pm Fri); 5pm-8pm Sun. Main courses £10.50-£18.75; bar meals £6.25-£8.75 (lunch only).
Closed	3pm-6pm. Open all day Sat & Sun.
Directions	From Danehill (A275) take School Lane towards Chelwood Common; pub on left 0.25 miles.

Meals	12.30pm-2.15pm (3pm Sun); 7pm-9.15pm (10pm Fri & Sat). Main courses £11.75-£19.50; set lunch £13.50 & £16.75; bar meals £4.90-£10.45.
Closed	3pm-5.45pm. Closed Sun from 4pm & Mon all day. Open all day Fri & Sat.
Directions	From Lewes A275; B2166 for East Chiltington.

Ian & Catherine Philpots
The Coach & Horses,
Coach & Horses Lane, Danehill,
Haywards Heath RH17 7JF
Tel +44 (0)1825 740369
Web www.coachandhorses.danehill.biz

Entry 708 Map 4

Bruce Wass
The Jolly Sportsman,
Chapel Lane, East Chiltington,
Lewes BN7 3BA
Tel +44 (0)1273 890400
Web www.thejollysportsman.com

Entry 709 Map 4

The Chimney House
Brighton

The Victorian corner boozer in arty Seven Dials has become a gastropub of note and new owner Helen Coggins plans to keep it that way. Taking its stylish lead from the bistro pubs of London it has not lost its community feel, so settle in to leather armchairs, scrubbed tables and an open kitchen from which classic British dishes flow. As you might expect, the produce is local and well-sourced, the sort of place where the ketchup is homemade. From the daily menu, tuck into butternut squash soup, sea bass with creamy chorizo sauce, and a prune and pecan nut crumble. Or pop in at lunchtime for a hot beef and horseradish sandwich – or just a bowl of hand-cut chips to soak up the excellent Harveys ales. Tables are filled on a first come, first-served basis – except on New Year's Eve and Valentine's Night!

The Ginger Pig
Hove

Everyone loves this smart pub minutes from the beach. The décor is fresh, contemporary and open-plan, and the food is consistently brilliant. Whether it's poached skate wing terrine or a blackboard special of slow-braised shoulder of lamb with spiced cabbage and garlic mash (or a simple chargrilled rib-eye with hand-cut chips) this is a serious destination for those who love real British food. In spite of clear gastropubby leanings, the friendly team has created a balanced mix of drinking bar frequented by locals and cool dining area decked with modern art. It's all down to experienced restaurateur Ben McKeller who, in transforming this building, has created the first in a proposed mini pub empire (note too The Ginger Fox, Albourne). The paved, sheltered garden is a little oasis.

Meals	12pm-2.30pm Tues-Fri (4pm Sat); 6pm-9.45pm; 12pm-6pm Sun. Main courses £10.95-£15.95; Sunday lunch £10.95.
Closed	3pm-5pm (Tues-Fri) & Mon all day.
Directions	In the Seven Dials area, on the corner of Upper Hamilton Road & Exeter Street.

Meals	12pm-2pm (12.30pm-3pm Sat; 12.30pm-4pm Sun); 6.30pm-10pm. Main courses £9.50-£18.
Closed	Open all day.
Directions	Southern end of Hove Street which runs between Church Road and the Kingsway (A259).

Helen Coggings
The Chimney House,
28 Upper Hamilton Road,
Brighton BN1 5DF

Tel	+44 (0)1273 556708
Web	www.chimneyhousebrighton.co.uk

Entry 710 Map 4

Ben McKeller
The Ginger Pig,
3 Hove Street,
Hove BN3 2TR

Tel	+44 (0)1273 736123
Web	www.gingermanrestaurants.com

Entry 711 Map 4

The Ram Inn
Firle

The road runs out once it reaches Firle village nestling beneath the South Downs... hard to believe now, but this quiet backwater was once a staging post. Built of brick and flint, the inn reveals a fascinating history – the Georgian part was once a courthouse and the kitchen goes back 500 years. Rescued from closure in 2006, the Ram Inn is once again thriving. Its three rooms have been decorated in rustic-chic style – bare boards and parquet, coal fires in old brick fireplaces, chunky candles on darkwood tables. Walkers stomp in from the Downs for pints of Harveys Sussex and hot steak sandwiches; foodies flock after dark for great fresh food, perhaps ham and pea broth, rump of Hankham Farm organic lamb with red wine jus, and sticky toffee pudding. Retire upstairs to quirky, individual rooms with bold colours, exposed beams, super comfortable beds, fluffy bathrobes in tiled bathrooms, and dreamy village or South Downs views. And there's a splendid flint-walled garden for peaceful summer supping. Handy for Charleston Farmhouse, country home to the Bloomsbury set.

Rooms	4: 2 doubles, 2 twins/doubles. £110-£145. Singles £60-£80.
Meals	12pm-3pm (3.30pm Sat; 4pm Sun); 6.30pm-9.30pm (6pm-9pm Sun). Main courses £9.95-£16.95; Sunday roast £11.95.
Closed	Open all day.
Directions	Pub & village signed off A27 east of Lewes.

Hayley Bayes
The Ram Inn,
The Street, Firle,
Lewes BN8 6NS
Tel   +44 (0)1273 858222
Web   www.raminn.co.uk

Entry 712 Map 4

The Sussex Ox
Milton Street

Tucked below the Downs, The Sussex Ox is a popular retreat with ramblers and A27 travellers – time it right and you'll catch a South Downs sunset from the garden. David and Suzanne have invested well in refurbishing the rambling old place, so expect a clean, uncluttered and civilised feel: creamy walls, wonky timbers, wood and worn-brick floors, painted panelling, big vases overflowing with lilies. Bag a cushioned pew at a scrubbed pine table in the Garden Room for the best of those long sweeping views. The chalkboard above the wood-burning stove lists the day's locally sourced choices – lunchtime sandwiches, warming soups, beef, ale and mushroom pie, white chocolate cheesecake, artisan cheeses. Ales come from the Dark Star and Harveys breweries, to be enjoyed in summer on the decked terrace.

Meals	12pm-2pm (3pm Sun in winter); 6pm-9pm; no food Sun eve in winter. Main courses £8.75-£15.
Closed	3pm-6pm.
Directions	Village & pub signed off A27, 3 miles west of Polegate.

	David & Suzanne Pritchard The Sussex Ox, Milton Street, Polegate BN26 5RL
Tel	+44 (0)1323 870840
Web	www.thesussexox.co.uk

Entry 713 Map 5

Giants Rest
Wilmington

Most East Sussex pubs are supporters of Harveys brewery in Lewes and this is no exception; local produce is on the menu, too. Adrian's wife Rebecca is chef, and her wild rabbit and bacon pie, home-cooked ham, sausages with bubble-and-squeak and fruit crumbles are just the ticket. It's not old by rural standards, but the high ceilings, the black and cream wallpaper, the pine dressers and the candlelight make a very respectable backdrop for a plate of Victorian trifle. Menus for Burns Night and New Year are offered at normal prices as a 'thank you' to the regulars, and served in front of a log fire. There are pews and pine tables at the long bar, and puzzles and games on the tables. Work up an appetite with a brisk stroll to view the impressive Long Man figure carved into the South Downs: it's no distance at all.

Meals	12pm-2pm; 6.30pm-9pm (12pm-9pm Sat & Sun). Main courses £9-£15; bar meals £3-£7.50; Sunday lunch £10.
Closed	3pm-6pm. Open all day Sat & Sun.
Directions	On A27 just past Drusilla's roundabout.

	Adrian & Rebecca Hillman Giants Rest, The Street, Wilmington, Polegate BN26 5SQ
Tel	+44 (0)1323 870207
Web	www.giantsrest.co.uk

Entry 714 Map 5

Sussex

The Tiger Inn
East Dean

In the flickering candlelight of a pub whose records go back nine centuries, new landlords are settling in. Big changes at this celebrated estate-owned inn: new kitchen, dining area and loos, and five bedrooms upstairs (watch this space!). Other than a lick of paint, little has changed in the bar, all low beams, stone floors, ancient settles and crackling fire – delightful to wash up here after a bracing walk on Beachy Head. Beside a cottage-lined green in a fold of the South Downs, the Tiger Inn is a supporter of the community: estate-brewed ales such as Legless Rambler, organic meat from the farm up the hill, local crab. There's traditional pub food at lunch – sandwiches, ploughman's, stews – and more inventive dishes served in the dining room in the evening. Mobbed in summer, it's a peaceful refuge in winter.

Sussex

The Cricketers Arms
Berwick

Walkers seek refuge from the breezy South Downs; so do visitors to Berwick Church and Charleston Farmhouse. The 500-year-old, brick and flint, creeper-clad pub is utterly unspoilt outside and in. An ale house for the past 200 years, it has three delightfully unpretentious rooms with beams and half-panelled walls dotted with cricket bats. Blazing log fires, scrubbed tables and wall benches on worn, quarry-tiled floors add to the pleasure of being here; all feels friendly and unhurried. Harveys ales are tapped from the cask in a back room and the food is perfectly straightforward pub grub, perhaps gammon steak and egg or a seafood platter. Try your luck at playing the Sussex coin game, Toad-In-Ye-Hole. Surrounded by a cottage garden resplendent with foxgloves and roses, The Cricketers is equally charming in summer.

Meals	12pm-3pm; 6pm-9pm. Main courses £4.95-£12.95.
Closed	Open all day.
Directions	0.5 miles from A259 at East Dean, in village centre.

Meals	12pm-2.15pm; 6.15pm-9pm (12pm-9pm Sat & Sun); all day in summer. Main courses £8.25-£16.95; set menu (2-course) £10 in winter.
Closed	3pm-6pm in winter. Open all day Sat & Sun.
Directions	Just off A27 Lewes to Polegate road near Berwick church.

Jo Staveley & Stuart Coot
The Tiger Inn,
The Green, East Dean,
Eastbourne BN20 0DA
Tel   +44 (0)1323 423209
Web   www.beachyhead.org.uk

Entry 715 Map 5

Peter Brown
The Cricketers Arms,
Berwick,
Polegate BN26 6SP
Tel   +44 (0)1323 870469
Web   www.cricketersberwick.co.uk

Entry 716 Map 5

Sussex

George Inn
Alfriston

You can't miss the ancient façade of The George as you stroll down Alfriston's pretty little High Street. Step inside the creaky old inn, first licensed in 1397, and things become even more historic, thanks to worn planked floors, head-cracking beams, thick standing timbers, a huge inglenook with a crackling winter fire, and hop bines strewn above the bar. It is the cosiest possible setting for some tasty pub food and a foaming pint of Greene King. Share a rustic board for two laden with charcuterie and breads, roasted garlic and warm olive oil, or tuck into a brie and bacon sandwich. Then there are hearty steaks, daily risottos, and, in the evening, dishes such as rump of lamb from Ashmore farm. Lunch in the flint-walled garden, explore the village, hike the South Downs Way.

Meals	12pm-9pm (10pm Fri-Sat). Main courses £4.95-£9.95 (lunch); £10-£16.95 (dinner).
Closed	Open all day.
Directions	Alfriston is signed off A27 between Polgate & Lewes, 4 miles west of Polegate.

Roland & Cate Couch
George Inn,
High Street, Alfriston,
Polegate BN26 5SY
Tel +44 (0)1323 870319
Web www.thegeorge-alfriston.com

Entry 717 Map 5

Sussex

The Lamb Inn
Wartling

Rob and Alison's rural dining pub continues to draw the crowds for good, homemade food, good beer and good cheer. There's a bar with a wood-burner, a beamy snug with chunky candles and fresh flowers, a dining room in the stables, and a lounge with comfy sofas and log fires... no music, no pool, just chatter. Specialising in fresh fish and local produce from Chilley Farm, the menu announces rib-eye of local Limousin beef with garlic and parsley butter; pancake of creamy garlic mushrooms glazed with stilton; fish pie. A good selection of cheeses will follow, along with temptations such as plum and blackberry sponge with cinnamon custard. Make a mental note of this secluded pub if you are planning a visit to Herstmonceux Castle: the drive across the Pevensey Levels is worth it.

Meals	12pm-2.15pm (2.30pm Sun); 7pm-9pm. Main courses £8.95-£17.95; bar meals £5.75-£12.95; set menu (2 courses) £11.95.
Closed	3pm-6pm, Sun eve & Mon.
Directions	A259 to Polegate & Pevensey; 1st exit for Wartling; on right after 3 miles.

Robert & Alison Farncombe
The Lamb Inn,
Wartling,
Hailsham BN27 1RY
Tel +44 (0)1323 832116
Web www.lambinnwartling.co.uk

Entry 718 Map 5

The George in Rye
Rye

Ancient Rye has a big history. It's a reclaimed island, a wealthy cinque port which once had its own army yet regularly fell into French hands. Henry James lived here, and the oldest working church clock in England chimes in a gracious square at the top of the hill. As for The George, it stands serenely on the cobbled high street. It was built in 1575 from reclaimed ships' timbers and its exposed beams and joists remain on display to this day. A contemporary revamp in classical style trumpets airy interiors, stripped floors, panelled walls and open fires – Jane Austen in the 21st century. There's a huge leather sofa in the bar by the fire, screen prints of the Beatles on the walls in reception, voile curtains and parquet floors in the restaurant. Divine bedrooms come in all shapes and sizes, but fabulous fabrics, Frette linen, flat-screen TVs and Vi-Spring mattresses are standard, as are Aveda soaps by the bath and cashmere covers on hot water bottles. Superb food in the restaurant – seared scallops, Romney Marsh lamb, Seville orange ice cream – can be washed down by local English wines. Exceptional.

Rooms	24: 12 doubles, 7 twins/doubles, 5 suites. £135-£175. Suites £225. Singles from £105.
Meals	12pm-3pm; 7pm-9.30pm. Main courses £12-£16; bar meals £5-£6.
Closed	Open all day.
Directions	Follow signs up hill into town centre. Through arch; hotel on left, below church. Parking at foot of hill.

Alex & Katie Clarke
The George in Rye,
98 High Street,
Rye TN31 7JT
Tel   +44 (0)1797 222114
Web   www.thegeorgeinrye.com

Sussex

The Gun
Gun Hill

Winding lanes lead to this 16th-century tiled and timbered farmhouse with glorious views across rolling countryside. Its name originates from the cannon foundries that were located at Gun Hill. Expect a neat open-plan interior with comfortably furnished alcoves, several log fires and an old Aga in the cosy main bar. Plank floors, thick candles on scrubbed tables, fresh flowers and bold artwork create a civilised feel, traditional menus champion local produce and every dish is freshly prepared. Kick off with a game terrine with red onion compote, follow with Speldhurst sausages with onion gravy, or pan-fried halibut with tarragon sauce, and finish with a warm chocolate fondant. Worth hunting down in all seasons, it has a terrace and lawn for lazy summer days. Pick up the 'Gun Walk' leaflet and explore the surrounding footpaths.

Sussex

The Star Inn
Old Heathfield

Built as an inn for pilgrims in the 14th century, with a rough honey-stone façade, The Star has gained a few creepers over the centuries and its atmospheric interior has mellowed nicely. Low-beamed ceilings, wall settles and panelling, huge log-fuelled inglenook — it's cosy, candlelit and hugely inviting. The appeal in summer is the peaceful award-winning garden, bright with flowers and characterful with hand-crafted furniture; the view 15 miles to the South Downs coast was once painted by Turner. The menu and chalkboard lists game pie, venison (from Heathfield Park), rack of lamb, salmon and leek risotto, warm treacle tart. To drink, try Harveys Sussex Bitter from Lewes. And visit the impressive church with its fine early-English tower — it's right next door.

Meals	12pm-3pm; 6pm-9.30pm (12pm-9pm Sun). Main courses £8.95-£17.20; set menu £10 & £12.
Closed	3pm-6pm in winter. Open all day Sat & Sun and in summer.
Directions	From A267 south of Horam, right after 0.25 miles for Gun Hill; pub after 0.5 miles.

Meals	12pm-2.30pm (4pm Sun); 6.30pm-9pm (9.30pm Fri & Sat); no food Sun eve. Main courses £9.50-£14; sandwiches £7.
Closed	Open all day.
Directions	From A265 east of Heathfield, left onto B2096, then 2nd right.

Martial Chaussy
The Gun,
Gun Hill,
Heathfield TN21 0JU

Tel +44 (0)1825 872361
Web www.thegunhouse.co.uk

Entry 720 Map 5

Jonathan Ritchie
The Star Inn,
Church Street, Old Heathfield,
Heathfield TN21 9AH

Tel +44 (0)1435 863570
Web www.starinnheathfield.co.uk

Entry 721 Map 5

Sussex

Worth a visit

722 The Ship Inn The Strand, Rye TN31 7DB
+44 (0)1797 222233

Former 16th-century smuggler's warehouse by the quay at the bottom of cobbled Mermaid Street. Explore pretty Rye, retreat to rustic bars with old beams, cosy nooks and blazing fires, daily papers and a quirky décor. Enjoy local ales and local food – reports welcome.

723 Blackboys Inn Lewes Road, Blackboys,
Uckfield TN22 5LG +44 (0)1825 890283

Splendid 14th-century black-weather-boarded pub overlooking an iris-covered pond. Rambling interior has bare boards, log fire, rustic benches and eclectic décor in the timeless bar. Extensive menus.

724 The Queen's Head Parsonage Lane,
Icklesham, Rye TN36 4BL +44 (0)1424 814552

Arrive early to bag a rustic garden bench in summer; in winter retreat to the beamed bar for pints of Dark Star or heady Biddenden cider. Traditional pub food too at this tile-hung 17th-century pub, set on a ridge with spectacular views across the Brede Valley to Rye.

725 Six Bells The Street, Chiddingly,
Lewes BN8 6HE +44 (0)1825 872227

Gary Glitter, Led Zeppelin and Leo Sayer have all played in this quirky little boozer renowned for its music and atmosphere. Log fires, Harveys on hand pump, boules in the garden, great value food.

726 Rose Cottage Inn Alciston,
Polegate BN26 6UW +44 (0)1323 870377

Close to the South Downs Way, this wisteria-clad pub is on a quiet lane to nowhere. Run by the Lewis family since 1960, it's a bolthole for foodies in search of cosy bars, cushioned pews, a decent pint and fresh fish and game.

727 The Dorset 28 North Road,
Brighton BN1 1YB +44 (0)1273 605423

A friendly, kooky, heart-of-Brighton pub ten minutes from the pier in the pedestrianised North Laines. Bare boards, scrubbed tables, eclectic music, decent ales and very tasty, very well-priced food. On the pavement or inside, a lovely vibe.

728 The Royal Oak Inn The Street, Poynings,
Brighton BN45 7AQ +44 (0)1273 857389

A pretty village location below the South Downs for Paul Day's revamped pub. Come for the lovely summer garden (great barbecues), the local Harveys bitter and the ambitious menus brimming with local foods.

729 The Fountain Inn Ashurst,
Steyning BN44 3AP +44 (0)1403 710219

Paul McCartney's *Wonderful Christmas Time* was filmed here, in the flagstoned, candlelit bar, aromatic with woodsmoke from its 16th-century inglenook. Raised decking overlooks the garden pond for a summery pint of Harveys Sussex ale.

730 The Half Moon The Street, Warninglid,
Horsham RH17 5TR +44 (0)1444 461227

Unpretentious brick and stone 18th-century pub just off the A23 south of Crawley – drop off for excellent modern pub food, Harvey's ales, decent wines, and a super summer garden.

731 The Chequers Slaugham,
Haywards Heath RH17 6AQ
+44 (0)1444 400239

Follow signs to sleepy Slaugham and the revitalised Chequers. Come for a cosy interior, great pub food and local produce, Sussex ales and a glorious summer garden with views across fields. New owners – one to watch!

732 Black Jug 31 North Street,
Horsham RH12 1RJ +44 (0)1403 253526

Victorian town centre pub owned and revamped by Brunning & Price. Expect classic wooden panelling, wooden floors, trademark bookcases and modern pub food served all day.

The Red Lion
Long Compton

Dogs are welcome in this ancient warren of a pub; dog sketches adorn the walls. The pub's own, Cocoa 'The Landlady', is often around. But that doesn't mean the whiff of wet canine. Instead you will get the mouthwatering aroma of excellent, imaginative cooking from Sarah Keightley, co-manager and chef, who has come from the Howard Arms at Ilmington. Crispy-battered cod and chips with caper berries and mushy peas are served here on *The Red Lion Times*(!), while herb-baked whole sea bass may be complemented by star anise and caramelised lemons. And you can stay, in five bedrooms that reflect the unfussy approach. With natural colours and crisp ginghams, their comfort and quality makes up for their size. In a place that goes back 250 years, bedrooms are not likely to be huge. Downstairs there's space for everyone, from the pool room to the restaurant to the beautiful flagged bar area warmed by a real fire and a wood-burning stove. The smart but sensitive refurb has not cost this village pub its character, nor its sense of community.

Rooms	5: 2 doubles, 1 twin, 1 single, 1 family room. £80–£110. Singles £55.
Meals	12pm-2.30pm; 6pm-9pm (12pm-9.30pm Fri-Sun). Main courses £10.50–£17.95.
Closed	2.30pm-6pm Mon-Thurs. Open all day Fri-Sun & Mon bank hols.
Directions	Beside A3400 between Chipping Norton & Shipston-on-Stour.

Lisa Phipps & Sarah Keightley
The Red Lion,
Main Street, Long Compton,
Shipston-on-Stour CV36 5JS

Tel	+44 (0)1608 684221
Web	www.redlion-longcompton.co.uk

Entry 733 Map 8

The Howard Arms
Ilmington

The Howard buzzes with good-humoured babble as well-kept beer flows from the flagstoned bar. Logs crackle contentedly in a vast open fire; a blackboard menu scales the wall above; a dining room at the far end has unexpected elegance, with great swathes of bold colour and some noble paintings. Gorgeous bedrooms are set discreetly apart from the joyful throng, mixing period style and modern luxury beautifully: one with a painted antique headboard and bleached beams, another more folksy (patchwork quilts, sunshine-yellow walls), while five new garden rooms come in elegant contemporary style with fancy bathrooms. All are individual, all huge by pub standards. The village is a surprise, too, literally tucked under a lone hill, with an unusual church surrounded by orchards and an extended village green. Round off an idyllic walk amid buzzing bees and fragrant wild flowers with a meal at the inn, perhaps seared scallops with a sweet chilli sauce and crème fraîche, then beef, ale and mustard pie, finally spiced pear and apple flapjack crumble. From a blackboard menu, the food is inventive, upmarket and very good.

Rooms	8: 5 doubles, 1 twin, 2 twins/doubles. £135–£150. Singles £95.
Meals	12pm–2.30pm (3pm Sun); 6.30pm–9.30pm (10pm Fri & Sat). Main courses £10.50–£16.
Closed	Open all day.
Directions	From Stratford, south on A3400 for 4 miles, right to Wimpstone & Ilmington. Pub in village centre.

Tim Churchman
The Howard Arms,
Lower Green, Ilmington,
Shipston-on-Stour CV36 4LT

Tel   +44 (0)1608 682226
Web   www.howardarms.com

Entry 734 Map 8

Warwickshire

The Fox & Hounds Inn
Great Wolford

The gorgeous, honey-coloured pub has been trading since 1540 and dozes contentedly in a tiny community on the edge of the Cotswold hills. On entering the bar through a low oak door the pub opens out, captivatingly, before you. Bunches of dried hops are tucked into ancient beams, there are candlelit tables on flagstoned floors, polished oak settles and a huge stone fireplace that crackles with logs in winter. Flames flicker in the copper bar counter as you order a pint of Hook Norton and study the blackboard menu announcing such treats as Gressingham duck with parsnip mousse and caramelised apple, and halibut with herb crust on chive and leek risotto. The menu is kept short and fresh and changes each day. It couldn't be cosier, or more welcoming – a perfect country pub. And there's also a good terrace for summer.

Meals	12pm-2pm (2.30pm Sat & Sun); 6.30pm-9pm; no food Sun eve. Main courses £12-£20.
Closed	2.30pm-6pm & Mon.
Directions	Off A3400 between Shipston-on-Stour & Long Compton.

Gill & Jamie Tarbox
& Sioned Rowland
The Fox & Hounds Inn, Great Wolford,
Shipston-on-Stour CV36 5NQ

Tel	+44 (0)1608 674220
Web	www.thefoxandhoundsinn.com

Entry 735 Map 8

Warwickshire

The One Elm
Stratford-upon-Avon

Stratford has a reputation for great pubs and drama – and was the birthplace of the first Slug and Lettuce. In the narrow building that The Slug once occupied stands The One Elm. Owned by Peach Pubs (of Warwick's Rose and Crown), it, too, is a cracker. The bar is light, airy and wooden-floored and the décor modern and stylish, with leather sofas and bar stools reminiscent of Giacometti sculptures. In the bar are good beers and great wines; outside, an attractive, sheltered terrace; at the back, the restaurant, with a private, secluded mezzanine and a short but mouthwatering menu. There's a chargrill section, a 'pie of the day' and a deli board that's available all day. Being slightly off the tourist trail this attracts a local crowd, and the friendly staff are on tap from breakfast until closing time.

Meals	12pm-10pm (9.30pm Sun). Main courses £9.75-£16.50.
Closed	Open all day.
Directions	In town centre on corner of Guild Street & Shakespeare Street.

Alex Marsh
The One Elm,
1 Guild Street,
Stratford-upon-Avon CV37 6QZ

Tel	+44 (0)1789 404919
Web	www.oneelmstratford.co.uk

Entry 736 Map 8

Warwickshire

The Chequers Inn
Ettington

New life has been breathed into this north Cotswold pub by new owners Kirstin and James – and how! A bold style of classic British meets country French thanks to rich tapestries, gilt mirrors, padded chairs, round tables and aged wooden flooring throughout. There is a proper glowing wood bar too with Old Hooky, Black Sheep and Betty Stoggs on tap; plus Stowford Press cider and several varieties of fizz for special occasions. The calm, elegant Provencal dining area at the back overlooks a well-planted and sheltered garden. Start with hot-smoked sea trout with pickled beetroot and horseradish cream, move on to grilled sea bream fillet, colcannon and crispy bacon and chive butter. The puds will also tempt, and then there's freshly ground coffee. Different, slightly decadent, and definitely worth a visit.

Warwickshire

Bell Inn
Welford-on-Avon

If things Elizabethan and Shakespearian entrance and inspire you, then the Bell will not disappoint, running alongside the village high street, set amongst the black and white timbered houses. There is a richness about the natural oak beams and settles, the stone floors partially covered with Persian rugs and the dog-grates cradling glowing embers. This is very much a historic village inn serving top-quality, locally sourced food, whether it be a simple pub favourite such as Lashford's pork and leek sausages on cheddar mash or, more adventurously, cajun swordfish steak with pineapple and spring onion salsa. If you're into food provenance, every supplier is listed on the back of the menu and they are almost all small independents – bakers, butchers, brewers. Just like this thriving free house.

Meals	12pm-2.30pm (12.30pm-3.30pm Sun); 6.30pm-9.30pm. Main courses £9.50-£16.95; sandwiches (lunch) from £5.50.
Closed	3pm-5pm, Sun eve & all Mon.
Directions	Off A429 11 miles south of Warwick, onto A422 east; pub at far end of village on left.

James & Kirstin Viggers
The Chequers Inn,
91 Banbury Road, Ettington,
Stratford-upon-Avon CV37 7SR
Tel   +44 (0)1789 740387
Web   www.the-chequers-ettington.co.uk

Entry 737 Map 8

Meals	11.45am-2.30pm (3pm Sat); 6.30pm-9.30pm (6pm-10pm Fri & Sat); 12pm-9.30pm Sun. Main courses £9.95-£16.95; bar meals from £5; Sunday roast £11.95-£13.75.
Closed	3pm-6pm. Open all day Sat & Sun.
Directions	Leave A3400 south west of Stratford on B439; continue to Welford; Bell on right through village.

Colin & Teresa Ombler
Bell Inn,
Binton Road, Welford-on-Avon,
Stratford upon Avon CV37 8EB
Tel   +44 (0)1789 750353
Web   www.thebellwelford.co.uk

Entry 738 Map 8

Warwickshire

The King's Head
Aston Cantlow

It is said that Shakespeare's parents had their wedding reception at The King's Head. One can imagine the scene at this long, low, rambling country inn with its small leaded windows, flagged floors and inglenook crackling with logs; perhaps they even tucked into the famous Duck Supper, a house speciality. More up-to-date delicacies join the menu today, and all is tasty, from the rare roast beef sandwiches with celeriac and horseradish to salmon, lemongrass and chive fishcakes, roast venison with calvados sauce, and the lemon cheesecake. Elderly ladies chat over pots of tea and diners come from miles around, notably well-heeled Brummies. In the bar, stylish with lime-washed beams, scrubbed pine and painted brick walls, are real ale and good wines. There's a small garden for summer and the walks start from the door.

Meals	12pm-2.30pm (12.30pm-3pm Sun); 6.30pm-9.30pm; no food Sun eve. Main courses £10-£15; bar meals £5-£8.
Closed	3pm-5.30pm. Sun eves after 7.30pm. Open all day Sat.
Directions	Off A46 for Aston Cantlow.

Peter & Louise Sadler
The King's Head,
21 Bearley Road, Aston Cantlow,
Henley-in-Arden B95 6HY

Tel +44 (0)1789 488242
Web www.thekh.co.uk

Entry 739 Map 8

Warwickshire

The Crabmill
Preston Bagot

The lovely, rambling building, with tiny leaded windows and wonderfully wonky beams, once contained a cider press. Later a pub, now it's a busy gastro haven with a dining room for every mood – one pistachio-green and scented with lilies, another deep red, its walls hung with plump nudes, and third a candlelit mushroom-cream. There's a steely bar with sandblasted glass panels, great flagstones and a winter fire. At the back, a split-level lounge with wooden floors, deep leather sofas and a garden that heads off into open countryside. For summer there's stylish decking outside. The food is popular and the dishes imaginative and colourful, from simple croque monsieur and Cornish pasty to roast halibut with parsley and shallot rösti, steamed greens and lobster sauce.

Meals	12pm-2.30pm (12.30pm-3.30pm Sun); 6.30pm-9.30pm. No food Sun eve. Main courses £9.95-£16.95; lunch £5.95-£6.95; Sunday lunch £12.75.
Closed	Open all day. Closed Sun eve from 6pm.
Directions	From Henley-in-Arden on A4189 towards Claverdon.

Sally Coll
The Crabmill,
Preston Bagot,
Henley-In-Arden B95 5EE

Tel +44 (0)1926 843342
Web www.thecrabmill.co.uk

Entry 740 Map 8

Warwickshire

The Rose & Crown
Warwick

Peach Pubs' flagship Rose and Crown opens with bacon sarnies for breakfast (rather good ones) and stays open all day. Enter a cheery, airy, wooden-floored front bar with red and white walls, big leather sofas, low tables and a crackling winter fire. To the back is the big and bustling eating area and a private room that can be booked for parties. Almost all of the staff trained at Raymond Blanc's Petit Blanc restaurants; the food is scrummy. Served all day, the tapas-style portions of cheeses, hams, marinated anchovies, mixed olives and rustic breads slip down easily with a pint of Fuller's London Pride or a glass of pinot, while hot dishes are modern British with a Mediterranean slant. On the menu may be baked sea trout; lemon and thyme couscous with chilli oil; pork loin with rhubarb confit, apple and cider jus. Lovely contemporary bedrooms above have large bath and shower rooms and overlook the square, filled on warm summer nights with a merry throng. It's young and fun and conveniently central for Warwick, which has history in spades.

Rooms	5: 2 doubles, 3 triples. £75-£85.
Meals	8am-10pm (9.30pm Sun).
	Main courses £9.75-£17.50; bar meals £4-£10.50.
Closed	Open all day from 8am.
Directions	In Warwick centre, on market place. Ask about parking.

Jeremy Kynaston
The Rose and Crown,
30 Market Place,
Warwick, CV34 4SH
Tel   +44 (0)1926 411117
Web   www.roseandcrownwarwick.co.uk

Entry 741 Map 8

Warwickshire

The Bluebell
Henley-in-Arden

Leigh and Duncan Taylor went to town updating this 500-year-old coaching inn, creating one of the most distinctive bistro-style pubs in the country. A clever combination of country casual and urban chic means atmosphere and style are delivered in spades: bold colours and striking furniture blend with ancient beams, flagstones and a big fireplace. Real ales, wines and an irresistible menu draw keen diners from far and near, ingredients are sourced with care and vegetables are grown on the owners' allotment. The menu combines colourful modern dishes — seared black pepper venison with rocket and parmesan, or open-style Scotch fillet steak Wellington with sautéed white truffle chard — with old favourites like steak and kidney pie; fishcakes; battered haddock with chips. In summer, lunch on the decked area is sublime.

Meals	12pm-2.30pm (3.30pm Sun); 6pm-9.30pm. No food Sun eve or Mon (except bank hols). Main courses £9.95-£17.95; sandwiches (lunch) from £5.95; Sunday roast £12.75.
Closed	Mon lunch (except bank hols).
Directions	M40 junc 16, follow A3400 south for 3 miles to Henley-in-Arden; pub in village centre.

Duncan & Leigh Taylor
The Bluebell,
93 High Street,
Henley-in-Arden B95 5AT

Tel	+44 (0)1564 793049
Web	www.bluebellhenley.co.uk

Entry 742 Map 8

Warwickshire

Red Lion
Hunningham

The 150 sandbags in the car park are a gentle reminder that the 17th-century Red Lion has been flooded twice in the past decade — but then it does stand next to the river Leam (with ancient bridge) and the river runs past the end of the garden. Owner Sam Cornwall-Jones originally wanted to be an illustrator and his passion for classic comics is evident from the walls, plastered with vintage copies of Fantastic Four, Batman and Supergirl. The food is honest, unfussy and sourced locally, perhaps a starter of salmon and smoked trout fishcake with horseradish mayonnaise followed by a Warwickshire fillet steak with Shropshire Blue butter and hand-cut chips. The old pub may be hard to find but you'll love it for its open fires, cheery bar staff, real ales and Sunday papers, guaranteed to put a smile on your face.

Meals	12pm-10pm (9.30pm Sun). Main courses £8.95-£15.95; bar meals £4.95-£8.95; Sunday roast from £12.95.
Closed	Open all day.
Directions	Off B4455 (Fosse Way) between Eathorpe and Offchurch east of Leamington Spa; pub is beside the River Leam.

Sam Cornwall-Jones
Red Lion, Main Street,
Hunningham,
Leamington Spa, CV33 9DY

Tel	+44 (0)1926 632715
Web	www.redlionhunningham.co.uk

Entry 743 Map 8

Warwickshire

The Case is Altered
Hatton

No food, no mobiles and a Sopwith Pup propeller suspended from the ceiling. This is a Warwickshire treasure. There's even a vintage bar billiards machine, operated by sixpences from behind the bar. In the main room are stone floors, leather-covered settles and walls covered in yellowing posters offering beverages at a penny a pint. Jackie does not open her arms to children or dogs; this is a place for adult conversation and liquid refreshment. Devotees travel some distance for the pork scratchings and the expertly kept beer. The sign used to show lawyers arguing but the name has nothing to do with the law; it used to be called, simply, 'The Case' and was so small that it was not eligible for a licence. It was made larger, whisky was introduced, the name was changed, and everyone was happy. They've been that way ever since.

Warwickshire

The Orange Tree
Chadwick End

The flagship dining pub of the Classic Country Pubs group has a striking interior. Be seduced by earthy colours, lime-washed low beams, open log fires, big lamps, deep sofas around low tables and chunky lightwood furnishings in airy eating rooms. A gorgeous Italian-style deli counter shows off breads, cheeses and vintage oils. This tastefully rustic-Mediterranean décor with oriental touches is matched by an ambitious, Italian-inspired menu, and diners descend in their droves for authentic fired pizzas and robust, full-flavoured meat dishes cooked on an in-view rotisserie spit. There are also homemade pasta dishes, delicious warm salads and fishy specials. Great wines by the bottle or glass, real ales, a heated patio dotted with stylish teak tables and all-day opening hours.

Meals	No food served.
Closed	2.30pm-6pm (2.15pm-7pm Sun).
Directions	Follow Rowington off A4177/A4141 junction, north of Warwick.

Meals	12pm-2.30pm (7pm Sun); 6pm-9.30pm; no food Sun eve. Main courses £8.95-£18.45.
Closed	Open all day.
Directions	On A4141 between Warwick & Solihull. On edge of village, 5 miles south of M42 junc. 5.

Jackie & Charlie Willacy
The Case is Altered,
Case Lane, Five Ways,
Hatton, Warwick CV35 7JD
Tel +44 (0)1926 484206

♿ ☕

Entry 744 Map 8

Paul Hales
The Orange Tree,
Warwick Road,
Chadwick End, Solihull B93 0BN
Tel +44 (0)1564 785364
Web www.theorangetreepub.co.uk

Entry 745 Map 8

Warwickshire

The Boot Inn
Lapworth

The Boot was here long before the canal that runs past the back garden. With its exposed timbers, rug-strewn quarry floors, open fires and daily papers it combines old-fashioned charm with rustic chic. Under the guidance of Paul Salisbury and James Elliot, the down-at-heel boozer became one of the first gastropubs of the Midlands nearly a decade ago, and has been pulling foodies in ever since. Menus have a distinct touch of Mediterranean and Pacific rim: crispy oriental duck salad, Moroccan lamb with red onion and coriander couscous, seared sea bass with peppers, crab and lemon aïoli. Ingredients are as fresh as can be and seafood dishes are a speciality. Eat in the bars or in the stylishly revamped dining room upstairs, and in summer go alfresco: there's a lovely terrace to the side.

Meals	12pm-2.30pm (3pm Sun); 7pm-10pm (9pm Sun). Main courses £9-£18.
Closed	Open all day.
Directions	Off M42 junc. 4 for Hockley Heath; Lapworth signed.

Paul Salisbury & James Elliot
The Boot Inn,
Old Warwick Road,
Lapworth, Solihull B94 6JU
Tel +44 (0)1564 782464
Web www.lovelypubs.co.uk

Entry 746 Map 8

Warwickshire

The Punchbowl
Lapworth

The Punchbowl looks pubby enough from the outside, and functions as such with a big fire and beamed bar dispensing Timothy Taylor's Landlord. So it's a surprise to discover that the building is new – the original burnt down 12 years ago. James Feeney has a flair for design, and from simple materials has created contemporary opulence: candelabra on long wooden tables, modern canvasses and ornate mirrors on bare brick, windows swept by crushed velvet. Food is a strength, menus are printed daily on paper and the cooking embraces many ideas: cumin-crusted tuna with sweet potato purée; spinach and tomato fondue; Thai red prawn curry; classic sirloin of beef with mushroom sauce. There's comfort food, too, in fish and chips and rack of lamb. And the glassed-in patio area has a conservatory feel.

Meals	12pm-2.30pm (3.30pm Sun); 6.30pm-9.30pm (10pm Fri & Sat; 9pm Sun). Main courses £9.95-£17.50.
Closed	Open all day.
Directions	Lapworth off B4439; pub near station.

James Feeney
The Punchbowl,
Mill Lane, Lapworth,
Solihull B94 6HR
Tel +44 (0)1564 784564
Web www.thepunchbowllapworth.com

Entry 747 Map 8

Warwickshire

The Almanack
Kenilworth

The innovative Peach Pubs people continue to reinvent the gastropub. This, their tenth venture, is a swish new-build beneath apartments in Kenilworth town centre. It opened in spring 2009 and business has boomed since. Although more trendy bar-restaurant than pub, there's a vast island bar, lots of spacious informal seating and local Purity ales on tap. Expect a cool retro feel, with vintage 60s and 70s armchairs and sofas and a colourfully eclectic décor throughout. Pop in for breakfast or coffee and cake and settle down to free WiFi – or graze from a modern pub menu. In the all-day, open-to-view kitchen, corned beef hash and BLT sandwiches are created, along with substantial lunches and suppers: a daily roast, coq au vin with creamy mash, a fish deli-board, duck with redcurrant jus. Young and fun.

Meals	Meals served all day from 12pm. Main prices £9.75–£20; Sunday lunch £11.50–£12.50.
Closed	Open all day.
Directions	On Abbey End, in front of Abbey End car park, next to the Clock Tower r'bout.

Jeremy Kynaston
The Almanack,
Abbey End North,
Kenilworth CV8 1QJ
Tel   +44 (0)1926 353637
Web   www.thealmanack-kenilworth.co.uk

Entry 748 Map 8

West Midlands

The Malt Shovel at Barston
Barston

No surprise that the car park holds some swanky motors. This is a smart, food-driven place that knows its market and caters to it well. Gastropubs may come and go but this is a favourite. Whether you're ensconced in the smart cream-and-green bar, on the trellis-shaded terrace or in the country-rustic restaurant, the food is to savour and the well-kept ales (Tribute, Old Speckled Hen) are matched by some decent wines. The menu covers global as well as pubby treats – Aberdeenshire rump steak, fishcakes, slow roast pork belly with plum and lemongrass sauce – and executes both with aplomb. The culinary innovation extends to the vegetarian options, perhaps a filo tart of crushed carrot topped with a poached egg, courgette strips and rocket pesto. A slick operation out in the country, that's also friendly and relaxed.

Meals	12pm-2.30pm (4pm Sun); 6pm-9.30pm; no food Sun eve. Main courses £10.95–£17.95; set menus £21.50 & £25.50.
Closed	Open all day.
Directions	Off A452; 1 mile beyond village.

Helen Somerfield
The Malt Shovel at Barston,
Barston Lane,
Barston, Solihull B92 0JP
Tel   +44 (0)1675 443223
Web   www.themaltshovelatbarston.com

Entry 749 Map 8

Wiltshire

The Royal Oak
Bishopstone

Passionately organic, delightfully unpreachy. In 2005 the simple pub in the idyllic village was taken on by farmer Helen Browning and has been flying the flag ever since. There's food bartering with locals, a wild garden with barbecues (they provide the ingredients, you do the rest) and open days with hay bales for kids to romp on: all part of the commitment to be a full-on local. The planked open-plan bar has a lovely feel with roaring fire and beams and the staff are friendly, but best of all is the menu that changes twice daily: crayfish from the Thames served with Bishopstone watercress, home-cured bacon from home-reared pigs, asparagus from Lotmead down the road, fish from day boats out of Newlyn, gooseberries from the garden. Perfect ingredients, perfect food, beer from Arkells and six wines by the glass.

Wiltshire

The Wheatsheaf
Oaksey

Ancient on the outside, inglenooked inside – the archetypal English country pub. Local drinkers are welcome, but, with cooking like this, it would be silly to come merely to booze. Peep around the corner from the bar and tradition ends – the dining room has pale wood and sisal floors, cream walls and modern prints, and good-looking food served on big white plates. Chef-patron Tony Robson-Burrell's imaginative country dishes reflect current trends, so whether you choose a pub classic like Hereford rump steak with parmesan and pesto salad and fat chips, or roast monkfish with gnocchi and braised leeks, you'll eat well (while dessert-lovers will relish the baked hot chocolate fondant with rum and raisin ice cream or Bailey's bread and butter pudding). Real ales include Butts ales and Sharp's Doom Bar, children and dogs are welcome.

Meals	12pm-2.30pm (3.30pm Sun); 6.30pm-9.30pm (8.30pm Sun). Main courses £8-£20; bar snacks £3.95-£6.50; Sunday roast from £12.50.
Closed	3pm-6pm. Open all day Sat & Sun.
Directions	In Bishopstone is 8 miles east of Swindon, take minor road off A419 just north of M4 junc. 15. Left onto Cues Lane; 50 yards on right. Car park at back.

Meals	12pm-2pm (2.30pm Sun); 6.30pm-9pm (9.30pm Fri & Sat); no food Sun eve or Mon. Main courses £5-£16.95; bar meals £5-£10.25.
Closed	3pm-6pm. Open all day Sat.
Directions	Oaksey signed off A429 at Crudwell, 5 miles north of Malmesbury.

Helen Browning
The Royal Oak,
Bishopstone,
Swindon SN6 8PP
Tel +44 (0)1793 790481
Web www.royaloakbishopstone.co.uk

Entry 750 Map 3

Tony Robson-Burrell
The Wheatsheaf,
Wheatsheaf Lane, Oaksey,
Malmesbury SN16 9TB
Tel +44 (0)1666 577348
Web www.thecompletechef.co.uk

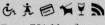

Entry 751 Map 3

Wiltshire

The Red Lion Inn
Cricklade

A stroll from the ancient North Meadow, famous for its spring show of wild fritillaries, the rambling old coaching inn lies off the Thames path. Bought by the Real Pub Food Company in 2008, specialising in seasonal, locally sourced and often organic food (along with The Clanfield Tavern near Bampton), it combines contemporary features with a charming 16th-century fabric. In the red-carpeted bar, all sagging beams, stone walls, ancient settles and log fires, treat yourself to a pint of ale; the choice is mind-boggling, from Ramsbury Gold to Cotswold Spring. Lunches involve the best of English classics: real burgers with triple-cooked chips, rabbit, bacon and leek pie, scrambled duck eggs with smoked salmon. Evening dishes, served at reclaimed wooden tables in the smart new restaurant, include tea-smoked salmon, pot roast pheasant with root vegetables, rhubarb and ginger crumble. The pick of the bedrooms are the two in the old stables with their stone walls and tiled floors, chunky, hand-crafted beds, crisp linen, and bathrooms that sparkle. Marvellous.

Rooms	5: 3 doubles, 2 twins. £65.
Meals	12pm-2.30pm (3pm Sun); 6.30pm-9pm (9.30pm Fri & Sat). No food Sun eve or Mon. Main courses £9.50-£20.95; bar meals £5.50-£10.25; Sunday lunch £13.95 & £16.95.
Closed	Mon lunch.
Directions	Cricklade is off A417 between Swindon and Cirencester; pub at lower end of High Street.

Tom Gee
The Red Lion Inn,
74 High Street,
Cricklade SN6 6DD

Tel	+44 (0)1793 750776
Web	www.theredlioncricklade.co.uk

Entry 752 Map 3

The Horse & Groom Inn
Charlton

The solidly elegant Cotswold stone house fronted by a tree-sheltered lawn stands well back from the road. Its long history as a coaching inn is documented in the framed prints that hang in the rustically atmospheric main bar, all exposed stone, assorted scrubbed tables and roaring log fire. Smart dining areas – gleaming tables, polished glasses – and bedrooms sparkling with style and panache await hungry and weary travellers. Expect padded window seats, chunky wood beds, herbal toiletries, earthy colours. Those in the eaves have painted beams, all have claw-foot baths; they're all great. Back in the bar, the kitchen team oversees well-priced menus that champion pub classics – homemade beefburger with chips and tomato relish, steak, mushroom and ale pie – alongside more innovative British dishes… shoulder of Cotswold lamb and wholegrain mustard mash; pan-roasted sea scallops with Jerusalem artichoke velouté; warm chocolate and walnut fondant. Cooked breakfast is a treat, everything is immaculate and there's a secret walled garden for civilised summer drinking.

Rooms	5 doubles. From £89.
Meals	12pm-2pm (2.30pm Fri & Sat; 3pm Sun); 6.30pm-9pm (9.30pm Fri & Sat; 6pm-9pm Sun). Main courses £8.95-£19.95; bar meals £4.50-£12.95.
Closed	Open all day.
Directions	M4 junc. 17, then A429 north for Cirencester. Right onto B4040 after 5 miles. On left in village after 1 mile.

	Dave Whitney-Brown
	The Horse & Groom Inn,
	The Street, Charlton,
	Malmesbury SN16 9DL
Tel	+44 (0)1666 823904
Web	www.horseandgroominn.com

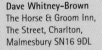

Wiltshire

The Potting Shed Pub
Crudwell

Jonathan and Julian, owners of the Rectory Hotel across the road, have transformed the village inn. As well as the open fireplaces and the stylish kilim sofas, you'll note a light fitting fashioned from a wheelbarrow, door handles from trowels, hand pumps from fork handles and old butchers' block tables; the large, airy dining room displays mix 'n' match antiques. As for the food, it is exuberantly British, from the homemade pork scratchings and rabbit terrine to the battered hake and lamb hotpot. Two acres of lawns and an apple orchard at the back have been turned into an organic vegetable patch, while local ales, ploughman's lunches and dog biscuits on the bar further reflect the focus on real-pub values and unpretentiousness. There's an excellent children's menu, and puds to warm your heart; try the spiced rice pudding. It's 21st-century pub heaven.

Meals	12pm-2.30pm (3.30pm Sun); 7pm-9.30pm; no food Sun eve. Main courses £10.75-£15.95.
Closed	Open all day.
Directions	In village centre on A429 between Cirencester & M4 junc. 17.

Local, seasonal & organic produce

Jonathan Barry & Julian Muggridge
The Potting Shed Pub,
Crudwell,
Malmesbury SN16 9EW
Tel   +44 (0)1666 577833
Web   www.thepottingshedpub.com

Entry 754 Map 3

Wiltshire

The Vine Tree
Norton

With a fine store of ales and over 40 wines by the glass the old watermill is a watering hole in every sense. It may be hidden away but the faithful return, for the food and the beer. On Sundays, memorable roast sirloin of beef from the neighbour's farm is served with all the trimmings. There's plenty of fresh fish, too, and local game in season, sautéed scallops with wild mushroom risotto, and rack of Cotswold lamb. Service is young and friendly and surroundings are inviting: deep red walls, candlelight and beams, a wood-burning stove; tables in the minuscule upstairs room are super-cosy. In summer, relax and gaze on the immaculate terrace – a delicious spot with urns of flowers and a fountain. This Vine Tree has a rich harvest for guests – and their dogs – to reap; no wonder Clementine the lab looks so content.

Meals	12pm-2.30pm (3.30pm Sun); 7pm-9.30pm (10pm Fri & Sat). Main courses £11.95-£18.95; bar meals £6.50-£12.50.
Closed	3pm-5.45pm. Open all day Sun in summer.
Directions	From M4 junc. 17 take A429 for Cirencester. After 1.5 miles left for Norton. There, right for Foxley. Follow road; on left.

Charles Walker & Tiggi Wood
The Vine Tree,
Foxley Road, Norton,
Malmesbury SN16 0JP
Tel   +44 (0)1666 837654
Web   www.thevinetree.co.uk

Entry 755 Map 3

Wiltshire

The Rattlebone Inn
Sherston

It was built in the late 17th-century and named after Saxon warrior John Rattlebone – when bones doubled up for armour! The village bar is all flagstones, beams and wood furniture with friendly Rob distributing Young's Bitter or St Austell Tribute. Behind, another carpeted area leads to numerous nooks and crannies from which to delve into the snack and main menus: homemade shepherd's pie; medallions of pork (with stilton sauce and spring onion mash and toasted cashews) plus interesting wines to go with your choice, as well as good cheeses and desserts. A wood-burner keeps it toasty in winter, there's a long, calm dining area for cosy meals, and outside, just off the High Street, two patio areas, two boules pistes and a skittle alley. On certain days you can even try Mangold hurling – an old West Country sport.

Meals	12pm-2.30pm (3pm Sun); 6pm-9.30pm. No food Sun eve. Main courses £9.50-£17.50; bar meals £7.95-£9.50; sandwiches from £4.75.
Closed	3pm-5pm. Open all day Sat & Sun.
Directions	On B4040 west of Malmesbury; pub in village centre.

Jason Read
The Rattlebone Inn,
Church Street, Sherston,
Malmesbury SN16 0LR
Tel +44 (0)1666 840871
Web www.therattlebone.co.uk

Entry 756 Map 3

Wiltshire

Quarrymans Arms
Box Hill

Though once a row of simple cottage dwellings, this has been a pub since the 18th century – a friendly, quirky little place. As the name suggests, it once served the stone miners from the local quarry. The mines may be long-gone, but history lingers in the shape of fascinating maps, photos and some lethal-looking stonecutting equipment hanging on the walls. In pride of place near the bar: a framed front page Box quarry story from a 1934 edition of the *Daily Sketch* asks: 'Is this the world's toughest job?'. Food on the changing blackboard menus is more traditional than gastropub, but is straightforward and tasty. Good Wiltshire home-cured ham, steak and ale pie, calves' liver with mustard mash and other staples are perfect fuel for walkers, cyclists and pot-holers intent on visiting the disused mines.

Meals	12pm-3pm; 6pm-9pm. Main courses £7.50-£16.95; bar meals £2.50-£7.95.
Closed	3pm-6pm. Open all day Fri-Sun.
Directions	Just off A4, on hillside to right of village; phone for directions.

John & Ginny Arundel
Quarrymans Arms,
Box Hill,
Corsham SN13 8HN
Tel +44 (0)1225 743569
Web www.quarrymans.plus.com

Entry 757 Map 3

The Pear Tree Inn
Whitley

A cool rustic chic flows effortlessly through The Pear Tree. This is a dreamy blend of French inspiration and English whimsy, a sweep of warm airy interiors that make you feel that you've washed up in country pub heaven. Step in under the beams, glide across the flagged floors, dive into an armchair and roast away in front of the fire. Keep going and you come to high-ceiling'd dining rooms where stripped floors are dressed in smart old rugs and agrarian artefacts hang from the walls. French windows flood the place with light and open up in summer for alfresco suppers. Gardens are manicured, staff are efficient. Bedrooms, up in the eaves or out in the barn, come in lime white and have suede headboards, upholstered chairs, Bang & Olufsen TVs and funky rugs for colour; bathrooms have robes and creamy tiles. As for the food, it's prepared from mostly local ingredients from an experienced team. Enjoy braised beef 'Jacob's Ladder' with buttery mash, chocolate and hazelnut brownies, delicious breakfasts. Smart locals flock at weekends, and there are wonderful walks from the door.

Rooms	8: 6 doubles, 2 family rooms. £125. Family rooms £160. Singles from £95.
Meals	12pm-2.30pm; 6.30pm-9.30pm (7pm-9.30pm Sun). Main courses £11.95-£20.95.
Closed	Open all day.
Directions	West from Melksham on A365, then right onto B3353 for Whitley. Through village, then left, signed Purlpit. Pub on right after 400 yards.

Lisa Penny
The Pear Tree Inn,
Top Lane, Whitley,
Melksham SN12 8QX
Tel   +44 (0)1225 709131
Web   www.maypolehotels.com/peartreeinn

The Compasses Inn
Tisbury

In the middle of a lovely village of thatched and timber-framed cottages, this inn seems so content with its lot it could almost be a figment of your imagination. Over the years, 14th-century foundations have gradually sunk into the ground. Its thatched roof is like a sombrero, shielding bedroom windows that peer sleepily over the lawn. Duck instinctively into the sudden darkness of the bar and experience a wave of nostalgia as your eyes adjust to a long wooden room, with flagstones and cosy booths divided by farmyard salvage: a cartwheel here, some horse tack there; at one end is a piano, at the other, a brick hearth. The pub crackles with Alan's enthusiasm; he's fairly new to the trade, but his genuine hospitality more than compensates. People come for the food as well: figs baked in red wine, topped with goat's cheese and chorizo, or grilled fish from the south coast. Bedrooms are at the top of stone stairs outside the front door and have the same effortless charm; thick walls, wonky windows, spotless bathrooms. And the sweet serenity of Wiltshire lies just down the lane.

Rooms	4 + 1: 3 doubles, 1 twin/double. 1 self-catering cottage for 4. £85-£90. Singles from £65. Cottage £100-£130.
Meals	12pm-2pm; 6.30pm-9pm (9.30pm Sat). Main courses £9-£22; bar meals from £5.
Closed	3pm-6pm (7pm Sun).
Directions	From Salisbury, A30 west, 3rd right after Fovant, signed Lower Chicksgrove, then 1st left down single track lane to village.

Alan & Susie Stoneham
The Compasses Inn,
Lower Chicksgrove,
Tisbury, Salisbury SP3 6NB

Tel	+44 (0)1722 714318
Web	www.thecompassesinn.com

Entry 759 Map 3

Wiltshire

The Tollgate Inn
Holt

All would pay the toll – were there one – to sample the delights of The Tollgate Inn. In a warm and convivial bar and lounge, lovely leather sofas, a log-burning stove, planked pine tables, newspapers and magazines encourage you to linger over a handpumped pint of Exmoor or a glass of sauvignon. The two dining areas have distinct personalities; the smaller off the bar with a traditional appeal, the upper, in the former chapel of the weavers who worked below, smart with high black rafters, open fire and an eclectic décor. Chef Alexander Venables' pedigree shines through in dishes that make the most of local produce (suppliers are named with the menu) and daily fish from Brixham. Light bites include omelette Arnold Bennett and set lunch is a snip at £12.50; try roast saddle of venison with stilton mash and port jus. Country-style bedrooms are in excellent order: oak beams, smart linen, lovely beds. For country views of goats and fields ask for one at the back. Breakfasts are as superb as all the rest, and there's a new farm shop in the renovated barn out back.

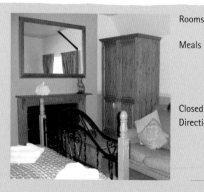

Rooms	4 doubles. £80–£100. Singles £50–£100.
Meals	12pm-2pm; 7pm-9pm (9.30pm Fri & Sat). Main courses £12.50–£18.80; bar meals £5.50–£8.95; set lunch from £12.50; set dinner (3 courses) £18.75.
Closed	3pm-5.30pm; Sun eve & Mon.
Directions	On B3107 between Bradford-on-Avon & Melksham.

Alison Ward–Baptiste
& Alexander Venables
The Tollgate Inn, Ham Green,
Holt, Trowbridge BA14 6PX
Tel +44 (0)1225 782326
Web www.tollgateholt.co.uk

Entry 760 Map 3

The Castle Inn
Bradford-on-Avon

On top of the hill that dips down to the mellow heart of Bradford-on-Avon, this heart-warming renovation of a neglected Bath stone inn is the work of Flatcappers, who, in their first foray into the world of real pubs, have struck gold. Enter a warren of planked rooms – one large, three small – in muted greys, reds and greens, lovingly and imaginatively restored. Imagine solid stone walls and little log fires, recycled chairs and long farmhouse tables, a leather sofa to sink into, books on the shelves and prints on the walls. Six ales from local breweries dominate the bar as locals pop in for a pint and the papers, and muted jazz plays. An all-day menu (soup with crusty bread; stilton and port terrine) stands alongside British pub classics, the specials are special (rabbit ragu with handmade pappardelle) and our Sunday sirloin with Yorkshire pud was heaven. Above, four equally characterful bedrooms have modish wallpapers and stylish hues, wonky door frames and period fireplaces, stunning walk-in bathrooms and wide-reaching views – of the church, or the White Horse on the Wiltshire hills.

Rooms	4: 3 doubles, 1 family room. £90–£140.
Meals	9am–10pm. Main courses £7.95–£18.95.
Closed	Open all day.
Directions	Entering Bradford-on-Avon on A363, pub is on mini-r'bout before turning for town centre.

Pierre Woodford
The Castle Inn,
Mount Pleasant,
Bradford-on-Avon BA15 1SJ

Tel	+44 (0)1225 865657
Web	www.flatcappers.co.uk

Entry 761 Map 3

Wiltshire

The George & Dragon
Rowde

Behind the unpromising exterior hides a low-ceilinged bar, its stone fireplace ablaze in winter, its half-panelled walls lined with old paintings, its antique clock ticking away the hours. Furnishings are authentically period, there are wooden boards in the dining room, painted walls and plenty of dark timber. The kitchen's chutneys and preserves are for sale, international bottled beers and organic ciders line the shelves and handpumped Butcombe Bitter announces itself on the bar. Experienced owners are maintaining the pub's reputation for fish delivered fresh from Cornwall — with the odd concession to meat eaters. There are specials such as delectable chargrilled scallops with black pudding brochettes and puddings to diet for. Rooms are charming and individual — Country, Classic or Funky — with wall timbers and wonky floors, contemporary wall coverings, White Company duvets and linen on wooden or brass beds and posh tiled bathrooms. Great value, a treat to come back to after a long walk along the Kennet & Avon Canal.

Rooms	3: 2 doubles, 1 family room. £55–£85.
Meals	12pm-3pm (4pm Sat & Sun), 7pm-10pm (from 6.30pm Sat). Main courses £9-£23; Sunday lunch £17.50.
Closed	3pm-7pm (4pm-6.30pm Sat & Sun).
Directions	On A342, 2 miles west of Devizes.

Chris Day & Michelle & Philip Hale
The George & Dragon,
High Street,
Rowde, Devizes SN10 2PN
Tel   +44 (0)1380 723053
Web   www.thegeorgeanddragonrowde.co.uk

Entry 762 Map 3

Wiltshire

The Red Lion
East Chisenbury

Unless you found yourself lost on Salisbury Plain, chances are you wouldn't stumble upon the Red Lion. You'd be missing much: this smart thatched village inn is both a local serving ale from Wiltshire microbreweries and a restaurant drawing food lovers from far and wide. New owner-chefs Guy and Brittany Manning have arrived with something of a star-spangled CV. Guy worked for three years at the Chez Bruce in London, both worked under Thomas Keller at the breathtaking Per Se in New York. The couple apply cutting-edge cookery techniques to simple rustic dishes and the results are very special. The menu changes every day – sometimes twice – so expect the likes of pheasant and ham hock terrine, mushroom tortellini, roast pollock with olive oil mash and New England cheesecake with rhubarb. The Sunday roasts are superb!

Wiltshire

The Outside Chance
Manton

Take a punt and swing off the A4: you'll not regret landing in this pretty village. Indeed, opportunity played a big part here as the finance for the recent revival came from backing a horse at 100-1. And you know you're in sporting country as soon as you step in the door: equine photographs and a Frankie Dettori racing silk complement a properly pubby feel. There are stone and oak floors, a brick fireplace, hop-hung beams, a golden oak bar, and brilliant staff. Wadworth's ales on tap deliciously match the freshly cooked modern British and traditional menu; try venison steak with rosemary-roasted potatoes, port jus and vegetables, and the Wiltshire ham with free-range eggs and chips. When the weather is fair, head for the smart patio or the garden, furnished with trees, chunky benches and tables.

Meals	12.30pm-2.30pm (3pm Sat & Sun); 6.30pm-10pm.
	£9.50-£14; bar snacks £6.50; Sunday roast £11.
Closed	3pm-6pm & Mon all day.
Directions	East Chisenbury is off A345/Salisbury Road.

Meals	12pm-2.30pm; 7pm-9pm (9.30pm Fri & Sat).
	Main courses £7.50-£15.95.
Closed	3pm-5.30pm.
	Open all day Sat & Sun.
Directions	Village signed off A4 just west of Marlborough.

Guy & Brittany Manning
The Red Lion,
East Chisenbury,
Pewsey SN9 6AQ
Tel   +44 (0)1980 671124
Web   www.redlionfreehouse.com

&. ☂ ⊟ ⋈ ⍭

Entry 763 Map 3

Howard Spooner & Guy Sangster
The Outside Chance,
71 High Street, Manton,
Marlborough SN8 4HW
Tel   +44 (0)1672 512352
Web   www.theoutsidechance.co.uk

☂ ⊟ ⋈ ⍭

Entry 764 Map 3

Wiltshire

The Bell
Ramsbury

Posh fish and chips! A generous fresh portion, a crisp beer-flavoured batter, great chips and real béarnaise sauce. The pub's food – sourced from Wiltshire and Berkshire and as seasonal as can be – is highly praised, though you don't have to come to eat: The Bell is also for drinkers, with a number of rooms to welcome you and several cosy nooks. There's a cheerful bar (rustic wooden floors, open fire, gilt-edged pictures, some stained glass) and a carpeted restaurant, comfortably stylish. The beer is well-kept with three Ramsbury brews on handpump, and there are many wines by the glass (pricey but praiseworthy). You can't help but go home happy, such is the atmosphere of the place. Lunch, by the way, is brilliant value. As for the village, it's very pretty; the pub, on the main square, is 100 yards from the river bank.

Meals	12pm-2.30pm; 7pm-9.30pm. Main courses £10.95-£19.95; set menus £12.50 & £16.50 (lunch), £15 & £20 (dinner); Sunday lunch £17 & £22.
Closed	3pm-6pm.
Directions	Ramsbury is off A4192, 6 miles east of Marlborough.

Jeremy Parke
The Bell,
The Square, Ramsbury,
Marlborough SN8 2PE
Tel +44 (0)1672 520230
Web www.thebellramsbury.com

Entry 765 Map 3

Wiltshire

The Malet Arms
Newton Tony

Formerly a bakehouse for a long-lost manor, the old flintstone pub draws walkers from miles. Expect cracking local ales, robust country cooking and a cheerful welcome from the Cardews. The low-beamed bar, cosy with rustic furnishings, blazing logs, old pictures and interesting bits and pieces, would be a nice spot for a pint of Stonehenge Heelstone. Hearty food, listed on boards above the fireplaces, reflects the rural setting, with local game (shot by Noel) a winter favourite. Fill your boots with a rich stew of pheasant and pigeon in Guinness, proper fish and chips or a local beefburger, and follow with Annie's speciality: an old English pudding (try the walnut and date tart). The pub cricket team play on the field opposite and there's a summer music festival in the paddock at the back – a true community pub.

Meals	12pm-2.30pm; 6.30pm-10pm (7pm-9.30pm Sun). Main courses £8.50-£15.
Closed	3pm-6pm (7pm Sun).
Directions	Off A338, 6 miles north of Salisbury.

Noel & Annie Cardew
The Malet Arms,
Newton Tony,
Salisbury SP4 0HF
Tel +44 (0)1980 629279
Web www.maletarms.com

Entry 766 Map 3

The Beckford Arms
Tisbury

You arrive in grand style: a fine sweep though the Fonthill estate and under the Triumphal Arch. Wash up at this country-house inn and expect to be seduced immediately. Outside, a half-acre garden is ridiculously pretty – hammocks in the trees, parasols on the terrace, church spire soaring to the heavens – but this Georgian house is equally sublime, an inn for all seasons. Inside, everything elates: a drawing room where facing sofas are warmed by a roaring fire; a restaurant with a wall of glass that opens onto the terrace; a bar with parquet flooring for an excellent local pint. Follow your nose and chance upon the odd chandelier, roaming wisteria, logs piled high inside and out, a rather grand mahogany table in the private dining room. Bedrooms are small but perfectly formed with prices to match: white walls, the best linen, sisal matting, super bathrooms. As for the food, there's much to please, perhaps marrow fritters with lemon mayo, local partridge with bread sauce, chocolate bread and butter pudding. There are film nights most Sundays, the cricket team comes to celebrate. Don't miss it.

Rooms	8: 6 doubles, 2 twins/doubles. £85. Singles £65.
Meals	12pm-2.30pm (3pm Sat & Sun); 6pm-9.30pm. Bar menu all day. Main courses £8-£15; bar meals £4-£10; Sunday lunch £11.50-£15.
Closed	Open all day.
Directions	Off B3089 between Hindon & Tisbury. From A303 take Fonthill Bishop exit; go to Fonthill Estate Arch and through estate.

Daniel Brod, Charlie Luxton
& Mark Blatchford
The Beckford Arms,
Fonthill Gifford, Tisbury,
Salisbury SP3 6PX
Tel   +44 (0)1747 870385
Web   www.beckfordarms.com

The Horseshoe Inn
Ebbesbourne Wake

The Ebble Valley and Ebbesbourne Wake have escaped the intrusions of modern-day life, dozing down tiny lanes close to the Dorset border. A bucolic charm pervades the village inn that has been run as a "proper country pub" by the Bath family for over 30 years. Climbing roses cling to the 17th-century brick façade, while the traditional layout of two bars around a central servery still survives. Old farming implements and country bygones fill every available cranny and a mix of rustic furniture is arranged around the crackling winter fire. Beer is tapped straight from the cask and food is hearty and wholesome, prepared by Pat Bath using local meat and vegetables, and game from local shoots. Tuck into steak and kidney pie, fresh fish bake, nursery pud, three roasts on Sundays (do book). Benches and flowers fill the garden.

The Forester Inn
Donhead St Andrew

Tiny lanes frothing with cowparsley twist down to this fine little pub in Donhead St Andrew. The revitalised 600-year-old inn sports rustic walls, black beams, a log fire in the inglenook and planked floors; colours are muted, there's not an ounce of flounce and locals still prop up the bar of a late weekday lunchtime. Foodies come from far for chef Tom Shaw's cooking – rib-eye steak with béarnaise, 'a trio of lamb chops' with bubble-and-squeak, goat's cheese omelette, tomato tarte tatin – and fine puddings cooked to order, slowly. Tom uses local Rushmore venison, Old Spot pork and specialises in fresh Cornish seafood – brill with shellfish bisque and mussels, skate wing with brown butter and capers. There's a pretty garden and terrace with views, three ales on tap, cider from Ashton Press and ten gorgeous wines by the glass.

Meals	12pm-2pm (2.30pm Sun); 7pm-9pm; no food Sun eve or Mon all day. Main courses £9.95-£15; bar meals £4.50-£11.95; Sunday roast £8.50.
Closed	3pm-6.30pm, Sun from 4pm & Mon until 7pm.
Directions	A354 south of Salisbury, right at Coombe Bissett; follow valley road for 8 miles.

Meals	12pm-2pm; 6.30pm-9.30pm. Main courses £10-£25; bar meals £7.50-£11.50; Sunday lunch £14.50.
Closed	3pm-6.30pm & Sun from 4pm.
Directions	A30 between Shaftesbury & Salisbury. Through Ludwell then left for Donhead; pub on right in 1.2 miles.

Anthony & Patricia Bath
The Horseshoe Inn,
The Cross, Ebbesbourne Wake,
Salisbury SP5 5JF
Tel +44 (0)1722 780474

Chris & Lizzie Matthews
The Forester Inn, Lower Street,
Donhead St Andrew,
Shaftesbury SP7 9EE
Tel +44 (0)1747 828038
Web www.theforesterdonheadstandrew.co.uk

The Lamb at Hindon
Hindon

The Lamb has been serving ale on Hindon's high street for 800 years, give or take a decade. It is a yard of England's finest cloth, a place where shooting parties come for lunch, where farmers meet to chew the cud. They come for huge oak settles, heavy old beams, deep red walls and roaring fires. A clipped Georgian country elegance lingers; you almost expect Mr Darcy to walk in, give a tormented sigh, then turn on his heels and vanish. There are flagstone floors and stripped wooden boards, window seats and gilded mirrors; old oils entwined in willow hang on the walls, a bookshelf is stuffed with aged tomes of poetry. At night, candles come out, as do some serious whiskies and the odd Cuban cigar, and in the restaurant you can feast on game terrine, Angus rump, then local cheeses. Bedrooms come with mahogany furniture, the odd four-poster, perhaps a sofa or a tartan carpet. Fishing can be arranged, or you can shoot off to Stonehenge, Stourhead, Salisbury or Bath. Return for a drink on the terrace and watch village life float by.

Rooms	17: 8 doubles, 6 twins/doubles, 2 singles, 1 suite. £99–£145. Singles from £70. Suite £190.
Meals	12.30pm–2.30pm; 6.30pm–9.30pm (7pm–9pm Sun). Main courses £9–£17.95.
Closed	Open all day.
Directions	M3, A303 & signed left at bottom of steep hill two miles east of junction with A350.

Adam Brierly
The Lamb at Hindon, High Street,
Hindon, Salisbury, SP3 6DP
Tel   +44 (0)1747 820573
Web   www.lambathindon.co.uk

Wiltshire

Fox & Hounds
East Knoyle

If you love beech trees and high ridges, make time for a walk with views over the vale before you land at the 17th-century thatched pub on the green. Enter to discover two areas: one bright and conservatory-like, with a great view, the other older and cosier, its fireplace flanked by small red leather sofas. There are warming ales from Youngs and Butcombe, and the inimitable Bishop's Tipple, and a well-presented wine card that tells you exactly what you'll get – which is what you'd expect from a no-nonsense landlord. Being a New Zealander, he cooks in an eclectic, untypical gastro style. Tuck into chorizo, bean and red pepper casserole in red wine with belly pork or sweet onion, ricotta and parmesan tart; follow with vanilla cheesecake… you'll stay till the pub closes, no hardship at all!

Meals	12pm-2.30pm; 6.30pm-9.30pm. Main courses £8.50-£16.
Closed	3pm-6pm.
Directions	Off A303 onto A350 to Blandford then follow signs to pub.

Murray Seator
Fox & Hounds,
The Green, East Knoyle,
Salisbury SP3 6BN
Tel   +44 (0)1747 830573
Web   www.foxandhounds-eastknoyle.co.uk

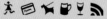

Entry 771 Map 3

Wiltshire

George Hotel
Codford

Boyd McIntosh and Joanne Fryer used to practise their art at the revered Howard's House in Teffont Evias. At the George, Boyd delivers dependable dishes from a compact modern menu: baked plaice with caper, chilli and garlic butter; beef, kidney, mushroom and ale pudding; wild mushroom risotto with basil oil; sandwiches made with home-baked bread. Joanne is a dab hand at front of house, and her influence is stamped over the understatedly contemporary interiors too. Floors are parquet, tiled or pale-carpeted, walls are warmly hued and the furniture is quirky and stylishly simple. The bar has a blond-wood counter, there are lush plants, mirrors and a cosy corner full of deep sofas. The vase of lilies on the bar adds a civilised touch, as do candles on tables. The winter fires are the icing on the cake.

Meals	12pm-2pm; 7pm-9.30pm. Main courses £8.95-£16.95.
Closed	Tues & Sun eves in winter.
Directions	Off A36 between Salisbury & Warminster.

Boyd McIntosh & Joanne Fryer
George Hotel,
High Street, Codford St Peter,
Codford, Warminster BA12 0NG
Tel   +44 (0)1985 850270
Web   www.thegeorgecodford.co.uk

Entry 772 Map 3

Spread Eagle Inn
Stourton

While Stourhead Gardens "echo with references to the heroes and gods of ancient Rome", this proper inn with rooms makes more than a passing nod to Bacchus. Mellow and old-fashioned it may appear but peep inside and you find slate or coir floors, Farrow & Ball colours and lovely jugs of garden flowers on old pine tables. In the bar a wood-burning stove is merry and the seats are comfy; you can eat here or in the restaurant that doubles as a sitting room. Red walls, large modern paintings, old prints, the odd game of scrabble create a mood that is cosy and warm. The higgledy-piggledy stairs are great if you're nimble and the bedrooms are peaceful – expect muted colours, white linen, original fireplaces, delightful views. Bathrooms are plain, not state-of-the-art, and spotless. Food is English and locally supplied: Wiltshire ham with sweet mustard, West Country fish soup, griddled organic salmon salad with anchovy mayonnaise. As for the estate: you can pretend that this stupendous example of a landscape garden with lake and follies is yours when the hordes have gone home (and to residents, entry is free).

Rooms	5: 2 doubles, 3 twins/doubles. £110. Singles £80.	
Meals	12pm-3pm; 7pm-9pm. Main courses £8.50-£16; bar meals from £5.50.	
Closed	Open all day.	
Directions	Turn off B3092 signed Stourhead Gardens. Spread Eagle is below main car park on left at entrance to garden. Private car park for inn.	

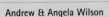

Andrew & Angela Wilson
Spread Eagle Inn,
Church Lawn,
Stourton,
Warminster BA12 6QE
Tel   +44 (0)1747 840587
Web   www.spreadeagleinn.com

Entry 773 Map 3

Wiltshire

The Bath Arms Crockerton
Crockerton

The rambling old pub stands on the Longleat Estate, minutes from Shearwater Lake and woodland walks, and draws an eclectic crowd: ramblers, tourists, foodies. With a culinary background that ranges from country-house hotels to The Ivy, Dean Carr presents a pub menu that's a cut above the norm. So expect wild sea bass with chorizo risotto alongside gammon and poached eggs, and rump steak with rocket pesto alongside shepherd's pie, all with a modern twist. There are classy baguettes too, like steak and horseradish, and nursery favourites like sticky toffee pudding. The setting is homely and traditional, the open-plan bar and dining area displaying beams, brasses and plain pine tables; arrive early to bag a bench by the lovely log fire and a pint of local Crockerton Classic. The bedrooms, just two, 'Left' and 'Right', are a big surprise; both are huge with a contemporary yet sumptuous feel. Be cheered by crisp linen on wooden sleigh beds, leather sofas, vast plasma screens, bold modern paintings and bathrooms combining 'wet room' showers with Gilchrist & Soames. Fabulous.

Rooms	2 doubles. £80–£110.
Meals	12pm-2.30pm; 6.30pm-9pm. Main courses £10.95-£14.95.
Closed	3pm-6pm. Open all day Sat & Sun in summer.
Directions	2 miles south of Warminster off A350 towards Shaftesbury.

	Dean Carr
	The Bath Arms Crockerton, Crockerton, Warminster BA12 8AJ
Tel	+44 (0)1985 212262
Web	www.batharmscrockerton.co.uk

Entry 774 Map 3

Somerset Arms
Maiden Bradley

Logs crackle and fat candles glow in the wood-floored bar, an atmospheric place to quaff a pint of 6X with the locals. The Somerset Arms lies between Longleat and Stourhead on the Duke of Somerset's estate, a Victorian pub that had lain untouched and unloved for 12 years. Former travel writers Lisa and Rachel took over in 2008 and have transformed the place with a mix of sumptuous furnishings and individual touches; now shelves groan with battered old Penguin paperbacks and the owners' Great Dane Henry wanders around, greeting customers with a doleful expression – there's much homely charm. Best of all, Rachel cooks modern British food using local produce, including meat from Stourhead's farm shop nearby, with delicious results – potted Devon crab, venison and redcurrant pie, slow-roast pork belly with cider sauce, pumpkin and pecan tart – all served at scrubbed tables in a rustic-chic dining room. Crisp cotton sheets, trendy motif wallpaper and slate-floored shower rooms add luxury to quirky bedrooms above – this is a brilliant retreat for walkers exploring the area.

Rooms	5 doubles. £85-£105.
Meals	12pm-3pm (3.30pm Sun); 6pm-9.30pm. No food Sun eve. Main courses £9.95-£17.95; set lunch £9.95 & £12.95.
Closed	3pm-6pm. Open all day in summer.
Directions	In village centre on B3092 between A303 at Stourhead & Frome.

Lisa Richards & Rachel Seed
Somerset Arms, Church Street,
Maiden Bradley,
Warminster BA12 7HW
Tel   +44 (0)1985 844207
Web   www.thesomersetarms.co.uk

Entry 775 Map 3

The Bath Arms at Longleat
Horningsham

A 17th-century coaching inn on the Longleat estate in a village lost in the country; geese swim in the river, cows munch the fields. At the front, a dozen pollarded lime trees shade a gravelled garden; at the back, two stone terraces soak up the sun. Inside are the best of old and new: flagstones and boarded floors, a stainless steel bar and Farrow & Ball colours. The feel is smart and airy, with a skittle alley that doubles as a sitting room (they show movies here) and shimmering Cole & Son walls in the dining room. Stop for caramelised onion tart, bavette steak with Lyonnaise potatoes, Pimms granita. They grow veg, keep pigs: produce makes its short way to the kitchen, and young guests may be given a small selection of vegetables to take home. Flashman, English Eccentric, Geisha... each of the bedrooms lives up to its name, some in the main house, others in the barn. The Kama Sutra room is heavily influenced by Lord Bath's own series of murals, and there's a spacious lodge overlooking Longleat House, perfectly private for a couple or a small family. The walk down to Longleat is majestic.

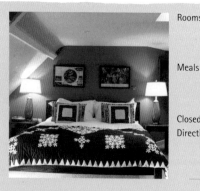

Rooms	15 + 1: 13 doubles, 2 twins. Self-catering lodge for 4. £95–£150. Singles from £85. Half-board from £75 p.p. Lodge £100.
Meals	12pm-2pm (2.30pm Sat & Sun); 7pm-9pm (9.30pm Fri & Sat). Main courses £16–£18; bar meals £4.50-£14.95.
Closed	Open all day.
Directions	A303, then A350 north to Longbridge Deverill. Left for Maiden Bradley; right for Horningsham. Thro' village, on right.

Sara Elston
The Bath Arms at Longleat,
Horningsham,
Warminster BA12 7LY
Tel   +44 (0)1985 844308
Web   www.batharms.co.uk

Wiltshire

The Angel Inn
Upton Scudamore

A blaze of summer colour on the smart, sheltered decked area that faces south west; beams and a huge log burner in the bare-boarded, terracotta-painted bar; sofas and contemporary art in the split-level restaurant. It's a comfortable and sophisticated environment for Tony and Carol Coates' menu and specials board that delivers straightforward modern food. Informality and decent sized portions are among the attractions, the menu changes frequently and the produce is sourced locally. Fish dishes star, in the form of roast halibut with haricot beans and vanilla, and smoked haddock with chive butter. A surprisingly light sticky toffee pudding makes a satisfying finish. There are Wadworth 6X and Butcombe on tap and several wines of the month chalked up on the board by the bar. Round off the treats with a visit to Longleat.

Meals	12pm–2pm; 6.30pm–9.30pm. Main courses £12–£22.
Closed	3pm–6pm.
Directions	Village signed off A350 Warminster to Westbury road & off A36.

Tony & Carol Coates
The Angel Inn,
Upton Scudamore,
Warminster BA12 0AG
Tel   +44 (0)1985 213225
Web   www.theangelinn.co.uk

Entry 777 Map 3

Wiltshire
Worth a visit

778 **Red Lion Inn** Kilmington, Warminster BA12 6RP +44 (0)1985 844263
The four-centuries-old farmhouse has become a quiet, traditional local. Accompany a great-value homemade cottage pie with a pint of Butcombe Bitter and a fabulous view of the South Wiltshire Downs.

779 **The Boot** High Street, Berwick St James, Salisbury SP3 4TN +44 (0)1722 790243
Lush gardens, great Wadworth beers and proper pub food (come for Sunday lunch) draw locals and walkers to this ex-cobbler's in the Wylye Valley.

780 **The Linnet** Great Hinton, Trowbridge BA14 6BU +44 (0)1380 870354
With enthusiasm, dedication and bags of talent, chef-patron Jonathan Furby has turned The Linnet into a cheerful pub-restaurant. Unusual combinations executed with panache, and great-value lunches.

781 **Rising Sun** 32 Bowden Hill, Lacock, Chippenham SN15 2PP +44 (0)1249 730363
Unpretentious stone pub high on a hill above Lacock. Escape the crowds for the terrace and unrivalled views, sup a pint of Moles as hot-air balloons drift across the sky on summer evenings.

782 **The Neeld Arms** The Street, Grittleton, Chippenham SN14 6AP +44 (0)1249 782470
True country boozer with friendly locals, two glowing inglenooks, fresh tasty food, good beers and drinkable wines. Four-poster beds upstairs, breakfast feasts.

Worcestershire

Butcher's Arms
Eldersfield

A small, two-room pub with a lovely big garden (and a cottage for let in the spacious car park!) the splendid Butcher's is still very much a place for regulars popping in for pints of Wye Valley Bitter straight from the cask and Herefordshire cider. It is also fast gaining a reputation for its food, and one of its attractions is a sensibly short menu. James has a hands-on philosophy and cooks single-handedly for just 18 covers a time, while Elizabeth does friendly front of house. He used to work with Alastair Little and his gutsy British dishes use local produce from named suppliers. Be adventurous and tuck into that traditional English delicacy Bath chap, served with potato scone and grain mustard, or loin and shoulder of lamb with braised lentils and leek and bacon mash. A great little place for some 'nose to tail' dining.

Worcestershire

The Live & Let Live
Bringsty Common

Well off the beaten track and reached down a stone road this 300-year-old thatched pub sits in splendid isolation. It was rescued by owner Sue Dovey after it had lain closed and unloved for 11 years; she spent an age restoring it, and restoring it beautifully – even the thatch is new. The single-room bar is a refuge for locals and walkers and is quaint with pale gnarled beams, flagstones, dusky pink walls, stoneware bottles and a wonderfully big fireplace. Upstairs is a dear little restaurant open at weekends. On sunny days, outside is best – a pretty little garden with superb views of the ancient common. Wherever you perch you can tuck into delicious beer, cider and perry from nearby, and good grub – Bringsty lamb chops, sausages from down the road, and, more surprisingly, Hungarian goulash: the sous chef is Hungarian.

Meals	12pm-1pm; 7pm-8.45pm; no food Sun eve & Tues lunch. Main courses £14.50-£18.50.
Closed	2.30pm-7pm & all day Mon.
Directions	From Tewkesbury, A438 west towards Ledbury; left on B4211 & follow signs for Eldersfield & Lime Street.

Meals	12pm-2pm (2.30pm Sat; 3pm Sun); 6.30pm-9pm. Main courses £6.75-£9.75 (lunch), £9.50-£20 (dinner).
Closed	2.30pm-5pm & Mon (except bank hols). Open all day Fri-Sun.
Directions	Bringsty Common is signposted off A44 between Knightwick and Bromyard. Look for cat and mouse on pub sign.

James & Elizabeth Winter
Butcher's Arms,
Lime Street,
Eldersfield, Gloucester GL19 4NX
Tel   +44 (0)1452 840381
Web   www.thebutchersarms.net

Entry 783 Map 8

Sue Dovey
The Live & Let Live,
Bringsty Common,
Bringsty WR6 5UW
Tel   +44 (0)1886 821462
Web   www.liveandletlive-bringsty.co.uk

Entry 784 Map 8

Worcestershire

The Talbot
Knightwick

It's run by two sisters, Annie and Wiz, chef-owners with a dedication to all things self-sufficient. Hops for their micro-brewed beers are grown here; organic produce comes from the farmers' market they host the second Sunday of every month. Their infectious commitment to using fresh local food pulls a crowd; the crab bisque, raised pies and spotted dick are legendary. Fresh fish comes from Cornwall and scallop beignets are wrapped in nori seaweed (not local, but delicious). The pot-roast lamb recipe is from Alnwick Castle in Northumberland, and the wild duck – drizzled with meat juices, a little grand marnier and served over mashed potato – suggests a touch of genius. Out of the way, on the bank of the Teme (you may fish with a permit): a superb place, well-run, and with a fire in the comfortable bar.

Worcestershire

The Chequers
Cutnall Green

On the site of an ancient coaching inn, The Chequers was rebuilt 70 years ago. You'd never know: its open fires, comfy sofas and snug little booths have evolved as smoothly as its menu. While the thirsty gather round the church-panel bar with pints of Timothy Taylor's, the hungry head for the dining room – cosy and candlelit with deep red walls, pale exposed beams and a huge display of wines. Make the most of a vibrant 'mod Brit' menu from award-winning chef Roger Narbett: the food bursts with flavour. There's potted duck confit with apricot chutney, roasted Cornish cod with leeks and cheddar mash, and mango syrup and coconut ice pavlova. And if the liqueur coffees catch your fancy, slip off and savour one in the Garden Room, whose sleek, striped, coffee-coloured curtains resemble an upside-down cappuccino.

Meals	12pm-2pm; 6.30pm-9pm (7pm-9pm Sun). Main courses £10-£20; bar meals £5-£16.
Closed	Open all day.
Directions	From Worcester A44 for Leominster; 8 miles on, through Cotheridge & Broadwas; right on B4197; on left.

Meals	12pm-2pm; 6.30pm-9.15pm (9.30pm Fri & Sat); Sun 12pm-2.30pm; 6.30pm-9pm. Main courses £8.95-£15.25; bar meals £4.25-£8.75.
Closed	3pm-6pm (3.30pm-6pm Sun).
Directions	3 miles north of Droitwich Spa on A442 towards Kidderminster. M5 exit 5.

	Annie Clift
	The Talbot,
	Bromyard Road, Knightwick,
	Worcester WR6 5PH
Tel	+44 (0)1886 821235
Web	www.the-talbot.co.uk

Entry 785 Map 8

	Roger & Jo Narbett
	The Chequers,
	Kidderminster Road, Cutnall Green,
	Droitwich WR9 0PJ
Tel	+44 (0)1299 851292
Web	www.chequerscutnallgreen.co.uk

Entry 786 Map 8

Worcestershire

Colliers Arms
Clows Top

Stocking up on local, seasonal food is easy here – they just nip into the garden. This pretty patch of Worcestershire countryside provides so much for the busy pub kitchen; even hazelnuts and artichokes are close to hand. There's still plenty of outdoor space for visitors too, with a pretty south-facing terrace and beer garden providing glorious views. Feast your eyes on Rock Church (largest Norman church in England), the local gallop – or just your plate. They aim high in this friendly yet unassuming place – all is pristine and traditional inside – and it works. Try aspirational stuff such as scallops, crab and chilli risotto or stick to fish and chips or beef stroganoff: it's all great. There are a couple of good cask ales to go with it – or even a local white wine (Astley Vineyard) if you fancy. A real find.

Meals	12pm-2pm (3pm Sun); 6.30pm-9pm (9.30pm Sat). No food Sun eve. Main courses £8.95-£15.95; set menu £10.95 & £13.50.
Closed	3pm-6pm & from 5pm Sun. Open all day Sat.
Directions	Beside A456 between Kidderminster & Tenbury Wells.

Michael Claydon
Colliers Arms,
Tenbury Road, Clows Top,
Kidderminster DY14 9HA
Tel   +44 (0)1299 832242
Web   www.colliersarms.com

Entry 787 Map 8

Worcestershire

Bell & Cross Inn
Clent

No cavernous interior here but a network of small, cosy rooms that reveal not just the roots of this 19th-century pub but the determination of its successive owners to maintain its integrity. And those cosy rooms decked in smart modern hues are usually full of happy diners; try excellent grilled sea bass with prawns and rocket or a lightly tweaked 'pub classic', faggots with cheese mash. Owner Roger Narbett – busy now at his other pub, The Chequers – is chef to the England football team and footie memorabilia decorates the corridors. Wife Jo runs a brisk yet friendly service; co-owner Paul Mohan is the classically trained chef. It's still a place for the locals though, and they crowd into the snug bar with its four real ales and open fire. At the foot of the Clent hills yet close to Birmingham – and a nice big garden and patio, too.

Meals	12pm-2pm; 6.30pm-9pm (9.30pm Sat); 12pm-7pm Sun. Main courses £8.50-£15.50; Sunday roast £13.50.
Closed	3pm-6pm. Open all day Sun.
Directions	Off A491 south-east of Hagley.

Roger & Jo Narbett
Bell & Cross Inn,
Bromsgrove Road,
Clent, Stourbridge DY9 9QL
Tel   +44 (0)1562 730319
Web   www.bellandcrossclent.co.uk

Entry 788 Map 8

Worcestershire

Nag's Head
Malvern

No beauty competition winner perhaps, but this low-slung white pub, converted from what was once a row of cottages, and with a timber-clad restaurant that was once a boxing gym, is worth seeking out. Tucked away in the side streets of lovely Malvern is a paradise for fans of whisky or real ale (fans of both tipples may have to be stretcher'd off). There are 25 single malts on offer and 18 beers, three of which are made at the pub's own brewery at Callow End. No wonder the homely bar with its deep-pink walls and living-room feel gets packed. This is a pub's pub. Stick to the bric-a-brac-strewn dining room for food, where ambitious restaurant-style fare (homemade chicken liver pâté, whole lemon sole) is proffered, and let the serious drinkers hog the bar. A great find.

Many backstreet boozers have been transformed, the fruit machines and beer-stained carpet being replaced by chalked-up menus and chunky tables. In the countryside, too, old-fashioned locals are being rejuvenated by landlords and chefs who believe that gastronomy is rooted in the soil and that food should be fresh, seasonal and sourced from the best local suppliers.

Meals	12pm–2pm; 6.30pm-8.30pm. Main courses £10.50-£17.50.
Closed	Open all day.
Directions	At the bottom of Bank Street.

Claire Willetts
Nag's Head,
Bank Street,
Malvern WR14 2JG
Tel   +44 (0)1684 574373

Entry 789 Map 8

The Fleece
Bretforton

"No potato crisps to be sold in the bar." So ordered Lola Taplin when The Fleece was bequeathed to the National Trust after 500 years in her family. It's the sort of tradition that thrives in the Pewter Room where you pitch up for fresh local food, ales from Uley and Fleece Folly cider. Local sausages with red onion marmalade and red wine gravy and locally culled rhubarb in pies and crumbles may tempt you but there is so much more: the Asparagus Festival commences in the courtyard of The Fleece with an auction on the last Sunday in May, summer festivals twirl with Morris dancers and the original farmyard is a gorgeous setting for hog roasts and live theatre. The black-and-white timbered building is as stuffed as a museum with historical artefacts, stone flagged floors, big log fires, ancient beams and a wonderful collection of pewter. The timbered bedroom, in the oldest part of the building, is small but perfectly formed, with seagrass flooring, oak panelling, antique mahogany bed and spotless bathroom. Leave the 21st century behind — by about half a millennium. Book the ancient barn for a wedding.

Rooms	1 double. £95.
Meals	12pm-2.30pm (4pm Sun); 6.30pm-9pm (8.30pm Sun). Main courses £7-£13.95; bar meals from £4.50.
Closed	3pm-6pm. Open all day Fri-Sun & every day June-Sep.
Directions	B4035 from Evesham for Chipping Campden. In Bretforton bear right into village. Opp. church in square.

Nigel Smith
The Fleece,
The Cross, Bretforton,
Evesham WR11 7JE
Tel   +44 (0)1386 831173
Web   www.thefleeceinn.co.uk

Worcestershire

Worth a visit

791 Royal Oak Kinnersley, Severn Stoke,
Worcester WR8 9JR +44 (0)1905 371482
New owners for the smart Royal Oak,
popular for its unassuming bar, pretty
little candle-dotted restaurant, real ales,
local ciders and heart-warming food.
Josephine Palmer is chef and co-owner
with husband Ben. Reports please.

792 The Monkey House Defford,
Upton-on-Severn WR8 9BW
+44 (0)1386 750234
One of the last four cider houses in
England – a curiosity. No signs guide you
to the thatched house set back from the
road but the locals will. Try Westons First
Quality or Woodmancote Dry cider
served through the hatch, and sit outside;
there's a shed if the weather's bad.

793 The Swan Worcester Road, Hanley Swan,
Worcester WR8 0EA +44 (0)1684 311870
Worth noting if heading for the Malvern
Hills – a smartly revamped local
overlooking the village green and pond.
Contemporary layout and décor, three
ales on tap and modern pub food.

794 Crown & Sandys Arms Main Road,
Ombersley WR9 0EW +44 (0)1905 620252
Richard Everton has revamped his grand
old coaching inn in beautiful Ombersley.
Ancient blends seamlessly with new in
rambling bars and dining areas. There's
an orangery, a smart patio, interesting
food and seven swish bedrooms.

795 Plough & Harrow Rhydd Road, Guarlford,
Malvern WR13 6NY +44 (0)1684 310453
Nice buzzy atmosphere and impressive
upmarket menus with an emphasis on
home-grown and local produce, in this
rambling 18th-century pub in the wilds
outside Malvern.

Yorkshire

The Cricket Inn
Totley

'Children, dogs, muddy boots welcome!' is
the legend over the door of this old stone
pub, next to the cricket pitch in a leafy
Sheffield suburb; the feel is rural. Local
restaurateurs Richard and Victoria Smith
have joined forces with Thornbridge Brewery
to create a laid-back, welcoming pub with
stone floors, tongue-and-groove walls, open
fires and wholesome, value-for-money food
flowing from Jack Baker's kitchen. Crispy
breadcrumbed belly pork with black
pudding mash, sweet and sour cabbage and
sage and scrumpy reduction is a signature
dish – along with steamed 'snake and pigmy'
pudding, roast carrots and creamy mash.
After a walk in the woods, pop in here,
put up your feet by the fire and pick up the
paper and a pint of specially brewed Jaipur.
Or take a ringside seat by the pitch in
summer. Marvellous.

Meals	12pm-2.30pm; 5pm-9pm. 12pm-9.30pm Sat; 12pm-8pm Sun. Main courses £10-£19; sandwiches from £5; Sunday lunch £12-£16.
Closed	Open all day.
Directions	On A621 south from Sheffield; in Totley take Hillfoot Road; left into Penny Lane; pub on right.

	Richard Smith The Cricket Inn, Penny Lane, Totley, Sheffield S17 3AZ
Tel	+44 (0)114 236 5256
Web	www.cricketinn.co.uk

Entry 796 Map 8

Yorkshire

King's Arms
Heath

Enter Heath and step back years. A string of wool merchants' houses, 100 acres of heathland, a couple of tethered ponies... who'd guess Wakefield was down the road? In the heart of Yorkshire's most unspoilt village is the equally unspoiled King's Arms. In a dark, rich network of tap rooms and snugs, softly hissing gas lamps cast an amber glow on oak-panelled walls, yellowed ceilings and low beams, while a magnificent Yorkshire range is the best of several open coal fires. It's no museum – just a superbly old-fashioned pub that serves Clarks Classic Blond, and Stella for non-believers. Traditional pub grub includes filled Yorkshire puddings and beef and ale pie. Attached is a serviceable restaurant, at the back is a conservatory that breaks the spell. The gardens have gentle moorland views.

Meals	12pm-2pm; 7pm-9pm (12pm-5pm Sun); no food Sun eve. Main courses £5.95-£9.95.
Closed	3pm-5pm in winter. Open all day weekends and in summer.
Directions	Heath signed off A655.

Andrew & Renata Shepherd
King's Arms,
Heath,
Wakefield WF1 5SL
Tel +44 (0)1924 377527

Entry 797 Map 12

Yorkshire

Butchers Arms
Hepworth

From the top of the hill in Hepworth you can almost see Norah Batty's wrinkled stockings in Holmfirth – this is the land of *Last of the Summer Wine*. But there's nothing quaint about Tim Bilton's refurbished pub on the windswept moors; he trained with Raymond Blanc, then ran the immensely popular Bibis in Leeds. Step into an interior of stone floors, beams and log fires – and if you think this is a typical Pennine boozer, just take a look at the menu, rooted in Yorkshire simplicity. Not only is there pot roast pheasant with braised red cabbage, air-dried bacon and pear purée but 'plate of pig' too: milk-fed belly of suckling pig cooked with its own sausage toad-in-the-hole style, and a pan-seared pork fillet with windfall apple sauce. You can bring the dog, sup a pint of well-kept Timothy Taylor's, read the papers.

Meals	12pm-2.30pm; 6pm-10pm; 12pm-6pm Sun. Main courses £13.95-£17.95; set menu £12.50 & £15.50.
Closed	Mon lunch.
Directions	7.5 miles south of Huddersfield;; off A616 Sheffiled Road.

Tim Bilton
Butchers Arms,
38 Towngate,
Hepworth, Holmfirth HD9 1TF
Tel +44 (0)1484 682361
Web www.thebutchersarmshepworth.co.uk

Entry 798 Map 12

Yorkshire

Three Acres

Shelley

A dining pub par excellence where everything ticks over beautifully. The bar is a work of art, brimful of bottles, pumps, flowers and old fishing reels and tackle hanging picturesquely above. Seating is comfy pub style, and there's a large solid fuel stove to warm the central space. Separate areas around the bar have a sea of tables set for dining (white linen, shining glasses); one area specialises in seafood. The overall feel is roomy yet intimate and hugely inviting, with plants, mirrors, old prints, a baby grand. Food is pricey, but the interesting menu lists dressed crab, roast grouse with game jus, steak, kidney and mushroom pie, and a hot seafood platter. There's also a private dining room. Well-kept beers on pump, scores of fine wines, over 50 whiskies, great sandwiches. Lovely.

Meals	12pm-2pm; 6.30pm-9.30pm. Main courses £15.95-£25.95; bar meals from £8.95; sandwiches from £5.95; Sunday lunch (3 courses) £25.95.
Closed	3pm-6pm.
Directions	5 miles SE of Huddersfield & off A629; signs for Kirburton on B6116; signs for Emley Moor Mast; 0.5 miles south of mast, on minor road above Shelley.

Neil Truelove & Brian Orme
Three Acres,
37-41 Roydhouse,
Shelley, Huddersfield HD8 8LR
Tel   +44 (0)1484 602606
Web   www.3acres.com

Entry 799 Map 12

Yorkshire

The Sair Inn

Linthwaite

Clinging to the side of the valley, The Sair oozes character with a warren of small rooms. Floors of rippling flagstone and scuffed boards carry tables, pews and chairs from The Ark. Massive winter fires ensure that Vulcan would feel at home; Pandora would be delighted by the artefacts and oddments. It's a Yorkshire treasure, enhanced by locals and traditional pub games; in the old pub Joanna allows impromptu entertainment, side rooms allow escape from the hubbub. Beers? – to die for, created in the brewhouse behind the pub; any or all of eight and more. Patrons flock from afar to soak up the atmosphere of this iconic idyll, so concerns about catering are the last thing on anyone's mind. It's uncompromising, not one for shrinking violets, 'grand' in the Wallace and Grommit sense, brilliant value and welcoming to all.

Meals	No meals served.
Closed	Mon-Fri lunch. Open all day Sat & Sun.
Directions	Off A62 in Linthwaite; up Hoyle Ing (past oil tanks painted with sheep; turn opposite); 400 yds up steep hill.

Ron Crabtree
The Sair Inn,
139 Lane Top,
Linthwaite,
Huddersfield HD7 5SG
Tel   +44 (0)1484 842370

Entry 800 Map 12

Yorkshire

The Old Bridge Inn
Ripponden

An ancient packhorse bridge and a little low inn… such is the setting. Family involvement over several decades has resulted in a thoroughly civilised, unspoilt little local; a friendly one, too. Three carpeted, oak-panelled, split-level rooms – suitably dimly lit – are furnished with old oak settles and rush-seated chairs. The small, green-walled snug at the top is atmospheric; the bar has a lofty ceiling with exposed timbers and a huge fireplace with log-burning stove; the lower room is good for dining. The buffet lunches are as popular as ever, while the evening menu announces sound English cooking (lamb shank with rosemary and red wine, sticky toffee pudding) featuring local produce and a modern slant. The bar is well used by local folk who come for Timothy Taylor's Best Bitter, Landlord and Golden Best; wines are good too.

Yorkshire

The Millbank
Mill Bank

Savour a pint and a rolling moorland view. The Millbank, clinging to the side of a steep hill, has a stripped-down, architect-scripted interior that combines flagstones and log fires with modern paintings and bold colours. Its friendly cosmopolitan style is echoed in the food, prepared by Chez Nico-trained Glenn Futter, who creates daily wonders with fresh local produce. There might be venison with roast beetroot and cumin sauce or haddock with chive sauce and tomato chutney. And then there are the spoiling puddings, the fine Yorkshire cheeses, the Yorkshire ales (Timothy Taylor's Landlord for one), the excellent wines, the malt whiskies and the first-class sandwiches in the bar. The steeply terraced garden has lead planters fashionably stuffed with box topiary and bamboo – and those views.

Meals	12pm-2pm; 6.30pm-9.30pm; no food Sat or Sun eve. Main courses £8.50-£12.50.	
Closed	3pm-5.30pm (5pm Fri). Open all day Sat & Sun.	
Directions	4 miles from junc. 22 M62 in Ripponden.	

Meals	12pm-2.30pm (4.30pm Sun); 6pm-9.30pm (10pm Fri & Sat; 8pm Sun). Main courses £9.95-£18.95; set menu, 2 courses, £13.95; sandwiches from £4.95.
Closed	3pm-5.30pm & Mon. Open all day Sun.
Directions	Off A58 between Sowerby Bridge & Ripponden.

Tim & Lindsay Eaton Walker
The Old Bridge Inn,
Ripponden,
Sowerby Bridge HX6 4DF
Tel +44 (0)1422 822595
Web www.porkpieclub.com

Entry 801 Map 12

Glenn Futter
The Millbank,
Mill Bank Road, Mill Bank,
Sowerby Bridge HX6 3DY
Tel +44 (0)1422 825588
Web www.themillbank.com

Entry 802 Map 12

Alma Inn & Fresco Italian Restaurant
Sowerby Bridge

High on the heather-clad moors this old boozer has a few surprises up its sleeve. The stone paved terrace is large and lovely and the bar is welcoming and warm – all flagged floors, stone walls, glowing fires, pine tables, old settles. Timothy Taylor's Golden Best and Landlord are on tap, along with 75 Belgian beers. Most surprising of all: the food is Italian, and fabulous. Vegetables come from the market, local meat is brought in on the bone and every last bit used in stocks and gravy. So tuck into *gamberoni all'aglio e burro* – that's prawns in garlic butter – or fillet steak, monkfish with pancetta, partridge with Parma ham, and big thin-crust pizzas from a wood-burning oven. Eat in the bar or in the fresh airy dining room, with its chunky chairs and open kitchen.

Travellers Rest
Sowerby Bridge

Beams, flagged floors and a huge open fire with cask ales and champagne cocktails: the integrity of this windswept moor-top pub has not been compromised. Old oak settles have faux fur throws and there's original art work on the stone walls; the bar is a cosy and cheery space. The recently revamped dining room is reborn as a chic bistro, with limed oak tables, leather chairs and a baby grand for the weekend. Chef/patron Mark Lilley has created a thoroughly modern menu that includes goat's cheese and lavender bruschetta, and duck confit with onion and berry marmalade. Mains are unpretentious – sea bass with braised fennel and star anise jus; chicken, lentil and chorizo casserole. Puddings are similarly hearty and homemade, and co-owner Caroline does front of house with charm and panache. It's a gem of a place where you'd least expect to find one.

Meals	12pm-9.30pm (10.30pm Fri & Sat). Main courses £7.95-£15.95.
Closed	Open all day.
Directions	A58 at Triangle Inn signed Cottonstones/Millbank - pub 1.5 miles from Triangle.

Meals	5pm-9.30pm Tues-Fri; 12pm-2pm & 5.30pm-9.30pm Sat; 12pm-7pm Sun. Main courses £10-£22; bar meals £10.
Closed	Mon all day, Tues-Fri lunch & 2.30pm-5.30pm Sat. Open until 7pm Sun.
Directions	West of Sowerby Bridge on A672; 5 miles west of Halifax. Signed.

David Giffen
Alma Inn & Fresco Italian Restaurant,
Four Lane Ends,
Sowerby Bridge HX6 4NS
Tel   +44 (0)1422 823334
Web   www.almainn.com

Caroline Lumley
Travellers Rest,
Steep Lane,
Sowerby Bridge HX6 1PE
Tel   +44 (0)1422 832124
Web   www.travellersrestsowerby.co.uk

Entry 803 Map 12

Entry 804 Map 12

Yorkshire

The Lord Nelson
Luddenden

Another hidden gem? Sitting squarely opposite a 400-year-old churchyard and a gurgling beck, this curious 17th-century pub was once a meeting place for artists and writers, including Branwell Brönte who worked as a clerk nearby. The interior hasn't changed much since his patronage: thick stone sills and mullion windows, old oak floors, open fire, ancient beams. Timothy Taylor's Landlord, Golden Best and IPA Green King are on tap today and there's no food other than snacks (and old-fashioned sweets) though plans are afoot to cater. Outside are two stunning levels of garden with plants spilling from every surface and basket; by the back door is a secluded flagged yard, and a narrow path opening onto a bark-covered area with wooden tables and deckchairs. Views swoop over the village to the hills.

Yorkshire

The Pack Horse
Widdop

This old whitewashed inn sags beneath weathered gritstone tiles in a gloriously remote spot. Once, water engineers had a whale of a time constructing reservoirs to slake the thirst of the local textile industry – the pub's stone walls sport old plans and photos of their endeavours. Today's thirsts are those of ramblers on the Pennine Way and riders on the Pennine Bridleway, which briefly meet right behind the pub. Four or five real ales to enjoy alongside whopping portions of crispy roast duck, rack of lamb and a whole side of grilled plaice ensure this is a popular spot. Two thickly beamed rooms off a passageway bar, with cavernous log fires, horsey ephemera and a comfy rag-tag of furnishings, invite you to unwind over a drink; this is a great pub with grand food, not a dining pub with good beer.

Meals	No food served.
Closed	Mon-Fri from 4pm. Open all day Sat & Sun.
Directions	A646 from Halifax towards Hebden Bridge; right signed Booth & Luddenden. Turn right down High Street, then left at fork; pub over bridge on left.

Meals	12pm-2pm; 7pm-9pm (9.30pm Fri; 10pm Sat). 12pm-8.30pm Sun. Main courses £5.95-£12.95.
Closed	Mon (except bank hols); weekday lunch Oct-Easter. Open all day Sun.
Directions	From A646 in Hebden Bridge take the road at the Fox & Goose, signed for Heptonstall & Slack. In Slack fork right for Widdop.

Debbie Collinge
The Lord Nelson,
15 High Street, Luddenden,
Halifax HX2 6PX
Tel +44 (0)1422 882176

Entry 805 Map 12

Andrew Hollinrake
The Pack Horse,
Widdop,
Hebden Bridge HX7 7AT
Tel +44 (0)1422 842803

Entry 806 Map 12

Shibden Mill Inn
Shibden

There's still a pubby feel to this rambling old inn – although it's known for its restaurant. Shibden Bitter, Theakstons and three rotating bitters keep beer drinkers happy in front of several open fires, the deep green valley setting within sound of the mill stream makes for idyllic summer drinking and the wine list is very impressive. An unstuffy integrity lies behind this venture, from the front-of-house warmth – the staff really are lovely – to the modern British kitchen from which delicious dishes flow: game pudding with tarragon jus; fish pie; confit pork belly with braised cheek, red cabbage and cider sauce; sticky toffee pudding (what better to come home to after a brisk valley walk?). There are cosy gate-leg tables and sofas in the bars, crisp white napery and candelabra in the restaurant, and most of the fruit and vegetables come from local suppliers; this is a special place to which people return. As for the bedrooms, all of which have been recently renovated, they are carpeted, comfortable, individual and equipped with everything. The Pink Room and the suite are huge fun.

Rooms	11 doubles/singles/suites. £90–£133. Singles £72–£90.
Meals	12pm–2pm; 6pm–9.30pm (12pm–7.30pm Sun). Main courses £9.95–£17.95; sandwiches from £5.45; Sunday roast £12.25.
Closed	2.30pm–5.30pm. Open all day Sat & Sun.
Directions	Off A58 Halifax to Leeds, near A6036 junction.

Simon Heaton
Shibden Mill Inn,
Shibden Mill Fold,
Shibden, Halifax HX3 7UL
Tel   +44 (0)1422 365840
Web   www.shibdenmillinn.com

Entry 807 Map 12

Yorkshire

The Old White Beare
Norwood Geen

Originally a farmhouse on the packhorse track, this handsome whitewashed pub in a pretty Pennine village was rebuilt following a fire in 1593 – using timbers from one of the 'Great Ships' in the Elizabeth I's fleet. Fast forward a few hundred years and the comfort quotient has improved! The place is instantly inviting, with its flagged floors, glowing oak settles and a roaring fire in the ancient snug, lovely in winter when Jack Frost is nipping at your nose; the beamed dining room bedecked with nautical ephemera is slightly more formal. Ales include Timothy Taylor's and Thwaites and the wine list is thorough, with lots by the glass. Homemade steak and ale pie vies with rack of three-Dales lamb and Lishman's black pudding in the food stakes; jam roly poly with crème anglais and apple tarte tatin bring up the rear.

Yorkshire

The Chequers Inn
Ledsham

Fires glow, horse brasses gleam... this honey-stone village inn could be in the Dales. In fact, you're a couple of miles from the A1. The panelled, carpeted rooms radiating off the central bar are cosy with log fires and plush red upholstery; faded sepia photographs are a reminder of an earlier age. Rare handpumped ales from the Brown Cow Brewery at Selby do justice to good English food of Yorkshire proportions: steaming platefuls of shin of venison and red cabbage, roast corn-fed chicken breast on a lentil bed... and just when you think you're replete, along comes a treacle sponge pudding. The pub has been welcoming travellers since the 18th century and still closes on Sundays; the tradition started in 1832 when the lady of Ledsham Hall, confronting a drunken farmer on her way to church, insisted they close on the Sabbath.

Meals	12pm-9pm (10pm Fri & Sat). Main courses £8.95-£18.50; sandwiches from £5.25.
Closed	Open all day.
Directions	M62 junc 26, take A58 towards Halifax, 3 miles to Norwood vllage.

Meals	12pm-9pm. Main courses £4.95-£19.95.
Closed	Sun.
Directions	From A1(M) at junc. 42, follow A63 Leeds to Selby road. Turn left & follow signs for Ledsham, 1 mile.

Andrew Krawec & Chris Blood
The Old White Beare,
Village Street, Norwood Geen,
Halifax HX3 8QG
Tel   +44 (0)1274 676645
Web   www.oldwhitebeare.com

Entry 808 Map 12

Chris Wraith
The Chequers Inn,
Claypit Lane, Ledsham,
Leeds LS25 5LP
Tel   +44 (0)1977 683135
Web   www.thechequersinn.com

Entry 809 Map 12

The Tempest Arms
Elslack

A 16th-century ale house with great prices, friendly staff and an easy style. Inside you find stone walls and old beams, settles and plump cushions, Yorkshire ales on tap and a smart beamed restaurant. An airy open-plan feel runs throughout with sofas and armchairs strategically placed in front of a fire that burns on both sides. Delicious traditional food is a big draw – the inn was packed for lunch on a Tuesday in April. You can eat wherever you want, so grab a seat and dig into Yorkshire puddings with a rich onion gravy, raised pork pie with homemade piccalilli, treacle tart with pink grapefruit sorbet. Bedrooms are just as good. Those in the main house are slightly simpler, but most are ten paces beyond in two newly built stone houses: rather swish with private terraces or balconies overlooking a babbling stream. They have hand-crafted furniture and L'Occitane toiletries, slate bathrooms and flat-screen TVs; a couple have decks with hot tubs to soak in and those at the back have views of the fells. Walkers pile in: the Dales are on the doorstep.

Rooms	21: 9 twins/doubles, 12 suites. £80. Suites £100–£140. Singles from £60.
Meals	12pm–2.30pm; 6pm–9pm (9.30pm Sat); 12pm–7.30pm Sun. Main courses £8.95–£15.95; bar meals from £5.95.
Closed	Open all day.
Directions	A56 west from Skipton. Signed left after two miles.

Martin & Veronica Clarkson
The Tempest Arms,
Elslack,
Skipton BD23 3AY

| Tel | +44 (0)1282 842450 |
| Web | www.tempestarms.co.uk |

The Wheatley Arms
Ben Rhydding

New life has been breathed into this fine old stone inn – and how! Oak floors, open fires, comfortable chairs... and it feels as if it's been like this for years. A labyrinth of rooms are linked by a vivid décor; bold textiles, original prints, clusters of mini-collections – something interesting at every turn. A wide range of well-kept ale will please the beer lovers, whilst a confident menu should please the rest. Carpaccio of tuna with pickled baby corn, pomegranate and balsamic reduction makes a robust start, followed by scampi in a basket (yes, it's back!). Puddings are impossible to resist; the pineapple tarte tatin with coconut and cardamon ice cream was divine. The same flair and care has been lavished on 12 sumptuous bedrooms, some with private roof terraces and wet rooms. All have luxurious beds, funky furniture, fabulous fabrics and high-spec audio technology. Statement wallpapers – a different one for each room – continue the film-set vibe. Bathrooms match the glamour: marble tiles, huge white vintage sinks. Refreshingly unpompous. Prepare to be wowed.

Rooms	12 doubles/twins. £89.99-£130. Singles from £79.99.
Meals	12pm-2.30pm (4pm Sun); 5.30pm-9pm (6pm-8.30pm). Main courses £9.95-£17.95; sandwiches from £5.95; set lunch/dinner, 2 courses, £9.95 (Mon-Thurs).
Closed	Open all day.
Directions	A65 from Leeds to Ilkley, left onto Wheatley Lane to Ben Rhydding.

Martin & Veronica Clarkson
The Wheatley Arms,
Wheatley Lane,
Ben Rhydding, Ilkley LS29 8PP
Tel   +44 (0)1943 816496
Web   www.wheatleyarms.co.uk

Ilkley Moor Vaults
Ilkley

A stone's throw from the centre of genteel, elegant, bustling Ilkley town is an establishment known for years as 'the Taps'. Though Joe McDermott and his loyal team have spruced it up you can still whet your whistle with a good pint of local ale; but there's so much more to enjoy. Joining the stone flagged floors, the scrubbed pine tables and the crackling fires are kitschy standard lamps with tasselled shades and a menu that promises robust dishes with a twist — and delivers. Out back is a smoker and kitchen garden, so air miles don't exist. Homemade smoked sausage, pickled peppers and mustard made a gorgeous starter plate, served with a slice of the sublime sourdough bread that Joe's wife Elizabeth makes daily; rhubarb and buttermilk pudding creates a silky-smooth finale. The vibe is young but completely inclusive. Don't hesitate, just go.

Pubs are also becoming more flexible as far as Sundays go, with many serving roasts up to 4pm – or later. What nicer than a lie-in and a late breakfast, a blustery walk and a slap-up lunch?

Meals	12pm-2.30pm (3pm Sat; 7pm Sun); 6pm-9pm (9.30pm Fri & Sat). Main courses £8.90-£15.50; bar lunches £4.50-£9.90; Sunday roast £9.90.
Closed	3pm-5pm & Mon all day. Open all day Sat & Sun.
Directions	Just off A65 towards Skipton; 5 mins walk from the town centre.

Joe McDermott
Ilkley Moor Vaults,
Stockeld Road,
Ilkley LS29 9HD

Tel   +44 (0)1943 607012
Web   www.ilkleymoorvaults.co.uk

Entry 812 Map

Yorkshire

The Fleece
Addingham

A gorgeous place run with flair and passion. The surroundings provide atmosphere, the licensees add something special, and the food is good. Bags of character comes from big open fires, solid tables and old settles, flagged floors, beamed ceilings, exposed stone. It's a big space that at peak times gets packed; in summer, the paved terrace handles the overflow. Chris Monkman has brought a refreshing enthusiasm for local, seasonal, rustic cuisine: Wharfedale lamb, roast partridge, confit duck, seafood chowder, and a delicious warm and sticky treacle tart. Even the children's menu is brilliant: home-battered fish, moules marinières. There's masses of choice and it's pretty good value. You're in glorious walking country, so enjoy the good tucker and a pint of Yorkshire ale after a yomp across the Dales.

Meals	12pm-2.15pm; 6pm-9.15pm (12pm-8pm Sun). Main courses £8.95-£17.
Closed	Open all day.
Directions	2 miles north of Ilkley on A65.

Chris Monkman
The Fleece,
152-154 Main
Street, Addingham, Ilkley LS29 0LY
Tel +44 (0)1943 830491
Web www.thefleeceaddingham.co.uk

Entry 813 Map 12

Yorkshire

Craven Arms
Appletreewick

Authentically restored, this ancient rustic, creeper-clad pub (built in 1548) stands among gorgeous hills overlooking Wharfedale. It's a favourite with walkers so you could end up chin-wagging with them alongside the glowing cast-iron range in the classic stone-flagged bar. Just plain settles, panelled walls, thick beams, nothing more; beyond, a snug with simple benches and valley views, and a homely dining room. The final treat are the Wharfedale ales — Folly Gold, Executioner. Head out back to the loo to take a peek at the amazing function room housed in a replica medieval barn; back in the bar, free of music and flashing games, there are hot sandwiches to be tucked into, and the legendary slow-roasted and minted lamb shoulder. Just the job after a blustery hike or cycle ride across the moors.

Meals	12pm-2pm (2.30pm Fri-Sun); 6.30pm-9pm (8.30pm Sun). Main courses £8.95-£15.25; bar meals £7.50-£10.50.
Closed	3pm-6pm (Mon & Tues). Open all day Wed-Sun.
Directions	A59 Skipton to Leeds; B6160 at Bolton Abbey towards Grassington; Appletreewick signed right.

Mark Cooper
Craven Arms,
Appletreewick,
Skipton BD23 6DA
Tel +44 (0)1756 720270
Web www.craven-cruckbarn.co.uk

Entry 814 Map 12

The Angel Inn
Hetton

The old drovers' inn remains staunchly, reassuringly traditional – but with a stylish restaurant and wines that have come, over the years, to rival the handpumped Yorkshire ales. There's even a 'cave' for private-party tastings. There are nooks, crannies, beams and crackling fires, and thought has gone into every detail, from the antique furniture in the timbered rooms (one with a magnificent oak-panelled bar) to the fabrics and the colours. Menus change with each season and include dishes ranging from filo 'moneybags' of seafood in lobster sauce – the fish comes fresh from Fleetwood – to Yorkshire lamb and rosemary sausage with juniper-scented red wine sauce. Or aubergine cannelloni stuffed with peppers, tomatoes and gruyère cheese. The glorious up-hill-and-down-dale drive to get here is part of the charm, and it is best to book.

The Falcon Inn
Arncliffe

Tucked into the top corner of Arncliffe in Littondale, one of the most remote and unspoilt of Yorkshire's dales. Several generations of Millers have been licensees here and they have preserved an inn and a way of life almost lost. The fine bay-windowed and ivy-clad building looks more like a private house than a village local... expect few frills and old-fashioned hospitality. The entrance passageway leads to a small hallway at the foot of the stairs – there's a tiny bar counter facing you, a small, simple lounge, a log fire and sporting prints on the walls. A sunny back room looks out across the garden to open fells. Beer is served, as ever, straight from the cask in a large jug, then dispensed into pint glasses at the bar. At lunchtime, call in for pie and peas, sandwiches and ploughman's lunches.

Meals	12pm-2.15pm (2.30pm Sun); 6pm-9.30pm (10pm Sat, 9pm in winter). Main courses £9.50-£17; bar meals £8.95-£16; Sunday lunch £23.95; Early Bird menus £13.95 & £16.95.
Closed	3pm-6pm. Open all day Fri-Sat (reduced choice menu).
Directions	North from Skipton on B6265. Left at Rylstone for Hetton. In village.

Meals	12pm-2pm. Snacks £2.50-£6.
Closed	3pm-7pm. Reduced winter opening times, phone to check.
Directions	Off B6160 16 miles north of Skipton.

Juliet Watkins
The Angel Inn,
Hetton,
Skipton BD23 6LT
Tel +44 (0)1756 730263
Web www.angelhetton.co.uk

Robin Miller
The Falcon Inn,
Arncliffe,
Skipton BD23 5QE
Tel +44 (0)1756 770205
Web www.thefalconinn.com

Entry 815 Map 12

Entry 816 Map 12

The Old Hill Inn
Chapel-le-Dale

A proper, wild-country tavern with terrific beer and food. It used to be a farmhouse, then a doss-house for potholers; now it's a comfortable old inn, a warm, safe haven in a countryside of crags, waterfalls and moors. Enter the unpretentious bar – a large, comfortable room with open-stone walls, wood floors, old pine tables and big log fire. Six pumps deliver ales in top condition – Black Sheep Bitter, Dent Aviator – while food is served in the candlelit intimacy of the diminutive dining rooms. From the family of chefs comes butternut squash risotto, lamb shank with dauphinoise potatoes and a rich lamb gravy, duck with prune, port and orange sauce, and homemade bread; from master confectioner Colin, warm chocolate pudding and lemon tart. His sugar sculptures alone are worth the trip.

The White Lion Inn
Cray

For centuries the White Lion has stood surrounded by moorland high in the Pennines, serving local farmers and cattle drovers. It still does, though walkers have replaced the drovers. In the main bar are wide upholstered settles and dark, plain tables – the ideal backdrop for straightforward soups, ploughman's lunches, pork casseroles, homemade lasagne and steak and mushroom pies, best washed down with a well-kept pint of Taylor's Landlord or Copper Dragon Golden Pippin. At quiet times the crackle of the logs on the fire and the ticking of the clock are all you hear and the owners' relaxed style permeates the place. There are plenty of spots for summer eating outside by the tumbling stream. Some of Wharfedale's footpaths pass by the door, and the views are all you'd hope for, and more.

Meals	12pm-2.30pm (3pm Sun); 6.30pm-8.45pm (from 6pm Sat). Main courses £10.95-£25; bar meals £5.25-£10.
Closed	3.30pm-6.30pm (4pm-6.30pm Sun) & all day Mon (except bank hols). Open all day Sat.
Directions	On the B6255 between Ingleton & Ribblehead.

Meals	12pm-2pm; 6pm-8.30pm. Main courses £7.50-£15.50.
Closed	Open all day.
Directions	20 miles north of Skipton on B6160.

Sabena Martin
The Old Hill Inn, Chapel-le-Dale, Carnforth, LA6 3AR
Tel   +44 (0)15242 41256
Web   www.oldhillinn.co.uk

Phil & Carol Lowther
The White Lion
Inn, Cray, Skipton, BD23 5JB
Tel   +44 (0)1756 760262
Web   www.whitelioncray.com

Entry 817 Map 12

Entry 818 Map 12

Yorkshire

The Wensleydale Heifer Inn
West Witton

Be lulled into a false sense of 'leather armchair by the fire' and 'mine's a pint of Black Sheep' security as you step off the street. Enter the Fish Bar and you're met with wall-to-wall seagrass and modish-naff touches. But the welcome is warm, and the food is sensational. Choose dressed crab with potato, capers and chive salad or Cornish fish stew with new potatoes, parsley and olive oil. As for the Whitby cod in crispy Black Sheep Bitter batter with peas and fat chips – it's the best fish and chips this side of Whitby's Magpie Café. Chef David Moss, ex-Crab & Lobster at Asenby, has achieved the impossible: a great fish restaurant as far from the sea as you can get. And there's a shiny, slightly more formal but still kitted-out-with-joke-crockery dining room – guaranteed to put a smile on your face.

Meals	12pm-2.30pm; 6pm-9.30pm (12pm-9.30pm Sat & Sun). Main courses £11.50-£22; bar meals (lunch) £4.50-£17; set lunch/early dinner £16.50-£18.95.
Closed	Open all day.
Directions	On A684 between Leyburn & Hawes.

David Moss
The Wensleydale Heifer Inn,
Main Street, West Witton,
Leyburn DL8 4LS

Tel   +44 (0)1969 622322
Web   www.wensleydaleheifer.co.uk

Entry 819 Map 12

Yorkshire

The Punch Bowl Inn
Low Row

The hamlet of Low Row clings to the hillside high above the Swale. The front of the pub is a suntrap, the views to the moors are superb and Gunnerside, Muker and Keld are a walk away. Inside, a contemporary-cum-traditional style is the order of the day, with regard to both food and décor. Walls are plain, interspersed with the odd tasteful picture or cream panelling, and scrubbed pine tables are married with matching chairs. It's not hugely pubby but it's spotless and stylish and feels pretty cosy when the fires are lit. There are real ales and good wines but the food is the draw and the menu is written on the mirror; try crab fishcakes served with a basket of warm bread, local lamb with homemade black pudding, and Yorkshire parkin with plum compote to finish… excellent fodder for walkers and shooters.

Meals	12pm-2pm; 6.30pm-9pm. Main courses £10-£15; Sunday roast £9.95.
Closed	Open all day.
Directions	From A1 take exit at Scotch Corner; A6108 to Richmond, then B6270 to Reeth; Low Row, 25m from main road on right.

Charles Cody
The Punch Bowl Inn,
Low Row,
Richmond DL11 6PF

Tel   +44 (0)1748 886233
Web   www.pbinn.co.uk

Entry 820 Map 12

Sandpiper Inn
Leyburn

Malt whisky lovers will eye the 100 bottles behind the bar appreciatively. In 1999, former Roux Scholar Jonathan Harrison swapped a slick city kitchen for an old stone pub in the Yorkshire Dales. In cosy alcoves beneath low black beams, locals and walkers put the world to rights over pints of Black Sheep and Theakston ale opposite chalkboards listing Jonathan's daily menus: fishcakes with herb sauce, club sandwiches, fish and chips in beer batter, braised beef in Guinness. Cooking moves up a gear in the simple stylish dining room as in-season game, Wensleydale heifer beef and home-grown herbs and veg come into play. Loosen belts before delving into Sunday lunch, which could be roast rib-eye of beef with Yorkshire pudding or Moroccan-spiced chicken with couscous – all of ours delicious, including the sticky toffee pudding with butterscotch sauce. Up a twisting stair at the back, two simple but charming bedrooms lie – fresh, warm and cosy to come back to after you've walked the legs off the dogs. Visit the falls at West Burton – or Middleham for the horses on the gallops.

Rooms	2 doubles. From £75.
Meals	12pm-2.30pm; 6.30pm-9pm (9.30pm Fri & Sat).
	Main courses £8.95-£13.95 (lunch), £9.95-£20 (dinner); bar meals £4-£6.95.
Closed	3pm-6.30pm (7pm Sun), Mon & Tues in winter.
Directions	From A1, A684 for Bedale; on for 12 miles; at edge of market place.

Jonathan & Janine Harrison
Sandpiper Inn,
Railway Street,
Leyburn DL8 5AT
Tel +44 (0)1969 622206
Web www.sandpiperinn.co.uk

Entry 821 Map 12

Yorkshire

The Oak Tree Inn
Hutton Magna

A tiny cottage at the end of a row, masquerading as a pub, the Oak Tree was snapped up by the Rosses, ready to swap London for the Dales. Alastair trained at The Savoy and together they have created a gem. The front bar has old wooden panelling and whitewashed stone, an attractive medley of tables, chairs and pews, newspapers, fresh flowers and an open fire. The dark green dining area at the back is softly lit, its tables separated by pews. All is delightful and informal. Locally shot game appears on the menu in season and the produce is as fresh as can be. Expect crab and sweetcorn risotto with home-cured salmon, seared duck breast with Cumberland sausage roll and carrot purée, peanut butter parfait with blueberries and Baileys sorbet. Booking is recommended.

Meals	6pm–11pm (5.30pm–10.30pm Sun), booking only. Main courses £17.50–£19.50.
Closed	Mon all day & Tues–Sun lunch.
Directions	Off A66, 6.5 miles west of Scotch Corner.

Alastair & Claire Ross
The Oak Tree Inn,
Hutton Magna,
Richmond DL11 7HH
Tel   +44 (0)1833 627371

Entry 822 Map 12

Yorkshire

The Blue Lion
East Witton

The Blue Lion has a big reputation locally; so big it followed our inspector round Yorkshire. Paul and Helen have mixed the traditions of a country pub with the elegance of a country house. This is a bustling place that serves superlative food and no one seems in a hurry to leave. Polished beer taps dispensing Yorkshire ale, stone-flagged floors, open fires, newspapers on poles, big settles, huge bunches of dried flowers hanging from beams, splashes of fresh ones. The two restaurants have boarded floors and shuttered Georgian windows, two coal fires and candles everywhere. Food is robust and heart-warming; local game, chargrilled beef fillet with shiraz sauce, braised marsala mutton with cumin sweet potato. East Witton has an interesting plague tale, Jervaulx Abbey is a mile away and there's an enclosed garden at the back.

Meals	12pm–2pm; 7pm–9.15pm. Main courses £10.50–£27.50.
Closed	Open all day.
Directions	From Leyburn, A6108 for 3 miles to East Witton.

Paul & Helen Klein
The Blue Lion,
East Witton,
Leyburn DL8 4SN
Tel   +44 (0)1969 624273
Web   www.thebluelion.co.uk

Entry 823 Map 12

Yorkshire

Black Sheep Brewery
Masham

Masham is a hugely appealing market town in Wensleydale, and has the added attraction of being the home of the Black Sheep Brewery. The visitor centre and bistro are integral here, at this handsome stone shrine to good ale. The guided tour is fascinating, and you may whet your appetite with a glass or two of bitter before settling down to lunch in the restaurant. Food is straightforward and tasty, perhaps pork medallions with black pudding, or braised lamb shank with root vegetables in Emmerdale beer. The coffee and snacks are delicious and there's a 'pub', of course, with old oak floors and all your favourite Black Sheep beers on tap. The spacious dining area on its mezzanine level has fabulous far-reaching views over the town to the hills beyond.

Meals	12pm-2.30pm; 6.30pm-9pm (Thurs-Sat). Main courses £7.50-£16.95.
Closed	Sun-Wed eves.
Directions	Centre of Masham on A6108 between Ripon & Leyburn.

Sue Dempsey
Black Sheep Brewery,
Wellgarth,
Masham, Ripon HG4 4EN
Tel   +44 (0)1765 680101
Web   www.blacksheepbrewery.co.uk

Entry 824 Map 12

Yorkshire

Freemason's Arms
Nosterfield

The Freemason's whitewashed exterior may suggest an ordinary village pub but over the years an unusual assemblage of items has been added to the traditional décor: 1900s enamel advertisements, agricultural implements, Union flags, miners' lamps, a piano, and beams littered with old bank notes. It's a low-beamed place with interconnecting rooms, some flagged floors, two open fires, pew seating, soft lighting, candlelight – traditional, unspoilt, cosy and intriguing. It's also a darn good pub, with four local cask ales on offer and a blackboard to tantalise the hungry: partridge in rowan berry sauce, pink liver and onions with bacon. Kris Stephenson enjoys buying locally and delivers with flair. Eat in the bar, or at one of the bigger tables in the far room, perfect for dining. Just the spot after a day at the Ripon races.

Meals	12pm-2pm; 5.30pm-9pm. Main courses £8-£16.
Closed	3pm-5pm. Open all day Sun.
Directions	On B6267 for Masham, 2 miles off A1.

Kristian Stephenson
Freemason's Arms,
Nosterfield,
Bedale DL8 2QP
Tel   +44 (0)1677 470548

Entry 825 Map 12

The White Bear
Masham

Minutes from the bustle of an ancient and quaint market square stands the Theakston family's face-lifted flagship inn. In the handsome public bar, an open fire throws golden light on old oak floors, whilst gleaming brass platters jostle for space with huge jugs of fresh flowers, newspapers and local magazines. Sit with a pint of Theakston's Best Bitter in the cosy tap room complete with dart board and cribbage, or wander through to the more formal and elegant dining room, where local and seasonal ingredients have prominence. Go for home made steak and ale pie, or rolled fillet of plaice with a cream dill sauce. To finish, banana butterscotch pancakes will fuel an afternoon tramp up into the heart of Wensleydale. On your return, 14 luxurious bedrooms await across the yard in what was once the Lightfoot brewery, but don't expect nostalgia here; the style is contemporary, with top class textiles, huge sumptuous beds and cutting edge bathrooms, warm tones and splashes of vibrant colour; some have lovely views across town. As a special treat, book the vast top floor penthouse with its beamed, raftered ceiling and swish bathroom.

Rooms	14: 13 doubles/twins; 1 suite. From £95–£175.
Meals	12pm-2.30pm (4pm Sun); light snacks 2.30pm-6pm; 6pm-9pm (8.30pm Sun). Main courses £9.95–£19.95.
Closed	Open all day.
Directions	From A1 north of Ripon take A684 for Bedale and follow signs for Masham; inn off Leyburn Road in town centre.

Sue Thomas
The White Bear,
Wellgarth,
Masham, Ripon HG4 4EN
Tel   +44 (0)1765 689319
Web   www.thewhitebearhotel.co.uk

The Black Horse
Kirkby Fleetham

Kirkby Fleetham: a tranquil village with old oak trees on a classic green edged with Georgian houses. The old boozer has been brought back to life; wooden settles, 'distressed' in pastel colours, are boldly upholstered, candy-stripe curtains and grandfather clocks add quaint touches, stone fireplaces, old beams and a snug with darts remain intact. Pub as hub, and dashes of humour too (the cushions embroidered "Be nice to your children: they choose your nursing home.") And good things are happening in the kitchen, where young chef Paul Waugh from Seaham Hall has joined forces with J Baker of the eponymous York bistro. The macaroni of ham shank with smoky Ribblesdale cheese and grain mustard is delicately comforting; the Whitby crab salad with vine tomatoes is the seaside on a plate; the treacle tart with orange blossom custard is irresistible. As for the bedrooms — just three — they will charm you, with their muted colours, oak floored bathrooms, picnic-hamper breakfasts and retro toasters. The two-room family suite sports cast-iron beds and Cath Kidston fabrics, fat floral eiderdowns and gingham-topped chairs.

Rooms	3: 2 doubles; 1 family room. £75–£100.
Meals	12pm-2.30pm; 5pm-9pm (9.30pm Fri & Sat). 12pm-8pm Sun (7pm banks hols). Bar food only Mon lunch.
	Main courses £8.95–£16.95; Sunday lunch £12.95 & £15.95.
Closed	Open all day.
Directions	Village signposted off A1

SPECIAL
AWARD
see pages 20-21

Pub with rooms

Deborah Whitwell
The Black Horse,
Lumley Lane, Kirkby Fleetham,
Northallerton DL7 0SH

Tel +44 (0)1609 749010
Web www.blackhorsekirkbyfleetham.com

Entry 827 Map 15

The Black Swan
Oldstead

In glorious isolation, tucked back from the road, the Black Swan goes back 400 years. The Banks family has farmed for almost as long, and they've pulled off a transformation. Open fires, stone flags and beams, candelabra and oak furniture; it's a cheerful and comforting space. The food, served off slate place mats on antique tables, is refined too, and delicious, and much comes from local farms; there's game terrine with Cumberland jelly and toasted brioche; haunch of venison with grain mustard risotto; rhubarb ice cream and burnt orange syrup. Take a pint of Copper Dragon to the blossom trees and gaze on the hills; don boots and set off from the door. Four luxury bedrooms furnished with antique pieces found on European travels have been created in a low stone building next to the pub; recline on French beds with satin throws and soak walker's limbs in a spectacular copper bath; the lovely bathrooms are heated underfoot. A secluded patio outside the door capitalises on the views — what a spot for a pre-prandial glass of something chilled. A classic in the making.

Rooms	4 doubles. £130-£170; weekends DB&B only £180-£230.
Meals	12pm-2pm (2.30pm Sun); 6pm-9pm. Main courses £9.50-£19.95; tasting menu (7 courses) £49.95; sandwiches £5.95.
Closed	3pm-6pm & Mon-Weds lunch. Open all day Sat & Sun.
Directions	A19 from Thirsk; left to Thirkleby & Coxwold, then left for Byland Abbey; follow signs left for Oldstead.

Anne Banks
The Black Swan,
Oldstead,
York YO61 4BL

Tel	+44 (0)1347 868387
Web	www.blackswanoldstead.co.uk

Entry 828 Map 12

Yorkshire

Fox & Hounds
Carthorpe

Part of this 200-year-old pub was once the village blacksmith's, serving the A1; now it draws locals and travellers in search of good food. Vincent and Helen have taken over from her parents, who first put this humble local on the culinary map. The L-shaped bar remains comfortably plush and cosy, with its warm red carpet, soothing classical music and glowing log fires, while the high-raftered dining room displays an interesting array of old smithy implements. Menus champion traditional British dishes cooked with skill and flair, with contemporary touches. There's ham hock terrine with homemade piccalilli, rack of lamb with redcurrant gravy, market-fresh fish... and a sticky ginger pudding served with orange sorbet and sugared nuts. Black Sheep Bitter is on tap and there are decent wines by the glass.

Yorkshire

The Hare
Scawton

If you've braved the vertical ascent of the infamous Sutton Bank and are in need of sustenance, come to The Hare. This absurdly pretty 13th-century pub is lovely outside and in. On sunny days, sit in the garden on cream wrought-iron French chairs and admire the distant view of Riveaulx Abbey; on damp ones, feel embraced by big fires, red walls and ancient beams. Chef/patron Geoff Smith thoughtfully sources his ingredients and presents them temptingly on the plate: the twice-baked cheese soufflé is exemplary, the risotto of Portland crab with parmesan is creamy, the roast rack of Sutton Bank lamb with tarragon is earthy and rich; and there's a great cheese selection, so save some space. Business partner Jan pulls a well-kept pint and chats to you like you're an old friend... brilliant after the North Yorkshire Moors.

Meals	12pm-2pm; 7pm-9.30pm. Main courses £10-£15; set menu £13.95 & £15.95.
Closed	3pm-7pm & Mon.
Directions	Carthorpe is 4 miles south of Bedale & 1 mile west of the A1.

Meals	12pm-2pm (4pm Sun); 6pm-9.30pm. No food Sun eve. Main courses £13.75-£19.50; light lunches from £6.75.
Closed	3pm-6pm, Sun eves & Mon.
Directions	Village signed off A170, 7 miles east of Thirsk.

Vincent & Helen Taylor
Fox & Hounds,
Carthorpe,
Bedale DL8 2LG
Tel +44 (0)1845 567433
Web www.foxandhoundscarthorpe.co.uk

Entry 829 Map 12

Geoff & Jan Smith
The Hare,
Scawton,
Thirsk YO7 2HG
Tel +44 (0)1845 597769
Web www.thehareinn.co.uk

Entry 830 Map 12

Yorkshire

Golden Lion
Osmotherley

Bustling with walkers doing the Coast to Coast in the day, humming with well-dressed diners at night, the old stone inn overlooking the green is run by young hands-on owners and a friendly staff. Arrive early to bag a smart pew in the brown-wood bar with raised open fire and flickering candles, and enjoy a pint of local bitter or a first-class wine as you choose from a refreshingly simple menu. The chef has a modern take on retro dishes – chicken Kiev, coq au vin, poached pear in wine with hot chocolate sauce – that stand the test of time. More contemporary dishes are free of flourish and fuss. And there's a fabulous gluten-free menu, from fish soup to calves' liver with onions and mash. The freshness of approach means you'll leave smiling, and the village is as unspoilt as any in the North Yorkshire Moors National Park.

Meals	12pm-3pm (Wed-Sun); 6pm-9pm. Main courses £7.95-£20.95.
Closed	3pm-6pm. Open all day Sat & Sun.
Directions	Off A19 10 miles north of Thirsk & Northallerton.

Christie Connelly & Belal Radwan
Golden Lion,
6 West End, Osmotherley,
Northallerton DL6 3AA

| Tel | +44 (0)1609 883526 |
| Web | www.goldenlionosmotherley.co.uk |

Entry 831 Map 12

Yorkshire

The Postgate Inn
Egton Bridge

This neck of the woods is best known for its 'Heartbeat' celebrity. Indeed, the Victorian stone pub sitting so handsomely at the bottom of the leafy Esk Valley – right by to the historic train line – is Heartbeat's 'Black Dog'. There's every reason to take the short trip inland from Whitby – for the big welcome, the homely feel (stone floors, beams, open fires) and the locally sourced ingredients brought together with such skill. Lamb noisettes with minted pea mash and a redcurrant and heather honey sauce are dense and toothsome; Whitby haddock and crab with gin crème sauce and white asparagus make the very best of the local catch. A terraced garden takes advantage of the views, making this a brilliant spot for lunch before stepping onto the steam train and rolling across the famous moors to Pickering.

Meals	12pm-2.30pm (3pm Sun). Main courses £10.95-£18.95.
Closed	3.30pm-6.30pm (5.30pm in summer).
Directions	Off A171 east of Whitby; go through Egton to reach Egton Bridge in the Esk Valley.

Mark & Shelley Powell
The Postgate Inn,
Egton Bridge,
Whitby YO21 1UX

| Tel | +44 (0)1947 895241 |
| Web | www.postgateinn.com |

Entry 832 Map 13

Yorkshire

The Birch Hall
Beck Hole

Two small bars with a shop in between, unaltered for 70 years. Steep wooded hillsides and a stone bridge straddling the rushing river and, inside, a glimpse of life before World War II. The Big Bar has been beautifully repapered and has a little open fire, dominoes, darts and service from a hatch; benches come from the station waiting room at Beck Hole. The shop (postcards, traditional sweets) has its original fittings, as does the Little Bar with its handpumps for three cask ales. The original 19th-century enamel sign hangs above the door. Food is simple and authentic: local pies, baked stotties or baps, homemade scones and delicious beer cake. Steep steps take you to the terraced garden that looks over the inn and across the valley. Parking is scarce so show patience and courtesy in this old-fashioned place.

Yorkshire

The Anvil Inn
Sawdon

The fact that this village is not on a bus route tells you one of two things; either you're in the back of beyond, or public transport is in a pretty state. Whichever; beat a path to this welcoming door, even if you have to hitch a lift. The Anvil was a working forge until the mid 1980s, the building is over 200 years old and the blacksmith's workshop – now the bar – forms a unusual centrepiece to a great little pub. Partner-chefs Mark and Alexandra have pulled the place up by its bootstraps and have created an environment you'll linger long in. Sit on an old oak pew or lounge in a leather tub chair with a pint of Daleside or Copper Dragon, and scan the tempting menu. Invention without pretension is the philosophy here, and thoughtfully executed, locally sourced food flows from the kitchen. A classic in the making.

Meals	11am-3pm; 7.30pm-11pm; all day in summer. Sandwiches & pies from £1.90.	
Closed	3pm-7.30pm, Mon eve & Tues in winter. Open all day in summer.	
Directions	9 miles from Whitby towards Pickering.	

Meals	12pm-2pm (3pm Sun); 6.30pm-9pm; no food Sun eve. Main courses £7.50-£15.45 (lunch), £9.50-£15.45 (dinner); Sunday lunch £8.75.
Closed	2.30pm-6.30pm & Mon.
Directions	Sawdon is signed north off A170 Thirsk road, 7 miles west of Scarborough.

Glenys & Neil Crampton
The Birch Hall,
Beck Hole,
Whitby YO22 5LE
Tel +44 (0)1947 896245
Web www.beckhole.info

The Anvil Inn,
Main Street, Sawdon,
Scarborough YO13 9DY
Tel +44 (0)1723 859896
Web www.theanvilinnsawdon.co.uk

Entry 833 Map 13

Entry 834 Map 13

The Wheatsheaf Inn
Egton

Unlike many pubs in this area, the family-run Wheatsheaf has avoided expansion and held on to its character. Indeed, it sits so modestly back from the village's wide main street you could pass it by. The first entrance brings you into the main bar, all low beams and cushioned settles, but the main treat is the bar with the original Yorkshire range – aglow most of the year. This drinkers' den takes 16 at a push and is a favourite of walkers, fishermen and dogs. (The river Esk at the foot of the steep hill is famous for fly-fishing, hence the angling memorabilia.) A range of cask ales ensures the chat flows, while the food sustains walkers: finnan haddock kedgeree, oxtail soup, local partridge in season, steaks from local farmers. Three quiet, cosy bedrooms have been freshly spruced up, so why not stay? After a day's yomp on the moors you can look forward to a soak in a Victorian roll top bath: two rooms have them. Fine cotton linen and sumptuous silk cushion top French cast-iron beds, oak furniture glows with the patina of age, and the views over the village to the hills are lovely.

Rooms	3 twins/doubles. From £85.
Meals	12pm-2pm; 6pm-9pm; no food Sun eve or all day Mon. Main courses £11-£16.95; bar meals £8.50; sandwiches from £4.
Closed	2.30pm-5.30pm & Mon lunch. Open all day Sat & Sun.
Directions	Off A171; 6 miles west of Whitby.

Nigel & Elaine Pulling
The Wheatsheaf Inn,
Egton,
Whitby YO21 1TZ
Tel   +44 (0)1947 895271
Web   www.wheatsheafegton.com

Entry 835 Map 13

The White Swan Inn
Pickering

Victor swapped the City for the North Yorkshire Moors and this old coaching inn; the place oozes comfort and style. Personality too: duck in through the front door to a tiny, cosy, panelled tap room serving real Yorkshire ales, with smart country furniture, fine wines and eager young staff. Best of all is the dining room and you'll find heaven on a plate when you dig into supper. Try seared, hand-dived king scallops with air-dried ham, Levisham mutton with Irish cabbage, poached rhubarb on toasted brioche and homemade ice cream. Menus change monthly and 80% of the ingredients are locally sourced, with meat coming from Levisham's celebrated Ginger Pig. Breakfast is just as good, and inspired one traveller to write a poem, now framed. Bedrooms come with pleasing colours, warm radiators, elegant fabrics, antique beds, maybe an armchair and a view of the pretty courtyard; bathrooms are small but classy. Don't miss the beamed club room for roaring fire, board games and an honesty bar. Castle Howard is nearby, the moors are wild and the steam railway is great fun.

Rooms	21: 14 doubles, 4 twins/doubles, 3 suites. £145–£175. Suites £200–£250. Singles from £110.
Meals	12pm–2pm; 6.45pm–9pm. Main courses £10.95–£19; Sunday lunch £15.95 & £21.
Closed	Open all day.
Directions	From North, A170 to Pickering. Entering town, left at traffic lights, then 1st right, Market Place. On left.

Victor & Marion Buchanan
The White Swan Inn,
Market Place,
Pickering YO18 7AA

Tel	+44 (0)1751 472288
Web	www.white-swan.co.uk

Entry 836 Map 13

Yorkshire

The Coachman Inn
Snainton

It's been an inn since 1776, and was the last staging post for the York mail coach before Scarborough. There's warmth in the Yorkshire welcome from David and Claire Chambers, and there's nothing dated about the food. Expect modern dishes from a bright young chef; even the breads, chutneys and puddings are homemade and the local ingredients – game in season, fish from Scarborough and Whitby – are impeccable. Dine elegantly on beetroot risotto with crispy parsnip chips, venison on black pudding mash with port sauce, and caramelised rice puddings with liquorice prunes. The lovely dining room, running the depth of the building, is broken up by double doors and sofas, its Georgian windows overlooking a pretty side garden. Perfectly situated for striding into the Yorkshire Moors.

Meals	12pm–2pm; 6.30pm–9pm (8.30pm Sun). Main courses £10–£16.50.
Closed	3pm–6pm, Mon all day & Tues lunch.
Directions	From A170 Pickering to Scarborough road, onto B1258 for Malton.

David & Claire Chambers
The Coachman Inn,
Pickering Road West,
Snainton, Scarborough YO13 9PL
Tel   +44 (0)1723 859231
Web   www.coachmaninn.co.uk

Entry 837 Map 13

Yorkshire

The Plough Inn
Fadmoor

It's been a welcoming refuge from the wintry moors for years. Catch sight of it from up high, smoke curling from the stack, and you feel irresistibly drawn. Inside The Plough all is as warm and reassuring as can be; the onetime row of cottage dwellings feels rambling but contained, the several small rooms immaculate with their gleaming wood, rosy upholstery and rugs on seagrass floors. The food is a major draw and there are six dining areas in all, the nicest being half-panelled; all have open fires. Dishes range from scallops pan-fried with black pudding and bacon to braised lamb shank with caramelised red onion mash and port gravy; the soups are very good, and we liked the crispy duck and mango spring rolls. Spill outside to bikes, boots, dogs and a pretty view of the village green in summer.

Meals	12pm–2pm (3.30pm Sun); 6.30pm–9pm. Main courses £8.95–£14.95; set menu, 2 courses, £10.
Closed	2.30pm–6.30pm. Closed Mon, Tues & Sun eve in winter.
Directions	From A170 Helmsley to Kirkbymoorside, left towards Fadmoor.

Neil & Rachael Nicholson
The Plough Inn,
Main Street, Fadmoor,
Kirkbymoorside YO62 7HY
Tel   +44 (0)1751 431515
Web   www.ploughrestaurant.co.uk

Entry 838 Map 13

Yorkshire

The Star Inn
Harome

You know you've hit the jackpot as soon as you walk into The Star – low ceilings, flagged floors, gleaming oak, a flickering fire. Andrew and Jacquie arrived in 1996 and the Michelin star in 2002. It's been a formidable turnaround for the 14th-century inn yet the brochure simply says: "He cooks, and she looks after you"... and how! Andrew's food is rooted in Yorkshire tradition, refined with French flair and written in plain English on ever-changing menus that brim with local produce (do book). Risotto of partridge with black trumpet mushrooms, mutton and caper suet pudding, gutsy desserts and a 'cheeseboard of the week'. There's a bar with a Sunday papers-and-pint feel, a coffee loft in the eaves, and their own deli across the road... even the schnapps is homemade. Exceptional.

Yorkshire

The Grapes Inn
Great Habton

In an unremarkable Yorkshire village, an unremarkable pub. Take heart, step inside. Adam and Katie have plans, when cash allows, to spruce up the exterior; in the meantime, enjoy what they've achieved in the short time they've been here. They deserve support in breathing life so beautifully into an old boozer in a sleepy village. Now there's dominoes, cricket, darts, a crackling fire to greet you, and exposed stone walls and fresh flowers to cheer up the old swirly carpets and retro moquette upholstery. And then there's Adam's cooking, which is modern and inventive. Meat, fish and vegetables are regionally sourced, and everything is made from scratch. May breast of pigeon on truffle mash with sloe gin jus inspire you! Add well-kept Ringwood Best Bitter and Jennings Lakeland Ale, and you know you've struck gold.

Closed	3pm-6.30pm (7.30pm Mon). Open all day Sun.
Directions	From Thirsk, A170 towards Scarborough. Through Helmsley, then right, signed Harome. Inn in village.

Meals	12pm-2pm (Wed-Sun); 6.30pm-8.30pm (Tues-Sun). Main courses £8.50-£19.95; Sunday lunch £7.25, £10.25 & £13.25.
Closed	3pm-6pm. Tues lunch & Mon.
Directions	Village signed off B1257 Malton to Helmsley road & A169 between Malton & Pickering.

Andrew & Jacquie Pern
The Star Inn,
High Street, Harome,
Helmsley YO62 5JE
Tel   +44 (0)1439 770397
Web   www.thestaratharome.co.uk

Entry 839 Map 13

Adam & Katie Myers
The Grapes Inn,
Great Habton,
Malton YO17 6TU
Tel   +44 (0)1653 669166
Web   www.thegrapes-inn.co.uk

Entry 840 Map 13

Pipe & Glass Inn
South Dalton

In the elegant estate village of Dalton, rejoicing in one of the highest church spires in the Wolds, is this 16th-century inn. The front garden has classic parkland vistas, the back is lushly lawned, the polished interiors glow with well-being. Turn right for a pubby pint, left for a leather sofa by the log-stacked fire. Eating and lounging areas are woody and stylish, window seats have chocolate cushions, customers cluck with pleasure as they head to their tables. Kate, front of house, and James, chef, cut their teeth at The Star at Harome, so the food is atune to the very best of seasonal, regional and humanely reared. Adventurous combinations include wild rabbit rissoles, braised Burdass lamb, mutton and kidney faggots – the website shares the recipes and the wines are from small producers. Overlooking woods and fields, two immaculately and plushly designed suites trumpet every modern thing. Be seduced by state of the art media systems, fabulously decadent bathrooms, huge sleigh beds, fat mattresses, quirky dressing tables. Breakfast is top class and brought to your door. We loved it all.

Rooms	2 doubles. £150.
Meals	12pm–2pm (4pm Sun); 6.30pm–9.30pm; no food Sun eve. Main courses £8.95–£19.95; Sunday roast £11.95.
Closed	3pm–6.30pm & Mon (except bank hols). Open all day Sun.
Directions	Village signed off A164 & B1248, 5 miles north west of Beverley.

James & Kate Mackenzie
Pipe & Glass Inn,
West End, South Dalton,
Beverley HU17 7PN

Tel   +44 (0)1430 810246
Web   www.pipeandglass.co.uk

Yorkshire

Bay Horse Inn
Burythorpe

Long, low and inviting, the old Bay Horse is the flagship of Real Yorkshire Pubs, and visitors and locals beat a path to the door for the food. Honest, wholesome English dishes are the order of the day, so expect whitebait with lemon mayonnaise, rump steak with hand-cut chips and all the trimmings fish pie, treacle sponge with toffee sauce, a local cheese board with apple oatcakes and cracking Sunday roasts. Meats and cheese are from local farms, fish is from Whitby and Hartlepool – all suppliers feature on the menu map. Warm colours are Farrow & Ball, 'scrubbed' pine tables are matched with comfortable leather dining chairs, and smart light oak floors merge into fine stone flags. A small fire burns in the alcove by the door and there are books and newspapers to browse. It's friendly, young and civilised.

Meals	12pm-2.30pm; 6pm-9.30pm. No food Sun eve. Main courses £8.95-£15.95; sandwiches from £4.25; Sunday lunch £11.50 (2 courses) & £13.95 (3 courses).
Closed	3pm-6pm, all day Mon & Tues lunch. Open all day Sun.
Directions	Kirkham Priory on right, sharp left towards Langton; 3 miles; signs for Burythorpe for 1.25 miles.

Dawn Pickering & Alison Thistleton
Bay Horse Inn,
Burythorpe,
Malton YO17 9LJ
Tel +44 (0)1653 658302
Web www.bayhorseburythorpe.co.uk

Entry 842 Map 13

Yorkshire

The White Horse Inn (Nellie's)
Beverley

You could pass the White Horse by: its brick front and old pub sign do not stand out on busy Hengate. Inside is more beguiling – be transported back 200 years. (The building itself is even older.) Known as 'Nellie's', it's a wonderfully atmospheric little place; your eyes will take a while to become accustomed, so dim are the gas-lit passages. Little has changed in these small rooms with their old quarry tiles, bare boards, smoke-stained walls and open fires. Furniture is a mix of high-backed settles, padded benches, marble-topped cast-iron tables, old pictures and a gas-lit, pulley-controlled chandelier. Food is straightforward and good value: sandwiches, bangers and mash, steak and ale pie, spotted dick with custard. The only concession to the modern age is the games room at the back with a pool table and darts.

Meals	11am-3pm; no food eve & all day Sun. Main courses £2.99-£6.
Closed	Open all day.
Directions	Off North Bar, close to St Mary's Church.

The White Horse Inn (Nellie's),
22 Hengate,
Beverley HU17 8BN
Tel +44 (0)1482 861973
Web www.nellies.co.uk

Entry 843 Map 13

Yorkshire

Yorkshire

St Vincent Arms
Sutton-upon-Derwent

Humming with happy chat, the traditional public bar is the heart of the place, sporting panelled walls lined with brass plates, warm red curtains, tartan carpeting. There are up to eight cask beers and no background music or electronic gadgetry – just an old radiogram. To the left of the lobby is a smaller, snugger bar decorated in pale green with matching tartan; this leads into several attractive small eating areas. Food ranges from crab sandwiches to chorizo and scallop risotto (delicious), steak, ale and mushroom pie, lobster with garlic butter, and sticky toffee pudding. And if you're not into ale there are several excellent wines by the glass. The St Vincent Arms is a great little local and the staff seem to enjoy themselves as much as the customers – you can't ask for more.

The Blue Bell
York

Unlike most city pubs, The Blue Bell is as it's always been – a timeless classic, a mecca for real ale fans. Its narrow brick frontage on Fossgate, not far from The Shambles, is easy to miss, but once you've found the old place, you enter a corridor that leads to the back. On the right, a tiny bar with red-tiled floor and high ceilings, panelling, Edwardian stained glass, a cast-iron and tiled fireplace, settle seating on two sides and iron-leg tables. 'Ladies only' were confined to the narrow back lounge; now the red carpet is trod on by all. Original fireplaces, polished panelling, interesting old pictures, ticking clocks and general clutter... all this and a terrific range of cask beers, at least seven, and wines too. No hot food but hearty sandwiches at lunchtime. Don't miss the annual beer festival in November.

Meals	12pm-2pm; 6.30pm-9.30pm. Main courses £8.50-£18.50.
Closed	3pm-6pm (6.30pm Sun).
Directions	On B1228, 8 miles south east of York.

Meals	12pm-2pm; 4pm-8pm. No food Sun. Sandwiches from £2.
Closed	Open all day.
Directions	In York city centre.

Simon, Philip & Adrian Hopwood
St Vincent Arms,
Main Street,
Sutton-upon-Derwent, York YO41 4BN
Tel +44 (0)1904 608349
Web www.stvincentarms.co.uk

Entry 844 Map 13

Jim Hardie
The Blue Bell,
53 Fossgate,
York YO1 9TF
Tel +44 (0)1904 654904

Entry 845 Map 13

Ye Old Sun Inn
Colton

A pretty, low-lying Yorkshire village, and a spick and span, 18th-century pub with a welcoming porch. Young enthusiastic owners have kept the bones – rustic beams and red brick fireplaces – but sprinkled a bit of bling here and there in sumptuous fabrics and tapestry cushions. There's an admirable dedication to good, local ingredients, too; rabbit from the Ledston estate finds itself in a pie (like poor Peter's father) with thyme, ginger and wild mushrooms, while trio of local Yorkshire pork might be crisp belly with red cabbage, toad in the hole, and pork fillet wrapped in smoked ham. There's a tiny deli round the back where you can buy homemade joys, and a rambling garden with views across open fields. The energetic McCarthys have recently turned the handsome Georgian house next door into a smart B&B with three bright bedrooms; snooze in a huge leather sleigh bed with faux fur throws and cushions, admire the well-lit 'hidden' dressing area, splash about in the swanky bathroom. In the summer, a huge hot tub in the leafy, private back garden is yours – perfect for lovers.

Rooms	3: 2 doubles, 1 double with private bathroom. £100–£120. Singles £100.
Meals	12pm-2pm (4pm Sun); 6.30pm-9.30pm. Main courses £5.50–£15.50 (lunch), £11.95–£14.95 (dinner); Sunday lunch £10–£17.
Closed	3pm-6pm & Mon lunch.
Directions	A64 towards York; follow signs to Colton.

Ashley & Kelly McCarthy
Ye Old Sun Inn,
Main Street,
Colton, Tadcaster LS24 8EP
Tel   +44 (0)1904 744261
Web   www.yeoldsuninn.co.uk

Entry 846 Map 12

Blackwell Ox Inn
Sutton-on-the-Forest

On the main road that runs through the trim Georgian village of Sutton-on-the-Forest, built in 1823 as a house for a certain Mrs Shepherd, the Blackwell Ox Inn has, in recent years, doubled in stature and size. The interior now is more country hotel than village pub, the walls bedecked with hunting prints and the odd sampler, the dining rooms spruce with cushioned window seats, stiff white napery and soft lights at night. Tom Kingston, an enthusiastic young chef, changes the menu daily and is passionate about local ingredients and rustic flavours. Seared pigeon breast comes with quince jelly salad; sea bream with bok choi, clams and pickled wild mushrooms; confit pork belly with scallops and a pea risotto. The North Yorkshire cheeses are delicious, the bread crusty and homemade, the wines fashionably listed by style. Handsome, spruced-up bedrooms, two with pretty views, promise Molton Brown toiletries in sparkling modern bathrooms while breakfasts are as first-class as all the rest. The bus stop just outside the inn is handy for York — and avoids hassles with car parking.

Rooms	7: 5 twins/doubles, 2 four-posters. £95–£110. Singles £65–£95.
Meals	12pm-2pm (4pm Sun); 6pm-9.30pm; no food Sun eve. Main courses £9.95–£16.75; bar meals £5.25–£8.75; set menu £10.95 & £13.95.
Closed	2pm–5pm. Open all day Sun.
Directions	Off B1363 7 miles north of York.

Jeff Ellis
Blackwell Ox Inn,
Huby Road, Sutton-on-the-Forest,
York YO61 1DT
Tel   +44 (0)1347 810328
Web   www.blackwelloxinn.co.uk

Entry 847 Map 12

The Durham Ox
Crayke

At the picturesque top of the Grand Old Duke of York's hill is an L-shaped bar of flagstones and rose walls, worn leather armchairs and settles, carved panelling and big fires. There are two more bars to either side, and a dapper wine-themed restaurant that draws all and sundry. Chalkboards above the stone fireplace and seasonal menus list game terrine with homemade chutney, pan-fried duck with parsnip mash, red cabbage and port sauce, and chocolate cake with vanilla yogurt ice cream. The Bar Bites menu and the Sunday roasts are inevitably popular. There's a coffee shop serving homemade truffles, and a garden with a marquee for summer frivolity. No need to drive home: the delightfully quirky rooms in the old farmworkers' cottages have been renovated in contemporary, country-house style. Expect original quarry-tile floors, warmly painted walls, beams and brass beds and re-vamped bathrooms. A smart new room, The Studio, is in the main pub with its' own outside staircase. The far-reaching views across the valley are stunning; in summer, flowers burst from stone troughs. Such peacefulness 20 minutes outside York.

Rooms	5 doubles. £100–£180. Singles £80.
Meals	12pm–2.30pm; 6pm–9.30pm (10pm Sat; 8.30pm Sun). Main courses £8.95–£18.95; bar meals from £6.95; Sunday roast from £13.95.
Closed	3pm–6pm. Open all day Sat & Sun.
Directions	Exit right off A19 York to Thirsk road. Through Easingwold to Crayke.

Michael & Sasha Ibbotson
The Durham Ox,
Westway, Crayke,
York YO61 4TE
Tel +44 (0)1347 821506
Web www.thedurhamox.com

Entry 848 Map 12

The Abbey Inn
Coxwold

Fifty paces from the door, majestic Byland Abbey stands defiant after 900 years. It was one of the first Gothic buildings to rise in the North. Yet in 1536 Henry VIII ordered the dissolution of the monasteries and over the years locals stripped its roof and looted its stone; still it shines. As for the inn, it dates to 1845 and once served as a farmhouse for the monks of Ampleforth. Refurbished by English Heritage and now with Melanie Drew (formerly at The Appletree), it's a perfect place with interiors that mix tradition, eccentricity and elegance. Characterful dining rooms have big fireplaces and carved oak seats on stone flags or polished boards; daily papers hang on poles. The food is British-based and interesting: sautéed scallops with cauliflower purée; venison with braised red cabbage and sloe gin sauce. Bedrooms upstairs sweep you back to long-lost days: beamed ceilings, panelled windows, fancy beds, a sofa if there's room. Downstairs, doors open onto a terrace that gives way to sprawling lawns. Bring your walking boots: the setting is stunning.

Rooms	3: 2 doubles, 1 suite. £100–£200.
Meals	12pm-2.30pm; 6pm-9.30pm. Afternoon tea 2.30pm-6pm. Main courses from £12 (dinner); lunch from £4.50.
Closed	Open all day. Closed Tues.
Directions	From A1(M) junc. 49, A168 for Thirsk, then A19 for York. Left for Coxwold after 2 miles. There, left for Byland Abbey. Opposite abbey.

Melanie Drew
The Abbey Inn,
Byland Abbey,
Coxwold, York YO61 4BD
Tel +44 (0)1347 868 204
Web www.theappletree.org

Entry 849 Map 12

The General Tarleton
Ferrensby

Chef-patron John Topham and wife Claire run the old coaching inn with an easy charm. The rambling, low-beamed, nooked and crannied brasserie-bar has been stylishly updated and mixes rough stone walls with smooth ones, there are leather chairs, muted heritage colours, and a roaring fire. You have Black Sheep Bitter on hand pump, 12 well-chosen wines by the glass and unfussy dishes based on the finest local produce. Here the menu ranges from classic ham and goose liver terrine to slow-braised Dales lamb, roast partridge with port wine jus and brilliant fish and chips. There's iced nougatine parfait for grown-ups, banana split for children, delightful staff and a great buzz. The cosy-chic dining room, formerly a stables, displays white napery; for warm days, there's a super terraced garden. If you're tempted to stay, the comfortable, well-equipped rooms are in a purpose-built extension and flaunt the best of contemporary... plus soft feather pillows, homemade biscuits and Molton Brown lotions. But the food is the thing – it's fabulous, and that includes the breakfasts.

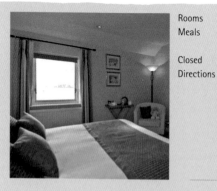

Rooms	14 twins/doubles. From £129.
Meals	12pm–2pm; 6pm–9pm (9.30pm Sat). Main courses £9.95–£19.95.
Closed	3pm–6pm.
Directions	From A1 junction 48; A6055 for Knaresborough; pub on right in Ferensby.

John Topham
The General Tarleton,
Boroughbridge Road,
Ferrensby, Knaresborough HG5 0PZ
Tel   +44 (0)1423 340284
Web   www.generaltarleton.co.uk

Entry 850 Map 12

Dawnay Arms
Newton on Ouse

The script on the lintel reads 1778. This stately Georgian building has been rescued from dereliction by Kerry and Martel Smith, who have taken one step sideways from their Leeds brasserie. Now the old boozer in the picture-postcard village is a shrine to modernity. Stone flagged floors and massive fireplaces have been kept, and chunky tables (constructed from timber pilfered from a post office in Durham) and old church pews sit stylishly in a pale palette, broken by splashes of colour from funky cushions and modern art in chubby rococo frames. Faultless food scrupulously sourced flows from a kitchen run by maestro Martel – perhaps steak and kidney pudding with root vegetables and ale sauce, and treacle tart with butterscotch ice cream. There's a glorious riverside garden for lazy summer days.

Meals	12pm-2.30pm; 6pm-9.30pm (12pm-6pm Sun); no food Sun eve. Main courses £7.95-£14.95 (lunch), £9.95-£16.95 (dinner); Sunday lunch £17.95.
Closed	3pm-6pm. Open all day Sat & Sun.
Directions	A19 from York towards Thirsk; left at Shipton following signs to Beningbrough Hall.

Kerry Smith
Dawnay Arms,
Newton on Ouse,
York YO30 2BR
Tel   +44 (0)1347 848345
Web   www.thedawnayatnewton.co.uk

Entry 851 Map 12

The Shoulder of Mutton
Kirkby Overblow

A few miles south of Harrogate, this handsome old inn has far-reaching views over the rolling hills towards the lovely Wharfe Valley; David and Kate having been here since 2004, and the pub is the hub of village life. Outside: a child-friendly garden and ancient trees for shade on a sunny day. Inside: a proper 'pubby' vibe, with oak floors and beams, wood-burning stoves and old prints on rough plaster walls. David's passion for beer is evident; guest ales feature week by week. There's dedication in the kitchen too, with pub classics updated for modern times; homemade chicken liver pâté comes with warm sodabread and red onion chutney, and haunch of venison with celeriac dauphinoise and mixed berry jus. This enterprising couple have also opened a shop next door, selling store cupboard staples alongside their own produce, including scrumptious pies and cakes.

Meals	12pm-2pm; 6pm-9pm (12pm-7pm Sun; 12pm-9pm bank hol Mon). Main courses £9.95-£16.95; set lunch Mon-Thurs £8.95 & £11.95.
Closed	3pm-6pm. Open all day Sun.
Directions	Off A61 & A658 3 miles S of Harrogate.

Community pub

David & Kate Deacon
The Shoulder of Mutton,
Kirkby Overblow,
Harrogate HG3 1HD
Tel   +44 (0)1423 871205
Web   www.shoulderatkirkbyoverblow.com

Entry 852 Map 12

The Timble Inn
Timble

Dick Turpin stayed here on his fateful journey between London and York. True or not, the story perfectly suits this charming, stone-built, listed pub in postcard-perfect Timble. Following a sympathetic makeover inside, the old flag floors are topped with oak settles covered in hunting jacket tweed and the exposed brick walls decorated with glass sconces and gothic gilt-framed mirrors. Locals prop up the bar accompanied by dogs and pints of Theakstons, and those who are hungry can choose from a pub grub menu of local-pork pies with mushy peas and mint sauce, steak and kidney pies cooked in beer, and fruit crumbles (and judging by the number of piping hot pies flowing from the kitchen, they're going down a storm). Seven spanking new bedrooms have had the same eye for detail passed over them – thanks to Marie, interior designer turned landlady. Expect big beds with fat mattresses, fabulous fabrics, high-tech audio/visual systems and cutting-edge bathrooms. Most rooms have long views over the delightful Washburn Valley, and the peace is a balm to the soul. A big treat.

Rooms	8 twins/doubles. From £99.
Meals	12pm-2pm (6pm Sun); 6pm-9pm. No food Sun eve. Main courses £8.95–£12.95; sandwiches from £5.95; Sunday roast from £11.95.
Closed	Sun eve, all Mon & Tues.
Directions	From Harrogate, A59 towards Skipton. Turn left at signs for Swinoty Reservoir, then Timble.

Paul Radcliffe & Marie Cooper
The Timble Inn,
Timble,
Otley LS21 2NN
Tel +44 (0)1943 880530
Web www.thetimbleinn.co.uk

Entry 853 Map 12

Crown Inn
Roecliffe

Is Roecliffe the prettiest village in Yorkshire? One of Roecliffe's greatest treasures stands alongside its immaculate green: this handsome window-box-tumbled old coaching inn. Inside are stone-flagged floors, beams and crackling fires, comfy gingham chairs and gleaming old oak; you almost feel you've stumbled into the home of a rather smart country couple who happen to have a bar in the sitting room! Above the pub, four elegant bedrooms await, each with its own character, though all have sumptuous beds, white duvets and polished antiques authentic and retro; pristine modern bathrooms sport L'Occitane smellies and free standing baths. Back downstairs there's good food too, the kitchen turning out the tasty likes of Scarborough lemon sole fillet with crayfish mousse and crab velouté, and Red Lincoln jugged beef shin with tarragon forcemeat and Wensleydale mash. Eat in the bar or the charming olive-green side room, or the more formal dining room. Or settle in the window with the paper and a hand-pulled pint of Old Speckled Hen – and take in that sweet village view.

Rooms	4 doubles. £110-£130.
Meals	12pm-2.15pm; 6pm-9.30pm; 12pm-7pm Sun. Main courses £9.95-£17.95 (bar); £14.95-£17.95 (restaurant); sandwiches £5.95; Sunday lunch (2 courses) £13.95.
Closed	3pm-5pm.
Directions	By village green, 2 miles west of Boroughbridge and A1M (junc. 48).

Karl & Amanda Mainey
Crown Inn,
Roecliffe,
York YO51 9LY

Tel	+44 (0)1423 322300
Web	www.crowninnroecliffe.co.uk

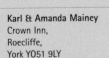

Yorkshire

The Malt Shovel
Brearton

The Bleikers of smoked fish fame took on this pretty 16th-century pub with their son and daughter-in-law in 2006; Jurg's in the kitchen, D'Arcy, Jane and Anna are front of house. Stone floors, open fires and beamed ceilings abound. Choose from three eating spaces – the bar with its salvaged church panelling and candles, the dining room stuffed with vintage finds, the conservatory complete with piano… D'Arcy and Anna are professional opera singers so get the night right and you'll be joined by Mozart or Mahler. Local ingredients are put to ambitious use in a long menu, with much of the veg and meat coming from the owner's new smallholding. There are several gruyère dishes on the bistro menu, while oxtail and kidney pudding is a winner on a damp Yorkshire day. Ales are well-kept, the wines are a cut above the norm.

Meals	12pm-2pm (3pm Sun); 6pm-9pm. No food Sun eve. Main courses £6.95-£12.95 (bistro); £14.95-£26.95 (restaurant); Sunday roast £13.95.
Closed	3pm-6pm, Sun eve, Mon & Tues.
Directions	Village signposted off A61, 5 miles north of Harrogate.

Jurg, Jane, D'Arcy & Anna Bleiker
The Malt Shovel,
Brearton,
Harrogate HG3 3BX
Tel +44 (0)1423 862929
Web www.themaltshovelbrearton.co.uk

Entry 855 Map 12

Yorkshire

Fountaine Inn
Linton

Imagine a village green with a stone bridge and a babbling stream – such is the setting for this 17th-century inn. In spite of some serious sprucing up last year, the Fountaine remains a classic Yorkshire village pub with glowing coal fires, slate floors, curved settles, old beams and cosy corners spread between interconnecting rooms. Weekend walkers arrive in droves for local Litton ales, all day thick-cut sandwiches and traditional burgers with relish and pickles. Wish to linger longer? Then settle into the dining room for a plateful of Kilnsey smoked trout or brisket beef cooked in port wine gravy. The green is well used in summer; for a seat and shade bag one of the smart benches and brollies out front. Note that The Tempest Arms in Elslack and The Mason's Arms in Cumbria are under the same excellent ownership.

Meals	12pm-9pm. Main courses £7.50-£13.99; sandwiches from £4.95.
Closed	Open all day.
Directions	Village signed off B6265 south of Grassington.

Chris Gregson
Fountaine Inn,
Linton,
Skipton BD23 5HJ
Tel +44 (0)1756 752210
Web www.fountaineinnatlinton.co.uk

Entry 856 Map 12

Yorkshire

Worth a visit

857 Whitelocks Turks Head Yard,
Leeds LS1 6HB +44 (0)113 245 3950
In Leeds' centre, an interior barely
changed since Victorian times: old
button-backed leather banquettes
with panelled mirrored dividers in a
tiny narrow bar. Come for the history
not the food, and the Deuchars.

858 The Blacksmith's Arms Front Street,
Lastingham, York YO62 6TL
+44 (0)1751 417247
Low black beams, glowing fires,
timeworn saddles, pints of Daleside
Blond and hearty traditional food –
all this from a rambling old pub,
a rural dream. The church sits next
door, the village is lovely, and
walks abound.

859 Queens Arms Litton, Skipton BD23 5QJ
+44 (0)1756 770208
Glorious walks onto the moors and
along the river from this homely
16th-century Dales inn. Head here
for warming fires, home-brewed
ales, hot food, stunning views.

860 The George Kirk Gill, Hubberholme,
Skipton BD23 SEJ +44 (0)1756 760223
Sympathetically updated but still
fairly basic Dales pub with good beer
and traditional pub food. J B
Priestley's favourite watering hole –
he's buried in the church opposite.

861 The Moorcock Inn Garsdale,
Sedbergh LA10 5PU +44 (0)1969 667488
Wild and remote, crouching in an
isolated moorland spot at the top end
of Wensleydale. There's a quirky
stylishness that is striking in such an
unworldly setting; plus local ales and
homemade pub grub.

862 Charles Bathurst Inn Arkengarthdale,
Richmond DL11 6EN +44 (0)1748 884567
Retreat after a bracing walk to the
Codys' wonderful inn tucked high
above Swaledale. Rustic pine-
furnished interiors; hearty dishes of
local produce; pints of Black Sheep.

863 The Red Lion Inn Langthwaite,
Richmond DL11 6RE +44 (0)1748 884218
A cluster of stone dwellings so
perfectly huddled that film
companies flock. All is carpeted and
cosy with wall seats around cast-iron
tables and a small snug. Black Sheep
and Riggwelter are served in
admirable condition, along with pies,
sausage rolls and sandwiches.

864 The Fat Cat 23 Alma Street,
Sheffield S3 8SA +44 (0)114 249 4801
In Sheffield and desperate for a pint?
Follow signs to the Kelham Island
Museum and this bustling backstreet
boozer. Great home-brewed beers
and six guest ales await. Good value
pub grub.

865 The Robin Hood Inn Greaves Lane,
Little Matlock, Stannington,
Sheffield S6 6BG +44 (0)114 234 4565
This 18th-century pub is tucked
away in English Nature woodland
close to the suburbs. Expect
interesting, good value pub grub and
a range of local beers including
Abbeydale and Kelham Island Bitter.
A bit of a gem.

Wales

Anglesey

The Seacroft
Holyhead

Big skies, sandy beaches, wheeling gulls, spectacular sunsets – that's what you find at the top of Anglesey. The Seacroft makes a great base. It stands 200 metres inland, its whitewashed walls sparkling in the summer sun. It's a very happy place, a pub to some (Tuesday night is quiz night), a restaurant to others (lightly battered calamari, pizzas, mussels from the Menai Strait). Outside is a decked terrace overlooking the lane; inside, New England interiors give an airy seaside feel. Conran lampshades hang above cool little dining booths, pints of Timothy Taylor wait at the American oak bar, dining tables circle a wood-burner that burns on both sides. Spin outside to explore the island and find the wide sands of Trearddur Bay, the coastal path, the sailing school, boats to hire, even a ferry across to Dublin – day trips are easy.

Meals	12pm-2.30pm; 5pm-9.30pm. All day in summer. Main courses £4.95-£20.
Closed	Open all day.
Directions	A55 north onto Anglesey for Holyhead. Exit at junc. 2, B4545 into village. Ravenspoint Road signed right after Spar. On right.

Patrick Flynn
The Seacroft,
Ravenspoint Road,
Trearddur Bay, Holyhead LL65 2YU
Tel   +44 (0)1407 860348
Web   www.theseacroft.com

Entry 866 Map 6

Anglesey

Ship Inn
Red Wharf Bay

The boatmen still walk across from the estuary with their catch. Inside the Ship, fires roar in several fireplaces and bars share nautical bits and bobs. There are pews and benches and bare stone walls, and huge blackboards where the daily specials change almost by the hour. At night, the menu proffers Welsh seafood based on the best the boats have brought in: grilled turbot served with lemon and seasonal vegetables; dressed crab. But the old Ship is so much more – a family-friendly public house where, for 30 years, regulars and visitors have been enjoying great ales and freshly prepared food, from 'brechdanau' – sandwiches – to 'pwdin'. Fine Welsh cheeses, too. These lovely people are as proud of their hospitality as they are of their language – and the vast sea and sand views from the front terraces are inspiring.

Meals	12pm-2.30pm; 6pm-9pm (12pm-9pm Sun). Main courses £7.95-£16.95; bar meals £4.75-£12.95.
Closed	Open all day.
Directions	Off B5025, north of Pentraeth.

Neil Kenneally
Ship Inn,
Red Wharf Bay,
Pentraeth LL75 8RJ
Tel   +44 (0)1248 852568
Web   www.shipinnredwharfbay.co.uk

Entry 867 Map 6

Anglesey

Ye Olde Bulls Head Inn
Beaumaris

This was a favourite haunt of Samuel Johnson and Charles Dickens and now attracts drinkers and foodies like bees to clover. In the rambling, snug-alcoved bar there's draught Bass on offer, while in the modern brasserie in the stables you have a choice of ten wines by the glass to match your sarnies, pasta or poussin (there's a long list of dishes). Spot the ancient weaponry and old ducking stool, which contrasts with the sophisticated remodelling of the intimate Loft Restaurant upstairs. Here, Welsh dishes are designed around seafood from the Menai Strait, and as much beef, lamb and game as the chefs can find on the island. The results: sticky short rib of Welsh black beef, breast of duck with purple figs, and fillets of local brill, seasoned as required with Anglesey sea salt. Service comes with warmth and charm.

Meals	12pm–2pm; 6pm–9pm. Main courses £8.65–£15.75.
Closed	Open all day.
Directions	Castle Street is main street in Beaumaris.

David Robertson
Ye Olde Bulls Head Inn,
Castle Street,
Beaumaris LL58 8AP
Tel   +44 (0)1248 810329
Web www.bullsheadinn.co.uk

Entry 868 Map 6

Carmarthenshire

The Brunant Arms
Caio

Miles from anywhere, the Vale of Cothi is a place of mystery and legend. In this lovely time-warp village, the pub feels warm, cared-for, cosy and at the community's heart. Owners David and Michael say, modestly, they do "good pub food", but what you get is succulent Welsh Black rump steak marinated in red wine and local seasonal game; dive into rabbit stew with herb dumplings or venison steak with pork, peppercorn and chocolate sauce. Expect delightful service, flickering candlelight and proper meals for children; walkers drop by for ploughman's and steaming bowls of cawl. In the bar are traditional tables and chairs, a couple of high-backed settles, logs in the grate, books and bagatelle and five ales on tap, perhaps Caio-brewed Jacobi Red Squirrel. And a lovely little garden with village views.

Meals	12pm–2pm; 6pm–8.30pm. Main courses £7.95–£12.25.
Closed	2.30pm–6pm. Open all day Sunday.
Directions	Signed from A482 midway between Lampeter & Llanwrda.

David Waterhouse
& Michael Edwards
The Brunant Arms,
Caio,
Llanwrda SA19 8RD
Tel   +44 (0)1558 650483

Entry 869 Map 7

Carmarthenshire

The Angel Inn
Salem

A warm, candlelit, unselfconsciously styled grotto of a place. Former Welsh chef of the year Rod Peterson rules the kitchen, but this isn't one of those restaurants masquerading as a pub; you'd feel as happy sinking into the sofa with a malty pint of Rev James. The bar has a quirky, homely charm — squishy sofas covered in throws, fairylights on corkscrew branches, the odd pot plant or Art Deco mirror — while the dining room is a revelation, its dark glossy floors broken up by lovely antique dressers and carved gothic arches. Staff are smart and attentive and the food divine; in the bar, ham hock ravioli with pea velouté; in the restaurant, pork tenderloin with apple and mustard purée and peppered cabbage. No designer vegetables here: portions are hearty and satisfying. Enchanting in every way.

Meals	12.15pm–2pm (Wed–Sun); 7pm–9pm (Wed–Sat); restaurant eves only. Main courses £9.95–£21.95; bar meals £4.25–£13.95.
Closed	Mon & Tues & Sun eve.
Directions	Off the A40 towards Talley, 3 miles north of Llandeilo.

Liz Smith
The Angel Inn,
Salem,
Llandeilo SA19 7LY
Tel +44 (0)1558 823394
Web www.angelsalem.co.uk

Entry 870 Map 7

Carmarthenshire

Y Polyn
Nantgaredig

The pub sits by a fork in the roads, one leading to Aberglasney, the other to the National Botanic Garden of Wales. This lot know their onions — Susan was head chef at the Worshipful Company of Innholders, Maryann chef-patron at the Four Seasons in Nantgaredig — and have jollied up the interior with bold colours, herringbone matting, local art, fresh flowers and candles. A wicker sofa and armchairs by the fire encourage you to loll, while the restaurant has a happy mix of tables and chairs. The short menu is pleasingly simple: fresh local ingredients well put together. Start with duck and ham hock terrine with piccalilli, move onto crispy roast pork belly with caramelised apples or Welsh lamb hotpot, finish with plum and frangipane tart or rhubarb fool. You are equally welcome to just pop in for a drink.

Meals	12pm–2pm; 7pm–9pm (9.30pm Fri–Sun). Main courses £9.50–£15.50 (lunch)' set menus (dinner) £23.50 & £29.50; Sunday lunch £17.50 (2 courses) & £22.50 (3 courses)
Closed	4pm–7pm, Sun eve & Mon all day.
Directions	Off junction of B4300 & B4310 between A48 & A40 east of Carmarthen.

Mark & Susan Manson, Simon & Maryann Wright
Y Polyn,
Nantgaredig, Carmarthen SA32 7LH
Tel +44 (0)1267 290000
Web www.ypolynrestaurant.co.uk

Entry 871 Map 6

Harbourmaster
Aberaeron

Lobster boats at lunch, twinkling harbour lights at dinner, real ale, well-chosen wines and dazzling service. The old harbourmaster's residence has become decidedly chic with an inspirational restaurant and bar. Step in to find a space that's cosy but cool: soft shades, blocked-oak tables. In the celebrated bistro, daily menus are studded with the best local produce and the dishes delight: Carlingford oysters, sea bass with roast pepper, anchovies and ratatouille, rack of Welsh lamb, chocolate fondant. In the bar tuck into local crab linguini with chilli and lime. The Heulyns' dedication to all that is best about Wales shines forth. If you're staying, wind up the staircase to super little bedrooms that come with shuttered windows, loads of colour and quietly funky bathrooms, or book one of the large, swish doubles in the adjoining converted warehouse. You get Frette linen, Welsh wool blankets and a hot water bottle in winter... cosy, characterful, contemporary, they're a pleasure to return to. There are even bikes to borrow: cycle tracks spin off into the hills, coastal paths lead north and south.

Rooms	13: 11 doubles, 2 singles. £110–£190. Suites £150–£250. Singles £60. Half-board from £80 p.p.
Meals	12pm-2.30pm; 6pm-9pm. Main courses £10–£22; bar food from £10.50; set lunch & Sunday lunch £14.50 & £18.
Closed	Open all day.
Directions	A487 south from Aberystwyth. In Aberaeron, right for the harbour. Hotel on waterfront.

Glyn & Menna Heulyn
Harbourmaster,
Pen Cei,
Aberaeron SA46 0BT
Tel   +44 (0)1545 570755
Web   www.harbour-master.com

The Queen's Head
Llandudno Junction

The old wheelwright's cottage has gone up in the world. It now has low beams, polished tables, walls strewn with old maps and a roaring fire in the bar. The food is good, the portions generous and you can see the cooks at work through the open hatch. This is home-cooked pub food with a modern twist that in summer might well include fresh Conwy crab and Great Orme lobster. Starters of foie gras and black pudding or squash and chestnut risotto are served by friendly, smartly turned-out staff. Follow with Jamaican jerk chicken or scrumptious steak and ale pie, finish with bara brith bread-and-butter pudding. Robert and Sally Cureton have been here for years, nurturing a country local that puts those of Llandudno to shame. Complete the treat by booking a night in the sweet parish storehouse across the road, recently converted into a retreat for two. A gallery bedroom under white-painted eaves, a bathroom lavishly tiled, a small private garden for breakfast coffee and fresh croissants – the perfect set up for a romantic break. *The Storehouse Cottage can also be booked for self-catering.*

Rooms	Cottage for 2. £100–£150.
Meals	12pm-2pm; 6pm-9pm (12pm-9pm Sat & Sun). Main courses £9.50–£16.50; Sunday roast £9.95.
Closed	3pm-6pm. Open all day Sat & Sun.
Directions	From A55; A470; right at 3rd r'bout for Penrhyn Bay; 2nd right to Glanwydden after 1.5 miles.

	Robert & Sally Cureton
	The Queen's Head,
	Glanwydden,
	Llandudno Junction LL31 9JP
Tel	+44 (0)1492 546570
Web	www.queensheadglanwydden.co.uk

Conwy

The Groes Inn
Conwy

The first licensed house in Wales (1573) is splendidly old-fashioned, with rambling bars, nooks and crannies, and low beams and doorways that demand heads be bowed. Painted stonework is hung with local prints and pictures, there are displays of teacups and Victorian postcards, a red carpet, a polished Welsh dresser, a wood-burner to keep things toasty. Our pint of Orme's Best – brewed by Justin's cousin – went down a treat, as did the prime-beef burger in its great toasted bap, with crisp mixed salad and delicious hand-cut chips. In the more elegant restaurant, 32 wines accompany award-winning dishes: baked field mushrooms, Conway crab and Anglesey oysters, sweet Welsh lamb with rich rosemary jus, chocolate-scented pancakes with sumptuous ice cream. For summer: a pretty garden with lovely mountain views. Excellent all round.

Meals	12pm-2.15pm; 6.30pm-9pm; 12pm-9pm Sun. No food Sun eve in winter. Main courses £9.65-£16.85 (bar); £13.25-£24.50 (restaurant); sandwiches (lunch only) from £5.75.
Closed	3pm-6pm. Open all day on Sun in summer.
Directions	A55 to Conwy, then B5106 south for 1.5 miles; hotel on right.

Dawn & Justin Humphreys
The Groes Inn,
Ty'n-y-Groes,
Conwy LL32 8TN
Tel   +44 (0)1492 650545
Web   www.groesinn.com

Entry 874 Map 7

Conwy

Pen-y-Bryn
Colwyn Bay

The interior shines like a film set: oak floors and bookcases, open fires and polished furniture – the make-believe world of Brunning & Price. No wonder the locals have taken to Pen-y-Bryn like ducks to water. Staff are well-informed and never too busy to share their knowledge of the food and its provenance. Menus are enticing and generously priced. Pan-fried squid is served with butter bean and chorizo; warming leek and potato soup comes with crusty bread. Pork and lamb is local, cheeses fly the Principality's flag and luscious mussels come from down the coast. You're high up on Colwyn Heights here but a few glasses of Orme Brewery's Cambria will soon warm your toes. Sturdy wooden furniture in the garden fits in well with the neighbourhood's residential air... but inside is best.

Meals	12pm-9.30pm (9pm Sun). Main courses £6.25-£16.95; bar meals £4.50-£9.25; Sunday lunch £10.25.
Closed	Open all day.
Directions	Follow B5113 south west of Colwyn Bay for 1 mile.

Graham Arathoon
Pen-y-Bryn,
Wentworth Avenue,
Colwyn Bay LL29 6DD
Tel   +44 (0)1492 533360
Web   www.penybryn-colwynbay.co.uk

Entry 875 Map 7

The Kinmel Arms
Abergele

In a tiny hamlet- yet easily reachable from the A55 – the Kinmel Arms shines like a culinary beacon. Lynn and Tim arrived nearly a decade ago, and their food continues to wow. Walk in to an open-plan space of cool neutral colours, hardwood floors and a central bar with new stained-glass feature above; then through to a conservatory-style restaurant, painted a cheery yellow, decorated with Tim's photographs. Seasonal brasserie-style menus champion local producers – try venison with port, redcurrant and vanilla jus, or roast hake with Conwy seafood chowder. The slate-topped bar dispenses top quality local ales and great value bin-end wines. Behind this striking stone building are four gorgeous suites, each with wide French windows to a decked seating area facing east and catching the morning sun. Summer breakfasts can be out here; goodies are left the night before in your fridge. Huge beds are topped with crisp linen, walls are fresh yellow, towels are vast. You're a hop from the stunning North Wales coast, and Snowdonia; great walks start from the door. *No children or dogs overnight.*

Rooms	4 suites. £115-£175.
Meals	12pm-2pm; 6.30pm-9.30pm. Main courses £10.95-£20.95; bar meals from £5.50.
Closed	3pm-6pm; Sun & Mon all day (except bank hols).
Directions	A55, junc. 24a from Chester, left up Primrose Hill to village; or junc.24 from Conwy, 1st exit at r'bout onto A547; 1st right towards St George; right onto Primrose Hill.

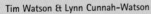

Tim Watson & Lynn Cunnah-Watson
The Kinmel Arms,
The Village,
St George,
Abergele LL22 9BP
Tel +44 (0)1745 832207
Web www.thekinmelarms.co.uk

Entry 876 Map 7

The Lion Inn
Abergele

A simple inn lost in the hills of North Wales, where you are more likely to hear birdsong, bleating sheep or a tractor than a car. The village was the setting for the first Cadfael novel, which is partly based on fact; St Winifred was buried at the priory here. In summer you can sit at colourful tables on the pavement and watch buzzards circle high in the sky, in winter you can sip your pint by a fire that burns on both sides in the bar. Downstairs, there are blue carpets and sprigs of hawthorn decorating stone walls. Upstairs, bedrooms are an unexpected tonic, warm and cosy, nicely stylish, super value for money. There are Farrow & Ball paints on old stone walls and Canadian pitch pine furniture, rustic wooden beds with crisp white linen and Welsh wool blankets, spotless bathrooms, DVDs for wintery nights. Big breakfasts set you up for the day – porridge, croissants, free-range eggs – so burn off the excess on Snowdon or ride your bike through local forests. The mobile reception is useless, the hospitality is magnificent, and Portmerion and Anglesey are close.

Rooms	5: 2 doubles, 1 twin, 1 single, 1 family room. £85. Singles from £53. Family room from £100.
Meals	7pm-8.30pm Fri & Sat. Main courses £8-£15.
Closed	Mon, Tues & Thurs. Open from 7pm Wed, Fri, Sat & Sun.
Directions	A55 to Abergele; A544 south to Llansannan; B5384 west to Gwytherin. In village.

Tim & Fiona Hughes
The Lion Inn,
Gwytherin,
Abergele LL22 8UU
Tel +44 (0)1745 860123
Web www.thelioninn.net

Entry 877 Map 7

Bryn Tyrch
Capel Curig

Bang in the heart of Snowdonia National Park: a no-nonsense mountain retreat for walkers and climbers. Its interior is well-worn, its style laid-back and, best of all, there's a great big blackboard over the fire displaying terrific walkers' food from a Romanian chef. The Hungarian goulash is fabulous – served in a mountain of a roll, washed down with a great pint of Orme ale. Evening blackboards suggest a generous approach to vegetarian and vegan dishes (such as woodland mushroom and chestnut wellington) alongside the delicious Welsh beef and lamb, the fish from Anglesey and the local sausages with cheese and chive mash; puddings will keep you going all day. Picture windows run the length of the main bar with carefully placed tables making the most of the view and there are big brown chesterfields by the fire – arrive early to nab one. Bedrooms are small but beautifully formed: super-comfy beds, big gleaming baths and showers, views worth waking up for; catch the mountains in snow and you'll imagine yourself skiing. Friendly staff know all the best hikes and climbs.

Rooms	12: 10 twins/doubles, 2 bunk rooms. £40–£110. Singles from £40.
Meals	12pm-2pm; 6pm-9pm. Main courses £10.95-£17.95.
Closed	Mon-Thurs lunch Nov-Mar. Open all day Fri-Sun.
Directions	On A5 near Plas-y-Brenin Mountain Centre, 5 miles west of Betws-y-Coed.

Rachel Roberts
Bryn Tyrch,
Capel Curig,
Betws-y-Coed LL24 0EL

Tel   +44 (0)1690 720223
Web   www.bryntyrchinn.co.uk

Entry 878 Map 7

Denbighshire

Pant-yr-Ochain
Gresford

A long drive snakes through landscaped parkland to this magnificent old country house sheltered by trees. It's multi-gabled with colourwashed walls pierced both by tiny, stone-mullioned and orangery-style windows. To one side a huge conservatory opens up views across terraces to the estate lake; within, a jigsaw of richly panelled rooms and drinking areas lures those who come to dine and those in search of the hop. Intimate corners, comfy alcoves and private snugs, with open fires, quarry tiles and bare boards below an eccentric ceiling-line. Everywhere, a cornucopia of bric-a-brac: penny slots and cases of clay pipes, caricatures and prints. It sounds OTT but it fits comfortably here, and the reliable Brunning & Price menus of home-cooked, locally sourced food are available. Beer aficionados revel in nine real ales.

Meals	12pm-9.30pm (9pm Sun). Main courses £7.25-£16.95.
Closed	Open all day.
Directions	Gresford signed off A483 Wrexham bypass.

Lindsey Douglas
Pant-yr-Ochain,
Old Wrexham Road,
Gresford, Wrexham LL12 8TY
Tel   +44 (0)1978 853525
Web   www.pantyrochain-gresford.co.uk

Entry 879 Map 7

Denbighshire

The Corn Mill
Llangollen

The 18th century has been left far behind in this renovated corn mill beside the swiftly flowing Dee. Not only is the interior light, airy and well-designed but the busy menu is laced with contemporary ideas. There are also gorgeous views onto the river whether you're quaffing your pint of Phoenix in the fabulous bar, or settling down to eat in one of the upper-floor dining areas. The decked veranda-cum-walkway is stunning, built out over the cascading rapids with a gangway overhanging one end beyond the revolving water wheel. Watch dippers and wagtails as you tuck into smoked haddock and mozzarella rarebit, Welsh pork sausages with spring onion mash, king prawn salad with chilli dressing. The Brunning & Price formula is known for its 'something-for-everyone' appeal, and the setting is supreme.

Meals	12pm-9.30pm (9pm Sun). Main courses £8.95-£16.50.
Closed	Open all day.
Directions	Off Castle Street (A539) just south of the river bridge.

Andrew Barker
The Corn Mill,
Castle Street,
Llangollen LL20 8PN
Tel   +44 (0)1978 869555
Web   www.cornmill-llangollen.co.uk

Entry 880 Map 7

The Hand at Llanarmon
Llangollen

Single-track lanes plunge you into the middle of nowhere, lush valleys rise and fall – pull on the boots and scale a mountain. Back at the inn, once frequented by 16th-century drovers, the pleasures of a country local are hard to miss. A coal fire burns on the range in reception, a fire crackles under brass in the front bar and a wood-burner warms the lofty dining room. There are exposed stone walls, low beamed ceilings, old pine settles and candles on the mantelpiece, a games room for darts and pool, a quiet sitting room for maps and books. Delicious food is popular with locals, so grab a table and enjoy seasonal menus – perhaps chicken liver parfait with fruit chutney and toasted homemade bread, duck with pancetta, black pudding and red wine, and autumn berry pudding. Stay and you'll get a lovely cooked Welsh breakfast. Bedrooms are just as they should be: not too fancy, cosy and warm, with crisp white linen and scrupulously clean. A very friendly place: Martin and Gaynor are full of passionate enthusiasm and have made their home warmly welcoming. Everyone loves this place.

Rooms	13: 8 doubles, 4 twins, 1 suite. £85-£120. Singles from £52.50. Half-board from £60 p.p.
Meals	12pm-2.30pm (12.30pm-2.45pm Sun); 6.30pm-9pm. Main courses £12.50-£20; bar meals £6-£10.50.
Closed	Open all day.
Directions	Leave A5 south of Chirk for B4500. Llanarmon 11 miles on.

Gaynor & Martin De Luchi
The Hand at Llanarmon,
Llanarmon Dyffryn Ceiriog,
Llangollen LL20 7LD

Tel	+44 (0)1691 600666
Web	www.thehandhotel.co.uk

Entry 881 Map 7

Flintshire

Glasfryn
Sychdyn

Drawing a hugely varied crowd, this solid red brick pub – a former judges' residence with an Arts & Crafts pedigree – sits on a south-facing slope with views over the town to the Clwydian range. A stunning makeover has led to acres of oak flooring, Indian rugs, book-lined walls and locally themed pictures and prints. Real ale aficionados will thrill to eight cask ales; Purple Moose's Snowdonia ale delivers a crisp, citrus beer whilst Flowers Original is, quite literally, brewing heritage in a glass. Foodies are not forgotten and can feast on mint-braised shoulder of lamb with mustard mash and broccoli or minced beef and onion pie with chips and peas. There are nearly 80 malts, every spirit imaginable and an Italian makes the coffee – need we say more? Yes, it's abuzz – and the staff couldn't be more helpful.

Meals	12pm-9.30pm (9pm Sun). Main courses £8.50-£15.95; sandwiches from £4.95.
Closed	Open all day.
Directions	Leave Mold on A5119, turn left to the theatre, pub on left.

James Meakin
Glasfryn,
Raikes Lane,
Sychdyn, Mold CH7 6LR
Tel +44 (0)1352 750500
Web www.glasfryn-mold.co.uk

Entry 882 Map 7

Flintshire

Stables Bar
Sychdyn

The approach towards Soughton Hall, a former Bishop's Palace, is worth the visit alone. The listed stables to one side have been startlingly transformed but preserve the memory of the racing occupants; now the cobbles are varnished and carry oriental rugs, the huge old blacksmith's bellows have become a fireside table, and a Beecher's Brook of a bar is fronted with metal bar stools. Honey Pot and Wizard's Wonder are beers not horses, and the posh pub grub flourishes local and seasonal specialities. Upstairs, through the impressive wine shop where South African bottles reign, is a restaurant with exposed brick walls under a huge raftered roof. Try pan-fried loin of venison served with crushed celeriac, crispy pancetta, and pommes Anna with a blackberry caramel. Super staff and fountain'd gardens make this a winner.

Meals	12pm-9.30pm (1pm-3pm; 7pm-9.30pm Sun). Main courses £7.50-£13.95 (lunch), £10-£18.95 (dinner)
Closed	Open all day.
Directions	Follow Northop sign from A55; A5119 through village; brown signs for Soughton Hall.

John & Rosemary Rodenhurst
Stables Bar,
Sychdyn, Mold CH7 6AB
Tel +44 (0)1352 840577
Web www.soughtonhall.co.uk

Entry 883 Map 7

Gwynedd

Penhelig Arms
Aberdyfi

It's small, friendly and rather smart, and the way things are done here is second to none. Village life pours through: old boys drop by for a pint, passing friends stop for a chat, families book in for a birthday lunch. Staff are friendly, and generous prices draw a loyal crowd. Fronting the inn is the tiniest harbour; along the quay come the fishermen, butchers, bakers and smallholders who deliver daily to the kitchen. The food is fabulous and the fish comes straight from the sea. Try hake stew with garlic and chorizo, or fillet steak with peppercorn sauce for carnivores; on sunnier days you can enjoy a refreshing drink and a snack at your chosen spot close to the harbour wall. Local art adorns the walls in the restaurant and a fire burns in the local's bar. Coast and hills beckon – bring the boots.

Passionate micro-brewers have been innovative and experimental, tapping into and promoting the rich vein of different beers that can be brewed without compromising on quality. There are now fantastic milds (dark and light), cracking bitters and a whole host of other beers, stouts, porters, fruit beers, wheat beers and craft lagers for the discerning beer drinker to discover.

Meals	12pm-2pm; 7pm-9pm (bar meals from 6pm). Main courses £8.95-£15.95; bar snacks from £4; set dinner £29; Sunday lunch £19.
Closed	3pm-5.30pm (5pm Sat & Sun). Open all day at peak times.
Directions	Through Machynlleth, then A493 to Aberdyfi. Inn on right entering village. Parking opposite.

Glyn Davies
Penhelig Arms,
27-29 Terrace Road,
Aberdyfi LL35 0LT

| Tel | +44 (0)1654 767215 |
| Web | www.penheligarms.com |

Entry 884 Map 6

Gwynedd

Y Beuno
Caernarfon

This old coaching inn faces squarely out to sea with the dramatic outline of the Yr Eifl Mountains behind. A long Welsh oak bar sits on square slate flags alongside worn polished floorboards, exposed stone and beams, small fires, cosy armchairs and a vibrant carpet in a snug that hosts that most authentic of pub pastimes, a dartboard. For the adventurous, Purple Moose's Mysterious Myrtle Stout has to be tried, as does Conwy Honey Fayre. The food comes with a Gallic twist courtesy of a Breton chef who does wonders with Caernarfon Bay seafood and lamb and beef from the mountains. The Welsh Black sirloin steak served in a rich mixed mushroom and garlic sauce will set you up for a long walk, as will the fish of the day, landed on the beach below. Sausages and burgers are homemade, bread is baked daily and a kitchen garden is abundant with vegetables and herbs. Just upstairs are a handful of good-sized, individually furnished bedrooms with solid wood furniture, and sumptuously elegant superior rooms with bathrooms to match: ask for one with a view across to Anglesey.

Rooms	7: 4 doubles, 2 twins, 1 four-poster. £85–£105. Four-poster £135.
Meals	12pm-2.30pm; 6pm-9pm. Light snacks 2.30pm-5.30pm. Main courses from £8.95; Sunday roast from £9.95.
Closed	Open all day.
Directions	In centre of village, set back from A499.

Ann Thomas
Y Beuno,
Clynnog Fawr,
Caernarfon LL54 5PB
Tel   +44 (0)1286 660785
Web   www.ybeuno.com

Entry 885 Map 6

The White Hart Village Inn
Llangybi

They say T S Eliot visited in 1935; this is his "white hart over the white well" in *Usk*. Between church, post office and blacksmith (the well is sadly defunct), it is now a food-centred inn, handsomely revamped. The bar area is traditional with exposed stonework and black-painted beams, and cushioned settles by the huge 16th-century fireplace. Pop in for a swift half or a meal in one of two rooms, one with dark tables and upholstered chairs, the other with a more contemporary feel. The day's specials are influenced by what's local and in season and our casserole with chicken falling off the bone and big chunks of apple was perfect for a winter lunch. The two cosy bedrooms are up a private side stair, with nice firm mattresses on attractively dressed pine beds, tub chairs in red leather, neutral-coloured fitted carpets and curtains, and a good bright shower room. There's a mini-kitchen (planning regs mean no chance of a skylight) for a continental breakfast that is brought up to you: croissants, cheeses, fresh fruits. So you may linger or leave early, take a local walk, return for Sunday lunch.

Rooms	2: 1 double, 1 single. £80.
Meals	12pm–2pm (2.30pm Sun); 6pm–9.30pm. Main courses £8.95–£15.45.
Closed	3pm–6pm; Sun eve from 5pm; Mon & Tues all day.
Directions	M4 junc. 25 onto B4596 (Caerleon Rd); through Caerleon village centre on High St, over r'bout onto Usk Rd. On to Llangybi.

David Pell
The White Hart Village Inn,
Llangybi,
Usk NP15 1NP

Tel	+44 (0)1633 450258
Web	www.whitehartvillageinn.com

Entry 886 Map 7

Monmouthshire

The Charthouse
Llanvihangel Gobion

At this cute little whitewashed roadside inn you'll find a charming welcome from Jane and Michael (she runs the show; he gets involved at weekends). At the back is an immaculate terraced garden, inside are three rustic-chic rooms with a nautical theme. The moment you get 'on board' you can look forward to being wined and dined in the woody Cabin downstairs – or on the carpeted Upper Deck, super-stylish with wood-burner, brick walls and cool yachting pics. It is modern, crisp and fresh, with a menu to match. So tuck into the best that Wales has to offer – succulent Welsh Black beef, ravioli of local goat's cheese, fish pie with homemade chips, glace nougatine – and scan the daily blackboard specials for seasonal dishes. Ales include Butty Bach; wines (21 bins) match the zippy feel.

Monmouthshire

Raglan Arms
Llandenny

An effortless combination of village local and excellent place to eat. In a bright, spacious bar with slate underfoot, anticipation mounts as you peruse the menu from leather sofas arranged around a log fire. These Anglo-Swedish co-owners prepare fairly priced dishes showcasing produce from the area. Savour chicken liver and pistachio parfait, brill with linguini, local samphire, mussels and chilli, or an upmarket open sandwich: slow-roasted shoulder of Gloucester Old Spot with apple sauce. To finish: pear and almond tart, a selection of cheeses. You can eat alfresco on the smart raised deck area, replete with planters and parasols, when the sun shines. Butty Bach is the only real ale; if this doesn't appeal, console yourself with the well-chosen modern wine list. It's worth the small detour to get here.

Meals	12pm-2.15pm (3pm Sun); 7pm-9.15pm. Main courses £6.20-£8 (lunch), £11.50-£18.50 (dinner).
Closed	3pm-6.30pm, Sun after 5pm, Mon & Tues all day.
Directions	Village is on B4598 between Abergavenny & Usk, just south of A40.

Meals	12pm-2.30pm (3pm Sun); 6.30pm-9.30pm. Main courses £6-£10 (lunch), £10-£19 (dinner).
Closed	3pm-6pm, Sun eve Mon & bank hols all day.
Directions	In the centre of Llandenny.

Michael & Jane Davies
The Charthouse,
Llanvihangel Gobion,
Abergavenny NP7 9AY
Tel   +44 (0)1873 840414
Web   www.thecharthouse-bar-bistro.co.uk

Entry 887 Map 7

Giles Cunliffe & Charlott Fagergard
Raglan Arms,
Llandenny, Usk NP15 1DL
Tel   +44 (0)1291 690800
Web   www.raglanarms.com

Entry 888 Map 7

The Beaufort Arms
Raglan

There's no missing the gracious old coaching inn on Raglan's High Street, with its south-facing terrace at the front. Inside, a big entrance hall of half-panelled walls and rippling glass takes you back to the 1920s. There are leather and wicker-arm chairs, open fires, slate floors and cosy corners, and a smart modern brasserie. The place is big enough to get lost in, just about everybody comes here and Eliot and Jana head a dedicated team. Choose from boarded menus in the big bar (lamb rump with mash and rosemary jus; beer-battered hake) or pick the brasserie for something more fancy, perhaps Cornish crab linguini with mussels, pernod and dill. To drink: local ales, Belgian beers, New World wines, French coffee. Bedrooms in the main house are inviting and stylish; the most recently refurbished are more contemporary. Most have lovely country and church views, all come with white linen, goose down duvets and pretty throws. (Note: the cheaper rooms in the old stables are far simpler.) Raglan's exquisite medieval castle is close, as are the mighty Brecon Beacons and the Wye and Usk valleys.

Rooms	15 + 1: 8 doubles, 5 twins, 2 singles. Apartment for 2. £60-£105.
Meals	12pm-3pm (5pm Fri-Sun); 6pm-9.30pm (8.30pm Sun). Main courses £8.95-£19.50; bar meals from £4.95; Sunday lunch £14.95 & £16.95.
Closed	Open all day.
Directions	At junction of A40/A449 between Monmouth & Abergavenny. 0.25 miles into village, opposite church.

Eliot & Jana Lewis
The Beaufort Arms,
High Street,
Raglan, Usk NP15 2DY
Tel   +44 (0)1291 690412
Web   www.beaufortraglan.co.uk

Monmouthshire

Clytha Arms
Clytha

The inn stands on the old coaching route into border country, in gorgeous surroundings. Sit outside in fine weather and enjoy cockles, crab sandwiches, tapas and a ploughman's with three local cheeses. Inside, two bars: one with button-back sofas and low tables, the other more rustic, with high ceiling, stripped floors and bar games; both have cheery fires. The restaurant is smart and homely with marbled walls, new stone floor, and white linen tablecloths. In the kitchen is Andrew Canning, the local genius who rustles up grilled tuna Sicilian style, herb-crusted hake, and steak and oyster pie. The monthly set menu is full of temptations such as lamb mixed grill with garlic jus and seafood stew. The wine list (11 by the glass) and the range of beers and cider are impressive, and there's homemade perry for the bibulously curious.

Meals	12.30pm-2.15pm (2.30pm Sun); 7pm-9.30pm (9pm Mon); no food Sun eve. Main courses £13-£19; tapas from £3.90; set menu £20 & £23.
Closed	3pm-6pm & Mon lunch. Open all day Fri-Sun.
Directions	6 miles east of Abergavenny off old Abergavenny to Raglan road.

Andrew & Beverley Canning
Clytha
Arms, Clytha, Abergavenny, NP7 9BW
Tel   +44 (0)1873 840206
Web   www.clytha-arms.com

Entry 890 Map 7

Monmouthshire

The Hardwick
Hardwick

After working in Marco Pierre White's kitchens, Stephen Terry runs his own show. In the shadows of the Black Mountains, the pub's proximity to The Walnut Tree – which Stephen also owned – has helped put this roadside inn on the gastropub map. The stripped-back-to-basics interior is a modest background for some seriously fine wines and astonishingly good food. While some of the ingredients are imported from Italy, most originate from closer to home – and that includes the Welsh beers on draught. The lengthy menu incorporates Blumenthalian marvels such as thrice-cooked chips, alongside comforting classics (a meltingly rich Longhorn beef pie with oxtail, kidney and ale). Try the set lunch (Tues-Fri), then walk off your indulgence among some of the best landscapes of Wales.

Meals	12pm-3pm; 6.30pm-10pm. Main courses £13.25-£23; Sunday lunch £11.50 & £18.50.
Closed	3pm-6pm, Sun eve & Mon all day.
Directions	One mile south-east from Abergavenny via A40 & B4598. Call for directions first.

Stephen Terry
The Hardwick,
Raglan Road,
Hardwick, Abergavenny NP7 9AA
Tel   +44 (0)1873 854220
Web   www.thehardwick.co.uk

Entry 891 Map 7

The Bell at Skenfrith
Skenfrith

The Bell stands by an ancient stone bridge in a little-known valley with hugely beautiful hills rising behind and a Norman castle paddling in the river a hundred yards from the front door. A sublime spot – and the inn is as good. It dates to the 17th century, but its crisply designed interiors ooze a cool country chic. In the locals' bar you find slate floors, open fires, plump-cushioned armchairs and polished oak. In summer, doors fly open and life decants onto the terrace at the back; priceless views of wood and hill are interrupted only by the odd chef pottering past on his way to a rather impressive kitchen garden. Stripped boards in the restaurant give an airy feel, so stop for delicious food served by young, attentive staff, perhaps roasted red pepper soup, breast of local duck, and fig tarte tatin with lemon and thyme ice cream. Finish with a fine cognac – the list is long. Bedrooms above are as you'd expect: dressed in fine fabrics, uncluttered and elegant, brimming with light, some beamed, others overlooking the river. Circular walks start from the front door and sweep you into blissful hills.

Rooms	11: 6 doubles, 2 twins, 3 four-posters. £110–£170. Four-posters £195–£220. Singles from £75 (Sun–Thurs).
Meals	12pm–2.30pm; 7pm–9.30pm (9pm Sun). Main courses £8–£15 (lunch), £16–£19 (dinner); Sunday lunch £19 & £23.
Closed	Open all day. Closed Tues Nov–Mar.
Directions	From Monmouth, B4233 to Rockfield; B4347 for 5 miles; right on B4521, Skenfrith 1 mile.

William & Janet Hutchings
The Bell at Skenfrith,
Skenfrith,
Abergavenny NP7 8UH

Tel	+44 (0)1600 750235
Web	www.skenfrith.co.uk

Monmouthshire

Hunter's Moon Inn
Llangattock Lingoed

Haydn Jones and his partner Jana run this deep-country inn just off Offa's Dyke with enthusiasm and passion. The original building, with its low ceilings and 1217-flagged floors, was constructed by stonemasons establishing a place to stay before building the neighbouring church. Book ahead; the 'table for the evening' policy ensures much care is taken with the locally sourced food. Specials may include 28-day aged beef, shank of lamb, or pork cooked in a sage, cream and apple sauce. The local and guest ales are well-kept, the wine list well chosen, there's Leffe on draught and a range of bottled ciders. In summer you sit out — under parasols overlooking the churchyard or in the beer garden. There's a drying room for walkers, too.

Pembrokeshire

The Old Point House Inn
Angle

Lonely, windswept, so close to the sea they're cut off at spring tide. Weary fishermen have beaten a path to the old inn's door for centuries; part-built with shipwreck timbers, it started life as a bakehouse for the ships' biscuits. The tiny, low-beamed bar, its bare walls papered with old navigation charts, is utterly authentic, the restaurant is cosy by night, and in fine weather you may sit out and devour vast prawn sandwiches. Everyone is welcome here, from weathered regulars meeting over pints of Felinfoel to families in for Sunday lunch. Naturally, menus favours fish, with local Milford cod, sea bass, and a delicious, peppery fish chowder chalked up on the board. Other crowd-pleasers include a pint of prawns and rib-eye steak with red wine sauce with piles of chips.

Meals	12.30pm-2.30pm (Sat & Sun); 6.30pm-9.30pm (Thurs-Sat). Main courses £8-£20.
Closed	Mon all day, Tues-Fri lunch, 3pm-6.30pm Sat (7pm Sun).
Directions	A465 Abergavenny to Hereford; for Skenfrith on B4521 thro' Llanvetherine. Signed left to Llangattock Lingoed.

Haydn Jones
Hunter's Moon Inn,
Llangattock Lingoed,
Abergavenny NP7 8RR
Tel   +44 (0)1873 821499
Web   www.hunters-moon-inn.co.uk

Entry 893 Map 7

Meals	12pm-3pm; 6.30pm-9pm (6pm-8pm Fri & Sat). Main courses £4.50-£12.75.
Closed	3pm-6pm. Closed Tues in winter. Open all day in summer.
Directions	From Pembroke follow signs for Angle. There, from Lifeboat Trust, cross beach to pub.

John Noble
The Old Point House Inn,
Angle Village,
Angle,
Pembroke SA71 5AS
Tel   +44 (0)1646 641205

Entry 894 Map 6

Stackpole Inn
Stackpole

In the lovely Stackpole National Park, a jolly, thriving, dining pub with owners who are infectiously enthusiastic and a chef with great local food connections: as much as possible is Welsh and all is cooked from scratch, so don't expect fast food. Ramble through several rustic rooms with a mix of exposed beams and stonework, carpets and slate floors, all warmed with wood-burners, freshly painted, softly lit and cosy. Daily specials (fresh sea bass, Welsh Black beef) compete with a sensibly priced menu: try Welsh blue cheese pots with crusty bread and local pork in an apple and cider cream sauce. There are several good single-malt whiskies to choose from, wine is plentiful by the glass and real ales include Rev James and Double Dragon. Bedrooms are in a separate building and all are light and airy with a contemporary feel; family rooms are excellent value. This is perfect for walking the coastal path, climbing cliff and rock faces, fishing from beach or boat, surfing those tricky beaches; each room has a locker downstairs for outdoor equipment and there's a cycle rack.

Rooms	4: 2 twins/doubles, 2 family rooms.£80–£90. Singles from £55.
Meals	12pm–2pm; 6.30pm–9pm. Main courses £10.90–£19.90.
Closed	2.30pm–6pm & Sun eve in winter. Open all day Sat & in summer.
Directions	B4319 south of Pembroke for 3 miles, then left for Stackpole. Through Stackpole Cheriton, up hill, right at T-junction. On right.

Gary & Becky Evans
Stackpole Inn,
Stackpole,
Pembroke SA71 5DF
Tel   +44 (0)1646 672324
Web   www.stackpoleinn.co.uk

Pembrokeshire

The Swan
Little Haven

Little Haven is jumbled into the seaward end of a narrow valley with glorious views across St Bride's Bay... trek up the cobbled path to reach the lovely old Swan, whose fabric and fortunes have been restored by Paul Morris. Original features abound in the uncluttered but snug side room and warm blue-painted dining room; imagine bare boards and stone, simple wooden furnishings and glowing stoves for wild winter days. Equally warming is the delicious food: at lunch, homemade sodabread topped with smoked salmon or traditional Welsh cawl with local Caerfai cheese; in the evening, venison with red cabbage and autumn fruits, and bitter chocolate tart. For summer there's a broad wall to lounge on and a tiny terrace, so settle in for the day with a foaming pint of Bass and enjoy the views – they're stupendous.

Meals	12pm-2pm; 6pm-9pm.
	Main courses £4.50-£9.90 (lunch), £5.90-£16.90 (dinner).
Closed	Open all day.
Directions	By the quay in the village centre.

Paul & Tracey Morris
The Swan,
Point Road, Little Haven,
Haverfordwest SA62 3UL

Tel   +44 (0)1437 781880
Web   www.theswanlittlehaven.co.uk

Entry 896 Map 6

Pembrokeshire

The Sloop
Porthgain

Perfectly in keeping with its seawashed setting, The Sloop has been welcoming fisherfolk since 1743. The village remains a fishing harbour – the landlord catches his own lobster, mackerel and crab and dives for scallops – but, until the Thirties, Porthgain was more famous for bricks and granite. Weatherbeaten on the outside, with a little seating area at the front, the old Sloop is surprisingly cosy within. Expect bare beams, some bare boards, a happy melée of furniture, a canoe suspended from the ceiling and a board announcing daily specials. Tuck into homemade mackerel pâté, lobster thermidor or Welsh Black steak; breakfast too (open to all) sounds a treat. Holiday-makers descend in summer but the rest of the year this is a community pub, with a proper games room and real fires.

Meals	12pm-2.30pm; 6pm-9.30pm (also 3pm-5pm in summer).
	Main courses £5.35-£18; snacks from £3.90-£6.10.
Closed	Open all day.
Directions	Village signed off A487 at Croesgoch between Fishguard & St Davids.

Matthew Blakiston
The Sloop,
Porthgain,
Haverfordwest SA62 5BN

Tel   +44 (0)1348 831449
Web   www.sloop.co.uk

Entry 897 Map 6

Pembrokeshire

Dyffryn Arms
Pontfaen

Miss the small sign peeping out of Bessie's well-tended garden and you'll miss the pub – which would be a shame, because it's a treasure. Bessie has been here half a century and nothing has changed in that time, including the outside loos. A trooper possessed of a dry wit she shows no sign of tiring, keeps the place spotless and serves from a hatch in the wall seven days a week. The bar has the proportions of a domestic front room so you'll fall into easy conversation with the locals: farmers, hunters and the like. Old quarry tiles on the floor, fresh flowers on the window sill, peanuts, crisps and Bass from the barrel – it's perfect. To the left of the pub is a garden with a bench under Bessie's washing line from which you may drink in the peace and the view: of the verdant little valley below, threaded by a silver river.

Meals	No food served.
Closed	Open all day.
Directions	Pontfaen is on the Gwaun Valley road off the B4313 east of Fishguard, second on left.

Bessie Davies
Dyffryn Arms,
Cwm Gwaun,
Pontfaen,
Fishguard SA65 9SG
Tel   +44 (0)1348 881305

Entry 898 Map 6

Pembrokeshire

Tafarn Sinc
Rosebush

The highest pub in Pembrokeshire is the quirkiest pub in the world – or a close contender. It was speedily erected in 1876 as a hotel on the GWR railway; now the giant, red-painted, corrugated zinc building oversees a tiny railway platform complete with mannequin-travellers and a Victorian pram. It is beautifully tended outside and in, with a prettily trellised garden and an arresting Alpine-panelled public bar. Hams and lamps hang from the ceiling, there's sawdust on the floors and two big wood-burners belch out heat. It's warm and welcoming and full of merry walkers. Hafwen, the perfect landlady, and husband Brian oversee the cosy, constant buzz and serve a solidly traditional menu (Preseli lamb burgers, faggots with onion gravy), and their own excellent beer. No further introduction is needed – just a visit.

Meals	12pm-2pm; 6pm-9pm; no food Sun eve in winter. Main courses £9.80-£16.50. Sandwiches from £3.50. Sunday lunch (3 courses) £12.95.
Closed	Open all day. Closed Mon in winter.
Directions	Rosebush is on the B4329 Haverfordwest to Cardigan road.

Brian & Hafwen Davies
Tafarn Sinc,
Rosebush,
Clynderwen SA66 7QT
Tel   +44 (0)1437 532214
Web   www.tafarnsinc.com

Entry 899 Map 6

Pembrokeshire

Nag's Head Inn
Abercych

Behind the vibrant orange exterior is a feast of bare wood and stone. The lighting is soft and warm, there's a rustic chicken-wire sideboard crammed with old beer bottles, a glass cabinet displaying the famous 'rat' of Abercych (a stuffed coypu) and a photo of old Emrys, the treasured regular after whom the home-brewed beer is named. The Nag's Head has a simple, tasteful charm, is full of old tales, curios and quirkery and serves the best kind of hearty pub food, from whitebait and fresh soups to steak and kidney pudding, treacle tart, and delicious Sunday roasts. Come with the family and explore the pushchair-friendly Clynfyw sculpture trail – it starts from here. There's a play area too, in the long, lovely riverside garden. By a bridge on the river bank, at the bottom of a steep hill, the setting alone is worth the trip.

Meals	12pm-2pm; 6pm-9pm. Main courses £8-£15.
Closed	3pm-6pm & Mon all day (except bank hols). Open all day Sun.
Directions	Off A4332 between Cenarth & Boncath.

Sam Jamieson
Nag's Head Inn,
Abercych,
Boncath SA37 0HJ
Tel   +44 (0)1239 841200

Entry 900 Map 6

Powys

Nantyffin Cider Mill Inn
Crickhowell

Diners pour in here for menus that spotlight pork, lamb, duck, guinea fowl, beef – exuberantly casseroled in farmhouse cider. A network of small suppliers provides the rest, while autumn brings mushrooms and game from a nearby estate. It started life in the 15th century as a drovers' inn and an old cider press occupies one end of the impressive, high-raftered restaurant in the old mill room. You can also sit in one of two intimate bars and choose from a bar menu and a specials board that is chalked up daily. Expect country cooking concocted with minimum fuss and maximum flavour – lamb with colcannon mash and rosemary garlic sauce, fish casserole – plus ales and ciders on tap, delicious wines by the glass, hot punch in winter and luscious lemonade in summer.

Meals	12pm-2.30pm; 6.30pm-9.30pm. Main courses £7.95-£16.95; Sunday lunch, 2 courses, £15.50 & £19.50.
Closed	3pm-6pm (7pm Sun), Sun eve in winter & all day Mon (except bank hols).
Directions	1 mile outside Crickhowell on the A40 to Brecon, at junc with A479.

Vic, Ann & Sharon Williams
Nantyffin Cider Mill Inn,
Brecon Road,
Crickhowell NP8 1SG
Tel   +44 (0)1873 810775
Web   www.cidermill.co.uk

Entry 901 Map 7

Bear Hotel
Crickhowell

Viewed from the square of this small market town, the 15th-century frontage of the old coaching inn looks modest. Behind the cobbles and the summer flowers, it is a warren of surprises and mild eccentricity – bars and brasserie at the front, nooks and crannies carved at the back – behind which is the family-and dog-friendly garden. The beamy lounge has parquet, plush seating and a mighty fire; settle in and savour their good beers, wines, whiskies and ports. There are two dining areas where at night you can feast on Welsh Black beef, Usk salmon, Brecon venison and locally grown seasonal vegetables and regional farmhouse cheeses. Homemade ice creams, mousses and puddings are equally sumptuous. We've never seen the place empty and Mrs Hindmarsh is still firmly in charge of an operation that rarely comes off the rails.

Meals	12pm-2pm; 6pm-10pm (7pm-9.30pm Sun). Main courses £5.95-£20.
Closed	3pm-6pm (7pm Sun).
Directions	In centre of Crickhowell, on A40 between Abergavenny & Brecon.

Judy Hindmarsh
Bear Hotel,
High Street,
Crickhowell NP8 1BW

Tel +44 (0)1873 810408
Web www.bearhotel.co.uk

Entry 902 Map 7

The White Swan
Llanfrynach

The front resembles the row of cottages this once was but the cavernous interior has been remodelled and its central bar is a split-level zone, making bar staff appear unnaturally tall as they serve Brains Bitter and other fine ales. The specials board majors in fish, so there could be bouillabaisse with aïoli and sea bass with tomato and artichoke mash – alongside confit shoulder and best end of local mutton with roasted shallots. The restaurant menu may include Hereford beef, Brecon lamb, local pheasant; the cheeses are Welsh and the ice creams and puddings homemade. There are farmhouse tables, leather sofas, big wood-burners and a trellised patio at the back – gorgeous in summer. You're spoilt for walks here, so stride off into the Brecon Beacons for the day. Or potter along the towpath of the Monmouthshire & Brecon canal.

Meals	12pm-2pm (2.30pm Sun); 7pm-9.30pm (9pm Sun). Main courses £10.95-£17.95.
Closed	3pm-6.30pm & Mon.
Directions	Signed from A40 3 miles east of Brecon on Crickhowell road.

Richard Griffiths
The White Swan,
Llanfrynach,
Brecon LD3 7BZ

Tel +44 (0)1874 665276
Web www.the-white-swan.com

Entry 903 Map 7

The Felin Fach Griffin
Brecon

It's quirky, homespun, utterly intoxicating and thrives on a mix of relaxed informality and colourful style. The timber-framed bar resembles the sitting room of a small hip country house, with sofas in front of a fire that burns on both sides and backgammon waiting to be played. Painted stone walls throughout come in blocks of colour. An open-plan feel sweeps you through to the restaurant, where stock pots simmer on an Aga; try roasted scallops, Welsh lamb, crème brûlée with Piña Colada, all of it delicious. Bedrooms above are warmly simple with comfy beds wrapped in crisp linen, making this a must for those in search of a welcoming billet close to the mountains. There are framed photographs on the walls, the odd piece of mahogany furniture, good books, no TVs (unless you ask). Breakfast is served around one table; wallow with the papers and make your toast on the Aga. A road passes outside, quietly at night, lanes lead into the hills, and a small organic kitchen garden provides much for the table. The Beacons are close, so walk, ride, bike, canoe – or head to Hay for books galore.

Rooms	7: 2 doubles, 2 twins/doubles, 3 four-posters.£110-£155. Singles from £75.
Meals	12.30pm-2.30pm (from 12pm Sun); 6pm-9.30pm. Main courses £4.90-£15 (lunch), £5-£18.90 (dinner); set lunch £15.90 & £18.90; set dinner £21.50 & £26.50.
Closed	Open all day.
Directions	From Brecon, A470 north to Felin Fach (4.5 miles). On left.

Charles & Edmund Inkin & Julie Bell
The Felin Fach Griffin,
Felin Fach,
Brecon LD3 0UB
Tel   +44 (0)1874 620111
Web   www.felinfachgriffin.co.uk

Powys

The Harp
Old Radnor

David and Jenny Ellison bring bags of experience (time spent at Bristol's Hotel du Vin) to this ancient Welsh longhouse tucked up a dead-end lane near the parish church. The wonderful interior is spick-and-span timeless: 14th-century slate flooring in the bar, tongue-and-groove in a tiny room that seats a dozen diners, crannies crammed with memorabilia, an ancient curved settle, an antique reader's chair, two fires and a happy crowd. Enjoy a pint of Shropshire Lass with a Welsh Black rump steak or a tagine of organic lamb with herb couscous, or pan-fried cod with pea and tarragon purée. Or take a ploughman's to a seat under the sycamore and gaze upon the spectacular Radnor Valley for total tranquillity. Life in this tiny village, like its glorious pub, remains delightfully unchanged.

Powys

The Talkhouse
Pontdolgoch

What was once a typical pub now serves 'niche boutique' wines. Stephen and Jacqueline have a winning formula in their 17th-century drovers' rest, combining attentive service with marvellous food. The first room you come into is a sitting room with comfy armchairs and sofa – just the place for pre-lunch drinks or after-dinner coffee. The bar has beams, log fire and sumptuous sofas; the claret-and-cream dining room has French windows that open to the garden in summer: dine outside. Classical, seasonal cooking – the lightest sweet potato and butternut soup; beef fillet with steak and kidney pudding and horseradish rösti; delicately cooked Welsh lamb – is a treat, the daily changing menu using the finest local produce. A small, perfect find in the rolling wilderness of mid-Wales. Booking is essential.

Meals	12pm-2pm (Sat & Sun only); 6.30pm-9pm. Main courses £7.95-£15; bar meals £4.25-£6.50.
Closed	Tues-Fri lunch, 3pm-6pm Sat & Sun & Mon all day.
Directions	From Kington A44; after 3 miles left for Old Radnor.

Meals	12pm-1.30pm Sun; 6.30pm-8.45pm Tues-Sat. Main courses £11.95-£19.95.
Closed	Tues-Sat lunch, Sun eve & Mon all day.
Directions	On A470 1 mile west of Caersws & 5 miles from Newtown.

	Jenny & David Ellison The Harp, Old Radnor, Presteigne LD8 2RH
Tel	+44 (0)1544 350655
Web	www.harpinnradnor.co.uk

	Stephen & Jacqueline Garratt The Talkhouse, Pontdolgoch, Caersws SY17 5JE
Tel	+44 (0)1686 688919
Web	www.talkhouse.co.uk

Entry 905 Map 7

Entry 906 Map 7

Powys

The Brigands Inn
Machynlleth

The Cambrian Mountains loom like vast waves over the Dovey valley and this big old coaching inn on an ancient drovers' path has been offering sustenance to travellers since the 15th century. The recent renovation has retained the integrity of the rambling building and as you step in to the big oak bar with its polished flagstones and waxed beams you feel that you've entered a well-run ship. Food is a mix of contemporary and classic Welsh cuisine. Best end of local Welsh lamb with baby veg, fondant potato and redcurrant jus stand alongside pan-fried fillet of bream with ratatouille, a sweet red pepper dressing and baby clams; make your choice as you sip a pint of Clogwyn Gold or Rev James. There's also a pretty view-filled garden, and a sofa'd snug in which to peruse the (rather tempting) wines.

Meals	12pm-9pm. Main courses £8.50-£16.50; sandwiches £5.50.
Closed	Open all day.
Directions	On r'bout where A470 meets A458, 10 miles east of Dolgellau.

Dawn Davies
The Brigands Inn,
Mallwyd,
Machynlleth SY20 9HJ
Tel   +44 (0)1650 511999
Web   www.brigandsinn.com

Entry 907 Map 7

Powys

Wynnstay Hotel
Machynlleth

Trucking through the gastronomic desert that is mid Wales, you'll be charmed to discover this rambling old coaching inn in quaint Machynlleth. It's rather more hotel than pub, but there's a cracking bar with traditional oak floors, low beams, scrubbed tables and candlelight. Bag a seat by the log fire in winter and peruse Gareth Johns's menus over a pint of Rev James. He applies his skills to fine local produce: Conwy mussels, Borth lobster, bass from Cardigan Bay, salmon and sewin from the river Dyfi, Welsh Black beef and lamb from the valley. Salt duck terrine with homemade chutney may precede hake with roasted vegetables and herb oil, or rib-eye of beef with chips; finish with Welsh cheeses. There are some wonderful wines from small Italian growers and, surprisingly, a traditional pizzeria at the back.

Meals	12pm-2pm; 6.30pm-9pm. Pizzeria 4.30pm-9.30pm (closed Sun). Main courses £7.50-£14.95 (lunch), £11.25-£15.50 (dinner).
Closed	2.30pm-6pm (bar only).
Directions	In the centre of Machynlleth.

Gareth & Paul Johns
Wynnstay Hotel,
Heol Maengwyn,
Machynlleth SY20 8AE
Tel   +44 (0)1654 702941
Web   www.wynnstay-hotel.com

Entry 908 Map 7

Swansea

Vale of Glamorgan

Pen-y-Cae Inn
Pen-y-Cae

Everything about the Pen-y-Cae is pristine, from the multi-levelled garden at the back to the claret leather sofas and wood-burner in the bar. They've even created a new upper floor, reached by a wooden staircase, supported by chunky beams. It's an exceptionally lovely interior, the best of old and new, and you feast under rafters. French windows open to the Brecon Beacons in summer, informed staff are delightful and there's food to match, from classic pub grub at lunch to liver with crispy pancetta on creamed potatoes at dinner. And rib-eye steaks with Lyonnaise potatoes (fabulous), and Welsh crumpety laverbread pikelets with leeks, cockles and white wine sauce. Wash it all down with a bottled beer from Tomos Watkin, Wales's fastest growing brewery, and trundle off home – charmed, well-fed and happy.

The Blue Anchor
East Aberthaw

Inglenooks and open log fires, stories of smugglers and derring-do – it's rich in atmosphere. Inside is a warm warren of little rooms and doorways less than five feet high. The Colemans have nurtured this 700-year-old place for 66 years and restored the pub to its former glory following a fire in 2004. Dine in winter on pheasant from their local shoot, in summer on sewin from Swansea Bay and salads from the vegetable garden. You can pop in for a bowl of mussels and a pint of Wye Valley – or dip into the chef's selection of regional cheeses. Under the eaves of a classic thatched roof, the restaurant delivers hake with chorizo and roasted red pepper risotto, duck with savoy cabbage, pancetta and redcurrant jus, lemon and sultana cheesecake, Sunday roasts (do book). It's pubby, good looking and wonderful at doing what it knows best.

Meals	12pm-2.30pm; 6.30pm-9.30pm. Main courses £7.95-£21; bar meals £4.95-£9.95; Sunday roast £8.95.
Closed	3pm-6pm, Sun eve & Mon all day. Open all day Sat.
Directions	On A4067 north of Abercraf, midway between Brecon & Swansea; near Dan-Yr-Ogof show caves.

Meals	12pm-2pm (12.30pm-2.30pm Sun); 6pm-9.30pm; no food Sun eve. Main courses £8.95-£10.95 (lunch); £12.50-£17.85 (dinner); set lunch (2 courses) £10.50.
Closed	Open all day.
Directions	2 miles west of Cardiff Airport just off B4265.

Anthony Christopher
Pen-y-Cae Inn,
Brecon Road,
Pen-y-Cae, Swansea SA9 1FA
Tel   +44 (0)1639 730100
Web   www.pen-y-caeinn.com

Jeremy Coleman
The Blue Anchor,
East Aberthaw,
Barry CF62 3DD
Tel   +44 (0)1446 750329
Web   www.blueanchoraberthaw.com

Entry 909 Map 7

Entry 910 Map 2

Vale of Glamorgan

Plough & Harrow
Monknash

Originally part of a monastic grange, and well off the beaten track, today's Plough & Harrow is hugely convivial. Ancient, low white walls lead you to the front door, then you dip into two dim-lit, low-ceilinged, character-oozing rooms, their rustic fireplaces filled with church candles or crackling logs. There are cheerful yellow walls, original floors, church pews, smiling staff and a small bar area with a big array of handpumps – up to 11 ales are served. Traditionalists will be relieved to see gammon and chips on the lunch menu while the more adventurous may plump for summer crab salad, moules marinières and roasted duck breast on potato fritters. A brilliant atmosphere, a great find, the kind of pub you wish was your local – and it is as friendly to single drinkers as it is to groups.

Wrexham

The Cross Foxes
Erbistock

It's set on a travellers' crossroads, as the highway crosses the waters of the Dee and both man and fish move in either direction, depending on the season. Rest on the terrace with a pint of Marston's Burton Bitter or Ringwood's Huffkin and soak up the views from this timeless spot. Inside, a log fire throws light on a well-carved bar front, polished wood tables and quarry tiles, while on the shelves glows one of the best whisky and armagnac collections for many a mile: cockle-warming stuff. The big blackboard at the end of the bar is scrawled with good things to eat, from Cumberland sausage with black pudding mash and onion gravy to venison and pheasant meat loaf with red cabbage and juniper sauce. Settle into the wood-panelled area, the fireside snug or the conservatory, and enjoy a genuine classic.

Meals	12pm-2.30pm (5pm Sat); 6pm-9pm (5pm-8pm Sun). Main courses £6.50-£14.95; bar meals £4-£9.50.
Closed	Open all day.
Directions	Village signed off B4265, between St Brides Major & Llantwit Major, 6 miles south west of Cowbridge.

Meals	12pm-9.30pm (9pm Sun). Main courses £9.50-£16.95; bar meals from £6.25; sandwiches from £4.75.
Closed	Open all day.
Directions	On A528 beside Overton Bridge, 7 miles south of Wrexham.

Gareth Davies & Alistair Jones
Plough & Harrow,
Monknash,
Cowbridge CF71 7QQ
Tel   +44 (0)1656 890209
Web   www.theploughmonknash.com

Entry 911 Map 2

Ian Pritchard-Jones
The Cross Foxes,
Erbistock,
Wrexham LL13 0DR
Tel   +44 (0)1978 780380
Web   www.crossfoxes-erbistock.co.uk

Entry 912 Map 7

Wales
Worth a visit

Cardiff

913 Gwaelod-y-Garth Inn Main Road,
Gwaelod-y-Garth CF15 9HH
+44 (0)29 2081 0408
Revamped former miners' pub in a village perched on the side of the Taff Valley. Walkers, cyclists and visitors to Castell Coch pile into the airy traditional bar to refuel on decent ales and Welsh produce; try the Gower saltmarsh lamb.

Carmarthenshire

914 White Hart Thatched Inn & Brewery
Llanddarog, Carmarthen SA32 8NT
+44 (0)1267 275395
An oddity for west Wales, a thatched pub whose low-beamed rooms ooze fairytale charm. Real log fires, real homemade pies and real beers (home brewed) – worth leaving the A40 for.

Conwy

915 The Lord Newborough Conway Road,
Dolgarrog LL32 8JX +44 (0)1492 660549
On the quiet side of the valley, yards from the river, this sky-blue-painted inn was a hunting lodge. Step in to an upbeat bar with yellowy hues, real fires and great-value homemade pub food. Great walks from the front door.

Denbighshire

916 The Wynnstay Arms Well Street,
Ruthin LL15 1AN +44 (0)1824 703147
More restaurant than traditional pub, it stands slap bang in Ruthin town centre. Come for the warm convivial vibe, the unpretentious atmosphere and the good-value meals.

Gwynedd

917 Pen-y-Gwryd Hotel Nant Gwynant,
Caernarfon, LL55 4NT +44 (0)1286 870211
Snowdonia's ex-Mountain Rescue HQ and training base for the 1953 Everest expedition. Spot their boots in the bar, eat by candlelight, soothe weary muscles in the (communal) Victorian bathroom. A treasure.

Gwynedd

918 Ty Coch Inn Porthdinllaen,
Morfa Nefyn LL53 6DB +44 (0)1758 720498
Find time to walk along the beach to the tiny beachside hamlet and this spectacularly sited pub. A warm Welsh welcome and simple food await – lovely. Drink beer with your feet in the sea.

Monmouthshire

919 Llanthony Priory Llanthony,
Abergavenny NP7 7NN +44 (0)1873 890487
Once only walkers knew Llanthony was here, now the abbot's cellar holds an atmospheric hotchpotch of tables and high-backed pews. Simple food, pints of Felinfoel, proper espresso, romantic views.

920 The Crown at Pantygelli Old Hereford Rd,
Pantygelli, Abergavenny NP7 7HR
+44 (0)1873 853314
Handsome 16th-century roadside pub with glorious rolling country views towards the Skirrid. A true community pub with farmers at the bar, local ales on tap and good food sourced from surrounding farms. Reports welcome.

921 The Newbridge Inn Tredunnock,
Usk NP15 1LY +44 (0)1633 451000
As darkness falls, the old stone bridge over the Usk is floodlit, the setting is seductive and this is all a gastropub should be: warm, inviting and beautifully turned out. Reports please.

Pembrokeshire

922 Cresselly Arms Cresswell Quay,
Kilgetty SA68 0TE +44 (0)1646 651210
The walls of this timeless old pub are hung with wisteria; pick an outside table and gaze onto the estuary and the woods. Inside, ale is poured from a jug – there's no truck with modern innovation here. Authentically plain.

923 Royal Oak Gladestry, Kington HR5 3NR
+44 (0)1544 260842
Stone-built local, smack on the Offa's Dyke Path beneath Hergest Ridge. Fills up with farmers and booted walkers in for pints of Woods, roaring fires and good value tucker here.

Have you enjoyed this book? Why not try one of the others in the Special Places series and get 35% discount on the RRP *

British Bed & Breakfast (Ed 14)	RRP £14.99	Offer price £9.75
British Bed & Breakfast for Garden Lovers (Ed 5)	RRP £14.99	Offer price £9.75
British Hotels & Inns (Ed 11)	RRP £14.99	Offer price £9.75
Devon & Cornwall (Ed 1)	RRP £9.99	Offer price £6.50
Scotland (Ed 1)	RRP £9.99	Offer price £6.50
Wales (Ed 1)	RRP £9.99	Offer price £6.50
Pubs & Inns of England & Wales (Ed 6)	RRP £15.99	Offer price £9.75
Go Slow England	RRP £19.99	Offer price £13.00
Ireland (Ed 7)	RRP £12.99	Offer price £8.45
French Bed & Breakfast (Ed 11)	RRP £15.99	Offer price £10.40
French Holiday Homes (Ed 5)	RRP £14.99	Offer price £9.75
French Châteaux & Hotels (Ed 6)	RRP £14.99	Offer price £9.75
French Vineyards (Ed 1)	RRP £19.99	Offer price £13.00
Go Slow France	RRP £19.99	Offer price £13.00
Paris (Ed 1)	RRP £9.99	Offer price £6.50
Italy (Ed 6)	RRP £14.99	Offer price £9.75
Go Slow Italy	RRP £19.99	Offer price £13.00
Spain (Ed 8)	RRP £14.99	Offer price £9.75
Portugal (Ed 4)	RRP £11.99	Offer price £7.80
India & Sri Lanka (Ed 3)	RRP £11.99	Offer price £7.80
Green Europe (Ed 1)	RRP £11.99	Offer price £7.80
Morocco (Ed 3)	RRP £9.99	Offer price £9.10

*postage and packing is added to each order

To order at the Reader's Discount price simply phone +44 (0)1275 395431 and quote 'Reader Discount PUB'.

If you have any comments on entries in this guide, please tell us. If you have a favourite place or a new discovery, please let us know about it. You can return this form or visit www.sawdays.co.uk.

Existing entry

Property name: _____

Entry number: _____   Date of visit: _____

New recommendation

Property name: _____

Address: _____

_____

Tel/Email/Web: _____

Your comments

What did you like (or dislike) about this place? Were the people friendly? What was the location like? What sort of food did they serve?

_____

_____

_____

_____

Your details

Name: _____

Address: _____

_____

_____   Postcode: _____

Tel: _____   Email: _____

Please send completed form to:
PUB7, Sawday's, The Old Farmyard, Yanley Lane, Long Ashton, Bristol BS41 9LR, UK

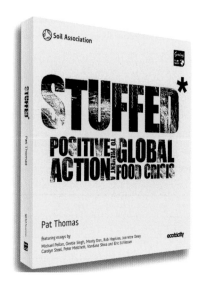

Stuffed – Postive Action to Prevent a Global Food Crisis   £9.74
(RRP £14.99)

Stuffed presents a global perspective on food production and agriculture with ideas for a fairly traded path we can follow to secure food for all and protection for the planet

With chapters on food in the kitchen through to global systems via the garden, schools, community, and an insight into food issues in cities and on farms, *Stuffed* takes a political and personal look the way that food systems influence, and can be influenced by, our choices.

Written by Patricia Thomas (former editor of The Ecologist), a preface by Michael Pollan, and with essays by Monty Don, Geetie Singh, Jeanette Orrey, Rob Hopkins, Carolyn Steel, Peter Melchett, Patrick Holden, Vandana Shiva and Eric Schlosser.

Also available in the Fragile Earth series:

Ban the Plastic Bag A community action plan £3.24 (RRP £4.99)
One Planet Living A guide to enjoying life on our one planet £3.24 (RRP £4.99)
The Little Food Book An explosive account of the food we eat today £4.54 (RRP £6.99)
What about China? A book to answer the sceptics £4.54 (RRP £6.99)

To order any of the books in the Fragile Earth series call
+44 (0)1275 395431 or visit www.sawdays.co.uk/bookshop

Climate Change
Our Warming World   £8.45 (RRP £12.99)

"Climate Change presents in a clear and unique way the greatest challenge facing humanity. It is illustrated with telling photography and sharply written text. It is both objective and passionate. To read it is to know that urgent action is needed at every level in all societies." Jonathan Dimbleby

Money Matters
Putting the eco into economics £5.30 (RRP £7.99)

This well-timed book will make you look at everything from your bank statements to the coins in your pocket in a whole new way. Author David Boyle sheds new light on our money system and exposes the inequality, greed and instability of the economies that dominate the world's wealth.

Do Humans Dream of Electric Cars?
£3.29 (RRP £4.99)

This guide provides a no-nonsense approach to sustainable travel and outlines the simple steps needed to achieve a low carbon future. It highlights innovative and imaginative schemes that are already working, such as car clubs and bike sharing.

The Book of Rubbish Ideas
£4.54 (RRP £6.99)

Every householder should have a copy of this guide to reducing household waste and stopping wasteful behaviour. Containing step-by-step projects, the book takes a top-down guided tour through the average family home.

The Big Earth Book
Updated paperback edition   £8.45 (RRP £12.99)

This book explores environmental, economic and social ideas to save our planet. It helps us understand what is happening to the planet today, exposes the actions of corporations and the lack of action of governments, weighs up new technologies, and champions innovative and viable solutions.

Cumbria

Masons Arms

Cartmel Fell

A perfect Lakeland inn tucked away two miles inland from Lake Windermere. You're on the side of a hill with huge views across lush fields to Scout Scar in the distance. In summer, all pub life decants onto a spectacular terrace – a sitting room in the sun – where window boxes and flowerbeds tumble with colour. The inn dates from the 16th century and is impossibly pretty. The bar is properly traditional with roaring fires, flagged floors, wavy beams, a cosy snug… and a menu of 70 bottled beers to quench your thirst. Rustic elegance upstairs comes courtesy of stripped floors, country rugs and muted walls in the first-floor dining room – so grab a window seat for fabulous views and order delicious food, anything from a sandwich to Cumbrian duck. Suites are contemporary and gorgeous, with cool colours, fabulous beds, gleaming bathrooms and Bang & Olufsen TVs. Self-catering cottages, equally immaculate, come with fancy kitchens (breakfast hampers can be arranged); best of all, you have your own private terrace, so order a meal in the restaurant and they'll bring it to you here.

Rooms	5 + 2: 5 suites. £75–£145. 2 cottages: 1 for 4, 1 for 6. Cottages £130–£175 per day.
Meals	12pm-2pm; 6pm-9pm (12pm-9pm Sat & Sun). Main courses £10.25–£14.95; bar meals from £5.95.
Closed	Open all day.
Directions	M6 junc. 36; A590 west, then A592 north. 1st right after Fell Foot Park. Straight ahead for 2.5 miles. On left after sharp right-hand turn.

John & Diane Taylor
Masons Arms,
Cartmel Fell,
Grange over Sands LA11 6NW
Tel   +44 (0)1539 568486
Web   www.strawberrybank.com

Entry 133 Map 11